D1587636

THE
SCOTTISH
JURISTS

THE
SCOTTISH
JURISTS

BY

DAVID M. WALKER,

Q.C., M.A., Ph.D., LL.D., F.B.A., F.R.S.E., F.S.A.Scot.,
Regius Professor of Law in the
University of Glasgow

EDINBURGH
W. GREEN & SON LTD.
LAW PUBLISHERS
1985

First Edition 1985

ISBN 0 414 00757 3

Printed in Great Britain by Oxford University Press

QUHATEVER I have done, I did it nocht to offend thee or to displease anie man, bot to provoke uthers to doe better.

SIR JOHN SKENE, To the Reader, in
De Verborum Significatione (1597)

PREFACE

ONE facet, and that not the least interesting one, of the study of the historical development of legal science, of the legal system of Scotland, and of the principles and rules and practices of all the branches of the substantive and adjective law of Scotland, is examination of the careers and works of those who, in their times, made by their writings what have proved to be valuable contributions to the development of the law and to contemporary and subsequent knowledge and understanding of the law and branches of it. Information about some of these men is fairly readily discoverable, about others much less easily found; some of their works are known, at least by title, to most of those who have essayed to study Scots law, others known only to antiquarians among lawyers and to bibliographers. But the attempt has not previously been made to look at them as a group, to discuss what they did, its value and importance, their influence on their successors and on the law itself, and their contributions to legal science. It is hard to say whether this enterprise should be considered as an essay in the history of ideas, or in historico-legal biography, or in the history of the law itself. It is offered as a contribution to the better understanding of the history of Scots law and the cultural history of Scotland.

It is desirable to stress that the biographical material is not in any case offered as a definitive Life, still less as a Life and Times, but only as a sketch depicting the background career of the man who wrote; we are more interested in what he wrote and in its importance. Nevertheless I have uncovered much new biographical information. Some of the jurists have previously been the subject of more or less adequate biographies, and some others should be made the subjects of biographical studies, but none, particularly the major figures, can be adequately portrayed in the space here available. I have included the few Scots who made names in branches of legal science other than those of the law of Scotland, but, save for brief mentions, I have excluded all persons still living; until a man has completed his work it is premature to attempt an assessment of him and of it.

The book is not to be regarded as the creation of a Scottish legal Pantheon or Hall of Fame; to have essayed this would have required consideration of the work of many judges and of some others. By no means all Scots lawyers who have published work are included. James Boswell, Henry Brougham, Walter Scott, Francis Jeffrey, Sir William Hamilton, John Wilson (Christopher North), John Gibson Lockhart and others have their places elsewhere; though lawyers they were notable as men of letters rather than men of law; others, such as Henry Cockburn, Fraser Tytler, Hill Burton and Mark Napier deserve mention under both heads. Others again, such as David Hume and Adam Smith, are figures of the very first importance in other contexts but of rather subsidiary importance among jurists.

The choice of whom to include and whom to exclude, particularly among the minor jurists, has not been easy but this book is not intended as a catalogue of Scottish legal writings nor a bibliography of Scots law and I have made no attempt to include everyone. I hope, however, that I have included all whose work has been at all significant in their own times and in the history of legal science in Scotland.

I am indebted to the Dean and Faculty of Advocates, the Director of the Scottish National Portrait Gallery, and the Pictures Committee of the University of Edinburgh, for permission to reproduce portraits of jurists which are in their possession. I am indebted also to Mrs Gillian Guthrie, Mrs Ruth McGregor and Mrs Moira Smith who typed the manuscript and to Miss Iris Stewart and Messrs W. Green & Son Ltd. for their co-operation and assistance at every stage of publishing.

DAVID M. WALKER

Department of Private Law
University of Glasgow
January 1, 1985

CONTENTS

ILLUSTRATIONS

(Between pages 224 and 225)

ABBREVIATIONS

A.D.A.	*Acta Dominorum Auditorum, Acts of the Lords Auditors of Causes and Complaints*, 1466–94 (ed. T. Thomson) (1839).
A.D.C., I	*Acta Dominorum Concilii, Acts of the Lords of Council in Civil Causes*, 1478–95 (ed. T. Thomson) (1839).
A.D.C., II	*Acta Dominorum Concilii, Acts of the Lords of Council in Civil Causes*, 1496–1501 (ed. G. Neilson and H. M. Paton) (1918).
A.D.C., III	*Acta Dominorum Concilii, Acts of the Lords of Council in Civil Causes*, 1501–1502/3 (ed. J. A. Clyde) (Stair Society: 1943).
A.D.C., Public	*Acta Dominorum Concilii, Acts of the Lords of Council in Public Affairs*, 1501–54 (ed. R. K. Hannay) (1932).
APS	*Acts of the Parliaments of Scotland*, 1124–1707 (ed. T. Thomson and Cosmo Innes), 12 vols. (1814–75).
Anderson, SN	William Anderson, *The Scottish Nation*, 3 vols. (1865).
Arbroath Liber	*Liber S. Thome de Aberbrothoc* (ed. C. Innes and P. Chalmers), 2 vols. (Bannatyne Club: 1848–56).
Brunton & Haig	George Brunton and David Haig, *Historical Account of the Senators of the College of Justice* (1832).
Calderwood	David Calderwood, *History of the Kirk of Scotland*, 1524–1625 (ed. T. Thomson and David Laing), 8 vols. (Wodrow Society: 1842–49).
C.S.P., Dom.	*Calendar of State Papers, Domestic Series* (1856–1924).
C.S.P., For.	*Calendar of State Papers, Foreign Series* (1861–1950).
C.S.P., Sc.	*Calendar of State Papers relating to Scotland*, 1509–1603 (ed. M. J. Thorpe), 2 vols. (1858).
C.Sc.P.	*Calendar of State Papers relating to Scotland*, 1547–1603 (ed. J. Bain and others), 13 vols. (1898–1969).
C.S.P., Spanish	*Calendar of State Papers, Spanish Series* (1862–1954).
Chambers, BDES	Robert Chambers, *A Biographical Dictionary of Eminent Scotsmen* (new edition by T. Thomson), 3 vols. (1870).
Complete Peerage	*The Complete Peerage*, by G. E. Cokayne (new ed. by Hon. V. Gibbs), 13 vols. (1910–59).
DNB	*Dictionary of National Biography.*
Diurnal	*Diurnal of Remarkable Occurrents*, 1513–75 (ed. T. Thomson) (Bannatyne and Maitland Clubs: 1833).
ESC	*Early Scottish Charters prior to A.D. 1153*, collected with notes by Sir A. C. Lawrie (1905).
Exch. Rolls	*The Exchequer Rolls of Scotland* (ed. J. Stuart and others), 23 vols. (1878–1908).
Fasti Aberdonenses	*Fasti Aberdonenses: Selections from the Records of the University and King's College of Aberdeen, 1494–1854* (ed. Cosmo Innes) (Spalding Club: 1854).
Fasti Ecclesiae Scoticanae	*Fasti Ecclesiae Scoticanae: The Succession of Ministers in the parish churches of Scotland from the Reformation*, by Hew Scott (revised ed.), 8 vols. (1915–50).
F.B.A.	Fellow of the British Academy.
F.R.S.	Fellow of the Royal Society of London.

F.R.S.E.   Fellow of the Royal Society of Edinburgh.

Grant   *The Faculty of Advocates in Scotland*, 1532–1943 (ed. Sir
                  Francis J. Grant) (Scottish Record Society: 1944).

H.M.C.   Royal Commission on Historical Manuscripts Reports.

History of James *The historie and life of King James the Sext* (ed. T. Thomson)
  the Sext   (Bannatyne Club: 1825).

Holdsworth   Sir William S. Holdsworth, *History of English Law*, 17 vols.
                  (1956–66).

J.F.   Sir Thomas Craig, *Jus Feudale*.

J.R.   *The Juridical Review*, 1889–.

Keith   Robert Keith, *History of the Affairs of Church and State in
                  Scotland*, 1527–68 (ed. J. P. Lawson), 3 vols.
                  (Spottiswoode Society: 1844–50).

Knox   John Knox, *History of the Reformation in Scotland* (ed. W. C.
                  Dickinson), 2 vols. (1949).

L.Q.R.   *Law Quarterly Review*, 1885–.

Melville   Sir James Melville of Halhill, *Memoirs of His Own Life*,
                  1549–93 (ed. T. Thomson) (Bannatyne and Maitland
                  Clubs: 1827).

Moysie   David Moysie, *Memoirs of the Affairs of Scotland*, 1577–1603
                  (ed. J. Dennistoun) (Bannatyne and Maitland Clubs:
                  1830).

Nau   Claude Nau, *History of Mary Stewart*.

Omond   G. W. T. Omond, *The Lord Advocates of Scotland*, 2 vols.
                  (1833).
                      The Lord Advocates of Scotland, Second series
                  (1834–80) (1914).

O.S.A.   *[Old] Statistical Account of Scotland*, 21 vols. (1791–99);
                  reprinted, 20 vols (1973–84).

P. & M.   Sir Frederick Pollock and Frederic W. Maitland, *The History
                  of English Law before the Time of Edward I* (2nd ed.), 2
                  vols. (1898).

Pitcairn   Robert Pitcairn, *Ancient Criminal Trials in Scotland*, 3 vols. in
                  7 (Bannatyne and Maitland Clubs: 1829–33).

Proc. B.A.   *Proceedings of the British Academy*, 1903–.

Q.A.   *Quoniam Attachiamenta*.

R.M.   *Regiam Majestatem*.

R.M.S.   *Registrum Magni Sigilli, The Register of the Great Seal of
                  Scotland* (ed. J. M. Thomson and others), 1306–1668; 11
                  vols. (1882–1914).

R.P.C.   *The Register of the Privy Council of Scotland*, First series,
                  1545–1625, 14 vols. (ed. J. H. Burton and others)
                  (1877–98).
                  Second series, 1625–60, 8 vols. (ed. D. Masson and others)
                  (1899–1908).
                  Third series, 1661–91, 16 vols. (ed. P. Hume Brown and
                  others) (1908–70).

R.R.A.N.	*Regesta Regum Anglo-Normannorum*, Vol. I (ed. H. W. C. Davis) (1913); Vol. II (ed. C. Johnson and H. A. Cronne) (1956); vols. III and IV (ed. H. A. Cronne and R. H. C. Davis) (1968–69).
R.R.S.	*Regesta Regum Scottorum*, Vol. I, Acts of Malcolm IV (ed. G. W. S. Barrow) (1960).
	Vol. II, Acts of William I (ed. G. W. S. Barrow and W. W. Scott) (1971).
	Vol. VI, Acts of David II (ed. Bruce Webster) (1982).
R.S.S.	*Registrum Secreti Sigilli, the Register of the Privy Seal of Scotland*, 1488–1584, 8 vols. (ed. M. Livingstone and others) (1908–82).
St. Andrews Register	*Liber Cartarum Prioratus Sancti Andree in Scotia* (ed. T. Thomson) (Bannatyne Club: 1841).
Scots Peerage	*The Scots Peerage* (ed. Sir J. Balfour Paul), 9 vols. (1904–14).
S.H.R.	*Scottish Historical Review*, 1904–.
S.H.S.	Scottish History Society.
S.R.O.	Scottish Record Office.
S.R.S.	Scottish Record Society.
S.L.T.	*Scots Law Times*, 1893–.
Sources and Lit.	H. McKechnie (ed.), *The Sources and Literature of Scots Law* (Stair Society: 1935).
Spottiswoode	John Spottiswoode, *History of the Church of Scotland* (ed. M. Russell and M. Napier), 3 vols. (Bannatyne Club and Spottiswoode Society: 1850).
Teulet	Alexandre Teulet, *Papiers d'état, pièces et documents inédits ou peu connus relatifs à l'histoire de l'Ecosse au XVI siècle*, 3 vols. (Bannatyne Club: 1852–60).
Thirds of Benefices	*Accounts of the Collectors of Thirds of Benefices*, 1561–72 (ed. G. Donaldson) (S.H.S.: 1949).
Trans. R.S.E.	*Transactions of the Royal Society of Edinburgh*, 1788–.
W.S.	Writer to the Signet.

CHAPTER 1

THE CONCEPT OF A SCOTTISH JURIST

THE word "jurist" does not bear a certain or clearly-defined meaning. It is sometimes used as a rather grandiloquent synonym for a lawyer of any kind, or sometimes for a judge. But it is on the whole more frequently used in a rather more restricted sense.

The word is of course of Latin derivation and had its origin in the titles *iurisconsulti, iurisprudentes*, applied to the succession of Roman lawyers who were concerned not merely nor so much to use and apply rules of law in the interests of clients in practical cases as to discover the underlying ideas, the principles behind the existing rules, to systematise the rules into an ordered scheme of rights and duties, to promote development of the body of law, and to write treatises rationalising and expounding the rules as a rational system.

Schulz[1] gives a rather wide meaning to the idea of a jurist:

"Our conception of 'legal science' (or 'jurisprudence' – we regard the terms as synonymous) embraces every vocational occupation with the law, its making, application, exposition and transmission. The term 'vocation' must not be restricted to activities directed to earning a livelihood or to some other economic purpose.... Thus for us 'legal science' or 'jurisprudence' embraces every form of vocational activity in the sphere of law, and 'jurist' covers all who dedicate themselves to such activities."

Under the Roman republic jurists, a class of men known as *iuris consulti* or *iuris prudentes*, began to be recognised. They were men who, particularly from about 100 B.C., advised the praetors on the introduction and modification of the formulae which they stated in their edicts they would recognise as giving a ground of action, who advised the lay judges on how they might interpret a rule or deal with a point of difficulty, advised orators on the line of argument they might present, or advised worried clients, or drafted, or advised on drafting, contracts, wills and other deeds, or sometimes argued cases themselves.[2] They also instructed young men and, very importantly, produced books which made their views available to their contemporaries and successors.[3] Though there were a few earlier ones, instructional texts became common in the second century B.C.[4] According to Cicero, one Brutus published books on the *ius civile*, and Quintus Mucius Scaevola, consul in 95 B.C., is said to have been the first who established the *ius civile*, reducing it to order in 18 books,[5] and it is known that others wrote books in private law in the first century B.C.[6] There were also works on the duties of a judge, practical collections of forms and collections of *responsa*.[7] Even at this stage there were clearly some who were making an attempt to sort legal rules into *genera* and to reduce the law into a coherent and comprehensible body of doctrine.[8]

The Roman jurists rose to the heights of their importance under the principate, the period from Augustus to Diocletian, the era of classical

Roman jurisprudence. It saw the fusion of the *ius civile* and the *ius honorarium*. The names of Iavolenus Priscus, Salvius Iulianus, Papinian, Paul, Ulpian, Modestinus, Gaius, Florentinus and Marcian are only the most notable among many.[9] They were consultants, teachers and writers, but not professional advocates or judges; some were high legal civil servants; the most important category of legal literature was the commentary on a text, on the Twelve Tables, republican or Augustan laws, and on the various edicts.[10] It was they who transformed a body of forms of actions into an ordered scheme of rights and duties, building on their experience and appreciation of real problems but creatively synthesising and rationalising.

In the dominate or bureaucratic period, from Diocletian to Justinian's codification at Constantinople in A.D. 534, jurists were prominent in the imperial council and chancery, in the law schools of Constantinople and Beyrout, and as advocates in the courts.[11] The commissions which produced the *Digest* and *Institutes* included legal members of the imperial council and law professors. The Law of Citations of Theodosius II and Valentinian III of A.D. 426 recognised the standing of some major jurists when it provided that all the writings of Gaius, Papinian, Paul, Ulpian and Modestinus were to have validity in court as authorities, and even the works of jurists cited by them were to have conditional authority.

Roman law continued to be studied in the West after the fall of the Western empire in A.D. 410 though public and systematic study disappeared until academic study of Justinian's texts, particularly that of the new-found *Digest*, was revived in Italy and France in the eleventh century.[12] The most famous and influential centre of the revived learning was the law school at Bologna.[13] Scholarly examination of legal principles began with the school of Glossators, founded by Irnerius about A.D. 1100, and glosses or marginal or interlinear annotations of texts were written, culminating in the Great Gloss of Accursius.[14] The authority of the gloss developed with its age, and by the fourteenth century it had begun to acquire an independent authority; then, as the gloss had supplemented the texts, the *communis opinio doctorum* was brought in to supplement the gloss, so that the opinion of an outstanding jurist such as Bartolus or Baldus came to have authority as much as the text or the gloss. To the Glossators succeeded the post-glossators or Commentators, who saw their special task as bringing the received doctrine into some relation with the conditions of the age. The greatest was Bartolus.[15] They based their work on the law of Justinian but gave more prominence to the medieval sources of law. They aimed at the production of methodical expositions, with divisions and subdivisions. Their great age was the fourteenth century.[16] It was the law of the Commentators, not of the *Corpus Iuris* which was received in Germany in the fifteenth and sixteenth centuries, whereby popular custom was subordinated to the modernised civil law.[17]

The Renaissance and the Reformation brought a breath of change to legal study.[18] The Humanists took a more critical attitude to the work of the Commentators. Cujas at Bourges was the first to try to relate legal texts and their rules to the society in which they had emerged and operated. The *mos Gallicus* became generally accepted in France, and also in Germany, and systematic textbooks proliferated, seeking to provide more intelligible and better-arranged statements of the principles of law than could be found in the *Digest*. Among the most famous of the attempts to sketch a new legal method was Leibniz's *Nova Methodus discendae docendaeque Iurisprudentiae* of 1667, which advocated the adoption by lawyers of the methods of reasoning used in mathematics and the new exact sciences.

The scholars of these different schools may all justifiably be called jurists; the Humanists in particular such as Cujas, Donellus, Brissonius and others, were distinguished for wide learning, legal acumen and elegant works of scholarship. By the seventeenth century much of the best work on law in general, and not least in Roman law, was being done in the Netherlands, by Grotius, Vinnius, Noodt, the Voets, and others.[19] In the eighteenth and nineteenth centuries the lead in Romanistic legal science passed to Germany, in the persons of Savigny, Jhering, Windscheid, Dernburg and others.[20]

Similarly from an early period in the history of the canon law an important part in explaining, criticising, rationalising and commenting on the authorised texts was played by decretists and decretalists.[21] The systematic collections of canons of church councils and ecclesiastical legislation of emperors began in the sixth century and several collections had been made in the West before A.D. 1000. Johannes Zonaras and Theodorus Balsamon were only the best known of the twelfth-century commentators on the canon law. Gratian's *Concordia Discordantium Canonum* (or *Decretum*) of *c.* A.D. 1140 was a masterly piece of juristic work and from the eleventh century the science of canon law was pursued as vigorously as that of the civil law, especially in the schools of Constantinople and Beyrout and at Bologna.

From the time of the Gregorian reformation of the church in the eleventh century papal laws and decisions, embodied in decretals, multiplied and were collected, annotated, discussed and taught, and were all the subject of intense juristic attention. After the Council of Trent (1545–63) there was a new impetus to the study of canon law but by this time half of Europe had repudiated the formal authority of the *Corpus Iuris Canonici*.

Feudalism originated in the kingdom of the Franks about the eighth century and spread rapidly, becoming part of custom and regulated by customary law, with variations emerging in different countries.[22] It never attained the universality nor was there the volume of legislation or juristic activity which grew up in relation to the civil and canon laws. Thinking and writing about feudal principles of government and landholding have been mainly works of emerging national legal systems.[23] The only literature of wide application were the *Libri Feudorum*, or Books of the Fiefs or Feus, composed by unknown writers, probably at Milan but receiving their final shaping at Bologna,[24] a work embodying the Lombard form of feudalism which attained great vogue in France and Germany as well as in Italy, was used in all the law schools and became semi-official when from the 13th century it came to be printed at the end of the *Corpus Iuris Civilis*.

From the earliest times, moreover, some men have been concerned with the legal aspects of more general speculation about the universe, man, man in society, the state or community, government and right and wrong. Legal thought has never been wholly distinct from social, political, or economic thought. These men too may reasonably be called jurists, and indeed this class of jurists comprises many sub-groups and very many individual scholars, many of whom have not been lawyers at all, in any professional or technical sense of that term, notably the natural-law school, men such as Grotius and Burlamaqui, the historical school, including such as Hugo and Savigny, the English analytical school, such as Hobbes, Bentham and Austin, the utilitarians and positivists, and more recently, social utilitarians, sociological jurisprudents, realists, economic jurisprudents and many more: *quot homines, tot sententiae*.

The word "jurist" has indeed sometimes been appropriated primarily to those who work in jurisprudence, in the narrow, modern, sense of legal philosophy, theories of and about law, and analysis of concepts.[25]

Cecil Fifoot's delightful Hamlyn lectures, *Judge and Jurist in the Reign of Queen Victoria*,[26] by implication distinguished the notable men of law of that era into two groups, both of whom in their different ways developed and expounded the law of England. In Anglo-American and associated systems of law the distinction is inevitable, necessary and important, but the dividing line is a shadowy one, not a great chasm. Fitzjames Stephen "became a judge because he was, or was thought to be, a jurist."[27] The problems discussed in those lectures show "that judge and jurist approach the law from different angles and with different aims."[28] The judge not merely decides specific disputed points but, by reason of the doctrine of *stare decisis*, legislates subordinately and interstitially. The jurist may also change the law as hitherto understood,

> "by detecting the raison d'être of the original decision and discovering both its current ineptitude and the way of escape from the tyranny of dogma. . . . The jurist has a second function. If the judge sees the law steadily, he cannot see it as a whole. It is for the jurist, at long range, to co-ordinate the immediate answers to fortuitous problems. . . . Though their opportunities and temptations thus diverge, judge and jurist are nevertheless complementary craftsmen. Together they can make law that is rooted in principle and yet pliant in the handling, at once tough and flexible."

In Anglo-American and Scots law some of the great jurists have also been working lawyers or judges; Coke and Blackstone in England, Story and Holmes in America, Stair and Bankton in Scotland. But more recently the mantle of the jurist has been worn more frequently by the incumbents of university chairs, largely cut off from active practice of the law, by Maitland and Pollock and Holdsworth and Winfield in England, by Erskine and Bell in Scotland.

The function and activity of the jurist may, it appears, accordingly be one or more of collecting and editing the texts of statutes or other legislative materials, collecting, classifying and editing reports of decisions, synthesising the materials of the law, either of a major field such as the private law, or of a smaller area such as the rules as to sale, and systematising the principles which underly the particular prescriptions and decisions, expounding and explaining the principles and rules on a particular subject-matter, exploring the historical origins and evolution of the institutions and principles of the system or branches of it, or examining the idea of law or particular problems of law from a philosophic standpoint.

Study of the personalities and work of great jurists has been pursued for a very long time,[29] but in a rather haphazard way. The volume entitled *Great Jurists of the World*[30] contains biographical sketches of 26 legal scholars from Gaius to von Jhering, but inevitably has many omissions; it includes no Scot. The list implies a broad meaning of the term jurist.

> "The collection includes jurists who were innovators, such as Grotius, distinguished practising lawyers, such as Zouche and Bynkershoek, reformers such as Mittermaier and Bentham; philosophic jurists, such as Leibnitz and Vico. . . . From the lists of the English and Scotch jurists several are wanting. Coke is omitted; so is Stair; so is Mansfield; so is Blackstone. The omission of Stair is particularly to be regretted. His *Institutions* stand out as a specimen of lucid exposition. . . ."[31]

In fact, apart from legal philosophers and theorists,[32] the careers and influences of great jurists are discussed mainly in the histories of particular systems of law, and there is still no history of Scots law.

Accordingly we come to the questions: what do we mean when we speak of a Scottish jurist? Who have been the Scottish jurists? Consistently with accepted meanings given to the term in the other legal systems which have historical and spiritual affinity with Scots law, a Scottish jurist can be described as a man who has devoted his energies, skill and understanding of the law and related subjects mainly, or at least substantially, to the collection and organisation of source-materials, the shaping of the law, its rationalisation, its interpretation, the systematisation of the principles, exploration of their implications, applications and difficulties, or has examined the historical or philosophic problems of the law in relation to Scotland, and who has thereby made a substantial contribution to Scottish legal literature. A jurist may be, and frequently has been also, a legal practitioner or a judge or law teacher or otherwise professionally involved in the working of the legal system. He is all the better for that. If such be the concept of a Scottish jurist, who have been the Scottish jurists whose works have been, and frequently still are, of interest, significance, value and importance?

NOTES

[1] *History of Roman Legal Science* (1946), pp. 1–2. The terms "legal science" and "jurisprudence" are themselves also of very indefinite connotation. The main meanings are probably: all knowledge of and about law; the knowledge of the more theoretical problems of law, as contrasted with knowledge of principles in force; and the systematic analysis and exposition of knowledge of and about law.

No apology need be made for using the word "science." It was only in the mid-19th century that the word without any qualifying adjective came to be restricted to the study and knowledge of natural phenomena. The word fundamentally means systematised knowledge and can properly be applied to such knowledge in any sphere and to the pursuit of it. In 1840 James Reddie of Glasgow published *Inquiries Elementary and Historical in the Science of Law*. Sir Frederick Pollock (*Oxford Lectures and Other Discourses* (1890), Lect. 1), distinguished between the practice of the law as an art, and the study of law as a science, and wrote (*Essays in Jurisprudence and Ethics* (1882), 237) on "The Science of Case Law," showing how the methods of the natural scientist and the legal scientist were not dissimilar. James Bryce (*Studies in History and Jurisprudence*, II, essay 12) discussed "The Methods of Legal Science." J. B. Ames ("The Vocation of the Law Professor," in *Lectures in Legal History* (1913), 354), observed that "law is a science, and as such can best be taught by the law faculty of a university." Huntington Cairns has written on *The Theory of Legal Science* (1941). The terms economic science, political science, moral science and social science are all common academic terms. The modern compendious term "the social sciences" is well established and there is ample warrant for including law among the social sciences.

[2] Jolowicz and Nicholas, *Historical Introduction to the Study of Roman Law* (3rd ed.), chap. 5; Schulz, *op. cit.*, pp. 40–48; Watson, *Law Making in the Later Roman Republic* (1974), pp. 102–106; F. de Zulueta, "The Development of Law under the Republic," *Camb. Anc. Hist.*, IX, chap. 21; de Zulueta, "The Science of Law," in C. Bailey (ed.), *The Legacy of Rome* (1923). See also J. P. Dawson, *The Oracles of the Law*.

[3] Schulz, *op. cit.*, pp. 55–58; Watson, *op. cit.*, pp. 108–109.

[4] Schulz, *op. cit.*, pp. 80–93; Watson, *op. cit.* pp. 134–142.

[5] Schulz, *op. cit.*, p. 94; Watson, *op. cit.*, p. 143.

[6] Watson, *op. cit.*, p. 159.

[7] Watson, *op. cit.*, p. 162.

[8] Kruger, *Geschichte der Quellen und Literatur des römischen Rechts* (1912), pp. 64–65.

[9] Jolowicz and Nicholas, *op. cit.*, chap. 22; Schulz, *op. cit.*, pp. 102–124: W. W. Buckland, "Classical Roman Law," *Camb. Anc. Hist.* XI, chap. 21.

[10] Schulz, *op. cit.*, pp. 183–223. See also H. Fitting, *Alter und Folge der römischen Juristen von Hadrian bis Alexander* (1908); A. M. Honoré, *Gaius* (1962); W. Kunkel, *Herkunft und soziale Stellung der römischen Juristen* (1967).

[11] Schulz, *op. cit.*, pp. 267–277; Laborde, *Les ecóles de droit dans l'empire d'orient* (1912); Collinet, *Histoire de l'école de droit de Beyrouth* (1925).

[12] Vinogradoff, *Roman Law in Mediaeval Europe* (1929), chap. 2; P. Koschaker, *Europa und das römische Recht* (1953); H. J. Roby "Roman Law," *Camb. Med. Hist.* II, chap. 3.

As to the East, see H. J. Scheltema, "Byzantine Law," in *Camb. Med. Hist.* IV(2), chap. 21; K. E. Zachariä von Lingenthal, *Geschichte des grieschich-römischen Rechts* (1892).

[13] H. Fitting, *Die Anfange der Rechtsschule zu Bologna* (1888); H. Rashdall, "The Mediaeval Universities," in *Camb. Med. Hist.* VI, chap. 17; H. Rashdall, *The Universities of Europe in the Middle Ages* (2nd ed., 1936).

[14] Vinogradoff, *op. cit.*; Hazeltine, "Roman and Canon Law in the Middle Ages," *Camb. Med. Hist.* V, chap. 21; *idem*, "Glossators," *Encyc. Soc. Sc.* VI, p. 679; J. W. Jones, *Historical Introduction to the Theory of Law* (1940); J. H. Wigmore (ed.), *General Survey of Continental Legal History* (1912); H. Kantorowicz and W. W. Buckland, *Studies in the Glossators of the Roman Law* (1938).

[15] Hazeltine, "Commentators," *Encyc. Soc. Sc.* III, p. 679; *idem*, "The Renaissance and the Laws of Europe," *Camb. Legal Essays* (1926), p. 139.

[16] M. Conrat, *Geschichte der Quellen und Literatur des römischen Rechts im frühen Mittelalter* (1891); W. Ullman, *The Mediaeval Idea of Law as represented by Lucas de Penna*, (1946).

[17] Below, *Die Ursachen der Rezeption des römischen Rechts in Deutschland* (1905).

[18] F. W. Maitland, *English Law and the Renaissance* (1901); W. S. Holdsworth, *History of English Law*, IV, p. 217.

[19] A. de Goede, *Nederlandse Rechtsgeschiedenis* (1949); J. W. Wessels, *History of the Roman-Dutch Law* (1908); R. W. Lee, *Introduction to Roman-Dutch Law* (1953); H. L. Hahlo and E. Kahn, *The South African Legal System and its Background* (1968) p. 548.

[20] H. Brunner, *Deutsche Rechtsgeschichte* (1897); H. Mitteis, *Deutsche Rechtsgeschichte* (1960); R. von Stinzing, *Geschichte der deutschen Rechtswissenschaft* (1880); E. Wolf, *Grosse Rechtsdenker* (1963).

[21] F. Schultz, *Geschichte der Quellen und der Literatur des kanonischen Rechts* (1875); A. L. Richter, *Lehrbuch des katholischen und evangelischen Kirchenrechts* (1886); E. Friedberg, *Lehrbuch des katholischen und evangelischen Kirchenrechts* (1895); I. A. Zeiger, *Historia Iuris Canonici* (1940–47).

[22] H. Mitteis, *Lehnrecht und Staatsgewalt* (1933); F. L. Ganshof (tr. Grierson), *Feudalism* (1952); M. Bloch, *Feudal Society* (tr. Manyon) (1961); *idem*, "Feudalism," *Encyc. Soc. Sc.*, VI; Vinogradoff, "Foundations of Society (Origins of Feudalism)," *Camb. Med. Hist.* II, Chap. 20; *idem*, "Feudalism," *Camb. Med. Hist.* VI, Chap. 18; see also F. W. Maitland, *Domesday Book and Beyond* (1897); Pollock and Maitland, *History of English Law* (1897).

[23] See J. H. Round, *Feudal England* (1907); F. M. Stenton, *The First Century of English Feudalism* (1932); G. O. Sayles, *The Mediaeval Foundations of England* (1948); G. W. S. Barrow, *Feudal Britain* (1956); S. F. C. Milsom, *The Legal Framework of English Feudalism* (1976).

[24] S. Villanueva, "Libri Feudorum," *Digesto Italiano*; Lehmann, *Consuetudines Feudorum* (1896); Laspeyre, *Über die Entstehung und die alteste Bearbeitung der Libri Feudorum* (1830).

[25] The modern series of books entitled *Jurists: Profiles in Legal Theory*, in which volumes have appeared dealing with John Austin, Lon L. Fuller, H. L. A. Hart and Max Weber, uses the word in this sense.

[26] (1959).

[27] p. 115.

[28] pp. 134–136.

[29] See, *e.g.* T. Diplovatatius, *De claris iuris consultis* (*c.* 1500; ed. H. Kantorowicz and F. Schulz, 1919); G. Panziroli, *De claris Legum Interpretibus Libri Quatuor* (1721); L. Justiniani, *Memorie storiche degli Scrittori Legali del Regno di Napoli* (1787); C. N. S. Woolf, *Bartolus of Sassoferrato* (1913).

[30] Ed. Sir John Macdonell and Edward Manson (*Continental Legal History Series*, Vol. II, 1913).

[31] Introduction by Sir John Macdonell, pp. x–xi.

[32] On them see F. Berolzheimer, *The World's Legal Philosophies* (1912); R. Pound, *An Introduction to the Philosophy of Law* (1922); M. Hamburger, *The Awakening of Western Legal Thought* (1942); H. Cairns, *Legal Philosophy from Plato to Hegel* (1949); C. J. Friedrich, *The Philosophy of Law in Historical Perspective* (1958).

CHAPTER 2

THE EARLY JURISTS

WE do not know who were the first jurists in Scotland. But there are
extant from the eleventh century grants of land to churches by Macbeth
and Queen Gruoch (1040×1057),[1] by King Duncan II to the monks of St.
Cuthbert (1094),[2] by King Edgar to the same monks (1100),[3] and from
the start of the twelfth century there is a swelling mass of surviving
charters.[4] These bring out several points. From the time of David I there
was a chancellor of Scotland who doubtless kept the royal seal and was
responsible for the production and issue of the main official documents
evidencing royal acts. Subordinate to him was a chancery staff, including
several *clerici regis*, and from the latter part of the reign of William the
Lion we have evidence of a master of the writing office and a clerk of the
seal.[5] The chancery staff were familiar with Latin and used it readily and
skilfully. Since David I introduced feudal ideas and offices on the models
he had seen in England it is probably not so far-fetched to surmise that he
may have brought a clerk or two from the English chancery. The senior
clerks were clearly well acquainted with the principles of feudal tenure of
land and offices, and skilled draftsmen. Several became bishops; at least
one became chancellor; they were not mere conveyancing clerks.

The extent of uniformity in the drafting of the documents which have
survived from the twelfth century plainly indicates that the chancery staff
were well accustomed to framing charters and other writs regularly. It
may be that they had and used a style book, or at least, a collection of
suitable phrases and words, or it may be that they had developed a
vocabulary of appropriate formulae and phrases, and passed these on to
juniors who joined the office. The tendency towards uniformity is mark-
edly more noticeable as the twelfth century progresses.

In the eleventh and twelfth centuries the royal documents were in
flexible rather than settled form and were rather the prototypes of what
would later be classified as brieves, writs or charters. Most of those
surviving from the twelfth century are in the writ-charter form, in which
the king's name is stated in the third person, his announcements are then
given in the text in the first person, and they are always authenticated by
the royal seal. The writ-charter form was derived from the Anglo-Saxon
royal vernacular writ, as adapted and latinised by the early Norman kings
of England. From the late eleventh century Latin is always used in
Scottish royal writs.[6] As the twelfth century progresses forms tend to
become more stereotyped.

Some writs are clearly the prototypes of charters. They are lengthy and
used for the more solemn and important grants, such as an original grant
of property or privileges in perpetuity, or a confirmation of a grant
previously made by the grantor's predecessor. The distinction between
an original grant and a confirmation[7] was well recognised in the twelfth
century; there are even confirmations of earlier royal confirmations.[8] A
splendid example is Malcolm IV's confirmation in 1161 to his Steward,
Walter son of Alan and his heirs in fee and heritage, the grants made to

him by David I, his office of stewardship and large holdings of land, to be held in chief for the service of five knights.[9]

Other writs are the prototypes of various legal and administrative brieves. The legal brieve *de nativis*, ordering the restoration of fugitive neyfs,[10] is practically identical with the English writ of naifty and had been adopted without modification from the English chancery,[11] though sometimes the Scottish clerks modified the wording from that used in England.[12] The brieve of protection[13] declaring that the grantee was in the king's protection and that no one was to cause him injury, varied substantially in wording according to circumstances and, as in England,[14] became elaborated in time. It was sometimes incorporated in more substantial charters of privileges. The brieve commanding payment of teind[15] sought to enforce that obligation. A number of miscellaneous administrative brieves also survive, usually commands to royal officers to see that the grantee obtains or is not prevented from enjoying some right earlier granted,[16] but occasionally grants of privileges to the burgesses of a burgh,[17] and grants of freedom from toll or, sometimes, cain, or of freedom to buy and sell.

The royal writs commence with the king's name, *David rex Scotiae*, or *Malcolmus* or *Willelmus rex Scottorum*, or a variant thereof, just as in the contemporary English style. The epithet *Dei gracia* sometimes appears, usually in the more solemn documents, but was added to the official style in 1173–74, following Angevin practice. This was followed by the address, which might be short and general, *e.g. omnibus probis hominibus suis totius terre sue*, or longer and more detailed, the latter showing many variations, the salutation, normally in the single word *salutem*, a feature which originated in classical Latin letters, the notification, usually in the form of *sciant* with accusative and infinitive or *sciatis* with the same construction, *e.g. sciatis me dedisse*. Occasionally this is followed by a harangue or rhetorical preamble. Then follows the text or body of the document, set out concisely and plainly, just as in the writs from the Anglo-Norman chancery, and finally the attestation in the form *Testibus* followed by the names, and frequently designations, of the witnesses in the ablative. The number of witnesses varies greatly but is frequently correlated with the importance and solemnity of the document; thus the great charter of Kelso[18] has 44 witnesses. But the number seems sometimes to have been due to the fullness of the assembly at which the grant was approved. Most royal acts have between two and six witnesses. The majority of witnesses were laymen but persons of importance. It is uncertain at this time whether the witnesses were witnesses to the fact of the king's decision or grant recorded by his brieve or charter, or authenticated the document itself, but it is probably the former, and indeed witnesses may have been named without being present at either the grant or the issuing of the document evidencing it, may have been, that is, consenters rather than witnesses in the modern sense. The most commonly-named witnesses, notably the Chancellor and the Steward, were generally present when the deed was passed for sealing.

Most writs state the place of granting but few bear a date until this became common at the end of the twelfth century. A few writs conclude with the word *valete*.

Royal writs were authenticated by a seal, a lump of wax bearing the impression of the two halves of the royal seal, affixed on a tag passing through slits in the folded foot of the parchment, or on cords passing through holes made in the foot, or on a tongue made by making a cut from near the right-hand bottom corner to within an inch or so of the left-hand bottom corner.[19]

A few twelfth-century royal writs[20] show traces of papal chancery influence.

> "The inference from the documents as a whole is that the King of Scots in the middle of the twelfth century was served by an efficient professional writing-office, whose staff was familiar with the best practice of the contemporary English royal chancery and had some knowledge also of the work produced by the clerks of the papal curia. . . . What the acts of David I, Earl Henry and Malcolm IV show beyond all doubt is that already in the first three-quarters of the twelfth century the government of Scotland, whether good or not, was government by writing . . . this expression of the king's will in written instruments was a continuous process. Royal favours, decisions and judgements were in constant demand."[21]

Another activity for which legal knowledge and capacity for drafting are required is the framing of legislation. There are printed in the first volume of the *Acts of the Parliaments of Scotland* two collections entitled by the editors *Assise Regis David*[22] and *Assise Regis Willelmi*,[23] but they cannot be accepted unquestioningly as attributable to these monarchs. But from the time of David I there does develop a body of legislation.

The collected acts of William I[24] include several items[25] which are or include material seemingly of a legislative rather than administrative character. Thus one[26] lays down that a person withholding teind is to be compelled to pay it with the forfeiture *secundum quod asisa fuit Regis David avi mei*; there are other provisions for penalty against a *transgressorem asise Regis David*. Apart from words redolent of legislation these writs are directed to large sections of the population, or even to all, as distinct from grants to or for particular grantees. The question arises whether the chancery clerks were also legislative draftsmen. The probability is that they were, as the differentiation between legislative and executive writs was not then drawn.

There was moreover a kind of legal renaissance in Western Europe in the twelfth and thirteenth centuries. One aspect of it was the revival in Italy from the later eleventh century of the study of the law, connected with the rediscovery of the *Digest*. But another was the appearance in many European countries of legal literature seeking to state the developing bodies of national law. Of this genre there are in England Glanvill's *Tractatus de Legibus et Consuetudinibus Angliae* (c. 1187), Bracton's *De Legibus et Consuetudinibus Angliae libri quinque* (c. 1250), *Brevia Placitata* (c. 1260), and other minor tracts, notably Britton and Fleta (both c. 1290), in France the *Très Ancien Coutumier de Normandie* (c. 1200–20), the *Grand Coutumier du pays et duchie de Normandie*, supposed to have been compiled about 1270, Philippe de Beaumanoir's *Coutumes de Beauvoisis et autres anciennes coutumes* of about 1283, in

Germany Eike von Repkow's *Sachsenspiegel* of 1220–30 and the *Schwabenspiegel* of about 1275. All these were unofficial productions, the work of private individuals. So too in Scotland individual jurists produced statements of the native law.

The earliest individual Scottish jurist whose work we know, even if we do not know about him, is the person who compiled the work known as *Regiam Majestatem*. It is possible indeed that more than one person was involved. *Regiam Majestatem*, so called from its opening words, is traditionally the earliest book of law in Scotland, the "auld lawis," and repeatedly[27] in the later medieval and early modern period the Scottish Parliament sought to take it as a fundamental statement of the law and the basis for its amendment. In 1567 commission was granted[28] to Sir James Balfour of Pittendreich[29] and certain others to examine "the bukis of the law ... beginnand at the buikis of the law called *Regiam Majestatem* and *Quoniam Attachiamenta*." In 1574 it was renewed to Balfour and Sir John Skene of Curriehill,[30] and a third commission was appointed by Parliament in 1578.[31] Skene began to work in June 1575.[32] Finally in 1609 Skene's edition of *Regiam Majestatem* and *Quoniam Attachiamenta* was published in two versions, in Latin and in Scottish. The Latin version has elaborate annotations, but the Scottish one has two appendices dealing with the Order of Process observed before the Lords of Council and Session, and a Treatise of all Crimes and of Judges in Criminal Causes.[33] There were later references to the *Regiam* in later commissions to revise the law[34] but nothing came of them.

The plan of the *Regiam* comprises a prologue, based originally on that of Justinian's *Institutions*, which was the model also for the prefaces to Glanvill,[35] Bracton[36] and Fleta,[37] and, in most MSS., four books, which again reflects the influence of Gaius and Justinian. Book I, usually entitled *De praeparatoriis Judiciorum*, sets out the jurisdiction of various courts by reference to subject-matter and explains the procedure in an ordinary action. Book II, *De Judiciis*, deals with a mixed bag of topics, serfdom, donations between spouses, legal rights and succession, homage, fealty and purpresture. Book III is headed *De Placitis Civilibus* or *De Debitis Laicorum* and deals with cautionary obligations and rights in security, the main consensual contracts and further procedural questions. Book IV is *De Placitis Criminalibus* and contains much miscellaneous material not properly integrated into the text.

The text of *Regiam Majestatem* has had an unfortunate history. It appeared in various manuscript collections of early Scottish legal materials[38] themselves frequently defective and not concurring in their readings, before a text was put together and printed by Skene in 1609. Skene was not, however, by modern standards, a careful or critical record scholar. He corrected some fairly obvious errors and made emendations which are probable, but suppressed pages inconsistent with his theory that the work was to be ascribed to David I, and introduced into the text glosses and additions, which were originally notes and incorporated in the text in the process of transmission and copying.[39] Another text was settled by Thomas Thomson and published in 1844.[40]

Thomson's text varies from Skene's in arrangement and chapter divisions, and he does not divide the chapters into verses as Skene does. He omits from Books I to III matter which Skene included and includes in Book IV matter which Skene printed under other heads of the "auld lawes" in his edition. Unfortunately Skene's edition was the one in use for well over two centuries and, moreover, during the period when most of the references to the *Regiam* were made, and it is accordingly Skene's defective text and references thereto which have become embodied in later cases and treatises. It is regarded as the authorised version. Though it is a better text, Thomson's text has not superseded Skene's. Lord Cooper's edition, published by the Stair Society in 1947, is based mainly on Skene's edition, because Skene's is the received text, but he relegates to an appendix 32 chapters attributed by Skene to early statutes or included in his text of *Quoniam Attachiamenta*, but included by Thomson in his much longer Book IV of the *Regiam*. The text is accordingly still not settled and probably could not be settled without some conjectural emendation of MS. readings.

It has been well known since at least the time of Skene[41] and Sir Thomas Craig in the early seventeenth century[42] that the major source of the *Regiam* is the *De Legibus et Consuetudinibus Angliae* ascribed to Ranulph de Glanvill, the justiciar of Henry II of England, but possibly truly written by his nephew Hubert Walter and dated to about 1187.[43] The anonymous author of the *Regiam* was, then, sufficient of a legal scholar to know of, and to have the use of a copy of, Glanvill, which by his time was at least half a century old, and possibly much older.

But the *Regiam* is not a straight copy of Glanvill. The compiler made significant changes,[44] clearly with the intention of adapting the English work to Scottish conditions and needs. The author, however, follows Glanvill's general pattern of exposition in setting out substantive law incidentally to a commentary on the procedure of the royal courts.

Seventy-five of the 190 titles in the APS text of the *Regiam* are not drawn from Glanvill; 30 of the titles in Glanvill have no corresponding passage in the *Regiam*.[45] At least seven titles have been drawn from legislation attributed to David I, William I and Alexander II.[46]

The compiler also knew and drew on much older native materials, such as the Laws of the Brets and Scots, probably of Celtic origin, but surviving into the fourteenth century.[47]

The compiler was clearly also familiar with Roman and canon law. The pattern of four books is reminiscent of Gaius and Justinian rather than of Glanvill (which has 14 books). There are four parts of the *Regiam* drawn from Roman law; Book I, 28–31, dealing with pacts and unilateral promises, Book II, 1–10 dealing with arbitration, Book II, 13–14, dealing with the effects of the ordination and manumission of serfs, and Book II, 15, concerning donations between husband and wife.[48] The section on pacts has close affinities with Azo of Bologna's *Summa Codicis*, II, 3,[49] that on arbitration is very similar to Azo's *Summa Codicis*, II, 55, and Tancred's *Ordo Judiciarius* I, 3,[50] and that on ordination and manumission of serfs has close resemblances to Raymond of Penafort's *Summa de Casibus*, III, 17.[50]

But the relevant text of the *Regiam* is even closer to the *Summa* of Hostiensis than to some of the passages in Azo or Tancred and there are parallels in Hostiensis for some passages for which there are no parallels in Azo or Tancred.[51] The only work, however, which offers close parallels to all the chapters in the *Regiam* founded on Roman and canon law, and moreover in the same order, is the *Summa in Titulos Decretalium* of Goffredo of Trani.[52]

The compiler of the *Regiam* made some changes of substance and abbreviated some passages but the verbal similarity is too close to be other than copying. Such copying and adaptation was however common in medieval times. Bracton also relied on Azo, Tancred and Raymond.[53] Identification of this source of the compiler's copying reinforces the view that prior to 1400 the main influence of Roman law on Scots law was through the medium of the canon law rather than directly. The influence appears to have been strongest in matters of legal procedure. The clerical lawyers, such as the compiler, regarded the procedural rules set out in the commentaries on the Decretals as having a general validity in the absence of any established local rule to the contrary.[54] There are also a substantial number of casual references to Roman and canon law in the *Regiam*, though at least some of these were probably incorporated into MSS. by copyists and were not in the originals.

There is also an excerpt from the English *Praerogativa Regis* in *Regiam Majestatem*, II, 46 (in APS, II, 40). This work has been dated to 1255.[55] But this is probably a later marginal note which has been incorporated into the text.[56] There is also a passage in Thomson's text as *Regiam Majestatem*, IV, 40, drawn from an English law tract found in fourteenth or fifteenth century collections and usually entitled *Articuli quae in narrando indigent observari*.[57]

As far as Book II, 15 (II, 12 in APS), the material from Glanvill and Goffredo appears to have been fully edited by the compiler and an attempt made to integrate the materials drawn from the various sources.[58] The basis is Glanvill but there are repeated interpolations of material from native and canonist sources and some significant omissions, notably passages about trial by combat. From II, 16 to IV, 8, the material is Glanvill taken over without much editorial change, though sometimes rearranged in order, and the remainder is a rather miscellaneous and disorderly collection of indigenous materials. Either the editorial work was not completed, or the compiler wearied or had his attention and energies diverted to other ends, so that the work could not be, or at least was not, as thoroughly done as in the earlier portion. In the fully edited parts of the *Regiam* all of the styles of writs given by Glanvill are omitted and in the rest of the work only a few remain, and these would probably have been deleted if editing had been carried further. Five however remain in II, 16 (II, 13 in APS) which seems hardly to have been revised at all. This policy of omission is understandable because Glanvill's styles are frequently cast in language only usable in English courts, because even by the later thirteenth century Scottish forms had diverged substantially from those in use in England.[59] Book II, 14, it has been contended,[60] may belong properly to Book IV, where it should follow IV, 41.

The date of the work is unknown, and a matter of dispute. The uncertainty is made greater by the doubts as to the true text. It is plainly later than Glanvill's *Tractatus* of *c.*1187. With two exceptions all the Scottish statutory material referred to antedates the reign of Alexander II

(1214–40). The two exceptions are the references to Alexander II, c. 9 (1214–40)[61] and Robert I, c. 19 (1318).[62] In favour of an early date, say 1230, are the facts that the compiler does not mention many matters which have been attributed with apparent justification to the reign of Alexander II and were relevant to topics dealt with in the *Regiam*. The Act Alexander II, c. 9, dealing with the right of sanctuary, could have been passed early in that king's reign and the reference to Robert I, c. 19, could have been a later copyist's interpolation. The references to Roman and canon law are almost certain later interpolations, from notes in various manuscripts. The most important evidence as to date is, however, the facts that trial by ordeal was condemned by the Fourth Lateran Council of the Church in 1215 and disappeared in England after about 1219[63] and that trial by combat was for practical purposes obsolete in England by the end of the thirteenth century,[64] though not formally abolished until 1819.[65] Glanvill expounded trial by combat at some length, but this account is omitted from *Regiam Majestatem*. Alexander II, c. 6, which is possibly to be dated to 1230, gave the option of the inquest or *visnetum* in lieu of the ordeal in all criminal cases, and Neilson[66] reached the view that the ordeal was abolished in Scotland in 1230, and that from about the same time the inquest was an alternative available in criminal cases and further that trial by combat fell into disuse in Scotland about the same time though there are traces of it more than three centuries later. The compiler's refusal to copy Glanvill on these points suggests that he was aware of the current state of the law in Scotland in 1230, and amended Glanvill's text accordingly. This suggests that the date is not earlier than 1230 but not necessarily much later. Indeed Neilson[67] suggested that *Regiam Majestatem* must have been completed before the date of Alexander II, c. 8, which he assigned to 1230. This dating of that Act, however, is not certain.

The fact that the Romano-canonical texts were almost certainly copied from Goffredo of Trani and that Goffredo's *Summa* was written between 1241 and 1246[68] suggests a date not earlier than 1250 or thereabouts for the *Regiam*. Richardson[69] regarded the earliest possible date as *c*. 1240 and thought that the probable date was 1240 × 1255.

The reference in *Regiam Majestatem* II, 46 (II, 40 in APS) to *Praerogativa Regis*, if it is original and not a copyist's interpolation, may indicate a rather later date, because this work has been dated to not earlier than 1255.[70] A possibly significant but not conclusive argument for an early date is the writer's reliance on Glanvill but total absence of reference to Bracton's *De Legibus Angliae* of *c*. 1250. But it could be that he had not got hold of a copy or decided not to use it.

Lord Hailes[71] drew attention to the text in the Cromertie MS. of *Regiam Majestatem* II, 56 (II, 50 in APS), tracing it to the passage in the Decretals of Boniface VIII (Pope 1294–1303) in the Sext I, 3, 8, which were not published until 1298. But the same passage recurs in Glanvill's *Tractatus* of 1187 at VII, 17. This cannot accordingly by itself be taken as evidencing a post-1298 date.

In favour of a late date, say 1320, is the reference to Robert I, c. 19 (1318) but this was only one chapter of a substantial body of important legislation[72] passed as part of the reconstruction after the Wars of

Independence and it raises the question why the writer, if he were writing in 1320, did not mention any other legislation or legal development between 1250 and 1320. It has been contended[73] that this reference cannot be an interpolation, that only two or three of the chapters of 1318 legislation were relevant, and that the book was an element in the reconstruction of the kingdom after the devastation and disorders of the Wars of Independence, an attempt at a post-war restatement, and accordingly falls to be dated about 1320. This may be supported by some of the verbal changes made by the compiler from Goffredo's text, which put points in an imperative, legislative, way, as by changing *Verius puto in hoc casu* into *In hoc casu volumus* . . .[74] and *illud autem non omitto* into *illud autem statuimus*.[75]

Whichever of these dates is correct, it is almost certain that the compiler was a cleric, a canonist rather than a civilian, and clear that he was an intelligent, scholarly man who deserves to be called a jurist. The significant fact is that he was acquainted with Glanvill, the *Corpus Juris Civilis*, Goffredo, and the *Corpus Juris Canonici*, and was trying to work elements from these sources into a synthetic text.

It is not certain either what his purpose was. But if the prologue is accepted the purpose was *ad totius regni notitiam* and the subject-matter was *quaedam in curia generalia et frequentius usitata*. It was intended as a practical book giving guidance on current law and practice compiled by one familiar with Scottish practice rather than a systematic treatise or, still less, a study in jurisprudence or legal history.

Controversy has raged over the authenticity of the *Regiam*, that is, over whether the law it states ever was in observance in Scotland, or whether the work is spurious like the *False Decretals*, passing off as law what was never our law, and the view adopted in this controversy necessarily implies a view as to the compiler. Two stories have enjoyed some credence, both of which are relevant to authenticity and authorship. The first is that the work was compiled by or by order of David I, to whom a great deal of legal innovation in Scotland is justifiably, and a great deal more unjustifiably, attributed. This was Skene's view. In many legal systems early works have been attributed without justification to great lawgivers, and it is not surprising that some in medieval Scotland attributed the *Regiam* to David I. In the light of modern knowledge it is impossible to accept that what Glanvill wrote about 1187 had been written in Scotland in the time of David I (1124–53), and even less possible to believe that the legislation of David I was the source and Glanvill the copyist, as has on occasion been argued.

The second myth is that *Regiam Majestatem* originated in the attempt of Edward I of England, while governing Scotland, to make and enforce a statement of Scots law. Thus Chalmers[76] suggested that the *Regiam* was the product of the instruction by Edward I in his *Ordinacio super stabilitate terre Scocie*[77] of 1305 that there should be rehearsed in the presence of the lieges the laws of King David with the amendments and additions of later kings, and that these should then be further amended in so far as against God and reason. Edward had done this in Wales in 1281 in the *Statutum Walliae*[78] and the *Ordinacio* contains parallels to the *Statutum Walliae* in prescribing the establishment of officials who were to administer the conquered territory and in making provision for the ascertainment of the native laws for amendment and application. But we have no evidence that the mixed Anglo-Scottish working party to review the laws of Scotland ever met or reported, and the working of the *Ordinacio* was frustrated by Bruce's murder of Comyn at Dumfries on February 10, 1306, his assumption of the crown, and subsequent coronation at Scone on March 27.

Nor is the variant theory acceptable that the *Regiam* was a draft prepared in London to assist the working party, and that it later came to be regarded as authentic. In fairness to Edward, he does not appear to have been trying to impose English law on Scotland but to have been trying to ascertain what the Scottish customs were, as a basis for restating them. This theory seems unacceptable; the English members of the joint working party would have recognised the *Regiam* as being mostly Glanvill; the Scottish members would have recognised it as not being a statement of existing Scots law.[79]

Neither theory of royal inspiration appears at all convincing and both can be dismissed. There is no convincing evidence that the work was compiled other than unofficially and privately.

The attitudes of the later Scottish jurists to the question of authenticity are worth considering. Balfour's *Practicks* is largely founded on the *Regiam* and cites it repeatedly. Craig initially attacked the plagiarist who had passed off Glanvill's *Tractatus* as a work on the law of Scotland[80] but in some 40 later passages he cites the *Regiam* as an authority[81] and at one point calls it *jus nostrum scriptum vetus*.[82] Hope in his *Major Practicks* accepted it and quoted it frequently. Stair unhesitatingly laid down that "those books called *Regiam Majestatem* are no part of our law."[83] Mackenzie[84] also accepted it, as did Dirleton.[85] Bankton[86] devoted space to asserting its authenticity. Lord Hailes reached the conclusion that the arguments for the antiquity of the *Regiam* were inconclusive.[87] Erskine in his *Principles*[88] stated the view that the *Regiam* was "a private transcript of Glanvill . . . altered so as to adapt it to notorious practice in Scotland and feigned to have been compiled by order of David I," but in his *Institute* (1773)[89] came to the conclusion that the more probable opinion was that the treatise is what it bears to be, and that the whole of Skene's collection, even if not technically authoritative, might be used in proof of our ancient customs and was of excellent use towards understanding the history and gradual progress of our law.

Walter Ross[90] in 1794 examined the issue carefully and asserted that independently of its aid, it would be impossible to understand anything of the history of our law. Hume[91] called it our oldest book of law and cited it repeatedly, and in his *Lectures*[92] accepted as conclusive reasons for withholding assent from the *Regiam* as a genuine work of the time of David I, but thought it was "undoubtedly an ancient compilation, not much later probably than the time of Alexander III, and never could have grown into that degree of credit which it had long ago gained with our people, and even with the legislature, unless it had borne a strong resemblance at least to the actual usages and laws of the country."

Ferguson,[93] though accepting that the *Regiam* was largely of foreign origin, founds heavily on it, but Riddell[94] thought that it could not fairly be trusted. Bell[95] dismissed it as spurious. Cosmo Innes,[96] however, was unconvinced. Chalmers[97] argued for it as a fourteenth-century compilation.

Among the modern scholars George Neilson,[98] David Murray[99] and Sir Philip Hamilton-Grierson[1] do not dismiss the work as spurious.

The fact that much of the text is admittedly copied from or adapted from Glanvill and other parts from other sources does not establish that the work is spurious. It is spurious and false only if it states as Scots law what was not in fact in use as law in Scotland. It is a perfectly understandable mode of setting down a statement of one's own law to copy verbatim or substantially from a foreign book if in fact that book states with general accuracy what one's own law and practice are, and merely to omit or alter the parts where there are differences, particularly at a time when plagiarism and infringement of copyright were not heeded. Moreover it is hard to ignore the fact that people only two or three centuries separated, and not, as we are, six or seven centuries away, from the law of the time represented, did not condemn the books. The Scottish Parliament did not regard the book as a fraud.

In 1471 and 1475 it was enacted[2] that persons on partial (*i.e.* not impartial) inquests or assizes should be punished after the form of the king's law in the first book of his majesty, *contra temere jurantes super assisam*, while in 1487 it was ordained[3] that persons convicted of maintaining or defending traitors and other trespassers should be punished after the form of the king's law and of *Regiam Majestatem*. The authenticity of the old book was clearly still believed down to the late fifteenth century. In the sixteenth[4] and repeatedly in the seventeenth and eighteenth centuries the *Regiam* was cited in debate. A visitor to the Parliament House in 1629 observed that "most of their law is Acts of Parliament and *Regiam Majestatem*."[5] In 1674 the *Regiam* was libelled in an indictment and its relevancy was upheld after challenge.[6]

"The fact which has too long been overlooked is that, whatever be the date and origin of the *Regiam*, it has actually been treated as an authentic repository of old Scots Law by many of our leading writers, and employed as a more or less reliable and authoritative source throughout the whole of the early formative period of Scottish legal principles and institutions. Such is the only conclusion which is indicated by the statute book from the earliest date from which the statutes are completely preserved, and by the reported decisions from almost the earliest period of our judicial records. However 'doubtful the quality of the brick',[7] the *Regiam* and its associated treatises have in fact been built into the structure of the law of Scotland; and no investigation into the history of that system would be adequate which did not assign an important place to the part played by the materials which Skene incorporated in his compilation of 1609."[8]

"The truth seems to be that Scoto-Norman law started from a point earlier than Glanvill, and by the close of the 13th century had reached a point far in advance of Glanvill, without necessarily, or even probably, having passed through the exact phase which Glanvill depicted. But to a fairly close approximation Glanvill provided an adequate account of the cardinal features of the system which Scotland was building up, and there was justification for choosing the *Tractatus* as the basis of a Scottish restatement of the law. In broad outline *Regiam Majestatem* must be near the truth. In detail it must always be examined with a critical eye. It is certainly neither accurate nor exhaustive as an account of the position which had been reached by 1300, but it cannot be very far out as a general description of things as they were about fifty or sixty years before."[9]

Modern practice is an unsafe criterion of authenticity, but the fact remains that the *Regiam* was referred to in the House of Lords in 1839 as "the most venerable of all authorities in the law of Scotland,"[10] and cited in the Courts of Session[11] and Justiciary[12] in 1934.

The fair conclusion probably is that sometime in the latter part of the thirteenth century an unknown cleric, who was a knowledgeable and competent legal scholar, compiled from various sources a reasonably accurate statement of the Scots law of his time.

Quoniam Attachiamenta, so-called from its opening words, is a tract repeatedly coupled with *Regiam Majestatem* in the early statutes as one of the ancient books of our law and as one of the bases for revision and restatement of the law. But it is in fact quite different from *Regiam* in origin and nature.

It is a systematic manual of procedure in baron and other feudal courts, and hence was sometimes sub-titled *Leges Baronum*. Its authenticity never seems to have been questioned. It seems to be original; at least no model is known. It is based not on any foreign text but on practical experience in the courts; it is a more mature work than *Regiam* and utilises a technical terminology which had developed after the time of the *Regiam*.

The work deals with attachments, or legal ties whereby a defender was compelled to stand to the law and answer a party complaining against him, citation, excuses and defaults by defenders, the defender who appears on the fourth day, payment of a debt due under decree, repledging, taking poinds for a disputed debt, who might give doom, how a man might defend himself against a claim by his lord or the king, who might speak in court, the rule that a free man might not be incarcerated, escheats, and the various brieves, including specimens of their wording.

The brieves discussed are the brieve of distress for debt, the brieve of convention (agreement), for releasing a cautioner, of mortancestor, of dissasine, on breach of the king's protection, of warranty, of serfdom and of right within burghs. Other brieves omitted by Skene from his text but included by Thomson are the brieve of safe-conduct, safe conduct for one or more seafarers, of living within burgh, and of caption.

All civil claims are treated as *placita de wrang et unlauch*: everything flowed from wrongdoing. There is no appreciation of the different grounds for civil claims which the Roman jurists had distinguished at least a millennium earlier.

The work does not occur in the earliest but only in the later manuscripts and therefore falls to be dated between about 1280 and 1380. Some of the styles run in the name of King Alexander, which indicates for them a date earlier than 1286 when Alexander III died. But the work as a whole probably belongs to the mid-fourteenth century.

It was first printed by Skene along with the *Regiam*, but his text of 101 chapters includes much miscellaneous material drawn from early statutes and other sources which is out of place in and totally obscures the coherence and shape of *Quoniam* as a manual of practice. Thomas Thomson's text[13] is much better and pretty certainly close to the original. Thomson, however, included a chapter on the regulation of fishing and hunting[14] and three styles of brieve which Skene had excluded. But as with the *Regiam* it is Skene's text of *Quoniam* which has been used and referred to by Scots lawyers and for this reason, as the authorised version, it was taken by Lord Cooper as the basis of his edition.[15]

The book is immensely valuable historically as a source of our knowledge of the procedure which was in operation from the fourteenth century until much later.

We have no knowledge of the author, but he would not necessarily have been a cleric nor acquainted with Roman or canon law. He was clearly an experienced practitioner in feudal courts and shows a detailed acquaintance with practice. He uses a technical vocabulary, gives specimens of oral pleading, styles for interlocutors and minutes of court.

These early works are of immense interest not merely because of their antiquity but because of the repeated references to them as the "auld lawis" and for the way they indicate the consistency of the emerging law of Scotland with that of Western European civilisation. The centre of interest is in procedure, the brieves or writs which assign cases to particular judges, the methods of proof, the king's peace and similar topics. But there are recognisable statements on topics which later become well-known matters of common law, contracts or pactions, dowries, legal rights in succession, agency, loan, sale and others. Many of what became settled principles of Scots law are identifiable, some in moderately developed forms.

The *Liber de Judicibus* is another source of early law, texts of which are also found in some of the MSS.[16] which contain *Regiam Majestatem*, but it was not included by Skene in his volume. It consists partly of passages from Glanvill which were also incorporated in the *Regiam*, but includes also some omitted from the *Regiam* and some other, rather miscellaneous, materials. It sometimes includes an edited version of a passage from Glanvill which is unedited in the *Regiam*. It appears accordingly to be largely founded on the same sources as the *Regiam*, and is rather a different version than a totally independent source of early law. It also is repeatedly cited as an authority in Balfour's *Practicks* but its origin and purpose is unknown. We have no knowledge of the compiler.[17]

Among the treatises printed by Skene in his Scottish (though not in his Latin) edition of *Regiam Majestatem* is one on *The Forme and Manner of Baron Court*. It extends to 18 pages and 81 short chapters (ignoring the jump from c. 20 to c. 38). There are many marginal cross-references to *Quoniam Attachiamenta*.

Belief that *Regiam Majestatem* at least, and frequently *Quoniam Attachiamenta* also, were authentic statements of older Scots law, is illustrated by the way they were repeatedly referred to as the basis for various projected restatements of the law in the later medieval period.

This theme requires an excursus. In March 1425–26 it was ordained[18] by the king (James I), and Parliament,[19] "that sex wise and discrete men of ilkane of the thre estaitis, the quhilkis knowis the lawis best, sal be chosyn, quha sen frande and gyll to help na man, sal se and examyn the bukis of law of this realm, that is to say, *Regiam Majestatem* and *Quoniam Attachiamenta*, and mend the lawis that nedis mendment." Nothing seems to have come of this and the MSS. later in date than 1425 continue to show considerable diversity of texts.

In 1447, 12 persons were to be chosen to examine all acts of Parliament and general council held in the king's (James II's) or his father's lifetime, to show those that were good for the next parliament.[20]

In 1469 Parliament referred to a commission of 12 to "avise and commone" upon "the reduction of the king's lawis, *Regiam Majestatem*, Actis, Statutis, and other Bukis, to be put in a volume, and to be autorizit, and the laif to be destroyit." There is no trace of any work of this commission[21] and neither the former, nor, fortunately, the latter part of its remit was acted upon.

In 1473 the lords and barons in Parliament, for the declaration of divers obscure matters that were now in our laws, requested the king to select two persons of wisdom, conscience and knowledge from each estate to clarify these matters and report to the next parliament, "and at that time there be a buke maid containing all the lawis of this realme that shall remain at a place where the laif may have copy, and that no other buke be used but of the copy of it, for the great diversity now found in divers books put in by divers persons that are called men of law. And they that will use practick that they use nane other lawis as for the lawis of this realme but them that are found in that book."[22]

Then in 1507 the art of printing was introduced into Scotland under royal auspices, for the purpose of "imprinting within our realme the Bukis of our Lawis, Actis of Parliament," and other works, and exclusive privileges were conferred on Chepman and Myllar, the first King's Printers, to encourage them in this work.[23] But there is no evidence that this part of their purpose was fulfilled, and not till 1541 were some Acts of James V printed.

In 1566 another commission was appointed by Queen Mary under the Great Seal, giving them full power and authority,

> "to Visie, sycht and correct the lawis of this Realme maid be Her and Her maist nobill progenitouris . . . beginnand at the bukis of the law called *Regiam Majestatem* and *Quoniam Attachiamenta* and swa consequentlie following be progress of tyme unto the dait of this commissioun. Swa that na utheris bot the saidis lawis sychtit mendit and correctit . . . salbe be Her privilege imprentit or have place, faith or autoritie to be allegit and reheirsit afoir ony Her Jugeis and Justices quwhatsumever in jugement and outwith."

This was the project which resulted in the publication of the volume known as *The Black Acts*.[24]

In 1567 Parliament agreed that a commission be given to sufficient persons, "to mak ane body of the civil and municipal lawis dividit in heads conform to the fashion of the law Romane. And the heads as they are reddy to be brought to the parliament to be confirmed."[25]

Then in 1574–75 came the appointment[26] of the commission including James (Balfour), commendator of Pittenweem, "to visite the Bukis of the Law, Actis of Parliament, and Decisions befoir the Sessioun, and draw the forme of the body of our lawis, alsweill of that quhilk is already statute, as thay thingsis that were meit and convenient to be statute . . . quhairthrow thair may be ane certaine writtin law to all oure Soverane lordis jugeis and ministeris of law to juge and decyde be." The result of the work of this commission was the book known as Balfour's *Practicks*.[27]

In 1578 yet another commission, which included one Thomas Craig, advocate, was appointed "to treat upoun the lawes,"[28] "to visie, sycht and considre the saidis lawis, and to reasone and confer thaireupoun," and to report to parliament, "Sua that they all in are voce may estableis the same as perpetuall lawes as salbe agreit hereafter thereupon."

In 1592 Parliament passed an Act[29] ordaining the Chancellor and others including Mr John Skene, advocate, and Mr Thomas Hamilton, apparent of Priestfield, "to visite the lawis and actis maid in this present Parliament, and all utheris municipall lawis and actis of Parliament bygane . . . and to consider quhat lawis or actis necessarlie wald be knawin to the subjectis, qubilkis suld be kepit and obeyit be thame" and authentic copies printed. The fruit of this was Skene's *Lawis and Actis* of 1597.

Then in 1598[30] to combat ignorance of the law the Lords of Session were to take order how the acts printed might be bought by all subjects of substance, and in 1607 an Act[31] provided for the printing of Skene's *Regiam Majestatem*.

To complete the tale of this perennial yearning for a restatement or codification of Scots law it is necessary to go on into the next century. In 1628[32] Charles I granted a commission under the Great Seal for surveying, recognoscing and considering of the laws, statutes and acts of parliament, printed and not printed, with the customs and consuetudes of the same. In 1630 a convention received a letter from Charles I for the opinion of the commissioners. It included[33] the request for an order "for proceeding according to our commission granted for reviewing the laws and practicks of that kingdom that all things necessary to be treated of in the next parliament may be the better prepared against that time." Persons were nominated[34] and their names approved in 1633.[35] Then a statute,[36] narrating the ineffective commissions since 1628, granted power and authority to a group, including Sir James Skene (Sir John's son), Sir Alexander Gibson of Durie, and Sir Robert Spottiswoode,

> "to read, recognosce and consider the whole laws, statutes, printed and unprinted, customes and consuetudes of the kingdom which are and have been observed as laws either in the civil or criminal judicatories, and which have been received in practice by the decreets of the lords of session or justice general . . . together with the books entitled *Regiam Majestatem* which contains ane record of the ancient lawis and customs observed within the said kingdom, And after due consideration thereof, to conclude and determine anent the true sense meaning and interpretation of all such lawis and acts of parliament which are unclear and doubtsome in the sense and

may receive divers interpretations . . . and to collect and sett down
the whole customs and generall consuetudes inviolably observed in
the said kingdom."

In 1639[37] there was another commission for surveying the laws, and in
1649[38] yet another, including Mr James Dalrymple, later Viscount Stair,

"to revise and consider all the laws statutes and actis of parliament of
this kingdom . . . and . . . all the consuetudes and practices of the
kingdom which have had the force of lawis And have been received
as practicks. . . . Together with the old registers of the buik called
regiam majestatem. . . . To the effect that . . . they may . . . draw up
and compyll ane formal modall and frame of a buik of just and
equitable lawis to be established and authorised . . . for governing of
the lieges in time coming."

Then in 1681[39] Charles II granted commission to persons to be named
to consider "the laws and customs and judicial practicks, and to collect
and digest the laws and acts of Parliament, customs, decisions and forms
of process into such order and methods as shall seem most fit and
expedient to them, and also to determine the true sense, meaning and
interpretation of all such laws, actis and practicks as are unclear or
doubtful in themselves."

Finally in 1695[40] a proposal was brought in for revising the laws and
practicques and after some debate delayed to the next parliament. It was
then enacted[41] that the King (William II, or III by English reckoning),

"nominate seven to revise the whole written lawes and acts of
Parliament of this kingdom, and reduce the same to the best order
for the direction and use of all concerned, as also to revise the whole
Acts of Sederunt and Decisions or Practiques of the said Lords of
Session since the institution of the College of Justice, and to take
notice and remark what Acts of Sederunt are in use and what
Decisions should be held for Practicques to be still adverted to in
judgment and what not . . . And generally to do all and sundry other
things that may best clear ascertain and establish the Practicque or
course of Decisions to be thereafter observed by the Lords of Session
in judgement."

This terminates the two-and-a-half century yearning for a revised and
consolidated restatement of the laws of Scotland. Most of the commissions proved abortive but what was produced, Balfour's *Practicks*,
Skene's *Lawis and Actis* and Skene's *Regiam Majestatem*, are immensely
valuable historical records, even if we arrogantly believe today that they
could and should have been better done.

To revert after this excursus to the Auld Laws. Other collections of
materials and short treatises on the law are found in some of the MSS.
They show that in the medieval period there were some lawyers with the
interest and the will to collect and write down these materials, though we
do not know who they were. The materials fall into two groups, collections of what purport to be legislation of early Scottish kings and rules set
down in something resembling the form of a treatise or text.

Several of the earlier MSS. contain the text of laws attributed to Malcolm MacKenneth,[42] who reigned from 1005 to 1034. The attribution cannot possibly be accepted as the laws refer repeatedly to officers of state, such as the Chancellor, Chamberlain, and Constable, who did not make an appearance till much later. It must be deemed a fourteenth-century collection, though embodying materials of an earlier date.

The *Leges Inter Brettos et Scots*[43] appear in three versions, in Latin, old French and Scots. It seems to have been a body of customary law which at one time prevailed widely but latterly applied only among the mixed peoples who inhabited Galloway. This body still had sufficient life for it to be expressly proscribed by Edward I's Ordinance for the Government of Scotland of 1305.[44] W. F. Skene[45] thought it was evidence that there existed at one time in Scotland a body of laws resembling that of other Celtic peoples. It certainly presents analogies to the Brehon Laws of Ireland in setting out a tariff of the payments due for the killing of one of various classes of the community, the tariff being related to the victim's status.

The *Assise Regis David*[46] comprises a body of legislation attributed to David I (1124—53) who has the reputation of having been a legislator. Many of the chapters commence, "Si quis ..." or "Statuit rex" or "Prohibuit rex" or "Decrevit et deliberavit rex." But whether they are authentic, or truly enactments of David I, is problematical. It cannot be all accepted without question or very critical scrutiny. Some of the MSS. and Skene include some of this material in *Quoniam Attachiamenta*.[46]

The *Assisa de Tolloneis* is a small piece but attested by a number of MSS.,[47] though not printed by Skene. It is attributed to David I and deals with customs duties levied by the king on various kinds of merchandise. Similarly the *Custuma Portuum*, comprising a prologue and four chapters, appears in several MSS.[48] but was not printed by Skene. It also is attributed to David I and deals with customs duties relative to ships. It seems in fact to be truly a version of the *Liber de Iudicibus*. To David I are also attributed the *Assise de Mensuris et Ponderibus*,[49] prescribing weights and measures, and the *Assisa Panis Vini et Cervisie*,[50] dealing with bread, wine and ale. The weight and values, however, relate to a later period; either a transcriber adjusted these to suit his own time or the collections are later than David I's time.

Skene also printed in his editions of *Regiam Majestatem* a text of the *Forest Laws*. Rules on this subject are found in various versions in many of the manuscripts containing also the *Regiam*,[51] and some of the clauses there have been borrowed from English *Consuetudines et Assisae Foreste*. This borrowing could have been from the late thirteenth century onwards. Edited versions, with the materials rearranged to some extent, include one in Balfour's *Practicks*.[52] Some of the rules may truly date from David I while others were probably introduced into Scotland by Edward I of England about the end of the thirteenth century.

The *Leges Quatuor Burgorum* or *Leges et Consuetudines Burgorum* appears in substantially the same form in many of the MSS. and in Skene.[53] Some of the manuscripts ascribe these to David I as "constitute per dominum David Regem Scotie," though they were rather collected and sanctioned in his reign than drafted or enacted by him. But they are the earliest collected body of customary rules known in Scotland. They represent the code of Berwick, Roxburgh, Edinburgh and Stirling, later regarded as authoritative generally. The collection is important as giving early information about the origins of burghal organisation and the privileges of burgesses. The rules are not, however, indigenous, and many of the customs have clearly been adopted from customs recognised in the boroughs of Northern England.[54] Nevertheless they give a basis for comparison of early Scottish burghal law with corresponding principles found in England and other European countries and they are enlightening about early mercantile law, property and rights in succession. The authenticity of the collection does not seem ever to have been questioned.

The *Statuta Gildae* appear in several MSS. with not great variations and Skene printed most of the chapters.[55] These are a supplementary code of burgh laws, originating at Berwick, and designed for the government of the gild merchant of that town. The date is probably about 1250.

Thomson and Innes printed[56] the Articles of Inquiry setting out the questions the Chamberlain Ayre was supposed, according to the use of Scotland, to pose when making a circuit of the Scottish burghs. This probably dates from the latter part of the reign of Robert I.

Iter Camerarii is a short text in 29 chapters setting out the functions and powers of the Chamberlain over burgesses and tradesmen of different kinds. These were extensive, and his functions may have antedated the burgh courts. This text is attested by a number of manuscripts[57] and a text was printed by Skene in his edition of *Regiam Majestatem*. It is probably later than the Articles of Inquiry, belonging to the end of the fourteenth century.

The *Ordo Justiciariae* is a short text of 12 chapters found in some manuscripts.[58] It deals with process in the justicier's ayre and gives styles of precepts applicable to some particular circumstances, such as a precept of summons to sheriffs on a brieve of novel dissasine. The writs run in the name of William, Earl of Orkney, who was justiciar in the reign of James II, but some of the procedure seems to belong to an earlier period.

The *Leges et Consuetudines Marchiarum inter Scotiam et Angliam*[59] are attributed to 1249. These rules are not so much legislation as treaty, having been established by a great assize of knights of both countries which met probably at Lochmabenstane in Gretna parish, Dumfriesshire. It embodies much which can be traced to the earlier laws of Scotland and England.

The *Assise Regis Willelmi* (*i.e.* William the Lion, 1165–1214) appears in many MSS. but Skene printed only a few chapters of it.[60] The authenticity of some of this material is doubtful and the validity of its attribution to William the Lion very doubtful. Some, such as c. XII, may well be authentic, and some, such as c. XXIII, very probably are.

The statutes of Alexander II (1214–49) appear in many MSS.[61] and some of this is probably justifiably attributed to him.

The statutes of Alexander III (1249–85/86)[62] are again more of the nature of treaty than legislation.

The so-called statutes of Queen Margaret (1285/86–90)[63] comprise only the agreement (in old French) of the magnates of Scotland with

Edward I of England, entered into at Brigham on March 17, 1289, relative to the proposed marriage of the young Margaret with Prince Edward (later Edward II).

The statutes of Robert I (Bruce) (1306–29) are included in many of the MS. collections[64] and are indeed, in many cases, preserved in the original or in good and early transcripts. Thus the important legislation of 1318 was copied into the Register of Arbroath Abbey,[65] probably at the instance of Bernard de Linton, the Chancellor and Abbot there. Some of the MSS. distinguish first and second collections of this king's legislation.

One man of note in this early period who deserves mention as a legal administrator is Bernard, usually but possibly wrongly called de Linton. He was "one of the really outstanding medieval royal chancellors."[66] He became Robert Bruce's chancellor in October 1308; about 1311 he was made Abbot of Arbroath, became Bishop of Sodor in 1328, relinquished the Chancellorship in 1328, and died in 1331. What little is known of his career suggests a strong personality, a vigorous supporter of Bruce and a strong leader. He probably went to Norway to conduct the negotiations which led up to the treaty of Inverness with Norway in 1312.

It is probable that the king's chapel or chancellor's office was restored very shortly after the end of the War of Independence.[67] Bernard both restored the practices in use under Alexander III and introduced new ones, such as an increase in the use of letters patent, which was less formal than the old charter, and the introduction of the inspection, a new writ used to confirm the titles of holders of old rights. Not least it became accepted that the king's chapel need not travel with the king but acquired a more or less fixed location, possibly at Arbroath Abbey. In consequence more use would have to be made of the Privy Seal, normally kept by an official with the king and authorising his immediate commands, while the Great Seal remained in the custody of the chancellor.

Under Bernard rolls again began to be kept containing copies of grants made by the king to supporters of property forfeited by his opponents, and some of these enrolments survive.

He may have participated in the drafting and the enactment of a set of statutes enacted at Scone in December 1318,[68] with the object of putting into effect part of the plans for reconstruction after the War of Independence. These include extension of the application of the brieve of mortancestor to claims to succeed a grandparent, a change adopting only part of an extension made to the corresponding English writ some 70 years earlier and effected without introducing the English terms and forms, and amending the brieve of novel dissasine but in a way which adopted some of the reforms adopted in England but not slavishly copying the English model. These and other reforms suggest that Scots law was developing about 70 or so years behind English and facing some of the same difficulties but showing an independent spirit and not sedulously copying the fictions, formalities and technicalities which were already enmeshing English law.

Stylistic argument suggests that Bernard was the draftsman, or at least the reviser, of five important state papers during the reign of Robert I, the

letter to Philip of France in 1308, the church's declaration for Bruce in
1309, the manifestoes regarding the succession to the throne in 1315 and
1318, and the peace terms of 1326.[69]

In 1320 Bernard was almost certainly the draftsman of the letter to the
Pope which is known to posterity as the Declaration of Arbroath,[70] and
was in attendance when peace was agreed, bringing to an end the War of
Independence, in 1328.[71]

There also survive from about the beginning of the fourteenth century
some collections of styles of writs made either by chancery clerks or legal
practitioners for their own use. They are always associated with collections of statutory provisions, statements of principle and other materials.
Among themselves they are quite consistent. Collections are found in the
Berne, Ayr and Bute manuscripts.[72] Those in the Berne MS. number 322
but are all entirely English, of the thirteenth century. The Ayr MS. was
considered by Cosmo Innes[73] as "the most purely Scotch of our ancient
collections of styles." The *Tabula* lists 81 brieves, but 35 are on pages
which have been lost at some time. This MS. dates from the early
fourteenth century and the practice which the styles disclose probably
spans the period 1280–1329. The Bute MS. styles comprise 109 brieves
which probably describe practice down to about 1375. Thirty-three of
these correspond closely to forms in the Ayr MS. and some 18 others are
consistent with the *Tabula* titles in the Ayr MS. There are, however, a few
new brieves and some further variants of others.

The *Register of Brieves* edited by Lord Cooper for the Stair Society
consists of the text of the Ayr MS. with an annotated calender of the styles
in the Bute MS. The forms given comprise firstly a number of conveyancing writs, such as of a crown charter of confirmation and of a charter of
resignation by a crown vassal, all of which are illustrated by actual deeds
now printed in cartularies and the *Regesta Regum Scottorum*. Secondly,
there is a large number of rather miscellaneous writs of an executive
character, such as safe-conducts and grants of trading privileges. Thirdly,
there is a large collection of forms of process, some 25 original brieves
intended to initiate legal processes and some 12 judicial brieves, which
are in effect interlocutory orders incidental to processes already pending.
The form of action most commonly mentioned is the *compulsio*, a writ
addressed to a judge ordering him to coerce a defender to do something.
There are also three grants of royal approval to the appointment of an
attorney to act for the grantee either in a particular matter or generally.
Some of these writs concerned with process have been adopted from
English practice, notably the writs of mortancestor and novel dissasine,
but they have been modified from the English model. That the collection
of styles is not complete is known from examples in other records of other
kinds of transactions, such as leases.

Another formulary, known as *Formulary E*,[74] contains many styles
similar to those in the Ayr and Bute MSS.

Many of the manuscripts containing the Auld Laws include also a text
sometimes entitled *De Composicione Cartarum*,[75] which contains advice
on the drafting of charters with observations on the legal effect of various
clauses, on impediments and defects, and warnings on how to avoid
certain dangers. There is material taken from English statutes, con-

veyancing handbooks and Bracton's *De Legibus*. It cannot be earlier than the fourteenth century.

The existence of these collections is clear evidence of the existence in early fourteenth-century Scotland of competent lawyers, cognisant of practice in England, but able and willing to adapt that knowledge to Scottish conditions.

NOTES

[1] ESC, No. 5.

[2] *Ibid.*, No. 12.

[3] *Ibid.*, Nos. 19–22.

[4] These are conveniently collected and printed in Lawrie, *Early Scottish Charters* (1905); *Regesta Regum Scottorum*, I (Malcolm IV), ed. G. W. S. Barrow (1960); *Regesta Regum Scottorum*, II (William the Lion), ed. G. W. S. Barrow (1971). There were certainly many charters and other writs which have perished, far more than have survived.

[5] RRS, II, 31–32.

[6] RRS, I, 60.

[7] *e.g.* ESC, Nos. 121, 178; RRS, I, Nos. 105, 132.

[8] *e.g.* RRS, I, Nos. 115, 141.

[9] RRS, I, No. 184.

[10] *e.g.* ESC, Nos. 70, 158.

[11] *e.g.* RRAN, Nos. 419 (1087 × 1099), 1799 (probably 1100 × 1117).

[12] *e.g.* ESC, Nos. 70, 209; RRS, I, Nos. 118, 195.

[13] *e.g.* ESC, Nos. 132; RRS, I, Nos. 14, 18, 24, 30, 145, 179, 181, 220. On these see Harding, "The medieval brieves of protection and the development of the common law," 1966 J.R. 115, which brings out that these grants of protection gave rise to the later procedures of trespass in England and wrang and unlauch in Scotland and consequently to the law of tort and delict in the two legal systems.

[14] RRAN, Nos. 1322, 1323.

[15] RRS, I, Nos. 162, 233, 258.

[16] *e.g.* RRS, I, Nos. 126, 177.

[17] RRS, I, No. 166.

[18] RRS, I, No. 131.

[19] On the seals see J. Stevenson and M. Wood, *Scottish Heraldic Seals*; W. de G. Birch, *History of Scottish Seals* (1905).

[20] RRS, I, Nos. 174, 195; Barrow, p. 82.

[21] Barrow, RRS, I, 89.

[22] APS, I, 212–213, 317–325.

[23] APS, I, 220–223, 369–392.

[24] RRS, II.

[25] RRS, II, Nos. 71, 124, 281, 406, 442, 475.

[26] No. 281.

[27] Statute Law Revision Act, 1425 (APS, II, 10, c. 10); Manswearing Act, 1471 (APS, II, 100, c. 9); Criminal Juries Act, 1475, (APS, II, 111, c. 4); Remit to Committee Act, 1487, c. 115 = 1469, c. 20) (APS, II, 97 c. 20).

[28] APS, I, 29; III, 40, c. 42.

[29] On him see Chap. 3, *infra.*

[30] APS, I, 30. On Skene see Chap. 4, *infra.*

[31] Commission on Law Act, 1578 (APS, III, 105, c. 18).

[32] Note in Skene's writing in the Bute MS: APS, I, 182.

[33] George Neilson found copies of both the Latin and Scottish editions with revisions and corrections in the editor's own hand: Neilson, "Sir John Skene's *Memorabilia Scotica* and revisals of *Regiam Majestatem*" (1924) Trans. Glasgow Archaeological Soc. VII.

[34] RPC (2nd ser.) II, 365; IV, 137; V, 9, 11, 32; Spottiswoode, *Practicks*, 368; APS, VI, (2) 299.

[35] Ranulph de Glanville, *Tractatus de Legibus et Consuetudinibus regni Angliae* (c. 1187): see the editions of G. E. Woodbine (1932) and G. D. G. Hall (1965).

[36] Henricus de Bracton, *De Legibus et Consuetudinibus Angliae Libri quinque* (c. 1250): see the editions of G. E. Woodbine (6 vols., 1915–42) and S. E. Thorne (4 vols., 1968–77).

[37] *Fleta, seu Commentarius Juris Anglicani* (c. 1290); see the edition of H. G. Richardson and G. O. Sayles (Selden Society, 3 vols, 1955–72).

[38] APS, I, 177. John Buchanan, "The MSS. of *Regiam Majestatem*" (1937) 49 J.R. 217. All of these MSS are two centuries or more later than the probable date of the original text, so probably represent more than one generation of copying with consequential errors. A. A. M. Duncan, "*Regiam Majestatem*: A reconsideration," 1961 J.R. 199 at p. 202,

considers that B.M. Add. MS. 18, 111 represents the earliest known version of the text.

³⁹ For criticisms of his work see Lord Hailes, *Annals of Scotland*, III, p. 279; Alexander Wight, *Elections* (1784), p. 21; Cosmo Innes, APS, I, 21. George Neilson, *Skene's Memorabilia Scotica* (1923), while critical, urged that Skene's services should be remembered rather than his imperfections, and Lord Cooper (*Regiam Majestatem*, (Stair Soc.), Intro., p. 20) observes that "Skene rendered to Scots law a service for which he is entitled to respectful gratitude rather than patronising censure or ill-natured abuse."

⁴⁰ APS, I, 597–641; this is based mainly on the Bute and Cromertie MSS., but omits the frequent references therein to the *Corpus Juris Civilis* and *Corpus Juris Canonici*, probably on the ground that these had probably been incorporated by later readers and copyists from notes made on copies and were not original. Neilson, *Trial by Combat* (1890), held that this text could not be accepted as definitive and final.

⁴¹ Skene's marginal notes to his Latin edition of 1609 give the references to Glanvill.

⁴² *Jus Feudale*, I, 108. See also Hale, *History of the Common Law of England* (1713), Chap. 10.

⁴³ The texts are set out in parallel in APS, I, 135 *et seq*. Glanvill and the *Regiam* are both printed in D. Houard's *Traités sur les Coutumes Anglo Normandes publiés en Angleterre* (4 vols., 1776). The best editions of Glanvill are that by G. E. Woodbine (1932) and by G. D. G. Hall (1965). On Glanvill see also P. & M. I, 162; Holdsworth, *H.E.L.* II; S. F. C. Milsom, *Historical Foundations of the Common Law* (2nd ed., 1981).

⁴⁴ The main passages are listed in *Regiam Majestatem* (ed. Cooper, Stair Soc.), p. 39.

⁴⁵ See the *Collatio* of the *Regiam* and Glanvill in APS, I, 135, 174.

⁴⁶ These are identified in Habakkuk Bisset's *Rolment of Courtis* (ed. Hamilton-Grierson), III, 18, n. 2. Lord Cooper (*Regiam Majestatem* (Stair Soc.), Intro., pp. 23–24) identifies 23 references in *R.M.* with early Scottish legislation.

⁴⁷ Edward I expressly proscribed these laws in his *Ordinacio super stabilitate terre Scotiae* of 1305; APS, I, 122, 178. But these chapters may be an addition to the original text.

⁴⁸ References to Stair Society edition. In the text in APS, I, 605 *et seq*. these passages are I, 29–32, II, 1–7, II, 10–11 and II, 12, respectively.

⁴⁹ The passages are set out in parallel for comparison in *Regiam Majestatem* (ed. Cooper, Stair Soc.), 30–31.

⁵⁰ The passages are set out in H. G. Richardson, "Roman law in the *Regiam Majestatem*" (1955) 67 J.R. 155.

⁵¹ P. Stein, "The Source of the Romano-canonical part of *Regiam Majestatem*" (1969) 48 S.H.R. 107, 109.

⁵² Set out in parallel columns in Stein, *loc. cit.*, pp. 113–123.

⁵³ F. Maitland, *Selected Passages from the Works of Bracton and Azo* (Selden Soc., 1895); F. Schulz, "Critical Studies on Bracton's Treatise" (1943) 59 L.Q.R. 172; "Bracton and Raymond of Penafort" (1945) 61 L.Q.R. 286; H. G. Richardson, "Bracton: The Problem of his Text" (Selden Soc., Supp. Ser. 2 (1965)), 18.

⁵⁴ Stein, *loc. cit.*, 112; see also Stein, "Roman law in Scotland," *Ius Romanum Medii Aevi*, V, 13b (1968).

⁵⁵ P. & M., I, 481; Holdsworth, I, 473, II, 223; Maitland, *Collected Papers*, II, 182.

⁵⁶ Duncan, *loc. cit.*, 202.

⁵⁷ Cooper's ed., Supp. No. 22 and note thereon.

⁵⁸ For specimens of the editorial work see Lord Cooper's introduction to *Regiam Majestatem* (Stair Soc.), 34–35, 38–40.

⁵⁹ Lord Cooper, *Register of Brieves* (Stair Soc.), intro., 6.

⁶⁰ Duncan, *loc. cit.*, 209.

⁶¹ Skene, Supp. 32; IV, 53 in APS ed.

⁶² Skene, I, 11; I, 10 in APS ed.

⁶³ P. & M, II, 598–599.

⁶⁴ Holdsworth, I, 308–310.

⁶⁵ Appeal of Murder Act, 1819, passed in consequence of *Ashford* v. *Thornton* (1818) 1 B. & Ald. 475.

⁶⁶ *Trial by Combat*, 113–116.

⁶⁷ *Trial by Combat*, p. 116.

⁶⁸ Schulte, *Die Geschichte der Quellen und Literatur des kanonischen Rechts* (1875), II, 89; Naz, *Dictionnaire de droit canonique*, V, 952, who gives the date 1241–43; *Enciclopedia Italiano; Dizionario Enciclopedica Italiano*.

⁶⁹ "Roman Law in the *Regiam Majestatem*" (1945) 67 J.R. 155.

[70] P. & M. I, 481; Holdsworth, I, 473; II, 223; Maitland, *Collected Papers*, II, 182.

[71] *Examination of some of the Arguments for the High Antiquity of Regiam Majestatem* (1769), 9–10.

[72] P. & M., I, 481; T. M. Cooper, "The first Law Reform (Miscellaneous Provisions) Act" (1944) 56 J.R. 1.

[73] Duncan, "Regiam Majestatem, a reconsideration," 1961 J.R. 199 at p. 210.

[74] R.M. II, 13 (II, 10, in APS, I, 609).

[75] R.M. II, 15 (II, 12, in APS, I, 609).

[76] *Caledonia*, II, 732.

[77] APS, I, 119.

[78] *Statutes at Large*, IX, Appx., p. 3.

[79] Pollock and Maitland (P. & M., I, 222–223) dismissed this theory in the words: "Of all the various theories that have been started, that which ascribes this book to Edward I will seem to an 'Englishman the most improbable."

[80] J.F., I, 8, 11.

[81] *e.g.* II, 17, 20.

[82] *Ibid.*, II, 22, 27.

[83] *Inst.*, I, 1, 16.

[84] *Works*, I, 177; II, 55.

[85] *Doubts*, 30.

[86] *Inst.*, I, 29.

[87] *Annals of Scotland* (1769), III, 278, App., and *An Examination of some of the Arguments for the High Antiquity of Regiam Majestatem* (1769), in *Tracts relative to the History and Antiquities of Scotland* (1800).

[88] I, 1, 13.

[89] I, 1, 32–36.

[90] *Lectures*, II, 64.

[91] *Crimes*, I, 554.

[92] I, 16; see also I, 360, where he calls it "clearly a forgery."

[93] *Consistorial Law*, xix.

[94] *Peerage and Consistorial Law*, I, xvi.

[95] *Comm.*, II, 431.

[96] APS, I, 21; *Scotch Legal Antiquities*, pp. 3, 16; and his Preface to *Ancient Laws and Customs of the Burghs of Scotland* (Sc. Burgh Records Soc., 1868).

[97] *Caledonia* II, p. 727.

[98] *Trial by Combat* (1890), pp. 82–104.

[99] *Property of Married Persons* (1891), p. 34.

[1] Introduction to Bisset's *Rolment of Courtis*, Vol. III.

[2] APS, II, 100, c. 9; II, 111, c. 4.

[3] APS, II, 176, c. 3.

[4] *Towris* v. *Barbour* (1501) ADC III, No. 159; *Acts of the Lords of Council in Civil Causes* (ed. Hannay, 1932), 137 (1518); *Sheriff Court Book of Fife* (ed. Dickinson, S. H. S.), 201, 305 (1520); RPC, IV, 688 (1591); Pitcairn, *Criminal Trials*, I, 313 (1594).

[5] H.M.C., 13 (7), p. 82.

[6] *Birnie* v. *McKenzie* (1674); *Justiciary Records* (ed. Scott-Moncrieff, S. H. S.), II, 212–217. See also *H.M. Advocate* v. *Douglas* (1667) *Justiciary Records*, I, 200.

[7] Craig, *Jus Feudale*, Lord Clyde's introduction, p. xxi.

[8] Cooper, *The Sources and Literature of Scots Law*, (1936), pp. 80–81.

[9] Cooper, *Regiam Majestatem* (Stair Soc.), intro., p. 47.

[10] *Earl of Kinnoull* v. *Presbytery of Auchterarder* (1839) MacL. & Rob. 220 at p. 229, *per* L. C. Cottenham, who, however, unfortunately said that the original source was Bracton.

[11] *Stewart* v. *Reid*, 1934 S.C. 69.

[12] *Sugden* v. *H.M. Advocate*, 1934 J.C. 103.

[13] APS, I, 647.

[14] Record ed., c. 31.

[15] *Regiam Majestatem and Quoniam Attachiamenta* (Stair Soc., 1947), pp. 307–384. See also Note, (1984) 5 J.L.H. 117–178.

[16] See Notice of the Manuscripts in APS, I, 175 *et seq.*

[17] See also T. M. Cooper, 1941 S.L.T. (News) 21; Note, (1984) 5 J.L.H. 176.

[18] APS, II, 10, c. 10.

[19] APS, II, 97, c. 20. Skene in his *Lawis and Actis* of 1597 ascribes this to a Parliament of 1487; so does Murray of Glendook.

[20] 1449, APS, II, 36, c. 10.

[21] Lord Clyde, in his introduction to Craig's *Jus Feudale*, p. xxi, suggested that this commission compiled a manuscript collection.

[22] 1473, APS, II, 105, c. 14.

[23] Privilege in APS, I, 28; RSS, III, 129.

[24] See further, Chaps. 3 and 4.

[25] (1567) APS, III, 40, Appx. 42.

[26] APS, I, 30; III, 89b.

[27] See further, Chaps. 3 and 4.

[28] APS, III, 105, c. 18.

[29] APS, III, 564, c. 45.

[30] APS, III, 116, c. 9

[31] APS, IV, 378, c. 16

[32] (1628) APS, I, 34 and narrative in APS, V, 46, c. 32.

[33] (1630) APS, V, 209, c. 3.

[34] *Ibid*, 225, 227, 228.

[35] (1633) APS, V, 39, c. 20.

[36] (1633) APS, V, 46, c. 32.

[37] APS, V, 611b.

[38] APS, VI (2), 299, c. 271: this narrates that previous commissions did never take the wished effect partly by reason of other important affairs and partly of the troubles of the times.

[39] (1681) APS, I, 35; VIII, 356, c. 94.

[40] (1695) APS, I, 35; IX, 362.

[41] (1695) APS, IX, 455, c. 57.

[42] APS, I, 252–253, 709–712.

[43] APS, I, 663–665.

[44] APS, I, 119, 122.

[45] *Celtic Scotland*, III, 217.

[46] APS, I, 212–213, 317–325.

[47] APS, I, 246–247, 667–670.

[48] APS, I, 246–247, 671–672.

[49] APS, I, 673–674.

[50] APS, I, 675–679.

[51] APS, I, 248–249. There are later texts edited by Thomson and Innes in APS, I, 687. The best modern edition is John Gilbert, *Hunting and Hunting Reserves in Mediaeval Scotland*, Appx. A (1979).

[52] pp. 138–142.

[53] APS, I, 214–219, 329–356. Also in *Ancient Laws and Customs of the Burghs of Scotland* (ed. Cosmo Innes, Sc. Burgh Records Soc., 1868), pp. 3–62.

[54] See parallel texts in APS, I, 39–41, and *Borough Customs* (ed. M. Bateson, Selden Soc., Vols. 18 and 21, 1904–06). See also D. Baird Smith, (1924) 21 S.H.R. 193.

[55] APS, I, 226–229, 431–438. Also in *Ancient Laws and Customs of the Burghs of Scotland, supra*, pp. 64–88.

[56] APS, I, 680–682.

[57] APS, I, 250–251, 693–702.

[58] APS, I, 252–253, 705–708.

[59] APS, I, 413–416. See G. Neilson, "The March Laws" (ed. T. I. Rae), in Stair Society, *Miscellany I* (1971), 12.

[60] APS, I, 220–223; 369–392. Some texts of William of a legislative character are printed in RRS, II, Nos. 71, 124, 281, 406, 442, 475.

[61] APS, I, 224–225, 395–410.

[62] APS, I, 419–428.

[63] APS, I, 441–442.

[64] APS, I, 230–231, 459–487.

[65] pp. 248–259.

[66] Barrow, *Robert Bruce*, p. 253.

[67] T. M. Cooper, *Supra Crepidam* (1951), pp. 48–59. A. A. M. Duncan, "The *Acta* of King Robert I," 32 S.H.R. 1.

[68] APS, I, 466; recorded also in *Arbroath Liber*, 248–259. See also T. M. Cooper, "The First Law Reform (Miscellaneous Provisions) Act," (1944) 56 J.R. 1.

[69] Lord Cooper, "The Declaration of Arbroath Revisited," in *Supra Crepidam* and *Selected Papers*, p. 324.

[70] Barrow, p. 378; J. Fergusson, *The Declaration of Arbroath* (1970), p. 15. The letter, mistakenly treated as a statute, is printed in APS, I, 474–475.

[71] Barrow, p. 365.

[72] All described in APS, I, 177–182. These MSS. contain also texts of *Regiam Majestatem* and other early materials of Scots law.

[73] *Scotch Legal Antiquities*, p. 42 (note). Cosmo Innes had a transcript of the "*Registrum Brevium*" prepared for his use (*ibid.*, p. 231). It is still in H.M. General Register House.

[74] Edited by A. A. M. Duncan from a MS. in Edinburgh University Library, and published as University of Glasgow Scottish History Department Occasional Paper (1976).

[75] J. J. Robertson, "*De Composicione Cartarum*," in Stair Society, *Miscellany I* (1971), p. 78, gives text and translation.

CHAPTER 3

SIR JAMES BALFOUR

SCOTTISH legal history has a relatively blank period between the early fourteenth century and the late fifteenth, or roughly the period from the death of Robert I (Bruce) in 1329 to the death of James III in 1488. Lord Cooper called it the Dark Age of Scottish Legal History[1] but made the period extend to 1650, which seems much too long. The period was not without important developments because Parliament became established[2] and legislation became common (and some of it was, and still is, important)[3] and the committees of Council for the dispensing of justice which ultimately developed in 1532 into the Court of Session were repeatedly appointed.[4] That there were lawyers is evident from the pleadings and opinions recorded in some of the monastic chartularies, and is implicit in the regulation of the costume of pleaders in 1455,[5] the growing number of notaries public, who from 1469, at least in civil courts, could only be appointed by the king[6] and whose protocol books survive in numbers from the late fifteenth century. The foundation of the three oldest Scottish universities in the fifteenth century included provision for teaching of civil and canon law.[7] But though we know of lawyers we have no knowledge of individual jurists or juristic activity.

Conditions changed in the early sixteenth century with the foundation of the College of Justice in 1532. There was now a permanent superior court, which made possible and indeed required a regular Bar. James V ordered a journal of decisions of the court to be kept, and the practical needs of judges and lawyers for collections of source materials became more pressing.

In the mid-sixteenth century the eruption of the Reformation in Scotland had a considerable effect on the law. The papal jurisdiction and authority were abrogated,[8] but the courts of the officials of the dioceses were not however abolished and continued to act, at least intermittently, and the ecclesiastical courts had been important, active and busy in the years before the Reformation and their law and procedure were well-known and had permeated the thinking of the lawyers of the time.[9] Several of the officials of the old ecclesiastical courts passed into the College of Justice.[10] It is therefore possibly not surprising that the first noteworthy jurist of the post-Reformation period came from the older ecclesiastical courts.

James Balfour[11] was the son of Sir Michael Balfour of Montquhanny[12] and was probably born about 1525. Several of his name attended St. Andrews University in 1539 or 1540[13] and he was probably one of them. Thereafter in 1544 he probably attended Wittenberg University.[14] Goodall states[15] that he studied divinity and law, the usual subjects for an aspirant to an administrative career. He was certainly referred to[16] as Maister, the title of a Master of Arts.[17] It is not certain, however, that he was ever in priest's orders, and there is no evidence that he ever became an advocate. When the Commissary Court of Edinburgh was established[18] he was designated Maister and Parson of Flisk, whereas two others appointed were, and were designated, advocates, which suggests that he was not.

By 1546 at latest he had been converted to protestantism[19] and, along with his father and brothers, was among those who killed Cardinal Beaton and took refuge in St. Andrews Castle, and there resisted the forces of the Queen Mother and regent, Mary of Guise. The castle, however, was forced to surrender and Balfour and others were taken prisoner. Like John Knox he was impressed by the French and had to serve as a galley slave.[20] Some time in 1548 he either escaped[21] or was released.[22]

In 1554 he was provided to, and in the following year, inducted to, the perpetual vicarage of Kilmany in Fife on the resignation of Alexander Balfour,[23] though the latter seems to have recovered the vicarage by March 1559/60.[24] At some time thereafter, he seems to have been prebendary of Snow Kirk in Aberdeen, a prebendal stall said to have been usually appropriated to the doctor of canon law in the University of Aberdeen.[25] By about February 26, 1554 he was made Official of Lothian, or judge of the ecclesiastical court of the archdeaconry[26] and he held this office until the ecclesiastical courts and their jurisdiction were abolished in 1560.[27]

When the Reformation erupted in Scotland Balfour at first supported the existing religion, but then joined the Reformers, it was said, to cause dissension among them and to spy on them.[28] Possibly as a reward for his services, possibly as a perquisite of his post of Official, he was made parson of Flisk in Fife.[29] He was probably non-resident and not actually serving as priest; the parish work would be done by a vicar. He continued to hold the benefice after the Reformation.[30]

In August 1561 Mary, Queen of Scots and recently widowed Queen of France, returned to Scotland and Balfour began to rise in public service. How he entered her service is unknown. In 1561 he was made an Extraordinary Lord of the Court of Session on the clerical side,[31] in place of the Abbot of Dunfermline. He is also mentioned as present at the Privy Council.[32] In 1563 he was promoted to an ordinary, permanent and salaried, seat on the Bench.[33] In 1564 the Commissary Courts were established to replace the former ecclesiastical courts, the jurisdiction of which had been abolished, and Balfour, as a former Official and hence familiar with the former jurisdiction was, not unreasonably, chosen chief of the four Commissaries of Edinburgh, with a salary of 400 merks,[34] but he seems to have contrived to keep his seat in the Court of Session also, and his salary.[35]

In October 1565 he resigned from his post as Chief Commissary.[36] By July 1565 he was a Privy Councillor,[37] though the Council was strongly Catholic, and close to the Queen, indeed said to be her Secretary[38]; it was said that the Queen was well served by her secretaries David (Riccio) and Balfour[39] and that "now except David no man so great with her and the whole governor of this estate."[40] He was an assiduous attender at Council and browbeat various leading Edinburgh citizens to make forced loans to the Queen's government.[41] He was spoken of as a potential Secretary of State and may indeed have been acting as such, and his relatives got grants of the escheat of the estates of rebels against the Crown.[42]

Darnley, the Queen's consort,[43] and his friends resented the intimacy Riccio and Balfour enjoyed with the Queen and their influence on her and sought to eliminate both. Riccio was murdered in the Queen's presence but Balfour escaped a similar fate because he had been allowed to withdraw from court at the time.[44] He had to hide while the conspirators were in command of the situation, but then emerged to become the Queen's leading assistant in the persecution of the murderers.[45] By way of reward he was knighted as Sir James Balfour of Pittendreich[46] and appointed Clerk Register in place of James McGill, who was outlawed for his part in Riccio's murder, with a grant of the escheat of McGill's property.[47]

Prior to 1566 the only parts of the statute law which had been printed were a selection of the Acts of some Parliaments of James V, published in 1541, and the Acts of a Parliament of Queen Mary of 1563, published in 1565. But now on May 1, 1566 a royal commission[48] was appointed under the Great Seal, appointing the Chancellor and various other persons, including Sir James Balfour of Pittendreich, Knight, Clerk of our Register, giving them full power and authority to visie, sight and correct the laws of this realm made by the Queen and her predecessors, by the advice of the three estates in Parliaments held by them,

> "beginning at the books of the law called *Regiam Majestatem* and *Quoniam Attachiamenta* and so consequently following by progress of time until the date of this commission. So that no others but the said laws seen, mended and corrected by her said counsellors and commissioners, or any six of them conjunctly, shall be by her privilege printed or have place, faith or authority to be alleged and rehearsed before any of her judges or justices whatsoever in judgment and outwith."

This commission's remit seems limited to legislation and it seems implied that the *Regiam* and *Quoniam* were deemed legislation, probably of David I.

In fact as appears from the preface to their published edition the commissioners thought it expedient to begin at the reign of James I in 1424, thereby evading the difficult questions of the texts of earlier legislation and the authenticity of each item.

The commissioners must have worked diligently but cannot have given much care to the collation and correction of texts. Within six months a text of the Acts from 1424 to 1564 was printed in black-letter by Lekprevik. This is known as the *Black Acts*. There are two editions, one dated October 16 and the other November 28, 1566. The difference is that certain Acts mainly concerned with suppression of reformed doctrines in religion were suppressed in the latter. Later editions contain Acts down to those of 1594.

The preface,[49] which appears to have been written by Edward Henryson, a Commissary (1563) and later (1565) an extraordinary Lord of Session, and a member of the commission,[50] pays tribute to two of the members particularly for the travail and diligence taken by them, John, Bishop of Ross, who had proposed the work, and Sir James Balfour of Pittendreich, "for his sincere, afald and glad concurrence to perfect the work, and exhibition of the originals out of the Register, and making of them patent at all times, on no wise regarding his own particular outer profit or glory, but only the common weal of the realm."

The project bears some resemblance to the *Codices* of the Roman law and to modern Statute Law Revision projects. But in fact there was little or no revision. Nevertheless it was a considerable achievement.

By the end of 1566 the Queen had come to hate Darnley, not least for his part in the murder of Riccio, and Balfour himself cannot but have harboured personal ill-feeling against Darnley. He was an active supporter of Bothwell, who wished to supplant Darnley as the Queen's husband. A plot developed to get rid of Darnley and an agreement was come to to murder him; Balfour is rumoured to have drafted the agreement[51] and he had custody of it as a friend of Bothwell and also as Clerk Register and later (from May 8, 1567) as captain of Edinburgh Castle, where the records were kept.[52]

Darnley conveniently contracted smallpox in January 1566/67 and had to be separated from the Queen and court, and was lodged at Kirk o' Field in Edinburgh.[53] Early in the morning of February 10, 1566/67 there was a violent explosion in Kirk o' Field which destroyed the building; Darnley's body was found 60 or 80 paces from the house in a garden, with his valet and a young page.[54] He had been strangled, probably when trying to escape.

The truth about the murder is very unclear, and there may have been more than one conspiracy; no theory wholly explains the facts. The common belief was that the Queen was fully cognisant of the intended murder. "The man who has the castle of Edinburgh was one of Bothwell's most trusted friends. . . . It is believed for certain that this man was one of the principal actors in the murder of the king."[55]

There is a good deal of evidence which casts grave suspicion on Balfour. The place of the murder, Kirk o' Field, was part of the provostry of Kirk o' Field which had lately been bought by Balfour[56] but recently transferred by him to his brother Robert,[57] possibly with a view to exculpating himself. Balfour assisted Bothwell to prepare the place for Darnley and indeed possibly induced the latter to go there, rather than to Craigmillar or Hamilton House, which would have been more suitable.[58]

He is said to have bought the gunpowder which caused the explosion[59] and passed it to one of Bothwell's men on the night of the explosion.[60] His brother Robert was present at the time of Darnley's death[61] and later that night Balfour himself left Edinburgh and returned three days later, having, he believed, established his alibi.[62] One of his servants was secretly killed and buried, lest he disclose anything.[63]

From the morning after the event Balfour was suspected to have been a deviser of the murder or one of the murderers[64] and he himself later conceded that there was a *prima facie* case against him in respect of the death.[65]

Current rumour certainly connected him and Bothwell with the death.[66] Official notices offered rewards for information about the murderers, but other posters appeared in Edinburgh plainly indicating that Balfour was involved.[67] He retracted an offer he had previously made to clear himself.[68] When, shortly after, he returned to Edinburgh he had to have a bodyguard of 30 horsemen and two months later he still thought it wise to keep indoors because he was at least unpopular, and possibly even in danger.[69]

Some of the evidence against Balfour must, however, be taken with caution. Confessions, possibly extracted under torture, said that he had signed the band for the murder,[70] and speeches on the scaffold by minor participants implicated him.[71] But Knox[72] named him first among those that "laid hands on the king to kill him," and he was named as first murderer by Lennox, Darnley's father.[73] Moray named Balfour, one of the Queen's secretaries, as one of the practisers of the King's death.[74]

Bothwell was tried for the murder of Darnley in a sham trial[75] and at it he produced a letter from Lennox, Darnley's father, to the Queen, naming Bothwell, Master James Balfour, Gilbert Balfour, his brother, and others as suspected murderers. Bothwell was aquitted and set up placards saying that he had been acquitted and if any gentleman would deny it, he gave him the lie in his throat and would fight him according to the law of arms.[76] But answers were affixed to the Cross at Edinburgh naming James, Gilbert and Henry Balfour as devisers of the murder.[77]

Balfour was indeed taken into custody by Moray and for a short time warded in Edinburgh Castle.[78] But the placards continued to appear naming, among others, Bothwell and Balfour, though an edict, quite probably drafted by Balfour and utilising the words of the Roman edict *de famosis libellis*, was published threatening the direst penalties.[79] Lennox, Darnley's father, accused Balfour as well as Bothwell[80] but Balfour was not charged.[81] He attended Parliament,[82] was made captain of Edinburgh Castle[83] and continued to support Bothwell, who took the Queen off to Dunbar.

Just before she married Bothwell on May 15, 1567, the Queen granted Bothwell and others a remission for their part in abducting her and for all other crimes whatsoever, a form of words which plainly covered Darnley's murder, and Balfour included his own and his brother's names in the remission.[84] Later Bothwell tried to break with Balfour and he was proposed for the post of ambassador to England to announce the Queen's remarriage[85] and an attempt made to supersede him as captain of Edinburgh Castle.[86]

Balfour was aware that to continue to support Bothwell was dangerous and a fortnight after the latter's marriage to the Queen he joined with the lords in a band to save her from Bothwell's thraldom,[87] and, while retaining the Castle,[88] he got rid of the Queen's supporters there.[89] The Queen did not apparently realise his change of allegiance and repeatedly sent him messages asking him to hold the Castle against the rebellious lords.[90] But he negotiated secretly with them and surrendered the Castle to them, being promised his life and a pardon. Balfour also arranged that a silver cabinet containing Bothwell's letters from the Queen fell into the hands of the lords.[91]

After Mary's defeat at Carberry Hill and her exile to Lochleven and abdication in June 1567, Balfour continued to associate with the rebel lords, participating in discussions with English representatives, and agreed to surrender Edinburgh Castle to Grange on "good composition."[92] When the Queen's half-brother Moray arrived from France in August to become Regent he granted a bond of maintenance under which Balfour was to use his good offices to pursue Darnley's murderers.[93]

The captaincy of Edinburgh Castle was to be given to Kirkcaldy of Grange but Moray, to detach Balfour from Mary's supporters, agreed to grant Balfour a remission for any crimes, make over the Priory of Pittenweem to him, pay a pension out of the Priory of St. Andrews for his son, and pay him a lump sum of £5000.[94] Balfour also agreed to surrender the office of Clerk Register to McGill, the previous holder, but to receive in return the office of Lord President of the Court of Session, the then holder, William Baillie, Lord Provand being put aside.[95] At the end of the year he was present in Parliament[96] and as one of the Lords of the Articles as Prior of Pittenweem.[97] He also signed an order justifying the conduct of the lords against the Queen.[98]

The following year, though there are suspicions that he had a hand in her escape,[99] Balfour supported the Regent Moray when the Queen escaped from Lochleven Castle. He was not a signatory of the band made before the battle of Langside favouring restoration of the Queen[1] and was present on the Regent's side at the battle.[2] Yet in the convention held at Perth in 1569 he was among those who supported the divorce of the Queen from Bothwell and her restoration.[3]

In 1567 and 1568 Balfour was present in Parliament and conventions and elected to the committee of Articles.[4] He was made a member in 1567 of a commission on the jurisdiction of the kirk.[5]

Balfour remained Lord President, certainly until 1569, and acted as a councillor, in Parliament,[6] and as an auditor of Exchequer.[7] But scaffold speeches repeatedly[8] implicated him in Darnley's murder and the governing group ultimately felt obliged to act against Lethington and Balfour.[9] Balfour and his brother Gilbert were arrested in Fife,[10] warded in Stirling and, very shortly after, in free ward in St. Andrews, having found caution of £20,000 not to practice with England.[11] He may have secured release by the Regent Moray's intervention, or by bribery of the Regent's secretary,[12] or by agreeing to give evidence against Lethington.[13] As late as 1579 his posterity were disinherited for the murder of Darnley.[14]

The assassination of the Regent Moray by a Hamilton in January 1570 decisively altered Balfour's position for the worse; Moray had been his protector. The new Regent was the Earl of Lennox, Darnley's father, who naturally bore an extreme grudge against Balfour and the Hamiltons. Shortly, despite oaths of loyalty to the Regent, he became an active and violent supporter of the Queen.

In August 1571 the Regent Lennox's government decreed the forfeiture of Balfour and the Hamiltons.[15] But shortly thereafter Lennox was murdered and Balfour had had a share of responsibility for this.[16] Lennox's successor, Mar, began to regrant the lands Balfour had acquired and Balfour, by secret negotiations with Morton which included giving away secret information about the Queen's party still holding Edinburgh Castle, purchased immunity from prosecution for the death of Darnley and for his resistance to successive regents.[17] Accordingly he received from Morton, who succeeded Mar as regent, a remission for his crimes, which, in any event, he denied, and a cancellation of his forfeiture of 1571.[18] Thereafter he aided Morton to achieve the Pacification of Perth which was ratified by Parliament.[19] Balfour was then reinvested in his lands and appointments; he resumed a seat in Parliament as Prior of Pittenweem and was made a member of committees to revise the laws and to consider church policy.[20]

In 1574 Morton, on the narrative of the absence of perfect policie by laws and constitutions setting out how the kirk should be governed, appointed a commission of 16[21] including Balfour, to put in form the ecclesiastical policie and order of the governing of the kirk and to report to the next convention so that it might be ratified and established as law. Nothing seems to have come of this commission but it may be that some investigation done for it accounts for the considerable space devoted to ecclesiastical matters in the *Practicks*.

Also in 1574, on March 5, 1574/75 the Regent Morton appointed a commission of nine,[22] including Balfour, to meet, call unto them such others of the Lords of Session or advocates as they thought expedient, and begin and "visit the books of the law, acts of parliament and decisions before the session, and draw the form of the body of other laws, as well as that which is already statute as the things that were meet and convenient to the statute. . . . Wherethough there may be a certain written law to all our sovereign lords judges and ministers to judge and decide by."

Hume of Godscroft[23] states that this task was "laid on Sir James Balfour and Master John Skeene, Clerk Register and Master of the Rolls.[24] The work (as I am informed) was well advanced, but when he [the regent Morton] quit his authority, they left off any further proceeding in it." The last words are probably incorrect inference.

That Skene, then aged about 33, continued to work on the project for some time seems evident, though he does not assert it himself. But in 1577 he received a grant of an annual pension out of the thirds of ecclesiastical benefices. It was ratified and confirmed in 1579.[25] Habakkuk Bisset refers[26] to Balfour's *Practicks*, "whereof there is some copies written by me in my lord Curriehill [Skene] or his brother Mr. John's hands but if the principal written by me might be had, the same is most correct . . . certain Notes of Chronicles and other ancient monuments of the Kingdom of Scotland that the late Sir James Balfour caused Andrew Moreson and me to write at Burleigh in the years of God 1582 and 1583 years or thereby." The "Notes of Chronicles" are the last title of the *Practicks*.

Just as the commission which resulted in the *Black Acts* bears some resemblance to the Roman *Codices*, so this commission's work bears some resemblance to the compilation of Justinian's *Digest*.

There seems little doubt that the work ultimately published in 1754 as Balfour's *Practicks* is the product of the work of Balfour, Skene and others, pursuant to the commission of 1575. The only alternative hypothesis is that the work of the commission came to nothing, or has been lost, and that Balfour, with assistance, was at the same time doing the same sort of work, and that his private work has survived. This seems unlikely. The most probable conclusion is that the commission never reported but the product of the labours of a few became known as Balfour's *Practicks*.

Balfour seems not to have been much in public in 1575–77 and may have been living in Fife and working on the *Practicks*.[27] In late 1578 he participated in a conference between representatives of Argyll and Atholl and representatives of Morton, which apparently effected a reconciliation.[28]

After a setback to his power in 1578–79 Morton fell from power but not before he had taken proceedings against Balfour and others. In May 1579 Balfour took refuge in France just as the government, relying on the forfeiture of 1571, ordered him to surrender his houses.[29] The forfeiture was renewed[30] and the king and council granted out the Priory and the lands of Burleigh, which had reverted to the Crown.[31]

In France, Balfour engaged in plots to overthrow Morton and restore Mary[32]; he engaged in correspondence with Mary.[33] In the meantime in Scotland young King James was wanting evidence from Balfour to use against Morton, evidence implicating Morton in Darnley's death, and by the beginning of 1581 he was back in Edinburgh.[34] Possibly to some extent relying on evidence provided by Balfour, Morton was at once charged with crimes including complicity in Darnley's death.[35] Balfour seems not to have produced any murder band implicating Morton,[36] though ultimately Morton was guillotined as guilty art and part of concealing Darnley's murder.[37]

Thereafter Balfour sought leave to state his case to the Council for rehabilitation[38] and a remission was granted for three years provided he stood trial for complicity in Darnley's death.[39] Whether he did so is uncertain, but he seems to have continued his work of restating the law.[40] The king made a declaration of protection in his favour, but had to concede that the protection did not extinguish the previous forfeiture and that he did not decide the issue of Balfour's guilt.[41] He seems to have regained possession of his lands because, according to Bisset, at Burleigh in 1582 and 1583 he was directing the transcription of ancient chronicles.[42]

He died in 1583.[43] His posterity were disinherited for his part in the murder of Darnley[44] but his feuars and tacksmen were allowed to enjoy their feus and tacks notwithstanding his forfeiture.[45]

In 1584–85 Parliament enacted that his forfeiture had been reduced in 1573 and that he remained a loyal subject until his death, so that his children might succeed to his lands,[46] and another Act in 1587, in favour of Lady Burleigh and her children, ratified the restitution of the late Sir James.[47] Another Act in her favour concerned land given for castles[48] and later she got a grant of the privilege of making salt for seven years.[49] His son Michael, was created Lord Balfour of Burleigh in 1607.[50] The family continued until the fifth Lord Balfour was forfeited after the rebellion of 1715.[51] His daughter married Alexander Bruce of Kennet. The title Lord Balfour of Burleigh was allowed by the House of Lords in 1868 and, the attainder of 1715 having been abrogated by statute in 1869, was restored to Alexander Hugh Bruce, a direct descendant of Alexander Bruce and Mary Balfour. He was a descendant of Robert Bruce (1718–85, advocate 1743), Professor of the Law of Nature and Nations at Edinburgh, 1759–64, and a judge of the Court of Session as Lord Kennet, 1764–85, and himself became Secretary for Scotland 1895–1903, Chancellor of St. Andrews University and Rector of Edinburgh University.[52]

Balfour's character presents the strangest contrasts. Queen Mary called him the man she could never forgive because of his treachery[53]; her secretary Nau described him as a traitor who offered himself to one party and then to the other[54]; and John Knox described him as blasphemous and a blasphemer.[55] Later historians have seen no cause to differ from these views.

Treacherous, self-seeking and corrupt to a high degree in an age when these vices were common, he nevertheless had great ability; several times he succeeded in reconciling violently opposing factions; he managed to stay alive during a time when many better men met violent death in one way or another. So far as is known he discharged his judicial functions adequately. And he appears to have had considerable legal ability and a genuine interest in law. The commissions given him and others could easily have been allowed to lapse unperformed, but at least the major ones were executed, in a matter for which later generations have reason to be grateful, even if, in the light of modern, more stringent, standards we are critical.

The work for which Balfour is mainly remembered in Scottish legal history is the book known as Balfour's *Practicks*. The term "practick" is clearly connected with "practice" and a practicks is a collection of materials for practice of the law, not a work on legal theory. Craig[56] observes that what we call *praxis* is custom of decided cases. One of Balfour's own headings[57] is, "Lawis and practiques anent tutorie," and later[58] he refers to an Act as "conform to the practique." Intrants seeking call to the bar in the sixteenth century had to study "practick,"[59] and a statute of 1669 refers to "the constant Practick of the Kingdom,"[60] and one of 1695[61] to "decisions or practiques" and to "practique or course of decisions." The word means practice in the sense of uniform customary mode of dealing with a problem rather than in the modern sense of rules of procedure,[62] though there too there is an element of uniform and customary mode of acting.

There are many works, some still in manuscript, some printed, called *Practicks*. A modern classification[63] distinguishes "decision practicks" or privately-made collections of notes of decisions, made contemporaneously, which were the forerunners of the modern law reports, and "digest practicks" or collected notes of materials from all sources, the Auld Lawes, statutes, decisions, which were the forerunners of modern general textbooks and encyclopedias. Balfour's is of the second category.

Contemporary, or near-contemporary, evidence is consistent that the attribution of the book to Balfour is justified. It is so referred to by Habakkuk Bisset, who was one of his "disciples" and who, with others, was engaged in the transcription of manuscript materials under Balfour's direction in 1582 or 1583.[64] It was so attributed without hesitation by Goodal in 1754. Modern re-examination of the problem has reached the conclusion that there are no good grounds for attributing the work to anyone else.[65]

That Balfour did have clerical assistance, from Andrew Moreson and Habakkuk Bisset[66] and possibly others, is certain, but the *Practicks* "is not the work of a number of commissioners, but one person, as appears by his speaking of himself now and then in the first person of the singular number."[67]

It is significant that the *Practicks* is in Scots, matter in Latin drawn from the Auld Lawes and the *Regiam* being translated. This plainly indicates that he had in mind the working lawyers of Scotland rather than the legal scholars of Europe.

The date of his book is generally stated as 1579, because the latest case cited by him is of that year,[68] but the printed text includes statutes of 1592 and 1597, and even some statutes passed after his death, as well as instructions to the commissaries of 1610. It seems accordingly that a clerk added material after Balfour had finished with it. As Goodall, the editor of the printed text, observes;[69] "for it is probable that he had begun to write or to make Collections, from the Time that he was joined in the Commission by the Queen for correcting the Laws." It is known that Balfour was out of public life from 1574, when he was appointed to revise the laws, until 1578; during this period he was probably working at Burleigh. From 1579 till the end of 1580 he was in exile in France and his property, possibly including his registers, had been seized by the treasurer.[70] He may not have been able to work on the book properly after 1579.

Moreover Habakkuk Bisset[71] refers to Notes of Chronicles and other ancient monuments ... that the late Sir James Balfour caused Andrew Moreson and him [Bisset] to write at Burleigh in the years 1582 and 1583 or thereby. These are probably among the miscellaneous topics at the end of the *Practicks*, and this suggests that Balfour was still at least adding to or correcting his work down to his death in 1583, and that his assistants may have added some later materials. The period of compilation should accordingly probably be taken as 1574 to 1583.

Furthermore, down to page 131 of the printed text statutes are quoted in full, but thereafter there are only titles and references; the change is indicated by the words on that page, *vide in libro impresso*, *i.e.* the Black Acts. This indicates either a change of plan, a decision to dispense with full transcription of statutes, or revision of the final text to that point and no further. As the text is not chronological and compilation of the material relevant to many if not all headings must have proceeded simultaneously, the more probable inference seems to be of revision to that point and no further, possibly even of the substitution of mere references for full texts in later pages.

A substantial number of manuscripts exist, some complete, some abbreviated, some incomplete, some alphabetically rearranged.[72] Two or three are near-contemporary; one is dated 1593; most are eighteenth-century.

The book was printed at Edinburgh in 1754 by Walter Goodal, (?1706–66),[73] sub-librarian of the Advocates' Library, who states in his title page that it has been "carefully published from several manuscripts" and in his preface that it was "after consulting all the Manuscript Copies we could find." He does not specify which manuscripts, nor say how he reconciled variant readings, but there are indications in some marginal notes of variations.[74] Goodal has the reputation of being a careful and meticulous scholar,[73] and his text has been the accepted version for over two centuries.

His edition, published by Ruddimans, is a large and stout quarto extending to 684 pages of text. In 1962–63 the Stair Society published, in two volumes, a facsimile reprint of Goodal's edition. After two centuries of citation little useful purpose would have been served by a laborious collation of the manuscripts, particularly when many later printed books and very many cases contain references to the work by Goodal's pagination. That is the received text even if it might have been improved on.

Goodal's edition does not, however, print the original preface which appears in the manuscripts, though it is not original but a copy of the preface which is found in Justinian's *Institutions*, Glanvill and *Regiam Majestatem*.[75] Goodal described the content of the work in these words:

> "In it are digested under proper heads, or titles, the Acts of Parliament, from the XIX year of King James I, the Books of the *Regiam Majestatem*, with the statutes of our Kings before James I and other Law treatises that are found in the Manuscript Copies to accompany the *Regiam Majestatem*; as also the Decisions of the Court of Session, as well before as after its more fixed and regular Constitution in the Reign of King James V."[76]

The selection of the heads or titles demanded a very competent knowledge of the law; this is itself evidence of an analytic mind and of substantial original thinking. The work of digesting and copying the materials must have been a very large one, all done by manual copying and mostly from manuscript sources. The statutes, in the *Black Acts*, would be the only sources printed; on the other hand those working on the enterprise were probably more familiar with reading medieval and early modern manuscripts than most modern scholars are.

The book comprises a series of 166 titles, such as Of Marriage, Anent Prescriptioun, Of Borrowing and Lending, under each of which is gathered a series of paragraphs each stating a proposition or a number of related propositions and each concluding with a reference to the Auld Lawes, or a statute or a case, by date, names of parties, and reference to tome and caput of the *registrum*, or some of these indications.

The titles are not arranged alphabetically, but appear to be grouped by reference to major headings. They can be generally classified as follows:

Public law, titles 1–12[77];
Private law – persons, titles 13–24;
       – things-heritable, titles 25–48;
       – things-moveable, titles 49–59;
       – succession, titles 60–69;
Courts, actions, evidence and procedure, titles 70–120;
Criminal law, titles 121–160;
Miscellaneous, titles 161–166.

This order shows some similarity to that used by Gaius and Justinian, namely persons, things and actions. Balfour's book is, however, a collection of propositions brought under headings rather than a systematically organised treatise. Within each title the paragraphs show no apparent pattern or order. It also bears some resemblance to Justinian's *Digest* as a collection of materials under headings, and some, but rather less, to a modern encyclopedia. It is not, even within particular titles or even paragraphs, a narrative text. It is very inadequate in the extraction and statement of principles of any generality. As is common in early law, practical classifications count for more than academic ones; much of the law of property is stated under heads of conveyancing and much substantive law under procedural headings.

While no doubt the law has changed and developed, it is very noteworthy how many titles in the *Practicks* are still familiar to the lawyer of four centuries later; there are titles about Procurators, Warrandice, Probation by oath, Probation by witnesses, Redemption of lands, and others. This is recognisably an earlier version of Scots law.

At the end of the *Practicks* there are four headings which do not fit into the pattern and seem to have been added later; some indeed must have been because they post-date his death. These topics are (a) a digest of sea laws drawn from the statutes, the practicks, the laws of Oleron and Wisby, and the constitutions of François, King of France of 1543 and 1557, the *registrum* and the Book of Kintore[78]; (b) the Order of the Chancellary, a commentary on the practice of the chancery with styles of brieves from chancery; no source is quoted for this, nor authorities cited[79]; (c) Commissariat, a collection of the instructions given to the Commissaries of Edinburgh, 1563, and of instructions to them on the execution of their functions[80]; these documents can all be traced to their original sources; and (d) a collection of Auld Lawes drawn from the Scottish chronicles and attributed to Scottish kings, some of whom, like Dornadilla, are certainly mythical but others, like Malcolm Canmore, historical.[81]

The main sources of Balfour's propositions are three: the Auld Lawes, *i.e.* statutes attributed to kings from Malcolm MacKenneth to Robert III, *Regiam Majestatem* and other old collections, the statutes from 1424, and decisions from about 1420.

It may be that Balfour excerpted from the main elements of the Auld Lawes, particularly *Regiam Majestatem* and *Liber de Judicibus*, directly, but an alternative view[82] is that he merely transcribed and, where necessary, translated an already existing digest of the Auld Lawes. Certain surviving manuscripts[83] may be copies of this early digest. It may have been a product of the commission of 1469, or Balfour's own work, made under the commissions of 1566 or 1574. He certainly cites a substantial range of the materials commonly included under the head of the Auld Lawes and printed by Thomson and Innes in Volume I of the Acts of the Parliaments of Scotland. It is significant that Balfour, who had great knowledge and experience, cites the Auld Lawes in the same way as what are certainly authentic Acts of Parliament and decisions of the Court of Session, and clearly regarded them as authentic sourcematerials. Whatever doubt has been cast by modern critical work on many elements of the Auld Lawes, Balfour did not share.

There are about 800 references to material in the Auld Lawes, some chapters of legislation being cited more than once.

In the second place he cites extensively the statute law, from the *Black Acts* of 1566, which was the first official collection of the Scots Acts,

1424–1564, compiled by a committee of which Balfour was the leading member, and reprinted with supplementary Acts until the 1590s. A few references are to post-1583 statutes and these must have been inserted in the manuscript after Balfour's death.

There are about 650 statutes cited, some of them more than once. As far as page 131 of the printed edition of the *Practicks*, statutes are quoted at length with the title in the marginal note, but thereafter the citation gives merely the king, the folio, the number of the Act and its date, and no marginal note.

Thirdly, he cites decisions of the Court of Session from what has been designated *registrum Scotie*,[84] or Balfour's register of Acts and Decreets.[85] This is not extant but the references indicate its nature. It comprised two volumes, both in digest form, arranged either alphabetically or by topics, the first covering 1469 to 1579 and including 1392 titles, and the second covering 1540[86] to 1577 and including 856 titles.[87] These are cited, *e.g.* 2 t. c. 319 (*i.e.* second *tomus*, *caput* 319).

Balfour may himself have compiled, or had compiled, these *registra* but they were more probably compiled from earlier decision-practicks than from the original acts and decreets of the courts. The ultimate source of all these collections is of course the manuscript acts and decreets of the Session and the Council. The starting date of 1469 coincides exactly with the beginning of a book of decreets handled by Sir Robert Spottiswoode in the seventeenth century and now lost.[88]

Some of these cases cited are cited from earlier manuscript collections; thus he refers to lib. Carneg.,[89] Ersk., Galbraith,[90] Kintor,[91] Purves, Scon[92] as well as *liber meus*.

Altogether there are about 1600 references to cases though about 300 are anonymous, cited only by date and, usually, reference to the *registrum*.

He refers to Acts of Council in the *registra*, which can be found in the modern printed editions of the *Acta Dominorum Concilii*, comprising both statutes of the Session, which came to be known in the seventeenth century as Acts of Sederunt, and Acts of the Privy Council.

There are also a few references to legislation of the provincial councils of the Scottish church,[93] and to other materials.

In what is a compilation rather than a treatise one cannot attribute to Balfour personally the views on law generally contained in the first title, Of the Law, but it is nevertheless instructive to see what statements he was able to collect and set down as at 1579 or at his death in 1583. The law is divided into three parts, the law of nature, the law of God, and positive law.[94] Parliament alone can make law or statutes.[95] The place of customary law and judicial law-finding is excluded: if any question shall happen to arise before any judges, which cannot be decided, by no clear written law, the decision and declaration thereof ought and should be referred and continued to the next parliament that a law may be clearly made by the Lords of the next parliament, how the said question should be decided and ruled in time to come.[95] Acts and statutes made by the three Estates in Parliament binds and obliges all the lieges of the realm, and has the strength of a law and ordinance after the first publication thereof in parliament, though not printed till later.[96] All the King's lieges must live and be governed under the King's laws and statutes of the realm only, and under no particular laws, nor special privileges, nor by any laws of other countries or realms.[97]

The state of the law revealed by the *Practicks* is of a corpus of propositions and rules, mostly of indigenous origin, partly embodied in statutory declarations or modifications of custom, partly expressed in decisions of specific cases. The influence of Roman law was not extensive,[98] though some had permeated the canon law and thereby influenced the consistorial law, which was just beginning to become part of the general law of the land.

The titles dealing with Public Law are concerned largely with the royal patrimony and the power to revoke alienations made during minority (a topic of perennial difficulty in Scotland in the fifteenth and sixteenth centuries).[99] There is quite a full treatment of local administration by the sheriff. Despite the Reformation, Balfour retained nearly all the pre-Reformation legislation relative to the church, qualified only by the abolition of papal jurisdiction and the mass, and seems to have regarded it as still applicable to the reformed church.[1] This is consistent with the view that initially the reformation was merely a reformation of the old church and not a root-and-branch destruction of the old and creation of a new church. He gives much space to the burgh laws[2] and gild laws.[3]

In respect of law of persons[4] many of the main rules of the matrimonial relationship had already emerged and the consequences on the property of spouses were already important. The distinctions between separation and divorce, and divorce and nullity had not emerged. Tutory and curatory were the only important topics in relation to children.

The group of titles dealing with law of things deals first with rights in heritage,[5] King's patrimony, the forest laws, patrimony of the kirk, teinds, alienation of heritage and lands, resignation, assignation, feus, tailzies and sasines. In this group is a title Of Obligation.[6] To Balfour an obligation was a written bond by which a man was bound by reason of any debt or contract; it should contain six principal parts. A conventional penalty in a contract or obligation might not be asked by any person but in so far as he was interested, hurt or skaithed. The basis for this view is the canonical condemnation of usury rather than the objectionable character of private penalties.

The following group of titles, concerned with moveable rights,[7] commenced with a title Anent Covenant and Pactioun.[8] C.1 concludes: "Besides, in so far as paction is called a consent of two or more persons, the same is understood from a hecht or simple promise, otherwise called *pollicitatio*, which is a promise of one man only to another." So ancient is the enforceability of promises as well as contracts in Scots law. There is a beginning of a theory of contractual obligation.

He then distinguishes pactions real and personal, and pactions profitable and unprofitable, and follows with titles on what we would call the specific contracts of loan, pledge and cautionry, deposit, hire, tack and assedation, buying and selling, and a title on money. The law of tacks or leases was quite well developed: withholding rent where the subjects were affected by *rei interitus* was recognised, and 40 days was already the standard period of warning to remove. But many matters of contract fell within the burgh laws and the admiralty law.

Delict, or the right of reparation, does not appear as such; harms to the person were regarded criminally rather than remediable civilly, but there are titles on skaith by and to animals, wrongful detention, and spuilzie and ejection.

The titles on succession[9] show legal rights accepted and testaments, executors, heirship moveables and the ward and marriage of heirs all well known. The group of titles concerned with courts, judges, procedure and evidence is a large one[10] and illustrates the way in which the technicalities of procedure and evidence bulk so largely in an immature legal system.

Similarly criminal law occupies considerable space.[11] A criminal action or cause is that which touches a pain of blood, of life or limb.[12] Theft was, as it still is, a big title.[13] The criminal law is mainly collections of rules about specific crimes with much about procedure. The general notion of criminal responsibility is quite undeveloped.

At the end there are some miscellaneous titles, on the chamberlain-ayre, the border laws, and taxation, the sea laws, the order of the chancellory, the commissariat, and the Auld Lawes contained in the Scottish chronicles.[14]

The importance and value of Balfour's *Practicks* has been and is very great. It is the earliest extant general compendium of the post-medieval law of Scotland comprising propositions and rules enunciated in the Auld Lawes, Acts of the Parliaments, and decisions of the Session and of the Council. For some of these sources Balfour is our sole authority.

> "His performance [of the commission to revise the laws] answered the general expectation concerning it, and continued to be used and consulted both by students and practitioners as the best of our Law books, till near a hundred years after his decease, that the Lord Stair's *Institutions* were published, which, by being set for a print, were more readily to be got, and more easily read than written books: However this Book always continued to be in great esteem; and as I have been told, still continues to be in as high Repute with all those who set themselves to pry more narrowly into the Grounds and ancient Practice of the Law of Scotland."[15]

When it was completed and circulating in manuscript it was, so far as known, the only substantially complete compendium of the source materials for legal advice and decision. "Balfour's *Practicks* stands as the pre-eminent written record of Scots Law until the publication of Stair's *Institutions*."[16] Even where, as frequently happens with Hope's *Major Practicks*,[17] Balfour and a later collector of materials cite the same authority, Balfour's is almost invariably the fuller and more detailed note on the point.

Hope and later writers cite Balfour extensively, though Stair does not, though it is impossible to believe that he did not know of Balfour's work; for one thing he cites Craig and Hope extensively and both quote Balfour; for another, manuscripts of Balfour must have been well known in Stair's time and one[18] may have belonged to him. Indeed he seems deliberately to have disregarded Balfour, sometimes finding authority in the Roman law though Balfour cites a Scottish authority to the same effect.[19]

It is not, of course, a narrative text and can hardly be read, but only looked into as a repository of source materials; it is "a compilation of every thing that could be collected."[20] There is little or no statement of principle as distinct from statements of particular propositions and rules. But it contains the seeds of the later textbooks in bringing together under heads the materials relevant to various topics. It is a work "of undoubted authority"[21] and the earliest or only authority on many matters. Balfour may have been a scoundrel but he and his helpers deserve our gratitude.

NOTES

[1] David Murray Lecture, Glasgow University, 1952, reprinted in his *Collected Papers*, p. 219.

[2] R. S. Rait, *The Parliaments of Scotland*, pp. 19 *et seq*.

[3] See legislation of David II (1329–70/71), Robert II (1370/71–90) and Robert III (1390–1406) in APS, I, 491–583.

[4] On them see *Acta Dominorum Auditorum in Civil Causes and Complaints* (1466–94); *Acta Dominorum Concilii in Civil Causes* (1478–95, 1496–1501 and (Stair Soc.) 1501–04); *MS Acta Dominorum Concilii* in Register House. See also J. J. Robertson, "The development of the Law," in J. M. Brown (ed.), *Scottish Society in the Fifteenth Century*, p. 136.

[5] (1455) APS, II, 43, c. 12.

[6] APS, II, 95, c. 6; see, also (1503) APS, II, 242, 250, c. 8; John Durkan, "The Early Scottish Notary," in *The Renaissance and Reformation in Scotland*, ed. Cowan and Shaw (1983), p. 22.

[7] In 1579 it was provided that advocates were not to be admitted without a testimonial of their proficiency in the law from the University of St. Andrews: APS, III, 180, c. 62.

[8] Papal Jurisdiction Act, 1560 (APS, II, 534, c. 2).

[9] Ollivant, *The Court of the Official* (1982).

[10] Ollivant, *supra*, Appx. II.

[11] DNB; Anderson, SN, I, 211; Chambers, BDES; Brunton & Haig, p. 110; Goodall, Preface to 1754 edition of Balfour's *Practicks*; P. G. B. McNeill, "Sir James Balfour of Pittendreich," 1960 J.R. I; McNeill, Introduction to *Balfour's Practicks* (Stair Soc., 1962). There is a farm called Pittendreich two miles SE of Milnathort, Kinross, not far from Burleigh Castle, and Balfour may have taken his customary designation from it. There is another Pittendreich near Lasswade, Midlothian, but no obvious reason for Balfour taking his title from it.

[12] *Scots Peerage*, I, 533; Montquhanny is five miles NW of Cupar, Fife.

[13] *Records of the University of St. Andrews*, 1413–1579 (S.H.S.), pp. 243, 245.

[14] Fostermann, *Album Academicae Vitebergensis*, 1502–60, S.216a, 7.

[15] Preface to 1754 edition.

[16] *e.g.* RSS V, 1633; Knox, *History of the Reformation in Scotland* (ed. Dickinson), I, p. 108; Pitcairn, *Criminal Trials*, I, p. 393.

[17] Patrick, *Statutes of the Scottish Church*, 88, n. 1.

[18] RSS, V, 1633.

[19] According to Knox, *History*, I, p. 93, Balfour later denied this, at a time when he was seeking appointment as Official of Lothian.

[20] C.S.P. For. VII, 480; Knox, *History*, I, pp. 97, 108. Knox says that Balfour later denied this too.

[21] Spottiswoode, I, p. 177.

[22] Knox, *History*, I, p. 111.

[23] *Bell Brander Writs*, (S.R.O.), 26, 27, 28.

[24] *St. Andrews Register*, I, 15.

[25] *Fasti Aberdonenses*, 87.

[26] *Evidence before Commissioners visiting Scottish Universities* III, St. Andrews, 336. In 1555 he appeared as Official in the Justice Court claiming immunity for a cleric: Pitcairn, I, 378.*

[27] APS, II, 534, c. 2.

[28] Knox, I, pp. 247, 257.

[29] Flisk is on the north coast of Fife overlooking the Firth of Tay.

[30] *Fasti Ecclesiae Scoticanae*, V, 155.

[31] *MS. Books of Sederunt*, II, 29. The Court of Session had consisted since its foundation in 1532 of 15 Lords, a cleric as President, and seven each of clerical and lay members, plus a number of "extraordinary" Lords, the number of whom was later fixed at four, two from each side.

[32] RPC, I, 188.

[33] *MS. Books of Sederunt*, II, 83.

[34] RSS, V, 1633; *Practicks*, 670. Others appointed were Edward Henryson, advocate, who was associated with Skene in the *Lawis and Actis*, and Clement Litill or Little, advocate, whose books are the foundation of Edinburgh University Library, and Robert

Maitland, Dean of Aberdeen. On Little see C. P. Finlayson, *Clement Litill and his Library* (1980); J. R. Guild and A. Law, *Edinburgh University Library*, 1580–1980 (1982).

[35] Parliament legislated against this pluralism; APS, III, 41, c. 50: commissaries were not to be Lords of Session or advocates or to have any other office, so that consistories should not be prevented by the sitting of the Session.

[36] RSS, V, 2396.

[37] RPC, I, 340, 367; C.Sc.P., II, 236; C.S.P. For., VII, 512.

[38] C.Sc.P., II, 211 (where he is said to be of no religion).

[39] C.S.P.Sc., I, 227.

[40] Knox, II, pp. 164, 167; also C. Sc, P., II, 211, 218, 236, 250; C.S.P. For., VII, 480, 482, 499; Teulet, *Papiers d'Etat*, II, 82, 106, 107.

[41] Knox, II, pp. 169–170; C.S.P. For., VII, 506.

[42] RSS, V, 2352, 2462, 2463.

[43] Queen Mary married Henry Stewart, Lord Darnley, son of the Earl of Lennox on July 29, 1565; C.S.P.Sc., I, 214; C.S.P. For., VII, 1298. He is frequently referred to as "the King" and is said (C.S.P.Sc., I, 214, Randolph to Earl of Bedford; *C.S.P. For.*, VII, 1326, Randolph to Bedford; VIII, 1331, Bedford to Cecil, and 1337) to have been proclaimed King, but there is no evidence that the title was ever legally conferred on him. This indeed was a matter of contention between him and the Queen.

[44] Melville, *Memoirs*, p. 149; Teulet, II, p. 114; Keith, II, pp. 417–418, III, 272; H.M.C. Salisbury, I, 334.

[45] Knox, II, p. 182; C.Sc.P., II, 269, 270.

[46] RSS, V, 2705.

[47] RSS, V, 2705; RPC, I, 436, 438.

[48] Printed in APS, I, 29 and prefixed to the *Black Acts*. See also Bisset, *Rolment of Courtis*, I, 72, 80.

[49] Printed in part in APS, I, 29 and in full in Bisset, *Rolment of Courtis*, I, 81.

[50] Henryson was given, by licence dated July 1, 1566, an exclusive privilege and licence to print and sell the laws and Acts of Parliament, that is to say, the Books of Law called *Regiam Majestatem* and the remaining auld Laws and Acts of Parliament, for 10 years: Bisset, *Rolment of Courtis*, I, 81–82.

[51] C.S.P. For., VIII, 393.

[52] The background is narrated in Antonia Fraser, *Mary Queen of Scots*, pp. 15–16.

[53] The site of Kirk o' Field is now occupied by the Old College of Edinburgh University.

[54] C.Sc.P., II, 312–313, C.S.P. Foreign, VIII, 174, 176. There is much further information in Pitcairn, I, 488*. See also R. H. Mahon, *The Tragedy of Kirk o' Field* (1930).

[55] C.S.P. Spanish, XIV, 673 (Guzman de Silva to the King of Spain).

[56] Knox, *History*, II, p. 201; *Thirds of Benefices*, 278.

[57] RSS, V, 3123 (Dec 9, 1566).

[58] C.Sc.P. II, 315.

[59] C.S.P. For., VIII, 182.

[60] Pitcairn, I, p. 511.

[61] Calderwood, VIII, p. 211.

[62] C.S.P. For., VIII, 182, 264.

[63] C.S.P. For., VIII, 211.

[64] C.Sc.P., II, 320, 321, 335. See also C.S.P.Sc., I, 419 (1581).

[65] C.Sc.P., IV, 461–462 (1573).

[66] C.S.P.Sc., I, 273; Omond, *Lord Advocates*, I, p. 31.

[67] RPC, I, 498; C.S.P.Sc., II, 320–321; C.S.P. For., VII, 178, 182; Keith, II, 519.

[68] HMC, VI, 642.

[69] C.S.P. For., VIII, 182, 211.

[70] C.S.P. For., VIII, 393; Pitcairn, I, 500, 511, 512.

[71] Calderwood, II, p. 401; Pitcairn, I, p. 511.

[72] *History*, II, p. 203; *cf.* Pitcairn, I, p. 500*.

[73] C.S.P.Sc., II, 488; Keith, II, 529–531.

[74] C.S.P. For., VIII, 184 (Forster to Cecil).

[75] C.Sc.P., II, 319; Pitcairn, I, p. 513*. For other trials arising from Darnley's death, see Pitcairn, I, pp. 35, 95, 101.

[76] C.Sc.P., II, 320.

[77] C.Sc.P., II, 320–321.

[78] C.S.P. For., VIII, 184.

[79] Spottiswoode, II, p. 48; Calderwood, II, p. 348.

[80] C.S.P.Sc., II, 319–321.

[81] Pitcairn, I, p. 489.

[82] APS, III, 3, 4, 30.

[83] CSP For., VIII, 223; Pitcairn, I, p. 479.

[84] RSS, V, 3511, 3512; Spottiswoode, II, p. 52; Pitcairn, I, p. 500*.

[85] C.S.P. For., VIII, 233.

[86] Melville, *Memoirs*, p. 180. On Balfour's changes of party see G. Donaldson, *All The Queen's Men* (1983).

[87] H.M.C. Rep., II, 183.

[88] C.S.P. For., VIII, 264.

[89] Calderwood, II, p. 362.

[90] Laing, II, pp. 106–109, 114.

[91] Knox, *History*, II, p. 212; R.P.C., I, 641; C.Sc.P. II, 730; Laing, II, 90; These were the famous Casket Letters, on which see T. F. Henderson, *Mary Queen of Scots* and *The Casket Letters and Mary Queen of Scots*; Andrew Lang, *The Mystery of Mary Stuart*; and the Henderson-Lang discussion in 5 S.H.R. 1, 160.

[92] C.Sc.P., II, 383.

[93] H.M.C. Rep., VI, 642.

[94] *Historie of James the Sext*, p. 18, HMC, VI, p. 646; *Diurnal of Remarkable Occurrents*, p. 120; Calderwood, III, p. 387; *Laing Charters*, 841.

[95] C.Sc.P., II, 350, 375; Pitmedden, I, 180.

[96] APS, III, 46.

[97] APS, III, 3, 46.

[98] C.Sc.P., II, 398.

[99] Spotiswoode, II, pp. 84–85.

[1] C.Sc.P., II, 403–404.

[2] C.Sc.P., II, 405; Melville, *Memoirs*, p. 202.

[3] R.P.C., II, 1, 8; C.Sc.P., II, 663, 667; C.S.P. For., IX, 107.

[4] APS, III, 3b, 4b, 30b, 46a.

[5] APS, III, 25a.

[6] APS, III, 49.

[7] E.R., XIX, 331, 374; XX, 27.

[8] C.S.P. For., VIII, 393; Calderwood, II, 401, Pitcairn, I, p. 511.

[9] C.S.P. For., IX, 120; *Diurnal*, 147.

[10] C.S.P.Sc., I, 273; C.Sc.P., II, 673–674; *Diurnal*, 148.

[11] R.P.C., II, 27; *Diurnal*, 149.

[12] C.Sc.P., III, 21; Melville, p. 221; Calderwood, II, p. 505.

[13] C.S.P. For., IX, 355; Melville, p. 220.

[14] APS, III, 137, c. 5.

[15] R.P.C., II, 114, 148n.; C.Sc.P., III, 668–669.

[16] C.Sc.P. III, 699–700; IV, 460–462; Calderwood, III, p. 257.

[17] C.Sc.P., IV, 195, 383, 430, 436, 462.

[18] *Ibid.*, IV, 461, 482, 490, 533.

[19] *Ibid.*, IV, 461, 495–498; RPC, II, 193–201.

[20] APS, III, 84, 89.

[21] APS, III, 89a.

[22] APS, I, 30; APS, III, 89b; RSS, VII, 1070, 1559, 1793.

[23] *History of the Houses of Douglas and Angus*, p. 358; Goodal, *Preface*, p. viii.

[24] On the latter see Chap. 5, *infra*.

[25] APS, I, 31.

[26] *Rolment of Courtis*, II, 275.

[27] McKechnie, "Balfour's *Practicks*" (1931) 43 J.R. 179.

[28] David Moysie, *Memoirs of the Affairs of Scotland* (1830), p. 19; C.Sc.P., V, 327.

[29] RPC, III, 174, 178; C.Sc.P., V, 339, 355.

[30] APS, III, 137, 166.

[31] RMS, IV, 2924, 2930, 2960; R.P.C., III, 519–520.

[32] C.Sc.P., V, 387.

[33] Calderwood, VIII, 31.

[34] C.Sc.P.,V, 387, 570, 577, 586; C.S.P.Sc.,II, 416.

[35] *Ibid.*, V, 571; VI, 23; Laing, II, p. 315; Hewitt, *Scotland under Morton*, p. 197.

[36] C.Sc.P., V, 587, 607.

[37] Calderwood, III, p. 558.

[38] RPC, III, 403.

[39] C.Sc.P., VI, 93.

[40] Calderwood, III, p. 576.

[41] RPC, III, 462, 514.

[42] Bisset, *Rolment of Courtis*, II, 275.

[43] RMS, V, 593, 614; RSS, VIII, 1550n, 1792; APS, III, 319 (c. 44); APS, III, 493 (c. 99); RSS, VIII, 1674.

[44] APS, III, 137, c. 5.

[45] APS, III, 166, c. 49.

[46] APS, III, 319, c. 44; III, 413, c. 55; C.S.P.Sc., I, 467; RSS VIII, 1674.

[47] APS, III, 493, c. 99.

[48] APS, III, 494, c. 100.

[49] APS, III, 495, c. 101.

[50] *Scots Peerage*, I, 536. Fragments of Burleigh Castle still stand beside farm buildings on A911 a short distance from Milnathort.

[51] *Ibid.*, I, 547.

[52] *Ibid.*, I, 553–555. The Bruces of Kennet also had connections with other well-known lawyers.

[53] Claude Nau, *History of Mary Stewart* (1883), p. 77.

[54] *Ibid.*, p. 44.

[55] *History*, I, pp. 112, 219.

[56] J.F., I, 8, 13; Lord Clyde's trans., I, p. 109.

[57] p. 114.

[58] p. 405.

[59] Hannay, *College of Justice*, pp. 139–142.

[60] APS, VI, 576, c. 39.

[61] APS, IX, 455.

[62] As in such titles as *Court of Session Practice*.

[63] McKechnie, "Practicks," in *Sources and Literature of Scots Law* (Stair Soc.), p. 28. See also D. B. Smith, "Practicks," 1962 S.L.T. (News) 147.

[64] Bisset, *Rolment of Courtis*, II, 275.

[65] McKechnie, "Balfour's Practicks," (1931) 43 J.R. 179.

[66] Bisset, *Rolment of Courtis*, II, 275.

[67] Goodal, preface, p. ix.

[68] A few dated later, such as of 1580 and 1590, are regarded as misprints for 1480 and 1490; Goodal, Preface, pp. x–xi.

[69] Preface, p. vii.

[70] RPC, I, 174, 178.

[71] II, 275.

[72] McNeill's *Preface to Balfour's Practicks* (Stair Soc. ed.), I, xxxiv.

[73] D.N.B.; Anderson, S.N., II, 316.

[74] *e.g.* pp. 267, 301, 373.

[75] McKechnie, *op. cit.*, p. 189.

[76] Goodal, Preface, p. ix.

[77] Balfour's titles are not, in fact, numbered. There is a numbered list in Stair Soc. ed. pp. cxviii–cxix.

[78] pp. 614–644. The Book of Kintore was a collection made by David Kintor, Vice-Admiral of Scotland.

[79] pp. 644–655.

[80] pp. 655–677.

[81] pp. 677–684.

[82] Buchanan, "The Mss of *Regiam Majestatem*" (1937) 49 J.R. 217.

[83] NLS Adv. Ms. 25.4.11 known as Ms. J; B.M. Add. Mss. 48000–48196, which belonged to Skene (see Nicolson, *Historical Libraries* (1736), II, p. 99) and was later at Elvethan Hall (HMC, II, 42, xxxvi).

[84] Wellwood, *Abridgment of All Sea Laws* (1613), *passim*.

[85] McKechnie, p. 183. Skene also cites cases from a *registrum* extending to the 1590s and many of his earlier cases are cited also by Balfour.

[86] Apart from three decisions of 1494, 1517 and 1534.

[87] Some of these titles appear to have been divided into *prima pars* and *posterior pars*.

[88] *Practicks*, x and 153; ADC, II, xcviii.

[89] Sir David Carnegie of Kinaird: see R.M., David II, c. 26.

[90] Robert Galbraith; see APS, I 192–193.

[91] David Kintor, Vice-Admiral of Scotland; see Wade, *Acta Curiae Admirallatus Scotiae* (Stair Soc. 1937), xv.

[92] The buke of Scone: Skene, R.M., 134; APS, II, 97.

[93] e.g. pp. 217, 219.

[94] 1, c. 1.

[95] 1, c. 3.

[96] 3, c. 7.

[97] 4, c. 12. This is, of course, without prejudice to the particular rules applicable to clergy, barons and burgesses.

[98] A noteworthy exception is the Act 1567, c. 8 (APS, II, 552) against infamous libels, clearly a paraphrase of the edict *de famosis libellis* of Valentinian and Valens.

[99] pp. 8–13.

[1] pp. 20–38.

[2] pp. 42–76.

[3] pp. 76–81.

[4] pp. 93–133.

[5] pp. 133–188.

[6] pp. 149.

[7] pp. 188–216.

[8] pp. 188–190.

[9] pp. 216–264.

[10] pp. 264–503.

[11] pp. 503–576.

[12] pp. 503, c. 1.

[13] pp. 521–529.

[14] pp. 576–684.

[15] Goodal, *Preface*, p. viii.

[16] McNeill, preface to *Practicks* (Stair Soc.), p. xxxix.

[17] Chap. 7, *infra*.

[18] Edinburgh Univ. Library, Laing, III, 410, bears the autograph "Stair."

[19] e.g. Stair, *Inst.*, I, 13, 1, 4 and Balfour, 198, on liability for negligence in deposit.

[20] *McNeight* v. *Lockhart* (1843) 6 D. 128 at p. 136 *per* Lord Justice-Clerk Hope.

[21] *Boettcher* v. *Carron Co.* (1861) 23 D. 322 at p. 331 *per* Lord Justice-Clerk Inglis.

CHAPTER 4

SIR THOMAS CRAIG

THOMAS Craig of Riccarton[1] was born in 1538, when the Court of Session was six years old. Authorities differ as to his ancestry. He went to St. Leonard's College, St. Andrews, in 1552 and in 1555 moved to Paris where he studied law under Petrus Rebuffus and Franciscus Balduinus, notable civilians. He possibly also attended Poitiers, Toulouse or Bourges and studied under Duarenus or Cujacius. On return to Scotland he passed advocate in 1563 and in the following year was appointed justice-depute at criminal trials in place of Archibald Campbell, Earl of Argyll, the hereditary justice-general.[2] In this capacity he presided at the trial in 1566 when Scott, sheriff-depute of Perth, and Yaire or Zaire, a priest and servant of Lord Ruthven, were condemned to death for subordinate parts in the murder of David Riccio, Queen Mary's secretary[3], and in 1568 he presided at the trial of Hepburn, Dalgleish, Hay and Powrie, who were similarly condemned for their parts in the murder of Darnley at Kirk o'Field.[4] Argyll, the Justice-general, however, sat in person at the sham trial at which Bothwell was acquitted of participation in that murder.[5]

In 1564/65 he got a gift, so long as he should be justice-depute, of the unlaws of any six persons unlawed in any justice court, to the limit of 120 pounds,[6] and several times was given gifts of the escheat of persons outlawed.[7] In 1569 he was before the Privy Council for letting one John Mosman go, and was ordered to apprehend him,[8] and was ordered a second time on pain of having to pay Mosman's penalty.[9]

About this time Craig married Helen Heriot, daughter of the Laird of Trabrown,[10] and in 1573 he was appointed sheriff-depute of Edinburgh and appears to have resigned his criminal judicial office. These were in any event part-time appointments and he continued in practice, and must have continued to study law. In 1579 he was appointed procurator for the collectory.[11] In June 1581 the king borrowed money from Craig and various other advocates and assigned to them the expected revenues of the "cunyiehouse" *i.e.* the mint.[12] Six months later he got a warrant for repayment.[13] This suggests that he was prospering in practice.

In 1587 he was made one of the commissioners for revising the laws,[14] and for printing the statutes.[15] In 1589 he was nominated with another *curatores ad lites* to the sons of the Earl of Bothwell for sundry actions.[16] He was in heavy practice before the Privy Council.[17] He was one of a committee which in 1589 was appointed to regulate the curriculum of the High School of Edinburgh and in that year sat in the General Assembly of the Kirk. In 1592 he appeared as counsel for the King, along with the King's Advocate and Mr. John Skene, in an action for the reduction of some alienations of the royal property made while in minority,[18] and in 1593 along with Skene and two others had to confer with MacGill, the Lord Advocate, on the sufficiency of a libel against three lords.

Craig went to London in 1603 when James VI succeeded to the throne of England, possibly being invited because he was known to be a strong supporter of closer union of the two kingdoms, a result much desired by the King, and he was one of the Scottish commissioners negotiating for union in 1604.[19]

He died in 1608, leaving three sons and two or possibly three daughters. His eldest son Lewis[20] became a judge (Lord Wrightshouses) and founder of the family of Riccarton. His third son, John,[21] became a distinguished physician and is said to have been the person who gave John Napier of Merchiston the first hint of what Napier developed as logarithms.

His elder daughter married Sir Alexander Gibson of Durie,[22] Lord President of the Court of Session, and a descendant was Sir James Gibson Craig, W.S.,[23] leader of the Scottish Whigs in the early nineteenth century, one of whose sons, Sir William Gibson Craig of Riccarton, was Lord Clerk Register, 1862–78.[24] Another son was James Thomson Gibson Craig,[24] a distinguished antiquary and friend of Scott, Jeffrey, Cockburn and Macaulay. Craig's younger daughter married James Johnston, a merchant in Edinburgh, and their son, Archibald Johnston of Warriston (1611–63, advocate 1633)[25] became Lord Advocate in 1646, Lord Clerk Register 1649–61, a judge of the Court of Session and an outstanding leader of the Presbyterians, while their daughter married Robert Burnet of the Crathes family (1592–1661, advocate 1617)[26], later (1661) a judge as Lord Crimond, and became mother of Gilbert Burnet,[27] Bishop of Salisbury and historian. Another descendant was James Craig (1672–1732, advocate 1701), first Professor of Civil Law (1710–32) in Edinburgh University, who by his second wife Christian Dundas of Arniston, had a son Robert,[28] who became a judge of the Commissary Court of Edinburgh about 1756.

Probably between 1600 and 1605 Craig wrote a *Treatise on the Right of James VI to the Succession to the English Crown*, in Latin, but published in English translation by James Getherer in 1703. This was a reply to the work by the Jesuit Parsons who, under the assumed name of Doleman, published in 1594 *A Conference about the next Succession to the Crown of England*, in which he gave support to the claim of the Infante of Spain, as a relative of Catherine of Aragon, Henry VIII's first and ill-used Queen (and in Catholic eyes, his only lawful wife). This work had been suppressed and the possession of a copy declared high treason. There were several other refutations of Doleman's arguments by other hands in the seventeenth century, including *Jus Regium* by Sir George Mackenzie in 1684.

In 1605 Craig wrote a tract *De Hominio*, intended to prove that Scotland had never done homage to England. This was translated after his death by George Ridpath and published under the title *Scotland's Soveraignty Asserted* in 1695 and 1698. The publication was prompted by the fact that Rymer, compiler of the *Foedera*, had revived the controversy by publishing what he called a Form of Homage for the Kingdom of Scotland performed by Malcolm III for Edward the Confessor. It provoked a reply by William Attwood entitled *Superiority and Direct Dominion of the Imperial Crown of England* in 1704.

About the same time he wrote a *De Unione Regnorum Britanniae Tractatus*. In 1604 he had been one of the Scottish commissioners

appointed to meet English commissioners in London to discuss closer
political union following James VI's accession to the English throne, and
he signed the Articles of Union agreed on by the delegates on December
6, 1604. The book is a detailed argument for union from the Scottish side,
and the only one, which indicates a lack of enthusiasm in Scotland for the
idea, which did not of course secure approval for a further century. The
De Unione was first published, with a translation, by the Scottish History
Society in 1909. It is a substantial but hardly well thought-out or well-
argued case. Craig was simply besotted with the thought of union and
devotes much space to classical analogies and historical examples. There
is a dearth of sober argument.

It is divided into 12 chapters, and the approach is indicated by the title
of Chapter 1: The Separation of the Crowns of the Island is the cause of all
the calamities that have befallen Britain. He discusses in Chapter 4 the
King's proposal and the recent assembly of commissioners of both
kingdoms in London. Particular interest attaches to Chapter 6, discussing
whether for the perfecting of the proposed Union the laws of the two
countries should be identical: With some remarks on the existing English
and Scottish systems. He cites many instances of unions which "prove
conclusively that to promote the union which we have in view, it is by no
means imperative that the two kingdoms should submit to identical laws
and systems. The revision of existing laws which have taken root in
national sentiment is, indeed, a fruitful source of trouble; for a change in
the laws governing a state often changes the character of the state
itself."[29]

He sees no difference between the two countries on the cardinal points
of religious doctrine.

> "I now affirm a similar harmony in the public laws of the two
> countries. Indeed I assert that at the present day there are no nations
> whose laws and institutions more closely correspond than England
> and Scotland. On fundamental principles of jurisprudence they
> agree perfectly, though in procedure they differ, a fact which by no
> means obscures the general resemblance between their systems of
> law. Though I am not deeply versed in English law, and much of it is
> beyond my knowledge, I should say, from such study as I have given
> the subject, that there is not that diversity between the two systems
> of law as is popularly supposed to exist."[30]

Craig either had a very superficial knowledge of English law, or, more
probably, was so carried away by the idea of union as to be blind to very
substantial differences, far greater then than exist now.

In the following pages, however, Craig, by remaining on the highest
level of generalisations concludes that in criminal matters the same laws
and procedures are used in both countries! The same is true of private
law!

> "Finally, decisions at law are founded, on the whole, on the same
> practice in the two countries. Both gave the first place to the
> provisions of statutory or Parliament-made law. . . . If statute law
> offers nothing to instruct a judicial decision, recourse is had in
> England to common law. . . . The following fundamental principles

of English common law show that it does not much differ from ours.... If neither statute nor common law avail to satisfy the judge on the issue before him, he has recourse to certain general maxims.... Failing the statute law, common law, and these general rules or propositions, recourse is had to local custom, *i.e.* the local principles and axioms of the district in which the case before the court arises.... If no guidance can be obtained from custom, general axioms, or prescription, then the precedents set by previous judicial decisions in similar cases, and particularly in the Court of King's Bench, must be followed, on which fresh cases when they arise must be decided if the circumstances are similar. Against a decision based on precedents there is no effective exception or reply other than proof that the circumstances of the two cases differ; and the smallest detail of difference frequently avails to break down the alleged similarity of fact.... No one therefore can fail to see that the origin, beginning and development of the systems of law of the two countries are identical; though the further we travel from their common origin the wider is the difference which can be detected between them.... I conclude as follows: There is not that difference between the laws of the two countries that is popularly supposed to exist. Nor is there any reason to despair of the possibility of so harmonising the legal systems of the two peoples as to fashion one body of law applicable equally to both, and thereby to promote the union of the two countries in one body politic."[31]

Of all this it must be said that Craig was totally deluded by similarities at the high level of generality and by ignorance of detail to see far greater similarity than in fact existed. He barely mentions, for example, the fundamental English division between common law and equity, King's Bench and Chancery, and shows no appreciation of the importance of the division of jurisdiction. By 1600 the systems were far apart and harmonisation would have been very difficult indeed.[32] Above all, Craig did not reckon with national pride and the spirit of independence.

His major work is, however, undoubtedly *Jus Feudale, tribus libris comprehensum, quibus non solum consuetudines Feudales et Praediorum quae in Scotia, Anglia, et plerisque Galliae locis obtinent continentur sed universum Jus Scoticum, et omnes fere materiae Juris exponuntur, et ad fontes Juris Feudalis et Civilis singula reducuntur*, completed in 1603.

In 1610 the Privy Council recommended to the King publication of the late Mr Thomas Craig's books,[33] and in 1612 the Estates conveyed to the King a recommendation of the late Mr Thomas Craig's works[34]; in 1633 the King and Estates, on a petition from his son Robert for printing the three volumes written by the late Thomas Craig entitled *De Feudis*, "in respect that the same would be very useful to the country and for the instruction of those who aspire to the knowledge and practick thereof" ordained them to be examined by Sir Thomas Hope of Craighall, Sir Alexander Gibson of Durie and two others, and thereafter to be printed, and granted the petitioner the sole privilege for printing and the whole benefit of the volumes for 20 years, and none of the said books to be imported and sold during the said 20 years without the petitioner's tolerance. Why Robert did not use his privilege is unknown.

The work was ultimately first published by Robert Burnet, later Lord
Crimond, whose wife was a grand-daughter of Craig, at London and
Edinburgh in 1655, and reprinted in 1665. It bears to be published
Impensis Societatis Stationariorum. It was printed again in a better text,
with a preface, by Luther Mencken at Leipzig in 1716, and a third edition,
the best, edited by James Baillie, was published by Thomas and Walter
Ruddiman in 1732. It included a short Latin life of Craig.[35] A translation,
with an appendix containing the Books of the Feus, by Lord President
Clyde (the first) was published in two volumes in 1934. There was also an
English abridgment entitled *A compend or Breviary . . . extracted furth of
the book of . . . D. Tho. Craig Treating of the Feudall Law*, about 1682.[36]

The work has from the start been divided into titles but the titles and
their headings vary in the different editions. Baillie divided the titles into
numbered sections and it is by his title and section numbers that the work
has been cited since 1732; he also added a summary of the contents of
each numbered section.

Though prominent in legal practice, Craig did not engage in political
and public life in the way many contemporaries did, still less engage in
their devious practices. He must have spent years in researching for and
writing his work, particularly the *Jus Feudale*. In the Epistle Dedicatory
to the *Jus Feudale* he states[37]:

> "For the last forty years I have been immersed in the work of our
> Scottish courts, and my practice there has taught me much. After I
> had, as I thought, acquired a competent grasp of the custom of
> Scotland and of the law observed in that country, as well as of the
> regular forms and procedure of our Scottish courts, I became curious
> to learn something of the ways and institutions of our neighbours in
> so far as that might be done by reading the commentaries of learned
> writers on English law; for I must confess that I have only the most
> distant acquaintance with English practice. From a study of these
> and other sources, I formed the definite conclusion that there exists a
> fundamental identity between the principles underlying the legal
> systems of the two countries; and in comparing them together, I
> found the closest affinity of method in legal argument, expression
> and analysis. Our Scottish forms of legal process and judicial pro-
> cedure are, no doubt, different from those in use in England; but,
> with all respect to our neighbours, I make bold to say, and to say
> advisedly, that the forms we use in Scotland are better than those
> used in any other country I know of."

Later[38] he observes:

> "There is small prospect of popularity for a commentary on feudal
> customs in these days. . . . I have attempted no more than a scientific
> formulation of our Scots Law (something thought to be vague and
> indefinite) by putting the custom of Scotland alongside the written
> Feudal Law. The only merit – such as it is – to which I may be entitled
> is that I am, I believe, the first of my countrymen to attempt this task;

but no wish is nearer my heart than that others, doing better than I, may succeed where I have failed."

Craig accordingly is important as the first Scottish jurist who tried to write a systematic treatise and to adopt a comparative standpoint, though his historical investigation was inadequate.

As is evidenced by the Leipzig edition, Craig's work had some European reputation and circulation, in those days aided by the fact that he wrote in Latin, the *lingua franca* of scholars and jurists. Mencken, his editor, described it as a work long sought after in Germany, and by the end of the seventeenth century the *Jus Feudale* was being lectured on in the universities of Utrecht and Leiden.[39] But this has not persisted and the modern authorities on feudalism in Europe do not mention Craig.[40]

There is little doubt that Craig had a political motive in writing, just as in the *De Unione Regnorum*. He had been impressed by the similarities between Scots law and English, which clearly pointed to a common origin, and now that there was one king on both thrones and at the head of both legal systems he wanted to use these similarities to urge the assimilation of the systems.

"With the object of laying a solid foundation for this union [of the two kingdoms] and of furthering its consummation, Your Majesty not long ago appointed a conference between men learned in the law of both countries, with instructions to examine the legal institutions observed in each, and to ascertain how far they agreed or differed, with the ultimate object of assimilating them as far as might be; and, as not a few of those who thus met together were misled into an attempt to persuade the uninitiated that the customs and institutions observed in the two countries are not merely different but diametrically opposed.... I determined, in the hope of removing misapprehension, to make a careful study of the original sources of the legal systems in force in the countries.... I formed the definite conclusion that there exists a fundamental identity between the principles underlying the legal systems of the two countries and, in comparing them together, I found the closest affinity of method in legal argument, expression and analysis."[41]

The major source of Craig's work was the general feudal law of Western Europe, which first began to be reduced to writing in constitutions promulgated by the Carolingian monarchs, and these were collected and digested into the *Libri Feudorum* in northern Italy by, according to tradition, Gerardus Niger, who may have been the same as Gerardus Capagistus, and Obertus of Orto.[42]

Only to a small extent does Craig cite Scots Acts and decisions. He mentions *Regiam Majestatem* but does not utilise the Scottish material contained in Balfour's *Practicks*, which he is unlikely not to have known of, or in Skene's *Actis and Lawis*, which was in print before he finished his writing. The oldest extant MS., the Nisbet transcript in the National Library of Scotland, has many references in the margin but it is unknown whether these are original, or additions made in that MS. The successive printed editions, particularly Baillie's third edition in 1732, added to these, and Baillie's references have been taken into the text of Lord

Clyde's translation, but references to commentators on the civil and feudal laws have not. But it is plain that Craig's sources and authorities were for the most part foreign. The Scottish references are rather local examples than main sources.

Craig (I, 8, 6) distinguished law into the law of nature, the law of nations and civil or municipal law:

> "Originally the term Civil Law was applied exclusively to the system which the Romans built up for their own use; but not only is that system now widely adopted by other peoples, but they use the term to denote their own native municipal laws. When therefore a controverted question in the Law of Scotland cannot be solved by appealing to the general principles of the Law of Nature or to those of the Laws of Nations, recourse must be had to the written law of our own country."

This rather reverses the proper priority, which would appeal to the law of nature or of nations only failing any principle of native law. Riddell[43] damned this as *nubes et inania*.

To Craig the prime source of Scots law was the Scots Acts. Their provisions must be searched for guidance in the solution of the difficulty before looking further afield; all the more so because in Scotland

> "we have no other body of positive written law of comparable authority" (I, 8, 9). "The Scots Acts are practically the only written source of genuine native law we have" (I, 8, 12). "If no assistance is to be had in that quarter, then the custom of Scotland as shown by the settled course of judicial decision (or practice as we call it) must be followed" (I, 8, 13). "When a question of novelty arises for decision which is not solved by anything in our written law, nor by the custom of Scotland, nor by any of the means above described, and an answer to it is discoverable in the Feudal Law, that answer should be preferred to any that may be drawn from Canon or Roman law. Speaking generally but none the less accurately, the Feudal Law is to be reckoned a part of the native law of Scotland. In saying this, I am not unduly stretching the connotation of native law; for feudalism is the source and origin from which most of the law in daily use in our courts, and all our legal usages and practice, are derived" (I, 8, 16). "So far then we have arrived at the general conclusion that, in the decision of controverted questions of Scots Law, the written law holds the first rank of authority, and that judicial precedent or custom (that is, the custom of Scotland) ranks next. That customary law should rank immediately after the written law of the land, is in accordance with the nature of the Feudal Law, for since the latter varies locally it necessarily sanctions the observance in each locality of its own local customs. After custom comes the written Feudal Law. But if neither a Scots Act, nor the custom of Scotland as evidenced by the decisions of the courts, nor the Feudal Law, provides the answer to a legal problem, we must betake ourselves to the Civil Law ... when however it is inconsistent with the Canon Law (and the points of difference between the Civil and Canon Laws have been collected by several writers) the Canon Law is preferred in

Scotland, especially with regard to the affairs of the Church, and matters of personal conduct where, as the canonists put it, the conscience is directly concerned" (I, 8, 16–17).

In Book I, Craig deals with the origin of the law in general, with the history of the civil, canon and feudal laws and of the introduction of the last into Scotland. Then he treats of the definition and classification of feus, and who may grant and take feus, and finally of the Crown's regalia or reserved feudal rights. Book II deals with the constitution of a new feu, charters, sasine, leases or tacks, succession, tailzied succession and related matters, and Book III with resignations and renunciations, apprising and adjudication, loss of feudal estate by felony or delict and ancient practice in feudal causes. It is accordingly a book on feudal landholding, particularly as understood and applied in Scotland, rather than a book on Scots law. Even allowing that land was the principal form of wealth and the most developed branch of the law, large tracts of law are not mentioned at all, or only in relation to the central topic, the feudal tenure of land. Burnet, in his preface to the first edition, observed that prior to 1603 Scots law was difficult to discover but then "our author rose, like another Justinian, and extracted light out of this legal darkness; and under the title of a treatise on the Feudal Law, embraced the whole body of our Scottish jurisprudence, discussing every important matter therein in a lucid and learned order, and reducing all to their original foundation of the civil and feudal law.' This is an overstatement. Craig's book is not a balanced examination of all the main branches of Scots law, but an examination of legal feudalism as worked out in Scotland, of Scottish feudal land law. Other topics are dealt with only incidentally. Marriage is discussed (II, 18, 17) incidentally to the question of succession by and to bastards. Contract is considered only in relation to the question whether a feu is a contract *bonae fidei* or one *stricti juris*. The only delicts are feudal ones; assythment is not mentioned and spuilzie only in relation to the brieve of ejection.

Craig was of the opinion (I, 8, 11) that *Regiam Majestatem* was not part of the authentic law of Scotland.[44] It was written by Ranulph de Glanvill.

"The version which is current in this country has been copied word for word from Ranulph's thirteen [sic] books except that the thirteen books have been rearranged so as to make four. It must have been the work of some obscure plagiarist . . . I intend making the *Regiam Majestatem* and the matter annexed to it the subject to a special monograph after I have completed the project of this work."[45]

Craig himself cited few authorities but these included Bartolus, Baldus, and Hotoman. Many additional references are given in the oldest extant transcript, inscribed *"ex libris* magistri Joannis Nisbet" (Qy. Sir John Nisbet of Dirleton), and Baillie added to his edition many references to the civil and canon laws, the Books of the Feus, Scots Acts, *Regiam Majestatem, Quoniam Attachiamenta* and *Leges Burgorum*, and commentators on the civil or feudal law, and also notes of changes in the law between Craig's time and his own day. In Lord Clyde's translation references are given for many of the passages cited. In particular Craig himself gave hardly any references to decided cases.

There is no doubt that Craig overstated the authority of the *Libri Feudorum* in Scotland. Fraser Tytler[46] pointed out that Craig's object was not to investigate the antiquities of Scots law or to describe its distinguishing and characteristic features but to establish the fact of similarity between the laws of Scotland and of England. His purpose was, indeed, partly political, to support his advocacy of union with England. Similarly he subordinated the reality of decisions and practice to the idealism of a great theoretical construct.

Burnet, his first editor,[47] remarked that Scots law was in a very confused state but then "our author arose, like another Justinian, extracted light from darkness and under the name of Three Books on the Feus, encompassed the whole of Scots law, and nearly all the materials of Law and expounded them clearly, lucidly and distinctly and drew everything to their sources in civil and feudal law." This panegyric is not wholly justified, because Craig was concerned with land laws only, not the whole of Scots law.

Walter Ross[48] was critical of Craig. He commented:

"The disposition [to neglect examination of the development of our own law in favour of external sources] which appears thus partially in Skene is seen complete in our first, as he may be justly termed, and favourite writer, the learned and elegant Sir Thomas Craig. He can scarcely bring himself to confess that we ever had any municipal law or custom, peculiar to ourselves: Everything, it seems, was regulated by the civil and canon codes, but more especially by the feudal law, which he dignifies with the title of 'the proper law of this kingdom.' Is it possible that this great writer could be ignorant of the laws by which the moveable property of his country was governed anterior to the reign of James V or the institution of the College of Justice, which happened only ten years before his own birth? And yet, he expressly acknowledges this ignorance.

'Is it credible' says he 'that the Judges of the old Session determined according to the civil and canon laws.' Can such a position be held by any man who reads even the statutes of that period, in every part of which he finds allusions to established customs, not only unconnected with, but sometimes opposite to, both these systems; and are not many of these usages existing in our law at this moment? With regard to the common law in heritage, did it not then, and does it not yet differ from, and stand in contradiction to, the written feudal law, in a great variety of cases? The further back we go, do not we find these differences grow wider? Sir Thomas Craig rejects the *Regiam Majestatem*, and treats with marked indifference almost every part of the old Scottish code published by Skene. If he doubted the authenticity of these evidences of national jurisprudence, would it not have been proper and natural for this great man to have had recourse to these unquestionable monuments of it, the public records, and the ancient deeds and instruments, with which the charter chest of every family was filled. . . . The brieves, or writs, of course, must be the foundation of the common law of any country which admits them. . . . A complete collection of the Scottish brieves would have been a record of a great part of our law. . . . If we look into the lives of the great lawyers and Judges of the Court of Session, which have been preserved, we shall find that they all studied in France and returned to their own country in quality of *Doctores utriusque juris*. Sir Thomas Craig himself studied only the languages and philosophy in Scotland; for the laws he went to France.... So little attention does this great man seem to have paid to his own country, that he does not even know, that both the civil and canon laws had, long before this time, been publicly taught in Scotland.... Influenced by his foreign education, Sir Thomas, in his elegant treatise, sets out with a fixed opinion, and is determined to persuade others, that the whole of our laws and usages are founded on the civil and canon laws; and thence alone their origin and principles were to be deduced. This freed our great author at once from the necessity of any material inquiry into the ancient common law of his country, or into the forms of our writs, public or private. He was certain of being able to explain everything contained in them upon the principles of the civil or the feudal laws; and thus it has most unfortunately happened, that the man, who from extensive learning, intense application, a taste for study, and who, from the circumstances of flourishing at an early period, was perhaps better fitted than any other, either of his contemporaries or successors, to give his country a complete system of her national jurisprudence, not only endeavoured to destroy the credit of the few books or evidences of the common law which were to be found, but has almost sunk them into oblivion, in favour of two foreign systems, the civil and the feudal laws.... What has been the consequence of this neglect of our ancient law and our records? Sir Thomas Craig quotes no styles, no deeds, no brieves, but the brieve of mortancestry, the charter and the seisine; and these he illustrates solely upon the principles of the written feudal law, without taking in the peculiarities which they derived either from our own consuetudes, or those of the people by whom it is said they were handed down to us."

Riddell similarly[49] denounced Craig's "unaccountable inaccuracy, even in the case of contemporary Scottish law, and facts."

Stair, however, thought well of Craig: "Our learned countryman, Craig of Riccarton, hath largely and learnedly handled the feudal rights of this and other nations, in his book *De Feudis*,"[50] and for that reason he concentrated on the developments since Craig's time.

Modern opinion rates Craig fairly highly. Cosmo Innes excepted from criticism

"Sir Thomas Craig, whose admirable book, the *Jus Feudale*, must always be spoken of with respect. But Craig wrote less as a Scottish lawyer, than as a learned student of the civil and canon and feudal law. He quotes cases that happened in his own day and a little before, in Scotland, but he had no care to distinguish the history of our law from that of any other feudal nation; and whenever he makes a general assertion, I think you will find that he draws it from the Roman law or the book *De Feudis* which, united, were in fact the common law – the law of civilised Europe in his time."[51]

It is true that the *Jus Feudale* is not so much a treatise on Scots law as a treatise on a field of law by a Scots lawyer illustrated by some reference to the application of that tract of law in and to Scottish conditions. He frequently disregards Scottish practice and does not adequately distinguish between the feudal law applied elsewhere and the feudal law as developed and applied in Scotland. But it is the first systematic, continuous narrative treatise in Scots law, albeit dealing with only one branch of the law; the exposition, moreover, is strongly based on a search for principles rather than on a mere collection of rules or instances or applications. Down to the twentieth century it has been repeatedly cited and referred to.[52] It is still a standard authority on the feudal system of his time, and Craig has generally been deemed the earliest of our institutional writers, whose work is considered of authority equivalent to that of a bench of judges.

He also wrote Latin verse of moderate quality, including *Genethliacon Jacobi Principis Scotorum, celebrating the birth of Prince James, later James VI and I,*[53] *Stephanoforia*, a long poem composed in honour of James's English coronation, and when he returned to Scotland in 1604 a Latin poem taking leave of his King and of the Muses.

NOTES

[1] DNB; Anderson, S.N., I, p. 687; Chambers, BDES; *Life* by Baillie, prefixed to 1732 edition of *Jus Feudale*; P. Fraser Tytler, *Account of the Life and Writings of Sir Thomas Craig of Riccarton* (1823). Riccarton is 1½ miles NW of Currie, Midlothian, and 6 miles SW of Edinburgh.

[2] Pitcairn, I, pp. 447* *et seq.*

[3] Keith, *History*, p. 334; Arnot, *Criminal Trials*, Appx. No. III. Pitcairn, I, p. 478*.

[4] Pitcairn, I, p. 490*; C.Sc.P., II, 572–573.

[5] Howell's *State Trials* (1809), I, p. 902.

[6] RSS, V, 1892.

[7] RSS, V, 1682, 2390, 2496, 2516; VI, 2440; VII, 1379; VIII, 878.

[8] RPC, II, 16.

[9] RPC, II, 27–28.

[10] George Buchanan's mother was Agnes Heriot of Trabrown. Thomas Hamilton, Earl of Haddington's mother was Elizabeth Heriot of Trabrown. The lands of Trabrown in East Lothian were granted by the Earl of Douglas to John Heriot about 1423. To this family belonged also George Heriot (1563–1624), James VI's friend "Jingling Geordie," founder of Heriot's Hospital in Edinburgh.

[11] RSS, VII, 2011.

[12] RPC, III, 393.

[13] RPC, III, 435.

[14] APS, III, 105b.

[15] APS, III, 520b.

[16] Tytler, citing Pitmedden MS.

[17] See numerous references to his appearances in RPC, II, III, IV, V and VI.

[18] Tytler, citing Haddington's MS. Decisions, I, 25, No. 126.

[19] APS, IV, 264a; RPC, VII, 457; List of Commissioners in Dicey and Rait's *Thoughts on the Union between England and Scotland* (1920), App. C.

[20] DNB; Anderson, S.N., I, p. 688; Brunton & Haig, p. 244.

[21] DNB.

[22] DNB; Anderson, S.N., II, p. 296; Brunton & Haig, p. 264.

[23] DNB; Anderson, S.N., I, p. 692.

[24] DNB.

[25] DNB; Anderson, S.N., II, p. 578; Brunton & Haig, 306; Omond, I, 148.

[26] Brunton & Haig p. 373, who give his date of call as 1642. But this was another Robert Burnett.

[27] DNB; Anderson, S.N., I, p. 489.

[28] DNB; Grant, *Story of the University of Edinburgh*, II, p. 364.

[29] p. 303.

[30] p. 304.

[31] pp. 320–328.

[32] On English law c. 1600 see Holdsworth, *History of English Law*, Vols. 4 and 5.

[33] RPC, IX, 572.

[34] APS, IV, 523, c. 75.

[35] Baillie ran into financial difficulties by reason of the cost of publication and on January 6, 1736, the Faculty of Advocates ordered an advance of £30 to him. "And it being further represented that the original book itself was one of the prime standard books of the Scottish Law, and that this edition was vastly more correct, and had several other advantages above the former editions; It was therefore warmly recommended to the members of the Faculty that they, as well for their own sakes as that of the publisher would purchase copies of it:" *Faculty of Advocates' Minute Book* (ed. Pinkerton, Stair Soc.), II, p. 156.

[36] See also John Spottiswoode's (6th) edition of Mackenzie's *Institutions* (1723), II, 6, 1, 113n.; George Law, "*Cragii Jus Feudale*" (1898) 10 J.R. 177, 334.

[37] Lord Clyde's ed., p. ix.

[38] Epistle, xii.

[39] Lord Clyde's introduction, p. xvii.

[40] See, *e.g.* Vinogradoff, "Foundations of Society: Origins of Feudalism," in 2 *Camb. Med. Hist.* 631; "Feudalism," in 3 *Camb. Med. Hist.* 458; F.L. Ganshof, *Feudalism* (1952); Marc Bloch, *Feudal Society* (1961).

[41] *Epistle Dedicatory*, p. ix. This is true in respect of original sources and the most general principles but Scottish land law and English real property had already, by 1600, diverged very considerably in detail.

[42] J. F., I, 6, 2–5. The *Books of the Feus* were frequently printed at the end of early modern editions of the *Corpus Juris Civilis*. They are translated as an appendix to Lord Clyde's translation of the J.F., Vol. 11, pp. 1079 *et seq.*

[43] *Inquiry into Scottish Peerages* (1842), I, p. 469.

[44] Baillie's footnotes, however, repeatedly refer to R.M.

[45] There is no evidence that this special monograph was ever written. If it was, no trace of it has survived.

[46] *Life of Craig*, pp. 156–157.

[47] *Ad Lectorem*, (1655 ed.), 3, reprinted in Baillie's 1732 ed., xi, translated also in Tytler's *Life of Craig*, p. 161.

[48] *Lectures*, II, p. 7.

[49] *Inquiry into Scottish Peerages* (1842), II, p. 1072.

[50] *Inst.*, II, 3,3.

[51] *Scotch Legal Antiquities*, pp. 2–3.

[52] Duff's *Feudal Conveyancing* and Rankine on *Land Ownership* cite Craig repeatedly in their footnotes.

[53] *Delitiae Poetarum Scotorum*, i, 221.

CHAPTER 5

SIR JOHN SKENE

SKENE has already been mentioned as a collaborator with Balfour but he became a notable jurist in his own right.

John Skene of Curriehill[1] was of an old Aberdeenshire family. He was probably born about 1543 (though some authorities[2] say 1549), and was a student at St. Mary's College, St. Andrews, in 1556 and a regent there in 1564–65.[3] His brother William appears to have studied at a foreign university and taken the licentiate *utriusque juris* there. After the Reformation William discoursed on Cicero's *Laws* and Justinian's *Institutions* in St. Mary's, and expounded to his students the practice of the Commissary Court of which he was chief judge.[4]

John Skene travelled in Scandinavia and became familiar with the languages of these countries, a capacity which later proved valuable to him, and he may have studied law in Paris.[5] In the preface to his Latin edition of the *Regiam* he says that he returned to Scotland from Wittenberg. On his return to Scotland he passed advocate in 1575.[6] He seems to have acquired a good practice from the start. Shortly after his call a commission was appointed "to visite the Bukis of the Law, Acts of Parliament, and Decisions before the Session and draw the forms of the body of our lawis"[7]: the commissioners included Balfour and, according to Hume of Godscroft,[8] the task was laid upon Sir James Balfour and Master John Skene, Clerk Register and Master of the Rolls.[9] This is almost certainly the work which resulted in the book known as Balfour's *Practicks*.[10]

For his work Skene was rewarded in 1577 by an annual pension of ten chalders of meal, granted for life from the revenues of Arbroath Abbey and the teind meal of various lands; it was renewed in 1579.[11]

From about 1578 onwards he is recorded as frequently appearing before the Privy Council[12] and was one of the advocates who lent the King money in June 1581.[13]

In 1587 he was named a member of a commission, along with Thomas Craig and others, or any three of them, the Chancellor always being one, appointed to "visite and consider the haill lawes actis and statuitis maid in the twa last parliaments. And how many of them necessarily would be imprentit. That according to their advise and declaration the Clerk of Register may gif furth an extract and copie to the prentare with sic guidlie diligence as may be used."[14] It is not clear what results followed from this commission's work. But Skene's appointment to these commissions indicates that he was regarded as a knowledgeable lawyer.

In April 1589 he was made Lord Advocate, jointly with David MacGill,[15] and is said to have been the first of the King's Advocates who was famous as a lawyer.

He was chosen to go with Sir James Melville when the latter was to go to Denmark to negotiate the marriage of Princess Anne of Denmark to James VI, because he had the necessary languages[16] and in 1589 did go with the Earl Marischal,[17] and was also an ambassador to Flanders,[18] some of the German states, seeking to promote peace in Europe,[19] and then in 1591 to the States-General in Holland.[20] "And knowing Mr. John Skene to be religious, learned and honest, having the Dutch and the Latine tongues, with great acquaintance with sundrie princes in Germanie and the chose of learned men about the princes there, therefore he thought it mete to joyne him with the Colonel [Stewart] trusting the same should well content her majestie cheflie upon her majestie's knowledge of the sufficientcie and good affection of Mr. Skene."[21] In August 1589 he was a party to the agreement between Scottish ambassadors and the Danish government about the Orkney Isles.[22]

In 1592 another commission was appointed by statute[23] ordaining the Chancellor, with the assistance of some distinguished lawyers including Master John Skene, advocate, and Mr. Thomas Hamilton, apparent of Priestfield (later first Earl of Haddington) "to visite the lawis and actis maid in this present Parliament, and all utheris municipall lawis and actis of Parliament bygane," to consider what should be known to the subjects, and to cause them to be copied and authentic copies delivered to the King's printer. The execution of this work seems to have been devolved on Skene.

In September 1594 he relinquished the office of Lord Advocate and was appointed Clerk Register[24] and also a judge of the Court of Session, as Lord Curriehill[25]; he was also an assessor at assizes and justice courts,[26] an auditor of exchequer,[27] and during the years 1596 and 1597 was one of the Octavians or eight Lords of Exchequer who managed the King's financial affairs.[28] As Clerk Register he sat in the Convention of 1596[29] and Parliament of 1596–98.[30]

The product of his work under the commission of 1592 appeared in print in 1597 as *The Lawes and Actes of Parliament*. To this was appended his *De Verborum Significatione*.

A royal privilege[31] gave Skene licence to have his work printed and therefore to sell and distribute the same, and to cause the same to be sold and distributed throughout our whole realm, to the effect that they may come to the better knowledge of all our lieges, and prohibiting others from doing so for ten years under pain of escheat and fine. An Act of 1598,[32] narrating the necessity for the whole lieges of knowledge of the laws and Acts of Parliament, "that be the ignorance of the same they pretend not an excuis for thair offence," remitted to the Lords of Session to consider how the said Acts already printed might be bought by such subjects within the realm as were of such substance and ability to buy the same, their conclusion to have the force of statute. The Privy Council also remitted to the Lords of Session to enforce the purchase by all of sufficient substance.[33] At this time Skene was regularly present in the Convention of Estates and the Privy Council.[34]

Thereafter he continued with the more difficult task of seeking to collect and print the ancient laws of the realm. A manuscript note in Skene's writing in the Bute MS. indicates that he had started work as early as June 1575.[35] It may be that Skene took the view that in implement of the 1592 commission it was easier, and possibly also more generally useful, to produce first an edition of the legislation from 1424, and then to deal with the earlier, and more difficult, material.[36] The fact that his *De Verborum Significatione*, an exposition of the terms and difficult words contained in *Regiam Majestatem* and other works, was published with the *Lawes and Actes* in 1597 also shows that before that date he had devoted considerable time and attention to the *Regiam* and other pre-1424 materials.

But his public duties continued. In 1598 he was one of a commission to treat of matters concerning the Isles[37]; in 1601 he was one of the commissioners appointed to assist the new Treasurer in the administration of his office,[38] a member of several other commissions,[39] including one to report on the disputes between the magistrates of Glasgow and the masters of the College thereof.[40] In June 1603 along with the Chancellor he inventoried the moveables in Holyrood.[41]

The work on the earlier materials was finally finished in 1607 and he laid the text of his labours before the Privy Council, which presented an address to the King,[42] recommending that, as the meanness of Skene's estate was not equal to his wit, genius and literature, the King should have the work printed at public expense. An Act[43] was accordingly passed, ordaining the manuscript to be printed, the expense to be met by a tax laid upon the judges and the members of the Estates, and a commission was granted in Skene's favour anent the printing in one volume of the auld lawes called *Regiam Majestatem* and other Acts and statutes.[44]

A royal letter of Februrary 2, 1608, to the Privy Council instructed them to have Skene's work advanced and forwarded. The Council granted commission to some of its number, including Thomas Hamilton of Priestfield and Sir Lewis Craig of Wrightslands (son of Sir Thomas Craig) to assist the commissioners to set down and modify a sum and make a division of it for printing of the said volume, and set down a stent roll among the persons who by the Act were ordained to pay the sum.[45] Skene also got from the Privy Council the services of the parish minister of Haddington, Mr. James Carmichael, for two months to help him in putting the book through the press.[46] A copyright licence was granted on December 6, 1608, but a dispute with Finlason, the printer, delayed work and on September 14, 1609, the Privy Council ordered Finlason to deliver the work within eight days.[47] The cost of the production, 20,000 marks or £1111 stg. was raised by an assessment levied by the commission appointed for the purpose, which assessed £638.16.8 Scots on Edinburgh and £100 Scots on Glasgow.[48] Burghs assessed for this purpose appear to have been given a copy of the work.[49]

In 1604 Skene was a commissioner along with Thomas Craig and others for treating of the proposed union with England[50] and in 1606 one of the Lords of the Articles.[51] In 1605, possibly when a commissioner for union, he was called to the English Bar, at the Middle Temple.[52] In 1607 with the rest of the Privy Council he took an oath required by a royal letter of April 1607, imposing an oath of allegiance and acknowledgment of royal supremacy, which was apparently intended as a new means of coercing the Presbyterians.[53] He was a member of several other commissions,[54] including one to make a visitation of the University of St. Andrews in 1609,[55] and busy on Council and committees thereof.[56]

One of his interesting tasks as Lord Clerk Register was to register[57] a copy of the decree of the Lord Chancellor of England (Lord Ellesmere, later (1616) Viscount Brackley) in *Calvin's Case* or the case of the *post-nati*.[58] The problem was whether, after the Union of 1603, Scots were alien in England, particularly persons born in Scotland after James's accession to the English throne. Calvin, or more correctly, Colville, was a child born in Scotland in 1606, and in a collusive action complained that he had been disseised of a free tenement in Shoreditch; the defendants pleaded that Calvin was an alien and could not hold freehold land in England, to which Calvin demurred. The matter was brought before courts both of law and equity and both cases were adjourned into the Exchequer Chamber and argued by Coke and Bacon. Ellesmere and a large majority of the judges held that the *post-nati* were natural-born subjects. The decision was very important not merely for Scots in England but as settling that there was a uniform status for natural-born subjects not only in England and Scotland but in the many lands later added to the King's dominions.

During the years 1609-13 Skene had as a clerk and assistant one Habakkuk Bisset, and Skene caused him to write "be his directioun, the formes of deductioun of all processis in civile actionis, presentlie used and observed befoir the lordis of his maiestais consell and sessioun, and utheris judges within his hienes Kingdom of Scotland," and to these he added a second part, comprising his own collections.[59] He died in 1616,[60] having in 1612 resigned his office of Clerk Register,[61] but his son, James, whom he had advised not to present the resignation unless he secured a promise of the office for himself, was not firm enough and Thomas Hamilton, later Lord Chancellor Haddington, got him to give in the resignation, and secured the office for himself; James abandoned any claim to the office, accepting in lieu a post as a Lord of Session.[62] In 1626 he succeeded as Lord President, also as Lord Curriehill, and held that office until his death in 1633.[63] In 1630 he was made a baronet of Nova Scotia. In 1633 he in turn was appointed a commissioner for revising the laws.[64]

Skene's work on the records gave to posterity three works, of which one is in two versions. The first is the *Lawes and Actes of Parliament, maid by King James the First, and His Successours Kinges of Scotland: Visied, collected and extracted furth of the Register*. It was printed by Waldegrave, the King's printer, in 1597 and is a stout folio. It contains the Acts from 1424 to its date (680 pp.), a large Table and Repertory of all special matters and heads contained in the said Acts, a Chronologie of all the Kings of Scotland from the beginning,[65] an Almanack for fifty years of the moveable feasts and other parts of the Kalendar, The Interpretation of the terms and difficult words used in the four Buiks of Regiam Maiestatem and others, in infeftments and practique of this Realme,[66] and a Catalogue of the Buikes conteinand the auld Lawes written before King James the First of gud memorie.

Like his predecessors under the royal commission of 1566 which produced the *Black Acts*, Skene did not think it expedient to go back to the earliest registers and authentic monuments. He also started in 1424 and brought the compilation down to 1597. He followed closely the edition of 1566, omitting a considerable number of statutes which he presumably considered unimportant and added a very few.

"In the choice of the materials for the subsequent part, he seems in a great measure, to have been directed by the successive publications already alluded to; and, throughout the whole, he would appear to have rarely consulted the original Records; and has, in many instances, adopted the errors of former editions with needless servility. With the exception of those statutes of most recent date, which had not been printed before, he cannot be said to have added much to the stock of public instruction. . . . The difficulties and hazards of the task must be, on all hands, admitted to have been great; though his own statement of them certainly seems to be tinged with much exaggeration."[67]

The Table of the Kings of Scotland starts with Fergus the First, whose reign is said to have begun in 330 B.C., and continues through many others, including Donald I, the first Christian king of Scotland, who succeeded in A.D. 199,[68] and so on to historical figures, Kenneth MacAlpin and finally to James VI. Most of this must be dismissed as unhistorical. The final three pages of the volume of *Lawes and Actes* is "Ane Admonition to the reader tuiching the buikes conteinand the lawes of his Realme and abbreviations used in the treatise proceiding." This is a short list of the law books prior to the time of James I, referred to by Skene in the *De Verborum Significatione*, and shows what materials he had found. He lists the *Leges Malcolmi Mackenneth; Regiam Majestatem*, "maid be King David the first;" *Quoniam attachiamenta; Modus tenendi curias Baronum*; *Leges burgorum*; *Statuta Willelmi regis*; *Statuta Alexandri*; *Statuta Roberti Bruyse*; *Assisa regis David*; *Statuta Roberti tertii*; *Leges Forestarum*, "whereof the author is not known to me;" *Iter camerarii*; *De maritagio*, "ane little treatise written be some private man and is no wais authentick;" *Statuta Gildae*; *Leges portuum*, "quhilk is nocht authentick;" *De iudicibus*, "ane lang and large Rapsodie, collected furth of all the buikes conteinand the civill law of this Realme. It is nocht authentick;" the *Actes of Parliament* of King James the First and his successors; and *Decreites given be the Lordes of the Sessioun and Councell*.

Another edition, in folio, was published by Finlason in 1611.

The same volume contained *De Verborum Significatione, The Exposition of the Termes and Difficill Wordes, conteined in the four Buikes of Regiam Maiestatem and others, in the Actes of Parliament, Infeftments, and used in practicque of this Realme with diverse rules and commoun places or principalles of the Lawes*. This runs to 139 pages. Skene got his title from the rubric of the second last title of Justinian's Digest (Dig. 50, 16), which is a collection of passages from Roman jurists explaining words. Skene's work is in fact our first legal dictionary[69] and explains terms even in his day unfamiliar and difficult and today wholly archaic, from Actilia, to Zemsel. His explanations of the words are lengthy, frequently of 20 or 30 lines; some, such as that of Breve, are articles on the subject, not mere definitions; he frequently attempts derivations, and gives references to places in the Auld Lawes where the word is found. Occasional references to Alciatus, Chassenaeus, Cuiacius, Tiraquellus and others indicate a scholar of some breadth of learning. Cosmo Innes however,[70] called it a "hasty, ill-considered work." In the *De Verborum* Skene frequently refers to a book of his brother William, probably in manuscript, and to a book of his brother Alexander, an advocate.

The *De Verborum* is a substantially original contribution to learning. It had no predecessors in Scotland and, in England, only Rastell. The work is of great value and every later dictionary looks to it. More modern scholarship would question some of Skene's statements and explanations, but he can hardly be criticised on that account. In 1681[71] Parliament passed a ratification of the order to print his treatise *De Verborum Significatione*.

The *De Verborum* was subsequently issued separately and reprinted many times. It was also appended to Robert Bell's *Dictionary of the Law of Scotland* (1808, 1815, and 1826).

Skene's third work appeared in 1609 as: *Regiam Majestatem, Scotiae Veteres Leges et Constitutiones, ex Archivis Publicis et Antiquis Libris Manuscriptis Collectae, Recognitae, et Notis Juris Civilis, Canonici, Nortmannici auctoritate confirmatis, illustratae, opera et studio Joannis Skenaei Regiae Majestati a Conciliis et Archivis Publicis*, published by Thomas Finlason. It comprised a Latin dedication to James VI, a royal grant of monopoly for the work for 20 years, a Latin discourse to the reader, various verses by various persons, including Thomas Craig, and the Latin texts of *Leges Malcolmi II Mackenneth, Regiam Majestatem, Quoniam Attachiamenta, Leges Burgorum, Curia Quatuor Burgorum, Statuta Gildae, Assisa de Ponderibus et Mensuris per Regem Davidum Primum*,[72] *Iter Camerarii, Iter Justitiarii, Statuta Wilhelmi, Leges Forestarum, Statuta Alexandri Secundi, Prima Statuta Roberti Primi, Secunda Statuta Roberti Primi, Statuta Davidis Secundi, Statuta Roberti Secundi, Statuta Roberti Tertii*, an *Index Rerum* and an *Index Verborum praecipue Barbarorum*. To some matters there is appended an "Annotatio." Many chapters have marginal notes explanatory or with references to later legislation.

In the same year the same publisher put out: *Regiam Majestatem, The Auld Lawes and Constitutions of Scotland, faithfullie collected furth of the Register and other auld authentick bukes, fra the dayes of King Malcolm the Second, until the time of King James the first, of gude memorie, and trewlie corrected in sindrie faults, and errours, committed be ignorant writers. And translated out of Latine in Scottish language, to the use and knowledge of all the subjects within this realm. With ane large table of the contents thereof, Be Sir John Skene of Curriehill, Clerk of our Souveraigne Lordis Register, Counsell and Rollis. Quhereunto are Adjoined Twa Treatises, The Ane, Anent the Order of proces observed before the Lords of Counsell and Session: The other of Crimes and Judges in criminal causes*. The contents, apart from being translated, are not quite the same. The dedication is omitted. The "To the Reader" of the Scottish edition is different from *Candido Lectori* of the Latin edition. The selection of Latin verses is different, and shorter. The Annotatio appended to many chapters in the Latin edition is omitted, and the marginal notes are different, not translations. The Lawes of Malcolm Mackenneth, *Regiam Majestatem* and *Quoniam Attachiamenta*, or the Baron Lawes are followed by The forme and manner of Baron Court,[73] The Burrow-lawes,

the court of the foure burrowes, the statutes of the Gilde, The
Chalmerlaine aire or court, Ane Short Forme of the Justiciar's Aire.
Then follows the legislation as in the Latin edition, Ane large table of all
maters, Ane treatise anent the order of proces observed before the Lords
of Counsell and Session, and Ane treatise of all crimes, and of Judges in
criminall causes: with ane short table concerning the samine. Both the
editions are large quartos.

In his "To the Reader," in the Scottish edition, Skene asserted that the
King commanded him to translate and convert the same auld Lawes furth
of Latin in English that the same might be known to all his subjects and
specially to them who were ignorant of the Latin tongue. The translation
is accordingly apparently his own. There was another edition of the Latin
version published at London in 1613 and another of the Scottish version
"printed conform to the First Edition in 1609" in 1774. It was "Printed for
John Wood, and sold by him, J. Bell and C. Elliot." It was a complete
reprint of the Scottish edition. There was a German reprint in 1971.[74]

The first additional treatise in the Scottish edition is *Ane Short Forme
of Proces presentlie Used and Observed before the Lords of Counsell and
Session*. It extends to 20 pages, and 36 chapters each comprising a number
of short numbered paragraphs. It is contemporary, containing references
to statutes of 1599 as well as to much earlier authorities, the Roman law
and some of the major commentators thereon, and may well be by Skene
himself. This work was the basis of Habakkuk Bisset's *Rolment of
Courtis*, which is substantially a revised and amplified edition of the *Short
Forme*, utilising Skene's own corrections and alterations of the original
text,[75] and it was reprinted by Thomas Thomson in 1809 in *A Compilation
of the Forms of Process in the Court of Session during the earlier periods
after its establishment*. The second treatise appended is entitled *Of Crimes
and Judge, in Criminall Causes, conform to the Lawes of the Realm*; it
runs to 50 pages and 16 titles, each divided into a number of very short
chapters which comprise two or three numbered paragraphs. It is a simple
but well-planned exposition, starting with the definition of a "Criminall
cause," then distinguishing capital crimes, pecuniary crimes, and crimes
neither capital nor pecuniary. The major part is concerned with who may
judge criminal causes, the justiciar general, sheriff, chamberlain, constables, earls, lords and barons, lords of regality, and extraordinary
judges, such as commissioners of justiciary. Most paragraphs have brief
references to statutory authority for the statement of the law. The date
cannot be much earlier than 1609 because there are references to statutes
of James VI. The author appears to have been Skene himself because
there is a reference:[76] "I have written at mair length in the treatise *De
Verborum Significatione, s. verb. Schiref* to the quhilk I remit the
Reader."

In the dedication prefixed to the Latin edition Skene made much of the
difficulty of his undertaking, which, it must certainly be conceded, was
very great. In the "To the Reader" in the Scots edition he more modestly
wrote:

> "Quhat I have done, I remit it to thy judgment and censure: I have
> travelled [travailed] meikill, ane lang time; but how profitable I
> cannot declare. I am the first that ever travelled in this mater, and

> therefore am subject to the reprehension on many quha sall follow after me; quhen I request maist friendlie to take in gude parte, all my doings. For my purpose and intention was to correct, interpret and reduce the auld lawes to their awin integritie, that they micht be understand with some frute be all Our Sovereign Lords lieges."

Skene's *Regiam* indeed received uncritical approval for a century and more. His accuracy as an editor was first seriously questioned by Lord Hailes in his *Examination of some of the Arguments for the High Antiquity of Regiam Majestatem*, published in 1769, where he said[75]:

> "I would not willingly derogate from the labours of others, but truth obliges me to observe, that, to all appearances, Skene was a careless, if not an unfaithful publisher. From what MSS. it was that Skene published his edition of *Regiam Majestatem*, no one can with certainty determine. Of the tenor and contents of those MSS. we can only judge by the MSS. which are still extant;[78] and if we judge by this rule, we must conclude that Skene was a careless, if not an unfaithful publisher."

Thomson and Innes concur.[77] Buchanan[80] concludes: "Skene's text is, therefore, untrustworthy."
Cosmo Innes[81] said that Skene,

> "being employed to collect the old lawes of Scotland, set his wits to make a respectable code of Scotch law, taking the materials wherever he could find them in lawyers' books, whether they were Scotch or English. Skene says very much of his labour in collecting and digesting his code, but it never occurred to him that the old laws of a country hitherto unpublished are to be found, or at least can best be tested and proved, in the written transactions of the people. I have tracked him and his manner of working, and I have not observed that he ever quotes an old charter, a brieve, or a step of old court procedure. He was satisfied with transferring to his work whole pages of the rambling note-books of nameless lawyers, and to attribute them to the legislation of fabulous kings from Malcolm Mackenneth downwards, while he put in his margin references to English books, wishing his reader to believe that they were borrowed from ours."

Walter Ross commented:[82]

> "Sir John Skene only collected and published a number of treatises from the MSS then in circulation, part of which were considered as authoritative; the remainder being the work of anonymous authors, composed upon particular branches of our law and practice, for their own amusement or instruction. Of these Sir John Skene published no more than he thought proper. This country, however, will ever be indebted to him for his labours. His notes upon the *Regiam Maiestatem*, and the statutes of our elder Princes, bear evidence of a knowledge in the statute laws of England, superior to what any of our lawyers have discovered since that time. He has marked the analogies of our statutes, and several of our customs, with ingenuity

and precision, while his treatise *De Verborum Significatione* exhibits an acquaintance with the antiquities of his country which seem to have been afterwards totally neglected. That little glossary keeps its ground among foreign antiquaries, and was all that we had to set up against a Camden, a Selden and a Spelman. In doing this justice to Sir John Skene, we must at the same time observe, that he has left a number of tracts unpublished, which would have been of the greatest use in illustrating the history and forms of our law. With regard to forms themselves, he has given us none but a few of the brieves which belong to the *Regiam Maiestatem*, and these neither in order nor complete. Of ancient deeds, there is only one or two to be found in his book *De Verborum Significatione*. This conduct in a lawyer who had a natural taste for antiquity, clearly indicated that the right path was about to be deserted. It was an error to consign these remains to destruction, if he found them, as he says, in such a confused and perishable situation. If any of these books were of ancient authority, they deserved to be preserved; and if others of them contained the old forms of Scotland, they could not be valuable to the antiquary, the historian, and the lawyer. . . . The reasons of Sir John Skene's conduct are apparent. The lawyers, even in his time, had deviated far from the right path. They had neither pleasure nor curiosity in the common law or usages of their own country, and were totally absorbed in the learning of the civil and canon systems, and in the endless subtleties and commentaries of the continental doctors of these laws. From such copious sources our lawyers found themselves furnished at once with inexhaustible arguments, and figured cases, which independent of the usage of their own country, supported their reasonings and oratory at the bar."

Skene's work has also been fairly harshly criticised by some later scholars, and undoubtedly it falls far short of modern scholarly standards. But it is fair to remember that he was working nearly four centuries ago, before modern methods or critical standards had been developed; also he was working in the intervals of manifold judicial and other public duties. He was not an academic with a research post, nor even a briefless advocate or retired judge. Indeed, how much he did personally must be doubted; he must have relied heavily on assistants. He should not be too harshly judged. He made a good attempt and deserves credit for what he achieved. "The services and studies rather than any imperfections of Sir John Skene should be kept in remembrance."[83] "Considering the difficulties of his task and the very limited information available to him as to medieval history in Scotland and England, Skene rendered to Scots Law a service for which he is entitled to respectful gratitude rather than patronising censure or ill-natured abuse."[84]

The most unfortunate thing is, however, probably the fact that by the time Hailes, and then Thomson and Innes, alerted lawyers and scholars to the defective quality of Skene's texts, reference to these texts had been made in countless books and cases. They had become the accepted, standard, text. Indeed so much is this the case that when Lord Cooper edited *Regiam* and *Quoniam* for the Stair Society in 1947 he adopted Skene's text with variations, but relegating to a supplement 32 chapters which Skene printed in *Quoniam* as legislation and Thomson and Innes printed as *Regiam*, IV, 10–53. We still do not have satisfactory texts of *Regiam Majestatem* and *Quoniam Attadiamenta*.

Habakkuk Bisset[85] lists among the things to be considered in the accomplishing and ending of his book, "the repartore of the foundamentall erectionis and mortificationis of all the kirk landis and benefices within the kingdom of Scotland for the time. Collected by Schir Johnne Skene beand in his sones handis with the sycht and inspection of all the Rollis and registeris thereanentis quhairunto the samin repertoir is relative etc." This may be another collection of materials made by Skene, but it does not appear to have survived.

NOTES

[1] DNB; Anderson, S.N. III, p. 472; Chambers, BDES; W. F. Skene, *Memorials of the Family of Skene of Skene* (New Spalding Club, 1887). Curriehill is about 6 miles S.W. of Edinburgh.

[2] Brunton & Haig, p. 230; Omond, *Lord Advocates*, I, p. 60.

[3] *Acta Facultatis Artium Universitatis Sancti Andree* (ed. Dunlop, SHS), II, pp. 423–424.

[4] *Early Records of St. Andrews* (ed. Anderson, SHS), p. 264; *Acta Facultatis Artium, supra*, I, lxvi, lxx; McCrie, *Life of Andrew Melville*, p. 364.

[5] Tytler, *Life of Sir Thomas Craig*, p. 239, says "probably at Bruges and Poitiers."

[6] Grant, *Faculty of Advocates*.

[7] APS, I, 30.

[8] *History of the Houses of Douglas and Angus*, p. 358.

[9] Skene was not in fact appointed Clerk Register until 1594.

[10] APS, I, 31; Chap. 3, *supra*.

[11] APS, I, 31; III, 89; RSS, VII, 1070, 1559, 1793.

[12] RPC, III, IV, *passim*.

[13] RPC, III, 393–394.

[14] APS, III, 520, c. 133; (1592) APS, III, 564b.

[15] RPC, V, 140; Omond, *Lord Advocates*, I, 60.

[16] C.Sc.P., X, 124, 126–127, 167; Melville, *Memoirs*, p. 366.

[17] APS, III, 567; RPC, IV, 430, 438; Moysie, *Memoirs*, p. 78.

[18] RPC, IV, 463.

[19] C.Sc.P., X, 305.

[20] C.Sc.P., X, 417, 425–426.

[21] C.Sc.P., X, 305, 311.

[22] RPC, IV, 823.

[23] APS, III, 564, c. 45. See also Bisset, *Rolment of Courtis*, I, 73.

[24] C.Sc.P., XI, 451; Omond, I, 65; Scott of Scotstarvet, *Staggering State of Scots Statesmen*, p. 121, attributes this to the interest of this brother-in-law, Lord Blantyre.

[25] Brunton & Haig, p. 230.

[26] RPC, V, 237, 755.

[27] RPC, V, 255, 289, 357.

[28] APS, IV, 98, 107, 113, 144; RPC, V, 245, 289.

[29] APS, IV, 101, 104, 106.

[30] APS, IV, 97, 118, 158.

[31] Printed in the preliminaries to the 1597 edition.

[32] APS, IV, 165, c. 9.

[33] RPC, V, 463.

[34] RPC, V and VI, *passim*.

[35] APS, I, 182.

[36] Thomas Thomson and Cosmo Innes, it may be remembered, did the same thing, deferring to the end the difficult Vol. I (which in any event replaced an earlier, unsatisfactory volume which was withdrawn).

[37] RPC, V, 455.

[38] RPC, VI, 292.

[39] RPC, VI, 308, 309.

[40] RPC, VI, 408.

[41] RPC, VI, 576.

[42] Printed in Brunton & Haig, pp. 232–234.

[43] APS, IV, 378–379, c. 16.

[44] RPC, VIII, 55.

[45] RPC, VIII, 55–56.

[46] RPC, VIII, 534. Carmichael had the reputation of being the most accurate of living Scottish scholars; he contributed one of the poems prefixed to the *Regiam*.

[47] *Ibid.*, p. 358.

[48] *Edinburgh Records Extracts* (1931), p. 41; *Glasgow Charters* (Burgh Records Soc.), p. 250.

[49] In 1625 the question arose in Peebles as to what had happened to their copy of the

Regiam: Peebles Records (Burgh Records Soc.), p. 366.

⁵⁰ APS IV, 264. List of Commissioners in Dicey and Rait's *Thoughts on the Union Between England and Scotland* (1920), App. C.

⁵¹ APS, IV, 280; RPC, IX, 369.

⁵² 17 S.H.R., 103.

⁵³ RPC, VII, 374–375.

⁵⁴ APS, IV, 303, 372, 374, 378, 409, 454.

⁵⁵ APS, IV, 442.

⁵⁶ RPC, VIII and IX, *passim*.

⁵⁷ RPC, VIII, 248, 558.

⁵⁸ (1609) 7 Co. Rep. 7b. On the history of this point see Holdsworth, *H.E.L.*, IX, pp. 74–91.

⁵⁹ *Rolment of Courtis* (ed. Hamilton Grierson, STS), I, 74. On this see further Chap. 6, *infra*.

⁶⁰ RPC, X, 540.

⁶¹ RPC, VII, 6, 9, 457, 740.

⁶² Spottiswoode, *History*, III, p. 215; Omond, I, pp. 66–67; Brunton & Haig, pp. 234, 253–254.

⁶³ Brunton & Haig, p. 254.

⁶⁴ APS, V, 47.

⁶⁵ Skene's Table of All the Kings of Scotland was reprinted in a small book edited anonymously by one John Monipennie, entitled *Certaine matters composed together. Genealogie of all the Kings of Scotland with a Description of Scotland*, published at London in 1597 and 1603 and several times later under varying titles. It is reprinted in *Somers Tracts*, Vol. 3. This may have been known to Shakespeare when he was working on Macbeth: Henry N. Paul, *The Royal Play of Macbeth* (1950), p. 220; Sir James Fergusson, *The Man Behind Macbeth* (1969), p. 27.

⁶⁶ This is the work known as *De Verborum Significatione*, frequently later reprinted separately.

⁶⁷ Thomson and Innes, APS, I, 32, Preface. See also Skene's dedication prefixed to the Latin edition of *Regiam Majestatem*.

⁶⁸ Habakkuk Bisset (*Rolment of Courtis*, I, 5), narrates that his patron and master, Skene, said in his hearing that if the monuments and registers of antiquities of Scotland might be got extant, that King Caractacus would be found the first Christian Scottish king, and that he was very careful otherwise to have gotten the true knowledge and certainty thereof but could not find the same by reason of the rest of the said registers and rolls.

⁶⁹ It antedates such famous legal dictionaries as Calvinus' *Lexicon Juridicum* (1600), John Cowell's *Interpreter* (1607); John Rastell's *Expositiones Terminorum Legum Anglorum* was earlier (1527).

⁷⁰ *Scotch Legal Antiquities*, p. 296.

⁷¹ APS, VIII, 389, c. 133.

⁷² This item is not included in the Scots edition.

⁷³ This is not in the Latin edition at all, nor was it old. It is not in any of the older MSS. According to Skene's preface to it, this treatise was written by some learned lawyer, not long time bygone, as the style of the same declares, and is published because it contains an interpretation of the treatise immediately preceding (c. 1., Q.A.), as is noted in the margin, and also, many profitable principles and rules of the laws of this realm, worthy to be remembered.

⁷⁴ *Die Versuche zur Herstellung eines schottischen Corpus Iuris in 15 und 16 Jahrhundert Einleitung zum Reprint der "Black Acts" von 1566 und der Sammlung "Regiam Majestatem" von 1609* (Mittelalterliche Gesetzbucher Europäischer Länder: 3, 4, 1971).

⁷⁵ George Neilson, "Skene's *Memorabilia Scotica*, 1475–1612, and Revisals of *Regiam Maiestatem*" (1923).

⁷⁶ Tit. 11, S.10.

⁷⁷ *Examination*, p. 4.

⁷⁸ On these see APS, I, 177–210, 211–265; John Buchanan, "The MSS. of Regiam Maiestatem" (1937) 49 J.R. 217.

⁷⁹ APS, I, 34, preface. Thomson and Innes produced a better text of the *Regiam* and *Quoniam*: APS, I, Apps. I and II, pp. 597–659, and also a collation of *Regiam* with Glanvill's *Tractatus de legibus et Consuetudinibus Angliae*; APS, I, 135–174.

⁸⁰ Buchanan, *op. cit.*, p. 227.

[81] *Scotch Legal Antiquities*, p. 3.

[82] *Lectures on the History and Practice of the Law of Scotland relative to Conveyancing and Legal Diligence* (1822), II, p. 5.

[83] George Neilson in "Skene's *Memorabilia Scotica*."

[84] Lord Cooper in Introduction to *Regiam Majestatem* (Stair Soc.), p. 20.

[85] Rolment of Courtis, II, 275.

CHAPTER 6

THE MINOR JURISTS OF THE SIXTEENTH CENTURY

THE outstanding importance of Balfour, Craig and Skene should not wholly obscure the careers and works of a number of lesser scholars, some of whom indeed, though now largely forgotten, had European reputations in their time, and many of whom made minor but not negligible contributions to the knowledge of Scots law of the time.

WILLIAM HAY

Insight into the teaching and study of a topic relevant to law is provided by the lectures on marriage delivered by William Hay in King's College, Aberdeen.[1] Hay (c. 1470–74 – c. 1542), friend of Hector Boece, may have studied at St. Andrews, studied at Paris under, among others, Erasmus, and returned to Aberdeen about 1497. He was well versed in theology and canon law, became sub-principal of King's College and lectured in theology there from about 1505 to 1537–38. He probably succeeded Boece as principal in 1536.[2] The complete course was concerned with the seven sacraments[3] of the Roman Catholic Church. It is founded on extensive reading and draws on and cites the Bible, Greek and Latin authors, Fathers of the Church, medieval theologians, Roman and, more heavily, canon law, and various miscellaneous sources.[4] Hay was teaching young priests and aspiring priests, not young lawyers, and he makes no reference to the College of Justice, statutes of the realm, practicks of the lawyers, or decisions of Officials' courts or of the Rota. He was looking at marriage from a different standpoint from that which would have been adopted by a law teacher. But what he taught to clerics in the early sixteenth century was familiar to the early reformers of the church, the early judges and officers of the new Commissary Courts established in 1563,[5] and the Reformation brought about no radical change in the concept of marriage or its requisites or incidentals. It introduced a new jurisdiction, and the concept of possible total dissolution (*divortium a vinculo matrimonii*) for adultery and, later for desertion. A very great deal of what Hay taught was not only pre-Reformation church and civil law but continued as part of the substance of the post-Reformation civil law. Betrothal followed by intercourse constituted a valid marriage,[6] and after the Reformation this became the form of irregular marriage by promise *subsequente copula*, competent until 1940.[7] Marriage might also be constituted by exchange of consent, which became the form of irregular marriage by declaration *de praesenti* (*matrimonio*), also competent until 1940.[7] Much of the canon law of marriage is discussed in terms of the impediments which vitiate apparent matrimonial consent, or render it illicit. Hay distinguished between diriment impediments, which are fundamental and nullify the purported marriage, and impedient impediments, which it is sinful to ignore but which do not affect the validity of the marriage.[8] This distinction became in Lord

Fraser's book[9] a distinction between irritant and prohibitive impediments. The former class included error as to the person, impotence, insanity, non-age (in which respect Scots law followed the canon law rule until 1929[10]), existing marriage, and relationship within the forbidden degrees, a topic on which there was very great and subtle extension of the basic rules contained in Leviticus, c. 18,[11] giving rise to a web of forbidden relationships from which relief could be had by papal dispensation.

Adultery was a ground for judicial separation (*divortium a mensa et thoro*) only, but much of Hay's teaching continued valid for centuries. Adultery was sinful and merited punishment.[12] It was a defence that the husband had made the wife prostitute herself against her will[13]; this is the basis of the modern defence of *lenocinium*. Condonation also is a defence.[14] The notion of protection of one spouse from intolerable behaviour by the other[15] was the basis of the later separation[16] and divorce[17] for cruelty. Desertion is not discussed by Hay, but legitimacy of children is mentioned incidentally.[18]

Making allowance for the differing standpoints of theologian and lawyer, viewing marriage as a sacrament and as a relationship giving rise to numerous obligations *inter se* and to others, there is clearly much in Hay's exposition relevant to later matrimonial law.

JOHN LAUDER

There survives from the earlier half of the sixteenth century an important collection of forms of deeds and writs. John Lauder was born about 1490, became a student at St. Andrews in 1504 and graduated bachelor in 1506 and master in 1509 and was later an examiner there. He was licensed by Andrew Forman, Bishop of Moray, and, appointed a notary by apostolic authority, was employed as such in Moray until at least 1516 and was admitted to the four minor orders. From 1517 to 1521 he was again at St. Andrews as secretary to Forman, who had since 1514 been Archbishop there. He held several benefices, having a dispensation to hold in plurality. After 1521 he was in Glasgow with Robert Forman, Dean of Glasgow, and Gavin Dunbar, Archbishop of Glasgow and Lord Chancellor, 1528–43. About 1536 he became parson of Morebattle and archdeacon of Teviotdale and about 1539 became secretary to Cardinal David Betoun, Archbishop of St. Andrews and Lord Chancellor, 1543–46.[19] He prosecuted in some heresy trials including that of George Wishart in 1546. His participation in it is described with bitterness by John Knox,[20] who describes how Lauder, "his face running down with sweat and frothing at the mouth like a bear, he spat at Master George's face, saying 'what answerest thou to these sayings, thou runagate, traitor, thief, which we have duly proved by sufficient witness against thee?'" He died in 1551.

Lauder is clearly identified as the compiler of a *Formulare instrumentorum ecclesiasticorum* preserved in St. Andrews University and printed by the Stair Society in two volumes in 1942–44 as the *St. Andrews Formulare, 1514–1546*.[21] It was compiled between 1521 and 1546 or possibly somewhat later. It is not a style book but a collection of copies of some 615 documents almost all in Latin, some transcribed specimens of writs in the archiepiscopal registers, some copies of deeds he had drawn in the course of his duty as archbishop's secretary or of his notarial practice, and some transcripts of writs concerning his own interest in various ecclesiastical benefices. Most are contemporary, from the period 1514–46 but a few are earlier, having been searched out as styles or of potential value as such. One is as early as 1417[22] and several date from the time of Archbishop Alexander Stewart (1504–13), Numbers 1–336 have a certain unity; nos. 337 to 391 are in approximately chronological order, dating from 1531–39, and nos. 392 to 554 are partly grouped, partly chronological and date from 1539–46.

The writs in Lauder's *Formulare* are not classified or grouped under headings, as is evident from his own alphabetical index of the types of documents.[23] It contains specimens of a variety of writs with very different purposes. There are writs relating to civil process, illustrating the working of the ecclesiastical courts shortly before they were radically affected by the development of the newly-created Court of Session (itself half-clerical in composition and influenced in its practice by that of the ecclesiastical courts). Under this head there are specimens of summonses, appeals and refutations of appeals, commissions to examine witnesses and execute other judicial proceedings.[24] There are brieves initiating claims.[25] There are writs relative to executry[26] and matrimonial questions,[27] matters which were shortly to be transferred to the new commissary courts. There are narratives of processes in both civil and criminal cases[28] and specimens of the submission of disputes to clerics' arbitration,[29] a practice which enlarged the influence of canon law. There is a writ appointing a procurator-fiscal and granting him powers[30] and some appointing procurators for cases raised and to be raised in the Roman curia.[31]

There are numerous conveyancing writs which indicate the breadth and importance of the church's position as a landowner,[32] and also the importance of the church courts as *fora* for the decision of disputes about land.[33] There are writs concerning disputed benefices,[34] teinds,[35] indulgences,[36] testimonials for pilgrims,[37] dispensation from vows of fasting[38] and numerous dispensations to clerics for defects of birth, minority, non-residence and plurality.[39] There are many examples of monitions, or charges, usually directed to parochial clergy to denounce persons who had offended the church in some way, by theft,[40] violence to clergy,[41] and a splended cursing and excommunication of Border reivers, in the vernacular.[42] Again there are instruments elucidating the procedure in the appointment of notaries public by apostolic authority.[43] It is accordingly a very wide-ranging collection of writs, many of which shed light on the state of development of the legal system, which had clearly attained a considerable degree of maturity.

PETER BISSET

Peter Bisset or Bissat or Bissart (?1500–1568)[44] was born in Fife, studied at St. Andrews and Paris, and settled in Bologna where he became a doctor of laws, professor of canon law and attained a high reputation as civilian, philosopher, poet and orator. His writings were published in quarto at Venice in 1565 as *Patricii Bissarti Opera Omnia, Poemata, Orationes, Lectiones Feriales et Liber de Irregularitate*, the last being a commentary on the part of the canon law concerned with the reasons for excluding certain categories of laymen from clerical office.

HENRY SCRIMGER

Henry Scrimger or Scrimgeour (1506–72),[45] born in Dundee and connected with the family of Scrimgers of Dudhope, hereditary standard-bearers of Scotland, and an uncle of James Melville, the reformer, studied at St. Andrews, and Paris and at Bourges under Eguinar Baro and Duaren. He was patronised by Ulric Fugger, who employed him to form his library at Augsburg. He later taught philosophy in Geneva and in 1565 opened a school there for teaching civil law. His friend George Buchanan tried to entice him back to Scotland.[46] He published in 1558 an edition of Justinian's *Novels* in Greek, a work highly regarded by jurists of the time. He also wrote notes on various Greek authors, which are believed later to have come into the possession of Isaac Casaubon. It was said of him that no man of his age had a more acute knowledge, not only of Latin and Greek, but of oriental languages, and that he had one of the most valuable libraries in Europe. Casaubon, Stephanus and other scholars of the time spoke of him with the highest regard.

EDWARD HENRYSON

Edward Henryson (?1510–?1590)[47] studied at Bourges under Eguinar Baro and was patronised by Ulric Fugger, who had previously patronised Scrimger. Then he was for several years professor of civil law at Bourges and numbered among the great European civilians of his time. He was author of a commentary on the title of Justinian's Institutions *De Testamentis* (*Inst*. II, 10), and after returning to Scotland about 1557 became one of the judges of the Commissary Court when it was established in 1563 and in 1565 was promoted an extraordinary Lord of Session. Shortly thereafter he became a member of the 1566 commission to revise and print the statutes and was engaged in supervising the publication of the *Black Acts*; he wrote the preface and was ostensibly the editor and obtained an exclusive privilege to print and sell the work for ten years from the date of publication. His son Thomas (?–1638)[48] became a judge as Lord Chesters in 1622 and was a commissioner for revising the laws in 1633.

ADAM BLACKWOOD

Adam Blackwood (1539–1613)[49] had for his mother the niece of Robert

Reid, Bishop of Orkney and second president of the Court of Session, who left a bequest for the foundation of a college in Edinburgh. He studied in Paris and Toulouse, and became a counsellor of the parliament of Poitiers and may also have been a professor of the civil law there. He wrote on the connection of religion and government, *De Vinculo Religionis* (1575). He is mainly remembered for his championing of Mary, Queen of Scots, notably his *Apologia pro Regibus, Adversus Georgii Buchanani Dialogum de Jure Regni apud Scotos*, published at Poitiers in 1581 and Paris in 1588, and dedicated to Mary and her son.[50] Blackwood was propounding an early version of absolutist monarchy, having an authority which could not be restricted in any way by human law. Blackwood's work was important because of its place in the development of political theories which would lead on to Louis XIV's concept of the state. He also published a work *Martyre de la Reyne d'Ecosse, Douarière de France* in 1588. He lived to see James VI succeed to the English throne and published Latin poetry in celebration of the event. His *Opera Omnia* were published in 1644, edited by Naudeus. His elder brother, Henry,[51] became dean of the faculty of medicine in Paris.

WILLIAM BARCLAY

William Barclay (*c.* 1546–1605)[52] spent his early years at the court of Mary, Queen of Scots, but in 1573, unhappy with the state of his country, he went to France, studied civil law at Bourges under Cujacius, Donellus, and Contius, and in 1578 became professor of that subject at the University of Pontamousson in Lorraine, a councillor of state and Master of Requests to the Duke of Lorraine. Jesuit pressure drove him to England in 1603. James VI and I offered him high office in England if he would become a protestant, but he refused, returned to France in 1604 and became professor of civil law at Angers. He wrote *De Regno et Regali Potestate, adversus Buchananum, Brutum,*[53] *Boucherum et Reliquos Monarchomachos* (1600), a counterblast to Buchanan's *De Jure Regni*, a wide-ranging attempt to provide the definitive case for absolute monarchy, *Commentarii in Titulos Pandectarum de Rebus Creditis et de Jurejurando* (1605), *De Potestate Papae*, (1609) and a commentary on Tacitus' *Agricola*.

He has sometimes been confused with Thomas Barclay (*fl.* 1620),[54] who became a professor of law at Poitiers.

He was the father of John Barclay (1582–1621),[55] poet and author of a Latin romance *Argenis*, a poetical fable with moral and political reflections of which several English and other translations were made, and of some historical works.

WILLIAM WELWOOD

William Welwood or Welwod[56] is thought to have been born about 1552, probably at St. Andrews, and is recorded as a master of arts at St. Mary's or New College there in 1578. He discovered the principle of the siphon and in 1577 he and a colleague received a patent under the Privy Seal for their invention, which he explained in a short pamphlet.[57] In 1598 Parliament granted them the sole right of making certain pumps for raising and forcing of water from mines.[58] He was at this time professor of mathematics and in 1580 he and William Skene, professor of law, were removed from New College to St. Salvator's College in face of opposition from the masters of the latter college, who alleged that these new professorships were superfluous. In 1583 the chancellor and officers of the university presented a supplication to the Privy Council against him, complaining that he had employed no diligence in the profession of mathematics that year and that the college funds were over-expended.[59] He was a friend and supporter of Andrew Melville, notably when Melville was cited to appear before the Privy Council for preaching a seditious sermon in 1583–84.[60]

About 1587 he transferred from the chair of mathematics to that of law, in succession to John Arthur, brother-in-law of Patrick Adamson, Archbishop of St. Andrews, who had succeeded William Skene and had not been removed.[61] He consequently incurred the enmity of the archbishop's party and in 1589 one of Adamson's retainers attempted to assassinate him in the High Street. In the fracas John Arthur's brother James was killed, and Welwood's brother John was sentenced to banishment.

In 1590 Welwood published a short treatise in 30 small pages, divided into 15 titles on *The Sea Law of Scotland*, "Shortly gathered and plainly dressed for the ready use of all seafairing men." It was printed by Waldegrave at Edinburgh. It was a very scarce book, and it is believed that only two copies exist, in the Bodleian and Cambridge University Library, but it was reprinted in the Scottish Text Society's *Miscellany* volume for 1933 and in facsimile by Theatrum Orbis Terrarum in 1969. Then in 1594 he published at Leyden in quarto a short *Juris Divini Judaeorum ac Juris Civilis Romanorum Parallela*, a sketch of the resemblances of the two systems and an early essay in comparative law. In the same year he published also at Leyden in quarto a work *Ad expediendos Processus in Judiciis ecclesiasticis Appendix Parallelorum Juris Divini Humanique*, dedicated to the ministers of St. Andrews, distinguishing the forms used in civil courts and those which should be used in ecclesiastical courts. This is of some importance because at that time the church had no established form of process. In this year also he published at Middelburg *Ars Domandarum Perturbationum ex solo Dei verbo quasi transcripti constructa*, dedicated to John Kennedy, fifth Earl of Cassillis. Welwood seems to have stayed at St. Andrews all this time, and to have published in Holland to avoid the interference of the Privy Council. But his views on ecclesiastical prerogatives had brought him into unfavourable notice and in 1597 royal visitors to the university removed him from office as having transgressed the foundation in sundry points.[62] The visitors declared that "the profession of the laws is no ways necessary at this time in this university." Two years later another set of visitors recommended looking for "a sufficient learned person in the laws, able to discharge both in the ordinary teaching of that profession in the said college, and of the place and jurisdiction of commissary within the diocese," but this recommendation was deleted by the King's special command. In 1600, however, the King ordered his restoration on giving sufficient bond and security for his dutiful behaviour; it is uncertain, however, whether he was ever in fact reinstated.[63]

In 1613 he published, at London, where he then was,[64] *An Abridgment of all Sea-Lawes*, in quarto, dedicated to James [VI and] I, comparing the codes of Oleron and Wisby with the Roman law. There was another edition (London, octavo) in 1636, and in 1686 it was reprinted, though without the author's name, in Gerard Malynes' *Consuetudo vel Lex Mercatoria*, which itself has been reprinted in modern times. In 1615–16 Welwood published in quarto a Latin version of the part concerned with the maritime supremacy as *De Dominio Maris Juribusque ad Dominium praecipue spectantibus Assertio brevis et methodica*; in this he supported the English claim to supremacy over the sea in the Channel. There was another edition at The Hague in 1653, to which Dirk Graswinckel replied in *Maris Liberi Vindiciae adversus G. Welwodum Britanniae Dominii Assertorem*, The Hague, 1653. This was the famous controversy about the freedom of the high seas to which the best-known contributions were Grotius' *Mare Liberum* of 1609 and Selden's *Mare Clausum* of 1635. It appears that this publication was prompted by the Queen (Anne of Denmark) to strengthen her monopoly of off-shore fishing licences.[65] Finally in 1622 he published at London in octavo a *Dubiorum quae tam in foro poli quam in foro fori occurrere solent, brevis expeditio*. He is not heard of after 1622.

His works have had no lasting importance and are remembered merely as historically interesting instances of scholarship. They do however, indicate an active man with an interest in comparative and commercial law. The *Abridgment* was the first treatise on maritime law in Britain and his participation in the controversy on the freedom of the seas cannot have been regarded as negligible when Graswinckel thought it called for a reply.

The Collectors of Decisions

Stair, in the Epistle Dedicatory to his *Decisions*, Part First (1661–71) published in 1683, narrates that James V, who instituted the College of Justice, "ordered one of the Lords to keep a Journal of their Decisions, with which Henry Sinclair, Dean of Restalrig was entrusted, and did so serve the same for the space of ten years, as Maitland, Hadingtoun, Hope, Balfour, Spotswood, Dury and several other since have done."

The Sinclairs

William Sinclair (?1401–80),[66] Earl of Orkney and Chancellor of Scotland, who was descended through his mother from the old royal line of Scotland, had two grandsons, Henry and John. Henry Sinclair

(1508–66),[67] Bishop of Ross, was third President of the Court of Session and is credited with effecting material improvements in the law. His brother John (?–1566), Dean of Restalrig, Bishop of Brechin, who had been an ordinary Lord since 1540, officiated at the marriage of Queen Mary to Darnley in 1565. He succeeded as fourth President of the Court but survived only a few months. The earliest surviving collection of decisions of the Court of Session, known as Sinclair's *Practicks*, covering the years 1540 to 1550, and still unprinted has usually been attributed to Henry, but should probably be attributed to John.[68] The reports are very brief and not easy to follow. Most of them were omitted from Morison's *Dictionary*. Both Sinclairs were notable book collectors and we have knowledge of each having substantial collections.[69]

MAITLAND OF LETHINGTON

Sir Richard Maitland of Lethington (1496–1586)[70] became an extra-ordinary Lord of Session in 1554 and an ordinary Lord in 1561, and later became Lord Privy Seal. He was a commissioner for revision of the laws in 1566.[71] He made a collection of decisions of the Court of Session from 1550 to 1565 in continuation of Sinclair's *Practicks*.[72] About a third of these are printed in Morison's *Dictionary*. Maitland is also noteworthy for having made a valuable collection of Scottish poetry, written much poetry himself, and written some historical works, *The History and Cronicle of the House of Seytoun* and a *Brief and Compendious Tabill or Catholog of the names of the Kings of Scotland, France and England*. His name was taken by the Maitland Club, founded in 1828 to print works illustrative of the antiquities, history and literature of Scotland. It published Maitland's *House of Seytoun* and *Poems*, Pitcairn's *Criminal Trials* and other valuable texts, coming to an end about 1860, having issued 77 volumes. His son William (?1528–73)[73] is better known as Secretary Lethington; he became an extraordinary Lord of Session in 1561 and an ordinary Lord in 1565. His second son John (1543–95)[74] later (1581) became a Lord of Session as Lord Thirlestane, in 1584 Secretary of State,[75] in 1586 Vice-Chancellor and in 1587 Chancellor.[76] His third son, Thomas, was a poet of some distinction.

COLVIL OF CULROSS

Alexander Colvil (?1530–97),[77] Commendator of Culross, younger brother of James, Lord Colvil of Culross, became a judge in 1575. He was one of the commission of 1578 appointed to revise the laws and made a Privy Councillor, and he made a manuscript collection of the decisions of the Court of Session covering 1570 to 1584. About a third of these were later printed in Morison's *Dictionary*.

HAMILTON OF PRIESTFIELD

Thomas Hamilton of Priestfield (1573–1637),[78] whose father was a judge (Lord Priestfield, 1607),[79] and whose mother was a collateral of Sir Thomas Craig's mother, became a judge as Lord Drumcairn in 1592 and then Lord Advocate 1596–1612. He was a commissioner for revision of the law, along with Skene, in 1592, a commissioner for union, along with Craig, in 1604, succeeded Skene as Clerk Register in 1612 and then became Secretary of State. From the situation of his Edinburgh home he was known as "Tam o' the Cowgate." When James VI visited Edinburgh in 1617 Hamilton entertained him there. He became President of the Court of Session (1616–27), being ennobled as Lord Binning (1613) and then Earl of Melrose (1619), a title which in 1627 he exchanged for Earl of Haddington. He is reputed to have amassed a large fortune mostly invested in land. He was a statesman and courtier but was also deemed a learned lawyer and left a substantial collection of decisions in three MS. volumes, containing over 3000 cases covering 1592 to 1624. This collection was frequently referred to by Stair but is still unprinted.

HABAKKUK BISSET

Habakkuk Bisset[80] is said to have been the son of Queen Mary's caterer. Little is known of his life, but he recorded himself that in 1582 or 1583 he was employed by Sir James Balfour as a research assistant and made several copies of Balfour's *Practicks*[81]. Before 1581 he had become a Writer to the Signet but in 1610 he was suspended by the society for living outwith Edinburgh and not wearing his gown.[82] Casual mentions of him in records of the time suggest a rather odd and quarrelsome character.[83] Bisset himself tells us[84] that Sir John Skene caused him in 1609 to 1613:

> "to write by his direction the forms of deduction of all processes in civil actions presently used and observed before the lords of his majesty's council and session and other judges, within his Highness' Kingdom of Scotland; together with the old forms and processes of falsing of dooms, the process of the brieve of perambulation, the process of the brieve of division, the process betwixt the lord and the tenant, the process of showing of holding and the process of purpresture, collected and extracted forth of the registers, laws, statutes and acts of the kingdom of Scotland, and statutes of the said lords of council and session, contained in their books and registers, called the sederunt books, wherein the said lords' acts and statutes are written and inserted, and are extracted furth thereof by the said clerk register, begun in March, the year of God, 1609; and revised and corrected by him, and me, the writer thereof; thereafter in December, and January, the year of God, 1612, foresaid. As the original warrant bears being noted and written by the said clerk register's own hand written on the margins thereof. Perused and

conferred together by him and me the writer foresaid, agreeing with the said registers, statutes and civil laws."

In 1613–22 Bisset made additional collections and intended to publish them and his treatise as a single work. He prepared a first draft in 1622 and subsequently a second correcting and amplifying the first. He explained their relation one to the other in a supplication he presented to the Privy Council in 1626.[85] It narrates that, as their lordships knew, he had been exercised these many years bygone in collecting and putting together in a book of eight quires of paper or thereby concerning all the most ancient monuments and antiquities of this kingdom, whereof by iniquity of time and other inconveniences the records thereof have been destroyed and decayed, and he accordingly petitioned for an allowance to assist him to complete his purpose.

His work is known as the *Rolment of Courtis*, from its opening words: "The rolment of courtis, containing the oldest laws, acts, statutes, constitutions, monuments and antiquities of the most ancient realm of Scotland as a free kingdom, conformed to the civil, canon, imperial and municipal laws, agreeing with the acts, statutes, and constitution of the said kingdom."[86]

The work opens with a "Preface or prolog to the godlie and Christiane Redare," many pages of inaccurate history which becomes important only when he reaches his own time and his work with Skene.[87] Book I comprises two divisions, one entitled "Ane Short Forme of Proces," and the other "Civil Process Used of Old," Book II deals with ecclesiastical erections and processes deduced before archbishops, bishops, their officials or commissaries and their jurisdiction in Scotland, Book III with prelacies and other religious places, Book IV of sea laws, Book V of burgh privileges and Book VI of the computation of times.

The "Short Forme of Process' is truly a revised and amplified edition of "Ane Short Forme of Proces, presentlie used and observed before the Lords of Council and Session," printed in the volume containing Skene's translation of *Regiam Majestatem, Quoniam Attachiamenta*, etc., of 1609, and reprinted by Thomas Thomson in 1809 in the volume entitled *A Compilation of the Forms of Process in the Court of Session during the earlier periods after its establishment*. It is, however, doubtful if Bisset was the author of the earlier version, though it was attributed to him by Thomas Thomson. Bisset never claims to have written it and his mis-translations and mistranscriptions made Hamilton-Grierson hesitate to credit him with sufficient scholarship to enable him to compose a treatise showing intimate acquaintance with Roman and canon law texts relating to procedure.[88] But though Bisset adhered to the arrangement of Skene's *Forme*, reproducing the substance of it and referring to the same authorities, he made additions, treating of topics omitted by the *Forme* and including public documents and parts of statutes and Acts of Sederunt. George Neilson, moreover, discovered a volume containing Skene's *Forme*, annotated by Skene himself, and points out that his corrections and alterations of the text, and the addition of rubrics to the chapters into which it is divided, were adopted with few exceptions by Bisset.[89]

The *Short Forme of Proces* deals only with civil procedure, though the distinction between civil and criminal, both in respect of substantive law and procedure, was shadowy in medieval times; both were concerned with wrongdoing or "wrong and unlaw," but in civil cases the penalty was a fine, in criminal it was a blood-penalty, death or mutilation. It comprises 40 titles, each divided into chapters, dealing with the parts of a process, summons, exceptions, probation, improbation of writs, sentence, execution of sentences, poinding and comprising of moveables and immoveables, suspension of decrees and reduction of decrees.

The second division of Book I, of "Civil Process Used of Old," comprises only six titles, dealing with falsing of dooms, the brieve of perambulation, the brieve of division, the process between lord and tenant, the process of showing of holding and the process of purpresture.

Book II is "anent ecclesiastical erections," processes deduced before ecclesiastics, their officials or commissaries and their jurisdiction. Particularly interesting is the narrative of the erection and instruction of the commissaries made and formed by Balfour of Pittendreich in March 1563/64,[90] and the form and order of process used before the Lords of Council and Session of the same date.[91]

Book III is about the erecting of prelacies and other religious places, the only interesting legal material being the process of four dooms and the forms of mortification and relative sasine.[92] Book IV deals with the admiral and sea laws.

Bisset's book, like Skene's, shows that early seventeenth century civil procedure owed much to Roman law and to canon law, and that the influence of the former source came mainly through the latter.

An interesting feature of the careers of several of these minor jurists of the sixteenth century is their European experience and reputations, showing the extent to which Scotland and Scotsmen were parts of the European intellectual milieu.[93]

NOTES

[1] Transcribed, translated and edited by J. C. Barry (Stair Soc. 1967), under the title *William Hay's Lectures on Marriage.*

[2] Biographical notes, in *William Hay's Lectures*, pp. ix–xiv.

[3] Baptism, confirmation, eucharist, penance, extreme unction, orders, and marriage.

[4] Sources used by Hay in his lectures, in *William Hay's Lectures, pp. xv–xxx.*

[5] Balfour, the first head of the Commissary Court of Edinburgh, had been Official of Lothian under a Catholic bishop.

[6] *Lectures*, p. 7.

[7] Marriage (Scotland) Act 1939, s.5.

[8] *Lectures*, p. 47. See also Stair, I, 4, 6; I, 17, 14; *Bliersbach* v. *MacEwen*, 1959 S.C. 43, at p. 49.

[9] Fraser, *Husband and Wife*, I, 49.

[10] Age of Marriage Act 1929.

[11] *Lectures*, pp. 193 *et seq.*

[12] *Lectures*, p. 61.

[13] *Ibid.*, p. 63.

[14] *Ibid.*, p. 63.

[15] *Ibid.*, p. 69.

[16] Fraser, *H. & W.*, II, 877.

[17] Divorce (Scotland) Act 1938, s.1.

[18] *Lectures*, p. 235.

[19] Herkless and Hannay, *Archbishops of St. Andrews*, II, pp. 224–230; III, pp. 256–257; *Early Records of the University of St. Andrews* (ed. Maitland Anderson, SHS), 93, 96, 198; *Acta Facultatis Artium Universitatis S. Andree, 1413–1588* (ed. Dunlop, SHS), 284, 292–293, 300, 302; RSS, I, 2072; III, 561, 2366; IV, 1438; RMS, III, 2741; V, 1191, 1548.

[20] *History of the Reformation in Scotland* (ed. Croft Dickinson), I, p. 27; I, p. 114, II, pp. 234–245 (Foxe's account of Wishart's trial and martyrdom).

[21] Transcribed and edited by Gordon Donaldson and C. Macrae.

[22] No. 286, analysed by R. K. Hannay in 13 S.H.R. 321–327; see also J. H. Baxter, *Copiale prioratus Sanctiandree*, lv.

[23] In *St Andrews Formulare*, II, 357–389.

[24] Nos. 56, 90–93, 140, 142, 167, 168, 193–216, 220–221, 225–226, 238, 269, 293, 303, 319.

[25] Nos. 217, 398, 523–524.

[26] Nos. 53, 68–74, 166, 177, 187, 203, 224, 259, 294, 553.

[27] Nos. 99–100, 319, 482, 552.

[28] Nos. 115, 167–168, 236–242, 272, 295–296, 303, 312.

[29] Nos. 42, 89.

[30] No. 13.

[31] Nos. 254, 270, 353–355, 385.

[32] Nos. 24–25, 77–79, 217, 243–250, 317–318, 390, 402, 436–437, 457, 472–473, 512–515.

[33] Nos. 88–89.

[34] Nos. 31–33, 36–37, 39–41, 97, 120, 158–159, 262.

[35] Nos. 123–133, 154, 160, 178–179, 256–257.

[36] Nos. 60, 62, 76.

[37] Nos. 297–298.

[38] Nos. 234.

[39] Nos. 14–15, 111–112, 183–184, 231, 275.

[40] Nos. 84, 191.

[41] Nos. 80–83, 86–87.

[42] Nos. 229.

[43] Nos. 491–493.

[44] DNB; Anderson, S.N., I, p. 305; Chambers, BDES.

[45] DNB; Anderson, S.N., III, p. 426; Chambers, BDES.

[46] Hume Brown, *George Buchanan*, pp. 334–335.

[47] DNB; Anderson, S.N., II, p. 465; Brunton & Haig, p. 132; Tytler, p. 269.

[48] DNB; Brunton & Haig, p. 265.

[49] DNB; Anderson, S.N., I, p. 316; Chambers, BDES; J. Plattard, "Scottish Masters and

Students at Poitiers in the Second Half of the 16th Century," 21 S.H.R. (1924) 82, which mentions also another Scot, Aelius Donatus Macrodorus as having gained a reputation in the law school at Poitiers.

50 On this see Figgis, *Divine Right of Kings*, pp. 133 *et seq.*

51 DNB; Anderson, S.N., II, p. 317.

52 W. Nicolson, *Scottish Historical Library* (1702), p. 12; DNB; Anderson, S.N., I, p. 245; Chambers, BDES.

53 *Brutus* was Hubert Languet, author of *Vindiciae contra Tyrannos* (1589).

54 DNB.

55 DNB; Anderson, S.N., I, p. 246, Lord Hailes wrote a life of John Barclay as a specimen of a *Biographia Scotica*, which was printed in 1782.

56 DNB.

57 McCrie, *Life of Andrew Melville*, pp. 392, 476.

58 APS, IV, 176.

59 McCrie, *op. cit.*, p. 77.

60 *Ibid.*, pp. 92, 462; See also 326, 329.

61 Melville, *Diary*, pp. 200–203.

62 McCrie, *op. cit.*, p. 206.

63 McCrie, p. 206, quoting Actis and Recesse of the King's Two Visitations of the University of St. Andrews.

64 McCrie, *op. cit.*, p. 326.

65 J. D. Alsop, "William Welwood, Anne of Denmark and The Sovereignty of The Sea," 59 S.H.R. 171.

66 DNB.

67 DNB; Forbes, *Journal of the Session, Preface*, p. 25; Brunton & Haig, p. 58; Tytler, *Life of Sir Thomas Craig*, p. 74.

68 DNB; Brunton & Haig, 63; Tytler, *op. cit.*, p. 86; A. L. Murray, "Sinclair's Practicks" in Harding (ed.), *Law Making and Law Makers in British History* (R.H.S., 1980) , p. 90.

69 J. Durkan and A. Ross, *Early Scottish Libraries*.

70 DNB; Anderson, S.N. III, 74; Chambers, BDES; Forbes, Preface to *Journal of the Session*, p. 25; Fraser Tytler, *Life of Craig*, p. 63; Brunton & Haig, p. 97.

71 APS, I, 29.

72 Forbes, Preface, pp. 25–26.

73 DNB; Anderson, S.N., III, 75; Chambers, BDES; Brunton & Haig, p. 106.

74 DNB; Anderson, S.N., III, p. 80, Brunton & Haig, p. 140.

75 Crawford, *Lives of the Officers of State*, p. 143.

76 On him see M. Lee, *John Maitland of Thirlestane and the Foundation of the Stewart Despotism in Scotland* (1959); Crawford, p. 147; Spottiswoode, *History of the Church of Scotland*, p. 364: Cowan, II, p. 140 (portrait in Vol. I).

77 DNB; Anderson, S.N., I. p. 671; Brunton & Haig, p. 160; Tytler, p. 266.

78 DNB; Douglas's *Peerage*, I, p. 678; *Scots Peerage*, IV, p. 309; Anderson, S.N., II, p. 440; Tytler, p. 258; Brunton &Haig, p. 221; Omond, *Lord Advocates*, I, pp. 69–87; Sir William Fraser, *The Earls of Haddington* (1889).

79 Brunton & Haig, p. 245.

80 Anderson, S.N., I, p. 305. Biographical note prefixed to *Habakkuk Bisset's Rolment of Courtis* (ed. P. J. Hamilton-Grierson, Scot. Text Soc., 3 vols., 1920–26).

81 *Rolment of Courtis*, II, 275.

82 *History of the Writers to H. M. Signet* (1936), p. 79.

83 Pitcairn, II, pp. 286, 298.

84 *Rolment*, I, 74–75.

85 RPC (2nd Ser.), VIII, 368.

86 *Rolment*, I, I.

87 *Ibid.*, I, 74.

88 *Rolment*, III, 2.

89 George Neilson, "Skene's Memorabilia Scotica, 1475–1612, and Revisals of Regiam Majestatem," 1923 (reprinted from *Trans. Glasgow Archeological Soc.*).

90 *Rolment*, II, 57.

91 *Ibid.*, II, 73.

92 *Ibid.*, II, 131–146.

93 There are numerous other instances of this, not least the cases of John Knox and George Buchanan, in sectors of scholarship other than the law.

CHAPTER 7

SIR THOMAS HOPE

IF the sixteenth century was marked by the Reformation and the religious strife it initiated, the seventeenth was marked by constitutional and political controversy, which was not however unrelated to the prior and continuing religious contention and intolerance. Yet it was a century of notable development in legal science in Scotland, the century of Hope, Stair, Mackenzie, and a number of others.

Thomas Hope of Craighall[1] was probably born about 1580. His great-grandfather is said to have come to Scotland from France in 1537 in the retinue of Madeleine, bride of James V, and his younger brother settled in Amsterdam. He passed advocate in 1605 and soon achieved prominence by his defence of six clergymen charged with declining the jurisdiction of the Privy Council over the General Assembly by convening a General Assembly without command or licence from the Crown. The ministers' action was legally unsupportable and they were sent into exile.[2] Later he appeared for Margaret Hartsyde, a lady of the Queen's bed-chamber charged with misappropriating the Queen's jewels[3] and for the advocates in the settlement of their taxation in the Privy Council.[4] In 1613–18 he was one of the four advocate assessors for Edinburgh.[5] Repeated mentions of him in the records show that he was in busy practice from 1610. Mackenzie, in his *Characteres Quorundam apud Scotos Advocatorum*,[6] praised him for founding argument on reason.

In the reign of Charles I, he became more prominent. In 1625 he drafted the King's revocation of his and his father's grants to laymen of ecclesiastical lands annexed to the Crown by the Act 1587, c. 29,[7] and in the following year was appointed Lord Advocate, jointly with Sir William Oliphant.[8] On his advice an action was begun to have the grants of church property declared null and void[9] but the action was abandoned and a commission, which included Hope, then appointed to examine the whole matter and value teinds and stipends.[10] In 1628 he was made a baronet of Nova Scotia for his work on this commission.[11]

In 1623 he was named one of the justices of the peace for Fife and Kinross.[12]

From 1619 Prince Charles had a council of his own at Edinburgh, distinct from the King's Council, though consisting mainly of members of that council, and from 1620 he had full power of managing all the property in Scotland constituting his principality. In July 1624 this council resolved to call in six advocates, of whom Thomas Hope was first-named, to advise them on the Prince's business.[13]

It has been recorded[14] that on July 1, 1626, the King communicated to the Lords of Session his pleasure that his Advocates (*i.e.* the Lord Advocate(s)) plead before them with covered heads. But Goodall recorded[15] the story that the King's Advocate used to plead uncovered; "but he [Hope] having two of his sons on the Bench, Sir John and Sir Thomas, the Lords indulged him the privilege of pleading with his hat on, which his successors in office have ever since enjoyed." But Sir John did not become a judge until 1632 and Sir Thomas (the younger) not until 1641. Goodall's story seems less well-founded than Balfour's.

In January 1628 Hope was admitted to be a member of the Privy Council.[16] He drafted the submission for the surrender of teinds[17] and was thereafter regularly present in Council and heavily involved in legal business of the Council.[18] He was involved in a long dispute with the Justice-Clerk about the precedence of their respective offices[19] and a committee was appointed to mediate between them.[20]

In accordance with an old claim of a privilege of Lord Advocate he was in November 1628 admitted to sit with the judges in cases in which he was not involved.[21] In Parliament the royal letters of prorogation were entrusted to him on each occasion between 1629 and 1633.

In February 1631 he was named to the renewed commission to survey the law,[22] and in March appointed to the new Privy Council.[23] Later in the same year he raised the question of the precedence of the Advocate and the Secretary.[24] In July 1633 a new commission for the surrender of teinds was appointed; Hope was a member and he and the Master of Requests protested about their precedence in the commission.[25] He drafted the indictment against John Elphinstone, Lord Balmerino, in 1634 for leasing-making, and appeared for the Crown at the trial.[26] From this time onwards Hope was far more a council adviser than a private lawyer and heavily engaged in council business. From about this time too he began to keep a diary.[27] It reveals a good deal about his character but little about his part in the events of the times.

In 1636 he was a party to the act of the Privy Council commanding the use of the Anglican-style service book (Laud's Liturgy),[28] but was not present at the resulting riot in St. Giles', and is indeed charged by Bishop Guthrie with having been privy to the rioting.[29] Later that year, however, he was alone of the Privy Councillors in refusing to sign the proclamation condemning opposition to the service book.[30]

He seems not to have taken any prominent share in the drafting of the National Covenant of 1637/38, nor to have signed it, though he gave an opinion supporting its legality.[31] With the rest of the Council he subscribed the Confession of 1580 as required by the King.[32] The King's commissioner, the Marquis of Hamilton, found him one of his greatest troubles, yet could not dismiss him.[33] Pretty clearly he supported the covenanters and his son, Thomas, served with their army, so that in January 1640 the King ordered him to remain at his country house, Craighall in Fife, during the King's pleasure.[34]

He was however present in Edinburgh to prorogue the Parliament in June 1640 and January 1641. But he refused without the King's authority to sign bills of indictment at the instance of the Estates against the opponents of the covenanters and despite the Estates' directions refused to prosecute them.[35] Later in the session his right to sit in Parliament as Lord Advocate but without sitting for a constituency was challenged, and he was permitted to be present only as an officer of State and to speak only if called upon by the house.[36]

In 1643 he opposed the proposal to summon a Parliament without any writ from the King and became re-established in the favour of the King's supporters.[37] At the General Assembly of that year he was royal commissioner[38] and upheld the King's policy despite lack of personal approval for it. Despite his pleas for delay and discussion with the King the Assembly adopted the Solemn League and Covenant.

Thereafter he performed the duties of his office despite opposition from the Estates and appeared in Parliament only if specially summoned. He died on October 1, 1646. He held the office of Lord Advocate until his death.[39] He had had a most successful practice and had bought estates in Fife, Stirlingshire, Midlothian, East Lothian and Berwickshire.

Two developments in legal doctrines have been attributed to Hope; the first was the use of clauses irritant and resolutive in entails. Fountainhall states[40] that these were a development of within the last 60 or 70 years, the first being the Laird of Calderwood's tailzie of his lands, advised by Sir Thomas Hope. In the *Minor Practicks*[41] Hope mentions such clauses as a new form, and Erskine[42] observed that entails containing such clauses appeared to have been first brought into use in Hope's time. The idea was not new, but he seems to have been the first who drafted a clause adapted to the purposes of an entail which was upheld as effective.[43] His second innovation was being the first to advise resort to a trust- adjudication, similar to the comprising on a trust bond familiar in Craig's time[44] as a method of compelling an unwilling superior to grant entry, to enable an heir, who was unwilling to enter, to challenge adverse deeds. This device is referred to[45] as having been "ofttimes advised as the remeid by Sir Thomas Hope and many since."

Of his children John (1605–54),[46] the eldest son, became a judge as Lord Craighall and one of Cromwell's commissioners for administration of justice in Scotland; his son Archibald (1639–1706) was also a judge (Lord Rankeillor);[47] Sir Thomas (1606–43)[48] the second son, became a judge as Lord Kerse and Lord Justice-General in 1641 and also wrote on the *Digest*, 18–24; Sir James (1614–61), the sixth son,[49] became a judge as Lord Hopetoun in 1649. From him are descended the Earls of Hopetoun (1703) and Marquesses of Linlithgow (1902),[50] and in different lines of descent from him James-Robert Hope-Scott who married Sir Walter Scott's granddaughter, Charles Hope of Granton, Lord Advocate (1801), Lord Justice-Clerk (1804) and Lord President (1811)[51] and his sons John Hope, Dean of Faculty (1830) and Lord Justice-Clerk (1841)[52] and James Hope, D.K.S., who married Elizabeth, daughter of Lord President David Boyle of Shewalton.[53]

Of his daughters, one, Mary, married Sir Charles Erskine of Alva; from them were descended Alexander Wedderburn, Lord Chief Justice of the Common Pleas in England (1780) later Lord Loughborough, Lord Chancellor (1793) and Earl of Rosslyn (1801),[54] Charles Erskine, later Lord Tinwald and Lord Justice-Clerk (1748),[55] whose son James became (1761) Lord Barjarg;[56] another, Anne, married David, second Lord Cardross; from them were descended in one line the fourth and later Earls of Buchan, Henry Erskine, Lord Advocate (1783 and 1806) and Dean of Faculty,[57] Thomas Erskine, Attorney-General of England (1786) and Lord Chancellor (1806)[58] and in a collateral line John Erskine of Carnock and Cardross, author of the *Principles* and the *Institute*.[59] In both lines there are many other members of the Faculty of Advocates. Sir Thomas was accordingly progenitor of several of the great noble and legal families of Scotland.

It was apparently Hope's habit from quite early in his career to make notes of cases which appeared to him to be of interest and importance, and these notes extend from 1608 to 1633 and provide the material for the *practicae observationes* in his *Major Practicks*. Many are concerned with cases in which he appeared as counsel. About 650 come from the years 1608 to 1624, and about 120 from 1625 to 1633; the substantial fall in average annual numbers probably reflects his increased involvement in public affairs from 1625 onwards.

Lesser writings by Hope included a Latin version of the Psalms and the Song of Solomon, a poem addressed to James VI when he visited Edinburgh in 1617, a Latin ode in praise of Charles I when that king made him Lord Advocate, and other verses, and a summary of Justinian's *Digest*, apparently prepared when Hope was preparing for the Bar, and dated 1602, 1603 and 1604. His historically significant writings are, however, the *Minor Practicks* and the *Major Practicks*.

The smaller is known as the *Minor Practicks*. It probably dates from about 1620–25, and has been printed twice, first in 1726 by Alexander Bayne of Rires, senior curator of the Advocates' Library in 1722 and from 1722 to 1737 the first professor of Scots Law in the University of Edinburgh. In the dedication prefaced to that edition Bayne describes it as "the most intirely Municipal, as well as one of the most valuable pieces of its kind and size, that any of our Lawiers have yet produced," and in his address to the reader he narrates that the *Minor Practicks* "was composed without any study or application, being dictated to his sons for their instruction, in mornings while he was dressing." Bayne states that he got this information from "some of the near relations of the family" so there may be some truth in it. If so the text must have been revised because it is remarkably well structured for extempore dictation. The second edition was published by John Spottiswood of that Ilk, advocate, in 1734. This edition, it appears from the preface, was being prepared by Alexander Spottiswood, advocate (grandson of John Spottiswood, Archbishop of St. Andrews and Lord Chancellor and author of *The History of the Church of Scotland*, and son of Sir Robert Spottiswood, Lord President of the Court of Session, 1633–41, and author of Spottiswood's *Practicks*), at the time of his death in 1675, and was completed by John, Alexander's son. The preface to this edition contains the statement that

> "my father [*i.e.* Alexander] thought he could not do a piece of better service to the public than by giving not only a correct edition of it, purged from the manifold errors that commonly creep into manuscript copies (in which it had hitherto appeared) through the negligence or ignorance of transcribers; but also to subjoin some Notes and Observations of his own, for illustrating such places as might create difficulties to ordinary readers, and more particularly for showing what alterations have been made in our law, by Acts of Parliament or otherwise, since the author's time."

This edition was accordingly begun substantially before, but completed and published after, Bayne's edition. Spottiswood subjoined an appendix (compiled by his father) giving an "Account of all the Religious Houses that were in Scotland at the time of the Reformation," a rather incongruous addition, a second listing the heirship moveables belonging to the heir of a prelate, baron or burgess, a third giving forms of three precepts to a superior, a fourth giving the method of expeding infeftments, and the fifth giving two forms of brieves.

The *Minor Practicks or a Treatise of the Scottish Law* is in Bayne's edition a small treatise in 26 titles and 370 paragraphs. It is misnamed in that it contains no references to statute or decision (though one or two cases are mentioned) nor any practical observations. The titles deal with The Form of Process before the Lords, Of Kirks and Bishops, Of Testaments, Of Moveable and Heritable Bonds, Of Heirs, Of Ward and Nonentry, Old and New Extent, Precepts directed to the Superior, Precepts of Sasine and Clare Constat, Tinsel of Superiority, Base and Publick Infeftments, Necessity of Confirmation, Of Wadsets, Reversions and Regress, Of the Nature of Reversions, Of Liferent Escheat, Of Signatures and Seals, Of Sasine and the Precept, Of the Inferior Jurisdictions, Of Judgments Possessory and Petitory, Of Apprisings and Adjudications, Of Comprisings, Of Reductions and Improbations, Of Warnings and Removings, Of the Diversity of Decreets, Of Assignations, Of Tailzies. There does not appear to be much pattern in this save that most of the topics are concerned with property. Bayne added to his edition A Discourse on the Rise and Progress of the Law of Scotland and the Method of Studying It, and an Alphabetical Index and Abridgment of the Acts of Sederunt 1661–1726.

Spottiswood's edition is entitled *Practical Observations upon Divers Titles of the Law of Scotland commonly called Hope's Minor Practicks*. It is arranged in 16 titles, some of those in Bayne's edition being omitted or altered. There are extensive notes, more voluminous than the text, and the paragraphs are numbered within each title.

The *Minor Practicks* must have been known in MS. during most of the seventeenth century. Stair refers to it once or twice. That there were two printed editions suggests that a need was felt for concise handbooks of the main topics of private law. Stair's *Institutions*, of which two editions had been printed before the *Minor Practicks* was, was too big for laymen and students.

Hope's other work, the *Major Practicks*, is a true digest *Practicks*. Though well known to Stair, who repeatedly cites materials contained in it, to Bankton and Erskine, it remained unpublished until edited by Lord President Clyde (the first) and published by the Stair Society in 1937–38.

Hope's original manuscript seems to have perished but there are a number of transcripts in existence,[60] at least one dating from 1656, which cannot be much later than the archetype.

Some doubt formerly existed as to the true authorship of the *Major Practicks*. W. M. Morison, compiler of the *Dictionary of Decisions*, incorporated therein something between a third and a half of the decisions noted in the *Major Practicks* but attributes them to "Kerse," *i.e.* to Sir Thomas Hope of Kerse, son of Sir Thomas Hope of Craighall. In the Advertisement to his *Dictionary* he states: "The decisions observed by Lord Kerse in his Law Repertory, (a valuable manuscript, which Lord Kames seems to have overlooked when compiling his Dictionary of

Abridged [sic] Cases; ... those reported by ... Sir Thomas Hope ... and some others, have never been printed." Morison clearly thought that one unprinted collection, entitled *Law Repertory*, was by Sir Thomas Hope of Kerse and was a different collection from an unprinted collection by Sir Thomas Hope of Craighall; but he does not cite any from the latter collection and failed to discover the identity of the two collections. Lord Kames, in the list of the collections of decisions from which his work was compiled, prefixed to his *Decisions of the Court of Session ... in the form of a Dictionary* (1741), does not include the name Kerse but does include the name Hope, and examination of the cases cited by Kames from "Hope" and by Morison from "Kerse" clearly indicates identity. Tait, in his *Index to the Decisions of the Court of Session* (1823) seems to have been confused by Morison because, in a note headed "Kerse" (p. 500), he says: "Kerse is the title; Hope the name," which happens to be true of the son but does nothing to clarify the confusion.

Moreover, in Lord Fraser's second edition (1866) of his *Law of Parent and Child*, at p. xxv, he narrates a controversy between himself and Lord Justice-Clerk Hope (1794–1858) arising out of the mention in his first edition of *Parent and Child* of 1846 of Hope's *Major Practicks* as an authority.

> "Though this book (Hope's *Major Practicks*) is entered in the Faculty's catalogue as the *Major Practicks* of Sir Thomas Hope, there may be reason to doubt whether this is correct. When the first edition of the present work was published, the late Lord Justice-Clerk Hope asked me to inform him where he could see the 'Major Practicks' which he found sometimes referred to in it, and, upon my stating that I had found a volume so described in the collection of the advocates' MSS., he informed me that this was a mistake; and added that 'I once intended to print the work of my ancestor, but gave it up on finding that no manuscript of it could be found.' The copy in the Advocates' Library (and the one I have myself from the Arniston Library and others) turned out to be by one of his sons – Sir Thomas Hope of Kerse, I think – and referred to my father's manuscript practicks. Lord Tweeddale may have a copy; but if not I do not know where any authentic manuscript is to be found. In the Advocates' Library, the manuscript called Sir T. Hope's Practicks is, like Balfour's Practicks, only a collection; and at all events was the compilation of Sir Thomas's son. Sir Thomas died in 1648–9.[61] I may mention that the opinions quoted from Sir Thomas's Major Practicks by Stair are not to be found in any manuscript now known. Erskine never saw the real Practicks!"

Lord Fraser concluded that "the reasons assigned by Lord Justice-Clerk Hope against accepting either volume[62] as the Major Practicks of Sir Thomas Hope are too cogent to be resisted." The Lord Justice-Clerk had indeed in 1843[63] expressed from the Bench, though *obiter*, similar views.

Despite Lord Fraser's acceptance of Lord Justice-Clerk Hope's view the evidence in favour of Sir Thomas Hope, the father's, authorship remains convincing. Stair was a regent at Glasgow University while Hope was still alive and was called to the Bar only two years after Hope died. He may have known some of the Hope sons and is likely to have known the contemporary attributions of the *Major Practicks* and the *Law Repertory*. In his *Institutions* of 1681 he cites "Hope" frequently and his references can readily be found in the text from which the *Major Practicks* was printed in 1937, though in the list of abbreviations prefixed to his (the fifth) edition of Stair of 1832 More explains "Hope" as "Hope's (Sir Thomas) practical observations upon various titles of the Law of Scotland, commonly called Sir Thomas Hope's *Minor Practicks*." But there are no decisions at all quoted in the *Minor Practicks* and Stair nowhere refers to the *Minor Practicks* by the bare abbreviation "Hope." Occasionally he does cite "Hope, *Min. Pr.*" More was as confused as Lord Justice-Clerk Hope, possibly even confused by him.

Similarly Mackenzie, another near-contemporary, in his *Observations on the Acts of Parliament* quotes Hope's *Major Practicks* frequently; so does Bankton (1751); so too does Erskine (1773), who sometimes refers to "Hope" followed by the title-heading, sometimes to "Hope, Maj. Prac." with the title-heading, and again his citations can be found in the now-printed text. In the first (posthumous) edition of Erskine the Note of Abbreviations includes Hope's *Minor Practicks*, cited from the 1726 edition, and, under the head of "Manuscript collections of decisions observed" there is "*Hop. Maj. Pr.* – by Sir Thomas Hope." But Badenach Nicholson, editor of the eighth (1871) edition of Erskine, in his list of abbreviations, explains "Hope" as "Hope's (Sir T. of Kerse) Decisions of the Court of Session, from 1610 to 1632" and to a reference in Ersk. III, 8, 36 to "(Hope, *Maj. Pr.*)" he appends the footnote: "See Fraser (Par. & Ch.), p. xxv," showing how he too had been led astray. No work under the name he gives seems to exist, but the dates of the father's *Practicks* are now taken to be 1608 to 1633 which suggests that the alleged Decisions was in fact the father's *Practicks*.

The confusion however persisted. The Mitchell Library, Glasgow, manuscript of the *Major Practicks*[64] is titled "Sir Thomas Hope of Craighall, advocat. regis, his greater practicks, 26 Sept. 1663," but a later hand has scored through "Craighall, advocat. regis" and interlined "Kerse, Justice-General." (Kerse was given the office of Justice-General in 1641 when he was made a Lord Ordinary.) Moreover the confusion infected the *Minor Practicks* also. One manuscript of the latter work[65] is entitled "Practiques . . . by Sir Thomas Hope of Carse, Knight, Advocate for his Majesty." A later hand has deleted "Carse" and substituted "Craighall." Kerse was never Lord Advocate. The writer of the article on Lord Kerse in the *Dictionary of National Biography* says of him: "He wrote the Law Repertorie." Sheriff McKechnie in his article on *Practicks*[66] treated the *Major Practicks* and the *Law Repertorie* as separate works.

There is indeed one manuscript[67] which bears on the first page the note: "This Law Repertorie was collected by the Lord Kerse who was a Lord of Session in the reign of King Charles the 1st., and son of Sir Thomas Hope of Craighall then Lord Advocate." The text is however that of the *Major Practicks*, not an independent work. Moreover some of the paragraphs of the first group within each title of the *Major Practicks* have appended to them the letters A, B, C, and Pa, and the *Law Repertorie* contains an *explicatio notarum* which includes the following:

My first book of practiques and the first part thereof	A.
the second part thereof	B.
Mr. James Balfour's practiques	B.Pr.
My second book of practiques	C.
My father's practiques	Pa.

The best explanation is that Lord Kerse wrote the *explicatio* which appears in all the later MSS. and that Kerse had himself collected two books of practicks, the first being in two parts, all apparently now lost, and that paragraphs from these sources were interpolated in a MS. of his father's *Major Practicks*. So too, Hope, the father, left at least one small collection of *practicae observationes*, other than the *Major Practicks*[68] containing cases dated between 1610 and 1619. A docquet on this collection by Sir Archibald Hope of Rankeillor, advocate, a descendant of Hope, and dated January 26, 1702, describes it as "some few practiques cited by his son Lord Kerse in his great practique observatio patris." Lord Clyde thought it hazardous to assert that any of the paragraphs marked "Pa" were drawn from the "few practiques," but it seems likely that it is from this source that they were incorporated in the early MS. of the *Major Practicks*. Consistent with this is the fact that most of the paragraphs so marked are placed at the end of the first group of paragraphs within a title though many would more appropriately have been fitted into the *practicae observationes*.

Similarly, though not explained in the *explicatio*, a few paragraphs are attributed to "Inst. Patr."[69] and "Resp. Pa."[70] The former have been traced to passages in the *Minor Practicks*. These also are pretty certainly interpolations by Lord Kerse, and Lord Clyde conjectured[71] that "It would seem as if Lord Kerse, in an excess of filial piety, had drawn a strained analogy between his father's Minor and Major Practicks on the one hand and Justinian's Institutes and Pandects on the other."

The best evidence that the *Major Practicks* were compiled by Hope the father, not the son, is provided by the dates of the cases noted and included in the fourth section of most of the titles. They cover the years 1608 to 1633, the years when Hope the father was in busy practice as an advocate; but Hope the son (Kerse) was born in 1606 and called to the Bar in 1631. Even in such a legal family he would not be likely to have been noting decisions at the age of two! If the work was the son's why do the materials stop at 1633 (when the father became immersed in public affairs) when the son was in full practice till 1641, when he was made a judge? Again there are instances, such as a case of 1626 noted at II, 1, 36, where the note concludes: "Quhilk caus I pleaded within the Barr in the inner house using the priviledge of the King's advocat." Hope the father became joint Lord Advocate on May 29th, 1626. Again Hope the son's (Kerse's) *Law Repertorie* invariably attaches the phrase "practicae observationes patris" as a heading of the section containing the notes of decided cases. This is consistent only with the *Law Repertorie* being

Kerse's transcript of his father's compilation, albeit with interpolations by himself from his own notes. The *Law Repertorie* is pretty clearly only another version of the *Major Practicks*, not an independent work.

The text edited by Lord President Clyde for the Stair Society is based on the only dated, and quite probably the oldest, transcript, one dated 1656, only therefore about ten years after Hope's death. This transcript pretty certainly contains interpolations made by Hope of Kerse in the original MS. or the archetype of the transcripts from his own collections of practicks.

The date when the collection stopped being compiled is clearly fixed as 1633. No entry in the sections comprising statutes, or Acts of Council and of Session, is later than 1633, and with a few doubtful exceptions the same is true of the *practicae observationes*.

The sources, as has been indicated, are very heavily native. There are hundreds of references to the Auld Laws, the statutes, Acts of Council and Session, Craig and Balfour. Hope clearly regarded the Auld Laws as authentic. At least 1000 cases are noted, practically all from the period 1608–33. There are only a few references to the Roman law and the canon law, and a few propositions the statement of which owes something to the Roman law, such as II, 3, 10 which reads "Titius oblidged himself to Seia in 500 marks provydeing she married with his consent. . . . The lords found that unless Titius . . ." But even such titles as De Empto et Vendito, De Mutuo et Commodato and De Locato et Conducto (II, 4–6), which plainly indicate some acquaintance with the Roman law, cite no Roman law material but only Scottish authorities. Clearly Roman law and canon law were unimportant sources, and sources only indirect, in so far as already incorporated into Scots law by statute or decision. There are very few, if indeed any, references to Roman or canon law as the direct and immediate authority for a proposition of Scots law.

The *Major Practicks* is not a connected or narrative treatise but a collection of notes on various topics. The work is divided into eight "parts" designated by Lord Clyde as follows: (1) Law and government civil and ecclesiastical; (2) Personal rights; (3) Real rights; (4) Wills and succession; (5) Courts and jurisdictions; (6) Actions and diligence; (7) Process and evidence; and (8) Crimes. The largest parts are that dealing with actions and diligence, followed by that dealing with real rights in land, and that dealing with law and government. The smallest are those concerned with personal rights and the personal and domestic relations. Each part is divided into a number of Titles, *e.g.* De Obligationibus, Of Superiors and Superiorities, De Minoribus, and each Title is divided into four groups of paragraphs, the first usually not headed, the second headed Acts of Parliament, printed and unprinted Acts being separately dealt with, the third headed Acts of Councell and Acts of Session and the fourth headed Practicae Observationes. The first group are drawn from *Regiam Majestatem*, Craig, and Balfour's *Practicks*. The second are brief statements of points of statute law, and have the year and chapter number of the Act given, the third are similar summaries of Acts of the Privy Council or Acts of Sederunt, and the fourth are points drawn from Hope's professional experience, usually giving the names of the parties to a case and the date; they frequently commence "In an action betwixt . . ."

or "Found. . . ." Not all four groups are found in every title.

The paragraphs are normally six to ten lines long, but some are shorter and some much longer. But they are all notes, not narrative text, and there is no explanation or criticism of rules or decisions.

The order of points within the first group is haphazard; no order is discernible. The notes on the statutes are generally chronological; those on the Acts of Council are not orderly; and the practical observations seem to be in roughly chronological order. Lord Clyde's edition helpfully supplies references where the sources referred to can be identified, as most of them can.

It has been observed that the biggest parts of the *Major Practicks* are those dealing with actions and diligence, with real rights and with government. It is noteworthy how little attention is given to husband and wife, marriage and divorce and parent and child; these topics arise only in relation to matters of property. There are no uses of phrases *jus mariti, jus relictae* and *legitim*. The doctrine of communion of goods is not mentioned. These matters were for the Commissaries. Personal rights and obligations take up little space and suggest a rather rudimentary state of the law. The titles on sale, loan, hire, pledge, deposit and mandate are brief; partnership or society is not mentioned; cautionry, assignation, payment and discharge are more substantial.

The collection and classification of this material must have been a very large undertaking, involving examination of everything in print in the early seventeenth century, the Black Acts or Skene's *Lawis and Actis*, Skene's *Regiam Majestatem*, and manuscripts of Balfour's *Practicks* and Craig's *Jus Feudale*, manuscript registers of the Privy Council and of the Acts of Sederunt, Pitmedden's MS. Abridgment of the Statutes of Session, and Hope's own MS. notes of cases. Considering that the compiler was a busy counsel and from 1626 a law officer it is hard to believe that he did not have a research assistant, possibly one of his own sons. (By 1630 three of his sons, who all later became judges, were aged 25, 24 and 16 and would be interested in the law; one or more of them may have helped; young Thomas, later Lord Kerse, may have been particularly involved.) But we can probably credit Hope the father with the arrangement and the headings, the shape of the work.

Whether he initiated the work for his private convenience, or the instruction of his sons, or with a view to publication, we do not know.

Hope was quite a different kind of jurist from each of his important predecessors. Balfour, despite his discreditable public life, was a careful collector of materials; Craig was a philosophic and comparative scholar, dealing with a European theme as exemplified in Scotland; Skene was an honest, but careless and confused and inadequate, antiquarian and record scholar. But Hope was an outstanding practitioner with the interest to note cases he observed or engaged in and to try to set down the materials for his work in orderly fashion.

Hope's two works are each of importance in different ways. The *Minor Practicks*, though a slight work and with no pretentions to being a systematic treatise is the first narrative text on some topics of Scots law, as contrasted with Craig's treatise on western feudal law as exemplified and applied in Scotland. The *Major Practicks* is the most important practical manual in the form of collected notes since Balfour's *Practicks* and differs in being based on the daily notes of a counsel in busy practice. It marks an advance on Balfour in point of arrangement; the grouping into eight parts is a step towards the systematic treatise.

Not least, Hope's works, coming a bare half-century before Stair's great work, are our main authorities for the state of the law shortly before Stair and for determination of the extent to which Stair, in stating the law, developed it and even made it.

NOTES

¹ DNB; Anderson, S.N. II, p. 492; Omond, *Lord Advocates*, I, p. 93; D. Stevenson, *The Scottish Revolution*, 1637–44. Craighall is about 3 miles SE of Cupar, Fife.

² *Diary of the Public Correspondence of Sir Thomas Hope of Craighall* (Bannatyne Club, 1843); *Letters of Sir Thomas Hope*, 1627–46, in S.H.S. *Miscellany*, Vol. I (1893); *Scots Peerage*, IV, p. 485; Lord President Clyde's introduction to his edition of *Hope's Major Practicks* (Stair Soc., 1937–38).

³ RPC, VIII, p. 80; Pitcairn, *Criminal Trials*, II, pp. 544–557. For sequel see RPC (2nd), I, xcvi. See also M. Lee, *Government by Pen: Scotland under James VI and I* (1980), p. 52.

⁴ RPC, XIII, 409.

⁵ *Edinburgh Burgh Records*, 1604–26, pp. 101, 120, 167, 182.

⁶ *Works*, I, p. 6.

⁷ On the Revocation edict see RPC (2nd), civ–cciii.

⁸ RSS, xcviii, 444; Burnet, *History of His Own Time*, I, p. 30; Omond, I, p. 102.

⁹ Connell on *Tithes*, III, App. xxxix; RPC (2nd), I, 398.

¹⁰ APS, V, 189–207; RPC (2nd), I, 509.

¹¹ RMS, VI, 1212.

¹² RPC, XIII, 346.

¹³ RPC, XIII, 545, 558.

¹⁴ Balfour, *Annals*, II, p. 139.

¹⁵ RPC (2nd), I, 314n. See also Omond, I, p. 146.

¹⁶ RPC (2nd), II, 180.

¹⁷ *Ibid.*, 245.

¹⁸ See indexes to RPC (2nd), II–VIII, *passim*.

¹⁹ RPC (2nd), II, 486, 490–491, 524–532, 547, 631.

²⁰ *Ibid.*, 490–491.

²¹ A.S., Nov. 19, 1628; Omond, I, pp. 104–105.

²² RPC (2nd), IV, 138: sequel, V, 227.

²³ *Ibid.*, 187.

²⁴ *Ibid.*, 273–276.

²⁵ RPC (2nd), V, 124.

²⁶ *State Trials*, III, 604; Omond, I, p. 109; *cf. Scots Peerage*, I, 564. Leasing-making was, broadly, sedition or making mischief between king and subjects. See Acts 1585, c. 10; 1594, c. 209. Balmerino was convicted by one vote, but pardoned.

²⁷ *Diary of the Public Correspondence of Sir Thomas Hope of Craighall* (Bannatyne Club, 1843).

²⁸ RPC, VI, 510. He was also one of the committee of Council, appointed to examine persons involved in the tumult in St. Giles': *ibid.*, 511, 528.

²⁹ Bishop Guthrie, *Memoirs*, pp. 17–20.

³⁰ Rothes, *Relation of Affairs*, p. 66.

³¹ *Hamilton Papers*, pp. 8, 9, 50–51.

³² RPC (2nd), VII, 74.

³³ Burnet, *Memoirs of the Dukes of Hamilton*, p. 92.

³⁴ Burnet, *supra*.

³⁵ APS, V, 307; Balfour, *Annals.*, III, pp. 1–3.

³⁶ APS, V, 324.

³⁷ Burnet, *Dukes of Hamilton*, p. 218.

³⁸ The only instance prior to the Disruption of a commoner being Lord High Commissioner to the General Assembly: *Acts of Assembly* (1638–1842) (1843 ed.), p. 1204.

³⁹ He is mentioned by name as Lord Advocate in May 1645; RPC (2nd), VIII, 47; and by title thereafter.

⁴⁰ Report of *Rothes v. Melville* (1677) 3 B.S. 168, 170.

⁴¹ Tit. 16, §11. See also *Preston v. Heirs of Entail of Valleyfield* (1845) 7 D. 305 at p. 322; *Laurie v. Laurie* (1854) 17 D. 181 at p. 193.

⁴² *Inst.*, III, 8, 25.

⁴³ In *Stormont v. Annandale's Creditors* (1662) Mor. 13994.

⁴⁴ J.F., II, 5, 6.

⁴⁵ *Glendonwyne v. Nithsdale* (1662) Mor. 9740.

[46] DNB; Brunton & Haig, p. 289. See also genealogical tree of the family of Hope in George Seton, *Memoir of Alexander Seton* (1882), App. II.

[47] Brunton & Haig, p. 444.

[48] DNB; Brunton & Haig, p. 306.

[49] DNB; Brunton & Haig, p. 321.

[50] *Scots Peerage*, IV, p. 485.

[51] DNB; Omond, Lord Advocates, II, p. 205; Brunton & Haig, p. 545.

[52] DNB.

[53] DNB; Brunton & Haig, p. 547.

[54] DNB.

[55] DNB; Brunton & Haig, p. 513.

[56] Brunton & Haig, p. 526.

[57] DNB; A. Fergusson, *The Hon. Henry Erskine* (1882).

[58] DNB.

[59] DNB; Chap. 13, *infra*.

[60] These are surveyed in Lord Clyde's introduction, pp. xviii–xix.

[61] This was a mistake; Hope died in 1646.

[62] *i.e.* the Advocate's Library copy (NLS Adv. MS. 24.3.10) or Lord Justice-Clerk Tinwald's copy (NLS Adv. MS. 6.2.20).

[63] *McNeight* v. *Lockhart* (1843) 6 D. 128 at p. 137.

[64] C. 187631.

[65] NLS Adv. MS. 24.3.8.

[66] *Sources and Literature of Scots Law* (Stair Soc.), p. 25.

[67] NLS Adv. MS. 6.1.2. It is probably an 18th-century copy.

[68] NLS Adv. MS. 6.2.9.

[69] *e.g. Maj. Prac.* I, 9, 27.

[70] *e.g. Maj. Prac.* II, 14, 9.

[71] Introduction, p. xxvi.

CHAPTER 8

JAMES DALRYMPLE, VISCOUNT STAIR

STAIR is a parish in Kyle, Ayrshire, about six miles east-north-east of Ayr and south of the Ayr-Mauchline road and the river Ayr. It was separated from the parish of Ochiltree in 1653 at the instance, it is said, of Sir James Dalrymple, who wanted a church nearer Stair House than that of Ochiltree, five miles away.[1]

In 1450 William de Dalrymple acquired the lands of Stair-Montgomery by marriage with Agnes Kennedy.[2] In 1603 the Crown granted to John Dalrymple of Stair in liferent and his eldest son James in fee 21 merklands of the lands of Stair-Montgomerie of old extent, which John had resigned.[3] Then in November 1620 the Crown granted anew to James Dalrymple of Drummurchie and Janet Kennedy his wife in conjunct fee the lands of Stair or Stair-Montgomerie, which James had resigned.[4] On June 1, 1624, the Crown granted to Andrew Dalrymple, notary in Mauchline, and Janet Dalrymple his wife and Charles Dalrymple their son the lands of Stair or Stair-Montgomery which James Dalrymple and Janet Kennedy his wife resigned, under provisions contained in a contract of impignoration of 1623 and relative backbond.[5] Andrew Dalrymple resigned the lands on November 26, 1647, and the Crown regranted them on March 1, 1648 to James Dalrymple and his wife Margaret Ross in conjunct fee.[6]

Stair House is pleasantly situated in a bend of the river Ayr, secluded in trees, and is still occupied. It is a symmetrical tower-house with crow-,stepped gables and a round tower at each angle.[7] The country at this point is quite heavily wooded and on both sides of the river the ground rises steadily from the river.

James Dalrymple, the future jurist later ennobled as Viscount Stair,[8] was born at Drummurchie or Dinmurchie in the Parish of Barr, Ayrshire[9] in May 1619, son of James Dalrymple and Janet Kennedy. The father died in 1625 and his widow later remarried. Stair's parents were both strongly attached to the reformed religion and his mother took care to have him well educated.[10]

He was educated at Mauchline Grammar School and in 1633 entered Glasgow University where he graduated Master of Arts in 1637, being named first in the list of laureates or graduates of July 1637.[11] Thereafter he went to Edinburgh but what he did there is unknown.

This was the time of Charles I's misguided attempt to force a service-book on the Kirk,[12] which gave rise to the famous riot in St. Giles in July 1637 and the reaction which gave rise to the National Covenant of 1638,[13] which was widely signed throughout Scotland. It was a very legal document, in effect an appeal to the rule of law, to precedent and to history, against the King's arbitrary actions and reliance on his prerogative. There is no evidence that young Dalrymple signed it, but it would not be surprising if he did. The General Assembly of 1638 met at Glasgow and condemned the King's ecclesiastical policy, the service-book, book of canons, book of ordination and the Court of High Commission, deposed and excommunicated the bishops and declared episcopacy to have been abjured and to be removed from the Kirk.[14]

A covenanting army was raised to defend the rights of the Kirk and marched to the Border, but without giving battle Charles agreed to the Scottish demands in June 1639 in the Pacification of Berwick. The following year the Scottish forces occupied Newcastle and insisted that they remain in occupation at English expense until a settlement was reached. Negotiations were begun at Ripon and a treaty agreed in August 1641. Charles had also been driven by the invasion to summon what became the (English) Long Parliament in November 1640. In these "Bishops' Wars" young Dalrymple commanded a company in the Earl of Glencairn's[15] regiment of foot.[16]

In March 1641, having been solicited by some of his former teachers to apply, and while still in uniform, he sought and obtained, by competitive examination, a post of regent in Glasgow University.[17] He probably taught philosophy, particularly logic, but according to Forbes[17] he studied hard the Greek and Latin languages and the history and antiquities of Greece and Rome, with a view to studying the civil law.[18] There survives[19] a volume of *Theses Logicae, Metaphysicae, Physicae, Mathematicae et Ethicae*, theses which students, to qualify for graduation, had to defend publicly before the examiners, their regents. Dalrymple presided on this occasion. In 1643 he resigned his office, as he was required to do, as he intended to marry, but he was immediately re-elected. His wife was Margaret Ross of Balneil in Wigtownshire. She was the widow of Fergus Kennedy, whom she had married in 1640; he was probably Dalrymple's first cousin, both being grandsons of the same maternal grandfather. He held the post until, probably, October 1647, when he resigned to go to be Bar.[20]

He had had no formal legal education, and indeed none was to be had in Scotland at that time. There were no treatises or textbooks on Scots law.[21] In 1646 and 1648 he was a member of the committee for war for the county of Ayr.[22]

On February 17, 1648, he passed advocate,[23] having doubtless satisfied the examiners in the Roman law, a requirement introduced before 1619[24] (an examination in Scots law was not required until 1750), but for over a year thereafter the sittings of the court were suspended because of the disturbed state of the country. Charles I was tried by his English subjects and on January 30, 1649, beheaded. On February 5 Charles II was proclaimed King of Scotland and on March 6 the Estates appointed commissioners to go to negotiate with Charles at The Hague in Holland; young Dalrymple was made secretary to the commission.[25]

Just before leaving for Holland, Dalrymple was appointed by Parliament one of a large commission to undertake the revision of the law.[26] There had been several similar commissions previously, in 1425,[27] 1469,[28] 1566,[29] (which prompted the publication of the *Black Acts*, the legislation from 1424 to 1566), in 1574[30] (which resulted in the compilation of Balfour's *Practicks* and Skene's *Lawes and Actes*), in 1592[31] and 1628, approved by Parliament in 1633.[32]

The commission of 1649 was given power to consider the customs and practices both of civil and criminal courts and "to order production of all records and registers, together with the old registers of the book called *Regiam Majestatem* in order that the Commissioners might compile a formal model or frame of a book of just and equitable laws to be established and authorised by his Majestie and Estates of Parliament, and might abrogate any byegone Acts of Parliament which had fallen into desuetude or become superfluous or unprofitable." There is no record of the commission having reported, or even of ever having met or done anything. As Fountainhall observed[33] this project was in imitation of that of Justinian, who employed Tribonian and other lawyers to review the books of law in his time, and from them they compiled the *Digest*.

On March 8, 1650 a fresh commission, again with Dalrymple as secretary, was appointed to visit Charles at Breda.[34] In connection with both commissions Dalrymple would meet Charles and may have acquired some favour in the King's eyes by siding with those commissioners whose demands on Charles were more moderate.

Whether on either of these visits to Holland Dalrymple met any of the great Dutch jurists, such as Paul Voet,[35] Arnold Vinnen (Vinnius)[36] or Antonius Matthaeus[37] is unknown,[38] but he is said[39] to have visited Salmasius[40] at Leiden, and he may have obtained copies of their and other Dutch jurists' books. He may have picked up some of the Dutch language.

At least since the Reformation there had been much coming and going between Scotland and Holland with Scottish settlements at Middleburgh and Campvere,[41] and Scottish congregations at many places.

In May, Dalrymple was appointed by Parliament with another to meet Charles and the Commissioners when they landed at Garmouth,[42] and he probably accompanied him to Falkland. He was not, however, with the Scottish army defeated by Cromwell at Dunbar (1650) or at Worcester (1651), after which Charles again took refuge in Holland.[43] Scotland became a conquered and occupied country and in October 1651 the Commonwealth government in London appointed eight commissioners for the administration of Scotland, stating that Scotland and England were henceforth to be one commonwealth. An ordinance for Union was not in fact passed until by the second Protectorate Parliament in April 1657. Under the Protectorate a council of state of nine, including two Scots, was operative from September 1655. The Scottish Parliament ceased to meet and Scotland was nominally represented by 30 members in the Commonwealth Parliament, most of whom were government nominees.[44]

The Court of Session ceased to sit after February 28, 1650 and on May 18, 1652 commissioners were appointed under the Great Seal of the Commonwealth for the administration of justice; they were seven, four English and three Scots, the Scots being Sir John Hope of Craighall, son of Sir Thomas Hope, Colonel William Lockhart, brother of Sir George Lockhart, President of the Court of Session, and John Swinton of Swinton.[45] Each judge took the chair for a week in rotation. The court sat as a body, the Outer House being abolished. Latin was replaced for legal purposes by plain English.[46]

In 1654 the leading advocates, including Dalrymple, refused the Tender or Oath of Allegiance to the Commonwealth and Abjuration of

Royalty, and withdrew from practice, but this did not last long and the Tender was not insisted in. Shortly thereafter Dalrymple was one of a small committee of the advocates appointed to represent to the judges that the Outer House be restored and this was done in 1655.[47] The reports of the *Decisions of the English Judges during the Usurpation* indicate that Dalrymple had a substantial practice. In 1654 the baron courts were abolished and new baron courts were to be set up. In 1656 justices of the peace were appointed in every sheriffdom. Dalrymple was made a commissioner for Wigtown and Kirkcudbright to collect the assessments imposed by Cromwell in 1656–57 and by Parliament in 1660.[48]

In 1657 one of the judges died. Monck, commander-in-chief in Scotland, proposed "one Mr. James Dalrymple as a person fit to be a judge, being a very honest man, a good lawyer, and one of considerable estate. There is scarce a Scotchman or Englishman who hath bin much in Scotland butt knows him."[49] Dalrymple was accordingly appointed and took his seat on July 1, 1657; on July 25 Cromwell confirmed his appointment.[50] His tenure of office was, however, short. The courts were closed between Cromwell's death in September 1658 and the Restoration. A new commission, comprising four English and six Scottish judges (the latter including Sir James Hope and James Dalrymple) was issued by the Council of State in Scotland in March 1660, but never became effective as they did not know in whose name and authority to direct their warrants, some being for a king, and some for the keepers of the liberty of England.[51] Testimony generally is that executive and judiciary under the Commonwealth were efficient, more so than previously.

Dalrymple seems to have been on intimate terms with Monck and they met the day before Monck marched on London, when Dalrymple recommended to him to call a free Parliament.[52] Monck reached London on February 13.

Charles II entered London on May 29, 1660. The Scottish Parliament met again in 1661 and Dalrymple, who had gone to London to pay his respects to the King, was well received. They probably talked of the old days of 1649–50 in Holland. Dalrymple was knighted, and he was named one of the judges when the Court of Session was restored in February 1661[53] and made a member of the new Commission for the Plantation of Kirks and Teinds and certain other commissions.[54] In the autumn he was appointed Vice-President of the court, to preside in the absence of the President, Sir John Gilmour. The Lord Chancellor from 1661 to 1664 was the Earl of Glencairn, Dalrymple's old commanding officer in the Bishops' Wars.

For the next 20 years Stair, as he may now be called, continued as a judge of the Court of Session, being appointed President in 1671 on Gilmour's resignation,[55] and also nominated a member of the Scottish Privy Council[56] But they were not peaceful nor uneventful years. Stair was a regular attender at the Privy Council and frequently a member of committees. This work must have taken up much time. From 1662 though the Earl of Rothes was Royal Commissioner in Scotland the effective power was in London, in Lauderdale as Secretary of State for Scotland.[57] Lauderdale in 1662 secured the passing of an Act[58] for the re-establishment of episcopal government of the Kirk, and an Act[59] required the taking of a declaration that it was unlawful for subjects to enter into leagues and covenants. Stair and three other judges had previously refused to take the declaration. Lord Glencairn as Chancellor wrote to Stair requiring him to take the declaration before January 19, 1663/64, under pain of losing his seat on the Bench. Stair resigned[60] and his seat was declared vacant, but the King summoned him to London and allowed him to make a qualified declaration,[61] and a royal letter to the court caused him to be readmitted. He was advanced to the rank of baronet[62] and resumed his seat on the Bench in June 1664. About the end of that year he was assaulted by apprentices in Edinburgh.[63]

In 1667 he was made one of the commissioners to receive the bonds of persons entitled to the benefit of the royal Act of Indemnity following the suppression of the Pentland Rising,[64] and in 1668 a commissioner for the shires of Renfrew and Ayr and of Wigtown and the Stewartry of Kirkcudbright for raising the militia.[65]

In 1669 there occurred a family tragedy. Stair's eldest daughter Janet married David Dunbar, son of Sir David Dunbar of Baldoon, Wigtownshire, on August 12 and died on September 12; her husband died before 1680,[66] or on May 28, 1682.[67] This incident became the basis for the story of Lucy Ashton in Scott's *The Bride of Lammermoor*, in which Lady Ashton is founded on Lady Stair. Scott's story is that Lucy Ashton tried to murder her husband on the wedding night.[68] In his own introduction to the novel[69] Scott tells the tale as he had it from connections of his own, that Janet Dalrymple had pledged herself to Lord Rutherford, but later another suitor, more acceptable to her parents, David Dunbar, had appeared, that she had reluctantly married him, knifed him on the bridal night, lost her reason and died three weeks later. Dunbar recovered from his wounds but died after a fall from his horse in 1682. Scott refers to versions of the story given him by Charles Kirkpatrick Sharpe[70] and other accounts. There is an elegy on Janet's death by Andrew Symson.[71] Agnew[72] gives as the true Galloway tradition that the bridegroom stabbed the bride sometime after the wedding. The story was adopted and further modified by Donizetti in his opera *Lucia di Lammermoor*, produced in 1835. Whatever the truth it was a family tragedy which must have caused the family acute pain.

In 1670 Stair was appointed by the King, under the authority of an Act of Parliament, to be one of the Scottish commissioners to meet English commissioners to discuss a union of the two kingdoms.[73] The points proposed by the King for discussion were: 1. The preservation to each kingdom of its laws, civil and ecclesiastical, unimpaired; 2. The inseparable union of the two kingdoms into one monarchy; 3. The union of the Parliaments; 4. The sharing of all trading and similar privileges; and, 5. The securing of the conditions of the union.[74]

Meetings took place at Somerset House.[75] The Scottish commissioners had private meetings at the lodgings of Rothes or Lauderdale. Some opposed union as destroying the fundamental sovereignty of Scotland and abolishing its Parliament, which they urged was *ultra vires*, but Stair and Lauderdale favoured union. Stair was a member of a sub-committee of the Scottish delegation which examined the first proposal, and recommended that in any union the separate systems of law be preserved and actions affecting Scots should be tried only in Scotland. The negotiations broke down on the issues of whether appeal should lie from the Court of Session to Parliament, and of the number of members to be sent from Scotland to a united Parliament.[76]

Though Stair himself did not live to see it, his son, the Master of Stair, was one of the main movers for bringing about the Union of 1707.

On September 21, 1669, the King nominated a commission, which included Stair,[77] to consider the whole matter of the Regulations of the three supreme courts then existing in Scotland, Session, Justiciary and Exchequer. The commission reported in March 1670, recommending for adoption certain rules, but without prejudice to what on more mature consideration they might propose as final settlement.[78] On June 4 the King ratified the report, ordered the rules to be observed, and the advocates to swear to them.[79] One rule imposed a limit on advocates' fees, which provoked them to refuse to swear to the Regulations and for a time some of them withdrew their services.

The commission continued and finally reported in 1672,[80] putting forward revised articles which were embodied by Parliament in the Act concerning the Regulation of the Judicatories.[81] The Regulations lay down many rules still accepted in civil practice. In relation to the Justiciary Court the office of Justice-Depute was abolished, and the Justiciary Court was to consist of the Justice-General, Justice-Clerk and five of the Lords of Session, as Commissioners of Justiciary, an arrangement which lasted until 1887; the robes of the Lords of Justiciary were prescribed as red faced with white, the Justice-General to have his lined with ermine. In relation to the Court of Exchequer provision was made for the fees of the Keeper of the Treasurer's Register and as to the Aeques or Exchequer Accounts of the Crown Vassals.

The work of the commission must be regarded as beneficial to the administration of justice. Stair is said[82] to have opposed the Act ratifying the Regulations, but in his *Institutions* he refers with approval to the Regulations. While this commission was at work Stair was appointed Lord President in place of Gilmour.[83]

In the Parliament of 1672 Stair sat as member for Wigtownshire and was made a member of the Committee of the Articles.[84] He may have had a hand in the notable number of reforms effected in private law by that Parliament, such as the introduction of adjudication of land in place of the older apprising[85] and improvements in the system of registration of deeds.[86] He again sat in the Parliament of 1673, in the Convention of 1678 and the Parliaments of 1681 and 1689–90.

Stair was clearly well-regarded as a judge, though in 1673 the Privy Council recommended to him to be careful that no suspensions be passed of decreets pronounced against persons guilty of being at conventicles and other disorders except *in praesentia* in Session time and by three of the Session in vacation.[87] Was he too tender to persons involved in conventicles? In 1676 the Common Council of Edinburgh ordered that his house rent, and that of his successors as President, be paid out of city revenues.[88] Lord President Forbes surrendered the privilege in 1741. He used the court's power of making Acts of Sederunt to effect improvements in the administration of the law, going beyond the merely procedural, such as having the public registers arranged and inventoried.[89]

It is difficult to know Stair's attitude to the government of Lauderdale during these years, the repression of the Covenanters, their revolt and defeat at Bothwell Bridge; in his *Apology*[90] he states that he secured alleviation of the Council's severity to them and disowned participation in the tortures ordered by the Council.

In May 1679 a royal letter named him with the Clerk Register,[91] Advocate,[92] Justice-Clerk[93] and Justice-General[94] to be sent to London to give a full account of the state of affairs "seeing from them we can have full information as well in matters of law as of fact,"[95] and in January 1680 the Council asked him and the other legal members of Council to meet and consider the condition of the Chancellary Office and what order the records thereof were in, and to report.[96]

Stair's colleagues on the Bench in these years after 1661 included many competent lawyers. Sir John Gilmour, Lord President 1661–71, collected *Decisions*, 1661–66, published with Falconer's *Decisions* in 1701; Sir John Nisbet, Lord Dirleton (1664–77) also collected *Decisions* and wrote Dirleton's *Doubts and Questions in the Law*, published together in 1690; Sir John Baird, Lord Newbyth (1664–81) compiled a manuscript *Practicks*; Sir Peter Wedderburn, Lord Gosford (1668–79) also collected *Decisions*; Sir Thomas Murray of Glendook (1674–81) printed folio and duodecimo editions of the statutes from 1424 in 1681–82; Sir David Falconer of Newton (1676–82) who became Lord President in 1682 in succession to Stair, also collected *Decisions*, published along with Gilmour's *Decisions* in 1701; Sir Alexander Seton of Pitmedden (1677–89) published in 1699 an edition of Mackenzie's *Law and Customs of Scotland in Matters Criminal* to which he annexed a treatise on *Mutilation and Demembration*; Sir Roger Hog, Lord Harcarse (1677–1700) collected *Decisions* of 1681 to 1692, published in 1757. Stair's colleagues were not all ignorant or inadequate; some have left no reputation or only a poor one, but the Bench was not staffed with incompetents.

The Parliament of 1681 had the King's brother, James, Duke of York (later James VII and II), a Catholic, who had been resident at Holyrood since 1679, as High Commissioner; Stair was a member. It passed an Act[97] ratifying all Acts in favour of the Protestant religion, and another[98] securing the indefeasible hereditary succession to the throne. Then was passed the Test Act.[99] This was ostensibly intended as protection to the Protestant religion following the Act securing the Duke of York's right of succession, but was truly intended to secure the submission of all in important positions in church and state to the royal supremacy in spiritual and temporal matters alike and to receive from them a repudiation of the Covenants. The Act imposed on all persons in offices and places of public trust, civil, ecclesiastical and military, the duty to publicly swear and subscribe an oath.

The oath prescribed asserted belief in Protestantism, obedience to the King, his heirs and lawful successors and further affirmed that the deponent judged it unlawful for subjects to enter into Covenants or Leagues or to convocate, convene or assemble in any councils, conventions or assemblies, to treat, consult or determine in any matter of state, civil or ecclesiastic without his majesty's special command or licence had thereto, Or to take up arms against the King or those commissioned by him, And that the deponent would never rise in arms or enter into such Covenant or Assemblies, And that there lay no obligation on him from the National Covenant or the Solemn League and Covenant or any other manner of way whatsoever, to endeavour any change or alteration in the Government, either in Church or State, as it was now established by the laws of this Kingdom. The oath finally affirmed that it was given in the plain genuine sense and meaning of the words without any equivocation, mental reservation, or any manner of evasion whatsoever, and that the deponent would not accept or use any dispensation from any creature whatsoever.

Some members had wanted an enactment more strongly for securing the Protestant religion than the first Act of the session which had ratified the former laws for the liberty of the Kirk and the security of the Protestant religion and of all Acts made against Popery.[1] The Test Act as drafted contained no definition of the Protestant religion which it professed to seek to protect. Stair carried an amendment that it should be described as the "religion contained in the Confession of Faith recorded in the first Parliament of James VI,[2] which is founded on and agreeable to the written word of God." This virtually nullified the government's purpose. He may have thought that this addition would lead to the Act being dropped but, according to Wodrow, few of the members had read the Confession of Faith and the Act was allowed to pass as amended rather than have no test at all. But more careful consideration indicated that the Act was full of inconsistencies, such that no man could honestly swear the oath.[3]

The Confession of Faith referred to is the Scots Confession of 1560, adopted by Parliament in 1560 but legally ratified only in 1567. It was a strongly anti-Roman document and condemned many of the major tenets of the Roman church. It remained the official doctrinal statement of the Church of Scotland until superseded (though not abrogated) by the Westminster Confession in 1647. At the Restoration the Rescissory Act cancelled the Westminster Confession's recently-acquired legal status and left the Scots Confession as the only one with the sanction of law. In 1581 the Negative Confession expressly acknowledged the Scots Confession and in 1638 the National Covenant incorporated the Negative Confession as its first section.[4]

Given that hereditary succession was accepted and that, failing the birth of a legitimate child to King Charles II,[5] the succession would pass to James, a Catholic, the oath never to consent to any change or alteration of the Protestant religion contrary to the Confession of Faith, never to take up arms against the King or to enter into Covenant or Assemblies contained a clear possibility of a conflict of duty when James succeeded.

The Test Act was at once put into force. The Privy Councillors subscribed the Test and it was then incumbent on them to enforce it on all those specified in the Act. Most of the advocates and Writers to the Signet, however, signed the Test.[6]

It is quite clear that the Test imposed was ambiguous and that some of those affected had reservations or were uncertain as to the meaning of what they were expected to swear to. The majority, though in many cases with reluctance, gave way, but many resigned offices rather than subscribe. Those who refused included the Duke of Hamilton, the Duke of Monmouth, and the Earl of Argyle. Argyle stated that he took the oath so far as it was consistent with itself and with the Protestant religion. He was imprisoned, charged with treason, and escaped.

On July 28, 1681, a Declaration that

> "we judge it unlawfull to subjects ... to enter into leagues and covenants or to take up armes against the King ... and that all these gatherings ... that were used in ... the late troubles were unlawfull and seditious and particularly that these oaths whereof the one was commonly called The National Covenant, as it was sworne and explained in the year 1638 and thereafter, and another entitled A Solemn League and Covenant, were and are in themselves unlawful oaths, and were taken by and imposed upon the subjects of this kingdom against the fundamental laws and liberties of the same, and that there lyeth no obligation upon us or any of the subjects from the said oaths or either of them to endeavour any change or alteration of the government either in Church or State as it is now established by the laws of this Kingdom,"

was signed by large groups of the clergy and nobility, and similar ones by the barons, including James Dalrymple, and the commissioners of the burghs.[7]

Stair was on October 21, 1681, required to take the Test before Lauderdale.[8] On December 17, 1681, Moray, Lord Secretary, reported to the Council that Stair, having quit all his public employments, had said he was under no statutory obligation to take the Test.[9]

Stair was "well pleased with the first part of it ... yet I could not sign the latter part of it."[10] Stair went to London seeking an audience with the King to show him that he could not take the test and to seek liberty to retire,[11] but the latter, warned by the Duke of York, declined to receive him and he returned to Scotland. Before he had even got to London he had been superseded as President by Sir George Gordon of Haddo, and he withdrew to his country house at Carscreoch.[12] In 1682 he protested against the conduct of Graham of Claverhouse who was engaged in suppressing conventicles in the area of Stair's estates.[13]

These Acts apart, the Parliament of 1681 passed some legislation important for private law, particularly one drafted by Stair and sometimes called Stair's Act, settling the law relative to the execution of deeds,[14] another applying the system of registration to burgh sasines and reversions,[15] another entitling the purchaser of a bankrupt's lands at judicial sale to enter with the superior on payment of a year's rent[16] and another confirming the privilege of doing summary diligence on foreign bills of exchange.[17]

In this retirement Stair busied himself with arrangements for the publication of his *Institutions*, which he had been working on for the last dozen or so years. Copies had been circulating in manuscript and Stair, whether or not he had originally intended to publish, thought it better to publish an authorised version than have more or less accurate transcripts circulating.[18]

His contract with Anderson, the printer, was dated March 26, 1681,[19] and he obtained a royal licence for printing the work on April 11. The work was probably published about the end of the year shortly before he left for Holland. On July 1, 1682, in a letter to the Marquis of Queensberry he states that he had ordered one of his books lately printed to be presented to his Lordship.

But he was not left in peace in Galloway. In January 1682 Graham of Claverhouse was commissioned by the Privy Council to enforce the laws against conventicles and in Wigtownshire came up against Stair and his son, who tried to protect their tenants from Claverhouse's exactions.

In September or October 1682 Stair, having been advised by Lord Advocate Mackenzie that he was not safe and free from danger of imprisonment,[20] went to Holland and established himself at Leiden.[21] Though the university was then just over a century old, it was the oldest in the Netherlands and had attracted many brilliant scholars including, in law, Noodt,[22] Schulting[23] and John Voet.[24] There were many Scots and English exiles. Stair and some of his sons enrolled as students at Leiden University. A young man who met him at Leiden was John Erskine, who read Hope's *Treatise on the Scots Law* (*i.e. Major* or *Minor Practicks*) and Stair's *Institutions* and later became the father of John Erskine, author of the *Institutes*.[25] Stair was not, however, wholly cut off from Scotland because at the end of 1683 he published at Edinburgh the first volume of his *Decisions of the Court of Session 1661–71*, with prefixed thereto the Acts of Sederunt from June 1661 to February 1681. It was dedicated to his former colleagues on the Bench. It is very significant as the first series of reports of decisions published in Scotland.[26]

On December 3, 1684, the Privy Council gave the Lord Advocate warrant to prosecute Stair and various others for treason[27] and a royal letter of December 24 gave the same order.[28] The Privy Council repeated the order on January 9, 1685,[29] and a further royal letter of March 8 repeated it.[30]

On January 5, 1686, the Council authorised payments to witnesses against Stair[31] and on May 7 granted commission for taking evidence about Stair.[32] On January 27, 1686, Stair was listed as one who did not attend His Majesty's service the time of the late rebellion.[33]

Though able to publish, Stair did not have a quiet time in Holland. The government made application to the authorities in Holland to expel Stair from their territories, but they declined to do so. Attempts were made to kidnap him, and he had to move his home several times. In December 1684 the Privy Council ordered Lord Advocate Mackenzie to commence a process for forfeiture for treason before the Duke of York and Parliament against Stair and some others and in March 1685 they were fugitated for treason before the Court of Justiciary,[34] and in May an indictment for high treason was read in Parliament,[35] Stair and most of those charged were by Act of June 15, 1685, remitted to the Court of Justiciary.[36] Some of his lands were forfeited.[37]

A servant of Argyle, under torture, deponed[38] that Stair and others had planned to raise an army in Scotland and to land at places where they hoped people would join with them.

In December trial took place (in the accused's absence) in the Court of Justiciary[39] but a necessary witness failed to appear and the case was adjourned several times until 1687, when it was dropped, not least because Stair's son John, the Master of Stair, was appointed Lord Advocate and in March secured a remission for Stair and his family.[40]

In 1685[41] while still at Leiden he published a work *Physiologia Nova Experimentalis*. It must have been projected, if not indeed written, by 1681, as the ratification of his contract with the printer[42] of that year mentions the *Institutions* "together with a Treatise containing four Inquiries concerning Humane Knowledge, Natural Theologie, Morality and Phisiologie."[43] It bears to be lately translated into Latin and the preface is addressed to the Royal Society of London,[44] and it was favourably reviewed by Pierre Bayle in the *Nouvelles de la Republique des Lettres* for December 1685.

The scope of the work is indicated to some extent by the title, saying: "In which the general notions of Aristotle, Epicurus and Descartes are completed, errors uncovered and amended." It is a treatise on natural philosophy or physics[45] but, whatever its merits, its thought was quickly superseded by Newton's *Principia*. Stair in any event rejected the heliocentric theory of the universe and had not grasped the principle of gravity. (Copernicus' *De Revolutionibus Orbium Coelestium* had been published in 1543 and been mentioned in English work from 1551; Kepler's *De Motibus Stellae Martis* appeared in 1609.)

The work should be considered, however, as a part in a complete system of philosophy, comprising knowledge of God, of the universe, and of the behaviour of men on earth. It reflects what had been his interest as a regent in Glasgow College nearly 50 years earlier, and connects with his view of law as ideally and ultimately divinely ordained.

While in Holland Stair was among those refugees there who looked to William of Orange, nephew and son-in-law of James VII and II, as the person to protect Protestantism from James and to secure constitutional government.[46] He became a confidant of William, sailed with William in his own ship in 1688 and landed at Torbay. He remained in London while William negotiated with the Convention Parliament, and he and other Scots refugees gathered in London pressed William to call a Scottish Convention of Estates on a wider franchise,[47] and he was the intermediary between this Convention and William, now King of England, himself.[48] His son, the Master of Stair, took a leading part in the Scottish Convention and moved the resolution that James had "forefaulted" the right to the crown of Scotland and that the throne had become vacant.[49] The reasons for the vote were embodied in the Declaration of the Estates containing the Claim of Right[50] and the Articles of Grievances.[51]

On the same day William and Mary were declared King and Queen of Scotland during their joint lives and the longest liver of them, and after their death the crown was to devolve on the heirs of the body of the Queen, whom failing the princess of Denmark[52] and the heirs of her body, whom failing the heirs of the body of William.[53]

When William appointed his officers of state in Scotland, Stair's eldest son, Sir John Dalrymple, the Master of Stair, was appointed Lord Advocate.[54] Lord President Sir George Lockhart was assassinated by a disgruntled litigant on March 31, 1689, and Stair was appointed to succeed him.[55] Stair was held responsible for the nominations of the new Lords of Session, who were described as "the dross of the nation,"[56] an unduly derogatory view.

On May 27, 1689, a fresh commission for Council was received from William; it named Stair and his son John, the Master of Stair, to it.[57] On October 11 the Council received a letter from the King anent the sitting of the Session, in which the King authorised them to appoint Stair, Baird of Newbyth[58] and Swinton of Mersingtoun[59] or any two of them, as persons formerly examined and tried, to examine and try the qualifications of the remaining persons named by the King as judges and admit them if the Council found them qualified.[60] The Council granted warrant accordingly.[61] On November 5 Stair produced the oath of allegiance taken by him in presence of the King on September 23, again took the oath and took his seat as a member of Council.[62] Thereafter he was again much involved in the work of the Council. He became a Commissioner of Exchequer.[63] He was named again when the Council was reconstituted in 1690.[64]

In the Parliament of 1689, in which Stair sat as a member for Ayr,[65] the opposition carried several resolutions detrimental to him, including one which declared that where there was a total vacancy in the Bench it should be filled up by the King's nominating fit and proper persons to be presented to Parliament, to be tried and admitted or rejected, and that the President of the College of Justice should be elected by the whole Senate thereof. A proposal that no temporal peer should be president of the Session was blocked only with difficulty.[66] The Dalrymples, father and son, were highly unpopular. An anonymous pamphlet strongly attacked Stair, charging him with illegally assuming the office of President on the nomination of Charles II contrary to the Act 1579, c. 93.[67] In reply Stair wrote a pamphlet entitled *An Apology for Sir James Dalrymple of Stair, President of the Session, by himself*,[68] "wherein he has fully vindicated himself from those misrepresentations made of his Lordship in the late pamphlet entitled *The Vindication of the Scotch Address*."[69] (The latter was attributed to one Hume, who was brought before the Council and committed close prisoner[70] but later released on bail.[71])

On May 1, 1690, Stair was ennobled as Viscount of Stair, Lord Glenluce and Stranraer,[72] and made a Visitor of all universities, colleges and schools.[73]

The latter years of Stair's life cannot have been happy. Lady Stair died in 1692. In the same year the Master of Stair incurred great odium by being largely responsible for the massacre of Glencoe. The Royal Commission which later investigated that act found that the killings were murder and that the Master of Stair had exceeded the King's instructions, and he was severely censured and deprived of office, though he soon after received a remission from the King.[74] The Court of Session was constantly and vehemently attacked, it being alleged that the Bench was filled with Stair's creatures, that a taint of corruption still attached to it, and that the judges showed favour to their relations and friends. Two Bills were tabled in 1693, one providing that no peer or Lord of Parliament should be an ordinary[75] Lord of Session, and the other that the

Crown might appoint one of the Lords to preside, any law or custom to the contrary notwithstanding. Stair wrote an Information to the Royal Commissioner and Estates[76] putting forward arguments against the Bills.

In 1693 Stair published a revised second edition of his *Institutions*.

In 1695 there was published in London a work entitled *A Vindication of the Divine Perfections, illustrating the Glory of God in them by Reason and Revelation, methodically digested into several meditations. By a Person of Honour*. This work has always been attributed to Stair, probably justifiably. It contains several references to his *Physiologia* and the style and reasoning are reminiscent of the *Institutions*. It is probably the work referred to under the name of an Inquiry concerning Natural Theology in his contract of 1681 with his printer. It had a preface by William Bates and John Howe, English nonconformists. Howe[77] had been in exile at Utrecht in 1686–89 and Stair had very possibly met him there. The book is divided into 18 meditations.

There are also in Glasgow University Library several anonymous pamphlets dated from 1689–90 commending the Revolution Settlement of these years, at least some of which may be attributed to Stair.[78] These may be thought of as similar to the *Federalist* papers, designed to commend a new constitution to the public.

He died at his house in Edinburgh on November 25, 1695, and was buried in St. Giles Church.

There is a statue of Stair, as representing law, on the façade of the National Museum of Antiquities in Queen Street, Edinburgh[79] and, as the keystones of the arches above the ground-floor windows of the hall of the Royal Faculty of Procurators in Glasgow,[80] there are 14 sculptured faces; on the long frontage to West George Street the five from left to right, represent Lord President Blair, Erskine, Stair (above the doorway), Kames and Lord President Forbes.

A memorial to Stair was unveiled in St. Giles Cathedral in 1906.[81] It takes the form of a brass tablet having a border of thistles with, in relief, the inscription: "In memory of Sir James Dalrymple, first Viscount Stair (Lord Glenluce and Stranraer in the Peerage of Scotland, P.C.) Lord President of the Court of Session. A distinguished lawyer and author of the Institutes [*sic*] of the Law of Scotland. Born May 1619. Died 23rd November 1695. Buried in this church."

In 1951 when Glasgow University celebrated the 500th anniversary of its foundation, the General Council, the general body of graduates, presented a handsome gateway and pair of wrought iron gates to the University. These bear in five rows of panels the names of some of the most distinguished Glasgow men and women of each of the five centuries in the life of the University. One of the six names for the seventeenth century is Stair.

In 1953 a memorial to Stair was unveiled in Glasgow University.[82] It is a stone tablet set into the wall of the entrance hall from which rises the staircase to the Court and Senate Rooms. The initiative for this memorial was taken by Professor A. Dewar Gibb. It takes the form of a large stone carved by Hew Lorimer[83] and bears the inscription:

"James Dalrymple/First Viscount Stair/Student in the College of Glasgow/1633–1637/Regent in the College/1641–1647/Senator of the

College of Justice/1661–1671/President of the Court of Session/1671–1681 and 1689–1695/A Supreme master of jurisprudence who in his Institutions/laid an imperishable foundation for the Law of Scotland."

It was unveiled by Lord President Cooper, who delivered an eloquent address in which he said:

"The two characteristics of Stair's work which it is fitting to stress on an academic occasion such as this are its originality and its universality. It is hardly an exaggeration to say that Stair created the modern Law of Scotland by presenting it for the first time as a complete and rational system. He appears among our legal writers as a veritable priest after the order of Melchisedech,[84] owing little or nothing to those who had preceded him except part of the raw material from which he picked and chose the wherewithal to construct a legal system. And the originality of his work is linked to its universality, for the *Institutions* are not so much a descriptive handbook of our municipal law as a treatise on universal jurisprudence, illustrated by reference to the Law of Scotland. Stair's subject, as he himself tells us, was 'material justice, the common law of the world, orderly deduced from self-evident principles', – words which seem to echo the methods of Plato and Aristotle and Thomas Aquinas, – and it was this insistence upon the philosophic approach and the common dictates of reason and natural justice that gave his work its universal appeal and its abiding influence upon Scottish legal thought."[85]

Stair's family attained distinction in many spheres.[86] Of his five sons, the eldest, John (1648–1707), was Lord Justice-Clerk 1688, later Lord Advocate and (1692) Secretary of State; in 1703 he became the 1st Earl of Stair, and his eldest son John (1673–1747), the 2nd Earl, became a Field-Marshal, and his youngest son George became a Baron of Exchequer. From him were descended the 2nd to 7th Earls. Stair's second son, James (1650–1719), became a Principal Clerk of Session and a baronet in 1697; he published *Collections concerning Scottish History* and his son John (1682–1743) succeeded him as Principal Clerk and the latter's son John (1726–1810) wrote *The Memoirs of Great Britain and Ireland*; from him are descended the 8th to 13th Earls. Stair's third son, Hew (1652–1737), became Dean of Faculty in 1695 and in 1698 became a baronet and succeeded his father as Lord President; from him were descended Hew Dalrymple (1690–1755), Lord Drummore (1726), and David Dalrymple (1714–84), Lord Westhall (1777). Stair's fourth son, Thomas (1663–1725), became first physician to the King in Scotland. Stair's fifth son, Sir David Dalrymple of Hailes (1665–1721), was Solicitor-General to Queen Anne, a baronet, and Lord Advocate 1700–11, 1714–20, and grandfather of Sir David Dalrymple (1726–92), Lord Hailes (1766), the distinguished antiquary and legal historian, author of the *Annals of Scotland* and other works.[87] A descendant in this line married the daughter of Lord President Boyle. Of Stair's remote descendants many made a mark in the law, and others in the army. The 8th Earl became Baron Oxenfoord of Cousland in the United Kingdom peerage in 1841. The 10th Earl was Chancellor of the University of

Glasgow. Stair also had four other daughters who all married persons of rank and distinction.

Stair's character and achievements deserve admiration. He was a scholar and an upright judge, a steady adherent to Protestantism and presbyterianism. That he was ambitious and did not lose opportunities to advance himself and his family is apparent but not discreditable. Despite being heavily engaged in Session, Privy Council and Parliament he made supremely valuable and important contributions to jurisprudence. Mackenzie's[88] estimate of him was:

> "And really Stair was a gentleman of excellent parts, of an equal wit and universal learning, but most remarkable from being so free from passion that most men thought this equality of spirit a mere hypocrisy in him. This weakness fitted him extremely to be a president, for he thereby received calmly all men's information, and by it he was capable to hear without disorder or confusion what the advocates represented; but that which I admired most in him was that in ten years' intimacy I never heard him speak unkindly of those who had injured him."

Balcarres in 1689 observed that: "the loyal party thought him too narrow and limited in principle for them, and the Presbyterians too moderate also for theirs ... a man of sense and law,"[89] and Bishop Burnet considered him "a man of great temper, and of a very mild deportment, but a false and cunning man."[90]

William Forbes, writing within 20 years of his death,[91] gave the following "short character of that great man:"

> "During the long time he was a judge, none could ever stain him with the least malversation or insolence in his great trust, at a time when it would have been thought obliging and good service to men of power, who wanted nothing more than the least ground to call him in question. He could not endure to be solicited, or impertinently addressed to in matters of justice. The memory of the many good regulations in the Form of Process before the Session owing to his Lordship will never be obliterated. He had a stiff aversion from being concerned in criminal matters, either as a judge or a lawyer. In the matter of civil government, he was always for sober measures. He thought it neither the interest nor duty of kings to rule arbitrarily: both king and people have their titles and rights by law; and an equal balance of prerogative and liberty being necessary to the happiness of a commonwealth. His judgment never led him to use or approve severity against those, who being sound in the fundamentals of religion, differed only in circumstantials. When he sat in the Privy Council, he always interposed so far as he could with safety, to resume the suffering Presbyterians from suffering the sharp edge of penal laws, to which they lay obnoxious in the reign of King Charles the II and suffered often publick reproach for his so doing. Where he gave it as his opinion, that the Privy Council, to whom the government and policy of the nation was committed, ought to be equally prudent and just in applying the severity of the laws: albeit judges in other courts are to walk by the letter of the law, however

rigorous or hard. He was a devout Christian, a sincere Protestant, and a true son of the Presbyterian Church of Scotland, though prudence allowed him not at all times to make a noise. He approved himself to be of steady principles, in thrice forsaking his honourable and profitable station, rather than comply with the corruption of the time. 1. He refused absolutely to take the Usurper's Tender, and contentedly sat down with the loss of a beneficial employment as an advocate, till it was dispensed with. 2. He risked his place of an ordinary Lord of Session, in the year 1664, before he would sign, without a commentary, the Declaration then imposed on all in publick trust. And 3. exposed himself to be shuffled out of his Presidency (as he was) in the year 1681, by his boldly standing up in defence of the Protestant interest. In the midst of the multiplicity of civil business, which his employment and character brought upon him, he always found time for the study of Divinity, wherein he arrived to a deep pitch of knowledge and directed everything else to it. In short he was indefatigable in business, even when he might have used the privilege of his age to lie by and withdraw from it. He knew not what it was to be idle, and took a strict account of his time: dividing himself between the duties of religion, and the studies of his profession, which he minded more than the raising a great fortune. He was sober, temperate and mighty regular. He duly prayed always and read a chapter of the Bible to his family before they sat down to dinner, and performed the like divine service after supper which he would not interrupt upon any consideration of business, how important soever. He had a great spirit, and equal temper in the harshest passages of his life: by the constant bent of his thoughts to what was serious or profitable, he knew how to divert them from any uneasy impression of sorrow. He was apt to forget, at least not to resent injuries done to him, when it was in his power to requite them.

"His excellent writings will carry down his memory to the latest posterity. His *Institutions of the Laws of Scotland*, wherein that is compared with the canon and civil laws, and the customs of neighbouring nations, are so useful, that few considerable families in Scotland, not to mention professed lawyers do want [*i.e.* lack] them. He hath therein so cleared up the springs and grounds of our law, that had been dammed up from observation by rust and rubbish, and reduced it into a sound and solid body (for which he deserves to be reckoned a founder and restorer of our law) that if it were lost, it might be retrieved and the tenor on't made up out of his excellent *Institutions*. He hath judiciously observed the Decisions of the Session from the Restauration of the Sovereignty, and re-establishment of the College of Justice to its ancient constitution and splendor, till August 1681: In which he hath not omitted any case of difficulty or importance determined when he was present on the Bench; without expressing his own opinion when different from that of the plurality of the Lords, out of modesty and deference to their judgment. He wrote them *de die in diem*, commonly before dinner when fresh in his memory: and was the more fitted to do it, that he was not a day absent during that period of 20 years, except the time of the summer session 1679 when he attended the king by his Majesty's special order. I have seen his *Physiologia Nova Experimentalis*. He wrote a treatise concerning the royal prerogative and the rights and privileges of the subject, and some sheets in vindication of the church government: but I don't remember to have seen either of these in print. He wrote also a *Vindication of the Divine Perfections*, which was published at London in the year 1695, with a Preface by Doctors W. Bates and J. Howe; wherein these learned divines give this character of the book: The clearness and vigour of the noble author's spirit are illustriously visible in managing a subject so deep and difficult. And in his unfolding the glorious and amiable excellencies of the blessed God, there is joined with the strength of argument, that beauty of expression, as may engage all readers, to be happy in the entire choice of God for their everlasting portion. Which performance shews it to be a thing not impracticable, as it is most praiseworthy, amidst the greatest secular employment, to find vacancy and a disposition of spirit to look with a very inquisitive eye into the deep things of God: which (if it were the author's pleasure to be known) would let it be seen, the statesman and the divine are not inconsistencies to a great and comprehensive mind."

Macaulay, however,[92] said that "he did not ... fall short of that very low standard of morality which was generally attained by politicians of his age and nation. In force of mind and extent of knowledge he was superior to them all ... the greatest jurist that his country had produced."

What is particularly noteworthy is the relentless regard for the law which drove him from 1660, despite the steady pressure of endless duties in Session, Parliament and Council (and doubtless many commitments consequential on these duties), to record and edit his two volumes of decisions, and to compose and revise his great treatise. All this was done too in politically turbulent times, in an atmosphere of plots and risings when resort to the sword and pistol were regular. Whatever his faults one cannot but admire his dedication to the law of Scotland and the supreme quality of his contribution to its jurisprudence.

Several factors combine to make Stair's *Institutions* a work of quite outstanding importance. It is the first narrative treatise stating systematically the whole private law of Scotland; it is the first text in Scottish legal history published and republished in a revised version by the author, and the text of which is not therefore dependent on manuscripts; it is a highly original and not a derivative work; it is based on general principles, with the more specific rules deduced therefrom.

It is significant to note Stair's title: it is *The Institutions of the Law of Scotland, deduced from its originals and collated with the civil, canon and feudal laws, and with the customs of neighbouring nations*. He used, for the first time in Scotland, the title "Institutions," plainly taken from Gaius' and Justinian's *Institutions* as the designation for a general, instructive work. Secondly, the law of Scotland was being deduced from its originals, or the propositions arrived at deductively from original or fundamental premises, and thirdly, the propositions thus arrived at were collated with, or set alongside and compared or contrasted with, the three great supra-national systems of medieval and early modern Europe, the civil law of Rome, the canon law of the Roman church, and the feudal law, and with the customs of neighbouring nations, of which the laws of Holland and of England were best known. It was not a matter of fitting Scottish rules and customs into the Roman framework, nor of adopting Roman and canon rules, but deducing the rules from fundamentals and seeing how they agreed with Roman, canon and feudal law.

A noteworthy feature of European legal history in the seventeenth and eighteenth centuries[93] is the writing in many countries, not of works expounding and interpreting the Roman law, the *jus commune* of Europe, and the canon law,[94] but examining the manner in which these systems agreed with, differed from or were modified by the local law of various European countries,[95] and passing into the periods when particular legal systems were commented on and described separately from the *jus commune*, yet in conformity with its general notions,[96] and finally the period when national legal systems became independent objects of legal study, the various vernaculars replacing Latin, a stage sometimes called *jus novissimum*,[97] *jus modernum*, *jus patrium* or national law. Roman law ceased to be the central topic of European legal science, being replaced by *droit français, deutsches Privatrecht, derecho español* and Scots law. The four stages were overlapping, not sharply distinguished, and particular legal systems attained them at different times. This movement was to some extent a product of the Reformation and the development of distinct nation-states.[98]

Hence there developed in many of the European states textbooks of national law, frequently called "Institutions," and strongly influenced in method and arrangement by the Roman law.[99] Though the Roman law had never been "received" in Scotland as it was in some continental countries, or officially recognised as subsidiary law, as in Germany in 1495, or applied as subsidiary common law, as in Holland,[1] it was studied and known and influential. Whether he realised it or not, the writing of Stair's *Institutions* was a development in accordance with the trend of jurisprudential evolution in the major countries of Western Europe, in particular with Grotius' *Inleiding*, Gudelinus' *De Jure Novissimo* and van Leeuwen's *Paratitla* and *Roomsch Hollandsch Recht*. Indeed passages in Stair seem to show the influence of Gudelinus.

It is uncertain what prompted Stair to write his *Institutions*. It may have been his study of the civil law and reading of Justinian's *Institutions*, prompting the thought: why not a Scottish *Institutions*? It may have been his membership of the reform commission of 1649, which was enjoined to "collect, draw up and compile a formal mode and frame of a book of just and equitable laws." It may have been the example of the work of the Dutch jurists, whose works he had probably seen in Holland, men such as Joost van Damhouder (1507–81, *Praxis rerum criminalium*, 1554, and *Praxis rerum civilium*, 1567, both later translated into Dutch), Peter Peckius (1529–89, *Tractatus de jure sistendi*, 1564, later translated), Petrus Gudelinus (1550–1619, *De Jure Novissimo*, perhaps the first attempt at a systematic exposition of the law of the Netherlands), but particularly Hugo Grotius (1583–1645, *Inleiding tot de Hollandsche Rechtsgeleerdtheyd*, 1621, and *De Jure Belli ac Pacis*, 1625). It may have been his experience as a commissioner for union with England in 1670, though it is known that manuscripts of at least parts of his book are dated earlier than 1670. It may have been an outstandingly able and diligent judge wanting, partly for his own satisfaction, partly for the improvement of the administration of justice, to set down in rational order the principles on which he wanted to lead his court to decide cases. A text is known to have been in existence by the mid-1660s, so that the writing cannot be wholly explained as prompted by his membership of the commission treating of Union in 1670. The writing and revision was probably proceeding *pari passu* with his noting of decisions.

In the Dedication to Charles II, prefixed to the first edition of 1681,[2] Stair professed to present to the King,

> "a summary of the laws and customs of your ancient kingdom of Scotland . . . you have governed this nation so long and so happily, by such just and convenient laws, which are here offered to the view of the world, in a plain, rational and natural method: In which material justice (the common law of the world) is, in the first place, orderly deduced from self-evident principles, through all the several private rights thence arising and, in the next place, the expedients of the most polite nations, for ascertaining and expeding the rights and interests of mankind, are applied in their proper places, especially those which have been invented or followed by this nation. So that a great part of what is here offered is common to most civil nations. . . . There is not much here asserted upon mere authority, or imposed for no other reason but *quia majoribus placuerunt*; but the rational motives, inductive of the several laws and customs, are therewith held forth."

In 1693 he wrote:

> "The former edition was collected by me in many years, and designed chiefly for my particular use, that I might know the decisions and acts of Session, since the first institution of it, and that I might the more clear and determine my judgment in the matter of justice. And to that end, I made indexes of all the decisions, which had been observed by men of the greatest reputation, and did cite the same: But considering that the ancient decisions were before these trodden paths, which have since come to be fixed customs, and that there were not authentic copies of these old collections; I thought fit, in this edition, only to relate to the later and more authentic and useful collections."[3]

As the work developed he must have thought of publication and it seems unlikely that anybody, setting down his working knowledge for his own use only, would be likely to have set it down at such length in such prose, but rather to have made notes, like a *Practicks*. The first versions may indeed have been notes, but these may have been later written out and reshaped into a continuous narrative text.

In his *Apology*[4] Stair said:

> "And I did write the *Institutions of the Law of Scotland*, and did derive it from that common law that rules the world, and compared it with the laws civil and canon, and with the custom of the neighbour-

ing nations, which hath been so acceptable that few considerable families of the nation wanted[5] the same, and I have seen them avending, both in England and Holland."

We do not know when Stair started to put down a text on paper. Probably the comparative calm and stability of the years after the Restoration both gave Stair the time and prompted the view that reasonable peace and quiet justified an attempt at a systematic statement of the whole private law. We know that he began to collect the decisions of the Court from 1661 and he probably began to put his notes into order from about the same time. There are manuscripts of at least parts or drafts of the book dated in the mid-1660s. "Then [1664] it was he began to compose a system of the civil law, intermixt with the law of Scotland, and practices and precedents of that sovereign court which makes the law intelligible and known to all the king's subjects there who can read English."[6] But the *Institutions* must have been several years in the writing. The start of the writing cannot be dated more closely than to the early and mid-1660s. By the 1670s manuscript copies were in circulation and generated pressure for him to publish it. "My modesty did not permit me to publish it, lest it should be judicially cited, where I sat: But now becoming old I have been prevailed with to print it, while I might oversee the press."[7]

So far as known none of the extant manuscripts is holograph of him or the original; all are transcripts. The only value of any of these manuscripts is in possibly indicating an earlier version of Stair's thought on a point. As we have two editions printed by his authority in his lifetime, the latter substantially revised, it is to the latter and not to any manuscript that we must look for his concluded views.[8]

He obtained from the King a Gift and Privilege for Printing, dated April 11, 1681,[9] which narrates confidence in the great benefit may arise to all our subjects by publishing the *Decisions* and *Institutions*, and ratifies and approves the contract between Stair and Agnes Campbell and Patrick Tailziefer [the heirs of Andrew Anderson] for printing, prohibiting all others from printing them for 19 years, without his permission, as the contract of March 26, 1681, bears. This is in substance a grant of copyright privileges.

The first printed edition was published by the Heir of Andrew Anderson in 1681 shortly before Stair withdrew to Holland. It comprises a Dedication to Charles II, an Index, or rather serial list, of Titles with summaries or headings of the sections. The text is divided into two parts with separate title-pages, the first comprising Titles I-XXII (pages 1 to 444), the second Titles XXIII-XXXI (pages 1 to 191). Some copies have, bound in, with a separate title-page, *Modus Litigandi*, or Form of Process observed Before the Lords of Council and Session in Scotland (pages 1 to 44). There is no general index.

The second edition bears to be "Revised, Corrected and Much Enlarged: With an alphabetical Index to the whole work" and was printed by the Heir of Andrew Anderson in 1693. It comprises an Advertisement, Index of the Titles, the text, now divided into four Books (pages 1 to 763), an Appendix dealing with some recently enacted

Statutes (pages 765 to 779), a list of printer's errors to be corrected, and an alphabetical index. The former first part had been divided into Books I and II, the second part had become Book III, and Book IV was a rewritten and greatly expanded version of the *Modus Litigandi*. The titles were now numbered serially within each book and now number 91 in all, of which 52 are in the new Book IV. Apart from the errors noted in the list of printer's errors there are a number of other errors in citations and references.

In the Advertisement, Stair points out that there had been various omissions and mistakes in the first edition, and that in this edition,

> "considering that the ancient decisions were before these trodden paths, which have since come to be fixed customs, and that there were not authentic copies of these old collections; I thought fit, in this edition, only to relate to the later and more authentic and useful collections.

> "Thirdly, in the former edition, I designed the treatise to be divided into three parts, as being most congruous to the subject-matter of jurisprudence. The first part, being concerning the constitution of original rights: The second, concerning the transmission of these original rights, amongst the living and from the dead: The third, concerning the cognition and execution of all these rights. Yet, finding it would be acceptable to divide the institutions of our law into four books, as the Institutions of the Civil Law are divided, and, especially because there is a more eminent distinction in our law betwixt heritable rights of the ground, and moveable rights; I have divided this edition into four parts: The first being of original personal rights: The second, of original real rights: The third, of the conveyance of both: And the fourth, of the cognition and execution of the whole."

He explains also that he had divided the long titles, divided the paragraphs, and joined them with the several titles accordingly.

> "Though indeed this edition be in a great part new, by occasion of new Statutes of Parliament, Acts of Sederunt, and Decisions since the treatise was written, and by an entire addition of the fourth part, which was resolved and expressed to be added. And yet, it is still the same treatise. . . ."

In the early eighteenth century Henry Home, Lord Kames, seems to have contemplated producing a new edition. In the preface to his *Remarkable Decisions*, Vol. I (1716–28), he says that his collection was at first undertaken "with a view to be ingrossed in a new projected Edition of the Viscount of Stair's *Institutions*," but it became too bulky and was published separately.

The third edition was undertaken, the preface to it tells us "with a view to remove, by the help of several manuscripts,[10] the obscurity which everywhere occurred in the former editions of this valuable system of law; and to add, in notes, alterations" introduced since 1693. It was begun by John Gordon, advocate,[11] and completed by William Johnstone, advocate[12] (who, having married an heiress, later called himself Sir William

Pulteney, Bart.), printed for G. Hamilton and J. Balfour and published in 1759. It comprises the Advertisement to the 1693 edition, Index (or serial list) of Titles in the four Books, the Dedication of the 1681 edition, the text of the four Books (pages 1 to 786) and the Appendix (pages 787 to 801), alphabetical index and a table of the pages of the 1693 edition with the corresponding pages of this edition. There are brief footnote annotations. The alterations in the text are printed in italics: "and such of them as have been made without the authority either of the manuscripts or of the decisions referred to in the book, are, besides, inclosed by crotchets; and the former reading is placed at the bottom of the page."[13]

The fourth edition was edited by George Brodie[14] and published as a tall folio by Thomas Clark, law bookseller, in 1826–27. It seems to have been planned as two volumes,[15] but is usually bound in one. Brodie professed to have constantly collated the three former editions with nine manuscript copies from the Advocates' Library and latterly with a tenth also, lent by David Laing. "But I must own that the chief advantage derived by me from the manuscripts, has been that of greater confidence in the accuracy of the edition of 1693, which, as published by the author himself after a careful revision, ought, in my opinion, to be adhered to, unless where it is obvious, from the sense or the decision referred to, that a slight inaccuracy exists."[16] Despite Brodie's assertion he did in some cases make changes in the text. The volume comprises the Advertisement to the 1693 edition, the Advertisement to Pulteney's edition, Indexes of the titles, the text (pages 1 to 832), Stair's Appendix (pages 833–845) and in some bindings Brodie's Supplement of 165 pages, 100 devoted to sale and the remainder to shipping, "comprising a treatise on mercantile law which I had prepared with a view to separate publication." There are editorial annotations, fuller in Book I, briefer in later books. Lord Cockburn[17] remarked: "His edition of Stair is a deep and difficult legal book. His style is bad and his method not good."

The fifth edition was edited by John S. More[18] and published in two large folio volumes by Bell and Bradfute[19] in 1832. It prints the Dedication of 1681, the Advertisements to the 1693 and 1759 editions, a lengthy Preface, Stair's Apology of 1690, and the text.

More observed:[20]

> "The text of the second edition seems, on the whole, the best; but as the third edition has been said by a very competent judge[21] to be 'deemed far preferable to the rest,' and as it is undoubtedly that which is best known, and has been most esteemed by the profession, the text of the present edition has been reprinted from it . . . and most of the material alterations between the text of the third edition and of the first or second, have been pointed out in marginal notes. So that the text of this edition embraces all the advantages of any of these three editions."

More's edition was the one normally cited between 1832 and 1981, and the unfortunate consequence has been that, since he reprinted Gordon and Johnstone's somewhat eclectic text rather than what he himself believed to be the best, Stair's own revised text, lawyers and courts during most of the nineteenth and twentieth centuries have accepted as the text of Stair a version which is not what Stair himself finally authorised.[22]

More added references to the pages in Morison's *Dictionary of Decisions* for many of the cases cited by Stair. But his footnotes do not distinguish citations given by Stair from those inserted by later editors.

More appended to each volume a series of lengthy notes, designated by letters of the alphabet, and extending to about the same total bulk as the text, explaining the developments in the law between 1693 and 1830. These are of considerable value and importance in themselves.[23]

In 1863 Patrick Shaw published a *Principles of the Law of Scotland in Lord Stair's Institutions, with Notes and References to Modern Law*, an abridgement intended to facilitate the use of the *Institutions* by students.

The sixth (Tercentenary) edition was edited by the present writer and published in 1981 by the Edinburgh and Glasgow University Presses jointly to mark the tercentenary of the publication of the first edition.[24] It comprises an Introduction, the Dedication of 1681, the Advertisement of 1693, the Index of Titles, and the text, reprinting the text of the 1693 edition. References to the *Acts of the Parliaments of Scotland*, the original reporter and Morison's *Dictionary*, and, where appropriate, to other sources are given for nearly all Stair's references. Subject to modernisation of spelling and punctuation this is as nearly as possible an exact reproduction of the text of 1693 and it is to be hoped that the text is now settled. The variations in the text printed in the different editions has on occasion caused problems. "And I may observe that the main passage in Stair, II, 1, 5, appears in form more different in the different editions than almost any other passage of equal length in the work; so much so that Mr. More gives in a footnote the version of it in the first edition."[25]

Whence did Stair draw his propositions, stating the law of Scotland as he understood it at 1681 and, in the revised edition, 1693? One must distinguish the historical sources, the events in legal history from which current rules had developed, and the formal sources, the statements by legislative or judicial authority which enunciate certain rules as valid, though Stair does not distinguish them.

Among historical sources Stair's view[26] was that *Regiam Majestatem* "are no part of our law, but were compiled for the customs of England in 13 books by the Earl of Chester, and by some unknown and inconsiderate hand stolen thence, and resarcinate into these four books which pass amongst us." Other historical sources certainly include Roman, canon and feudal law and our ancient customs.

As to formal sources Stair observed[27] that

> "we are happy in having so few and so clear statutes. Our law is most part consuetudinary, whereby what is found inconvenient is obliterated and forgot. . . . We are not involved in the labyrinth of many and large statutes, whereof the posterior do ordinarily so abrogate and derogate from the prior, that it requires a great part of a life to be prompt in all these windings, without which no man, with sincerity and confidence, can consult or plead, much less can the subjects, by their own industry, know where to rest, but must give more implicit

faith to their judges and lawyers than they need, or ought, to give to their divines."

The law of each society of people is called the civil law.[28] Our customs have arisen mainly from equity or natural law, and also from the civil, canon and feudal laws from which much is borrowed, and these have great weight with us, where a custom is not yet formed. But none have with us the authority of law but are received only according to their equity and expediency.[29]

> "We are ruled in the first place by our ancient and immemorial customs, which may be called our common law[30].... In the next place are our statutes, or our acts of parliament, which in this are inferior to our ancient laws that they are liable to desuetude.... But there is much difference to be made betwixt a custom by frequent decisions, and a simple decision, which hath not the like force. Yet frequently agreeing decisions are more effectual than acts of sederunt themselves, who do easily go into desuetude. Where our ancient law, statutes and our recent customs and practiques are defective, recourse is had to equity, as the first and universal law, and to expediency, whereby laws are drawn in consequence *ad similes casus*.[31]

The hierarchy of formal sources according to Stair is accordingly ancient custom or common law, declared by frequent decisions of the Lords, statutes, acts of sederunt, recent customs and practices as evidenced by recent decisions, and failing these, equity or natural law. Decisions by themselves were not to him authoritative, or sources, but merely evidence of ancient custom or common law, or of recent custom and practices.

The sources most commonly referred to in the *Institutions* are decisions of the Court of Session, drawn very largely from his own volumes of *Decisions* and some of the then unprinted *Practicks*, principally of Spottiswoode, Hope and Haddington.[32] Some other *Practicks* are cited though, surprisingly, not Balfour's, though it is hard to believe that Stair did not know of or use it. Next are statutes of the Scottish Parliament, cited from Skene's *Lawes and Actes*.[33] A long way behind these in frequency are Craig[34] and the Dutch jurists, particularly Grotius; there are numerous references to the Bible, to the Roman law[35] and, to a much lesser extent, to the canon law.[36] There are some comparative references to English law.[37] It is plain accordingly that Stair's book is mainly built from indigenous materials, and that the references to other sources are historical and comparative. It is not a textbook of Roman, or any other, law adapted to Scottish conditions.

In default of Scottish authority Stair clearly drew mainly from Roman law.[38] This is particularly apparent in his treatment of obligations.[39] But he stressed (I, 1, 12) that Roman law was not acknowledged as a law binding for its authority, yet being, as a rule, followed for its equity. Neither he, nor his book, could, in a technical sense, import any rule of Roman law into Scots law, but in default of native rule he sometimes suggested the Roman rule as the standard or a guide for conduct and a court's decision. He is seeking to discover the natural or equitable rule, to mention systems, notably Roman law, as exemplifying or diverging from the natural rule, and to see how the rule established in Scotland by custom, statute and decision accords with the natural rule.[40]

In some cases Stair thinks that a Roman rule should be adopted in Scots law, *e.g.* the rules as to fraud (I, 9, 9), the praetorian edict *nautae caupones stabularii* (I, 13, 3), the rules on *depositum miserabile* (I, 13, 9), the rule of *damnum infectum* (II, 7, 7) and in some other cases. In each case the reason is that the Roman rule seems consistent with nature and equity. In some cases too he appears to be considering the consistency of Roman rules with natural law and to have reservations about their adoption.[41]

Apart from comparision with Roman rules and possible adoption of some of them, Stair refers extensively to Roman law, sketching its history (I, 1, 12), giving accounts of its institutions for comparison (I, 8, 3; III, 4, 15), accepting definitions (I, 3, pr.; I, 4, 6) or quoting maxims drawn from Roman law (I, 7, 14; I, 9, 15; III, 1, 42; III, 2, 1; IV, 39, 4; IV, 23, 20; IV, 41, 1). On some topics, *e.g.* acquisition by accession (II, 1, 34), his approach is clearly influenced by that of the writers on Roman law. He refers sometimes generally to "the civil law," sometimes to the text, sometimes he quotes the text, sometimes the Latin, sometimes a translation. At least some of his references seem to have been drawn from Gudelinus's *De Jure Novissimo* (1620), a basic treatise of the Roman-Dutch law.

The references to canon law are, in comparison, not numerous.[42] He admits that canon law has in the past been an important historical source of principles, particularly in relation to marriage, and concedes (I, 1, 14) that "so deep hath the canon law been rooted, that, even where the Pope's authority is rejected, yet consideration must be had to these laws ... as ... containing many equitable and profitable laws." In Book IV the main stages of Scottish civil procedure, as explained by Stair, in fact follow the main stages of canonical procedure, itself derived from Roman procedure. There are a number of comparative references to the attitude of the canon law. Probably not surprisingly for a strong Protestant, Stair does not appear anywhere to seek to import canon law or utilise it to fill a gap in Scots law. His general approach is that canon law is an historical source, whose influence is now spent, and interesting for comparison.

In Stair's time real rights in interests in land were the most important forms of property, and Stair very largely accepted the principles of feudal law as understood and expounded by Craig in his *Jus Feudale*, and indeed professed (II, 3, 3) to deal fully only with what had been clarified or altered as to feudal law since Craig's time; this included such matters as the role of positive prescription and the establishment of the registers of land writs.

Clearly from the Scoto-Norman era of the twelfth century onwards the feudal system had been the main, almost the sole, historical source of Scots law in this branch, and Craig's version and explanation of it had been accepted as the prevailing theory. Stair provided a restatement of this, taking account of the important statutes and decisions since Craig had written, *e.g.* on bounding title, registration and prescription. His dependence on Craig was substantial, but by no means total. Moreover his restatement was more concise, ordered and disciplined than Craig's had been, and displays a better grasp of essential principles. He frequently relies on decisions of the Session in preference to Craig's view.

Here again the source had historically been very important, but was now substantially spent; the sources of the law Stair expounded were Scottish statutes and decisions building on that foundation.

English law was not a formal source for Stair.[43] He clearly had an adequate acquaintance with English law, and mentions it a number of times[44] by way of comparison. Historically many of the customs he refers to, our ancient and immemorial customs, were in Anglo-Norman law before they appeared in Scoto-Norman law. But Stair was well aware of the very different courses of evolution native custom and Norman practices had taken since the eleventh century, that in consequence there were by the seventeenth quite fundamental differences, and nowhere does he cite English custom, still less statute or decision, as authoritative or suggest that English rule or practice be adopted.

It is important to observe that while in a broad and general sense Stair was clearly influenced by the structure of Justinian's *Institutions* he did not by any means copy the structure or arrangement of that work.[45] The structure of that work is:

Book I,	titles 1–2:	Justice and law: the law of nature, the law of nations and the civil law.
	titles 3–26:	Persons and family law.
Book II,	titles 1–25:	Things, property rights and wills.
Book III,	titles 1–12:	Intestacy.
	titles 13–29:	Obligations by contract and quasi-contract.
Book IV,	titles 1–5:	Delicts.
	titles 6–18:	Actions.

In his revised edition, he wrote,[46]

"I designed the treatise to be divided into three parts, as being most congruous to the subject matter of jurisprudence. The first part, being concerning the constitution of original rights: The second, concerning the transmission of these original rights, among the living and from the dead: The third, concerning the cognition and execution of all these rights. Yet finding it would be acceptable to divide the institutions of our law into four books, as the Institutions of the Civil Law are divided, and, especially, because there is a more eminent distinction in our law betwixt heritable rights of the ground and moveable rights; I have divided this edition into four parts: The first being of original personal rights;[47] The second, of original real rights: The Third of the conveyance of both:[48] And the fourth, of the cognition and execution of the whole. Fourthly, In the former edition I made the titles as comprehensive as I could, that congenerous matters might be handled in the same titles; and therefore the whole treatise was contained in 31 titles: But now I have divided the long titles in the first book, and put them under more special titles, and have divided the paragraphs, and joined them with the several titles accordingly."

This different structure follows from his recognition that the Roman law taken up for its object Persons, Things, and Actions and according to these orders itself, but these are only the extrinsic object and matter, about which law and right are versant.[49] "The formal and proper object of law are the rights of men."[50]

> "But the proper object is the right itself, whether it concerns persons, things or actions: and according to the several rights and their natural order, the order of jurisprudence may be taken up in a threefold consideration, First, in the constitution and nature of rights; Secondly, in their conveyance, or translation from one person to another, whether it be among the living or from the dead; Thirdly, in their cognition, which comprehends the trial, decision and execution of every man's right by the legal remeids."[51]

This is beautifully logical and explains the structure of the *Institutions* which is:

Book I,	titles 1–2:	Common principles of law: liberty.
	titles 3–18:	Obligations as limitations on liberty, creating personal rights, conjugal, quasi-contractual, delictual, and contractual.
Book II,	titles 1–12:	The creation of rights (continued): Real rights in objects of property, particularly land.
Book III,	titles 1–9:	Transfer of rights *inter vivos* and transmission on death.
Book IV,	titles 1–52:	The cognition of rights. Forms of process, proof, decreets and execution thereof.

"Here already we have something different from Justinian, a universal plan for the exposition of rights, whatever their subject-matter, the excogitation of which indicates a high degree of abstract jurisprudential thinking. Whether it is of Stair's own devising I have not been able to discover. This is the 'master-plan' of Stair's *Institutions*."[52]

The second pattern is that of Justinian's *Institutions*, treating successively of persons, things (including inheritance and the kinds of incorporeal things called obligations, discussed in the order: contracts, quasi-contracts, delicts and quasi-delicts) and actions. In a general sense Stair accepted this pattern but he turned it from a pattern of objects of law (law as to persons, things and actions) into a pattern of substantive rights (rights against other persons, rights over things, and rights of action). The Roman pattern is based on the object about which law and right are versant; Stair's view is that the proper object of examination is the legal right, which may exist in relation to persons, to things or to actions.

There is also a third pattern discernible in Books I and II. In I, 1, 18 Stair says that "the first principles of right are obedience, freedom and engagement" and at I, 1, 23 he says,

"Whereby the whole method may be clearly thus: First, of the nature
of those several rights; and because liberty standeth in the midst
betwixt obligations of obedience, which are anterior, and of
engagement, which are posterior (both which being of the same
nature must be handled together), therefore liberty must have the
first place;[53] then next obligations obediential,[54] and then conventional;[55] and after these, dominion in all its parts;[56] and, in the
second place, shall follow the conveyance of these several rights;[57]
and lastly the cognition of all by judicial process and execution."[58]

This explains why in Book I the titles deal with liberty and servitude,[59]
obligations in general (which are all restrictions on liberty, by law or
convention) and the various kinds of obligations, conjugal, parental,
curatorial, restitutionary, reparative[60] and contractual.[61] This is why,
unlike Justinian, Stair deals with obligations before things or property,
and why he deals first with restitution and recompense (corresponding to
the Roman quasi-contractual obligations), then with reparation (corresponding to the Roman delictual obligations) and finally with conventional obligations created by promises, pactions and contracts. In Book I
accordingly his pattern does not entirely accord with his other plans. The
source of this third pattern, considering obligations as qualifications of
liberty, is unknown, but Professor Campbell observed that it accords
closely with the pattern of Books 2 and 3 of Pufendorf's *De Jure Naturae
et Gentium*, published in 1672, which takes the primary idea of liberty,
considers natural law as imposing duties which restrict man's liberty, and
then general duties of reparation and duties created by agreement.
Pufendorf also examines obligations before property. But Stair's work
was substantially written before 1672. It may be that both Stair and
Pufendorf were influenced by some earlier writer. In Hobbes' *Leviathan*
(1651), Chapter 14, Hobbes adopted a generally similar approach,
discussing obligation as contrasting with and as a restriction on liberty,
and Pufendorf in *De Officio Hominis et Civis* (1673) also founded his
treatment of moral duty on the freedom of the individual will limited by
obligation.

It is plain from comparison that Stair did not follow the layout of
Grotius' *Inleiding* and he does not even refer to it. He possibly could not
read it, in Dutch, but might have known of it from Vinnius' commentary
on the *Institutes*.[62]

Stair's arrangement of his material represents an advance on Justinian;
he saw that there was something more important than rules about
persons, things and actions. The fundamental subject for examination
and exposition was the legal right, or legally recognised and enforceable
claim against another or others generally and the counterpart duty on that
other or them. His basic scheme is accordingly the rights of persons
concerning other persons, concerning things, and actions to declare and
enforce rights.

Though his book is primarily a treatise expounding private law, Stair
commences with an essay in jurisprudence, an analysis of the nature of
law. He believed that Scots law could be shown to be a rational system

only if it were consistent with the general notions of law as commonly accepted in Europe. As was common in the seventeenth century, Stair followed the mathematical model, arguing from fundamental axioms down to particular propositions, from fundamental moral principles to divine and human law, and then to the law of the particular society concerned.[63] Stair defined law[64] as "the dictate of reason, determining every rational being to that which is congruous and convenient for the nature and condition thereof; and this will extend to the indifferency of all rational beings."

The absolute sovereign is divine law, which is also the law of all rational creatures; it is also called the law of nature. Correspondent to those dictates of reason (wherein law consists) which are in the understanding, there is an inclination in the will of man to observe and follow those dictates, which is justice; and justice is distributive or commutative. The laws by which private rights are constituted, conveyed or destituted are either divine or human.[65] Divine law is the law of nature known without reasoning or experience, written in the hearts of men.[66] It is also called conscience,[67] equity[68] or the moral law.[69] It is impressed in our hearts and expressed in the word of God.[70] This natural, necessary and perpetual law is accordingly the moral basis of all forms of law among rational men. God had also given men voluntary and positive laws, such as the ceremonial laws,[79] and notably the Judicial law prescribed by the ministry of Moses to the people of Israel.[71] These were, however, not written in the hearts of men, nor deducible by reason from any such principle.

Human law is that which, for utility's sake, is introduced by men, by tacit consent, by custom, or by express will or command of those in authority, having the legislative power. These were written or unwritten according to origin. The law of men are either common to many nations, the law of nations,[72] or proper to one nation, or peculiar to some places or incorporations in the same nation.[73] Stair does not detail the principles which are deducible from the law of nature, but other passages suggest that he considered that they included such as that undertakings should be performed, reparation made for harm done, restitution made for the avoidance of unjust enrichment, and the like principles.

"The law of each society of people under the same sovereign authority, is called the civil law, or the law of the citizens of that commonwealth; though that now be appropriate to the civil law of the Roman commonwealth or empire, as the most excellent. And because of that affinity that the law of Scotland hath with it . . . that though it be not acknowledged as a law binding for its authority, yet being, as a rule, followed for its equity,[74] it shall not be amiss here to say something of it," and he gives a short historical account of the Roman law.[75]

There are also the feudal law, which took rise among the Lombards and has now spread over most of the world,[76] and the canon law of the Roman church.[77] He gives short historical sketches of these too. Human laws are added, he continues, not to take away the law of nature and reason, but some of the effects thereof, which are in our power; men's laws are nothing else but the public sponsions of princes and people; which, therefore, even by the law of nature, people ought and must perform. They are introduced for clearing and condescending on the law of nature and of reason. Such laws declare equity. But for men to enjoy their rights securely they need more detailed rules than inferences from natural law. There are five reasons justifying human positive laws. Human law is needed to make precise the application of principles of natural law in particular circumstances. It establishes also what parts of natural law can be enforced by legal proceedings. In the interests of security and to avoid error and fraud, human laws must settle the forms required for such transactions as contracts and conveyances. Human laws modify the law of nature in respect of rights of succession. Penalties for crimes too may be altered from time to time according to the inclinations of people. These reasons show how necessary human laws are. Those peoples are most happy, he continues, whose laws are nearest to equity (reason or natural law) and most declaratory of it, and least altering of the effects thereof. They are most happy too whose laws have entered by long custom, wrung out from their debates on particular cases until it came to the consistence of a fixed and known custom. Those statutes are best which are approbatory or correctory of experienced customs.[78]

The customs of Scotland "have arisen mainly from equity [natural law] and from the civil, canon and feudal laws, from which the terms, tenors and forms of them are much borrowed, and therefore these (especially the civil law) have great weight with us, namely, in cases where a custom is not yet formed. But none of these have with us the authority of law, and therefore are only received according to their equity and expediency, *secundum bonum et aequum.*" The law of Scotland at first could be no other than *aequum et bonum*, equity and expediency. "Next to equity, nations were ruled by consuetude, which declareth equity and constituteth expediency, and in the third place positive laws of sovereigns became accustomed, customs always continuing and proceeding, so that every nation under the name of law understand their ancient and uncontroverted customs, time out of mind, or their first and fundamental laws." Scots are ruled first "by our ancient and immemorial customs, which may be called our common law; though sometimes by that name is understood equity, which is common to all nations, or the civil Roman law, which in some sort is common to many."[79] In the next place are our statutes or acts of Parliament which are inferior to our ancient law in that they are liable to desuetude and acts of sederunt. Lastly there are recent customs and practices declared by the Session. "There is much difference to be made betwixt a custom by frequent decisions and a single decision which hath not the like force. Yet frequently agreeing decisions are more effectual than acts of sederunt themselves, which easily go into desuetude." Failing all these recourse is had to equity, as the first and universal law, and to expediency. "The law of Scotland in its nearness to equity, plainness and facility in its customs, tenors and forms, and in its celerity and dispatch in the administration and execution of justice, may be well paralleled with the best law in Christendom."[80]

Stair then digresses briefly[81] to discuss the question, whether law may or should be handled as a rational discipline, having principles from whence its conclusions may be deduced. He criticises the confused order of the civil (Roman) law and the commentaries on it. He answers his own question affirmatively, giving three justifications, that law is reason itself, as to its principles about the rights of men, and is therefore called the law of reason, that God has given men reason to distinguish matters of legal right, and that God argues with men from common principles of righteousness and law should be expounded as deduced from them. Positive law is only to declare equity (natural law) and make it effectual; equity is the body of the law and the statutes of men only the ornaments and vestiture thereof.

Stair then sets out three most general principles of equity or natural law, that God is to be obeyed by man, that man is a free creature, having power to dispose of himself and all things, in so far as, by his obedience to God, he is not restrained, and that this freedom of man is in his own power, and may be restrained by his voluntary engagements, which he is bound to fulfil,[82] in short, obedience,[83] freedom[84] and engagement,[85] and three prime principles of the positive law, whose aim and interest is the profit and utility of man, namely, society, property and commerce. "The principles of equity are the efficient causes of rights and laws: the principles of positive law are the final causes or ends for which laws are made and rights constitute and ordered. And all of them may aim at the maintenance, flourishing and peace of society, the security of property, and the freedom of commerce."[86] If he performs his duty to God, man is free unless he restricts himself by contract, and the three principles of positive law can be regarded as the products of such a contractual restriction.

Stair's view is accordingly that divine law or the law of nature or conscience or equity or the moral law is the supreme law. There is also human law, of nations, of particular nations, and of societies in the same nation, deducible from natural law. Much of this hearks back to older views of the nature of law.[87]

Aristotle[88] distinguished natural law, which he said was the same everywhere and had equal validity everywhere, and was common, and man-made law. This was taken up by the Stoics, whose ideal was life according to Nature, and by Cicero, who regarding the universality of a principle as a proof of its naturalness and accordingly of its validity, because the law of nature was not an ideal but a binding rule and no human enactment could prevail against it.[89] He identified the law of nature with the *ius gentium* in the sense of the principles of law common to all nations.[90]

The distinction between natural law and human law was taken over by the Romans, but not much discussed though adapted in practical use. In classical and post-classical times the distinction was more discussed.[91] Gaius' *Institutions* similarly distinguished *ius gentium* and *ius civile*,[92] and Justinian's *Institutions*[93] distinguished the natural law common to humans and animals, and human law, divided into the law of nations and the civil law of particular nations, the latter distinguished into written and unwritten: the laws of nature are fixed and immutable, but the laws of individual states are liable to change.

The rise of Christianity introduced modifications and throughout the Middle Ages legal thought was coloured by a belief in the existence of a law of nature based on reason and binding all men. It was generally agreed that the ultimate source of the law of nature was in God.[94] The

Corpus Juris Canonici emphasised the superiority of natural law to all human law. St. Thomas Aquinas[95] defined law as a rule or measure of action, but the rule and measure of human action is reason. He distinguished[96] the eternal law, as the rational guidance of created things on the part of God, the natural law, or participation in the eternal law by rational creatures, and human law, and these three are further elucidated.[97] Human law is subordinate to natural law, and may be divided into *ius gentium* and *ius civile*. He then discussed the powers of human law, and its mutability.[98] The scholastic tradition of thinking about natural law reached its final development in the Spanish jurist theologians, notably Suarez.[99]

From the end of the fifteenth century, however, the law of nature was less closely identified with the will of God, and reason came to mean human reason.[1] Grotius was the founder of the modern theory of natural law, which he made the foundation of his formulation of international law. His theory did not break away from the scholastic theory of natural law in content, but only in method, bcause his aim was to construct a system of laws acceptable in an age which was less convinced by Catholic and scholastic argument.

The only one of these whom Stair expressly mentions is Grotius, whom he clearly regards as the great authority, but he seems to cling to the older tradition, regarding natural law, conscience or equity as divinely ordained. This is consistent with his early philosophical studies, his intimacy with divines, and his frequent citation of scripture. Grotius owed much to the scholastics, particularly the later ones, the Spanish jurist-theologians, Suarez, Vitoria and Molina.[2] Stair's thought is accordingly conservative and traditional, rather than advanced; he cannot be regarded as a precursor of the Enlightenment. He does not accept the view which Hobbes championed not much later, that law, justice and rights have their source and justification in utility and expediency, a view which led on to Bentham and Austin.

Stair similarly shows his philosophic background in his next, important, paragraph. "As to the object thereof [*i.e.* of the common principles of law] the formal, and proper object of law are the rights of men. A right is a power, given by the law, of disposing of things, or exacting from persons that which they are due. This will be evident if we consider the several kinds of rights, which are three, our personal liberty, dominion and obligation,"[3] and he goes on to explain further these three concepts, and to distinguish personal right from obligation and real right of dominion. "The Roman law," he continues,[4] "taketh up for its object, persons, things and actions, and, according to these, orders itself; but these are only the extrinsic object and matter, about which law and right are versant. But the proper object is the right itself, whether it concerns persons, things or actions; and according to the several rights and their natural order, the order of jurisprudence may be taken up in a threefold consideration; 1st, in the constitution and nature of rights; 2ndly, in their conveyance or translation from one person to another, whether it be among the living or from the dead; 3rdly in their cognition, which comprehends the trial, decision and execution of every right by the legal remeids." Finally he distinguishes public rights which concern the state of the commonwealth, and private rights, which are the rights of persons and particular incorporations.[4]

Stair was certainly the first in Scotland and is, even yet, practically the only one of the writers on positive law in Scotland to have examined the general concepts he used and tried to clarify his usage of them. Today this is left to the jurisprudents. In his first paragraph he observes: "I have therefore begun with the common principles of law, ... and have explained the general terms commonly made use of in law. And there is no term of which men have a more common but confused apprehension, than what law is: and yet there be few terms harder to be distinctly conceived or described. The clearest conception of it, I can find, is thus: Law is the dictate of reason, determining every rational being to that which is congruous and convenient for the nature and condition thereof; and this will extend to the determination of the indifferency of all rational beings." As well as Law he seeks to elucidate other major concepts.[5]

The formal and proper object of law, Stair said,[6] are the rights of men. Rules of law, that is, are directed to defining and securing the rights of men; a legal order is an order of rights, distinct from an order of behaviour. This is a fundamental point. He continues:

> "A right is a power, given by the law, of disposing of things, or exacting from persons that which they are due. This will be evident if we consider the several kinds of rights, which are three, our personal liberty, dominion and obligation. Personal liberty is the power to dispose of our persons, and to live where, and as we please, except in so far as by obedience or engagement we are bound. Dominion is the power of disposal of the creatures in their substance, fruits and use. Obligation is that which is correspondent to a personal right, which hath no proper name as it is in the creditor, but hath the name of obligation as it is in the debtor, and it is nothing else but a legal tie, whereby the debtor may be compelled to pay or perform something, to which he is bound by obedience to God, or by his own consent and engagement. Unto which bond the correlate in the creditor is the power of exaction, whereby he may exact, obtain or compel the debtor to pay or perform what is due; and this is called a personal right, as looking directly to the person obliged, but to things indirectly, as they belong to that person. So dominion is called a real right, because it respecteth things directly, but persons, as they have meddled with these things. By which it is clear, that all rights consist in a power or faculty; the act whereof is possession, enjoyment or use; which is a matter of fact, and no point of right, and may be where no right is, as right may be where these are not."[7]

This is a valuable exegesis of right, as a legally-backed power, and *ius* was used in this sense in Roman law, *e.g. ius testamenti faciendi*, though the main use of the word is to designate a legally-recognised claim, while modern analysis[8] distinguishes rights into claims, privileges, powers and immunities and their respective correlatives[9] duty, inability or no right, liability and disability. Moreover Stair is surely correct in contending that the act of possessing, enjoying or using is a matter of fact, and independent of right, moral or legal. What a man may or should do is quite different from what he actually does. This view of rights as the proper object of law is, moreover, fundamental to his account of the whole law by reference to constitution of rights, transfer of rights and cognition or enforcement of rights.

He says further that the several kinds of rights or powers were three, liberty,[10] dominion[11] and obligation.[12] This fitted his scheme of exposition, covering control of oneself, other people and things, but is too limited; legally-recognised rights (claims, privileges, powers, immunities) can exist in respect of a much wider range of objects than these.

The concept of duty is hardly mentioned by Stair. It is subsumed in his concept of obligation, and obligation (duty) is inadequately distinguished from obligation meaning a link or bond relating two legal persons.[13]

By liberty Stair means "that natural power which man hath of his own person . . . a natural faculty to do that which every man pleaseth, unless he be hindered by law or force."[14] Its opposites are restraint and constraint.[15] It is not absolute but limited by the will of God and our obligations to him and to men by his ordinance, by punishment for delinquency, by engagement, as by imprisonment for debt, by subjection to authority, and by bondage, slavery or servitude.[16] Every engagement by voluntary obligation is a diminution of a man's freedom.[17] Stair tends accordingly, and, it is submitted, rightly, to treat liberty as an element of man's estate or status.

Dominion, Stair says,[18] is the power of disposal of the creatures in their substance, fruits and use. This view may be based on the idea of Genesis I, 28–29, of the God-given dominion of man over all the creatures of the earth, air and sea, but it gives inadequate place to rights in land, which is surprising in view of the phrases *dominium ex iure Quiritium, dominium directum* and *dominium utile* and rights in things other than animals.

Stair's use of the concept obligation seems initially to confuse two senses of that word, firstly obligation as meaning the duty or burden or liability incumbent on a person, corresponding to the personal right or claim inhering in another, that is, what we now call duty,[19] and, secondly, obligation as meaning a relationship, legal bond or tie linking two or more distinct legal persons, by which we may be constrained by pay or perform something.[20] In the latter sense obligation is equally applicable to both parties.

He adverts[21] to the quadruple classification of obligations in the Roman law[22] into obligations *ex contractu, quasi ex contractu, ex maleficio* and *quasi ex maleficio*, but observes that obligations can be better distinguished "according to the principle or original from whence they flow, as in obligations obediential,[23] and by engagement,[24] or natural and conventional."[25] This is a more rational distinction; obligations are imposed by law, or assumed voluntarily. He further distinguishes obligations natural and civil, principal and accessory, and pure, conditional and to a day.[26] Obediential or legal obligations cover those to others within the domestic relations, to those unjustifiably harmed, and to those who will be unjustifiably prejudiced unless restitution be made; obligations by engagement or conventional include those by promises or by contracts.

Stair does not discuss some concepts, notably legal personality, persons, and personal status.[27] Nor does he examine conduct, acts and events, nor the mental states with which acts may be done or neglected.[28] But to criticise thus is to demand too much. Judged by the standards of his predecessors and contemporaries Stair was very far advanced in explicitly seeking to clarify and explain his use of basic technical terms and ideas fundamental to his exposition of the principles and rules. That he did so to the extent which he did emphasises what a strongly jurisprudential mind he had applied to his writing. His analysis, moreover, was not in the abstract; it was done to clarify and explain his doctrinal exposition of the positive law of Scotland.

The *Institutions* was and is not merely a narrative book, expository of settled law, but a creative book. It is a creative book in two distinct respects. In the first place it was creative in that it, for the first time, presented the materials of Scots law not as a series of distinct strands but as woven together into a piece or, to vary the metaphor, not as a heap of materials but as a structure with a clear plan, shape and form.

In the second place it was creative in that where there were gaps, in the sense of situations for which no rule had been accepted or laid down for the solution of the difficulty, he suggested an appropriate solution. Thus his formulation of the principles of restitution for the avoidance of unjustified enrichment[29] established the principles applied to this day. His creative function was probably exercised mainly in the field of obligations, in Book I of the *Institutions*. There was less scope for creative work, for judicial or juristic legislation, in the areas of property or remedies and procedure. Nor should Stair be criticised for doing so. At the stage of development Scots law had reached in the 1670s and 1680s the best thing to do when discovering a gap was to suggest a solution and the most obvious quarry from which to dig out a principle was the Roman law, the *jus commune* of Western European countries. "Our customs . . . are also from the civil, canon and feudal laws, from which the terms, tenors and forms of them are much borrowed: and therefore these (especially the civil law) have great weight with us, namely, in cases where a custom is not yet formed."[30]

The magnitude of Stair's achievement and the advance made by him on the existing state of legal literature and legal knowledge can only be appreciated if one remembers that when the *Institutions* were first published there were in print and available to judges and lawyers in Scotland, apart from imported foreign books, only a small number of printed books, the *Black Acts* (1566), Welwood's *Sea-law of Scotland* (1590), Skene's *Lawes and Actes* (1597), Skene's *Regiam Majestatem* (1609), Craig's *Jus Fendale* (1655), and Mackenzie's *Pleadings* (1672–73), *Laws in Matters Criminal* (1678) and *Science of Heraldry* (1680).[31] Glendook's Acts appeared in 1681–82. There were also various *Practicks* circulating in an unknown but necessarily limited number of manuscript copies. Of these Welwood and Craig dealt with limited areas of the whole field of private law. Mackenzie dealt only with criminal law. Stair's *Institutions* was accordingly the first book dealing with the whole private law. Moreover it was not, as might have been expected of the first book to appear, a sketchy tentative formulation; it was a mature, narrative text with a clear pattern, expounding the law systematically and supported by many references to cases and statutes.

The extent of the advance in analysis and exposition of particular topics can be judged by comparing the text of Stair on a particular matter with the texts of his predecessors on the same matter, then unpublished and only later made generally available in print, namely Balfour's *Practicks* (1574), Hope's *Major Practicks* (1633) and Durie's *Decisions* (1642, published 1690). If one considers the common contract of sale: Balfour, under Anent buying and selling, has four pages, much of it single-line summaries of the effect of Acts. Craig does not treat of this. Hope has three entries, extending in all to 20 lines, two being quotations from *Regiam Majestatem* and one a case of 1621. Durie indexes under Emptio and Vendito a few cases. Stair, apart from consideration of contracts generally (I, 10), has a substantial discussion of sale (I, 14), including treatment of the passing of the property, the risk, and conditions attached to the contract. Similarly as to liability for personal harm or injury: Balfour collects points under such heads as Ravishing, Assythment, Injury, but all from the criminal standpoint. Craig is again silent. Hope has a series of titles, Blood, Mutilation, Murder, Ravishing of Women, Slaughter and Assythment, all relevant to the topic but dealing with the topic from the criminal standpoint. Durie has little or nothing on it. Stair gives an extended examination in I, 9, distinguishing criminal and civil liability and treating of individual modes of causing harm, notably assythment, and moreover exploring the issues of concomitant accession and of joint and several liability. Such examples could readily be multiplied. On every topic Stair's examination is longer, fuller and more thorough than any previous one and, above all, it is a systematic reasoned exposition, supported by references to relevant authorities, not just a collection of points or examples.

From its first publication Stair's *Institutions* has been regarded as a work of the very highest quality, importance and value.[32] In the first place, apart from Craig's *Jus Feudale*, which covers only part of the private law and is a treatise on feudal land law, particularly as understood and applied in Scotland, rather than a text primarily on Scots law, it is the first continuous prose text, expounding the private law, as distinct from notes of statutes and decisions and practical observations, or reports of decisions or other collected notes.

In the second place, the whole subject-matter is presented from a philosophic standpoint, as deductions of principles from more fundamental principles.

In the third place, in each branch the relevant law is stated in the form of basic principles, which are then elaborated, exemplified, explained, the exceptions set out and so on. Thus in relation to injury to the person he states: "So the life of any person being taken away, the damage of those who were entertained and maintained by his life, as his wife and children, may be repaired. So likewise the loss any man hath in the expense of his cure, or the loss of his labour, and industry in his affairs, is also reparable."[33]

Again in relation to contracts:

"Both parties have quoted largely from the writings of jurists and commentators on the civil law. But the speculations of these learned authors are so much at variance as to make them of but little use as guides in such a question. And fortunately in Scotland we have those general principles of the law of contracts, which have been adopted in this country, stated in a very lucid manner by a most eminent jurist, who, after having taught philosophy as a professor in one of our Universities for several years, was distinguished as a practising lawyer and a most eminent judge for a period of about half a century, and who, as he himself informs us (Preface to More's Stair, p. 22), as to his Institutes [sic] of the Law of Scotland, 'did derive it from that common law that rules the world and compared it with the law civil and canon, and with the custom of neighbouring nations.' I am referring of course to Lord Stair; and it is in his Institutes [sic] I have looked for, and found, these principles of the law of Scotland, on which I have founded my opinion in this case."[34]

In many respects one cannot but wonder at the modernity of the work, which reveals a perceptive and organising mind which sees far beyond the individual cases and the decisions of them. In relation to delinquences, which we should now call delicts or harms, Stair distinguishes them not merely by name, nor by the kind or mode of harm done, but according to the interest of the person injured, which is deemed legally protected and for the infringement of which action lies. "According to our several rights and enjoyments, damages and delinquences may be esteemed. As, first, our life, members and health ... next to life is liberty, and the delinquences against it are restraint and constraint.... The third is fame, reputation and honour.... The fourth interest that may be damnified, is our content, delight and satisfaction, and especially by the singular affection to, or opinion of the value of worth of anything that the owner hath.... The last damage is in goods and possessions...."[35]

Not the least of the achievements of the *Institutions* is that by writing and publishing it, Stair probably contributed very materially to preserving Scots law from extinction at the time of the Union in 1707, only 26 years after his first and 14 years after his second edition. If the *Institutions* had not been in print, as evidence of the systematic and ordered nature of Scottish private law and of the substance of its principles and rules, it would have been very easy for the English commissioners to have said that there was no distinct system of Scots law, or if there was, nobody could say what its rules were.[36] The protective Article 18 of the Union of 1707 – "that no alteration be made in laws which concern Private Right except for Evident Utility of the subjects within Scotland" – could not have had much effect if one could not have said what the existing laws concerning private right were. Ignorance of Scots law in the House of Lords (as an appellate court) and in Parliament in the eighteenth and early nineteenth century was great enough; it would have been nearly total if Stair's book had not been in existence.

The esteem in which the *Institutions* has been held can be seen firstly from the number of times it has been cited in argument and in decision, as supporting an argument or as authority.[37] The work was being relied on in Stair's own lifetime. An act of the Privy Council of February 17, 1691, gave the Council's reasons "as is clearly particularly by Stair, title 18, para. 35, McKenzie's *Institutions* title Teynds, and by Act of Parliament. . . ."[38] The *Institutions* were cited in a case in 1683[39] and Stair himself cited this case in his second edition.[40] Fountainhall's reports contain many references to Stair. Citation of the work was common from the early eighteenth century,[41] though it is fair to remember that reports were not readily available until the mid-eighteenth century and books must have been cited as containing examples as well as for their statements of principle. Stair was cited in the House of Lords in *Schaw* v. *Schaw and Houston*.[42] In the mid-eighteenth century he is cited more frequently than Bankton, though towards the end of that century there is more frequent reference to Erskine than to Stair.

In *Campbell* v. *McKellar*[43] there was reference in argument to "our best institutional writers," those mentioned being Stair, Bankton, Erskine, and Bayne's Notes to Mackenzie. In *Dalrymple* v. *Dalrymple*[44] Stair was thoroughly discussed in a case before Lord Stowell in the London Consistory Court. In *Routledge* v. *Carruthers*[45] the Lord President observed: "these questions Lord Stair, that oracle of the law of Scotland, has long ago answered." In *Ross* v. *Heriot's Hospital*[46] Lord Justice-Clerk Boyle said, with reference to Stair, Bankton and Erskine, that: "I am not bold enough, for one, to set my opinion against the great luminaries of our law, even if I differed from them." By 1840 Stair's reputation was such that a Lord Ordinary almost felt impelled to report the case to the Inner House before declining to follow Stair.[47] In 1878 Lord Justice-Clerk Moncreiff observed*: "The authority of Lord Stair, however, on this question is of predominating weight . . . because. . . ."[48] In modern practice Stair is always reckoned among the writers whose works are authoritative.

Secondly it is noteworthy to what extent subsequent writers refer to Stair as an authority. The attitude of the later writers is naturally influenced by the view of the judges. In the 1720s someone, usually considered to be Lord Elchies,[49] wrote notes on Stair, showing a close and detailed acquaintance with the work. In 1726 Bayne, first professor of Scots Law at Edinburgh,[50] observed: "What is it then that we do not owe in matter of law to the labours of . . . my Lord Stair, when we consider that even this textbook [Mackenzie's *Institutions*] has sprung out of this larger commentary?" Bankton, in his Preface,[51] refers to Stair as "That great judge and lawyer" and to the *Institutions*, the method of which he followed "because . . . it is most just and natural, and therefore a good model . . . and . . . in the hands of all persons conversant in our laws." Kames, who at one time thought to do an edition of Stair,[52] speaks of him as "our capital writer on law,"[53] but he was critical of Stair.[54] Erskine sometimes cites Stair, sometimes does not follow him, and sometimes gives greater weight to decisions. Walter Ross was distinctly critical of Stair.[55] Hume as Professor of Scots Law told his students in 1821:[56] "He who has done most for us, and stands certainly in the highest place, is Lord Stair, an acute reasoner certainly and a profound and intelligent lawyer, who has given us a complete system of our law, from which all later authorities have drawn, and were obliged to draw, a great part at least of what is most valuable in their works." Bell, similarly frequently cites and regularly follows Stair. Thereafter, increasingly, Stair is treated not only as an authority, but as the supreme authority.

Occasionally his view is out of line with other authoritative writers. "... I have some doubt whether Lord Stair intended to lay down the doctrine in the full and explicit manner which perhaps his words as literally construed would imply. On the other hand Craig ... Erskine, too, entirely repudiates Stair's doctrine in respect to the minor regalia, and Mr. Bell in his *Principles* (sec. 754) lays down the opposite doctrine...."[57]

Thirdly, there are express statements by later lawyers and judges regarding the work. Thus in *Dalrymple* v. *Dalrymple*[58] Lord Stowell referred to Stair as "a person whose learned labours have at all times engaged the reverence of Scottish jurisprudence." In the same case the evidence of several distinguished Scots lawyers, taken on commission, pays high tribute to the *Institutions*. David Hume said[59] that "he considers Lord Stair as by far the ablest and most profound of the writers on the law of Scotland and his *Institutes* [sic] as a work of higher authority than any of the other systems of that law,[60] not excepting Sir Thomas Craig's work *De Feudis*." Similar views were expressed by Henry Erskine (later Lord Advocate and Dean of the Faculty of Advocates) – "an author of the very highest authority ... in the court ... the greatest deference has always been paid to Lord Stair's authority;" Ilay Campbell (late Lord President of the Court of Session) – "both Lord Stair's and Mr. Erskine's *Institutes* are books of authority on the law of Scotland;" Robert Hamilton, Professor of the Law of Nature and Nations at Edinburgh – "the authority of Lord Stair, which is justly considered as of great weight in the law of Scotland;" and John Clerk of Eldin – "Lord Stair's *Institutes* [sic] is a work of very high authority in the law of Scotland."

In *Drew* v. *Drew*[61] Lord Benholme observed: "When on any point of law I find Stair's opinion uncontradicted I look upon that opinion as settling the law of Scotland." "Stair, Erskine and Bell are cited daily in the courts, and the court will pay as much respect to them as to a judgment of the House of Lords, though it is bound to follow a judgment of the House of Lords whatever the institutional writers may have said."[62] Stair's *Institutions* "has long been accepted as the fountain-head of Scots law. Its outstanding feature is the emphasis consistently laid upon first principles, and the systematic development of these principles in harmony with the most enlarged and comprehensive views of comparative jurisprudence.... He ranged in a spirit of philosophic eclecticism over an immense field of enquiry, extending from the basic axioms of religion and ethics to the intricacies of the early Scottish forms of process, and reduced the whole to an orderly and scientific system which has furnished the model and basis for all subsequent treatises of its kind."[63]

Stair's *Decisions of the Lords of Council and Session in the most Important Cases debate before them. Part First*, contains the decisions from 1661 to 1671 and was printed by the Heir of Andrew Anderson and published in 1683. It is a stout folio and the decisions extend to 720 pages. There are about 1200 cases reported. The cases are in chronological order, the date of each is given and the narrative frequently extends to half-a-page or more. The actual decision is always clearly stated, in such a phrase as: "The Lords found. . . ." There are indices of parties' names and by subject-matter.

Stair had made his contract with the Heir of Anderson on March 26, 1681, and on April 11, 1681, obtained a royal Gift and Privilege[64] for printing his *Institutions, Acts of Sederunt* and *Decisions of the Lords of Session*, in which the King, "being confident of the great benefit may arise to all our subjects of that our ancient kingdom, by publishing of the said *Decisions* and *Institutions*," ratified and approved the contract to publish, and prohibited others from doing so without Stair's permission for 19 years. On June 10 that year Stair disclosed his intention to the Lords and intimated the King's allowance and approbation, and the Lords, "considering that the Lord President has been at extraordinary pains, in Observing and Collecting these Decisions, and that the publishing thereof will be of great use and advantage, not only to the College of Justice but to the whole lieges," approved his resolution to print and thanked him for undertaking the work.[65]

The Epistle Dedicatory, dated from Leiden October 30, November 9, 1683, contains interesting observations on the importance of decisions as sources of law:

"and therefore the best expedient to give this most desirable security, is to show that Judges . . . make not law like the Delphick Sword, bowing or bending to the several Parties, but as a firm and stable rule, which will ply to no obliquity, but whatever must be regulate by it, must be applyed to it, and be straight like it, and so quadrat one to another, which can be no way better known than by the publishing and comparing of Decisions, whereby it may be seen that like cases have like events, and that there is no respect of persons in Judgment."

He continues:

"I did form this Breviat of these Decisions, in fresh and recent Memory, *de die in diem* as they were pronounced; I seldom eat, before I observed the Interlocutors I judged of difficulty, that past that day and when I was hindered by any extraordinary occasion, I delayed no longer then that was over. It was neither feazable nor fit that I should set down the large Pleadings, or the Written Informations of Parties, I did peruse them thoroughly, and pitched upon the Reasons which were of moment, as to the points determined, whereas in the same Informations, there were many obvious clear Points insisted on, which I omitted."

The Epistle Dedicatory, concludes:

"I had the best opportunity to make these observations, being scarce a day absent in any of these sessions, from the 1st of June 1661 to the first of August 1681, and I was not one day absent from the 23rd of January 1671 when it pleased His Majesty to appoint me to be constant President of the Session in place of my Lord Craigmillar, who then demitted, except the Summer Session of 1679, when I was absent by his command."

The Decisions of the Lords of Council and Session in the Most Important Cases Debate before Them. Part Second (1671–81) was printed in folio by the Heir of Andrew Anderson and sold by George Mosman "Finely Bound and gilded, for Six Rix Dollers" in 1687. It comprises 896 pages; there are about 1200 cases reported; the reports are in the same style but tend to be longer, and there are indices as in the first part.

Most of Stair's cases are reprinted in Morison's *Dictionary* but over 200 are omitted, but most of these were printed in his Supplemental Volume; a few are duplicated.

The writing of the *Institutions* and the compilation of the *Decisions* were clearly accordingly complementary parts of a single enterprise.

His *Decisions* were later attacked for their obscurity, and in his *Apology*[66] Stair replied:

> "I may say without vanity, that no man did so much to make the law of this kingdom known and constant as I have done, that not only bred lawyers, but generally the nobility and gentry of the nation might know their rights; for I did carefully and faithfully observe the debates and decisions of the Lords of Session, during all the time I was in it, expressing mainly the reasons that the Lords laid hold on in all important cases, which were not come to be incontroverted as a beaten path, or were obvious to common capacities; and I did seldon eat or drink, and scarcely ever slept, before I perused the informations that passed every sederunt day, and set down the decisions of the Lords (though sometimes not in the same terms as they were marked by the clerks; for at that time the interlocutors were all upon their trust, without being revised and signed by the President, as now they are) while they were fresh in my memory, which were published in two volumes after my removal; but not being present at the time they were printed, there are many escapes in printing, but seldom is there any thing of the sense unclear."[67]

NOTES

[1] OSA, XI, p. 573; *Third Statistical Account*, Ayrshire, p. 713; erection of the new kirk was ratified by Parliament in 1690: APS, IX, 219, c. 91. There are also a parish and village of Dalrymple in Ayrshire.

[2] For further details of the Dalrymple ancestry see Anderson, SN, II, p. 5; Crawfurd, *Peerage*, p. 451; Douglas, *Peerage*, II, p. 519, *s.v.* Stair; *Scots Peerage*, VIII, 114.

[3] RMS, VI, 1478.

[4] RMS, VIII, 94.

[5] RMS, VIII, 626.

[6] RMS, IX, 1940.

[7] Engraving in Graham, *Annals of Stairs,* I, p. 6, See also APS, VII, 585.

[8] DNB; Anderson, S.N., II, p. 7; Chambers, BDES; William Forbes, Preface to *Journal of the Session*; Ae. J. G. Mackay, *Memoir of Sir James Dalrymple, First Viscount Stair* (1873); J. M. Graham, *Annals and Correspondence of the Viscount and the First and Second Earls of Stair* (2 vols., 1875); Crawfurd's *Peerage*, p. 451, *Scots Peerage*, VIII, p. 114, s.v. Stair; *Complete Peerage*, XII, p. 201, s.v. Stair; (1906) 14 S.L.T. 21 (portrait); J. Thomson, "The First Viscount Stair" (1924) 36 J.R. 33; J. L. Duncan, "Life and Times of Viscount Stair" (1934) 46 J.R. 103; D. M. Walker (ed.), *Stair Tercentenary Studies* (Stair Soc., 1981).

[9] All the older authorities call it Drummurchie. Drummurchie had belonged to James Dalrymple who made over the lands of Stair to his uncle James, by contract dated October 12, 1620. James the uncle became the father of James the jurist. The family probably moved from Drummurchie to Stair in 1620 or 1621. As to Drummurchie see *Statistical Account, Ayrshire*, p. 409. It cannot now be identified but there is a Dinmurchie Loch on the Albany burn about two miles SE of Barr, which is inland from Girvan. Groome's *Ordnance Gazetteer, s.v.* Barr, gives Dinmurchie farm near the village of Barr as the birthplace.

[10] Preface to Forbes, *Journal of the Session*, p. 30.

[11] *Munimenta Almae Universitatis Glasguensis*, III, 22. It is uncertain whether the names are in order of merit or not, but they are not alphabetical.

[12] Proclamations authorising the Book of Common Prayer and the Preface to it are in Dickinson and Donaldson, *Source Book of Scottish History*, III, pp. 90–93.

[13] Text in Dickinson and Donaldson, *supra*, III, p. 95 and Donaldson's *Scottish Historical Documents* (1970), pp. 194–201. See also G. D. Henderson, "The idea of the covenant in Scotland," in *The Burning Bush*, pp. 61–74. On the whole period see D. Stevenson, *The Scottish Revolution, 1637–44* (1973).

[14] Texts of Acts of Assembly in Dickinson and Donaldson, *supra*, III, pp. 106–13, and Donaldson, *supra*, pp. 202–206.

[15] William Cunningham, 8th Earl of Glencairn (*c.* 1610–64), was the leading landlord in Cunningham district of Ayrshire, and later (1646–49) Lord Justice-General of Scotland and (1661–64) Lord Chancellor of Scotland. He was Chancellor of Glasgow University, 1660–61. On him see DNB; *Scots Peerage*, IV, p. 247; Cowan, *Lord Chancellors*, II, p. 222 (portrait).

[16] Glencairn's Regiment was still in existence some years later; see *Papers Relating to the Army of the Solemn League and Covenant* (ed. C. S. Terry, S.H.S.), Introduction.

[17] Forbes, Preface, p. 30.

[18] The place in which he taught was, of course, not the modern University, nor even the Old College in High Street, but in the Pedagogy and the Arthurlie House on the east side of the High Street. The Old College was built in 1632–59.

[19] G.U. Library, Sp. Coll. 623.

[20] One of his students who later achieved distinction was John Snell, who later became clerk to Sir Orlando Bridgman, then Crier to the Court of Common Pleas and, when Bridgman became Lord Keeper of the Great Seal in 1667, Seal Bearer, and who founded the Snell Exhibition under which outstanding Glasgow graduates go on to Balliol College, Oxford. On Snell see E. L. G. Stones in *Stair Society Miscellany*, II (1984). Aeneas Mackay in 1873 states (*Memoir*, p. 16) that notes taken by one of Stair's students had been preserved; these unfortunately cannot now be traced. So too Graham, *Annals*, I, p. 7.

[21] Lord Cooper, "The Scottish Lawyer's Library in the Seventeenth Century" (1954) 66 J. R. 1, and *Selected Papers*, p. 276.

[22] APS, VI (1), 562; VI (2), 34.

[23] SRO CS1/5 f. 182 v. His oration on passing advocate is printed with facsimile in S.H.R. 13, pp. 380–392.

[24] A.S., February 12, 1619, in Ilay Campbell's *Early Acts of Sederunt*, 75; *Minute Book of the Faculty of Advocates*, I, 9 (November, 7, 1664).

[25] APS, VI (2) 232, 435; Baillie's *Letters*, III, p. 507.

[26] APS, VI (2), 299, c. 271.

[27] APS, II, 10, c. 10.

[28] APS, II, 97, c. 20.

[29] APS, I, 29; III, 40.

[30] APS, I, 30; III, 89b; see also III, 105.

[31] APS, III, 564, c. 45.

[32] APS, V, 46.

[33] *Decisions*, I, p. 155.

[34] Baillie, *Letters and Papers*, III, p. 524.

[35] (1619–67), Professor at Utrecht, author of works on Roman law.

[36] (1588–1657), Professor at Leiden, author of *In IV Libros Institutionum Commentarius* (1642).

[37] (1601–54), Professor at Utrecht, a distinguished jurist.

[38] Grotius had died in 1646.

[39] Mackay, *Memoir*, p. 55.

[40] Claude de Saumaise (1588–1653), French humanist and an outstanding scholar in law and later in theology; he succeeded Scaliger at Leiden in 1631. In 1649 he wrote a *Defensio regia pro Carolo I* upholding the divine right of monarchy, which provoked a reply from John Milton, *Defensio pro Populo Anglicano* (1650).

[41] See J. Davidson and A. Gray, *The Scottish Staple at Veere* (1909); M. P. Rooseboom, *The Scottish Staple in the Netherlands* (1910); S. G. E. Lythe, *The Economy of Scotland in its European Setting, 1550–1625* (1960); T. C. Smout, *Scottish Trade on the Eve of Union, 1650–1707* (1963).

[42] Balfour, *Annals*, IV, p. 18, See further, S. R. Gardiner, *Letters and Papers illustrating the relations between Charles II and Scotland in 1650* (S.H.S., 1894).

[43] On this episode in Charles's career see Antonia Fraser, *King Charles II*, Chaps. 6–8.

[44] On this topic see further F. D. Dow, *Cromwellian Scotland, 1651–60* (1979); C. H. Firth, *Scotland and the Commonwealth* (S.H.S., 1895); C. H. Firth, *Scotland and the Protectorate* (S.H.S., 1899); C. S. Terry, *The Cromwellian Union* (S.H.S., 1902).

[45] C.S.P. Dom., 1651–52, 210, 439, 448; *The Cromwellian Union* (ed. C. S. Terry, S.H.S., 1902), pp. 174, 176, 180. See also Orders issued by the Judges (1653) in C. H. Firth (ed.), *Scotland and the Commonwealth* (S.H.S., 1895) p. 276.

[46] *Acts and Ordinances of the Interregnum, 1642–60* (ed. C. H. Firth and R. S. Rait, 1911), II, p. 455.

[47] Forbes' Preface, pp. 16, 31.

[48] APS, VI(2), 841, 854, 884.

[49] Thurloe, *State Papers*, VI, pp. 367, 372.

[50] Thurloe, *ibid.*, p. 402. See also list of judges in Scotland in C. H. Firth (ed.), *Scotland and the Protectorate*, p. 385.

[51] Nicol's *Diary*, p. 278.

[52] Forbes, Preface, p. 32.

[53] APS, VII, 124 and App. 33.

[54] APS, VII, 48, 92, 295; RPC (3rd), II, 528–530.

[55] Royal letter quoted by Mackay, p. 91; commission dated January 7, 1671: Edin. Univ. Lib., Laing MSS., II, 521; Fountainhall's *Journals* (ed. Crawford, S.H.S.), pp. 213–214.

[56] RPC (3rd), III, 277. He was again included when the Privy Council was reconstituted in June 1674 (RPC (3rd), IV, 186) and again in July 1676 (RPC (3rd), V, 6). On the background see R. H. Campbell, "Stair's Scotland: Social and Economic Background," 1982 J.R. 110; G. Donaldson, "Stair's Scotland: The Intellectual Inheritance," 1982 J.R. 128.

[57] On Lauderdale see W. C. Mackenzie, *Life and Times of John Maitland, Duke of Lauderdale (1616–82)* (1923). On his policy see Julia Buckroyd, *Church and State in Scotland, 1660–81* (1980).

[58] APS, VII, 372.

[59] APS, VII, 472.

[60] MS. Books of Sederunt, 1661–74, quoted in Mackay, p. 77; Letter to Glencairn: SRO Misc. Gifts and Deposits GD1/520/i.

[61] Stair, Apology, p. 4; Brunton & Haig, 366.

[62] RMS, XI, 593.

[63] RPC (3rd), I, 702.

[64] RPC (3rd), II, 349, 351.

[65] RPC (3rd), II, 528, 530. The militia had been offered by the Estates in 1663; APS, VIII, 480.

[66] Scots Peerage, VIII, p. 147.

[67] Mackay, p. 82, quoting Maidment's Scottish Pasquils, p. 198.

[68] Bride of Lammermoor, Chap. 34.

[69] O.U.P. Ed., 1909.

[70] In his edition of the Rev. Robert Law's Memorials, 1638–84 (1818), Sharpe gives two versions; in the first the husband lost his reason and attacked the bride; in the second the bride attacked the bridegroom.

[71] Large Description of Galloway, App. 192.

[72] Hereditary Sheriffs of Galloway (1864), pp. 367–369.

[73] Mackenzie, Discourse Concerning the Three Unions between Scotland and England (in Works, II, p. 637) – The Third Union (p. 659); Mackenzie, Memoirs; Lists of Commissioners in C. S. Terry (ed.), The Cromwellian Union (S.H.S., 1902), p. 189; Dicey and Rait, Thoughts on the Union between England and Scotland (1920), App. C.

[74] Terry, supra, p. 197.

[75] For minutes of these see Terry (ed.), The Cromwellian Union, pp. 187 et seq.

[76] Terry, supra, p. 206.

[77] Inst., IV, 2, 6; Forbes, Preface, p. 33.

[78] Articles for Regulating of the Judicatories set down by the Commissioners thereto authorised by His Majesty under the Great Seal (1670); Adv. Lib. Pamphlets, 2, 5, 19.

[79] See APS, VIII, 80.

[80] Dalrymple must have been absent from some sittings of the commission when he was in London on the Union Commission.

[81] APS, VIII, 80.

[82] Mackenzie, History, p. 234.

[83] Commission dated January 7, 1671; Edin. Univ. Lib., Laing MSS, II, 521; Fountainhall's Journals (ed. Crawford, S.H.S.), pp. 213–214.

[84] APS, VIII, 57, 235.

[85] APS, VIII, 93, c. 45.

[86] APS, VIII, 69, c. 16.

[87] RPC (3rd), IV, 61.

[88] Stair lived in Potterrow, near the junction with Bristo Street.

[89] A.S., July 4 and July 14, 1676.

[90] p. 5. On this policy see Julia Buckroyd, Church and State in Scotland, 1660–81.

[91] Sir Thomas Murray of Glendook.

[92] Sir George Mackenzie of Rosehaugh.

[93] Sir Thomas Wallace of Craigie.

[94] Sir George Mackenzie of Tarbat.

[95] RPC (3rd), VI, 194–195. Lauderdale's conduct was in question: see Wodrow, III, p. 168.

[96] RPC (3rd), VII, 374.

[97] APS, VIII, 238, c. 1.

[98] APS, VIII, 238, c. 2.

[99] APS, VIII, 243, c. 6. Text in Dickinson and Donaldson, Source Book of Scottish History, III, p. 186; text of oath in Donaldson, Scottish Historical Documents, p. 243.

[1] Wodrow, III, p. 298.

[2] The Act 1567, c. 4 (APS III, 14) to which is appended "The Confession of the Faith and Doctrine believed and professed by the Protestantes of the Realme of Scotland . . . and . . . authorised as a doctrine groundit upon the infallibill word of God."

[3] I. B. Cowan, The Scottish Covenanters, p. 108.

[4] G. D. Henderson, "Scots Confession, 1560," in The Burning Bush (1957), p. 23; see also "The Idea of the Covenant in Scotland," ibid., p. 61; J. H. S. Burleigh, A Church

History of Scotland (1960), p. 154. For text of the Negative Confession see Dickinson and Donaldson, *Source-Book*, III, p. 32; of the National Covenant, *ibid.*, III, p. 95.

[5] Charles by this time was 51; his queen, Catherine of Braganza, had had only miscarriages and was now highly unlikely to have a child.

[6] RPC (3rd), VII, 718–723.

[7] Misc. P.C. papers in RPC (3rd), VII, 705–706.

[8] RPC (3rd), VII, 233.

[9] RPC (3rd), VII, 295.

[10] *Apology*, p. 4.

[11] *Apology*, p. 5.

[12] C.S.P. Dom., 1680–81, 516, 534.

[13] RPC (3rd), VII, xvi-xvii.

[14] APS, VIII, 242, c. 5.

[15] APS, VIII, 248, c. 11.

[16] APS, VIII, 351, c. 17.

[17] APS, VIII, 352, c. 20.

[18] It is important to remember how little Scottish legal materials and literature were in print then. There were the *Black Acts* of 1566 and some subsequent legislation, Skene's *Lawes and Actes* of 1597, and Skene's *Regiam* in Latin and Scots versions of 1609, and his *De Verborum Significatione*. Various volumes of *Practicks* circulated in manuscript. Editions of, and texts on, the Roman law, the canon law, and the feudal law, and commentators thereon, published in Europe were also in print. Grotius' *De Jure Belli*, for example, had been published in 1625. Petrus Gudelinus' *De Jure Novissimo*, said to be the first systematic exposition of the law of the Netherlands, appeared in 1620 and Grotius' *Inleiding* (Introduction to Roman-Dutch law) in 1631.

[19] Printed in Dallas's *Styles* (1st ed., Pt.II, 152); (2nd ed.; Vol. I, Pt. II, 76).

[20] *Apology*, p. 5.

[21] C.S.P. Dom., Jan.–June 1683, 371; Coltness Papers (Maitland Club), p. 78; Hist. MSS. Com., Drumlanrig MSS., I, 175.

[22] Gerard Noodt, (1647–1725),

[23] Antony Schulting (1659–1734).

[24] (1647–1713).

[25] John Erskine of Carnock's *Journal* 1683–87 (ed. Macleod, S.H.S.).

[26] None of the volumes of *Practicks* (which are not in any event truly comparable) were published till later. Durie's *Decisions* relate to an earlier period (1621–42) but were not published till 1690.

[27] RPC (3rd), X, 46, 90.

[28] *Ibid.*, 97.

[29] *Ibid.*, 102.

[30] *Ibid.*, 554–555.

[31] RPC (3rd) XI, xxxii.

[32] *Ibid.*, 36.

[33] *Ibid.*, 513.

[34] Fountainhall, *Decisions*, I, p. 353; Howell, *State Trials*.

[35] APS, VIII, App. 32.

[36] APS, VIII, 490, c. 52.

[37] APS, VIII, 646, c. 71.

[38] Fountainhall, *Historical Notices of Scotch Affairs*, p. 552; Fountainhall, *Decisions*, I, p. 301.

[39] Fountainhall, *Decisions*, I, p. 370.

[40] Fountainhall, *Decisions*, I, pp. 447–448; APS, VIII, 490, App. 32; RPC (3rd), XIII, xv. *Historical Notices*, II, pp. 629, 686, 783.

[41] The title-page bears the date 1686.

[42] *Supra*.

[43] We have no knowledge whether the first three were ever written. Stair's *Treatise on the Divine Perfections*, published in 1695, may be, or be part of, the Inquiry concerned Natural Theology.

[44] The Royal Society had been founded in 1662, at least partly at the instance of one Sir Robert Murray or Moray, a friend of Stair and Lord Justice-Clerk 1667–73. The MS. of the first book of Newton's *Philosophiae Naturalis Principia Mathematica*, dedicated to it, was presented to the Royal Society in April 1686, though not published until 1687.

45 It is summarised in Mackay, *Memoir*, pp. 201–206. See also Lord Cooper, "Stair the Scientist" (1955) 67 J.R.1.

46 A fascinating speculation is whether Stair, while in exile, ever met John Locke, who was in Holland from 1683 to 1688. From Utrecht Locke wrote his *Letters on Toleration* in 1686.

47 APS, IX, 3: *Proceedings of the Estates in Scotland, 1689–90* (ed. Balfour Melville, S.H.S.), II, App.

48 *Leven and Melville Papers* (Bannatyne Club), p. 79.

49 APS, IX, 38.

50 APS, IX, 37; Dickinson and Donaldson, *Source Book*, III, p. 200.

51 APS, IX, 38; Dickinson and Donaldson, III, p. 207.

52 *i.e.* Anne, who had married Prince George of Denmark.

53 APS, IX, 40. For their oath on acceptance see *Nat. MSS. Scot*: III, cvii, Dickinson and Donaldson, III, p. 208.

54 He had been Lord Advocate from February 1687 and then an Ordinary Lord and Justice-Clerk since February 1688. In 1692 he became a Secretary of State but had to resign after the Massacre of Glencoe: Brunton & Haig, p. 430; Omond, pp. 225, 236.

55 Brunton & Haig, pp. 419, 425. On the trial of the murderer, Chiesely of Dalry, see Arnot's *Criminal Trials*, p. 150 (2nd ed., p. 163). On the activities of Stair and his son John in these years see P. W. J. Riley, *King William and the Scottish Politicians* (1979).

56 *Leven and Melville Papers*, p. 23. For final appointments see *ibid.*, p. 307; *Proceedings of the Estates in Scotland*, II, 37.

57 RPC (3rd), XIII, 378–379.

58 Brunton & Haig, p. 391; he was a judge 1667–81.

59 Brunton & Haig, p. 431; he was a judge 1681–1700.

60 RPC (3rd), XIII, 404; *Proceedings of the Estates in Scotland, 1689–90* (ed. Balfour Meville, S.H.S.), II, pp. 35, 41.

61 *Ibid.*, 456.

62 *Ibid.*, XIV, 459; *Proceedings, supra*, II, 48.

63 RPC (3rd), XIII, 379; XIV, 459; C.S.P. Dom. 1689–90, 154, 350; *Leven and Melville Papers*, p. 313.

64 *Ibid.*, XV, 286.

65 *Proceedings*, II, 69. His election was disputed: *ibid.*, II, 137. He sat on the committees for settling the church government, on fines and forfeitures, etc., and for the visitation of the universities, colleges and schools: *ibid.*, II, 161, 223, 227, 266.

66 NLS MS. 7012, 87.

67 APS III, 153, *c.* 38.

68 Reprinted by the Bannatyne Club, 1825 (Publications, No. 12), in More's edition of Stair's *Institutions*, pp. xix–xxiv and in Graham's *Annals*, I, p. 344. There are said to have been two versions, one for England recommending an episcopalian settlement in Scotland, one for Scotland supporting presbyterianism: House of Lords Record Office, Wilcocks MSS., 61, David Hay to Tweeddale.

69 *Proceedings*, II, 124.

70 *Ibid.*, II, 125.

71 *Ibid.*, II, 127.

72 APS, IX, 112; *Proceedings of the Estates*, II, 122, 153.

73 APS, IX, 139, 164, 200.

74 *Papers Illustrative of the Condition of the Highlands*, p. 149.

75 As contrasted with Extraordinary, not in the modern sense of Lord Ordinary.

76 Printed in Graham, *Annals*, I, pp. 361–364.

77 1630–1705; see DNB and authorities there cited.

78 See also G. M. Hutton, *The Political Thought of Viscount Stair* (unpub. Ph.D. thesis, Birmingham University, 1971).

79 The museum was designed by Robert Rowand Anderson and built in 1890.

80 The hall was designed by Charles Wilson and built in 1854.

81 (1906) 14 S.L.T. 24.

82 1953 S.L.T. (News) 139.

83 Grandson of Professor Lorimer, on whom see Chap. 23, *infra*.

84 See Gen. XIV, 18–20; Psalm XC; Matt. XXII, 42.

85 For further expressions of Lord Cooper's view of Stair see "Some Classics of Scottish Legal Literature" Lord Cooper's *Selected Papers* (1957), 39, 42; and *The Scottish Legal*

Tradition (Saltire Society, 4th ed., 1977) and *Selected Papers*, 172, 177.

[86] *Scots Peerage*, VIII, 114, 118; Seton, *Memoir of Chancellor Seton*, genealogical tree in Appx. II, No. 3; Murray Graham, *Annals*.

[87] On Lord Drummore see *Hutchison* v. *Hutchison* (1872) 11 M.229 at p. 233, *per* Lord President Inglis. On Hailes see Chap. 16, *infra*.

[88] *History*, p. 214.

[89] Balcarres, *Memoirs touching the Revolution in Scotland*, 1688–90 (Bannatyne Club), p. 50.

[90] *History of His Own Time* (1823 ed.), I, p. 369.

[91] *Journal of the Session* (1714), Preface, p. 38. There must have been many lawyers alive in 1714 who remembered Stair, so that Forbes's estimate is probably substantially accurate. It never appears to have been challenged. Moreover at the end of the preface Forbes mentions as among those who had given him information about Stair and other persons mentioned Sir Hugh [*sic*] Dalrymple of North Berwick, Lord President of the Session [Stair's third son] and Sir David Dalrymple of Hales [*sic*], late Queen's Advocate [Stair's fifth son].

[92] *History of England*, III, p. 264.

[93] K. Luig, "The Institutes of National Law in the Seventeenth and Eighteenth Centuries," 1972 J.R. 193.

[94] This stage is extensively illustrated by the European works of the glossators, postglossators and humanists, the decretists and decretalists, and the feudalists, but not at all by Scottish juristic activity.

[95] *e.g.* G.A. Struve, *Jurisprudentia Romano-Germanica Forensis* (1670); Juan Sala, *Institutiones Romanae-Hispanae* (1795). This stage is illustrated in Scotland by Skene's mention in his preface to *Regiam Majestatem* (Latin ed., 1609), p. 2, where he speaks of *peregrina cum domesticis conjungere* and by Burnett in the preface to Craig's *Jus Feudale* (1732 ed.), where he speaks of Gibson of Durie *in iure civili cum iure Scotico maritando*.

[96] Craig's *Jus Feudale* (1605) may be taken as an example of this stage.

[97] *e.g.*, Gudelinus, *De iure novissimo* (1620); Simon van Leeuwen, *Paratitla iuris novissimi* (1652); M. Guarini, *Historia Juris* (1796), Book 4: *De Jurisprudentia Novissima*.

[98] In international law the full existence of nation-states is traditionally accepted as having been recognised by the Treaty of Westphalia (1648).

[99] *e.g.* in France Guy Coquille, *Institution au droit français* (1607); G. Argou, *Institution au droit français* (1692); Claude Serres, *Les Institutions du droit français* (1753); in Germany J S. Putter, *Elementa iuris Germanici privati* (1748); J. G. Heineccius, *Elementa iuris Germanici* (1735); J. H. C. von Selchow, *Institutiones iurisprudentiae Germanicae* (1757); in Holland, H. Grotius, *Inleiding tot de Hollandsche Rechsgeleertheyd* (1620); S. van Leeuwen, *Het Roomsch Hollandsch Recht* (1664); in Spain, I. J. de Asso y del Rio and M. de Manuel y Rodrigues, *Instituciones del derecho civil de Castilla* (1771); in Italy, Oronzio Fighera, *Institutiones iuris Regni Neapolitani* (1766); N. Valletta, *Elementi del diritto del regno napoletano* (1776); C. Fimiani, *Elementa iuris privati neapolitani* (1782).

Although the Roman law influence was much lesser, the final stage is illustrated in England also, by J. Cowell, *Institutiones Iuris Anglicani ad methodum et seriem Institutionum Imperialium compositae et digestae* (1605); Francis Bacon, *Elements of the Common Lawes of England* (1639); E. Coke, *Institutes of the Laws of England* (1628–44); W. Bohun, *Institutio Legalis* (1708–09); and T. Wood, *An Institute of the Laws of England* (1720).

[1] Thus Scotland has no book on the same lines as Johannes Voet's *Commentarius ad Pandectas* (1698–1704).

[2] 6th ed., p. 59.

[3] Advertisement to 2nd ed. (6th ed., p. 64).

[4] p. 6 (More's ed., p. xxii).

[5] *i.e.* lacked, were without, or in want of.

[6] *Somers Tracts* (ed. Sir Walter Scott), XI, p. 550.

[7] Dedication to 1681 ed. (6th ed., p. 63).

[8] As contrasted with classical and Biblical texts and other texts not printed by the author, where the earliest MS., that nearest to the author's time and presumably nearest to what he wrote, is the basis for a modern printed text, in the case of a book printed by the author, the latest edition known to have been revised and authorised by him, in this case the second edition, must be taken as the copy-text.

[9] Printed in Stair's *Decisions*, Vol. I, after the Epistle Dedicatory to the King.

[10] The value of looking at readings of manuscripts, none, so far as known, being the

author's autograph, is very limited when the author himself had put out two printed editions, the second substantially revised. Surely his last printed edition must be taken to represent his *ultima verba* and to supersede all manuscripts. It would be otherwise if the work had never been printed in Stair's lifetime.

[11] 1715–75, advocate 1737, joint professor of civil law at Edinburgh University, 1753–54.

[12] 1729–1805, advocate 1751.

[13] The editors, that is, admit to having altered the text without warrant from manuscript or decision.

[14] 1786–1867, advocate 1811, Historiographer-Royal for Scotland, 1836; see DNB.

[15] There are separate title pages bearing to be Vol. I, Vol. II, Part III and Part IV.

[16] Notice, p. iv.

[17] *Journal* (1874 ed.), II, p. 113.

[18] On him see Chap. 24, *infra*.

[19] A firm founded in 1734, the predecessors in business of W. Green & Son Ltd. Their name is still fixed high upon the wall of W. Green's premises in St. Giles Street.

[20] Preface, p. xvi.

[21] There is a reference to a footnote: "See Dodson's Report of the Judgment in *Dalrymple* v. *Dalrymple*, p. 1 (of Appendix)." This is a serious mistake. The proper reference is to (1811) 2 Haggard's Consistorial Rep. 54; 161 Eng. Rep. 665, and the dictum was not pronounced by the judge, Lord Stowell, sitting in the London Consistory Court, but appears in the Appendix to the report, p. 42 (161 Eng. Rep. 802) in the answers of Robert Craigie, advocate, to interrogatories administered to him as to the law of Scotland relative to the matter in issue. It is evidence, not judicial dictum. In any event it was stated when only the first three editions had been published and the first and second were then already scarce. This is no authority for preferring Gordon and Johnstone's text to any other.

[22] Thus in *Carmichael* v. *Carmichael's Exrx.*, 1920 S.C. (H.L.) 195, which was decided on careful exegesis of a passage in Stair, I, 10, 5 the House of Lords decided it on the basis of More's text, in ignorance of differences between that and the text of the second edition. See Smith, *Studies Critical and Comparative* (1962), p. 182; Cameron, "*Jus Quaesitum Tertio*: The True meaning of Stair, I, x, 5," 1961 J.R. 103; Rodger, "Molina, Stair and the *Jus Quaesitum Tertio*," 1969 J.R. 34, 128; McCormick, "*Jus Quaesitum Tertio*: Stair v. Dunedin," 1970 J.R. 228.

[23] The Notes have often been cited as authorities. In *Fortington* v. *Kinnaird*, 1942 S.C. 239, Lord Justice-Clerk Cooper and Lord Jamieson attached importance to the views expressed in More's Notes (pp. 265, 289) and Lord Mackay (p. 276) said that the Notes "carries almost the authority of a separate Institution."

[24] The tercentenary was also marked by a conference held at Glasgow University on March 28, 1981; the text of the papers given by the four leading speakers is printed in 1981 J.R. 101–176. There was also an exhibition, entitled "A Gentleman of Excellent Parts," displaying many items illustrating the life and times of Stair, held in the Hunterian Museum, Glasgow University, and later in the Canongate Tolbooth, Edinburgh. The Stair Society published, as its volume for 1981, *Stair Tercentenary Studies*.

[25] *Fergusson* v. *Shirreff* (1844) 6 D. 1363 at p. 1365, *per* Lord Justice-Clerk Hope.

[26] I, 1, 16; *cf.* III, 4, 27.

[27] Dedication of 1681 edition (6th ed., p. 60).

[28] I, 1, 12.

[29] I, 1, 16.

[30] I, 1, 16, instancing legitim, rules of succession, terce and courtesy.

[31] I, 1, 16.

[32] He cites some 3000 cases, some more than once.

[33] He cites some 300 statutes, some many times.

[34] J. M. Halliday, "Feudal Law as a Source," in *Stair Tercentenary Studies*. p. 136.

[35] W. M. Gordon, "Roman Law as a Source," in *Stair Tercentenary Studies*, p. 107; Gordon, "Stair's Use of Roman Law," in Harding (ed.), *Law Making and Law Makers in British History* (R. Hist. S., 1980). There are about 1000 references or allusions to Roman law about half of them in Bk. I.

[36] J. J. Robertson, "Canon Law as a Source," *ibid.*, p. 112. Many of the references are general and not to specific sources.

[37] W. D. H. Sellar, "English Law as a Source," *ibid.*, p. 140. There are about 50 references to English law and practice.

[38] P. Stein, "Influence of Roman Law on the Law of Scotland," 1963 J.R. 205.

[39] There are, on average, about three references to Roman law per page in Bk. I of the *Institutions*, about one per page thereafter, about 1000 in all.

[40] This pattern of exposition is clearly exemplified in I, 9, and III, 4.

[41] *e.g.* I, 8, 3–5, on *negotiorum gestio*; I, 14, 7, the rule that the buyer takes the risk in sale from the conclusion of the contract.

[42] The references, direct and indirect, probably do not exceed 100.

[43] W. D. H. Sellar, "English Law as a Source," in *Stair Tercentenary Studies* p. 140, concentrates on English law as an historical source.

[44] He mentions John Cowell's *Institutiones Juris Anglicani ad Methodum et Seriem Institutionum Imperialium compositae et digestae* (1605, trans. 1651).

[45] See also D. M. Walker, "The Structure and Arrangement of the Institutions," in *Stair Tercentenary Studies* p. 100.

[46] Advertisement to second edition.

[47] Personal rights arising from domestic relations, and from obligations, quasi-contractual, delictual and contractual.

[48] This, logically but rather awkwardly, places assignations of personal rights between real rights and dispositions and the conveyances of real rights.

[49] I, 1, 23.

[50] I, 1, 22.

[51] I, 1, 23.

[52] A. H. Campbell, "The Structure of Stair's Institutions" (David Murray Lecture, Glasgow, 1954), p. 11.

[53] I, 2.

[54] I, 3–9.

[55] I, 10–18.

[56] II, 1–12.

[57] III, 1–9.

[58] IV, 1–52.

[59] I, 2.

[60] I, 3–9.

[61] I, 10–18.

[62] See T. B. Smith, "Scots Law and Roman Dutch Law: A Shared Tradition," in *Studies Critical and Comparative* (1962), 46, 50; R. Feenstra and C. Waal, *Seventeenth Century Levden Law Professors and their Influence on the Development of the Civil Law* (1975), p. 84.

[63] See generally P. G. Stein, "Stair's General concepts in the Theory of Law," in *Stair Tercentenary Studies* p. 181.

[64] I, 1, 1; *ef.* Grotius, I, 1, 10.

[65] I, 1, 2; Grotius, I, 1, 13.

[66] I, 1, 3.

[67] I, 1, 5.

[68] I, 1, 6.

[69] I, 1, 7.

[70] I, 1, 8.

[71] I, 1, 9. Similarly the theologians distinguished the laws of God, published by Moses, into moral, ceremonial and judicial: Aquinas, *Summa Theologiae, I, IIae, 89*; Calvin *Institutes. IV, 20, 14.*

[72] I, 1, 10–11. At this time Grotius' influence was changing the meaning of the law of nations from the law common to all nations to the law applying between nations, *i.e.* what we now call international law.

[73] I, 1, 10 and 12.

[74] This does not mean "usually followed" but "as a norm or standard, followed."

[75] I, 1, 12.

[76] I, 1, 13.

[77] I, 1, 14.

[78] I, 1, 15.

[79] Instancing primogeniture, degrees of succession, legitim, terce and courtesy.

[80] I, 1, 16.

[81] I, 1, 17. See also D. N. MacCormick, "The Rational Discipline of Law," 1982 J.R. 146.

[82] I, 1, 18.

[83] I, 1, 19.

[84] I, 1, 20; I, 2.

[85] I, 1, 21; I, 3.

[86] I, 1, 18.

[87] See also G. M. Hutton, "Stair's Philosophic Precursors," in *Stair Tercentenary Studies*, 87.

[88] *Eth. Nicom.*, V. 7, 1.

[89] *De Republica*, III, 22, 33.

[90] *De Officiis*, III, 5, 23; *De Har. Resp.*, 14, 32.

[91] See further, Schulz, *History of Roman Legal Science*. pp. 72–75, 136, 336.

[92] Gaius, I, 1.

[93] *Just. Inst.*, I, 2, pr. i; *cf. Dig.* I, 1.

[94] J. W. Jones, *Historical Introduction to the Theory of Law*. p. 104.

[95] *Summa Theologiae.*, I, IIae, Q. 90.

[96] *Ibid.*, Q. 91.

[97] *Ibid.*, Qq. 93, 94, 95, respectively.

[98] *Ibid.*, Qq. 96–97.

[99] *De Legibus et Deo Legislatore* (1619), Lib. II, Grotius quotes Suarez with respect.

[1] Grotius, *De Jure Belli ac Pacis* (1625), Prolegomena, and Book I, Chap. 1, 10(6). Pufendorf continued to speak of the law of nature as in some sense coming from God: *De Jure Naturae et Gentium* (1671), II, Chap. 3. See also Thomasius, *Fundamenta Juris Naturae et Gentium* (1705); Burlamaqui, *Principes du Droit Naturel* (1747); Christian Wolff, *Institutiones Juris Naturae et Gentium* (1750); Vattel, *Droit des Gens ou Principes de la Loi Naturelle* (1758), who all move further from theology. Natural law is a purely rational construction, though paying homage to a remote notion of God. A link between the older and the newer schools of natural law is provided by Hooker's *Laws of Ecclesiastical Polity* (1594). On the whole subject see J. Bryce, "The Law of Nature," in *Studies in History and Jurisprudence* (1901), II, p. 556; H. S. Maine, *Ancient Law* (1861), Chap. 3 and 4; Gierke, *Natural Law and the Theory of Society*. trs. Barker (1934); A.P. D'Entreves, *Natural Law* (1951); Sir F. Pollock, "History of the Law of Nature," in *Essays in the Law* (1922). With the later development of natural law thinking we are not, at this point, concerned.

[2] Molina is mentioned by Stair in I, 10, 4, but not the others. On these thinkers see B. Hamilton, *Political Thought in Seventeenth Century Spain*; R. Williams, *The Social and Political Theory of Francisco Suarez* (1963); Q. Skinner, *Foundations of Modern Political Thought*. II, pp. 135–184.

[3] I, 1, 22.

[4] I, 1, 23.

[5] See further D. N. McCormick, "Stair as Analytical Jurist," in *Stair Tercentenary Studies*. p. 187.

[6] I, 1, 22. The terminology of "formal and proper object" is derived from Aristotelian metaphysics; the formal object or formal cause is a thing's essential feature, as distinct from the efficient cause which may bring it into being, and its final cause, that which is supposed to justify its coming into or being in existence.

[7] I, 1, 22.

[8] *e.g.* Hohfeld, "Fundamental Legal Conceptions as Applied in Judicial Reasoning" (1913) 23 Yale L.J. 16; 26 Yale L.J. 712; Kocourek, *Jural Relations*. These build on earlier work by Windscheid (1862), Thon (1878), Bierling (1883) and Salmond (1902).

[9] It is most interesting that Stair used the word "correlate" while the 20th-century thinkers use "correlative."

[10] I, 1, 18 and I, 2; see also IV, 45, 17. It is interesting to note that Hobbes in *De Cive* took as two of his major heads liberty and dominion.

[11] I, 1, 20 and 22; II and III.

[12] I, 1, 90 and I, 3–18.

[13] See *infra* as to Obligation.

[14] I, 1, 1; I, 3, 1.

[15] I, 3, 4.

[16] I, 3, 5–16.

[17] I, 3, 7.

[18] I, 1, 22.

[19] *e.g.* I, 1, 22; I, 3, 1.

[20] *e.g.* I, 3, 1; *cf.* Justinian, *Inst.* III, 13, pr.: *Obligatio est iuris vinculum. . . .*

[21] I, 3, 2.

[22] Justinian, *Inst.* III, 13, 2.

[23] On the term "obediential" see Stair's *Institutions*. (6th ed.), Introduction, p. 33. On what is included therein see *Inst.* I, 3, 3–4.

[24] I, 3, 3; I, 10, – I, 18.

[25] *i.e.* arising *ex conventione*.

[26] I, 3, 5–9.

[27] He does mention the idea of *persona standi in judicio*; IV, 52, 22; IV, 52, 38.

[28] He does distinguish *dolus* and *culpa lata*: I, 9, 11.

[29] *Inst.*, I, 7 and 8. Other instances are deposit (I, 13) and partnership (I, 16).

[30] *Inst.*, I, 1, 16. It is in Bk. I that the majority of the references to the civil law occur.

[31] On what else had been printed before 1700 see H. G. Aldis, *List of Books Printed in Scotland before 1700* (1904; revised ed., 1970).

[32] See also D. M. Walker, "The Importance of Stair's Work for the Modern Lawyer," 1982 J. R. 161.

[33] I, 9, 4. These are the fundamental statements of, respectively, the claim of damages for the wrongful death of a close relative, and the claim of damages for wrongful personal injury (not resulting in death).

[34] *Thomson* v. *James* (1855) 18 D. 1 at p. 23, *per* Lord President McNeill.

[35] I, 9, 4. The "interest theory" was not fully worked out until the work of von Jhering, Pound and Stone in the 19th and 20th centuries.

[36] But for the *Institutions* there would only have been Skene's, Craig's and Mackenzie's works, and various manuscripts.

[37] See also J. W. G. Blackie, "Stair's later reputation as a Jurist," in *Stair Tercentenary Studies*, p. 207.

[38] R.P.C. (3rd), XVI, 134.

[39] *Creditors of Ruthvan* v. *Ker* (1683) Harcarse 1. References in pre-1681 cases are probably later interpolations in the report rather than reference to manuscripts of the *Institutions*.

[40] III, 2, 54.

[41] Unfortunately the 18th century reporters (*e.g.* Kilkerran, Kames, Hailes) usually do not disclose what were cited in argument as authorities but the reports in *Faculty Collection* more frequently do so.

[42] (1718) 1 Rob. 203.

[43] March 2, 1808, F.C., at p. 122, At this time "institutional" meant only "writer of a systematic instructional work," not, as it now does, "authoritative."

[44] (1811) 2 Hagg. C.R. 54.

[45] May 19, 1812, F.C., at p. 588.

[46] June 6, 1815, F.C., at p. 412.

[47] *Barbour* v. *Halliday* (1840) 2 D. 1279 at p. 1284.

[48] *Burt* v. *Home* (1878) 5 R. 445 at p. 491.

[49] This work seems to have been first cited in *Ross* v. *Heriot's Hospital*, June 6, 1815, F.C.; 6 Paton 640; and it was published in 1824. For a doubt as to the authorship see Bell, *Comm.*, I, 24.

[50] *Discourse on the Rise and Progress of the Law of Scotland and the Method of Studying It* (bound with Bayne's edition of Hope's *Minor Practicks* (1726)), p. 169.

[51] (1751) pp. v, vi.

[52] *Remarkable Decisions*, I, (1716–28), Preface.

[53] *Principles of Equity* (3rd ed.), p. 301.

[54] *Elucidations*, Preface and *passim*.

[55] *Lectures*, Preface, p. xxi, and p. 207.

[56] *Lectures* (Stair Soc.) I, p. 14.

[57] *Duke of Richmond* v. *Earl of Seafield* (1870) 8M. 530 at p. 540, *per* Lord Justice-Clerk Moncreiff. See also p. 547.

[58] (1811) 2 Hagg. C.R. 54, 88; 161 Eng. R. 665. (The case in fact relates to the alleged marriage of a descendant of Stair.)

[59] *Ibid*; App. 42, 77; 161 Eng. R. 802.

[60] By this time the "systems" of Mackenzie, Forbes, Bankton and Erskine were in print.

[61] (1870) 9 M. 163 at p. 167.

[62] Lord Normand, "The Scottish Judicature and Legal Procedure," (Presidential address, Holdsworth Club, Birmingham University, 1941).

[63] Lord Cooper, "Some Classics of Scottish Legal Literature," (1929) *Scottish Bankers*

Magazine XXI, 259, reprinted in *Selected Papers*. pp. 39, 43–44.

[64] Printed in *Decisions*. Vol. I, after the Epistle Dedicatory.

[65] A.S. June 10, 1681, printed in *Decisions*. Vol. I, after royal Gift.

[66] p. 6 (More's ed., p. xxii).

[67] *Apology*, 6 (More's ed., p. xxii).

CHAPTER 9

SIR GEORGE MACKENZIE

GEORGE Mackenzie[1] was of the family of Mackenzie of Kintail. His grandfather became Lord Mackenzie of Kintail in 1609 and the latter's eldest son became first Earl of Seaforth; his fourth son, by his second marriage, Simon of Lochslin, sat in Parliament in 1640–41 and became father of George Mackenzie, who was born at Dundee, probably in 1636, but possibly in 1638. On his mother's side he was related to Sir Peter Wedderburn of Gosford (?–1679, advocate 1642), a Lord of Session (1668) and Clerk of the Privy Council.[2] Young Mackenzie attended King's College, Aberdeen, from 1650 and, from 1653, St. Leonard's College, St. Andrews. He studied thereafter at Bourges, which was famous for law.[3] On his return to Scotland he was called to the Bar in 1659 and readmitted in 1661, after the Restoration.

He rapidly won a place at the Bar, distinguishing himself by his bold defence of Argyll in 1661. He was made a justice-depute and became at once engaged in trying cases of witchcraft.[4] By the time he resigned that office in 1663[5] the rash of witch-hunting had abated and it may be that he and the other deputes had done something to discourage the practice.[6] In 1664 he appears as prosecutor, as substitute to the King's Advocate[7] but also appeared sometimes for the defence.[8] From 1663 onwards he is found regularly appearing in the Privy Council and the criminal courts.[9] Sometime about 1666 he was knighted.[10]

In 1669 he obtained a seat in Parliament as member for Ross-shire and from the start boldly and persistently opposed the policy of Lauderdale, the King's Commissioner in Scotland, and his corrupt administration. Lauderdale even thought of unseating him.[11] He opposed a proposal in 1669 for an incorporating union with England. In 1674–76 he was involved in the secession of the advocates, when the Earl of Dunfermline sued the Earl of Callendar and the latter, having had a procedural issue decided against him, intimated an appeal to Parliament.[12] The judges treated this as a contempt of court; Mackenzie and three others prepared a paper explaining the nature of the proposed appeal; the judges summoned the four before them, censured them and complained to the King, who commanded the advocates never to mention appeals. Most of the Bar left Edinburgh. Mackenzie persuaded the seceding advocates to return,[13] and moved over to a position of support for the Crown and the administration. He was made a member of the Privy Council.

In August 1677 Nisbet (Dirleton) was dismissed from the office of Lord Advocate and Mackenzie was appointed.[14] The prosecution of covenanters was zealously pursued, but the forms of justice were reasonably observed and he formulated rules requiring greater specification as to time and place in drawing indictments, which were probably fairer to the accused.[15] He is said to have secured that the choice of the jurors was by the judges, that the defender had the last word to the jury, except in treason cases, and to have excluded the clerk of court from the jurors' deliberations.[16]

After the battle of Bothwell Bridge (June 1679) the treatment of covenanters became even more severe, and the government relied on him both for the legislation against covenanters and the application of the law.[17] Graham of Claverhouse hunted down the covenanters and Mackenzie prided himself on ensuring that few escaped the penalties. He declared: "No king's advocate has ever screwed the prerogative higher than I have. I deserve to have my statue placed riding behind Charles II in the parliament close." He came to be called "Bloody Mackenzie." In 1680 he declared to Lauderdale that he had never lost a case for the King.[18]

A matter of some consequence is his use of torture. This has been frequently imputed to him. In his later *Vindication* he defended its legality, and its use at that time was undoubtedly competent and frequent. He seems undoubtedly to have strained the law to secure convictions, notably in the case of James Mitchell, who in 1668 sought to assassinate Archbishop Sharp. He was taken prisoner in 1674 and confessed his guilt.[19] At his first trial in 1674[20] Mackenzie had been his counsel and Mitchell withdrew his confession and the Lord Advocate (Nisbet) deserted the diet, but Mitchell was kept in prison. At his second trial in 1678[21] Mackenzie was prosecuting and proved Mitchell's guilt by the confession; Mitchell's defence was that he had made the confession in return for a promise that his life would be spared, but at the second trial Lord Chancellor Rothes, Lauderdale, Halton and Archbishop Sharp all denied that any such promise had been given, though Lockhart, for the defence, produced a copy of the Act of Council recalling the promise of life (thereby admitting that it had been given). Mitchell was hanged.

An equally flagrant case of stretching the law to secure conviction was the case of the Earl of Argyll, who was indicted in December 1681 for leasing-making, on account of a reservation made when making the declaration under the Test Act. Argyll was sentenced to death but escaped. In 1685 he was captured after an unsuccessful attempt to promote a rising. Mackenzie advised that he be not tried, but that the old sentence of 1681 be enforced.[22]

Mackenzie, who was elected Dean of Faculty in 1682, played a large part in establishing the Advocates' Library, since 1925 the National Library of Scotland.

In July 1680 a report to the Faculty of Advocates pointed out that if advocates who had failed to pay their entry-money could be coerced to do so there would be between £3000 and £4000 in cash which could be employed on the best and finest lawyers' and other rare books conform to a catalogue to be condescended on by the Faculty that the same may be a fund for any Bibliothek whereto many lawyers and others may leave their books.[23] In December the President (Stair) told the Dean for the Faculty's further encouragement towards a Bibliothecque that the Lords would concur that they might have the bygone protestation money lying in the Clerk of the Bills' hands if they would petition for it.[24] On the same day the Dean of Faculty recommended to a committee to report to the Lords the Faculty's resolution for employing part of their stock on a Bibliothecque and to desire their Lordships to interpose with the town of Edinburgh that a convenient Bibliothecque with a chamber and waiting room might be afforded in Thomas Robison's new Buildings.[25]

In June 1681 the Dean reported that the Lords would authorise the act of the Faculty imposing 500 marks on intrants in order to their Bibliothecque and that the town of Edinburgh in their new buildings should bigg to the Faculty ane large room with convenience for a Bibliothecque.[26] In January 1682 the Faculty elected Sir George Mackenzie Dean.[27] In March the Faculty authorised taking rooms to keep their books in, to repair the house and put up shelves or presses for their books and to advertise for books, and remitted to the Dean and any quorum of his council to consider what books were fit to be bought.[28]

In March 1689, shortly before he left Edinburgh, Mackenzie delivered a Latin inaugural address at the opening of the library. It was printed as *Oratio Inauguralis habita Edinburgi de Structura Bibliothecae Juridicae*.[29] The library's first catalogue, of 1692, gives the holdings as 3140 volumes, already a substantial collection.

In the difficulties over the Test Act, Mackenzie subscribed the required declaration[30] and avoided the trouble which affected Stair.

The bitterness between the government and the covenanters was exacerbated by the threat published by Renwick and others in 1684 to retaliate against their persecutors. Mackenzie in reply secured the passage of an enactment that "any person who owns, or will not disown the late treasonable declaration on oath, whether they have arms or not, be immediately put to death, this being done in the presence of two witnesses, and the person or persons having commission to this effect."[31] This inaugurated what became known as the Killing Time, when troops of dragoons shot down persons who merely refused to answer their questions.

In 1684, when the Privy Council was reconstituted, he was reappointed.[32] After the accession of James VII and II and the passing in 1686 of the Act abrogating the penal laws against Catholics,[33] Mackenzie was dismissed from the office of King's Advocate,[34] and for a time actually vigorously defended covenanter prisoners. In February 1688, however, he resumed his former office. Thereafter however, he prosecuted less violently than previously.

In the Convention Parliament of March 1689 he opposed the resolution moved by Sir John Dalrymple (Stair's son) that James VII had forefaulted the crown, arguing that his acts were protected by the declaration of Parliament that he was an absolute monarch, and he voted against the resolution.[35] Thereafter he was totally out of favour.

Shortly thereafter he went to England[36]; he found it impossible to continue in Edinburgh; despite attempts to have him punished for having decamped, no proceedings were in fact taken. In June 1690 he was admitted a student of Oxford University. In 1691 his *Institutions* were cited in Council as justifying a decision.[37] He died in London on May 6, 1691, and was buried in Greyfriars' Churchyard, Edinburgh. Mackenzie's first wife, Elizabeth, died in 1669 and he remarried in 1670. His widowed second wife about 1700 married his kinsman Roderick Mackenzie of Prestonhall (?–1712, advocate 1666), who was Lord Justice-Clerk 1702–04, an ordinary Lord of Session (Prestonhall) 1703–10, and thereafter Sheriff of Ross. From his eldest daughter, by his first marriage,

are descended the Marquises of Bute[38] and the Earls of Wharncliffe.[39]
His second daughter Elizabeth married Sir Archibald Cockburn of
Langton (?–1702, advocate, 1686) and then Sir James Mackenzie
(1671–1744, advocate 1698), third son of the Earl of Cromarty, a Lord of
Session (Royston) and of Justiciary, 1710–44.

Mackenzie had a reputation for his social gifts and his wit. He
undoubtedly fanatically hated the covenantors and pressed legal forms
and rules to their limits in his eagerness to secure convictions. On the
other hand he was devoted to literature and learning, and the steady
stream of his publications shows an underlying scholarly temperament.
Not least his foundation of the Advocates' Library is an act for which he
deserves eternal credit.

> "He was a gentleman of a pleasant and useful conversation, but a
> severe opposer of vicious and loose principles in whomsoever he
> found them. He was a great lover of the laws and customs of his
> country, and from his many excellent writings upon them it appears,
> that no man understood the law of nature, the law of nations, the
> civil law and the laws of his own country better than he did. He was
> regardless of riches and popularity, frugal in his expenses, and
> temperate in his diet, being a great enemy to all sorts of extrava-
> gances and debaucheries. He was a faithful friend, a loyal subject, an
> able statesman, a constant advocate for the clergy and university, a
> zealous defender of piety and religion, in all companies and on all
> occasions, against the attacks of atheists, deists and all sorts of
> sectaries that differed from the Church of England, of which he was a
> true and faithful son. His abilities in his profession were great, being
> a great master of eloquence, as it appeared in all his pleadings at the
> bar, which were constantly accompanied with all these hidden and
> wandering beauties that never fail to charm and captivate the
> affections of mankind, and which he never exerted but with the
> greatest integrity, being a person of strict honour and justice in all his
> actions. His natural parts were extraordinarily good, which he
> improved by indefatigable pains, and made himself thoroughly
> acquainted with all the best writers ancient and modern. The gaiety
> of his fancy, and fertility of his invention, were corrected by so exact
> a judgement, that he is copious upon all his subjects, and yet very
> close and pertinent; all his thoughts are clear and coherent, and his
> most serious discourses have such variety of curious remarks and
> observations, as render them very pleasant and diverting. . . . He
> was acquainted with most of the learned men in Britain, particularly
> with those of the University of Oxford, and of the Royal Society, that
> were alive whilst he was residing in England; nor was he less famous
> amongst the learned men abroad, especially amongst the learned
> lawyers in France and Holland. In one word, as he was a great
> ornament to his country, so he was a great honour to the noble family
> of which he was descended."[40]

His first published work was a novel, *Aretina*, in 1661,[41] followed in
1663 by *Religio Stoici*,[42] which showed that he was not in sympathy with
the covenanters, *A Moral Essay, Preferring Solitude to Public Employ-*

ment (1665),[43] *Moral Gallantry, a Discourse proving that the Point of Honour obliges a man to be Virtuous* (1667),[44] and *A Moral Paradox proving that it is much easier to be Virtuous than Vicious and a Consolation against Calumnies* (1667).[45] All of these moral writings went into second editions.

Then in 1672 he published *Pleadings in some remarkable cases before the Supreme Courts of Scotland since 1661, to which the Decisions are subjoined.*[46] It was reprinted in 1673 and 1704. These include his speech for the late Marquis of Argyle, and other genuine specimens, though one suspects that like Cicero's speeches for the defence, they were polished for publication. Some, such as For Maevia, accused of witchcraft, and For Titius, accused before the Secret Council for beating his wife, seem rather exercises than discourses delivered in actual cases.

In November 1672 the Privy Council granted named stationers a monopoly of reprinting and importing the book for 11 years.[47]

In 1675 he published *Observations upon the Act of Parliament 1621 against Dispositions made in Defraud of Creditors.*[48] Like a modern statute annotated, the commentary proceeds by careful examination of each successive important phrase in the Act, such as "to any conjunct and confident person." The explanations are detailed and mention numerous cases, sometimes without date or other identification but sometimes with their date. An unusual authority, several times cited, is the *Basilica.*[49]

In 1678 there was published in small octavo *A Discourse upon the Laws and Customs of Scotland in Matters Criminal*, a squarish small octavo of 581 pages. There were three editions by different printers in this one year and there was a new edition in tall octavo in 1699.[50] Mackenzie had practised mainly in the criminal courts all his career and must have been very familiar with criminal law and practice from personal experience. It was fulsomely dedicated to Lauderdale. In August 1677 the Privy Council granted Brown, Swinton & Glen the monopoly of printing and selling the works for 19 years.[51]

It was the first book in Scotland specifically about the criminal law. It is divided into two parts, the first dealing with crimes in general and specific crimes, the second with criminal jurisdiction and procedure. These are subdivided into 36 and 31 titles respectively. The first part is notable for commencing with an examination of crimes in general, how far dole or design is necessary to committing crimes, and of the capacity of minors, persons asleep or drunk, and of corporations to commit crimes. Conduct is a crime if it is declared such by express statute, or transgresses any municipal law which prohibits that which either the law of God or the civil law punishes criminally, or if the public peace is immediately disquieted or the law of nature is violated, as by incest or rape, or if long custom has punished it by corporal punishment or by a pecuniary mulct.[52] This is the first attempt in Scotland to arrive inductively at a concept of crime in general.

He observes that the law of God is the first fountain of our criminal law; "the decisions of our criminal court, as of all our other, do bind the same or succeeding judges, rather out of decency than necessity."[52] He observes further that we follow the civil law in judging crimes and that the fourth branch of our criminal law are the books of *Regiam Majestatem* which are *in Criminalibus* looked upon as authentic.[53] It is Mackenzie's "opinion that King James I[54] hath brought down some of these collections from England with him. Nor do I find these books cited before this time."[53] The sources of the criminal law are accordingly the law of God, decisions (*i.e.* common law), the civil law and *Regiam Majestatem*.

He discusses thoroughly the element of *dolus* or wicked design as a requisite of crimes.[55] The will is the only fountain of wickedness, but in some cases *dolus* may be inferred from conjectures and presumptions. He discusses drunkenness as a defence.[56]

In Title II he discusses the division of crimes, and then proceeds to the specific crimes; these include blasphemy, heresy, simony and barratry, treason, sedition, poison, fire-raising, witchcraft, murder, duels, self-murder, parricide, incest, sodomy, bestiality, rapes, adultery, bigamy, theft, theftboot and reset, hamesucken, usury and others.

There are many references to the civil law, European jurists and to decided Scottish cases. He again cites the *Basilica*, Theophilus and the Greek scholiasts because he concluded them the best interpreters of Justinian's texts.[57]

The Second Part deal with the jurisdiction of Parliament, the High Constable, the High Chamberlain, the Privy Council, the Exchequer, the Lords of Session, the Admiral, the Commissaries, Regalities, sheriffs, barons, justices of peace, and then deals with procedure and proof. Title 18 deals with Torture – "Torture is seldom used with us. . . . And the Council are so tender in Torture that . . ." Title 21 deals with the requisites of libels (*i.e.* indictments), and later titles deals with assisers, probation by confession, by oath, by writ and by presumptions, by witnesses, remissions and punishments.

Matters Criminal is a well-arranged, lucid and highly instructive book. When it was published it must have been absolutely invaluable to all who had anything to do with the criminal law. There was nothing before it, and *Matters Criminal* gave a thorough, systematic and detailed exposition of the whole of that branch of the law. It is still immensely interesting and valuable historically, and by no means to be neglected in discovering the rule in even a modern case. It is a most important and valuable work.

Then came *Observations upon the Laws and Customs of Nations as to Precedency: With the Science of Heraldry, treated as a part of the Civil Law and Law of Nations* (1680).[58] *Precedency* deals in nine chapters with the precedency of kings and commonwealths, that due to the Kings of Scotland, that the crown of Scotland was not subject to England, the debates between various kings, the precedencies amongst commonwealths, of the Electors and princes of the Empire, of churchmen, of subjects, and of women, and is followed by discussion of 44 questions concerning precedency. While not of much present value, there is much in this of historical interest and value.

Though the science of heraldry is broadly common to all the countries of Western Europe there are material variations in practice in Scotland as compared with other countries. Not least, heraldry has been precisely regulated by statute since well before the Union.[59] In 1324 King Robert I granted the office of Marischal of Scotland and the lands of Keith-Marischal to Keith and those bearing the name and arms of Keith.[60] A Scottish king of arms is mentioned in statute of 1482[61] and the title Lyon King or Lyon Herald is applied to the king's herald as early as 1377.[62] The earliest writing on heraldry was a short treatise by Bartolus da Sassoferrato, *Tractatus de Insigniis et Armis* of about 1356. Mackenzie's was the first Scottish work on the subject and it is still deemed authoritative both by later writers on the subject[63] and by the courts.[64] It is a substantial treatise, illustrated by numerous engravings of arms. Mackenzie lays down the general law of arms and comments on the statutes; in doing so he shows an extensive acquaintance with the European authorities from Bartolus onwards. In his preface, he says that "hearing, when I was beyond seas, Heraldry looked upon as the Science of Gentlemen and finding it taught as such in the Academies. I resolved to know somewhat of it, upon design rather to serve my country than to satisfy my curiosity: For it was justly admired, that we only of all nations had never published any thing to let the world know what marks of honour our predecessors had gained."

Later institutional writers say little or nothing of the law of heraldry and certainly add nothing to what has been said by Mackenzie. Though armorial bearings are a form of heritable property, Mackenzie is the only Scottish jurist who has studied the science which underlies the grant of arms.

His next work came out in 1681, *Idea eloquentiae forensis hodiernae*,[65] later translated by R. Hepburn as *An Idea of the Modern Eloquence of the Bar* (1711).

In 1683 appeared his *Vindication of the Government in Scotland during the reign of King Charles II against misrepresentations made in several scandalous Pamphlets*;[66] to which is added the *Method of proceeding against Criminals, as also of the Fanatical Covenants*,[67] as they were printed and published by themselves in that reign. There seems to have been a reissue in 1691.

In 1684 there appeared his *Institutions of the Law of Scotland*.[68] In his dedication to the Earl of Middleton,[69] Mackenzie observes that:

"The natural way of learning all arts and sciences is to know first the terms used in them, and the principles upon which they are founded, with the origins of the one and the reasons of the other. A collection of these terms and principles is, in law, called Institutions, and the natural and easy way of writing these, is by going from the first principle to a second, and from that to a third, the admired method of Euclid and his *Elements*, though much neglected by all who have written Institutions of Law ... I have therefore in these my Institutions treated of nothing save terms and principles ... in all which I have proceeded, building always one principle upon another, and expressing every thing in the terms of the civil law, or in the stile of ours respectively; so that if any man understand fully this little treatise, natural reason and thinking will easily supply much of what is diffused through our many volumes of treatises and decisions ... and I have often observed, that more lawyers are ignorant, for not understanding the first principle, than for not having read many books. . . ."

Mackenzie clearly had a rather different object in mind from that which Stair had, not to deduce law from its originals and compare it with other systems, but to define the terms and state the leading principles of Scots law concisely. There are no philosophical disquisitions but rather the approach of a skilled and scholarly practising lawyer, trying to set down the leading principles concisely. Compared with Stair's work this is a slight production, a small pocket-size duodecimo. It is in four books dealing with law, jurisdiction, courts and persons (Book I), heritable rights (Book II), obligations and succession (Book III), and actions, probation, sentences and execution, and crimes (Book IV). It is however a concise, clear and straightforward statement of principles: thus

> "Our municipal law of Scotland is made up partly of our written, and partly of our unwritten Law. Our written Law comprehends, First, our statutory law, which consists of our Statutes or Acts of Parliament. Secundo, the Acts of Sederunt, which are statutes made by the Lords of Session . . . Tertio, the Books of *Regiam Majestatem*, which are generally looked upon as part of our Law; which with the *Leges Burgorum*, and the other Tractates joined by Skeen to them, are called the Old Books of our Law, by many express Acts of Parliament. Though the Books of *Regiam Majestatem* were originally but works of one private Lawier, writing by way of Institution and are now very much abrogated by custom.
>
> "Our unwritten Law, comprehends the constant Tract of Decisions, past by the Lords of Session, which is considered as Law; the Lords respecting very much their own Decisions; and though they may, yet they use not to recede from them, except upon grave consideration. Secundo, our Ancient Customs, make up part of our Unwritten Law which have been universally received among us. The tacit consent of King and People operating as much in these as their express concourse does in making law. . . ."[70]

There are marginal references to statutes but no cases are cited.

The statement of principles is similarly concise and plain. "A contract is an agreement entered into by several persons, inducing an obligation by its own nature; and the obligations arising from contracts are divided and distinguished according as they are perfected, either by the sole consent of the contractors, or by the intervention or tradition of things; or lastly, by word or writ."[71]

Mackenzie was clearly influenced as to his order of treatment more by Justinian's *Institutions* than Stair was,[72] and indeed his work is closer in size, style and approach to Justinian than was Stair's. His view of law is positivist: law is the science which teaches us to do justice; it is divided into the law of nature, law of nations and the civil or municipal law of each particular country. The law of nature comprises all these common principles which are common to man and beast, innate, instinctive rather than positive law. The law of nations is peculiar to mankind and is divided into the primary law of nature flowing from right reason and the secondary law of nature, consisting of those general conclusions in which ordinarily all nations agree, including obligations arising from promises or contracts and the like. Civil or municipal laws are the particular laws and customs of every nation or people who are under one sovereign power.

The civil law of Rome "is much respected generally, so it has great influence in Scotland, except where our own laws or customs have receded from it. And by the common law in our Acts of Parliament is meant the civil law of the Romans." The canon law is yet much respected among us, especially in what relates to conscience and ecclesiastic rights.[73]

Mackenzie put out a revised edition in 1688. Later editions bear to be revised, corrected and augmented. Thus in the fourth edition (1706) the bookseller states that he got Mr William Forbes to revise Lord Whitelaw's short marginal notes, add some others, explain things not so clearly expressed, correct some of the citations and set down the innovations since the author's time. An edition with notes by John Spottiswoode appeared in 1723. The seventh edition (1730) bears to be revised and corrected by Alexander Bayne JMP.[74]

The book clearly proved popular and useful; it had reached an eighth edition by 1758, apart from a London edition of 1694 and the edition included in the folio *Works*, and was taken as the textbook generally used by young men studying law until the publication of Erskine's *Principles* in 1754. For that purpose it was excellent, more suitable than Stair's ponderous, philosophic discourse.

The same year saw the appearance of *Jus Regium, or the Just and Solid Foundations of Monarchy in general and more particularly of the monarchy of Scotland; against Buchanan,*[75] *Naphthali,*[76] *Dolman,*[77] *Milton,*[78] *etc.,*[79] an answer to Buchanan's *De Jure Regni Apud Scotos*, and other works such as the fanatical manifesto *Jus Populi Vindicatum* by James Stewart, published in 1669 and advocating the hanging of bishops and the enforcement of presbytery in Scotland and England. There were three editions in the year of publication, which indicates that it aroused considerable interest. In effect Mackenzie was arguing for a high view of monarchical power against those who contended for limited monarchy.

On the Discovery of the Fanatick Plot (1684) was followed by *A Defence of the Antiquity of the Royal Line of Scotland in answer to William Lloyd, Bishop of St. Asaph,*[80] *with a True Account when the Scots were governed by the Kings in the Isle of Britain* (1685),[81] which defends the mythical line of Scottish kings against aspersions. It was followed by *The Antiquity of the Royal Line of Scotland further cleared and defended against the exceptions lately offered by Dr. Stillingfleet in his Vindication of the Bishop of St. Asaph* (1686)[82] which, translated into Latin, was published at Utrecht in 1689.

Next year (1686) there appeared *Observations on the Acts of Parliament made by James I and his successors to the end of the reign of Charles II.*[83] This is a major work, a tall quarto of nearly 500 pages, noting in respect of each Act, whether it is in desuetude, abrogated, limited or enlarged, what decisions have been given in relation to it; some undecided matters are discussed and parallel citations from the civil, canon, feudal and municipal laws and the laws of other nations adduced for explaining these statutes. The Acts are cited sometimes from Skene, sometimes from Glendook. The explanations are clear and workmanlike, and the work must have been of great utility. It is still valuable as near-contemporary commentary on the legislation. Mackenzie himself sought a monopoly of printing and selling the work.[84]

Then came *A Memorial to the Parliament by two persons of Quality* (1689),[85] his *Oratio Inauguralis* (1689),[86] *Reason, An Essay* (1690),[87] and *The Moral History of Frugality and its Opposite Vices* (1691).[88]

A *Treatise of Tailies*[89] is a short treatise but of interest, being from the pen of the man credited with framing the Entail Act 1685. A *Treatise of Actions*[90] is also a short treatise but clear and plain. It is our first text entirely concerned with remedies and the legal procedure to obtain them.

In 1699 there appeared posthumously a folio *On the Act of James VI against Dispositions made in Defraud of Creditors*. This seems to be a reissue of his book of 1675 on the Bankruptcy Act 1621.

There was a continuing demand for Mackenzie's writings and in 1716–22 were published, in a subscription edition, in two tall folios *The Works of that eminent and learned Lawyer, Sir George Mackenzie of Rosehaugh, Advocate to King Charles II and King James VII*.[91] This edition omits *Aretina* and the *Fanatick Plot* and prints one or two minor works for the first time, particularly the *Discourse concerning the Three Unions between Scotland and England*.[92] The three which he distinguishes were the union which ensued as the proper and natural effect of King James's succession to the Crown of England, the union which was the product of the treaty 1604, and the third is to be that union designed by King Charles II in 1667. The consideration of the first embodies much detailed historical discussion, mainly designed to establish that England did not take over Scotland. Mackenzie clearly supported the proposed union of 1670.

Also very interesting and apparently printed for the first time in the *Works*[93] is his *Characteres Quorundam apud Scotos Advocatorum*, a series of sketches (in Latin) of some of the leading advocates of his time, Gilmour senior and junior, Nisbet (Dirleton), Nicholson Junior, Wedderburn (Gosford), Kerr, Lockhart, Cunningham and some others.

His *Memoirs of the Affairs of Scotland*, a long-lost fragment of a *History of the Affairs of Scotland from the Restauration of King Charles II, 1660, to 1691*,[94] which is said to have been submitted to Lauderdale for his revision,[95] was published in 1821 and an *Account of the Law and Government of Scotland* was printed in 1908 in *Macfarlane's Geographical Collections*, Volume III.[96] *A Collection about Families in Scotland from their Charters* is still in manuscript, and he also collected a *Genealogy of Families of Scotland*.[97]

An inevitable observation is of amazement that a man, busily engaged as a Privy Councillor, in practice, and particularly as chief prosecutor for the Crown, and with such a deplorable reputation for vindictive prosecution, should have produced such a steady stream of publications, including at least half-a-dozen which are noteworthy and have proved of permanent value and importance. His *Matters Criminal, Precedency and Science of Heraldry, Institutions* and *Observations on the Acts of Parliament* are still very valuable authorities. His *Jus Regium* is a minor classic in the history of political thought and his *Memoirs* is a valuable historical source. His *Idea Eloquentiae Forensis Hodiernae* earned acclaim from the professors at Bourges, from John Voet of Leiden, Ulric Huber of Franeker, John Hixdorf of Dantzig and Doujat of Paris[98]. These works display very extensive scholarship and acquaintance with continental sources. Even assuming amanuenses to help him, Mackenzie must have devoted considerable time and thought regularly, despite the calls of other commitments, to research and writing. He clearly was well-read, and had very broad interests in law and a very deep interest in its elucidation and exposition. And not least, his achievement in establishing the Advocates' Library can never be forgotten.

NOTES

¹ DNB; Anderson, SN., III, pp. 20, 22; Chambers, BDES; biography, probably by Ruddiman, in folio edition of Mackenzie's *Works*; Andrew Lang, *Sir George Mackenzie of Rosehaugh, His Life and Times* (1909); Omond, *Lord Advocates*, I, p. 200; Taylor Innes in *Contemporary Review* (1871), pp. 18, 248; J. W. Barty (ed.), *Ancient Deeds and Other Writs in the Mackenzie-Wharncliffe Charter Chest* (1906); (1901) 9 S.L.T. 1 (portrait). Many mentions of his forensic appearances are in *Records of the Proceedings of the Justiciary Court*, 1661–78 (ed. Scott-Moncrieff, S.H.S., 1905). He should not be confused with his second cousin Sir George Mackenzie of Tarbat (1630–1714), a judge as Lord Tarbat (1661–64), later Lord Justice-General (1678), Lord Clerk Register and an Ordinary Lord of Session (1681), Viscount Tarbat (1685), Lord Clerk-Register again (1692–95), Earl of Cromarty (1703) and Lord Justice-General again (1705–10). He was one of the original Fellows of the Royal Society. On him see DNB; Brunton & Haig, p. 356; *Scots Peerage*, III, 69; Sir William Fraser, *The Earls of Cromartie* (2 vols., 1876); Earl of Cromartie, *A Highland History* (1979). A son of the third Earl raised the 73rd Highlanders, later the 71st, and later the 1st Battn. Highland Light Infantry.

² Brunton & Haig, p. 394.

³ In the preface to his *Heraldry* he refers to having had intimacy with the most learned advocates at Bourges in France.

⁴ RPC (3rd), I, 11, 17, 26.

⁵ RPC (3rd), I, 470.

⁶ In the chapter on Witchcraft in his *Laws and Customs of Scotland in Matters Criminal* (1678), pp. 80–108, he narrates some personal experiences with alleged witches and indicates lack of personal conviction in the existence of witchcraft.

⁷ *Records of the Justiciary Court* (S.H.S.), I, 97.

⁸ *Records*, I, 117, 129, 134; RPC (3rd), II, 231.

⁹ RPC (3rd), II–XII, *passim*.

¹⁰ Laing, p. 325. He became known as "of Rosehaugh." This was an estate built up from various properties around Avoch and Fortrose in the Black Isle: Barty, p. 51. The place was previously known as Petconachy (or variants thereof) and Mackenzie imposed the new name Rosehaugh (*a valle rosarum*) from the large number of wild roses which bloomed there and which gave him much pleasure: W. J. Watson, *Place Names of Ross and Cromarty* (1904), p. 132. A grandiose Victorian house was built in the 19th century but has now been demolished.

¹¹ Mackenzie, *History*, p. 173.

¹² RPC (3rd), IV, 284.

¹³ RPC (3rd), IV, 309, 395.

¹⁴ RPC (3rd), V, 232. Thereafter he was a regular attender at Council and various committees thereof.

¹⁵ Mackenzie, *History*, pp. 322–323.

¹⁶ Life, in *Works*, I, p. vii.

¹⁷ RPC (3rd), V, 255–256.

¹⁸ *Lauderdale Papers*, III, 192.

¹⁹ Mackenzie's pleadings are in *Works*, I, pp. 118–121.

²⁰ For the first trial see *Records of the Justiciary Court* (ed. Scott-Moncrieff, S.H.S.), II, 255.

²¹ For the second trial see *Records of the Justiciary Court,* II, App.

²² It is fair to remember that in those days prosecutors took a more vigorous line than they do today; they were expected not to present the case but to secure a conviction. Compare for example, Sir Edward Coke's approach at the trial of Sir Walter Raleigh and Judge Jeffrey's Bloody Assizes, dealing with those captured after Monmouth's rebellion in 1685.

²³ Faculty of Advocates Minute Book (ed. Pinkerton, Stair Soc.), I, p. 47.

²⁴ *Ibid.*, I, p. 51.

²⁵ *Ibid.*, I, p. 53.

²⁶ *Ibid.*, I, p. 57.

²⁷ *Ibid.*, I, p. 58.

²⁸ *Ibid.*, I, 59. Further entries relative to the library are on pp. 60, 61, 65, 66, 83. The first recorded gift was by Mackenzie, the *Tractatus Tractatuum*, in 12 vols., folio.

²⁹ *Works*, I, p. 1. Translated by J. H. Loudon, *Trans. Edinburgh Bibliographical Soc.*

(1946), 11, 275. See also W. K. Dickson, "The Advocates' Library" (1902) 14 J. R. 1, 113, 214; "The National Library" (1928) 40 J.R. 172; "David Hume and the Advocates' Library" (1932) 44 J.R. 1.

[30] RPC (3rd), VII, 708, 719, 799, 803.

[31] RPC (3rd) IX, 156.

[32] RPC (3rd), IX, 33; XI, 13.

[33] APS, VIII, 579–581; Wodrow, II, App. cxxix and cxxxiv; cf. RPC (3rd), XIII, 123–124, 156–158.

[34] RPC (3rd), XII, 221, 228.

[35] Balcarres, Memoirs, p. 35.

[36] RPC (3rd), XIV, 93.

[37] RPC (3rd), XVI, 134.

[38] Scots Peerage, II, 298, 300. Mackenzie's estates passed via Sir Archibald Cockburn of Langton to James, second Earl of Bute.

[39] Scots Peerage, II, 303.

[40] Life, in Works, I, pp. xvii–xviii.

[41] It is summarised in Lang, pp. 26–30; it is not reprinted in the Works. There is a Bibliography of the writings of Sir George Mackenzie, Lord Advocate, Founder of the Advocates' Library, by P. S. Ferguson in Papers of the Edinburgh Bibliographical Society, Vol. 14.

[42] Works, I, pp. 39–74.

[43] Works, I, pp. 77–97.

[44] Works, I, pp. 99–121.

[45] Works, I, pp. 121–140.

[46] Works, Legal Treatises, I, pp. 9–102.

[47] RPC (3rd), III, 606.

[48] Works, II, pp. 1–50. A second edition "corrected and in several paragraphs much enlarged" was published with the second edition of Matters Criminal in 1699.

[49] A compilation in Greek, made about A.D. 900 under the instructions of the Eastern Roman Emperor Basil I and completed by his son Leo VI the Wise. It is in 60 books and became the foundation of Byzantine jurisprudence. It was first generally published only in the 17th century. See also Collinet, "Byzantine Legislation," Camb. Med. Hist. (1923) IV, Chap. 20; Scheltema, "Byzantine Law", Camb. Med. Hist. (1967) IV (2), Chap. 21; F. H. Lawson, "The Basilica" (1931) 46 L.Q.R. 486; (1932) 47 L.Q.R. 536.

[50] Works, II, pp. 49–275. To the second edition is added by way of Appendix a Treatise on Mutilation and Demembration and their Punishments, by Sir Alexander Seton of Pitmedden, Bart.

[51] RPC V, 218–219.

[52] Tit. I, sec. 3.

[53] Tit. I, sec. 3.

[54] i.e. James I of Scotland (1406–37), not James VI and I (1567–1625).

[55] Title I, sec. 4.

[56] Title I, sec. 7.

[57] The Author's Design, prefaced to the work (Works, II, 51).

[58] Works, II, pp. 511–573 and 575–635.

[59] e.g. Lyon King of Arms Acts, 1592 (APS, III, 554, c. 29); 1662 (APS, VII, 404, c. 53); 1663 (APS, VII, 458, c. 15); 1672 (APS, VIII, 123, c. 47).

[60] APS, I, 482–483.

[61] APS, II, 143, c. 1.

[62] Exchequer Rolls, II, 553.

[63] e.g. J. H. Stevenson, Heraldry in Scotland (1914); T. Innes of Learney, Scots Heraldry (1956). Stevenson's book contains plates of the armorial achievement of Sir James Balfour of Pittendreich February 6, 1566/67 (p. 88), and of the arms of Sir James Dalrymple of Stair, Lord President (later Viscount Stair), February 21, 1673 (p. 152).

[64] e.g. Stewart Mackenzie v. Fraser Mackenzie, 1922 S.C. (H.L.) 39; Maclean of Ardgour v. Maclean, 1941 S.C. 662.

[65] Works, Legal Treatises, I, pp. 103–137.

[66] Works, II, pp. 341–354.

[67] This is probably the work reprinted in Works, II, p. 351, as A true Account of the Forms used in Pursuits of Treasons.

[68] *Works*, II, pp. 277–340. John Reid printed the *Institutions* and in March 1684 secured from the Privy Council a monopoly in the work for 19 years: RPC (3rd), VIII, 410.

[69] *Works*, II, pp. 277–278.

[70] I, 1.

[71] III, 1, 5.

[72] See I, 2, 1.

[73] I, 1, 3–8.

[74] *Juris Municipalis Professor*. Bayne was Professor of Scots Law in Edinburgh University. In 1731 he published *Notes for the Use of Students of the Municipal Law in the University of Edinburgh. Being a supplement to Sir George Mackenzie's Institutions.*

[75] George Buchanan (1506–82), in *De Jure Regni apud Scotos* (1578), justified the dethronement of Mary, Queen of Scots. Kings, he asserted, exist only for public purposes, and powers given to a king can be taken away. On Buchanan's views in this work see P. Hume Brown, *George Buchanan*, p. 268; W. S. McKechnie, "De Jure Regni Apud Scotos," in *George Buchanan, Glasgow Ouatercentenary Studies*, 1906; I. D. McFarlane, *Buchanan*, p. 392; J. W. Allen, *History of Political Thought in the Sixteenth Century*, p. 336; Q. Skinner, *Foundations of Modern Political Thought*, II, p. 342.

[76] A Presbyterian clergyman, Stirling, published in 1667 *Naphtali, or The Wrestling of the Church of Scotland for the Kingdom of Christ*, a violently Covenanting work. On legal matters he had the assistance of James Stewart (1635–1715) later (1692) Lord Advocate. It was answered by Andrew Honyman, Bishop of Orkney (1619–76) in his *Survey of the Insolent and Infamous Libel entitled Naphtaly*, in two parts (1668–69). To this in turn Stewart rejoined in *Jus Populi Vindicatum, or the People's Right to Defend Themselves, and their Covenanted Reign vindicated* (1669) and then had to flee the country. On Stewart see further Chap. 10, *infra*. One Andrew Kennedy was tried in 1672 for publishing *Naphtali* and *Jus Populi Vindicatum*, "treasonable pamphlets", and put to the horn: *Records of the Justiciary Court* (ed. Scott-Moncrieff, S.H.S.), II, pp. 109–110.

[77] Robert Parsons (1546–1610), Jesuit missionary, published in 1594, under the name Doleman, a *Conference about the next Succession to the Crown of England*, contending that the powers of a monarch should always be limited by law. Kings exist for the welfare of their subjects. Parliament made it high treason to possess a copy. See DNB and authorities there cited; Allen, *supra*, p. 260.

[78] John Milton (1608–74), the poet, as secretary to Cromwell's Council of State wrote *The Tenure of Kings and Magistrates* (1649), *Eikonoklastes* (1649), and *First* (1651) and *Second* (1654) *Defences of the People of England*, justifying the Puritan revolution and the dethronement and execution of King Charles I.

[79] *Works*, II, pp. 439–483.

[80] Lloyd had published a work *An Historical Account of Church Government* (1684), which offended Mackenzie's nationalist spirit by denying the antiquity of the Scottish monarchy. In fact Lloyd was substantially right historically and Mackenzie seriously wrong. On the controversy see Fountainhall, *Historical Observes*, p. 155.

[81] *Works*, II, pp. 355–396.

[82] *Works*, II, pp. 397–438.

[83] *Works, Legal Treatises*, I, pp. 165–443.

[84] RPC (3rd), XII, 140, 143.

[85] Not in *Works*. The two were Mackenzie and the Earl of Seaforth.

[86] *Works, Legal Treatises*, I, pp. 1–6.

[87] *Works*, I, pp. 167–192.

[88] *Works*, I, pp. 141–165.

[89] *Works*, II, pp. 484–491.

[90] *Works*, II, pp. 492–510.

[91] In this edition Vol. I contains his poems, a life (probably by Thomas Ruddiman) and the moral essays, and separately paginated, some of his legal writings. Vol. II, also separately paginated, contains legal writings only.

[92] *Works*, II, pp. 637–670.

[93] *Works, Legal Writings*, I, pp. 6–7.

[94] This work is mentioned in proposals issued in 1714 for the publication of Mackenzie's *Works* and an advertisement in the second volume of his *Works* (1722) stated that this manuscript was in the hands of some of the author's relations who did not think it ready for the press until revised and it was to appear as an Appendix to that volume, but never did.

The MS. of parts of it turned up in a collection of waste paper in 1816 or 1817 and was printed by Thomas Thomson.

[95] *Lauderdale Papers*, III, p. 219.
[96] ed. Mitchell and Clark (S.H.S., Vol. 53), 1908.
[97] At Blairs College: H.M.C. 2nd Rep., App. 201.
[98] Life, in *Works*, I, p. x.

CHAPTER 10

THE MINOR JURISTS OF THE SEVENTEENTH CENTURY

THE seventeenth century is undoubtedly dominated by Hope, Stair and Mackenzie. But there were others who made contributions to legal literature which were significant in their time and deserve to be remembered. Their works can be considered under six heads, editions of the statutes, compilations of practicks and collections of decisions, narrative texts, compilations of styles or forms, and writings on other matters related to law.

AN EDITOR OF THE STATUTES

Throughout most of the seventeenth century judges and lawyers used the *Black Acts* or Skene's *Laws and Acts* as their text of the Statutes. Sir Thomas Murray of Glendoick or Glendook (?–1684, advocate 1661)[1] was elevated to the Bench in 1674 and became a baronet in 1676. By the influence, it is recorded, of the Duchess of Lauderdale he was appointed Clerk Register in 1677. In 1679 he was granted a licence to print an edition of the statutes, with the exclusive privilege of doing so for 19 years and prohibition of others from doing so under penalty of £500 Scots.[2] When Lauderdale fell from power he lost both his judgeship and the office of Clerk Register, which latter office was conferred on Sir George Mackenzie of Tarbat.

Glendook's edition appeared in a large folio in 1681 and in two thick duodecimo volumes in 1682–83. The folio edition is a large handsome book, well printed, with engravings of the pre-Union royal arms and of portraits of the monarchs. It contains the statutes from King James I to King Charles II, and the Acts of the Conventions of 1665, 1667 and 1678. There are sometimes bound in with these *An Abridgment of the Acts of Parliament digested into Heads, in alphabetical order*, compiled by Sir James Stewart of Gutters or Goodtrees (45 pages),[3] a Table of all the Kings of Scotland from Fergus the First, said to have reigned in 330 B.C., to Charles II, Skene's *De Verborum Significatione* "now reprinted by His Majestie's special command," and the Acts of the first Parliament of James VII of 1685–86. The materials bear to have been "Collected and Extracted from the Publick Records of the said Kingdom."

The duodecimo edition bears to be in two parts: Part 1 (Volume 1) contains the statutes from James I to James VI; Part 2 (Volume 2) contains the Acts of Charles I, the submissions and surrenders of teinds and the King's decreets arbitral following thereon, the Acts of Charles II, the Acts of the Conventions, and an Index or Abridgment of the whole Acts of Parliament and Conventions, dated 1685. Uniform with these two volumes is a volume containing the Acts of James VII, Acts and Orders of the meeting of the Estates of 1689, the legislation of William and Mary and of Anne, down to the final adjournment of the Parliament of

Scotland, all printed by Robert Freebairn and Co., His Majesty's Printers, in 1731.

Cosmo Innes observed[4] that Glendook's edition "is copied implicitly from that of Skene in 1597, and from the subsequent sessional publications. This is the more unpardonable, that he professes to have extracted the work from the original Records of Parliament; whereas, in fact, even the more accurate and ample edition in 1566 does not appear to have been consulted. Yet it is this edition, that, for more than a century, has been usually quoted in all our Courts of Justice as a correct and genuine code of the Laws of Scotland." He also observed[4] that the folio edition "is the least inaccurate; having been purged of some of the more palpable typographical errors of Skene's edition, which had been retained" in the duodecimo. Glendook accordingly deserves little credit for the work. Even since the publication of the more accurate Record edition, by Thomas Thomson and Cosmo Innes (12 volumes, 1834–75) Glendook's edition has been too frequently referred to, and many references to the statutes in cases and books are to his text and numbering of the statutes rather than that of the Record edition (the *Acts of the Parliaments of Scotland*).[5]

An abridgment of the statutes seems also to have been made by Charles Maitland, Lord Halton (?–1691), ordinary Lord 1669,[6] brother of the second Earl of Lauderdale and himself third Earl. In Lord Fountainhall's library catalogue there appears, under the date 1678, an entry: "Lo. Halton on Statuts and acts of parliat. 12 pence."[7] No copy of this work seems to have survived. In the next century there were several other abridgments.[8]

In 1672 Parliament[9] ratified a royal grant of 1671 to Andrew Anderson for 41 years of the sole right of printing the Acts of Parliament, Proclamations, etc., and "books of the common and civil law." Anderson worked in Edinburgh, 1653–57, in Glasgow 1657–61, and in Edinburgh 1661–76. He had been appointed printer to the Town and College of Edinburgh in 1663. He died in 1676. His widow continued the business with or on behalf of their son and heir, James, and sought vigorously to enforce her monopoly privilege.[10] In 1687 the Town Council gave Anderson's widow the right to establish her presses in the College below the Library and she remained in business there until her death in 1716.[11]

The imprints Heir of Andrew Anderson, Heirs of Andrew Anderson, Relict of Andrew Anderson, successors of Andrew Anderson, and Heirs and Successors of Andrew Anderson, appear between 1676 and 1716. Anderson and his widow, heirs and successors, as a group were printers of hundreds of books, including many legal works, over these years.[12]

THE COMPILATIONS OF PRACTICKS

Though most of the manuscripts are entitled *Practicks* a distinction must be drawn between those who compiled digest-Practicks, including materials drawn from all kinds of sources, the Auld Laws, statutes, Acts of Council and of Sederunt, and decisions, and those who made notes of decisions only. The first group in the seventeenth century comprises not only Hope's *Minor Practicks* and his *Major Practicks* but others.

An anonymous MS., once in the possession of Charles Erskine, Lord Justice-Clerk Tinwald, contains a digest-Practicks which includes decisions from at least 1501 to 1606. The compiler is unknown but the guess has been hazarded[13] that it is the work of Alexander Seton (1555–1622, advocate c. 1577), successively an Extraordinary Lord (Pluscarden) (1586), an Ordinary Lord (Urquhart) (1587), Lord President (1593), a peer as Lord Fyvie (1598), Lord Chancellor of Scotland (1604–22) and first Earl of Dunfermline in 1606.[14]

Sir William Oliphant of Newton (1551–1628, advocate 1577)[15] was justice-depute and depute-advocate for Sir Thomas Hamilton in 1604. He was made a judge in 1611 and Lord Advocate in 1612 in room of Hamilton. In 1626 he was removed from the Bench in consequence of the King's resolution that no officer of state should be an Ordinary Lord of Session. He made a collection of decisions, statutes and customs.[16] His son John, advocate 1608, was an ordinary Lord 1629–32.[17]

Thomas Hamilton of Drumcairn (c. 1563–1637, advocate 1587)[18] became an ordinary Lord in 1592 and was named along with Skene on the commission for printing the Acts of Parliament. He then became first joint (1596) and then sole (1597) Lord Advocate, was a commissioner for union in 1604, Clerk Register in 1612 in succession to Skene, then Secretary of State, and in 1613 a peer as Lord Binning. In 1616 he became Lord President and as such entertained King James when he visited Edinburgh in 1617; in 1619 he became Earl of Melrose, a title which in 1627 he exchanged for that of Earl of Haddington. In 1626 he resigned the office of Lord President, and in 1627 the office of Secretary, becoming Lord Privy Seal. He is said to have amassed a large fortune, mostly invested in land. From him are descended the modern Baillie-Hamiltons, Earls of Haddington. One of his descendants became the mother of Sir David Dalrymple, Lord Hailes.[19] To him are attributed two collections under alphabetical heads covering 1609–13 and 1622–23, and, more valuable, a collection of notes of decisions covering 1592–1628 in three folio volumes, one being an index of subjects. Stair makes frequent reference to cases collected by Haddington, and Morison in his *Dictionary* printed about a quarter of these cases. He also transcribed parts of the Exchequer Rolls and of the Register of the Privy Council, and some of his State Papers were published by the Abbotsford Club in 1837.

John Spottiswood(e), Spotiswood or Spotswood (1565–1639)[20] became an extraordinary Lord of Session in 1610 and then was Archbishop of St. Andrews 1615–39 and Lord Chancellor 1635–39. He was King James's great instrument for introducing episcopal government into the church in Scotland, and consequently hated by the Presbyterians, and was author of the *History of the Church and State of Scotland from 203 to 1625*, first published in 1655. His second son Robert (1596–1646)[21] became a Privy Councillor, an extraordinary Lord in 1622 and an ordinary Lord as Lord New Abbey in 1626 and was promoted President in 1633 in succession to Sir James Skene. He was taken prisoner at Philiphaugh and executed by the Covenanters in 1646. He compiled a thin *Practicks of the Law of Scotland*, published, with a memoir of him, by his grandson John (1665–1728, advocate 1696)[22] in 1706. The decisions are arranged under subject-headings along with extracts from

Justinian, Craig, the Scots statutes and other sources. The reports are brief and not very informative but Stair cited them frequently from a MS.

Sir George Lockhart of Carnwath (?1630–1689, advocate 1656),[23] son of Sir James Lockhart of Lee (?–1674), judge (1646) and Lord Justice-Clerk, 1671–74,[24] served as Advocate to the Protector in 1658–61 and, in consequence, though pardoned at the Restoration, had to express contrition to Charles II. He became an eloquent pleader, rivalling Sir George Mackenzie. In 1672 he became Dean of the Faculty of Advocates. In 1685 he succeeded Sir David Falconer as Lord President. In 1689 he was shot in the High Street in Edinburgh by John Chiesley of Dalry for having decided in favour of Chiesley's wife in an action for aliment. He left a MS. *Compend* of Durie. His brother Sir John Lockhart of Castlehill, (?1632–?1700, advocate 1656), Lord of Session in 1665,[25] is mentioned by Forbes[26] as one who digested decisions under alphabetical heads of law.

His son George (1673–1731)[27] was a prominent Jacobite and author of *Memoirs of the Affairs of Scotland from Queen Anne's Accession to the commencement of the Union of the two Kingdoms of Scotland and England in May 1707*. His *Papers on the Affairs of Scotland* including his *Memoirs* and other materials was published in 1817 and is a valuable historical source.

Sir Thomas Wallace of Craigie (?–1680, advocate c. 1660)[28] was a Lord of Session from 1671 to 1680 and Lord Justice-Clerk from 1675. To him are attributed a MS. *Law Repertorie and Collection*.

There exists also in MS. an anonymous three-volume *Observations on the Practicks* of Durie, Hope, Balfour, Spotiswoode and Haddington, which belongs to the latter seventeenth century.

THE COLLECTORS OF DECISIONS

The group who collected decisions in the seventeenth century was a substantial one. Apart from the collections which can be assigned to their collector there are several anonymous collections.

Alexander Gibson (?–1644)[29] married the eldest daughter of Sir Thomas Craig of Riccarton, became a clerk of session in 1594 and was in 1621 elevated to the Bench, taking the title of Lord Durie; he was knighted some time before 1628. In 1633 he was one of the commission appointed to review the laws[30] and, during the period when the office of President was elective, he was twice so elected and was regularly vice-president. During the years he sat as judge, 1621–42, he noted the decisions of the court and these were published by his grandson[31] in 1690 by warrant of the Court as *The Decisions of the Lords of Council and Session in Most Cases of Importance, Debated and brought before them: from July 1621 to July 1642*. It bears to be corrected and revised by W.A.J.C., *i.e.* William Alexander, Juris Consultus. It is a big volume of 900 pages, dedicated to Stair and the 13 other judges. The reports are chronological and substantial, not mere notes, and explain the points at issue. Stair frequently refers to Durie. An interesting feature is the mention of the counsel involved. These are the reports of cases earliest in date as distinct from the mere notes of cases contained in *Practicks*.[32] Some are reprinted in Morison's *Dictionary*, Supplement Volume. Forbes[33] characterises Durie as "a man of a penetrating wit and clear judgment, polished and improved by much study and exercise. He is said to have been constantly studying the civil law." His eldest son, of the same name (?–1656)[34] became Clerk Register in 1641 and a judge in 1646, taking the same title.

Haddington's substantial collection of cases (1592–1628) has already been mentioned when discussing his *Practicks*.

Sir Thomas Nicolson of Carnock (1609–56, advocate 1632)[35] was Lord Advocate from 1649 to 1656; he was an eloquent pleader eulogised by Mackenzie[36] and made a collection of decisions still unprinted. They number 620 and are grouped according to subject-matter.[37] The termini are 1610 and 1632. A few of them are reprinted in Morison's *Dictionary* and the rest in Brown's *Supplement*, Volume I.

Sir John Gilmour of Craigmillar (?–1671)[38] passed advocate in 1628 and was one of Montrose's counsel in 1641. When the Court of Session was re-established in 1661 he was appointed Lord President and played a prominent part in public life until he resigned in 1670. Mackenzie[39] described him as a man of rough eloquence and powerful common sense, but little learning, but the publisher of his *Decisions*[40] said he had obtained the character of The Honest President. *The Decisions of the Lords of Council and Session in Sundry Important Cases, plead before them from July 1661 to July 1666. Observed by Sir John Gilmour of Craigmillar, at that time President of the College of Justice* was published in a small octavo, along with Falconer's *Decisions*, in 1701 by John Spottiswood of that Ilk, advocate. There are 188 cases in 136 pages, set down chronologically. They are merely records of the contentions and the decisions and not very informative.

John Nisbet (?1609–1687)[41] was a grandson of Margaret, sister of Sir Thomas Craig of Riccarton, and a son of Patrick Nisbet, Lord Eastbank. He passed advocate in 1633 and in 1641 defended Montrose. In 1664 he was appointed Lord Advocate and also raised to the Bench as Lord Dirleton, being the last person to hold these posts concurrently. He was a harsh persecutor of the covenanters and sometimes acted unscrupulously to secure convictions. In 1670 he was a commissioner anent union with England and opposed the disappearance of the separate Scottish Parliament. In 1677 he was forced to resign office, being succeeded by Mackenzie. There was published in quarto in 1698 *Some Doubts and Questions in the Law Especially of Scotland, as also, Some Decisions of the Lords of Council and Session, Collected and Observed by Sir John Nisbet of Dirleton, Advocate to King Charles II*. The *Doubts* are under alphabetical headings. The usual form is a statement of an uncertain point, followed by *Quaeritur*, whether.... There is some discussion of the difficulty, but an answer is usually not hazarded. The *Doubts* were written without any order but the work was brushed into form and method by Sir William Hamilton of Whitelaw, Lord Justice-Clerk.[42] The *Decisions*, which are in the same volume but separately paginated, cover December 1665 to June 1677 and are frequently substantial reports of 462 cases, noted chronologically. The book was published by Robert Bennet, advocate.

Burnet[43] describes him as "one of the worthiest and most learned men of his age" and as a man of great learning, both in law and many other things; he is said to have been devoted to the study of Greek. Mackenzie described him as pleading cases with the utmost learning and consummate eloquence.[44]

Sir James Stewart of Gutters or Goodtrees (1635–1713, advocate 1713)[45] wrote an *Answers to Dirleton's Doubts in the Laws of Scotland* which were not published until 1715 and 1762.

Sir David Falconer of Newton (1640–86)[46] passed advocate in 1661, later became one of the commissaries of Edinburgh and was knighted. In 1676 he became a judge and President of the Court in 1682. The publisher of his *Decisions*[47] says he was reckoned "One of the most painful [painstaking] Lawyers in his time." He made a small collection of decisions from November 1681 to January 1686 which were published in a small octavo along with Gilmour's *Decisions* in 1701. They extend to only 80 pages and 114 decisions and are undistinguished in quality as reports. His third daughter married Joseph Hume of Ninewells in Berwickshire and became mother of David Hume the philosopher.

Sir Roger Hog (?1635–1700)[48] became an advocate in 1661 and a judge as Lord Harcarse in 1677 but was removed from the Bench in 1688 by James VII. He left a *Decisions of the Court of Session collected by Sir Roger Hog of Harcarse, One of the Senators of the College of Justice, from 1681 to 1691*, published in 1757. It is a tall quarto of nearly 300 pages. The cases are collected under headings arranged alphabetically in the manner of a *Practicks*. The reports are concise, frequently no more than the decision. The volume contains also a brief Particulars of the Life and Character of Harcarse, who is described as "in high esteem with all the great lawyers of his time, for his judgment and industry. . . . Both in his public and private capacity, [he] was spoken of by all parties with honour, as a person of great knowledge and probity." One Robert Pittilloch, Solicitor-General in 1655,[49] published in 1659 some tracts, *The Hammer of Persecution, Scotland Mourning*,[50] and in 1689 *Oppression under the Colour of Law*,[51] attacking Harcarse for partiality in judgment. Fountainhall[52] mentions the lawsuits with Pittilloch as one of the reasons for the removal of Harcarse from the Bench.

Sir Patrick Lyon of Carse (1637–94, advocate 1671)[53] had been professor of philosophy at St. Andrews and was later Admiral-depute. He was a Lord of Session from 1683 to 1688. He is said[54] to have compiled a *Decisions of the Court of Session*, 1682–87, which has not been printed nor is even now identifiable, and to have left a *Collection of Genealogies*.

Sir Patrick Home of Renton or of Lumsden (?–1723, advocate 1667),[55] son of Sir John Home of Renton, Lord Justice-Clerk, 1663–71,[56] created a baronet of Nova Scotia in 1682 and Member of Parliament for Berwick 1702–07, also left a manuscript collection of notes of about 1200 decisions, 1673–77 and 1681–88, in three folio volumes. A committee of the Faculty of Advocates in 1705, considering what encouragement should be given to William Forbes's proposal to collect the Lords' decisions, commended Forbes for his making up the interlocutors wanting in Sir

Patrick Home's collection.[57] The collection has not been printed but about a third of the cases were printed in Morison's *Dictionary*.

Sir John Lauder of Fountainhall (1646–1722)[58] graduated at Edinburgh in 1664, then travelled on the Continent, staying at Poitiers from 1665 to 1668 and then briefly at Leiden. He passed advocate in 1668 and was one of the advocates who seceded from Edinburgh. Later he defended Argyll in 1681. He was a member of the Estates in 1685, 1690–1702 and 1702–07 and also of the Privy Council. In 1688 he supported the revolution and in 1689 was promoted to the Bench as Lord Fountainhall. In 1692 he declined the office of Lord Advocate. In 1706 he opposed the union with England. He was not of particular distinction as a lawyer or judge but from early in his career he kept a record of the decisions of the courts.

In 1738 Thomas Ruddiman sought the leave of the Faculty of Advocates to print and publish Lord Fountainhall's Collection of Decisions at his own expense. The Faculty approved and appointed seven members, including James Boswell and Henry Home (later Lord Kames), to revise the Decisions with a view of their being printed by Ruddiman.[59] The *Decisions of the Lords of Council and Session from June 6, 1678, to July 30, 1712, collected by the Honourable Sir John Lauder of Fountainhall, one of the Senators of the College of Justice, containing also the Transactions of the Privy Council, of the Criminal Court, and Court of Exchequer and interspersed with a variety of Historical Facts and many curious Anecdotes* were ultimately printed for G. Hamilton and J. Balfour and published in two folio volumes in 1759–61.

His *Historical Observes of Memorable Occurrents happening either in Church or State from 1680 to 1686* were printed by the Bannatyne Club in 1840, and one Robert Mylne, an Edinburgh lawyer, made extracts, partly abridged, and with additions, portions of which were published by Sir Walter Scott in 1822 under the title *Chronological Notes of Scottish Affairs from 1680 to 1781, being chiefly taken from the diary of Lord Fountainhall*. *Historical Notices of Scottish Affairs selected from the Manuscripts of [The Decisions of] Sir John Lauder of Fountainhall* was also published by the Bannatyne Club in two volumes in 1848. It covers 1661–88. Both are very important sources for the history of his times. His *Journals* 1665–76, including a chronicle of events connected with the Court of Session 1668–76, was published by the Scottish History Society in 1904.

Fountainhall's *Decisions* rather resemble a diary in that under dates he records decisions of Privy Council, Session, Justiciary and Exchequer, but includes many interesting comments and observations. Even if not of great value as reports the *Decisions* is a most readable and interesting account of legal life in the stirring times he lived through, with mentions of torture and executions, Craig, Stair and Mackenzie cited as authorities as well as many Continental jurists, and a case when "The Lords desired to hear his point more fully, ere they laid down a general rule to be a leading case in all time coming."[60] He records James, Duke of Albany,[61] being proclaimed King of Great Britain at Edinburgh in 1685,[62] Mackenzie being restored as Lord Advocate in 1688,[63] Archbishop Sharp being murdered,[64] and the ·arrival of the King's yacht from London with Popish trumpery for the Abbey.[65]

The second volume contains separate indices of historical affairs and of the names of the parties to actions but no index of legal subjects discussed.

Fountainhall's *Journals*[66] also contains interesting mentions of the books he possessed, which included several volumes of *practicks* and collections of decisions.

Morison's *Dictionary of Decisions* and Brown's *Supplement to the Dictionary of Decisions* print a number of cases found in seventeenth century manuscript collections and, at least as yet, not printed separately. Morison distributed the cases under the appropriate heads of his *Dictionary* but Brown prints the cases of each collection as a block, in chronological order. The authors of these collections are Sir George Auchinleck, Lord Balmanno,[67] covering 1627–37, Robert McGill, Lord Foord,[68] covering 1649–50, Sir John Baird, Lord Newbyth,[69] covering 1664–67 and Sir Peter Wedderburn, Lord Gosford,[70] covering 1668–77. Wedderburn also made an epitome of part of Sir Thomas Nicolson's *Practicks*.

During the Cromwellian Commonwealth the Court of Session was replaced by Commissioners for Administration of Justice. In 1762 there was published *The Decisions of the English Judges*[71] *during the Usurpation from the year 1655 to his Majesty's Restoration and the sitting down of the Session in June 1661*. It is a tall quarto of 233 pages. The editors are anonymous; occasionally they make a brief editorial comment at the end of a report.

TEXT-WRITINGS

Alexander Seton (?1639–1719, advocate 1661)[72] came of a very ancient family, was knighted in 1664, became a Lord of Session as Lord Pitmedden in 1677, a Lord of Justiciary in 1682 and a baronet of Nova Scotia in 1684 but was removed from office in 1686 for opposition to James VII and declined to be reinstated at the Revolution. A remote collateral was Alexander Seton, Lord Pluscarden (Extraordinary Lord) (1586), Lord Urquhart (Ordinary) (1587), Lord President (1593) and Earl of Dunfermline and Lord Chancellor of Scotland (1604). Pitmedden wrote *A Treatise of Mutilation and Demembration and their Punishment* as an appendix to the second (1699) edition of Mackenzie's *Criminal Law* and also an *Explication of the xxxix Chapter of the Statutes of King William concerning Minors* (1728). One of his sons was one of the commissioners who negotiated the Union of 1707, and wrote several works supporting the Union.

From another Seton who in the sixteenth century assumed the surname of Tytler were descended Alexander Fraser-Tytler (1747–1813, advocate 1770, FRSE 1783), author of *Elements of General History* (1801), the third and fourth volumes of Kames's *Folio Dictionary*, and the *Memoir of Lord Kames* (1807), who became a judge as Lord Woodhouselee in 1802[73] and whose grandson, James Stuart Fraser-Tytler, W.S. (1802–91), became Professor of Conveyancing in Edinburgh University (1866–91).[74]

Pitmedden records[75] that he was solicited by one Symson, a retired minister turned bookseller, to bring out a new edition of Mackenzie's *Matters Criminal* with some addition and pitched upon the crimes of mutilation and demembration as those on which least had been written and yet afforded variety of matter both profitable and pleasant. It is divided into two parts, the first dealing with the names and nature of these crimes and showing how they can only be committed on proper members of the body. It includes some general directions for framing a libel, the most remarkable defences, methods of probation and "some pertinent passages of history, to divert the reader." This part extends to 26 pages, divided into 98 numbered paragraphs. It contains a good deal of recondite learning, garnished with citations from jurists from Aristotle onwards and mentions of some unreported cases. Much of it today can only be regarded as irrelevant and tedious hair-splitting detail.

In the second part, extending to a further 33 pages and a further 95 paragraphs, he considers the punishments of these crimes, adducing the testimonies of physicians, divines and other authors as well as numerous jurists. Much space is devoted to retaliation which he sees as founded on natural equity. It is apparent that the civil and criminal aspects of bodily injuries had not separated, as Pitmedden tells us that the Lords of Justiciary were in use to decern a sum of money to be paid by the pannel or delinquent to the party injured, either for damages or punishment, except the delinquency be very atrocious.

The *Explication* was posthumously published in 1728 with notes by A. Bruce in a sextodecimo of 112 pages. It is similarly tediously long.

COMPILER OF A BOOK OF STYLES

George Dallas (1635–1701, W.S. 1661)[76] of St. Martin's, Ross-shire, became a Writer to the Signet and after 1660 Depute-keeper of the Signet. Later he was a Member of Parliament. He compiled a *System of Stiles as now practicable within the Kingdom of Scotland*, made between 1666 and 1688 but not published until 1697. It is a substantial folio of 900 pages, divided into six parts concerned with 1. Real and Personal Diligence; 2. What passeth the Privy Seal only; 3. Summonds passing the Signet; 4. What letters pass the Signet and such Precepts in Latine as upon Signatures pass also the Signet and whole Seals, except the Quarter-Seal; and what passes the Great-Seal *per saltum*; 5. All Securities, Contracts of Marriage, Tailzies, Mortifications, Liferent-Rights, Provisions of Younger Children, Excambions and the Like; 6. Services, Tutories, Summonds of Error and others. The styles are full and complete precedents and must have been extremely valuable to conveyancers. They are now of great value as exemplifying the forms of writs in use at the time. Some are specimens of real deeds such as the King's ratification of 1681 of the contract between Stair and his printers for printing the *Institutions*. There was a second edition in two smaller octavo volumes in 1774 by John Wood, who proposed to publish a supplementary volume but seems not to have done so. Wood's preface describes them as "not only been almost universally followed by the writers to the signet, and other conveyancers, but also appealed to by the lawyers in their private practice and public pleadings, nay, even cited as authorities by our best historians."[77]

WRITERS ON OTHER MATTERS RELATED TO LAW

Samuel Rutherford (?1600–61)[78] Professor of Humanity at Edinburgh (1623), minister of Anwoth in Galloway (1627–36) and later Professor of Divinity at St. Mary's College, St. Andrews (1639), then Principal of that college (1647) but deprived in 1661, wrote books against Arminianism and, more importantly, *Lex Rex, a Dispute for the Just Prerogative of King and People* (1644), a treatise intended as a reply to a book by one John Maxwell, excommunicated Bishop of Ross, in support of absolute monarchy. In it he contended, in substance, for the superiority of the rule of law over personal absolutism.

At the Restoration the Estates ordered *Lex Rex* to be burned at the crosses of Edinburgh and St. Andrews and any in possession of copies to be punished. It is now a largely forgotten work, but it entitles Rutherford to a minor place among the writers on political thought and as an early writer on constitutional law.

Sir James Steuart or Stewart, of Gutters or Goodtrees (1635–1713, advocate 1661),[79] was son of a niece of Sir Thomas Hope, and her husband was Lord Provost of Edinburgh during the Commonwealth. In support of a clergyman, Stirling's, work *Naphtali* (1667), recounting the grievances of the covenanters, to which Bishop Honeyman of Orkney replied in *A Survey of Naphtali* (1668), Stewart wrote *Jus Populi Vindicatum* (1669) under an assumed name and for his own safety, left Scotland for some years, and lived in France and practised law in London for a time. He returned in 1679 and became regarded as the ablest man at the Bar. In 1681 he again had to take refuge, in Holland this time, being suspected of involvement in Argyll's expedition. In 1692 he was made Lord Advocate and is credited with many legal reforms; he was a member of the commission inquiring into the Massacre of Glencoe and probably wrote the report. He lost office in 1709 but held the office again 1711–13. His only son was Solicitor-General for Scotland for a time and father of Sir James Steuart or Steuart Denham (1712–80, advocate 1735)[80] who joined Prince Charles's rebellion in 1745 and in consequence had to take refuge on the Continent. He returned home in 1763 and wrote *An Inquiry into the Principles of Political Economy* (2 vols., 1767)[81] and other works, mostly on economics. His *Inquiry*, though totally overshadowed by Adam Smith's *Wealth of Nations*, is an important analysis of economic relations.

NOTES

[1] DNB; Brunton & Haig, p. 403.

[2] Ratified by Parliament in 1681 (APS, VIII, 388, c. 133).

[3] On him see further, Chap. 18.

[4] APS, I, 35.

[5] Comparative tables of the chapter numbers of the Acts are available in *The Acts of the Parliaments of Scotland 1424–1707: Second revised edition* (HMSO, 1966) and appended to the annual *Chronological Table of the Statutes*.

[6] DNB; Anderson, S.N., II, 635; Brunton & Haig, 396.

[7] Fountainhall, *Journals* (S.H.S.), App. II, p. 296.

[8] Chap. 18, *infra*.

[9] APS, VIII, 206, c. 147; see also RPC (3rd), III, 425, 596–599.

[10] APS, IX, 269, c. 19.

[11] W. J. Couper, "Mrs. Anderson and the Royal Prerogative in Printing," *Proc. Royal Phil. Soc. Glasgow*, 48 (1916–17).

[12] H. G. Aldis, *List of Books Printed in Scotland before 1700* (revised ed., 1970).

[13] H. McKechnie, "Practicks," in (Stair Soc.) *Sources and Literature of Scots Law*, pp. 26, 35.

[14] On him see DNB; Anderson, S.N., II, p. 104; Brunton & Haig, p. 198; Cowan, II, p. 171; G. Seton, *Memoir of Alexander Seton, Earl of Dunfermline* (1882) (portrait).

[15] Brunton & Haig, p. 252; Omond, *Lord Advocates*, I, p. 87.

[16] Forbes, *Journal of the Session*, Preface, p. xxiii.

[17] Brunton & Haig, p. 282.

[18] DNB; Anderson, S.N., II, p. 394; Brunton & Haig, p. 221; Omond, *Lord Advocates*, I, p. 69; *Scots Peerage* IV, 309; Sir William Fraser, *The Earls of Haddington*, (2 vols., 1889), I, pp. 34–188. Forbes, *Preface to Journal of the Session*, pp. 26–27, considered him a very astute judge. On Haddington's political role see M. Lee, *Government by Pen: Scotland under James VI and I* (1980), *passim*.

[19] Chap. 16, *infra*.

[20] DNB; Anderson, S.N., III, pp. 496, 497; Brunton & Haig, p. 250; Cowan, II, p. 189; *Life* prefixed to his *History* (1655 ed. and Spottiswoode Society ed. 1851); M. Lee, *Government by Pen* (1980), *passim*.

[21] DNB; Anderson, S.N., III, p. 499; Brunton & Haig, p. 266; *Memoir* in his *Practicks*; papers in Spottiswoode Miscellany I (Spottiswoode Soc., 1844), pp. 185, 197.

[22] DNB; Anderson, S.N., III, p. 496. On John see further Chap. 18, *infra*.

[23] DNB; Anderson, S.N., II, p. 683; Fountainhall's *Historical Notices* and *Historical Observes*; Mackenzie's *Memoirs*; Burnet's *History of his Own Time*; Brunton & Haig, p. 419; Omond, *Lord Advocates*, I, p. 168; *Archaeologia Scotica* IV (1857).

[24] DNB; Anderson, S.N., II, p. 681; Brunton & Haig, p. 319.

[25] Brunton & Haig, p. 392.

[26] *Journal of the Session*, Preface, p. xxiii.

[27] Anderson, S.N., II, p. 684; Omond, *Lord Advocates*, I, p. 301.

[28] Brunton & Haig, p. 399.

[29] DNB; Anderson, S.N., II, p. 296; Brunton & Haig, p. 264. Tytler's *Life of Sir Thomas Craig*, p. 323 and App. II.

[30] APS, V, 309, 464.

[31] DNB.

[32] Stair's *Decisions* were published earlier than Durie's but are of cases of a later period.

[33] *Journal of the Session*, Preface.

[34] DNB; Anderson, S.N., II, p. 296; Brunton & Haig, p. 317.

[35] Omond, *Lord Advocates*, I, pp. 121, 154.

[36] *Characteres Quorundam Advocatorum Scotorum*, in *Works*, I, p. 6.

[37] Forbes, *Journal of the Session*, Preface, p. xxiii.

[38] DNB; Forbes, *Journal of the Session*, Preface, p. xxviii; Anderson, S.N., II, p. 305; Brunton & Haig, p. 350.

[39] *Idea Eloquentiae Forensis*.

[40] *To the Reader*, p. 1.

[41] DNB; Anderson, S.N., III, p. 255; Brunton & Haig, p. 389; Omond, *Lord Advocates*, I, p. 186.

42 Forbes, *Journal of the Session*, Preface.

43 *History of his Own Time*, p. 275.

44 *Characteres Quorundam*, in *Works*, I, p. 6.

45 On him see *infra* and Chap. 18.

46 DNB; Anderson, S.N., II, p. 188; Brunton & Haig, p. 405.

47 *To the Reader*, p. 1.

48 DNB; Forbes, *Journal of the Session*, Preface, p. xliii; Brunton & Haig, p. 407.

49 Omond, *Lord Advocates*, I, p. 167.

50 Reprinted in 1827 as *Tracts Legal and Historical*.

51 Subtitled *My Lord Harcarse his New Practicks*.

52 *Chronological Notes*, p. 247.

53 Brunton & Haig, p. 418.

54 Forbes, *Journal*, Preface, p. xxiii; Hailes, *Catalogue of the Lords of Session, Notes*, p. 27; Brunton & Haig, p. 418.

55 Anderson, S.N., II, p. 485; *Fac. of Adv. Minute Book, passim*. He was active in the life of the Faculty. He is frequently called Home of Renton.

56 Brunton & Haig, p. 383.

57 *Faculty of Advocates Minute Book*, I, p. 257.

58 DNB; Forbes, *Journal of the Session*, Preface, p. xliii, Anderson, S.N., II, p. 631; Brunton & Haig, p. 442; Tytler's *Life of Lord Kames*; Life by David Laing in preface to *Historical Notices*; Omond, *Lord Advocates*, I, pp. 221, 242. Portrait in *Historical Observes* and *Journals*.

59 *Faculty of Advocates' Minute Book* (ed. Pinkerton), II, p. 168.

60 *Decisions*, I, p. 537 (1692).

61 *i.e.* James VII and II.

62 I, p. 339.

63 I, p. 499.

64 I, p. 47.

65 I, p. 429.

66 ed. Crawford (S.H.S., 1904), Apps. I, II.

67 Anderson, S.N., I, p. 168; Forbes, *Journal of the Session*, Preface, p. xxiii; Brunton & Haig, p. 273.

68 Brunton & Haig, p. 339.

69 Forbes, pp. xxiii and xl, describes him as "a judge of long experience, a good humanist and well seen in the belles lettres." Brunton & Haig, p. 391, also ascribe to him practicques from 1664 to 1681 with an appendix to 1690, the MSS. of which are in the Advocates' Library. His collection was chronological.

70 Brunton & Haig, p. 394. Mackenzie, *Characteres Quorundam* in *Works*, See also Fountainhall, I, p. 48; Forbes, pp. xxiii and xlii, who describes him as a man of great eloquence and literature, and other bright parts. He was also sole clerk of the Privy Council.

71 The judges were some English, some Scottish. Stair became one of them in 1657.

72 DNB; Anderson, S.N., III, p. 440; Brunton & Haig, p. 406; genealogical table in G. Seton, *Memoir of Alexander Seton, earl of Dunfermline*, p. 15. The Great Garden at Pitmedden in Aberdeenshire has in recent years been restored by the National Trust for Scotland.

73 Brunton & Haig, pp. 545; Anderson, S.N. III, p. 587. On him see further, Chap. 25, *infra*.

74 Turner, *History of the University of Edinburgh* (1883–1933), p. 412.

75 "To the Reader."

76 DNB. There is a portrait in the Signet Library, Edinburgh.

77 The footnote cites Dr. Robertson, David Hume, Esq., etc. Sir Walter Scott also refers to Dallas's *Stiles*.

78 DNB; Anderson, S.N., III, p. 393; Chambers, BDES; Alexander Whyte, *Samuel Rutherford and Some of his Correspondents* (1894); R. Gilmour, *Samuel Rutherford* (1904).

79 DNB; Omond, *Lord Advocates*, I, pp. 243, 295.

80 DNB.

81 Reissued with introduction by A. S. Skinner in 1967.

CHAPTER 11

WILLIAM FORBES

A SIGNIFICANT development of the early eighteenth century was the revival or introduction of the teaching of law in the older Scottish universities and the consequent appearance of university teachers among the jurists. William Forbes was born about 1675, son of a physician in Aberdeen, and called to the Bar in 1696.[1] He served as clerk of Faculty in 1702–03 and again from 1706.[2] He married Margaret Lindsay, daughter of an Edinburgh merchant and they had a son Thomas, who became an advocate in 1723,[3] and a daughter.[4] Forbes seems to be the first, or at least the first notable, advocate who either could not get a practice and turned to reporting and text-writing, or was more interested in scholarship and writing and found in that some outlet for his abilities and industry. But the Bar was overcrowded in the early eighteenth century; only a third could gain their bread by practice.[5]

His first publication appears to have been a small book *The Law of Election of Members of Parliament* (1700 and, enlarged, 1710).

His *A Methodical Treatise concerning Bills of Exchange* was published as a slim sextodecimo in 1703, and there was a second improved edition in octavo in 1718. In November 1703 the Privy Council granted Forbes the sole privilege of printing, vending and selling the book for 19 years, and Forbes assigned his privilege to John Russel, writer in Edinburgh, for whom the book was printed.[6] It is divided into chapters, some of which are divided into sections, comprising numbered paragraphs, and quotes specimens of bills. The preface and footnotes indicate acquaintance with Marquhardus, Marius, Molloy and other early authorities on the subject and there are references to the Scottish cases.

The Duty and Powers of Justices of Peace in this Part of Great Britain called Scotland, a slim sextodecimo of only 72 pages dedicated to Sir David Dalrymple of Hales, appeared in 1703 and again in 1707. Again Forbes got a grant of monopoly for 19 years. The book deals with the justices' powers, their constables and customs and excise duties. There is an appendix concerning weights and measures.

In 1705 he published *A Treatise of Church-lands and Tithes*, a small but stout sextodecimo of 450 pages. For this book too Forbes got a monopoly of printing and selling from the Privy Council for 19 years. Part I deals with the temporality of benefices, with ecclesiastical property, superiorities, tithes and ann, Part II with the spirituality, with churches, churchyards, manses, glebes and tithes. The book exhibits much learning in history and the works of the canonists, as well as in the law of Scotland. There was a second edition in 1707. Forbes again shows acquaintance with European jurists, with Selden's work. The work is still of value on this intricate subject and it was being cited in judgment for a long time.[7]

In 1705 a committee of Faculty appointed to consider what encouragement should be given to Mr. William Forbes's proposal to collect the Lords' decisions favoured the proposal and proposed that he be made conjoint Bibliothecus and given 700 merks yearly for collecting the Lords' decisions.[8] The Faculty approved the report and gave effect to it.[9] This was the first official appointment by the Faculty of a reporter of decisions. Forbes continued in office until he resigned in July 1714, having been appointed professor of law at Glasgow. His successors as reporters were, in order, Bruce, Edgar and David Falconer.[10]

In 1708 he put forward to the Faculty of Advocates another proposal:[11]

"In pursuance of a design to write a complete body of the law of Scotland, containing the harmony thereof with, and differences from the civil and feudal laws; and shewing how far the Scots and English laws do agree and differ; with incident comparative views of the modern constitutions of other nations in Europe. Having endeavoured to clear up the dark and untraced subjects of the Scots law by three distinct books already published, viz ... *bills of exchange* ... *Church lands and tithes* ... *Justices of the Peace* ... And having sessionally since February 1705 observed and collected the decisions of the Lords of Session, under the title of the Journal of the Session; he is resolved, if incouraged by the Government, not only to make up these decisions wanting *ab ante* from December 1681 where the Viscount of Stair left of down to the commencement of his own journal. But also is designed to handle the consistorial, maritime and criminal parts of law, by way of district treatises; And then to set about the grand work of compiling a complete body of the law of Scotland.

"Since the happy union of the two kingdoms into one monarchy, such a complete body of the law of Scotland, as is proposed, may now be justly reckoned among the Desiderata, or things that are wanting, towards settling and maintaining a fair understanding and correspondence betwixt the judicatures in north and south Britain, and for facilitating the dispatch of justice; In which Judges and persons of all ranks will find their account.

"An earnest desyre to serve these good ends in some measure, and not any ambition or design to appear more learned than others, doth lead Mr. Forbes to set his shoulders to this vast undertaking which those of more approved abilities would not perhaps find leisure to compass and go through with."

At a meeting on November 16, 1708,[12] the Dean and Faculty considered the proposal and

"were of opinion that the performance thereof would be of universal use, and very satisfying to all British subjects in general and to members of parliament, statesmen, judges and lawyers in particular. And being sufficiently convinced of the said Mr. William Forbes's ability to accomplish such a work from their particular knowledge of his learning and industry, in the fair and ample specimens he has given of both, in clearing the difficult parts of our law, viz. church lands and tithes, bills of exchange and the duty and powers of Justice of Peace, by three distinct learned and useful treatises already published. They were of opinion that he deserved publick incouragement to prosecute and finish with all expedition, that vast and useful undertaking wherein much of his time would be spent.

And they ordered their Dean to sign this their opinion in their name and presence which was accordingly done. And gave orders to their Clerk to record the forsaid proposal with this their recommendatory approbation in the Faculty's books."

Forbes did undertake his Herculean task and in large measure accomplished it. To judge from the preface to his *Institute* he was still writing the *Great Body* until the mid-1720s. The *Great Body* was unfortunately never published. It still exists in a massive, neatly-written manuscript, partly in one hand, partly in another, in Glasgow University library,[13] bound in seven tall volumes, presented to the University by a Mrs. Carmichael, Forbes's daughter, in 1786. The full title is *A Great Body of the Law of Scotland containing the Harmony thereof with and Differences from the Civil and Feudal Laws: and shewing how far the Scots and English Law do agree and differ, with incident comparative views of the modern Constitutions of other Nations in Europe.* Despite this title it is predominantly about Scots law and not substantially comparative. Volume I, comprising 1949 folios bound in three volumes, deals with Private Law, and commences with a consideration of law generally, as the command of sovereign power, and as a science or collection of the precepts of sovereign power, and then continues with seven Parts dealing respectively with: 1. "Persons" (337 folios); 2. "Estates, or Rights to Things consisting of Possession or Property, the several kinds of estates and the general ways how these may be acquired" (232 folios); 3. "Of Real and Heritable rights" (204 folios); 4. "Of Obligations or Engagements and Personal Rights" (322 folios); 5. "How Property may be transmitted and passed over by progress to singular successors" (289 folios); 6. "How Estates or property may be transmitted by progress to universal successors" (190 folios); 7. "The Ways of Determining Civil Controversies in point of right or possession about Estates" (373 folios). Each Part is divided into Books, subdivided into Chapters, and these into Titles.

Volume II comprises volume 4 and part of 5 of the bound MS. It comprehends the Criminal Law and comprises two parts: 1. "Concerning crimes and offences and the punishment thereof" (667 folios); 2. "Of Criminal Jurisdiction" (324 folios).

Volume III, comprising the rest of volume 5 of the MS, comprehends the Public Law and comprises two parts: 1. "Of matters relating to the Government and General Policy of the State and order thereof" (including taxation and commerce) (162 folios); 2. "Concerning the Administration of Justice" (51 folios). This volume as a whole and some topics in this volume have not been completed.

An Appendix contains brief histories of the laws of France, of England and of Scotland, an "Account of those who have written the History of the Laws and customs of the several nations," "Concerning the King's negative voice in passing Acts of Parliament," a substantial "Terms of the Law of Scotland with the corresponding Terms of the Law of England," and some supplementary notes. The whole manuscript runs to something like one million words.

There is bound in at the beginning a printed pamphlet containing Forbes's proposal setting out his intention, also a letter from "An

Eminent Scots Lawyer" to Forbes on the utility of the work, making the point that, in view of the Union, courts in South Britain might have from time to time to apply Scots law, an approbation of the project from the Lords of Council and Session, and the recommendation and approbation by the Dean and Faculty of Advocates.

Why this great work was never published is unknown. It was probably prevented by the formidable size and consequent expense of the undertaking. Moreover at that time an author bore the outlay and commercial risk of his publication. We shall see that Forbes had to publish his *Journal of the Session* at his own risk, and we have also seen that Robert Baillie, the editor of Craig, put himself in financial difficulties by that edition.[14]

It is, however, a very great pity that the *Great Body* never appeared in print. It is logically arranged, clearly expressed, and if it had appeared, might well have held the field against Bankton and even Erskine. The volume on criminal law is fuller than Mackenzie's *Matters Criminal* and would possibly have superseded that work and held the field until Hume. The volume on the public law would have been the first of its kind and particularly interesting and valuable, but is very incomplete. Forbes may have been prevented from completion by his academic duties in Glasgow, or by diverting his attention to his *Institute*.

On June 11, 1712,[15] Forbes reported to the Faculty that he had collected the decisions from 1705 to 1712 and was ready to print them, that it had been resolved to print them at the expense of the Faculty but the Faculty had no money at that juncture to spare to that end, and that accordingly he proposed that the Faculty allow him to print his decisions at his own risk and charges and take the profit. The Faculty agreed. He also reported that he had brought "the first volume of his body of the laws of Great Britain nigh to a period and wanting only to complete it the use of a number of sixteenth and seventeenth century English books requested a recommendation to the curators of the library to buy them to enable him to complete his work." This too the Faculty recommended. The Lords of Session on July 7, 1713,[16] allowed and approved of his printing and publishing the work and on December 8, 1713,[17] similarly approved his publishing the continuation to November 1713.

A Journal of the Session Containing the Decisions of the Lords of Council and Session in the Most Important Cases Heard and Determin'd From February 1705 till November 1713 was published in 1714. It is a tall quarto of 720 pages with over 100 pages of indices. The cases are reported chronologically, frequently at considerable length. They set out the arguments, sometimes the books and authorities founded on and are the best of the reports published down to that time. Most of the cases were reprinted in Kames' and Morison's *Dictionaries* and some of the omitted ones in Morison's *Supplemental Volume*. Forbes tells in his Preface[18] what prompted him to record the decisions and Acts of Sederunt. The fact that he records both is his justification for the title *A Journal of the Session*. "Law is the Rule of Right and Property" he observes,[19]

"But the decisions of judges, those *Leges loquentes*, are applications of that rule in various cases, and the best explanations thereof, where it is obscure or doubtful. They furnish notions of things for determining parallel cases, without the expense of that time and thought imployed in hitting upon them at first. Judges do thereby see, not only with their own eyes, but also with the eyes of their learned and judicious predecessors, whose observations they (who being raised upon the other's shoulders, can see farthur) may improve to the best advantage. It's ridiculous to think that the subject of Decisions is exhausted; when we daily see so great variety of cases, out of which the rich invention of lawyers do always discover something new, that falls not directly under former precedents, but must be determined by analogy. . . .

"Whatever latitude the Lords might have taken in deciding contrary to former unprinted decisions, which were known only to lawyers; Yet they have always approved themselves very tender to alter printed decisions; especially in determining cases happening after such precedents were published, upon the faith whereof the lieges might have probably transacted their rights, or contracted, and settled their interests. And as it is advisable for the Lords to regard their own decisions, that others may pay the more respect to them: so it is certainly better to have an ill rule than no rule at all; at least to alter an established rule, though attended with some little inconveniencies, is a snare to the lieges, doth marr commerce and confound human society."

The Preface of 48 pages[20] is particularly valuable, giving much information about the Court of Session, many of the recent judges, the reports of decisions and the collectors of them, and related matters, particularly valuable since Forbes was nearly contemporary with many of the persons concerned. He was called to the Bar the year after Stair died, and much of his information must have come from observers who had themselves seen and heard the events in question. At the end of the Preface he acknowledges information from Lord President Hew Dalrymple, Fountainhall, Seton of Pitmedden and others, so that his information can be taken as authentic.

When Glasgow University was founded in 1451 the Bull of Pope Nicholas V granted it the privileges, liberties, honours, exemptions and immunities granted to the University of Bologna, which in the twelfth century had achieved distinction as the leading centre for the study of Roman and canon law. The Bull expressly authorised the teaching of law, civil and canon, and Bishop Turnbull, the founder, established teaching in law from the outset and envisaged the creation of a law school as part of the programme of development.[21]

Civilians and canonists, particularly the latter, were among those active in the university from the outset.[22] There was a lectureship in canon law in 1463, a succession of possible teachers of civil law, while men of distinction in the law faculty included Robert Henryson, the poet, and William Elphinstone, a lawyer of distinction, later Bishop of Aberdeen and founder of the King's College there. Later, Gavin Dunbar was a distinguished student of law and ultimately became Chancellor of Scotland. The readership in canon law, however, foundered in 1513,[23] though there was a move to revive the subject later in the century. The study of canon law finally died at the Reformation. The First Book of Discipline envisaged the revived teaching of civil law and municipal law in St. Andrews, Glasgow and Aberdeen but this was never put into effect.

In 1573 a possible re-foundation by the town council made no provision at all for teaching law[24] but under the Nova Erectio of 1577 it was contemplated and there was a scheme at the beginning of the seventeenth century with a proposal to appoint a professor of the laws. After the Restoration commissioners for visitation of the university in 1664 seriously canvassed the creation of a chair in civil and canon law.[25] Nothing came of these plans and in Stair's time there, both as student and as regent, there was no teaching of law.

In 1712 the University resolved that law and medicine had been too long neglected and obtained from the rector, Sir John Maxwell, Lord Justice-Clerk, an opinion that the time was propitious and it resolved to petition Queen Anne for the establishment of a chair of law and a chair of medicine. Principal Stirling and Professor Morthland journeyed to London to petition the Queen. In 1713 the Queen acceded to the petition and created a chair of civil law, assigning for it a salary of £90 a year. Alexander Dunlop, professor of Greek, was sent to Edinburgh to consult Maxwell and others about the selection of a suitable person, and brought back a report that William Forbes was strongly recommended and in January 1714 the professors appointed him. It was provided that the professor of law should teach nothing but civil, feudal, canon and Scots law. This was not so much to exclude English, French, Islamic and other systems as to secure the fields of study of existing professors; the law of nature, for instance, was probably deemed already appropriated to the teachers of moral philosophy.[26] Provision was also made for law students being stented for the library by the professor, so that the collection of law books might be improved. The university also recommended that Forbes see that his students were duly prepared for law by acquiring a previous adequate knowledge of languages and philosophy.[27] It also decided, having regard to the practice of other universities, that in point of precedence the professor of law should rank second only to the professor of divinity and have precedence over the professor of medicine.

Forbes was a sound choice; he had shown, by an already substantial volume of publication, that he was a good scholar, and an able and diligent expositor of law, with a major work in hand. He gave his inaugural lecture on February 18, 1714, in Latin, on the nature, history, dignity, utility and authority of the (Roman) civil law. The subject is well treated.[28] He is said to have had one student in his first session and three in his second. Forbes held the chair until 1745 and is believed to have taught civil (Roman) and Scots law. It is said that he refused to teach the civil law except on exorbitant fees.[29] He had no legal colleagues and there was no Faculty of Law. He pretty certainly lectured in Latin, at least on the civil law, because ten years after his death his second sucessor, Lindsay, began to lecture on Justinian in English and the Faculty of Advocates requested the university to restore the old practice of teaching the civil law in Latin. The university declined.[30] There is in the university library a manuscript of a commentary on Justinian's *Institutions* which has been attributed to him.[31] It is plain from the preface to the work next to be considered that he taught Scots law as well, presumably in English. To have lectured on Scots law in Latin would seem inconvenient pedantry, particularly when the books, statutes and cases were in English.

Forbes is also mentioned frequently in the university records as having been active in the life of the university and the management of its affairs. In his last two or three years he was in ill health and unable to lecture and the class was taken by his assistant, Hercules Lindsay (?–1761, advocate 1745),[32] who had studied at Leiden, for a time taught law privately in Edinburgh and succeeded to the chair in 1750, having done the work from 1745 to 1750 during the nominal professorship of William Crosse (1711–75, advocate 1735), who was also sheriff-depute of Lanarkshire and never lectured.

In 1722 Forbes published *The Institutes of the Law of Scotland, Volume First comprehending the Private Law*, a pocket-sized sextodecimo of 260 pages.

In the preface he observes:
> "Having made the Study of the Laws the business of my whole life, I did, some years ago, set about the compiling of *a great Body of the Law of Scotland: Containing its Harmony with, and Differences from the Civil and Feudal Law: and showing how far the Scottish and English Laws do agree and differ; with incident Comparative Views of the Modern Constitutions of other Nations in Europe*. Which was to consist of Two Volumes. In the first I designed to treat of the Private Law, which mainly respects private property; the interests and differences of particular persons among themselves. The second volume was to set forth the Publick Law, which contains all matters that have any relation to the Order of the State. . . . And lastly, the Criminal Law.[33] Out of both these Volumes, when finished, I propounded to draw a comprehensive *Institute of the Law of Scotland*, consisting also of two volumes, in the same Order and Method with that of the Great Body, for the use of such as shall study law under my care and direction in the University of Glasgow.
>
> "The first volume of the Great Work, wherein the private law is handled, being in some measure finished, and a good advance made in the other: The first volume of the Relative Institute doth now come forth to publick View, to be followed by the other in its due time.
>
> "In so doing, I not only copy after the learned John Voet, late Professor of Law in the University of Leyden, whose Compendium of the Roman Law was published before his Commentary came to light: But also have before me the Example of the Great Justinian, by whose order his Institutes, composed after the Pandects, were promulgated before them. I have nothing less in view, than to derogate in the least from the value of Sir George Mackenzie's Book, which is got into most hands, and hath hitherto been useful to initiate persons in the study of our law: But several things notwithstanding moved me to think of such a composure. 1. Great Alterations have been made in the Law of Scotland, since that learned man writ; and several points controverted in his time, are now cleared up, and established by a Tract of Uniform Decisions. 2. Some matters of the Private Law, and many of the Publick, are not

taken notice of by him at all; and others only in a word or two *en passant* so as the student can reap but little instruction from thence. 3. Though Sir George's authority goes a great way with me, I cannot help differing from his opinion in some points. 4. Seeing every one has a peculiar method of digesting his thoughts, as well as a certain turn of thought and notion, I found myself concerned, in the discharge of my academical function, to reduce and range the fundamentals of our law in such order, as I conceived most natural, and adapted to teaching."

He goes on to outline his classification. There is first a preliminary dissertation on law in general and the several kinds of it. Then the private law is cast into four parts, namely persons in their natural and relative or civil capacities; the latter comprises family and domestic relations. The second part deals with possession and property, real and heritable rights, and obligations and personal rights of all kinds. The third part deals with transmission of property, to singular successors, including trusts, and to universal successors, by succession. The fourth part deals with the determining of civil controversies, extrajudicially and by proceedings in courts.

Of law in general he observes that the word is taken in a twofold sense, for the precept or command of a supreme power, obliging subjects to act, or not to act, under a penalty, and for a science or collection of such precepts.[34] He then discusses in the conventional way law of nature and positive law, divine and human, the latter distinguished into law of nations and a civil law, which is "what the Sovereign Power in every nation, whether monarchical, aristocratical or democratical, hath made for their own peculiar conveniency, to govern the people united by the ties of society under such authority.[35] Law considered as a science "is a science directing us to know and do justice, for the well ordering of society. Justice, which is the end of law, is a constant and perpetual desire of giving to every one his due. There is no authorised collection of the laws of nature and nations anywhere, save in the books of the Roman law.[36]

The municipal law of Scotland is built on 11 foundations, the law of nature, the revealed law of God, the law of nations, the civil law, the canon law, the feudal law, upon some old books,[37] on Acts of Parliament and of Convention of Estates, ancient customs, Acts of Sederunt and Decisions of the Court of Session,[38] by-laws or statutes of particular corporations, or bodies politic.[39]

In 1730 appeared *The Institutes of the Law of Scotland, Volume Second, Comprehending the Criminal Law*. It is a sextodecimo, uniform with the first volume, but extending to 374 pages. In his preface Forbes observes that nobody has been at pains to explain our criminal law, except Mackenzie and Seton of Pitmedden's appendix thereto. Nor had anybody set forth the decisions of the Court of Justiciary, "which obliged me, in order to accomplish the present work, to peruse all the criminal records, and to excerp what I found to the purpose." This, assuming its truth, itself represents a major effort.

The book falls into two parts, dealing with crimes and offences both in general and the particular crimes, and the punishment thereof, and the administration of criminal justice, and criminal procedure. There are footnote references to statutes but no discussion of decided cases.

The *Institutes* is in both volumes a good, clear exposition of the law, but never seems to have attained popularity. Mackenzie's works continued to be used until Erskine's *Principles* swept the field on the civil side. Forbes' work is rarely later referred to. Its explanation of judicial procedure is still historically useful and valuable for assisting understanding of the judgments of the court of the early eighteenth century.

After he took up his duties in Glasgow, Forbes remained active in the life of the Faculty of Advocates. In 1725 he was one of a committee to look into a proposal that Lawrence Dundas, Professor of Humanity in Edinburgh, demit office in favour of the son of a member of Faculty but be conjoined with him for his lifetime, or absolutely in favour of that person.[40]

Part of the interest which attaches to Forbes is that he is the first of the Scottish jurists who was a professor of law; another part is that, without abandoning the idea of the wide-ranging general book dealing with the whole of the law, he essays what is the predominant modern form of the text-writer's art, the treatise on a distinct but limited branch or area of the whole field, in his case, elections, bills, churches and tithes, and justices of the peace, and we know that he contemplated works on other branches.

Forbes was well thought of in his time. The Lords' Act of Sederunt of July 7, 1713,[41] approving of his publishing the *Journal*, states that the Lords "considering that Mr. William Forbes, advocate, hath given sufficient evidence of great Learning and Judgement, by former treatises published by him, which have been very acceptable and useful to the publick; and that he . . . hath been enabled to observe with exactness and accuracy their Lordships decisions. . . ."

Forbes has been unfortunate. His smaller works have been superseded and largely forgotten; his *Journal* is looked at by legal antiquaries only; his small *Institute* does not seem to have "caught on" as a textbook or replaced Mackenzie's, which in any event was overtaken by Erskine's *Principles*, and his major *Great Body* never saw the light of day in print. Today he is largely forgotten. But he was clearly a learned lawyer, a good scholar, and a diligent text-writer and reporter, and seems to have been a competent professor.

NOTES

[1] Grant, *Faculty of Advocates: Faculty of Advocates' Minute Book* (ed. Pinkerton), I, p. 166. Forbes does not appear to be mentioned in any of the standard biographical books of reference.

[2] *Ibid.*, I, pp. 229, 241, 251; II, pp. 1, 4.

[3] *Ibid.*, II, p. 64.

[4] There is a little about his family affairs in *Forbes* v. *Knox* (1714), in his own MS. reports and *Forbes* v. *Kincaid* (1735) Craigie Session Papers, Vol. X.

[5] Forbes, *Journal of the Session*, preface, vii (170 constantly attending the House); Letter, Sir James Agnew to the Earl of Stair, in Graham, *Annals of Stair*, II, pp. 381–382.

[6] Printed at the end of the *Treatise*.

[7] *e.g.* *Burt* v. *Home* (1878) 5 R. 445 at pp. 481, 491.

[8] *Faculty of Advocates' Minute Book*, I, p. 257.

[9] *Ibid.*, I, p. 261.

[10] On these see Chap. 18, *infra*.

[11] *Faculty of Advocates' Minute Book* (ed. Pinkerton), I, p. 277.

[12] *Faculty of Advocates' Minute Book* (ed. Pinkerton), I, p. 276.

[13] G.U.L. MS. Gen. 1246–52.

[14] *Faculty of Advocates' Minute Book*, II, p. 156.

[15] *Faculty of Advocates' Minute Book*, I, p. 298.

[16] A.S., printed in *Journal*, p. xlviii.

[17] A.S., printed in *Journal*, p. xlix.

[18] p. xlv.

[19] The Preface was reprinted in the Supplemental Volume to Morison's *Dictionary*.

[20] p. xlvii.

[21] J. Durkan and J. Kirk, *The University of Glasgow, 1451–1577* (1977) p. 13.

[22] *Ibid.*, p. 128.

[23] *Ibid.*, p. 132.

[24] *Ibid.*, p. 253.

[25] *Ibid.*, p. 331 and App. J.

[26] In 1714 the teaching of Moral Philosophy, Logic and Natural Philosophy was shared among the Regents. In 1727 distinct chairs were instituted and Gerschom Carmichael became first professor of moral philosophy. See further Chap. 18 , *infra*.

[27] Coutts, *History of the University of Glasgow, 1451–1909*, p. 193; David Murray, *Memories of the Old College of Glasgow* (1927), pp. 213–218; *Munimenta Almae Universitatis Glasguensis*, I, 467; II, 408, 480.

[28] See reproduction of the title-page of his Inaugural Lecture in Murray, *op. cit.*, p. 216; see also A. D. Gibb, "Law" in *Fortuna Domus* (1951), p. 157.

[29] Wodrow, *Analecta* (1842–43), III, 332.

[30] Murray, *op. cit.*, p. 220.

[31] Murray, *op. cit.*, p. 216.

[32] Forbes had married a Lindsay and Hercules Lindsay may have been a relative of hers.

[33] He seems to have abandoned the idea of writing on the public law as well. In any event this volume was never fully written.

[34] *Prelim. Diss.*, p. 1.

[35] *Ibid.*, pp. 2–3.

[36] *Ibid.*, p. 4.

[37] These are defined (*ibid.*, p. 13) as the laws of King Malcolm II, *Regiam Majestatem, Quoniam Attachiamenta* and other old pieces of our law translated and published by Sir John Skene of Curriehill.

[38] "Decisions of the Lords of Session, sometimes called *Practiques*, are the determinations or resolutions upon particular points of right or form contested before them. Which if they continue uniform for some considerable time, have the force of a law": *ibid*, pp. 15–16.

[39] *Ibid.*, pp. 4–5.

[40] *Faculty of Advocates' Minute Book*, II, p. 90.

[41] *Journal*, p. xlviii.

CHAPTER 12

ANDREW McDOUALL, LORD BANKTON

THE McDoualls or McDowalls are a branch of the MacDougalls, particularly those of Galloway. Andrew McDouall (1685–1760),[1] son of Robert McDouall of Logan, studied at Edinburgh, passed advocate in 1708 and was promoted to the Bench in 1755, taking the judicial title of Lord Bankton.[2] His career seems to have been rather uneventful.[3] He is recorded as having been married five times.

He published in 1751–53 in three tall and stout quartos, totalling 1500 pages, apart from tables and indices, *An Institute of the Laws of Scotland in Civil Rights with Observations upon the Agreement or Diversity between them and the Laws of England, in Four Books, after the General Method of the Viscount of Stair's Institutions.* The title-page of Volume I does not disclose the author but those of the second and third do.[4] He justifies his work on the ground that since Stair's revised edition "our law has undergone many alterations and received great improvements since that time, and therefore another system thereof seems to be much wanted."[5] He followed the general method of Stair's *Institutions*, "because, in my apprehension, it is most just and natural, and therefore a good model."[6] But Bankton varied the pattern, adding titles on "The State and distinction of Persons," and "The Division and quality of Things," "a general notion of persons and things being preliminary to the knowledge of rights incident to them," and making other variations. Another particular was

> "in my apprehension, of the highest consequence to the improvement of the work. I have subjoined at the end of each title of the first three books, and in divers titles of the fourth, a kind of parallel between our laws and those of England, in relation to the subject of such title, showing the conformity or disconformity betwixt the one and the other. The Lord Stair had no occasion to observe anything of this kind, nor was it of great use in his time; but now, since the union of the two kingdoms, there is such intercourse between the subjects of South and North Britain, that it must be of great moment, that the laws of both be generally understood, and their agreement or diversity attended to; so that people in their mutual correspondence, may regulate themselves accordingly; and the respective laws and usages may likewise receive some light from the comparison."[7]

For his observations on the law of England, Bankton tells us[8] that he depended, among others, on Danvers[9] and Viner's *General Abridgment of Law and Equity*,[10] and on Bacon's *New Abridgment of the Law of England*,[11] and submitted his observations to the review of gentlemen learned in the laws of England who made such alterations as they thought proper. Bankton had been in correspondence with Lord Chancellor Hardwicke, to whom he dedicated the second volume of the *Institute*, and Hardwicke greatly admired the work.[12] Hardwicke's interest helped to secure his promotion to the Bench.[13]

The work is divided into four books, each subdivided into titles and these into numbered paragraphs. The structure of his *Institute* is accordingly:

Book I – Personal Rights, comprising common principles of law, the state and distinction of persons, division and quality of things, personal rights or obligations in general, marriage, parent and child, guardianship, restitution, gift and recompense, reparation arising from crimes or delinquencies, obligations conventional and the major kinds of agreements. There is a long note[14] on the settlement of the feudal law in Scotland, and another[15] on the authority of the books of the *Regiam Majestatem*, etc. The first takes the view that feudalism was derived from the ancient Goths, not from England, and was introduced by King Fergus, founder or restorer of the Scots monarchy. The second accepted that the *Regiam* was authentic, composed by order of King David I: "in my humble judgment, the *Regiam Majestatem and Quoniam Attachiamenta* are an authentick system of our old laws and customs, especially in feudal questions."[16] The treatise of Glanvill "seems indeed, for the most part, to have been transcribed from the *Regiam Majestatem*."[17] Both views must be dismissed as incorrect.

Book II deals with rights real, including fees, superiority, liferents, servitudes, tacks, security rights, tithes and other rights in land.

Book III is concerned with the transmission of rights, personal and real, succession, heirs and executors.

Book IV deals with actions, including titles on the High Court of Parliament, jurisdiction, advocates and proctors, notaries, the courts of session, justiciary, exchequer and admiralty, the commissary court, the inferior courts. The final title, following Justinian's *De Regulis Juris*, deals with rules of the civil law, illustrated and adapted to the law of Scotland.

The book is written mostly in short paragraphs, each dealing with a distinct point. Each paragraph has a note in the outside margin indicating the topic dealt with therein and summarising the statement, and in the inside margin are brief references to the sources of the propositions in the text. Cases are cited usually by the date, and the pursuer's name alone, which renders them, certainly today, difficult to find,[18] but also frequently by the reporter's name and the number of the case.

The observations on the law of England appended to each title are substantial statements, not mere notes though less full than the statements of the Scots law, and are supported by references to authority as much as are the Scottish propositions. Bankton was clearly quite adequately competent in English law, even if his work on these points was revised and possibly amplified by English legal friends.

He makes much less reference to the Bible, law of God or of nature, or to Grotius and the civilians, than did Stair, though there are frequent marginal citations of the Roman law. It is clear that the book had been written by reference mainly to the Scots statutes and decisions.

It is apparent that while Bankton has in general followed the pattern of Stair he has not done so slavishly, but intelligently, with variations and improvements. He is of course less philosophic than Stair. He regards law as "the rule of voluntary actions of rational beings, prescribing what ought to be done or forborn; what it commands is just, right and good and what it forbids is unjust, wrong or evil; but such actions as are not commanded nor forbidden are indifferent, neither good nor evil, but left to the freedom of man's will."[19] Only voluntary actions are subject to laws. Law in a proper sense is the law of nature, and the particular law of a nation. The laws of every state though given to men by men ultimately derive their authority from the universal law of mankind or the law of nature given by God to all men.[20] The law of nature is peculiar to rational beings.[21] The dictates of nature are laws in the properest sense.[22] Like Stair he equates the law of nature, the law of reason, equity and the moral law.[23] "From many of our statutes it appears, that our legislators had great regard to the civil and canon laws, as being common to most nations . . . our judges ought to direct themselves by the civil and canon laws, as a rule,[24] where our own statutes and customs fail, or where the question, tho' concerning a feudal subject, is not decided by our feudal customs."[25]

The political law of a nation either relates to public or private right.[26] Our civil or municipal law consists of our ancient and immemorial customs,[27] divers principles and maxims founded on these inveterate customs,[28] our statutes or Acts of Parliament[29] and acts of sederunt.[30]

"The decisions of the court of session serve to explain our laws, and ascertain our customs, in the same manner as the judgments of the sovereign courts of other nations do theirs. Where there is a tract of such judgments and precedents uniform upon the same point, it is justly esteemed as law, and ought to be followed in all time thereafter in parallel cases; but otherwise the rule is, that *non exemplis sed legibus iudicandum*. Not one or two precedents, but the prescription of the law is to govern the decisions of courts of justice."[31]

"The old books of law, called *regiam majestatem* and *quoniam attachiamenta*, from their initial words, with the baron laws, and other small treatises and certain old statutes, by some of our ancient kings, thereto adjoined, were undoubtedly of old part of our law; for first, they are expressly termed our law; and next, reference is made to them as such."[32]

"My business, at present, is to treat of our laws in relation to civil and private rights. A right is what belongs to one by law, or can be exacted by him: in an extensive sense, it comprehends what is one's due by the law of nature, or positive law, and it is taken here for what is due by our law. As the subject of law is the voluntary actions of men, which it regulates and governs: so when taken for jurisprudence, the object of law (according to Justinian) is persons, things and actions at law."[33]

Having contrasted the methods of Stair "our learned judge and lawyer" (based on rights) and Justinian (based on objects of rights) Bankton states that he will follow Lord Stair's method without altogether neglecting the emperor Justinian's.[34]

In the immediately following Observations upon the Law of England in relation to the premises, there is another interesting long note[35] on the pretended ancient communication of the English laws to Scotland examined.

In some respects Bankton's treatment of a topic represents a distinct advance on Stair's. His title[36] on the State and Distinction of Persons, really a consideration of status-groups, is valuable, and deals also with corporations as public persons.[37] So too the title on the Division and Quality of Things[38] is a useful survey of the subject as a preliminary to later examination of rights in things and shows a sound appreciation of the concepts involved.

In relation to reparation arising from crimes or delinquencies[39] Bankton fails adequately to distinguish crimes or public wrongs from delicts or private wrongs; he recognises some delinquencies as civilly cognoscible,[40] and treats of damage as *damnum injuria datum*, repaired by the *Lex Aquilia*,[41] *viz.* a damage occasioned by some fraud or fault of the committer; "The smallest fault or neglect of the offender subjects him to the damage thereby occasioned. . . . It hath as many branches as there are ways whereby our valuable and repairable interests may be damnified, whereof divers instances are given in the title of the Digests, *ad leg. Aquil.*"[42] The most important, and too frequent instance of damage is by fire, when a house is burned. He comes close in this branch of the title to recognising a general liability for negligence.

On conventional obligations Bankton's account is clearer and fuller than Stair's. He distinguishes promises, without any mutual obligation or valuable consideration,[43] from a contract or bargain "when persons agree to pay or perform something to others, or to a third party, for a valuable consideration, either already given, or to be given or performed to the party contracter, or to a third person."[44] He distinguishes the various kinds of contracts and gives rules for the interpretation of writings, again a novel element,[45] and, before treating of the particular contracts, touches on the common requisites of all contracts,[46] such as capacity, legality and possibility. He devotes a separate title[47] to bills of exchange, and one[48] to the obligations on innkeepers, stablers and shipmasters. There is discussion of insurance,[49] interest of money,[50] partnership,[51] arbitration,[52] and cautionry.[53] He appreciates the distinction between compensation and retention.[54] This all represents a considerable advance in exposition beyond any previous work.

Book IV on Actions commences with an interesting account of Parliament[55] and then proceeds to an analysis of jurisdiction,[56] and gives an account of the advocates,[57] clerks of court, clerks to or writers to the Signet,[58] and notaries,[59] all of which are of considerable historical value, before coming to the jurisdiction and authority of the Court of Session,[60] the Court of Commission for Plantation of Churches and Valuation of Tithes,[61] the Court of Justiciary,[63] the High Constable of Scotland,[63] the Court of Exchequer,[64] the Court of Admiralty,[65] the Commissary Court,[66] the Sheriff or stewart-court,[67] courts of bailies or stewards of regalities,[68] baron courts,[69] justices of peace,[70] commissioners of supply,[71] jurisdiction of royal burghs,[72] dean of guild courts,[73] the Lord Conservator's jurisdiction,[74] and finally ecclesiastical jurisdiction.[75] Then he treats of actions at law in general,[76] and proof or evidence.[77] He does not, as Stair does, deal with all the individual forms of action, nor does he give styles for summonses. It is a wholly original account, and full of interest.

The very last title (IV, 45) is a novel feature, the Rules of the Civil Law, illustrated and adapted to the Law of Scotland. There are 54 such rules and the title extends to over 60 pages. This is clearly founded on Dig. 50, 17, *De Regulis Juris Antiqui*. Each point consists of a Latin rule, with free translation, and several paragraphs of commentary thereon with references to the places where the point has been dealt with in the text. "This also is an Essay, the first of the kind with us, and tends to the perfection of the work since, as shall appear in the progress, we regard the civil law very much, where our own statutes and customs fail."[78]

An Appendix touches on some matters of recent legislation.

Bankton would seem rather less an original thinker than Erskine, and very much less so than Stair. He makes few express references to his predecessors and their opinions, sometimes departing from Stair's view without naming him.[79] While he has in general adopted Stair's order of treatment it is greatly mistaken to think of Bankton's as merely an updated version of Stair's work. It is clearer and more readable than Stair though less philosophic and profound. But there are many matters on which he says original and valuable things. Thus he deals at I, 1, 76–83, with salient points of international private law and treats bills of exchange as a distinct type of contract.[80]

Bankton's book has always enjoyed a good reputation. In 1773 when James Boswell was on his Highland jaunt with Dr. Johnson he found at Ullinish in Skye a copy of Bankton on the head of an escritoire.[81] In the latter part of the eighteenth century, while Erskine's work is the most commonly cited in the reported cases, as the most recent, Bankton is cited frequently, though rather less than Stair. But it has never been regarded as in quite the first rank of treatises.

It is slightly difficult to say why Bankton's book has never been regarded as of quite the first rank in authority or value. It is well arranged, written in a clear, straightforward style and the propositions are clearly presented. It is an unjustifiably neglected book. But by the end of the eighteenth century it had become somewhat dated, and had not been revised or annotated, whereas Erskine had, and by the mid-nineteenth century this was more so. Hume, in his introductory lecture,[82] does not mention Bankton among the important writers. Bell, in his *Principles*, very rarely refers to Bankton, which may have contributed to his being regarded as somewhat second-rate. But Bankton was being regularly referred to in court in the late eighteenth and the early nineteenth century, though decreasingly as time went on and it became more outdated in comparison with Erskine and Bell, whose works were regularly updated by editors.

Why it has never gone into a later edition is probably to be explained by the sheer bulk and weight of the book. Even 20 years later, just before Erskine's *Institute* appeared, to have undertaken a revised edition of Bankton would have been a most formidable undertaking both in scholarship and in money. To have revised the English material as well as the Scottish would have been beyond the capacity of most scholars.

NOTES

[1] DNB; Brunton & Haig, p. 521. His name sometimes appears as McDougal.

[2] Bankton was a mansion NW of Tranent near Prestonpans Station, at the end of the battlefield of Prestonpans (Sept. 21, 1745). It belonged to Colonel Gardiner, who was killed in that action, before being acquired by McDouall, and was destroyed by fire in 1852. For an assessment of Bankton as a judge see Ramsay, *Scotland and Scotsmen in the Eighteenth Century*, I, pp. 128, 323–327, 343–350.

[3] Mentions in the *Faculty of Advocates' Minute Book* (ed. Pinkerton), show him as taking a regular part in the affairs of the Faculty. Latterly he was regularly a member of the Dean's Council.

[4] In the Preface, p. xii, Bankton indicates that he published in his lifetime only because he was prevailed on to do so. In a preface to Vol. II he remarks: "And as it hath so happened that the Author is as generally known as if his Name had been originally prefixed to the Work, it is now added in the Title, to avoid the imputation of an affected Modesty, by pretending longer to conceal the same." Each volume has a separate dedication.

[5] Preface, p. vi.

[6] *Ibid.*, p. vii.

[7] *Ibid.*, pp. ix–x.

[8] Preface, p. x.

[9] Knightly D'Anvers, *General Abridgment of the Common Law*, (3 vols., 1705–37).

[10] Charles Viner, *General Abridgment of Law and Equity*, (23 vols., 1741–53).

[11] Matthew Bacon, *New Abridgment of the Law*, (5 vols., 1736–66). On these works see Holdsworth, *H.E.L.*, xii, pp. 162–75.

[12] British Library, Hardwicke, Add. MSS. 35448, fo. 273, 280.

[13] A. Murdoch, *The People Above* (1980), p. 57. See also J. S. Shaw, *The Management of Scottish Society, 1707–1764* (1983) p. 54.

[14] *Inst.* I, 1, 41 (p. 13). To judge from the indices to the work in Vol. III, Bankton chose to have his work cited, not by book, title and section, as in the cases of Stair and Erskine, but by volume, page and section number.

[15] I, 1, 75 (p. 29).

[16] p. 29.

[17] p. 30.

[18] The only ways to find cases thus referred to, *e.g.* Feb. 9, 1672, *Wood*, are by trying the Index of Parties in Kames' *Folio Dictionary* and in Tait's *Index to Morison's Dictionary*.

[19] I, 1, 1.

[20] I, 1, 15.

[21] I, 1, 19.

[22] I, 1, 20.

[23] I, 1, 24–25.

[24] *i.e.* as a norm to be obeyed.

[25] I, 1, 42.

[26] I, 1, 54.

[27] I, 1. 59, instancing legitim, heirship moveables.

[28] I, 1, 59.

[29] I, 1, 60. He deals in sections 61–66 with rules of interpretation.

[30] I, 1, 73.

[31] I, 1, 74.

[32] At this point Bankton inserts his long note on the authority of the books of *Regiam Majestatem*, etc., ascribing its composition to the order of David I. R.M. and Q.A. he holds to be authentic and seem to have been written by the same hand. In all this Bankton is unfortunately wrong. But he has not deferred to the views of Craig or Stair on the matter.

[33] I, 1, 85.

[34] I, 1, 86.

[35] p. 38.

[36] I, 2.

[37] I, 2, 17.

[38] I, 3.

[39] I, 10, 1. This seems to be the first use of the term "reparation" which became a standard Scottish term for this category of obligation, though appropriate to the remedy rather than the obligation.

[40] I, 10, 13.

[41] I, 10, 40.

[42] *Ibid.*

[43] I, 11, 1–5.

[44] I, 11, 6.

[45] I, 11, 53–62.

[46] I, 11, 66.

[47] I, 13.

[48] I, 16.

[49] I, 19, 38–46.

[50] I, 21.

[51] I, 22.

[52] I, 23, 7–24.

[53] I, 23, 25–50.

[54] I, 24, 34.

[55] IV, 1.

[56] IV, 2.

[57] IV, 3.

[58] IV, 4.

[59] IV, 5.

[60] IV, 7.

[61] IV, 8.

[62] IV, 9.

[63] IV, 10.

[64] IV, 11.

[65] IV, 12.

[66] IV, 13.

[67] IV, 14.

[68] IV, 15.

[69] IV, 16.

[70] IV, 17.

[71] IV, 18.

[72] IV, 19.

[73] IV, 20.

[74] IV, 21.

[75] IV, 22.

[76] IV, 23–24.

[77] IV, 25–32.

[78] Preface, p. ix.

[79] *e.g.* I, 19, 35 and 26; II, 1, 36.

[80] I, 13.

[81] F. A. Pottle and Charles H. Bennett (ed.), *Tour to the Hebrides with Samuel Johnson*, p. 198.

[82] Baron Hume's *Lectures*, 1781–1822 (ed. Paton, Stair Soc.), I, 8, 14.

CHAPTER 13

JOHN ERSKINE

UNTIL the early eighteenth century there was no provision for public instruction in law in Edinburgh, notwithstanding that the town was the seat of the Parliament, the Privy Council, the Court of Session, and some lesser courts. Robert Reid (?1495–1558), abbot of Kinloss and Bishop of Orkney and second President (1548/9–58) of the Court of Session,[1] bequeathed 8000 marks for an institution leading towards the study of the civil and canon laws.[2] This he may have intended, not as a university, but as a school of "Arts and Jure" of the kind contemplated by the Education Act 1494 of James IV. His ideas were however, wholly frustrated.[3] In 1574 the Regent Morton stressed the need for theoretical instruction in law, and it was again recommended that an academic training be required of all pleaders in the courts.[4] In 1582 the Privy Council empowered Edinburgh to seek to recover Reid's legacy and put it under an obligation to spend the money on a college within a year after recovery.[5] Ultimately only 2500 marks were recovered, by instalments. Shortly thereafter King James granted a charter confirming a gift of the land of Kirk o' Field and empowering the town council to erect buildings to accommodate studies in Arts, Theology, Medicine, the Laws or any other liberal branch of knowledge.[6] An embryonic college accordingly took shape. In 1564 the Lords of Session had had a grant from Queen Mary, and they were now prepared to hand over £1000 of the surplus to endow a teacher and professor of the laws in the college, if the town paid an equal sum and the King ratified his mother's gift. The advocates, however, not having been consulted, declined to contribute a third £1000. In 1590 the Lords of Session, having obtained royal confirmation of gifts conferred since 1542 on the College of Justice, appointed Sir Adrian Daman and in 1595 one Adam Newton, but the town council, not having been consulted, refused to pay him. Both holders taught Latin only and the advocates' opposition got the professor's duties limited to Latin. The professorship was abandoned in 1597.[7]

In January 1684 the Faculty of Advocates, considering how necessary it was now to have a professor of the laws in this kingdom, to save gentlemen the expense of studying abroad, unanimously agreed that there should be a professor of the laws in this place and recommended to the Dean and Council to make overtures towards condescending upon some learned and qualified person to be professor of the laws in this kingdom and how to establish a competent salary on him.[8] The town would not find the money, even when the College of Justice offered to maintain a professor or two in return for its immunity from local taxation.[9] Discussions between the Faculty and the town were held in 1695 about the proposal[10] and some members of Faculty applied to Parliament for a settlement of a professor of law. An Act providing for a monthly cess for two or more professors of law in this kingdom was printed[11] but was never enacted.

In 1698 one Alexander Cunningham petitioned Parliament[12] for an allowance of £200 per annum for six years to enable him to complete a work in four folio volumes on the civil law, the first two containing the text of the civil law accurately settled, with notes on 2000 passages requiring elucidation, the third to contain the Reconciliations of the Opposite Laws[13] "written in such a method, that this part of the study of the Civil Law will become pleasant, useful and necessary," and the fourth a System of the Digests by way of Principles and Consequences. The Committee for Security of the Kingdom, to whom the matter was remitted, recommended that he be appointed professor of the civil law in this kingdom, and sent abroad to complete his studies of the subject,[14] but his professorship seems to have been a nominal one; he had no real connection with the Town's College and he never taught. Statute[15] added to sums charged against tunnage on foreign ships £150 as the salary for five years of Mr. Alexander Cunningham as Professor of the Civil Law, nominated and designed to that profession, and this was renewed in 1704 for five years.[16] The contemplated great work never seems to have appeared, though he produced editions of Horace and Virgil.[17]

In 1707 Queen Anne allotted £150 a year to establish and settle a foundation for a Professor of the Public Law and the Law of Nature and Nations and Charles Areskine (1680–1763, advocate 1711),[18] Professor of Philosophy (*i.e.* one of the regents) at Edinburgh, was appointed. Though a course by him on the law of nature and nations was advertised in 1711,[19] his only teaching is believed to have been his inaugural lecture, and he used the salary to study law at Utrecht with a view to becoming an advocate, which he did in 1711. He remained nominal professor until 1734.

In 1710 Sir Archibald Sinclair (1664–1719, advocate 1686) petitioned the Faculty to the effect that he had a design to teach the civil and municipal laws and craved the Faculty's approbation of his undertaking and recommendation of him as a person capable to discharge the function, which the Faculty duly did.[20]

About this time too various lawyers were teaching law privately in Edinburgh. John Spottiswoode (1667–1728)[21] grandson of Lord President Sir Robert Spottiswoode, whose *Practicks* he published in 1706, great-grandson of Archbishop Spottiswoode, and Keeper of the Advocates' Library 1703–28, opened a school in his own house for teaching Roman and Scots law and continued to do so extra-murally for 26 years. Robert Craigie (1685–1760, advocate 1710) also lectured on the civil law.[22] Others did the same, including one James Craig (1672–1732, advocate 1701), son of Lewis Craig of Riccarton, advocate, and great-great-grandson of Sir Thomas Craig, who had been lecturing privately on civil law for some years before he was, in 1710, appointed by the town council Professor of Civil Law, but without salary. Craig gave two courses, one on *Institutions*, one on Pandects, using as textbook for the latter Van Eck's *Principia*. From 1717 he received a stipend.

In 1722 statute[23] renewed provision for his stipend and provided for payment of £100 per annum for a Professor of Scots Law. It also prescribed the mode of filling the chairs of Civil Law, Scots Law and Universal History. In case of a vacancy the Faculty of Advocates were to nominate and present to the town council two names, from which the council was to choose one and appoint him to the vacant professorship.[24]

In November 1722 accordingly the Council appointed Mr. Alexander Bayne of Rires (?–1737, advocate 1714),[25] who had been lecturing privately on Scots law in the city and had in a petition "represented how much it would be for the interest of the Nation and of this City to have a Professor of the Law of Scotland placed in the University of this City, not only for teaching the Scots Law, but also for qualifying of Writers for His Majesty's Signet."[26]

Boswell records that Lord Kames told him

> "that a Mr Bayne of Logie, known by the name of Logie Bayne, was the first regular Professor of Scots Law here. He was first an advocate at this bar but did not succeed. He then went to London and resided for some years, thinking to try the English bar. But that would not do either. He returned to Scotland in low circumstances and knew very little law. But such was the effect of a grave countenance and a slow, formal manner, a neatness of expression and the English accent, that the advocates sent a deputation to ask him to accept of being professor, which he did most readily. Stirling of Keir was once invited to dine with him. One o'clock was then the hour. When he went in to Mr Bayne's study, Mr Bayne took no notice of him at first, but kept his eye intent looking through a telescope to the clock of the Tron Church. Then, suddenly rising, said, 'You're welcome, Sir. It is precisely one o'clock.' He was a sort of musical composer but of no taste in music, for he was quite inattentive to the finest pieces at the concert till his own performances were played, and then he fell to the harpsichord and was all alive. He was a kind of mechanic too, and tried to boil snuff in place of roasting it. I found Lord Kames held Bayne very cheap."

Bayne died in 1737 and was succeeded by John Erskine.

John Erskine came of an ancient family with extensive ramifications and connections with the law.[28] It originated with Sir Thomas Erskine of that Ilk, sixth in descent from the proprietor of the barony of Erskine in the time of Alexander II. In the senior line of descent from him were the Earls of Mar, of whom the fifth was guardian of Queen Mary and a Lord of Session in 1532 and the sixth Regent of Scotland. The Earldom of Mar was re-erected in 1620 for the seventh Earl. From his eldest son were descended the later earls, including the 15th Earl who is 1829 became also 11th Earl of Kellie.[29] This line included James Erskine (1679–1754, advocate 1705), who became Lord Grange in 1707 and Lord Justice-Clerk 1710–34.[30]

The seventh Earl's third son Henry was father of David, second Lord Cardross, who married Anne, fifth daughter of Sir Thomas Hope of Craighall.[31] Their son was the ancestor of David Stewart Erskine (1742–1829), sixth Earl of Buchan, founder of the Society of Antiquaries of Scotland,[32] of Henry Erskine (1746–1817, advocate 1768), Lord Advocate in 1783 and 1806 and Dean of Faculty in 1786,[33] and of Thomas (1750–1823), called to the English Bar in 1778, Attorney-General in 1786, Lord Chancellor and Lord Erskine of Restormel Castle in 1806,[34] both of whom were renowned pleaders. David, second Lord Cardross, married secondly Mary, daughter of Sir George Bruce of Carnock,[35] and the third son of this second marriage was Colonel John Erskine (1662–1743),[36] whose son was John Erskine of Carnock and Cardross, who became Professor of Scots Law at Edinburgh and author of the *Principles* and the *Institute.*

The seventh son of the seventh Earl of Mar, Sir Charles Erskine of Alva,[37] married, first, Mary, third daughter of Sir Thomas Hope of Craighall. Their great-grandson in one line, John Erskine (?–1767, advocate 1734), married Janet Wedderburn, whose brother Alexander Wedderburn (1733–1805)[38] was called to the Scottish Bar in 1752, left it and joined the English Bar in 1757, and became Solicitor-General of England (1771), Attorney-General (1778), Chief Justice of the Common Pleas as Lord Loughborough (1780–93), Lord Chancellor (1793–1801) and Earl of Rosslyn (1801); further direct descendants in that line became second and later Earls of Rosslyn. In the other line their grandson was Charles Erskine or Areskine (1680–1763, advocate 1711),[39] first Regius Professor of Public Law at Edinburgh (1707–34), later Solicitor-General for Scotland (1725), Lord Advocate (1737), a judge as Lord Tinwald (1744), and Lord Justice-Clerk (1748-63), whose son James (1723–96, advocate 1743)[40] became in 1761 Lord Barjarg and later Lord Alva.

Sir Charles Erskine of Alva married, second, Helen Skene of Currie-hill, daughter of Sir James Skene, Lord President[41] and they had a son, Colonel John Erskine (1660–1737), who married as his third wife Euphemia Cochrane (?1693–?1721), and their daughter Euphemia Erskine (1718–66)[42] married Alexander Boswell (1707–82, advocate 1729),[43] later (1754) Lord Auchinleck, and their son was James Boswell (1740–95, advocate 1766, barrister 1786)[44] the friend and biographer of Dr. Samuel Johnson.[45] Hence John Erskine the jurist and James Boswell had a common ancestor in John, 7th Earl of Mar.

This Colonel John Erskine is not to be confused with the other Colonel John Erskine, father of John Erskine the jurist. The tenement now called the Palace of Culross, a property of the National Trust for Scotland, consists of two adjoining but separate houses built in 1597 and 1611 by Sir George Bruce of Carnock. It passed by judicial sale in 1700 to Colonel John Erskine of Carnock, the jurist's father, who became Governor of Stirling Castle. Boswell's grandfather, Colonel John Erskine, was the Deputy Governor. The tradition is that Colonel John, the Governor, lived in half of the Bruce palace and rented the other half to the Deputy Governor. People in Culross knew them as "the black Colonel" (the Governor) and "The white (or fair) Colonel" (the Deputy), and the palace as "the Colonel's Close."[46]

Boswell was a devotee of Erskine's works. In Holland in 1763 he read the *Principles*[47] which Lord Auchinleck, his father, thought well composed.[48] In 1764 he planned to translate Erskine's *Principles* into Latin,[49] and in 1774 he and his friend Charles Hay were studying Erskine's *Institute.*[50] But he does not seem ever to mention, or possibly to have realised, that they were remote kinsmen with a common ancestor. It is hard to think that Boswell would not have made much of the relationship, if he had known of it.

The Erskine family tree includes numerous other advocates and many Erskine wives came of legal families; they include not only Hope but a Stewart of Goodtrees, a Dalrymple and a Dundas of Arniston.

To come, however, to the one from this complicated family who mainly interests us, John Erskine[51] was born in 1695, son of the Hon. Colonel John Erskine of Carnock.[52] The father (1662–1743) contemplated the Bar as a career and his *Journal* narrates happenings in the Scottish courts in the early 1680s and mentions his reading Hope's *Minor Practicks* and Stair's *Institutions* among other works. In 1685–86 he studied law in Holland and accompanied William of Orange to England in 1688. He was later Lieutenant Governor of Stirling Castle (1701) and of Dumbarton Castle (1702) and a Member of Parliament 1702–10. He married four times and young John Erskine was a son of the second marriage, to Anna, daughter of William Dundas of Kincavil (?–1700, advocate 1665).

Young John Erskine was called to the Bar in 1719[53] but does not appear to have achieved any special distinction in practice. In 1732 the Faculty, having voted openly by roll call, sent up to the town council the names of Thomas Dundas and John Erskine as a short leet from which the magistrates and town council were to choose a person to be professor of civil law in the College, vacant by the death of James Craig.[54] The town council chose Dundas. But in 1737 the chair of Scots law fell vacant by the death of Alexander Bayne. "The roll being called and votes marked, it was found that Mr. John Erskine and Mr. James Balfour, Advocates, were the two that had the majority of votes."[55] The short leet submitted to the town council accordingly consisted of John Erskine and James Balfour.[56] Erskine was appointed by the town council. He seems to have taught mainly by commenting on Mackenzie, and he is reputed to have been successful as a teacher of law.[57] In 1746 he purchased the estate of Cardross in Menteith, near Port of Menteith, about 12 miles west of Stirling, which had formerly belonged to his grandfather David Erskine, Lord Cardross. Cardross House, still occupied, is a substantial plain mansion standing in good farming country, well planted with mature trees, facing south, looking over the stripling Forth, only a few hundred yards away.[58] In 1765 he resigned his chair to devote his time to the completion of his *Institute*. He died at Cardross in 1768.

Erskine's son, John (1721–1803),[59] became a minister, latterly at Greyfriars where he was the colleague of Principal Robertson, and leader of the Evangelical party in the Church of Scotland. He wrote extensively and corresponded with Kames and Hailes as well as with many leading divines.

In the 1730s and 1740s admission to the Faculty of Advocates by trial on the civil law was looked on as more honourable and made the intrant more respected than trial on Scots Law.[60] The great majority of those admitted in the first half of the century passed trials in the civil law.[61]

It was not until 1750 that the Faculty of Advocates required intrants to undergo a trial of their knowledge of the municipal law as well as the civil law, and the trial in the former could take place only after the lapse of one year from the trial in the latter. Thereafter the candidate had to undergo the public trial by publishing a thesis on the civil law and defending it before the Faculty.[62] But it is plain that long before this knowledge of the municipal law was in fact required prospective advocates had sought, and got, instruction in the municipal law privately and in the universities.

As professor, Erskine seems initially to have used Mackenzie's *Institutions* as the class textbook but in 1754 he published *The Principles of the Law of Scotland: In the Order of Sir George Mackenzie's Institutions of that Law*. The title-page does not give his name, but that appears at the end of the Advertisement. It bears on the title-page to be two volumes but these are normally bound in one, making a small octavo of 509 pages. His Advertisement points out that Mackenzie's compend was excessively condensed and is not so useful at present as formerly because of the many and considerable alterations which the law of Scotland has undergone since its publication. "The following sheets," he continues, "are designed to supply these defects; and by exhibiting a more full and complete view of the principles and general system of our law, to prepare the Reader for deeper researches into that study."

The *Principles* is divided into four books, the first dealing with laws in general, jurisdiction and courts, persons and the domestic relations (seven titles), the second with heritable rights and land law (12 titles), the third with personal rights, obligations and succession (10 titles), and the fourth with actions, probation, sentences and their execution and with crimes (four titles). Each book is divided into titles and these into numbered paragraphs.

Hume[63] regarded Mackenzie's order of treatment, which was followed by Erskine, as having

"generally been accounted somewhat unfortunate in this important article. On that account, and certainly on that only, I do not make use of Erskine's lesser work – his *Principles of the Law of Scotland* – as a text-book to be commented upon and expounded from this Chair. That treatise is, however, certainly one of the most useful law books that we have and comprises within very moderate bounds a great deal of sound intelligent doctrine and accurate information; and I mean therefore every day before dismissing to direct you to those passages of it where the subject of next day's study is to be found. On certain matters . . . I shall content myself with a more brief exposition of the law, or simply refer you to Erskine, or to those treatises, for a more minute acquaintance with it."

It represents a distinct advance on Mackenzie's *Institutions* and on Forbes's *Institute* in being less condensed but fuller and yet much more readable. The style is plain and direct, and the expression of principles clear. There are marginal titles to each numbered paragraph. There is a moderate citation of authority, mostly of statutes and cases, cited by date and pursuer's name. It must have been from the outset an admirable introductory work for students, clearer and easier to read than any preceding book.

Erskine adopted a positivistic view of the nature of law.

"Law is the command of a sovereign, containing a common rule of life for his subjects. It is divided into the law of nature, the law of nations, and civil or municipal law.[64]" "The law of nature is that which God, the Sovereign of the universe, has prescribed to all men, not by any formal promulgation, but by the internal dictate of reason alone. . . . The law of nations is also the result of reason, and has God for its author. . . . Civil or municipal law is that which every sovereign kingdom or state has appropriated to itself."[65] "The law of nature . . . is immutable, and cannot be controlled by any human authority."[66] "The municipal law of Scotland, as of most other countries, consists partly of statutory or written law, which has the express authority of the legislative power; partly of consuetude or unwritten law, which derives force from its presumed or tacit consent."[67]

The books of *Regiam Majestatem*, he says,

"are a system of Scots law, written by a private lawyer at the command of David I . . . none of these remains are received as of proper authority in our courts; yet they are of noble use in proving and illustrating our most ancient customs."[68] "The civil and canon laws, though they are not perhaps to be deemed proper parts of our written law, have undoubtedly had the greatest influence in Scotland . . . the Roman law continues to have great authority in all cases, where it is not derogated from by statute or custom, and where the genius of our law suffers us to apply it."[69] "An uniform tract of the judgments or decisions of the court of Session is commonly considered as part of our consuetudinary law, and without doubt, where a particular custom is thereby fixed or proved, such custom of itself constitutes a law: but decisions, though they bind the parties litigating, have not in their own nature, the authority of law in similar cases; yet where they continue uniform, great weight is laid on them. Neither can the judgments of the house of peers of Great Britain reach farther than to the parties in the appeal, since in these the Peers act as judges, not as lawgivers; nevertheless, where a similar judgment is repeated in the court of last resort, it must have the strongest influence upon the determinations of inferior courts."[70]

The *Principles* appears to have been an immediate success, so much so that there were no more editions of Mackenzie's *Institutions* after 1758. Erskine published revised editions in 1757 and 1764. There were four more editions of Erskine before the end of the eighteenth century, and 12 more in the nineteenth century, and a 20th and 21st in 1903 and 1911. After Erskine's death it was edited by Joseph Gillon, Professor John Schank More, Guthrie Smith, William Guthrie, Norman Macpherson and Sir John Rankine. Every edition has revisions and corrections, which in the course of time became more extensive and voluminous; whole new titles were added by editors to make the book more comprehensive and useful, while the citation of authority, particularly case law, was made fuller. In its last editions "little Erskine" was "now frankly nothing but a modern treatise with an archaic flavour due to the original authorship."[71] W. M. Gloag and R. C. Henderson in 1927[68] remarked that: "Since its publication in 1754 Erskine's *Principles*, as revised and brought up to date by various editors, has held a leading place as a textbook in the classes of Scots Law in the Universities. . . . In the later editions Erskine's original work had been extensively altered by the inclusion of new material rendered necessary by the development of the law," and they accordingly had thought it better to write a new book rather than try again to re-edit Erskine. But a life of 170 years for a textbook is remarkable and Erskine's approach initially shaped the view of law of thousands of Scottish lawyers. Though intended as a students' textbook it was repeatedly cited in court, and quoted from: "so also, in Erskine's Principles, in which it has long been understood that our Scottish law is very accurately, though briefly, explained, it is thus stated. . . ."[73]

Erskine resigned his chair in 1765 and devoted his remaining years to the composition of his *Institute*. He died in 1768. In 1773 there was published *An Institute of the Law of Scotland in Four Books. In the Order of Sir George Mackenzie's Institutions of that Law*, in two volumes quarto[14] (frequently bound in one) extending to 758 pages. It is not known who prepared the MS. for the press; that edition states that "a few notes have been added, referring to later decisions which occurred to the gentlemen who took the trouble to revise the manuscript." The books, and the subjects and arrangement of the titles, are the same as his *Principles*. The treatment of every topic is however fuller and more discursive. It is a less philosophic but much more readable work than that of Stair.

There were seven further editions, in 1784 by Alexander Fraser Tytler, later Lord Woodhouselee,[75] in 1793 and in 1805 by Joseph Gillon, the fifth by William Maxwell Morison,[76] compiler of the *Dictionary of Decisions*, in 1812, the sixth by James (later Lord) Ivory[77] in 1828, the seventh by Alexander Macallan[78] in 1838 and the eighth by James Badenach Nicholson[79] in 1871. In all the editions the text has been reprinted unaltered but annotations have been added. Ivory's edition contained much fuller and better annotations than any of the previous editions.[80] Badenach Nicolson omitted many of the notes of earlier editions but only a few of Ivory's, reprinting the great bulk of them verbatim, and added substantial and very valuable notes of his own, commenting both on the text and on Ivory's notes, and in effect brought the text up-to-date to 1871.

There are no problems about the text of Erskine's *Institute*. All the editions reprint the text of the first edition, which was printed posthumously, though it is known that the persons who prepared the MS. for the press made some minor changes on the text which Erskine left.[81]

The plan of the *Institute*, as of the *Principles*, is avowedly that of Mackenzie's *Institutions* and consequently that of Justinian's *Institutions*. The four books deal (Book I) with laws in general, jurisdiction and courts, persons and domestic relations (seven titles), in Book II with the division of rights and heritable rights (12 titles), in Book III with personal rights by obligation and succession (10 titles), and in Book IV with actions, probation, sentences and execution, and with crimes (four titles). Unlike Stair, Erskine did not try to develop a plan based on rights, but analysed the private law on the basis of its objects. "The objects of law, or the matters of which it treats, are three: 1st, persons; 2dly, Things, or Rights which persons are capable of enjoying; 3dly, Actions, by which the persons entitled to those rights make them effectual."[82] Later he distinguishes real rights[83] and personal rights.[84] But nowhere does he try to analyse a right.

Erskine begins by distinguishing law in the scientific sense, a statement of what regularly happens in the material world, from law in the strict meaning, "sometimes denoting the science which teacheth what things are or are not just, styled by the Romans *jurisprudentia*; and sometimes what is contained in that science; or, in other words, the particular rules to which the science is applied. In this last acceptation, *law* may be defined, the command of a sovereign, containing a common rule of life for his subjects, and obliging them to obedience. By a sovereign is understood the supreme power, whether it be lodged in the hands of one or of many."[85] This is totally different from Stair's natural law theory; this is a positivist view consonant with the approach of Bodin and Hobbes,[86] and foreshadowing the approach of Bentham and Austin. But he goes on to say that as the end of law is an equal distribution of justice, all laws ought to be in themselves just. "This character is inseparable from the laws of God, who is justice itself; and human laws, when they prescribe anything repugnant to natural justice, have no coercive force."[87] This seems some importation of natural law views.

Justice consists in the conformity of one's actions to law, whatever the person's motives to action.[88] When laws have a tendency to promote the real happiness of the subjects, that alone creates an obligation to obedience called by Heineccius and others the internal obligation of law. But there must also be sanction, express or implied.[89]

Law is divided, Erskine says, into the law of nature, the law of nations, and civil or municipal law. The first is, as Grotius stated, the dictate of reason. "That there is such a law cannot be denied, without denying the essential attributes of the Deity." "The law of nature, therefore, has the God of nature for its author and it is . . . impressed on our minds by the internal suggestion of reason."[90] The observance of the law of nature is strongly enforced by conscience.[91] It is divided into primary and secondary, the former regarding men in their state of nature, previous to any human act or establishment, the latter arising from the nature of society, and from the necessities of mankind as members of it.[92] From the latter arises the right of property; it is nothing more in effect than the first and most obvious principles of natural law applied to the state of civil society.[93]

The law of nations comprises the duties owed by one state to another and also rules generally received by sovereign powers for regulating their mutual relations.[94]

Some laws of nature are not enforced by positive law, such as benevolence, charity or gratitude, but left entirely to conscience,[95] but it is necessary for the power in states to superadd certain rules for explaining its true extent and adapting it to the several exigencies of the state.[96] The law which is superadded to the law of nature "is called civil and sometimes positive or municipal."[97] The right of legislation is vested in the supreme power of the state[98] which may not only superadd but circumscribe or set bounds to the law of nature, without violating its authority. "What the law of nature has commanded cannot be forbidden, or even dispensed with, by positive law; and, in like manner, what it prohibits, cannot be commanded, or even permitted, by human authority. The law of nature being indeed the command of God . . . no earthly lawgiver who is himself subject to that law, hath a right of abrogating or controlling it. Obedience, therefore, to any enactment which is plainly adverse to the perceptive law of nature, is rebellion against God."[99]

Erskine accordingly theoretically regards the law of nature as an ultimate overriding regulative force; he is by no means a pure or total positivist. But he gives no hypothetical example, still less cites any instance, of the law of nature being held to overrule positive law.[1]

He continues by distinguishing mere civil law, which derives its whole force from the arbitrary will of the lawgiver without any obvious foundation in nature, as the Roman laws of adoption and most of those of the feudal system, and mixed civil law, founded on the law of nature but adding to or varying it, such as the laws of marriage, testaments and contracts.[2] Positive or civil law may also be divided into divine, such as the judicial law of Moses, and human.[3] Among systems of human law notable examples are the Roman law[4] and the canon law.[5] Positive law may be divided into public and private.[6]

Erskine also interestingly observes[7] that "when mention is made of *The Common law* in our statutes, the Roman is understood, either by itself, 1540, c. 69;[8] 1585, c. 18;[9] 1587, c. 31;[10] or in conjunction with the Canon Law, 1540, c. 18;[11] 1551, c. 22.[12] When the expression is fuller, *the Common laws of the realm*, our ancient usages are meant, whether derived from the Roman law, the feudal customs, or whatever other source, 1503, c. 79;[13] 1584, c. 131,[14] etc. The epithet of *Common law* is used by English nearly in this last sense, to denote their most ancient customary law anterior to statute."

In the sense of historical sources Erskine distinguishes the municipal law into written or statutory and unwritten or customary.[15] As to the statutory law he doubts the authenticity of the laws of Malcolm Mackenneth,[16] and discusses the problem of *Regiam Majestatem*, which he considers to have been probably compiled by order of David I,[17] but discusses at length the objections to that view,[18] and the question what authority the works in Skene's collection have had or now ought to have in the Scottish courts. None, he concludes, ought to be received as of proper authority. But they may be produced for illustrating or even proving our ancient customs and are of excellent use towards understanding the history and gradual progress of our law.[19]   In the sense of formal or authoritative sources Erskine includes under written law Scots and British statutes from the time of James I onwards,[20] Acts of Sederunt,[21] and Roman law:

> "great weight is to be laid on the Roman law in all cases not fixed by statute or custom, and in which the genius of our law will suffer us to apply it: and as we have few statutes in the matter of contracts, transactions, restitutions, servitudes, tutories and obligations, the knowledge of it must be singularly useful in determining controversies arising from these heads of the law. Yet where any rule of the Roman law appears to have been founded on a subtilty peculiar to their system, it were absurd to pay the smallest regard to it."[22] "The Canon law must have been at least of as great authority in Scotland as

the Roman before the Reformation . . . but since the Reformation it has declined fast in its authority, so that it is now little respected except . . . where the canons are consistent with Protestant principles."[23]

Roman law and, even more so, canon law were clearly by 1773 of diminished authority. The Bible was to him an historical source only.

Unwritten law is that which without express enactment derives force from tacit consent, presumed from the inveterate or immemorial usage of the community.[24] The most essential articles of customary law such as the title of primogeniture are notorious and require no proof, nor declaration by court.[25] Our customary law is universal, applicable to the whole country, or local, such as udal rights in Orkney and Shetland.[26]

> "An uniform series of decisions of the court of session, i.e. of their judgments on particular points, either of right or of form, brought before them by litigants, and anciently called 'Practics' is by mackenzie §10, *h.t.*, accounted part of our customary law. . . ." "Great weight is to be laid on their later decisions, where they continue for a reasonable time uniform upon points that appear doubtful, *l. 38, De legibus*.[27] But they have no proper authority in similar cases . . . judgment ought not to be pronounced by examples or precedents, *l. 13, C. De sent. et int.*[28] Decisions, therefore, though they bind the parties litigating, create no obligation on the judges to follow in the same track, if it shall appear to them contrary to law. It is, however, certain that they are frequently the occasion of establishing usages, which, after they have gathered force by a sufficient length of time, must from the tacit consent of the state, make part of our unwritten law. What has been said of decisions of the court of session is also applicable to the judgments pronounced upon appeal by the House of Lords . . . their judgments, though they are final as to the parties in the appeal, cannot introduce any general rule which shall be binding either on themselves or inferior courts. Nevertheless, where a similar judgment is repeated in this court of the last resort, it ought to have the strongest influence on the determinations of inferior courts."[29]

It is very interesting to note this view of 1773, that a series of decisions makes customary law, and that decisions, even of the House of Lords, are not binding on the court or inferior courts. The rule of *stare decisis* was clearly not accepted.

When one examines Erskine's text the authorities cited *in gremio* are the statutes, and decisions, cited normally by date and pursuer's name, sometimes with the addition of the reporter's name, sometimes the reporter's name and the number of the decision only.[30] There are references to the Roman and canon law, the *Libri Feudorum*, to *Regiam Majestatem*, *Quoniam Attachiamenta*, Craig, Stair, Mackenzie and Kames.

Though Erskine repeatedly cites Stair, whom at one point he calls "that great lawyer,"[31] and other earlier writers he sometimes differs from them, even from all of them, as in his view that rights of reversion are not *stricti juris*,[32] or when he criticises two court decisions as being founded on an "erroneous assumption" as to the effect of the Act 1661, *c*. 51.[33] He sometimes relies on "nature" as a ground for differing from Stair, *e.g.* when he asserts that a father's power over a child ends with majority on the ground that it is "better founded in nature."[34] Or he may assert that a contrary opinion "appears to have no foundation in nature or in law."[35] Or he may doubt Stair as where he observes that certain children "are not, in the opinion of Stair, bastards.... If this opinion be well founded...."[36] Clearly he was a man of independent judgment who would not slavishly defer to his predecessors or to authority.

He has himself, of course, sometimes been criticised. Thus in *Smith* v. *Burns*[37] Lord President Boyle said that Erskine misunderstood the decision he relied on, Lord Mackenzie was not satisfied that the rule he laid down was supported by the decisions, and Lord Fullerton said that, looking at the decisions, he had no authority for his law on the point in issue.

It has repeatedly been observed[38] that mercantile topics were rather summarily treated by Erskine, indeed more summarily than by Stair. But as Bell pointed out in the Preface to his *Commentaries*, commercial enterprise and the law relative thereto received a stimulus after the Restoration, of which symptoms were the foundation of the Bank of Scotland and the Darien Scheme, but thereafter there was a setback evidenced by the failure of the Darien Scheme and the Jacobite rebellions of 1715 and 1745.

> "All the learning of the feudal law came more immediately to be called into use; and the professional success, as well as the character of a lawyer, was estimated chiefly according to his skill in the Law of Heritable Property. The jurisprudence of mercantile dealings, fitted for times of a different complexion, was almost entirely abandoned. In the work of Mr. Erskine, published after this era, there is very little to be found concerning Commercial Law; and the valuable learning governing Contracts, and the principles of Mercantile Jurisprudence in general, to be found in the *Institutions* of Lord Stair, shrinks in the *Institute* of Mr. Erskine into a very narrow compass."[39]

This is slightly surprising because by the time Erskine died the quickening of commerce had certainly begun; the Glasgow tobacco trade for example was substantial from 1745 and indeed peaked in 1775. The Industrial Revolution is usually dated as being under way from 1760.

As Badenach Nicolson observed:[40]

> "Other institutional writers, it may be acknowledged, have excelled Erskine in some one particular, – one in philosophical grasp of principles, another in subtlety of analysis, a third in precision of statement, a fourth in style. But though not, perhaps, preeminent in any one of these gifts or acquirements, he possessed them all in such sufficient measure that, combined with his great learning and his exceeding good sense, it is no wonder that for a century his writings have held so distinguished a place in the legal literature of his country.

"Erskine was in many respects fortunate in the time at which he wrote. In the middle of the Eighteenth century the law of Scotland, in both of its great divisions, – the one resting on the Roman law,[41] the other adapted from the Feudal customs,[42] – had reached the highest development of which it probably was capable. The views of the Scottish lawyers had been enlarged and their power of expressing them had been improved by their intercourse with their brethren on the other side of the Tweed; but yet there had been scarcely any attempt to introduce changes by means of Imperial legislation. The pedantry of former times had largely disappeared; but as yet the redundancy of modern writers was unknown. It was possible then, it is probably impossible now, to compose within reasonable limits an Institutional work on our law. The changes did not come violently or in great number at first. But beginning with the action of the House of Lords when cases went there on appeal – widening with the increasing activity of the Imperial legislature, and the demands of an increasingly commercial people, – fostered by the great respect paid to the judgments of English courts and the views of English writers, – these changes have gone on till, at the present day, the body of our law is not more bulky in size than it is heterogeneous in material."

The extent to which Erskine's major work won acceptance in the courts can be judged by scrutiny of the reports of the period. In the volumes of *Faculty Collection* for the last two decades of the eighteenth century Erskine appears to have been cited at least as much as Stair. By the early to mid-nineteenth century Erskine appears to have been relied on rather more, probably partly because it was more up-to-date.

In considering Erskine's contribution to Scottish legal scholarship one must consider the *Principles* and the *Institute* separately. The *Principles* was from first to last a moderate-sized survey for students, a plain statement of leading principles, not a practitioner's reference book nor a treatise to invoke to persuade a court, though it was undoubtedly sometimes used for both these purposes. It is indeed sometimes referred to in nineteenth-century cases as "lesser Institute," though it was commonly known as "little Erskine." In its time, and for some time after it should have been replaced, it was excellent, and it may sometimes still be looked at with profit. To have lasted 170 years is a great record for a legal textbook.

The *Institute* on the other hand is the fully extended and matured statement of his views. It is not so original as Stair's work, but a masterly restatement. It embodies the final development of the older common law largely embodying Roman and feudal law, and Erskine is supreme as the final and most authoritative expositor of the older law. It is detailed, exhaustive and accurate.

"He does not, and probably could not, display the philosophic breadth of Stair or the bold insight of Bell. His attitude is cautious rather than subtle, exact rather than profound. His style – be it said in all humility – sets the standard of the undistinguished pedestrian prose only too familiar to the reader of the modern textbook. But the name of Erskine is still one for reverence. Than Erskine's *Institute* no other volume in Scottish legal literature has been accorded a respect more nearly approaching that due to verbal inspiration. Within his limits he is unshaken and unassailable. But limits he had; for Erskine failed to realise that, even as he was writing, the centre of interest in legal study was rapidly shifting from the Law of Property to Commercial Law, which in his work received scant consideration and very imperfect treatment."[43]

NOTES

[1] DNB; Brunton & Haig, p. 14.

[2] RPC, II, 528.

[3] Grant, *History of the University of Edinburgh*, I, p. 167.

[4] APS, III, 178.

[5] RPC, III, 472.·

[6] RMS, V, 688.

[7] *Extracts from Burgh Records of Edinburgh*, V, 115–116, 131, 134. See also W. C. Dickinson, "The Advocates' Protest against the Institution of a Chair of Law in the University of Edinburgh" (1926) 23 S.H.R. 205.

[8] *Faculty of Advocates' Minute Book*, I, pp. 65–66.

[9] *Ibid.*, I, p. 77 (1687); see also *ibid.*, p. 133 (1694).

[10] *Ibid.*, I, p. 140.

[11] *Ibid.*, I, p. 159–161.

[12] APS X, App. 27.

[13] This is reminiscent of Gratian's *Concordia Discordantium Canonum*.

[14] APS, X, App. 28.

[15] Tunnage Act 1698 (APS, X 176, c. 37). This Act also authorised payments to John Adair, geographer, for maps, John Slezer, for *Theatrum Scotiae*, and Alexander Nisbet to enable him to publish his *Treatise on Heraldry*.

[16] Duty on Foreign Shipping Act 1704 (APS, XI, 203, c. 9).

[17] Grant, *op. cit.*, pp. 283–284 and App. I.

[18] He was later M.P. (1722–41), Solicitor-General (1725), Lord Advocate (1737), a judge as Lord Tinwald (1744) and Lord Justice-Clerk (Tinwald) (1748–63). See DNB; Tytler, *Life of Kames*, I, p. 37; Brunton & Haig, p. 513; Omond, *Lord Advocates*, II, p. 1; Lorimer, "Story of the Chair of Public Law in the University of Edinburgh" (1888) 4 L.Q.R. 139.

[19] Omond, II, p. 1.

[20] *Faculty of Advocates' Minute Book*, I, 287.

[21] DNB. See also Spottiswoode, *A Discourse Showing the Necessary Qualifications of a Student of the Laws* (1704); *The Form of Process*, preface.

[22] DNB; Brunton & Haig, p. 517; Tytler, *Life of Kames*, I, p. 41; Omond, *Lord Advocates*, II, p. 3. He was later Lord Advocate, 1742–45, and Lord President, 1754–60.

[23] Edinburgh Beer Duties Act 1722.

[24] On this system working see *Faculty of Advocates' Minute Book* (ed. Pinkerton), II, 164. This system continues save that consultations now take place between representatives of the Faculty and of the University Court, who submit names, with an agreed preference, for the Faculty formally to nominate to the Curators of Patronage (who are representatives of the University Court and of the Town Council). In practice the University has the real decision. Appointment to the Regius Chair of Public Law remains in the gift of the Crown.

[25] On Bayne, see further Chap. 18, *infra*. See also Bayne, *To the gentlemen who have attended his college of prelections* (a broadsheet, Edinburgh, 1725).

[26] Grant, *op. Cit.*, I, p. 288.

[27] C. M. Weis and F. A. Pottle, *Boswell in Extremes, 1776–78* (1971), p. 213.

[28] Anderson, S.N., II, p. 143; Genealogical trees in Seton, *Life of Chancellor Seton*, App. II, and Fergusson, *The Honourable Henry Erskine*, p. 535.

[29] Anderson, S.N., II, p. 593; III, p. 108; *Scots Peerage*, V, 590.

[30] Brunton & Haig, p. 484; Omond, *Lord Advocates*, I; he married a daughter of John Chiesly of Dalry who assassinated Lord President Sir George Lockhart in 1689.

[31] *Scots Peerage*, II, p. 366.

[32] On him see DNB; Anderson, S.N., II, p. 164; *Scots Peerage*, II, 278; *Complete Peerage*, II, 382; Bell (ed.), *The Scottish Antiquarian Tradition*.

[33] DNB; Anderson, S.N., II, p. 166; Chambers, BDES; *Scots Peerage*, II, 277; Fergusson, *The Honourable Henry Erskine* (1882); Omond, *Lord Advocates*, II, p. 163.

[34] DNB; Anderson, S.N., II, p. 171; Campbell, *Lives of the Lord Chancellors*, ch. 176; *Scots Peerage*, II, 277; *Complete Peerage*, V, 107. One of his great-grandsons was Sir

Thomas Erskine Holland (1835–1926), distinguished scholar in jurisprudence and international law.

[35] *Scots Peerage* II, 366.

[36] See *Scots Peerage*, II, 366; *Journal of the Hon. John Erskine of Carnock* (ed. W. Macleod, S.H.S., 1893).

[37] *Scots Peerage*, V, 622.

[38] DNB; *Complete Peerage*, XI, 172; Campbell, *Lives of the Lord Chancellors*. The Wedderburns' great-grandfather was Sir Peter Wedderburn (1616–79, advocate 1642), Lord Gosford, maker of a collection of decisions covering 1668–77, and their father was Peter Wedderburn (?–1756, advocate 1715), Lord Chesterhall; Brunton & Haig, pp. 394, 521.

[39] DNB; Brunton & Haig, p. 513; Omond, *Lord Advocates*, II, p. 1.

[40] Brunton & Haig, p. 526.

[41] Her first husband was Robert Bruce of Alva (?–1652, advocate 1631), Lord Broomhall (1649), and her third was Sir James Dundas of Arniston. See *Scots Peerage*, III, 488; V, 622.

[42] Her sister Mary married the Rev. Alexander Webster (1707–84), author of the first modern British census: see J. G. Kyd (ed.), *Scottish Population Statistics* (S.H.S., 1975).

[43] DNB.

[44] DNB; F. A. Pottle, *James Boswell: The Earlier Years, 1740–69.*

[45] Genealogical tree in C. Ryskamp and F. A. Pottle (ed.), *Boswell: The Ominous Years*, p. 377. See also F. A. Pottle, *James Boswell: The Earlier Years, 1740–69*, pp. 11–12 and 454–455.

[46] D. Beveridge, *Culross and Tulliallan* (1889), *passim.*

[47] F. A. Pottle (ed.), *Boswell in Holland*, p. 31.

[48] *Ibid.*, p. 63.

[49] *Ibid.*, p. 239.

[50] W. K. Wimsatt and F. A. Pottle (ed.), *Boswell for the Defence*, pp. 286, 332.

[51] DNB; Anderson, S.N., II, p. 158; Chambers, BDES.

[52] On the father see *Scots Peerage*, II, 366; *Journal of the Hon. John Erskine of Carnock, 1683–87* (ed. W. Macleod, S.H.S., 1893). Carnock is three miles WNW of Dunfermline. It is the next parish to Culross. Young Erskine lived at Newbigging, later a farmhouse, in the summers for about 30 years, until he bought Cardross in 1746. O.S.A., Carnock, 139.

[53] *Faculty of Advocates' Minute Book*, II, 27.

[54] *Ibid.*, II, 137.

[55] It must be assumed that the gentlemen concerned had made known their willingness to be put on the leet.

[56] *Ibid.*, II, 164.

[57] There are extant students' notes of his lectures which were on the same lines as his own *Principles* and *Institute*: NLS MS. 3862; Signet Library MS. 106. 38. See also D. B. Smith, "Mr Erskine's Lectures," 1962 S.L.T. (News) 74.

[58] There is an old photograph of the house in *Erskine of Carnock's Journal* (S.H.S.), p. xliv. See also *Memoirs of Sir David Erskine of Cardross, KCVO* (ed. Mrs. Steuart Erskine, 1926).

[59] DNB; Anderson, S.N., II, p. 159; Chambers, BDES; Henry Moncrieff Wellwood, *Life of Dr. John Erskine*; Cockburn's *Memorials*, p. 49; Kay's *Edinburgh Portraits*, I, 67, 171, 175.

[60] Spottiswoode, *Form of Process*, xlv. There was also a differential entry money favouring civil law candidates.

[61] J. S. Shaw, *The Management of Scottish Society, 1707–64* (1983), p. 27.

[62] *Faculty of Advocates' Minute Book* (ed. Pinkerton), II, 239, 241–242. Examination in the civil law had been required since 1610.

[63] *Baron Hume's Lectures, 1786–1822* (Stair Soc.), I, 9.

[64] *Prin.*, I, 1, 1.

[65] *Prin.*, I, 1, 2–4.

[66] *Prin.*, I, 1, 5.

[67] *Prin.*, I, 1, 11.

[68] *Prin.*, I, 1, 13.

[69] *Prin.*, I, 1, 15.

[70] *Prin.*, I, 1, 17.

[71] Sir John Rankine's preface to 21st (1911) ed. (the last one).

[72] *Introduction to the Law of Scotland* (1st ed.), preface.

[73] *Tennent* v. *Tennent's Trs.* (1868) 6 M. 840 at p. 865, *per* Lord Ardmillan.

[74] There is a separate title-page for Vol. II, comprising Books III and IV.

[75] 1747–1813, advocate 1770, Lord of Session 1802–13.

[76] ?–1821, advocate 1784.

[77] 1792–1866, advocate 1816, Lord of Session 1840–62.

[78] ?–1840, advocate 1825.

[79] 1832–99, advocate 1855; (1899) 7 S.L.T. 84 (portrait).

[80] In *Fortington* v. *Kinnaird*, 1942 S.C. 239, at p. 265, Lord Justice-Clerk Cooper attached importance to Lord Ivory's Notes.

[81] In *Heddle* v. *Baikie* (1841) 3 D. 370, at p. 373 Lord Moncreiff observed *obiter* that Erskine's *Principles* "as published by himself, is his work of highest authority." In *Kirkpatrick* v. *Kirkpatrick's Trs.* (1873) 11 M. 551, at p. 563, Lord Deas observed: "Mr. Erskine, it is well known, never himself revised his great work for publication, and he seems just to have transferred to it, in the above passage, the loose language of the report in the Faculty Collection." The lack of final revision by the author has accordingly detracted a little from the book's authority.

[82] I, 2, 1.

[83] II, 1, 1.

[84] III, 1, 1.

[85] *Inst.*, I, 1, 1–2.

[86] He cites Hobbes, *De Cive*, Lib. 14, §8 in I, 1, 5, and in I, 1, 14.

[87] I, 1, 3.

[88] I, 1, 4.

[89] I, 1, 5.

[90] I, 1, 7.

[91] I, 1, 10.

[92] I, 1, 12.

[93] I, 1, 13.

[94] I, 1, 14–15.

[95] I, 1, 16.

[96] I, 1, 17.

[97] I, 1, 18.

[98] I, 1, 19.

[99] I, 1, 20.

[1] The same is true of English law: see J. W. Gough, *Fundamental Law in English Constitutional History*, (1955).

[2] I, 1, 25.

[3] I, 1, 26.

[4] I, 1, 27.

[5] I, 1, 28.

[6] I, 1, 29.

[7] I, 1, 28.

[8] APS, II, 356, c. 1.

[9] APS, III, 396, c. 25.

[10] APS, III, 439, c. 14.

[11] APS, II, 357, c. 4.

[12] APS, II, 487, c. 17.

[13] APS, II, 252, c. 24.

[14] APS, III, 293, c. 4.

[15] I, 1, 30.

[16] I, 1, 31.

[17] I, 1, 32.

[18] I, 1, 33–35.

[19] I, 1, 36.

[20] I, 1, 37–39. He discusses interpretation of statutes in I, 1, 49–60.

[21] I, 1, 40.

[22] I, 1, 41.

[23] I, 1, 42.

[24] I, 1, 43.

[25] I, 1, 45. Feudal law is not expressly mentioned but many principles were clearly by this time embodied in customary law.

[26] I, 1, 46.

[27] Dig. I, 3, 38.

[28] The Code says, "*Cum non exemplis, sed legibus judicandum sit.*"

[29] I, 1, 47.

[30] There is a Note of Abbreviations, which indicates what treatises and collections of decisions he referred to. This indicates also that he referred to the manuscript collections of Haddington, Gosford, Forbes and Tinwald and to Hope's *Major Practicks*, and Bruce, later printed, and observed some decisions after 1719, which are neither to be found in any printed collection, nor in Kames's *Dictionary of Decisions*.

[31] II, 10, 30.

[32] II, 8, 5.

[33] III, 6, 10.

[34] I, 6, 55.

[35] II, 1, 4.

[36] III, 10, 6.

[37] (1847) 9 D. 1344 at pp. 1346–1347.

[38] *e.g.* by Badenach Nicolson, prefatory note to 8th ed., p. vii.

[39] Bell, *Comm.*, Preface.

[40] Prefatory note to 8th ed., p. v.

[41] *i.e.* obligations and moveable property.

[42] *i.e.* heritable property.

[43] Lord Cooper, "Some Classics of Scottish Legal Literature," in *Selected Papers* (1955), 39, at pp. 48–49.

CHAPTER 14

HENRY HOME, LORD KAMES

THE latter part of the eighteenth century was a brilliant period in Scottish literature and thought and not the least of the stars of this time was Lord Kames. Henry Home[1] was the son of George Home of Kames, in Eccles parish, Berwickshire,[2] and was born there in 1696. His ancestry on his father's side included Sir John Home of Renton, Lord Justice-Clerk 1663–71,[3] and his mother was a Walkinshaw of Barrowfield[4] and a granddaughter of Robert Baillie (1599–1662) who was Principal of Glasgow University, 1660–62, and author of the *Letters and Papers*.[5] His mother's sister became grandmother of Lord President Ilay Campbell.[6] He was tutored at home and never went to a university.

After service in a Writer to the Signet's office and attending James Craig's law lectures, possibly extra-murally, he became a pupil, probably of Patrick Grant (1691–1754, advocate 1754), later (1732) Lord Elchies, before being called to the Bar in 1723. At first he was not very successful in practice but his abilities were recognised after the publication of his *Remarkable Decisions* in 1728. In 1736 he was of counsel for Captain Porteous, who had ordered his men to fire on the Edinburgh mobs at the execution of the smuggler, Andrew Wilson. Porteous's later pardon caused the famous riot.[7]

According to Tytler,[8] in his oral pleading he eschewed oratory and rhetoric but concentrated on the principle on which he apprehended the decision ought to rest and endeavoured to show its application to the question in discussion.

In 1732 he sought appointment to the chair of civil law at Edinburgh in succession to James Craig[9] but was unsuccessful.

He was friendly with numerous bright young men of the town[10] and, more importantly, with Lord Deskford, later Earl of Findlater, Oswald of Dunnikier, a leading Member of Parliament, and from about 1739, David Hume, the philosopher.[11] In 1741 he inherited his father's estate of Kames and also married Agatha, daughter of James Drummond of Blair near Stirling. They had a son, George, and a daughter Jean; Kames brought into his Edinburgh household as tutor to George a young man, John Millar, a former student of Adam Smith, who later became pro-fessor of law at Glasgow.[12] James Boswell, whom Kames befriended, was friendly with George and committed adultery with Jean.[13] Boswell planned to write a life of Kames and asked him for notes for it, which Kames said he would give if Boswell would write it before his death, and that he wanted it done in a flattering manner.[14] If begun it was never completed.

He took a leading part, as co-founder, general manager, and from 1769 for many years president, of the Edinburgh Philosophical Society, which had originated in 1718 in a group calling themselves an Association for Improving Each Other in Classical Lore, reorganised in 1731 as, or possibly succeeded by, the Society for the Improvement of Medical Knowledge, which in turn became the Edinburgh Society for the

Improvement of Arts and Sciences. After the 1745 rebellion this was revived by Kames, Hume and Alexander Munro *primus* as the Edinburgh Philosophical Society and Kames became President in 1769. In 1783 it was chartered as The Royal Society of Edinburgh.[15] It is uncertain if Kames was a member of the Rankenian Society, but he was of the Select Society.[16] To the Philosophical Society he contributed a paper, "Of the Laws of Motion."[17]

In 1752 he was appointed a judge and took the judicial title of Lord Kames, and in 1763 was appointed a Lord of Justiciary also.[18] He is reported as being well esteemed by Bench and Bar.[19] Repute also attributes to him an eagerness to secure convictions.[20] According to the practice then obtaining in the High Court of Justiciary it was part of the judge's duty to examine the witnesses and dictate their evidence to the clerk, who engrossed it in the record of the court.[21] In this Kames was said to be particularly skilful. He is said, moreover,[22] to have been the first, or at least one of the first, to introduce in criminal trials the practice of charging the jury, of summarising the evidence and stating the points of law involved after counsel had concluded their addresses, and this soon became a generally accepted practice. It was sanctioned by statute within a year of Kames's death.

Throughout his mature years Kames maintained extensive connections with men of letters and science. He acted too as a kind of father-figure to David Hume, Adam Smith and James Boswell. He probably encouraged David Hume to become a man of letters and philosopher and in 1739 they seem to have nearly collaborated in a periodical.[23] Certainly in his earlier years David Hume did not publish anything without consulting Kames. For years Thomas Reid, the philosopher, spent summer vacations with the Kameses at Blair Drummond. Kames entertained Benjamin Franklin in 1759 and 1771 and maintained a friendship and correspondence with him for many years thereafter.[24]

He encouraged Adam Smith to give in 1748–50 the lectures on rhetoric and belles lettres[25] which presaged his appointment to the chairs successively of logic (1751) and moral philosophy (1752) in the University of Glasgow. Their friendship probably gave rise to some mutual influence of thought. He prompted Hugh Blair to lecture on the same subject, which led to his being elected in 1760 Professor of Rhetoric and from 1762 also of Belles Lettres in the University of Edinburgh.[26] He got young John Millar[27] to join his household in 1758–60 as tutor to his son: "The tutor of the son became the pupil and companion of the father; and the two years before Mr. Millar was called to the Bar, were spent, with great improvement on his part, in acquiring those enlarged views of the union of law with philosophy, which he afterwards displayed with uncommon ability in his academical lectures on Jurisprudence."[28] Kames and Adam Smith supported Millar's application for the chair of law at Glasgow, to which he was appointed in 1761.

In 1755 Kames was made a member of the Board of Trustees for the Encouragement of the Fisheries, Arts and Manufactures of Scotland. This was a board established by letters patent in 1727 to expend on the purposes named the sum, known as the Equivalent, paid by England to Scotland under Article 15 of the Treaty of Union of 1707.[29] In 1762–63 this board took up the project of a Forth and Clyde Canal and work was begun in 1768.

In the same or following year he was made one of the commissioners for management of the Forfeited Estates, which had been annexed to the Crown after the suppression of the rebellion of 1745.[30] Kames was a diligent member of both boards, frequently acting as chairman.

In 1766 Mrs. Drummond[31] succeeded to the estate of Blair Drummond,[32] six miles west of Stirling, on the death of her brother, and Kames took over the management of the estate and began to make agricultural improvements on a substantial scale. The most notable was his project of floating off the moss from the Kincardine Moss into the Forth, thereby uncovering the underlying soil for cultivation by some of the Highland families he had settled on the land for that purpose.

He sat on the Bench until about a week before his death, which occurred on December 27, 1782. He was 86. He is buried in the churchyard of Kincardine, Stirlingshire, near Blair Drummond. There is a Gothic monument to Lord Kames and Mrs. Drummond, part of the Blair-Drummond memorial in the churchyard, replacing an earlier monument about which nothing is known.

Kames's publications evidence industry and high professional competence, a breadth of scholarship and a lively, inquiring mind.[33]

His first book was a slim folio, published in 1728, entitled *Remarkable Decisions of the Court of Session* covering the period 1716–28. It is usually found bound with reports by Alexander Bruce, the Faculty reporter, and titled on the spine as *Bruce and Home's Decisions*. In "To the Reader" Kames observes that, "This Collection was at first undertaken, with a view to be ingrossed in a new projected Edition of the Viscount of Stair's *Institutions*: But the work turning bulky, it was thought more convenient to publish it separately . . . no decision is taken notice of, but wherein some new point is established; or which in some other shape, may contribute to make the intended edition of the *Institutions* more compleat." Kames was encouraged to collect the decisions by Lord President Sir Hew Dalrymple and he attributes any degree of perfection it attained to Dalrymple's directions. There are 107 decisions, occupying 287 pages. They state the point at issue clearly, usually narrate the arguments, and always state the decision, but not the judges' speeches or reasons. There was a later edition in 1790 with different pagination. The cases are all reprinted in Morison's *Dictionary*. David Hume, professor of Scots law in Edinburgh, commended the *Remarkable Decisions* to his students.[34]

This was followed in 1732 by *Essays upon Several Subjects in Law, viz Jus Tertii, Beneficium cedendarum actionum, Vinco vincentem* and *Prescription* based on cases in which he had been employed and which had raised these issues.[35] They "procured to their author the character of a profound and scientific lawyer."[36] In consequence his practice steadily developed and he became a rising advocate.

In 1741 he published in two folio volumes *The Decisions of the Court of Session from its institution to the present time, abridged and digested under proper heads in the form of a Dictionary*. This was a major work which must have involved enormous labour over a substantial number of years.[37] It was the first time that the decisions of more than two centuries had been abridged and reduced to their essentials and, more importantly, classified and grouped under headings, though some precedent for this had been provided by some of the *Practicks*.

"The classification of the Reports in the *Dictionary* is regulated by the *ratio decidendi*[38] or rule of law on which the judgment rests. Every head or title, therefore, is an illustration of some legal principle, by a series of adjudged cases regularly methodised; which by their order and connexion, exhibit a clear analysis of the general doctrine, and reconcile all its apparent anomalies. Thus the *Dictionary of Decisions* is not only to be valued as a great collection of authorities or precedents drawn from the practice of the court, and therefore of consummate utility to the barrister and practitioner, in the daily course of business, but is fitted, from the nature of its plan, to furnish instruction in the law as a science. The examination of various cases, which turn upon one common *ratio decidendi*, familiarises the mind, in all points of doubt, to recur immediately to a principle; and this habit of reference will not only be found of the utmost benefit when any abstruse or intricate question is the subject of discussion; but it tends, from the agreeable and vigorous exercise it affords to the intellectual powers, to give to jurisprudence that dignity as a science which it merits, and to render the study of the laws, instead of a servile drudgery, the manly employment of a philosophic mind."[39]

The "List of the Several Collections of Decisions from which this Work is taken" comprises eight printed collections (Durie, Gilmour, Stair, Dirleton, Falconer, Forbes' Journal, Bruce and Kames's own *Select Decisions*) and 17 manuscript collections (Sinclair, Maitland, Colvil, Haddington, Erskine of Inverteil, Newbyth, Gosford, Fountainhall, Hew Dalrymple, Forbes, Bruce, Harcarse and "Spotiswood, Balfour, Hope, Balmanno, Nicolson, Collected in form of a dictionary, and the decisions they observe are before the Restoration." (Some of these manuscript collections have subsequently been published.) To have deciphered and examined all these, summarised them, and put the slips for all the individual decisions into order must have been a most formidable undertaking. Without enormous labour it cannot be determined whether every decision recorded in any of these collections has been incorporated in the *Dictionary* though McGrugor, editor of the supplement of 1804 to the *Dictionary*, says in the advertisement to his volume that the omissions are considerable and in Fraser Tytler's third and fourth volumes also many cases have been overlooked.

Cases are stated concisely in a few lines and the reference given in the form of the reporter's name, the date and the names of the parties, *e.g.* "Haddington, January 16, 1610, Spence contra executor of Reid. The like, Maitland, May 6, 1553, Cunningham contra Lady Semple." The cases are grouped under main headings, such as Executor, Implied Condition and Minor, and under each heading marginal notes indicate sub-headings.

There is much of interest in the Preface.

"In the first place, decisions upon arbitrary question, points of form, and such like, ought to have the utmost weight and authority: For, with regard to matters of this nature, it is of great importance, that there should be a fixed rule publicly known but of very little importance what the rule be.

"As to cases which ought to be determined from principles universally agreed upon, I acknowledge that decisions ought there to have no authority. If the deduction upon which the decision is founded be fair, the decision is just; but then reason is the authority, not the decision. If the decision be founded upon wrong principles, or concludes falsely from true principles, it can signify nothing: And in these matters every man must judge for himself."

Other decisions, "tho' they have of themselves no authority, yet when collected with judgment and accuracy, they may be considered as so many regular treatises upon particular subjects." Whether they were technically authoritative or not Kames clearly regarded decisions as a valuable source of law; a scholar could inductively arrive at general principles from examination of decisions. But valuable is his affirmation that reason is the authority, not the decision. This is the point which has been forgotten as the principles of *stare decisis* have developed and become rigid since the mid-nineteenth century. Today a *ratio decidendi*, if discoverable, however contrary to reason, may be binding or persuasive and we must disregard reason and seek merely the principle of the decision.

Not long before Kames died Boswell asked him:[40] "Pray how long time did the *Dictionary* cost you?" Kames: "I don't like to recollect." Boswell: "I have heard your Lordship tell that the scheme of it was thought of by MacEwan the bookseller,[41] and he employed poor Bruce,[42] who blocked it out." Kames: "Yes. And after he had advanced a great deal of money from time to time, it was like to stop by which he would have lost much. So he applied to the Faculty to see if they would authorise its being published. Some of us were appointed to consider it,[43] and really from compassion I undertook to smooth it over so as it might pass. But when I came to set about it attentively, I found it was like taking down an old ruin: I should bring it about my ears. So I had to begin it anew. I employed Peter Haldane,[44] Archie Murray,[45] and William Grant[46] to abridge Durie's *Decisions* for me, as I could not trust to Bruce there. But what they did was so short, I was obliged to do it all over again. Pitfour[47] did some which were well done. The difficulty was to trace the steps which led to each decision, find out a *ratio decidendi* and place it under a head." Boswell: "Ay, there was the genius." Kames: "I have been ten hours studying one decision to fix its proper principle and place." "But, my Lord, there is some difficulty in finding out the head under which a decision is placed unless one is acquainted with the *Dictionary*. A man must be a good lawyer to be able to consult it." Kames: "No doubt it is of no use but to one acquainted with it."

There was a supplemental volume in 1780 by Fraser Tytler (later Lord Woodhouselee). A second edition appeared in 1790 and in 1797 a two-volume supplement was issued by Fraser Tytler, Kames's biographer, "to whom the task was committed by Lord Kames himself, and carried on under his own eye."[48] These are labelled Volumes 3 and 4. They are based on the Session Papers and the collections of Edgar, Clerk

PLATE 1.   Sir Thomas Craig of Riccarton
(*Frontispiece to the third edition of* Jus Feudale)

George Jameson

PLATE 2. Sir Thomas Hope of Craighall
(*In the collection of the Faculty of Advocates*)

Artist unknown

PLATE 3.   James Dalrymple, Viscount Stair
(*In the collection of the Faculty of Advocates*)

Sir Godfrey Kneller

PLATE 4.   Sir George Mackenzie of Rosehaugh
(*In the collection of the Faculty of Advocates*)

Artist unknown

PLATE 5.   John Erskine
(*In the collection of the Faculty of Advocates*)

David Martin

PLATE 6.   Henry Home, Lord Kames
(*National Galleries of Scotland, Edinburgh*)

Sir Henry Raeburn

PLATE 7.   David Hume
(*In the collection of the Faculty of Advocates*)

Sir Henry Raeburn

PLATE 8.   George Joseph Bell
(*In the collection of the Faculty of Advocates*)

John H. Lorimer

PLATE 9.   James Lorimer
(*By permission of the University of Edinburgh*)

Sir John Lavery

PLATE 10.   John McLaren
(*National Galleries of Scotland, Edinburgh*)

D. Alison

PLATE 11.   Sir John Rankine
(*By permission of the University of Edinburgh*)

PLATE 12.   William Murray Gloag
(*From a photograph in the possession of the author*)

Home, Kilkerran, Falconer, Kames's *Remarkable* and *Select Decisions* and the *Faculty Collection*. The summaries of the decisions are fuller than in the original work. A supplement to Volumes 3 and 4, was published by Thomas McGrugor[49] in 1804. It sought to supply the omissions in the two last volumes and bring the work down to 1796.

Later correspondence between Kames and Boswell casts some doubt on the accuracy of the Dictionary. In October 1770 Boswell wrote to Kames, "putting a combined question of law and conscience.

> "'You know it has been questioned by some nice philosophers whether the practice of the law be consistent with strict moral rectitude'. This question had come home with peculiar force on Boswell's looking up a principle in Kames's *Dictionary of Decisions* and then going down to the Advocates' Library to consult the original manuscript report on the sixteenth-century case cited in the Dictionary. He found that the latter was 'totally different' from what the Dictionary said. 'Now, my good Lord, what ought I to do? The *Dictionary of Decisions* is a book of authority in our court . . . I know your Lordship is not answerable for the exactness of every decision in the *Dictionary*, as you have told me a part of it was done by another hand'. 'Friend Boswell', wrote Kames in reply, 'I have not been much accustomed to answer casuistical queries, especially of such a squeamish nature. What business has your officious Honour to pry into secrets – was not the *Dictionary* sufficient authority without going farther? Take what you have got for your peeping'. Then relaxing he went on to give Boswell some very good legal advice (perhaps what Boswell was in part angling for) and ended, 'Yours affectionately, Henry Home.'"[50]

The Court of Session did not sit between August 1745 and July 1746 on account of the Jacobite rebellion,[57] and Kames withdrew to his house of Kames and employed his time in writing a small book of 220 pages, published in 1747, entitled *Essays upon Several Subjects concerning British Antiquities*, comprising five short dissertations, "On the Introduction of the Feudal Law into Scotland," "On the Constitution of Parliament," "On Honour and Dignity," "On Succession or Descent," and "Appendix on the Hereditary and Indefeasible Right of Kings."[52] There were later editions in 1749, 1763 and 1797. This work shows a shift of Kames's interests from strictly legal subjects to an historical approach to the study of law. "But he confesses, he has at heart to raise a spirit among his countrymen, of searching into their antiquities, those especially which regard the Law and the Constitution. . . ."[53] It is a useful early essay on legal history. Some of the essays have political overtones. He rejected as improbable the view that feudalism had been introduced into Scotland in the reign of Malcolm II (1005–34) and preferred to assign it to the reign of Malcolm Canmore (1058–93), in part attributable to the example given by the Norman Conquest of England. The essay on Parliament is largely directed against the view that the Scottish Parliaments were agencies of freedom; rather their constitution, and particularly the institution of the Lords of the Articles, gave power to the Crown.

The British Parliament, continuing English practice, was better at resisting the Crown. Kames was clearly arguing to reconcile Scots to the Union of 1707.

In "Succession or Descent" Kames emphasised the association of feudal tenure with war, which hindered commercial use of land, and indicated by reference to the course of social change in Europe since the Middle Ages that feudalism had little future; commerce, and a contractual, not a tenurial nexus between parties was the future pattern. The preference for males and the rule of primogeniture were not natural principles, but rules convenient for a system based on capacity for war. He touches also on two of his pet antipathies, the use of fictions to preserve outdated rules and the existence of entails to maintain land in one line.[54] In "Honour and Dignity," he discusses the change from titles associated with territory to those personal, annexed to families. He found rank acceptable when associated with the ownership of land or with political power. In the "Appendix on the Hereditary and Indefeasible Right of Kings" he contends, by reference to the development of government, that government exists for the good of mankind, that no particular form is necessary, or preferable to any other, save in so far as it has a greater tendency to promote the good of the society. He attacks the notion of the divine right of kings, and the views of the Stuarts in particular, and his conclusion is truly an appeal to the Jacobites to see where the peaceful interests of their country truly lay.

David Hume commended the *Essays*; he wrote that he had "read them with great satisfaction, the reasonings are solid, the conjectures ingenious, and the whole is instructive. The Stile is also very good; correct and nervous and very pure; only a very few Scotticisms as conform for conformable, which I remarkt. You do me the Honour to borrow some Principles from a certain Book.[55]"[56]

The *Essays* went through three editions in Kames's lifetime and a fourth, posthumously, in 1797.

Kames had for many years been interested in philosophic topics and had had in 1723 a correspondence with Samuel Clarke whose *Discourse concerning the Being and Attributes of God, the Obligations of Natural Religion, and the Truth and Certainty of the Christian Revelation*, based on sermons at St. Paul's in 1704 and 1705, reached a fourth edition in 1716, and one with Andrew Baxter, whose detailed examination of Berkeley's doctrines, *An Enquiry into the Nature of the Human Soul*, appeared in 1722.[57] In 1737 he visited Butler, whose *Analogy of Religion* had been published the previous year, and later corresponded with Butler about points in his sermons.[58] Ultimately the results of Kames's thinking and discussions with these philosophers and with his intellectual circle in Edinburgh came to light.

In 1751 appeared *Essays on the Principles of Morality and Natural Religion*, seeking to prove that the great laws of morality, which influence the conduct of man as a social being, have their foundation in the human constitution and are as certain and immutable as those physical laws which regulate the whole system of nature. He looked particularly at David Hume's view that utility was the chief foundation of morals. This also shows his interests broadening and moving away from law alone. He begins by stressing sympathy as a mainspring of human nature, and its existence leads him to commit himself to the doctrine of final causation. We have, he contends, a moral sense which distinguishes the different kinds of human actions, some of which are indispensably obligatory on us, and others merely arising from benevolence or generosity. Kames was attacked for his views, as savouring of scepticism and impiety,[59] was threatened with being cited before the General Assembly of the Kirk,[60] and driven to reply anonymously in *Objections against the Essays on Morality and Natural Religion Examined* (1756) and to modify his views in the third edition of the *Essays* (1779).[61] The leading moderates in the Assembly easily rebutted the charges of heresy, but the matter caused much discussion in the press and rumbled on for several years. The principle involved was of great importance, nothing less than that of freedom for intellectual investigation, the cardinal idea of the Enlightenment. Kames's book in time became a standard text in the Scottish common-sense philosophy. Thomas Reid read the *Essays* and became a friend of Kames; his own works are a more philosophically developed version of the main propositions advanced by Kames.[62]

Some reference books attribute to Kames a *Principles of the Law of Scotland* of the year 1754. But this is a mistake, an erroneous attribution to Kames of the anonymous first edition of the *Principles* of Erskine.

His next work, published in 1757, was *The Statute Law of Scotland Abridged with Historical Notes*, designed to do for the statute law what he had done for the decisions of the court, to bring together all the enacted law under general titles. These are arranged alphabetically, from "Abbreviate" to "Yeoman." The order was intended to be as nearly as possible that of the *Dictionary of Decisions*, though there are headings not found in that work. It draws on enacted law from the earliest times, from the *Regiam* down to the union with England, and is particularly important for its valuable historical notes (pp. 407–440). To some extent Kames was following the trail blazed by Mackenzie's *Observations on the Acts of Parliament from 1424* and Stewart of Goodtrees' *Index or Abridgment of the Acts of Parliament*.[63] It differed from Swinton's *Abridgment of the Public Statutes* in starting from *Regiam Majestatem* (which also shows Kames's antiquarian bent), whereas Swinton commenced at the union of the kingdoms. A number of the entries, such as on "Commerce," "Jurisdiction," "Liberty of the Subject" and "Police" are enlightening and of considerable interest and value today. There is recognition of the need to interpret Scots legislation liberally, and of the principle of desuetude. There was a second edition in 1769 and a third in 1778.

Kames was very sensible of the inconvenience, particularly in commercial relations, of the differences between the legal systems of Scotland and of England, and he favoured a measure of assimilation. Having put his ideas in the form of separate short essays on certain branches of the law of Scotland he sent them to Lord Chancellor Hardwicke,[64] who made some suggestions.[65] Prompted by these Kames published his *Historical Law Tracts* in 1759. His Preface begins:

> "The history of man is a delightful subject. A rational enquirer is no
> less entertained than instructed, in tracing the progress of manners,

of laws, of arts, from their birth to their present maturity. Events and subordinate incidents are, in each of these, linked together, and connected in a regular chain of causes and effects. Law in particular, becomes then only a rational study, when it is traced historically, from its first rudiments among savages, through successive changes, to its highest improvements in a civilised society. . . . Such neglect of the history of law is the more strange, that in place of a dry, intricate, and crabbed science, law treated historically becomes an entertaining study. . .''

He goes on to regret the divergence between the laws of Scotland and of England, and observes that he has chosen topics which permit of comparative treatment. The *Tracts* number 14, and treat of criminal law, promises and covenants, property, securities upon land for payment of debt, privilege of an heir-apparent in a feudal holding to continue the possession of his ancestor, regalities and the privilege of repledging, courts, brieves, process in absence, execution against moveables and land for payment of debt, personal execution for payment of debt, execution for obtaining payment after the death of the debtor, limited and universal representation of heirs, and old and new extent. An appendix contains specimens of old legal forms, such as a letter of slains, and letters of four forms. The book is interesting and shows Kames's sociological interests, that he was concerned not only to look at the evolution of legal doctrines but to examine their connection with manners and politics. This approach is not novel today; it was in 1758.

David Hume thought a man might as well think of making a fine sauce by a mixture of wormwood and aloes as an agreeable composition by joining metaphysics and Scotch law, but that the book had merit though few people would take the pains of diving into it.[66] This proved, however, a misjudgment. It was popular and ran into four editions. More importantly, it was a significant contribution to the emerging science of historical inquiry, which was being practised at about the same time by Hume, Robertson, Gibbon and, further away, Voltaire[67] and Kant.[68] Dugald Stewart later stressed the special interest of the men of the Scottish Enlightenment in which he called Theoretical or Conjectural History, by which he meant an attempt "to account, from the changes in the condition of mankind, which take place in the different stages of their progress, for the corresponding alterations which their institutions undergo." The first attempt was made by Montesquieu[69] but: "The advances in this line of enquiry since Montesquieu's time have been great. Lord Kames, in his *Historical Law Tracts*, has given us some excellent specimens of it, particularly in his Essays on the History of Property and of Criminal Law, and many ingenious speculations of the same kind occur in the works of Mr. Millar."[70]

Kames followed Hardwicke's advice in dealing first with the history of the criminal law, but he treated the subject in a broad and philosophical way. Criminal law is based on resentment of injury; punishment vents resentment and revenge, but gradually revenge came to be transmitted into public punishment. He presents what is truly a psychological theory of criminal law.

Kames's general attitude was that the laws of Scotland and of England had been the same at the stage of customary and feudal law and had diverged, but there would be great advantages in bringing about a closer union, even a complete union. Hardwicke also took up the question of entails, to which Kames was strongly opposed, as is apparent from the way he deals critically with them in his *Sketches*, the *Historical Law Tracts* and again in his *Elucidations*.

The *Historical Law Tracts* proved an influential book; it was a major element in leading Adam Smith to make the remark, "We must every one of us acknowledge Kames for our master."[71] Principal Robertson acknowledged in his "View of the Progress of Society in Europe," part of his Introduction to *The History of The Reign of the Emperor Charles V*, his indebtedness to Kames's *Historical Law Tracts* for material and ideas about public and private jurisdictions in Europe. The Swiss jurist Daniel Fellenberg (1736–1801) got Kames to join a Society of Citizens organised from Berne with the purpose of perfecting moral science and the science of legislation. A French scholar Mathieu-Antoine Bouchard (1719–1804) made a partial translation.

Kames's views were welcomed by legal reformers. William Eden[72] concurred with Kames in seeing the development as one from the gratification of private resentment to control of that instinct by law and government. Jeremy Bentham[73] received the *Tracts* with enthusiasm, treating them as a splendid corrective to Blackstone's complacency.

Historical Law Tracts was, however, severely criticised by Walter Ross[74] in his *Lectures on the History and Practice of the Law of Scotland Relative to Conveyancing and Legal Diligence* (1792) for having more than once built on a hypothesis and reasoned convincingly from it, but erroneously. But he concedes: "Although, by trusting to his own strength of reasoning, in place of deliberate inquiry, Lord Kaims [sic] has often gone wrong, yet, upon the whole, it would be the height of ingratitude not to acknowledge, that I have been more indebted to him for assistance and materials, than to all other writers on our law."[75]

The significance of the *Historical Law Tracts* as a contribution to historical understanding was fourfold; it showed the application of the technique of comparative analysis to legal history; it related those techniques to inquiries, of the kind initiated by Montesquieu, into human motivation and cultural differences attributable to environment; it showed how institutions were modified and evolved in response to changes in human activities; and it sprang from a philosophy of history which stressed the mode of subsistence and the belief in human progress. Moreover it first revealed Kames's essentially sociological interest, concerned to trace not only the development of legal principles but their connection with manners and politics.[76] Similarly Kames's view of the final purpose of legal history was that it indicated the need for legal change by demonstrating the antiquated nature of inherited legal practices.[77]

Kames had also been looking at the differences between the legal systems of England and of Scotland and in particular at the phenomenon, then very marked and well established in the former system, the existence of parallel bodies of rules of common law applied in the king's courts of

King's Bench, Common Pleas and Exchequer, and of principles of equity applied in the Chancellor's Court of Chancery. Frequently these two bodies of rules conflicted, frequently a litigant resorting to one had to be referred to the other, and frequently serious injustice was avoided only by the manner in which equity supplemented, moderated and corrected rules of strict law.

The origin of the principles of equity in English law lay in the medieval practice of litigants petitioning the king for relief in circumstances not covered or not adequately covered by rules of law applied by the common law courts, of these petitions being referred to the Lord Chancellor to do what was fair in the circumstances and the practice gradually developing of Chancellors regularly dealing with such petitions and building up a body of practice on such matters. By the mid-eighteenth century equity was a substantial and systematised body of principles, not an interference with law on a vague and uncertain basis of natural justice but a regular body of principles.[78]

In Scotland, however, there had never been such a dual system of administration of justice. Kames had pointed out in his *Historical Law Tracts* that the Court of Session was a court of both law and equity and it had never been hindered, as had the English courts of common law, by the premature development of strict forms of action, from doing justice by applying principles founded on natural justice and reason. The Roman law, basis of much of Scots law, had similarly been familiar with rules introduced by praetors to supplement and correct principles of strict law. Scots law accordingly, partly from Roman law principles and partly from indigenous principles developed on the basis of natural justice, had incorporated many principles of an equitable character. But it had never developed Equity in the sense of a distinct body of principles administered, as it was in England down to 1875, in a distinct court, a distinct jurisdiction. Moreover many of the principles of English equity were known to Scottish common law, though frequently under other names.[79]

In 1759 Kames sent to Lord Chancellor Hardwicke an "Introduction to the Treatise upon Equity" discussing the different concepts of equity, as equality or abstract justice, as natural justice and reason as contrasted with the rigidity and possible injustice of strict law, and as a distinct body of principles contrasted with and sometimes conflicting with principles of common law. Hardwicke agreed with Kames's view on the origins of the equitable jurisdiction of the Chancellor and encouraged him in his study of the subject.

In 1760 Kames published his *Principles of Equity*. He divided it into an historical and philosophical introduction and three Books dealing respectively with powers of a court of equity founded on the principle of justice, powers of a court of equity founded on the principle of utility, and application of equitable powers to several important subjects. This reflects his propositions that two great principles, justice and utility, govern the proceedings of a court of equity. Book I is divided into three Parts, each subdivided into chapters, some of which are further subdivided into sections, and runs to 172 pages. Book II in six chapters is much smaller – a mere 15 pages, and Book III in eight chapters extends to 100 pages.[80]

In his Introduction Kames makes the significant observation[81] that

"in England, where the courts of equity and common law are distinct, the boundary betwixt equity and common law, where the legislature doth not interpose, will remain always the same. But in Scotland, and other countries where equity and common law are united in one court, the boundary varies imperceptibly. For what originally is a rule in equity, loses its character when, gathering strength by practice, it is considered as common law. Thus the *actio negotiorum gestorum*, retention, salvage, etc. are in Scotland scarce now considered as depending on principles of equity."

In substances there are many principles based on equity recognised in Scots law and administered as part of common law. Equity in Scotland is not by any means confined to the *nobile officium* of the Court of Session. This is a very valuable and valid observation.

He sketched the development of the Court of Chancery in England but appreciated that while a distinct Court of Chancery or equitable jurisdiction had never developed in Scotland this did not mean that equitable tempering of rules of strict law was unknown in or foreign to Scottish jurisprudence, because, firstly, many Roman law principles of an essentially equitable character had been incorporated into Scottish common law and, secondly, in Scotland the King's privilege in Council to give relief in any case not covered by common law had never been delegated to a Chancellor or other officer, nor assigned to a particular tribunal. From the early days of the Court of Session equity was administered as part of common law; it was an inherent moderating force, not as in England an external power. Kames favoured an undivided jurisdiction administering law and equity.

He considered also the important question: whether a court of equity ought to be governed by any general rules? The whole trend of English equity had been to move from formless discretion to discretion exercised in accordance with settled principles, and in the development of these principles Lord Chancellor Nottingham, Kames's correspondent Lord Chancellor Hardwicke and, later, Lord Chancellor Eldon contributed very substantially.

Kames gives marginal references to a few authorities, mostly drawn from English equity decisions, and to a few Scottish cases. But his work should not be viewed as a textbook but as an exploration of an historical and jurisprudential problem, sparked off by his quest for similarities in Scots and English law. At the end he gives an index of the principles explained or mentioned in the work, which is reminiscent of the lists of maxims of equity found in the older English books on that subject, such as "He that demands equity must give equity." There is also an Explanation of Scotch Law terms.

In writing his *Equity* Kames was, for Scotland, breaking new ground. None of his predecessors had dealt with the topic save Bankton, who in his comparative observations on Scots and English law made many valuable points, not least that the Court of Session had an extensive jurisdiction of an essentially equitable character and foundation as part of its ordinary jurisdiction as well as the extraordinary equitable jurisdiction called the *nobile officium*. There were, of course, English books[82] and some volumes of reports of cases in Chancery but even Kames had to accept that historical origins, concepts, terminology, and procedure for invoking the jurisdiction were quite different. The English books and cases might provide suggestive analogies for him but could not provide direct guidance for Scottish courts.

Kames's *Equity* attracted considerable attention in both countries. Hardwicke himself in a long letter to Kames of June 30, 1759,[83] though expressing a preference for divided jurisdictions conceded that there were powerful agreements for a unified system, as Kames contended. Lord Chief Justice Mansfield commended *Equity* highly[84] and Benjamin Franklin regarded it as an excellent work.[85]

Blackstone, however,[86] denied that equity was a science of which it was possible to ascertain the principles and at several points expressly criticised Kames and Mr. Justice Story[87] regarded judicial discretion according to conscience as dangerous.

Equity went through five editions down to 1825 but deserves to be remembered more as an essay in historical jurisprudence than as a treatise on equity as a body of principles administered in either system. It is, however, probably Kames's most important contribution to legal theory. Kames himself seems to have been proud of it. Braxfield observed to Boswell: "Kames thinks nothing of any law book but *Principles of Equity*."[88]

In the later eighteenth and earlier nineteenth century *Equity* was treated as a work of authority and frequently cited in court. Bell in his *Commentaries* (1810) and *Principles* (1829) refers to it with respect. In 1885 in *Cassels* v. *Lamb*[89] Lord Rutherford Clark said that Kames's authority stood very high, though Lord Fraser[90] was more doubtful. In 1889 in *Kennedy* v. *Stewart*[91] it was observed during the debate: "The principles of equity as systematised by Lord Kames I look upon as the equity law of Scotland." But in *Tennent* v. *Tennent's Trs.*[92] Lord Ardmillan observed:

> "I am not quite prepared to adopt to their full extent the views expressed by Lord Kames in the first book of his *Principles of Equity*, which have been urged for the pursuer. They are very broadly and unqualifiedly put; and I think they have not been altogether recognised as law, and have been subjected to some qualifications. Still there is much truth and power in many of the remarks on the great principles of justice according to which the law reads all contracts. I agree with Lord Kames, that... ."

In the *Gordon Peerage Case* (1929) Lord Dunedin said: "He is an authority, though rather a wild one." *Equity* was cited in *Burmah Oil Co (Burma Trading)* v. *Lord Advocate*.[93]

After *Equity* Kames turned next to a different theme and published a small volume in 1761, entitled *An Introduction to the Art of Thinking*. This is an elementary book intended for young people, "suited to the minds of children when reason first begins to open, and should be calculated to serve at once the purposes of improving the understanding and cultivating just notions of morality." It is divided into two parts, the first containing a series of moral maxims, some culled from ancient and modern moralists and some original, and the second illustrations of these maxims by fictitious stories or historical anecdotes.

Some of the maxims in the first part are probably too advanced for most children and even young adults. The book is now largely forgotten but Benjamin Franklin thought well of the plan and of the execution of it.[94] Franklin and his son had been in Scotland in the autumn of 1759 and spent some time with Kames at his estate in Berwickshire, and this led to a lifelong friendship and correspondence. In a letter of May 3, 1760,[95] Franklin wrote: "I am now reading with great pleasure and improvement your excellent work, *The Principles of Equity*. It will be of the greatest advantage to the judges in our colonies, not only in those which have Courts of Chancery, but also in those which, having no such courts, are obliged to mix equity with the common law. It will be of more service to the colony judges, as few of them have been bred to the law. I have sent a book to a particular friend, one of the Judges of the Supreme Court in Pennsylvania."

For a considerable time Kames had also been thinking about the causes of the pleasure which men derive from specimens of the fine arts, poetry, painting, sculpture, music and architecture. Aristotle had written on *Rhetoric* and a *Poetics* and there had been others among the ancients. More recently Francis Hutcheson had in 1725 published *An Inquiry into the Original of our Ideas of Beauty and Virtue*, Thomas Edwards his *Canons of Criticism* in 1748, Hogarth *The Analysis of Beauty* in 1753, Burke his *Inquiry into the Origin of our Ideas of the Sublime and Beautiful* in 1756–57, and Alexander Gerard *An Essay on Taste* in 1759. Kames's own *Elements of Criticism* appeared in three volumes octavo in 1762.

It was prompted by the remarkable efflorescence of literary, historical and philosophical writing in Scotland in the mid-eighteenth century. It had clearly been contemplated for a considerable time as materials on the main theme, the interaction between psychology and literature, are to be found in a common-place book dating from the 1730s. It is by far his most important non-legal work and brought him considerable prestige. He described his subject as "the science of rational criticism." His major proposition was that the impressions made on the mind by specimens of the fine arts are a subject of reasoning as well as of feeling, and that the pleasant emotions stirred by seeing or hearing an aesthetically pleasing object of sensation depend on certain principles common to the whole species of mankind though possessed in greater measure by some rather than by others. He based his *Elements* on a "science of man" in Hume's sense, and made substantial use of the concept of association of ideas which Hume believed was the most original feature of his *Treatise of Human Nature*. The method was empirical, analysing instances into parts and then synthesising these into a rational structure of laws and rules of artistic composition[96] and may owe something to Stair's and Mackenzie's *Institutions*, developing from one principle to the next. Chapters 1 to 15 deal with fundamental rules of human nature and how they give rise to aesthetic principles. Chapters 16 to 24 show how aesthetic principles might be used in practice and in Chapter 25 Kames treats of the standard of taste involved in apprehending and maintaining critical judgments.

Apart from anything else, the *Elements* shows a very extensive acquaintance with literature, ancient and modern, with gardening and architecture, and Kames cites numerous examples and instances to illustrate his
contentions.

Benjamin Franklin regarded it as an "excellent work ... in which I
found great entertainment: much to admire, and nothing to reprove".[97]
Dr. Johnson, who usually took a jaundiced view of anything Scottish,
conceded that at least the method was right[98] and that "it is a pretty essay
and deserves to be held in some estimation, though it is chimerical."[99]
Adam Smith, however,[1] said it was Kames's worst work and Voltaire
derided it. There has been attributed[2] to it and to Kames's work at Blair
Drummond the widespread interest from the 1760s in gardening as an art
form.

The *Elements* was clearly popular and very widely read and studied. It
went through 13 editions in 75 years, and there were at least 32 editions
published in the United States and a German translation, repeatedly
reprinted. Kames has been said to have founded a school of philosophical
criticism. His followers included George Campbell, Professor of Divinity
at Marischal College, Aberdeen, and author of *The Philosophy of
Rhetoric* of 1776. Hugh Blair, first holder of the chair of English Literature and Rhetoric at Edinburgh, published his *Lectures on Rhetoric and
Belles-Lettres* in 1783, which shows the influence of Kames. The influence
was lesser in the Reverend Archibald Alison's[3] *Essay on the Nature and
Principles of Taste* (1790), but continued in Kames's friend, William
Smellie's, articles on taste and beauty in the early editions of the
Encyclopaedia Britannica (1771, 1778–83 and 1797) and in Dugald Stewart's *Philosophical Essays* (1810). In the United States the *Elements* was
a standard college text until the mid-nineteenth century. In Germany the
Elements attracted considerable interest and Herder, Lessing and possibly Kant knew Kames's work well.[4] It has been a major work in its field
and made Kames's name known and respected far outside his own
country and primary field of expertise.

In 1766 Kames returned to his main subject and published a further
volume of *Remarkable Decisions*, reports of 130 cases covering the years
1730 to 1752. He had himself, he tells us in the Preface, been engaged as
counsel in all the cases noted, and had deposited in the Advocates'
Library the Session papers in the cases. The reports are careful and
detailed and some of the cases are of much interest. The cases are all
reprinted in Morison's *Dictionary*, save two which are in Morison's
Supplemental Volume. The volume has sometimes been criticised as by
Lord Justice-Clerk Hope[5] where he describes a report as "characterised
with all the peculiarities which render the *Remarkable Decisions* more
specimens of speculation than accurate reports."

In the same year there appeared *Progress of Flax Husbandry in
Scotland*,[6] a pamphlet which reflects the work in which he participated of
the Board of Trustees for the Encouragement of Fisheries, Arts and
Manufactures in Scotland.

For some years in the 1760s and early 1770s Kames had been collecting
historical, anthropological and sociological information for a natural
history of man. He may have got some inspiration from Buffon's *Histoire*

naturelle, générale et particulière (1744–1804). He was doubtless displeased when Lord Monboddo to some extent anticipated him by publishing in 1773 the first of ultimately (by 1792) six volumes *Of the Origin and Progress of Language* but Kames's *Sketches of the History of Man* appeared in 1774. It developed some of the ideas first enunciated in *British Antiquities, Morality and Natural Religion, Historical Law Tracts* and *Elements of Criticism*. It is in three books dealing respectively with the progress of men independently of society, the progress of men in society, and the progress of the sciences. The first sketch deals with the Diversity of Men and Languages and Kames struggles with the question whether there had been separate creations of men at different places, or men had been scattered over the world and consequently developed differently towards maturity. He discusses the origin of property, the origin and progress of commerce, the origin and progress of the arts, the progress of woman (and Kames supported the right of women to a position of importance in society, though still subordinate to men), the development of luxury. A major theme of the second book is the need for patriotism if society is to survive. He treats of government, the progress of states from small to great, public finances, and much more. The third book examines the progress of the sciences, divided into the mental and moral branches and theology. He got Thomas Reid, professor of moral philosophy at Glasgow, to contribute an account of Aristotle's logic, which indicates Kames's sympathy with the common-sense school of philosophy. In an Appendix he adds three sketches concerning Scotland, dealing with entails, which he wished to see abolished as withdrawing land from commerce and hindering development, with reform of the government of the royal burghs, which he wished to see made accountable to the Court of Exchequer in Scotland, and with the improvement and preservation in order of the highways in Scotland, which he thought required the appointment of commissioners in each county to survey roads and raise road taxes for their repair and maintenance.

The book initially had a rather mixed reception but nine more editions were called for by 1819; there was an American version of part of Book I and a German translation.

The book also presents Kames's final views of his moral theory[7] which was inspired principally by Francis Hutcheson's moral theory.[8] Man discerned the moral character of actions through his moral sense or conscience, and its dictates could be construed as laws of nature. He distinguished morally just actions from merely morally correct ones; in the former the individual is under a duty to act. This view of justice was adopted by Adam Smith[8] in his *Theory of Moral Sentiments*, who refers back[9] to Kames. The distinction was relevant to legal theory in several ways: justice was unlike other moral virtues and the rules of justice were accordingly susceptible of precise formulation in a way other moral precepts were not; the distinction between justice and other virtues was also relevant to the historical treatment of legal practices; and because justice was essential for any effective social existence its social utility could be easily and clearly observed. This did not however mean that justice could be explained in entirely utilitarian terms.[10]

From the 1750s Kames was a vigorous member of the Board of Trustees for Fisheries, Manufactures and Improvements in Scotland and one of the Commissioners for the Forfeited Estates.[11] In 1776 his interests as a reforming landlord, an "improver," found expression in *The Gentleman Farmer, being an attempt to improve agriculture by subjecting it to the test of rational principles*, dedicated to Sir John Pringle, President of the Royal Society of London, which reached a sixth edition. It is based on his own experience as laird of Kames and then of Blair Drummond, on observation, reading, experiments, correspondence with and the work of various scientific friends; it is a practical book and is believed to have had a considerable influence on agricultural improvement and agricultural education. In an Appendix he sketched a plan for a Board of Agriculture to survey the state of husbandry in the different counties, develop plans of instruction for improving husbandry, offer prizes and rewards for improvements and initiate a programme of research and experiments. Such a board was set up in England in 1793 under the direction of Sir John Sinclair of Ulbster,[12] himself a great improver, with Arthur Young[13] as secretary. It came to an end in 1822 without having had significant effect. It seems probable, moreover, that Kames's work encouraged a greater project initiated by Sir John Sinclair, the *Statistical Account of Scotland, drawn from the communications of the ministers of the different parishes*, published in 21 volumes over the years 1791–99.[14]

Then in 1777 appeared *Elucidations respecting the Common and Statute Law of Scotland*, dedicated to Henry Dundas, Lord Advocate and Dean of Faculty and later Viscount Melville. There was a second edition in 1800. This volume was intended, the author said in his preface, to vindicate the municipal law of his country from the reproach it had incurred from the writings of the older jurists, of comprising a mass of propositions, rarely connected either with premises or consequences. Kames was concerned to advocate rational principle in opposition to practice and blind deference to authority.

> "No science affords more opportunity for exerting the reasoning faculty than that of law; and yet, in no other science is authority so prevalent. What are our law-books but a mass of naked propositions, drawn chiefly from the decisions of our supreme courts, rarely connected either with premises or consequences? ... Lord Stair, our capital writer on law, was an eminent philosopher; but as he was not educated to the profession of law, his Institutes [*sic*] consist chiefly of decisions of the court of session; which with him are all of equal authority, though not always concordant; nor are the works of our later writers much more systematic.... Were law taught as a rational science, its principles unfolded, and its connection with manners and politics, it would prove an enticing study to every person who has an appetite for knowledge."[15]

Kames was very critical of the teachers of law of his time – "nothing is presented to the young gentlemen but naked facts" – but in a footnote, he excepted from censure "John Millar, Professor of Roman Law in the College of Glasgow." The volume contains 42 distinct topics of discussion, including a large number of difficult and abstruse doctrines such as the active and passive representation of heirs, special and general services of heirs, and the rules for the ranking of creditors on a bankrupt estate. Kames also revised and republished in this volume the greater part of the material which he had published in 1732 under the title of *Essays on Several Subjects in Law*.

In 1780 he published his *Select Decisions of the Court of Session* comprising a selection of the cases which had come before the court between 1752, when Kames became a judge, and 1768. There are 264 reports. Sometimes Kames indicates the substance of his own judgment, or his own doubt as to the decision. Publication was delayed because, he admits, it would have had an insolent air of challenging the court, in so far as he dissented from judgments, and he accordingly delayed until none of the judges concerned, himself apart, was still alive. There are two editions of this volume also, but with the same pagination. Morison reprinted most of these decisions in his text, all the rest bar two in his Appendix, Part I, and the remaining two in his supplemental volume.

His last publication, in 1781, was *Loose Hints upon Education, Chiefly concerning the Culture of the Heart*, of which an enlarged edition came out in the following year, shortly before his death. It shows considerable insight into child psychology and educational method, and advocates the kind of education which would help children develop their sensibility. Like many of his works it provoked a reply, in the form of a poem which charged him with lack of respect for Christianity, but required a further edition in the next year, the year of Kames's death.

Kames is a fascinating person; but so many and varied are the facets of his personality and his achievements that he is difficult to evaluate justly. He was a leading figure in the Scottish Enlightenment, he was jurist and judge, author and literary critic, philosopher and improving landlord. He counselled and encouraged David Hume and Adam Smith, had a hand in securing the academic appointments of Adam Smith, William Cullen the physician, Joseph Black the physicist, and John Millar, and participated in the circle of literary, historical and philosophical scholars comprising Hume, Adam Smith, Robertson and others. To Hume, Adam Smith, Boswell and Millar he was a father-figure, even a father-substitute.

Kames was clearly a man of very broad interests and active, inquiring mind and, bearing in mind that all he wrote was in the spare time of a busy advocate and, later, of a Lord of Session and Justiciary and public figure, shows a high degree of application; only a man of driving energy could have kept up this steady production of books on diverse subjects. He was not merely a jurist, but also legal historian, moralist, anthropologist and several other roles. Boswell once admonished himself (as he not infrequently did): "Never desist an hour from plan. Be always like Lord Kames, doing something."[16]

It is worth observing that most of his legal writings appeared before he was 65 (in 1761) and, apart from the *Essays on the Principles of Morality and Natural Religion*, all his non-legal works appeared after that date. This indicates a shifting and broadening of his interests and possibly also a feeling that, to some extent, he had made his contribution to the science he practised and could justifiably devote time to other interests.

As public figure and public servant Kames was associated with many activities of public benefit, as a Commissioner for the Forfeited Estates from 1755 or 1756 to 1782,[17] amongst other acts prompting Walker's[18] and Wight's[19] tours and surveys of large tracts of Scotland, as a Trustee of the Board of Trustees for Fisheries, Manufactures and Improvements in Scotland from 1755 to 1782, which largely transformed the country from a backward one to an advanced one,[20] as a promoter of improved transport facilities, notably the Forth and Clyde Canal[21] and a protagonist in the 1750s and 1760s of the schemes to erect the North Bridge, drain the Nor' Loch, and begin the development of the New Town of Edinburgh.[22]

Kames's reputation as a jurist in the narrow sense rests on his three volumes of reports, the *Folio Dictionary*, the *Principles of Equity* and his historico-legal essays and tracts. The reports are good and better than most previous ones, while the *Folio Dictionary* must have been an invaluable working tool for Bench and Bar. *Equity* and the essays and tracts are not properly to be compared with the work of Bankton and Erskine, Hume and Bell, because he was not seeking to expound and systematise, but to hypothesise, probe, criticise and, to a substantial extent, provoke reform. Many of those works show his concern to rationalise, systematise and put in order. To him law was very much a number of connected principles, not a collection of arbitrary rules to be memorised. He was a protagonist of law reform, particularly the abolition of entails.[23] One must consider him also as historical jurist and philosophical jurist.

Kames was not an historian in any strict sense, like Hume or Robertson, but he had a keen sense of the fact that humanity and its institutions develop and evolve, and that an historical approach to many issues was illuminating. "Events and subordinate incidents are linked together in a regular chain of causes and effects. Law in particular becomes then only a rational study when it is traced from its first rudiments among savages through successive changes to its highest improvement in a civilised society."[24] Again the theoretical-historical approach he adopted was not original to him, nor unique at the time; Hume, Robertson, Adam Ferguson and Millar all adopted it, but the ideas appeared earlier in Kames than in the others named and some of these rather younger contemporaries acknowledged their indebtedness to him. Moreover, Kames applied his approach to law generally and to legal institutions much more extensively than any of his predecessors had done. Thus he examines the evolution of reparation for wrongs from revenge and retribution to composition by fine or damages by reference to many ancient and medieval law codes. The approach to history coming into vogue in his time, and to some extent initiated by him, was what Dugald Stewart called "theoretical" or "conjectural" history,[25] examining evolution and development of institutions, laws, languages and other aspects of society rather than merely facts in sequence, and bringing in also a comparative consideration. "We must be satisfied with collecting facts and circumstances as they may be gathered from the laws of different countries: and if these, put together, make a regular system of causes and effects, we may rationally conclude that the progress has been the same among all nations, in the capital circumstances at least, for accidents of the singular nature of a people, or of a government, will always produce some peculiarities."[26] This approach he shared with Hume, Robertson, Ferguson and Millar but it appeared early in his work, and before it was common. Younger men acknowledged his lead in this matter. Also he applied it to legal institutions much more thoroughly than any predecessor had done, but yet cautiously and sensible of its uncertainties, of the danger of drawing conclusions for Scotland from foreign evidence.

As a philosopher[27] he was a follower of Shaftesbury and Butler and in accord with the other Scottish thinkers of the time in being less interested in metaphysics and epistemology than in social and moral philosophy, and in accord with the "common-sense" school;[28] of which the founder was Thomas Reid, in his *Inquiry into the Human Mind on the Principles of Common Sense* (1764). Kames indeed has been credited[29] with the distinction of marking out the lines which Scottish philosophy was to follow, his *Essays on the Principles of Morality and Natural Religion* foreshadowing Reid's work. Kames was not, however, a systematic nor a deep philosophic thinker. Like others of the Scottish philosophers of the time he had a sociological bent in his thinking, recognising that a man was a member of a community, and his behaviour influenced by a great variety of social factors, many of them historically shaped. In this he was at one with Adam Smith, Ferguson, Millar and others. So too his approach to principles of morality is primarily psychological, finding the foundations of morality in human nature itself. The real drives to human action are passions, which are many and varied.

So far as concerns philosophy of law[30] Kames considered the existing major expositions of Scots law to be both inadequately philosophical and insufficiently historical, neither reducing the rules to general principles nor seeing them as adaptations to constantly changing society. To him, Stair's *Institutions* consisted chiefly of the decisions of the Court of Session, which to Stair were all of equal authority, though not always consistent, and hence insufficiently philosophical, while Mackenzie's *Institutions* failed to integrate the principles and classifications of the Roman law with modern Scots law. Neither criticism is wholly fair yet not wholly unfounded.

Kames did not anywhere explicitly expound his own philosophy of law but his views can be gathered from his *Equity*, the prefaces to various works, and numerous scattered observations. It can probably safely be stated as follows: Law is a body of norms or rules for regulating the conduct of men in society, enforceable by public authority, and includes the institutions, such as courts, and the machinery for applying the rules, to cases. The end of law is justice and orderly relations among persons in society. Though mainly a development from custom it must ultimately have a moral foundation and be based on human nature and the nature of society. To be understood, effective and fairly administered, the rules of law must be reduced to an ordered system and to their underlying principles, and related to one another, to the other social controls operating in the society, to prevailing moral standards and to the total state of society. But specific rules may vary greatly from one country to another, which requires their comparative examination. To accord with constantly developing society and changing circumstances law and legal institutions must be changed and adapted and reinterpreted, which requires historical consideration. The administration of law must always be tempered by equity to avoid undue rigour or the inflexibility which begets injustice.

The natural law-based legal philosophy of the seventeenth century had not in Kames fully given way to the eighteenth century utilitarian view, still less to the emergent positivism of the nineteenth century. The law of nature was to him still an important basis for law.

He was very insistent that law be scientifically approached. The rules of law had to be classified and put into systematic order, reduced to their underlying principles and viewed in relation to the society in which they were intended to function, and consequently adapted to the constant changes taking place in society. His insistence on reducing the body of law and the major particular rules to principles was a persistent element in Kames's work, in his practice and in his writings, not mere principles in the sense of very general propositions of law but principles founded on human nature, on the nature of society and on essential rationality which Kames regarded as part of the natural order.

It is interesting that in Kames the phrase, and the notion of, *ratio decidendi* seems first to make its appearance in Scotland. Decisions, that is, were important and valuable for, and in so far as they evidenced, a principle or proposition of law applied to a set of facts justifying the court's decision of the controversy.

Kames was a man with many facets to his character and many interests and was esteemed by many in his own generation. Lord Chancellor Hardwicke, with whom Kames corresponded on legal reforms, treated him with considerable regard. Thomas Reid wrote:[31]

> "His genius and industry in many different branches of literature will, by his works, be known to posterity. His private virtues and public spirit, his assiduity through a long and laborious life in many honourable public offices with which he was entrusted, and his zeal to encourage and promote everything that tended to the improvement of his country, in laws, literature, manufactures and agriculture, are best known to his friends and contemporaries."

John Ramsay of Ochtertyre summed up:[32]

> "But be Lord Kames's speculative opinions what they would, he was universally esteemed a man of great talents and taste, who thought and acted for himself. In fact the ardour and industry with which he promoted the cultivation and improvement of polite literature and the useful arts in Scotland was almost apostolical. By living to a great age, he had the satisfaction to see his own labours and those of his associates crowned with all the success he could desire; and what was highly flattering, himself looked up to as an umpire in literary questions and matters of taste."

James Boswell characterised him:[33]

> "Lord Kames is a man of uncommon genius, great application and extensive knowledge, of which his various works are a standing

proof. It is indeed astonishing to find a man so much master of Law, Philosophy and the Belles Lettres, and possessed of so great insight into human nature and, at the same time, a good companion, cheerful and lively. Although he is now and then a little whimsical and impatient of contradiction, he is honest, friendly and public spirited and is, on the whole, a great character."

Dr. Johnson did not think so highly of him. On an occasion in 1768 when he was depreciating the Scots, Boswell said to him: "But, Sir, we have Lord Kames." "You have Lord Kames," said he, "keep him, ha! ha! ha! We don't envy you him."[34] Then years later Johnson told Boswell he had been reading Kames's *Sketches of the History of Man* and criticised it.[35] On the other hand he said to Boswell that, "Lord Kames's *Elements* is a pretty essay and deserves to be held in some estimation, though it is chimerical."[36]

Smellie, the printer, stated that, "in the supreme court the law writings of Lord Kames are held in equal estimation and quoted with equal respect as those of Coke and Blackstone in the courts of England.[37] This verdict would have pleased Kames, but it is an over-statement.

Kames and his works were well known to, and well regarded by, leading political and legal figures in the young United States, by John Adams,[38] Thomas Jefferson, who recommended many of Kames's books as important in a young lawyer's education,[39] James Madison, and James Wilson, born in Fife and a student at St. Andrews, an original Associate Justice of the Supreme Court and a teacher at the young University of Pennsylvania who in the introductory lecture to what was, with one exception, probably the earliest course of lectures on law ever given in an American college, stated that he intended in the series to do little more than offer a commentary on the principles of law laid down by Lord Kames, along with Francis Bacon and Lord Bolingbroke.[40]

The better part of a century later, opinion still ranked Kames high. In 1847 James Reddie wrote: "From the middle of the [eighteenth] century the study of law as a science made considerable progress. Lord Kames had, in a great measure, the merit of originating this study."[41]

Professor Hume, though he commended Kames's *Remarkable Decisions* to his students, "particularly the first, as the best series of Law Essays in our language. Much instruction can be drawn from the details there given of the pleadings in the cases," in his latter years warned his students that Kames

"was curious also of the antiquities of our law, and knew how to turn his researches to the best account. It is right, however, to mention to the young student that we cannot in every instance rely upon his doctrines (ingenious and instructive though they always are) as a faithful picture of the actual state of practice. His impressions of what ought to be the law were so lively on some occasions as to influence his judgment of what was truly done or meant on the Bench."[42]

Judicial views of Kames have varied; in *Cassels* v. *Lamb*[43] Lord Rutherford Clark said:

"Again, I am charged with having cited, in support of my opinion, a passage which, it is said, has become one of the curiosities of our legal literature. It is taken from the writings of Lord Kames. I always conceived that Lord Kames was a great lawyer, and that his authority stood very high. He was sometimes quaint in his expression, and in this instance his metaphor is perhaps not happy. But his meaning is clear. . ."

NOTES

[1] DNB; Anderson, S.N., II, p. 486; Chambers, BDES; Brunton & Haig, p. 515; *Scots Magazine* 53 (1791); H. H. Brown, "A Master of Equity" (1905) 20 L.Q.R. 308; W. Smellie, *Literary and Characteristic Lives* (1800), p. 119; J. Ramsay of Ochtertyre, *Scotland and Scotsmen in the Eighteenth Century* (ed. Allardyce), (1888); H. G. Graham, *Scottish Men of Letters in the 18th Century* (1901), p. 172; W. F. Gray, *Some Old Scots Judges* (1914), p. 1; Kay's *Edinburgh Portraits* I, 14, 323; A. Fraser Tytler (Lord Woodhouselee), *Memoirs of the Life and Writings of the Honourable Henry Home of Kames* (2 vols.) 1807 and supp. 1809; W. C. Lehmann, *Henry Home, Lord Kames, and the Scottish Enlightenment* (1971); I. S. Ross, *Lord Kames and the Scotland of his Day* (1972).

[2] Home sold Kames in 1775 but the mansion house of his time, a gabled house of the old Scottish style, still stands not materially changed. See sketch in Ross, *op. cit.* p. 7.

[3] Brunton & Haig, p. 383.

[4] His mother's older brother, John Walkinshaw of Barrowfield, had 10 daughters, one of whom, Clementina, became mistress of Prince Charles Edward Stewart and mother of his only child, the Duchess of Albany. D. Daiches, *Charles Edward Stuart* (1973), pp. 188, 287, 289–300; M. Foster. *The Rash Adventurer* (1973), pp. 230, 288; F. J. A. Skeet, *The Life and Letters of H. R. H. Charlotte Stuart, Duchess of Albany* (1932).

[5] Bannatyne Club, 3 vols (1841–42).

[6] Tytler, pp. 1–2. Ilay Campbell of Succoth (1734–1823, advocate 1757) was Lord Advocate 1784, and Lord President 1789–1808.

[7] *The Trial of Captain Porteous* (ed. W. Roughead, 1909). See also Scott's *Heart of Midlothian.*

[8] pp. 44–47. See also J. A. Inglis, "Eighteenth century Pleading" (1908) 24 J.R. 42.

[9] *Culloden Papers* 125 (letter to Lord Advocate Duncan Forbes).

[10] Tytler, pp. 57–71.

[11] *Ibid.*, pp. 71–105.

[12] Chap. 15, *infra.*

[13] F. A. Pottle, *James Boswell; The Earlier Years 1740–1769*, pp. 78–79, 93, 478.

[14] C. Ryskamp and F. A. Pottle, *Boswell, The Ominous Years*, 1774–76, p. 68; I. S. Lustig and F. A. Pottle, *Boswell, The Applause of the Jury*, 1782–85, pp. 53–54.

[15] Tytler, *op. cit.*, I, p. 184; II, p. 86; Edinburgh Philosophical Society, *Essays and Observations, Physical and Literary*, I (1754), Preface; *Trans, R.S.E.* I (1788), 3–100; Neil Campbell and R.M.S. Smellie, *The Royal Society of Edinburgh, 1783–1983* (1983). The Faculty of Advocates strongly supported the founding of the R.S.E. and the inaugural meeting was chaired by Thomas Miller, Lord Justice-Clerk, and attended by Principal Robertson, Professor Adam Ferguson, Ilay Campbell, Solicitor-General, Robert Cullen, John Maclaurin and William Nairne, Advocates and Adam Smith, Commissioner of Customs. Invitations to join were sent to the Lords of Session, Barons of Exchequer and Professors of each of the four Universities. The Duke of Buccleuch was elected the first President. Lawyers who served as Presidents have been Sir Walter Scott (1820–32), Lord Moncreiff (1879–84), and Lord Cameron (1973–76), while a number of distinguished lawyers have been elected Fellows. Original Fellows included Lord Abercromby, Lord Bannatyne, Robert Blair (later Lord President), Sir George Buchan Hepburn (Baron of Exchequer), Ilay Campbell (later Lord President), Lord Stonefield, Lord Craig, Lord Cullen, Henry Dundas (later Viscount Melville), Lord President Dundas, Robert Dundas (later Chief Baron of Exchequer), Lord Pitfour, Charles Hope (later Lord President), David Hume (later Baron of Exchequer), Lord Dreghorn, Lord Meadowbank, Lord Justice-Clerk Miller, Lord Glenlee, Sir James Montgomery (Chief Baron of Exchequer), Lord Dunsinnan, Fletcher Norton (Baron of Exchequer), Lord Eskgrove, Lord Robertson, Adam Smith, Lord Woodhouselee, Lord Elliock.

[16] Lehmann, p. 53; Ross, p. 177.

[17] *Essays and Obervations, Physical and Literary Read before a Society in Edinburgh* (1754).

[18] On the wire-pulling to secure these appointments, see Lehmann, *op. cit.*, p. 32; Ross, *op. cit.*, p. 295.

[19] Ramsay, *op. cit.*, I, p. 202.

[20] Ross, *op. cit*, p. 304.

[21] This is discontinued in 1783.

[22] Ramsay, *op. cit.* I, p. 189, citing the trials of Katharine Nairn in 1765 and of William

Keith in 1766. See also William Roughead, *Twelve Scots Trials* (1913), pp. 128, 149–150, 156.

[23] Ross, *op. cit.*, p. 81.

[24] Ross, *op. cit.*, p. 197; J. B. Nolan, *Beniamin Franklin in Scotland and Ireland 1759 and 1771* (1938).

[25] For these see W. R. Scott, *Adam Smith as Student and Professor* (1937), Chap. 5; Adam Smith, *Lectures on Rhetoric and Belles Lettres* (ed. J. C. Bryce, 1983). Smith may also have given lectures which were the basis of his later lectures on jurisprudence: Ross, *op. cit.*, p. 93.

[26] Tytler, p. 196; *op. cit.*, p. 94.

[27] On whom see Chap. 15.

[28] Tytler, p. 199.

[29] Tytler, I, p. 202; Lehmann, Chap. 7. In 1764 the Commissioners instructed Dr. John Walker to make a survey of the Western Isles (Tytler, II, p. 12), and his reports have been published as *An Economical History of the Hebrides and the Highlands* (2 vols., 1808), and *Report on the Hebrides* (ed. M. M. McKay, 1980).

[30] *Ibid.* See also H. Hamilton, *Economic History of Scotland in the Eighteenth Century*; J. Shaw, *The Management of Scottish Society* (1983), p. 77.

[31] It was not until 1907 that wives of Lords of Session were entitled to the courtesy style of "Lady."

[32] The original mansion-house was demolished in 1866 and the present house was built in 1868 and rebuilt after a fire in 1919, on a site not far from that of the original. See print in Ross, *op. cit.*, p. 354. The estate, sold by the Home-Drummonds in 1911, is now a safari park.

[33] Full bibliography in DNB; Lehmann, *op. cit*, p. 341; Ross, *op. cit.*

[34] *Lectures* (ed. Paton, Stair Soc.), I, p. 15.

[35] The essays are analysed in Tytler, *op. cit.*, pp. 48–56. The latter three essays were republished in amended form as his *Elucidations respecting the Law of Scotland*.

[36] Tytler, *op. cit.* p. 56.

[37] In 1730 he was authorised to borrow Fountainhalls's *Decisions* from the Library for use in making the *Dictionary*; *Faculty of Advocates' Minute Book* (ed. Pinkerton), II, 125, 126; see also 168.

[38] The use of this term, and the concept itself, as early as this is noteworthy. Kames used the phrase himself, in *Cumming* v. *King's Advocate*, 1756, *Select Decisions*, 159, in his *Principles of Equity* (1760), p. 25 and in the Preface to his *Remarkable Decisions* (1766). Did he originate it? It is also used in *Paterson* v. *Speirs*, Nov. 29, 1782, F.C.

[39] Tytler, p. 114.

[40] I. S. Lustig and F. A. Pottle, *Boswell, The Applause of the Jury*, 1782–85 (1982), p. 18.

[41] James MacEwan in 1718 founded the *Edinburgh Evening Courant*, a Whig journal. In 1752 he succeeded the poet Allan Ramsay as proprietor of the principal bookshop in Edinburgh and the first lending library in Scotland.

[42] Alexander Bruce (?–1729, advocate 1702) succeeded William Forbes as Faculty Reporter and ultimately produced the *Decisions of the Lords of Council and Session* for November 1714 to July 1715 in 1720. These are frequently bound up with Vol. I of Kames's *Remarkable Decisions of the Court of Session*, 1716–1728, and backed as *Bruce and Home's Decisions*. Further, reports by Bruce of 1716–17 are printed in Vol. 3 of the *Faculty Collection* (1760–64).

[43] *Faculty of Advocates' Minute Book* (ed. Pinkerton), II, 17, 20, 39 (committee appointed, July 1721), 92, 112 (committee, including Kames appointed July 1728). Bruce was constantly petitioning the Faculty for financial assistance and died in 1729 without leaving enough to defray the cost of his funeral.

[44] Probably Patrick Haldane of Gleneagles (1683–1769, advocate 1715, barrister (Middle Temple), Professor of Church History, St. Andrews, 1709–18, M.P. 1715, Solicitor-General 1746–55).

[45] ?–1773, advocate, 1718, Sheriff of Peebles 1760, father of Alexander Murray, Lord Henderland.

[46] 1701–64, barrister (Middle Temple) 1721, advocate 1722, Lord Advocate 1746, Lord Prestongrange 1754–64: Omond, *Lord Advocates*, II, p. 29; Brunton & Haig, p. 518.

[47] James Ferguson (1700–77, advocate 1722), Dean of Faculty, 1760, Lord Pitfour 1764–77: Brunton & Haig, p. 527.

[48] Tytler, p. 115.

[49] (?–1810, advocate 1786).

[50] W. K. Wimsatt and F. A. Pottle, *Boswell for the Defence*, 1769–1774 (1960), p. 25.

[51] Tytler, p. 117.

[52] These are discussed *seriatim* by Tytler, pp. 118–122.

[53] Kames's *Introduction*.

[54] The Heritable Jurisdictions Act 1747 and the Tenures Abolition Act 1747, went some way to achieving what Kames desired.

[55] *Treatise on Human Nature*, probably from Bk. III.

[56] *New Letters of David Hume* (ed. R. Klibansky and E. C. Mossner, 1954), p. 27.

[57] Ross, *op. cit.*, pp. 60–66.

[58] Ross, *op. cit.*, pp. 35–36.

[59] The main attack was by the Rev. George Anderson in a book entitled *An Estimate of the Profit and Loss of Religion Personally Stated*, supported by the Rev. John Bonar in a pamphlet *An Analysis of the Moral and Religious Sentiments Contained in the Writings of Sopho* [Kames] *and David Hume Esq*; see Ross, *op. cit.*, 152–165.

[60] Tytler, pp. 138–145.

[61] See his Preface to the third edition.

[62] Ross, *op. cit.*, pp. 98–100.

[63] Tytler, I, p. 208, saw a resemblance also to J. Cay's *Abridgment of the Public Statutes* (1739). It anticipated Daines Barrington's *Observations on the Statutes* (1766).

[64] Philip Yorke (1690–1764), Chief Justice of the King's Bench, 1733–36, Lord Chancellor 1736–56, in which capacity he did much to systematise equity and make it a coherent body of doctrine.

[65] Letter printed in Tytler, pp. 211–214.

[66] Letter to Adam Smith, April 12, 1759, in *Correspondence of Adam Smith* (ed. E. C. Mossner and I. S. Ross, 1977), p. 34.

[67] *Essai sur l'histoire générale et sur les moeurs et l'esprit des nations* (1765).

[68] *General History of Nature and Theory of the Heavens* (1755).

[69] David Hume much admired Montesquieu's *L'Esprit des Lois* and Adam Ferguson's *Essay on the History of Civil Society* was influenced by it and it was the model for Sir John Dalrymple's *Essay towards a General History of Feudal Property in Great Britain*.

[70] Dugald Stewart, *Works of Adam Smith*, V, p. 452. On conjectural history see further J. W. Burrow, *Evolution and Society* (1966), p. 10.

[71] Tytler, I, 160.

[72] *Principles of Penal Law* (1771), pp. 1–3.

[73] *A Comment on the Commentaries and A Fragment on Government* (ed. J. H. Burns and H. L. A. Hart, 1977), pp. 313, 330, 430.

[74] Chap. 17, *infra*.

[75] p. 16.

[76] D. Lieberman, "The legal needs of a commercial society: the jurisprudence of Lord Kames," in I. Hont and M. Ignatieff, *Wealth and Virtue* (1983), p. 203.

[77] *Ibid.*, p. 210.

[78] H. Ballow, *A Treatise of Equity* (1737); Chief Baron Gilbert, *History and Practice of the High Court of Chancery* (1758); G. Spence, *Equitable Jurisdiction of the Court of Chancery* (2 Vols., 1840–49); D. M. Kerly, *Historical Sketch of the Equitable Jurisdiction of the Court of Chancery* (1890); Holdsworth, H.E.L., II, 344; V, 215, and references there.

[79] D. M. Walker, "Equity in Scots Law" (1954) 66 J.R. 103, summarising unpublished Ph.D. thesis (Edin. Univ. 1952).

[80] See further analysis by H. H. Brown in (1903) 10 S.L.T. (News), pp. 94, 111, 127, 159, 173, 181.

[81] p. xiii.

[82] Particularly St. Germain, *Doctor and Student* (1530); R. Francis, *Maxims of Equity* (1728); H. Bellow, *A Treatise of Equity* (1737); Anon., *Grounds and Rudiments of Law and Equity* (1749); Chief Baron Gilbert, *History and Practice of the High Court of Chancery* (1758).

[83] Tytler, I, pp. 237–249.

[84] Ross, p. 237.

[85] Ross, p. 245.

[86] *Commentaries* (1st ed., 1765), I, Intro. §2, 3.

[87] *Commentaries on Equity Jurisprudence* (1836), 2nd English ed. (1892), p. 7.

[88] J. W. Reed and F. A. Pottle, *Boswell, Laird of Auchinleck*, 1778–82, p. 385.

[89] (1885) 12 R. 722, at 755.

[90] *Ibid.*, at p. 749.

[91] (1889) 16 R. 421, 430.

[92] (1868) 6 M. 840, 867.

[93] 1963 S.C. 410, at p. 424, *per* Lord Kilbrandon; affd. 1964 S.C. (H.L.) 117 (decision overruled by War Damage Act 1965).

[94] Letter to Kames quoted in Tytler, I, p. 262.

[95] Tytler, I, p. 268. For a later letter see Tytler, II, p. 10.

[96] H. W. Randall, *The Critical Theory of Lord Kames* (1940), p. 24; Ross, *op. cit.*, p. 262.

[97] Tytler, II, p. 21.

[98] Boswell, *Life of Johnson*, October 16, 1769.

[99] F. A. Pottle, *Boswell's London Journal* (1950), p. 255.

[1] J. W. Reed and F. A. Pottle, *Boswell, Laird of Auchinleck*, 1778–82, 385.

[2] M. Plant, *The Domestic Life of Scotland in the Eighteenth Century* (1952), p. 74.

[3] Alison was the father of Archibald Alison, the jurist, on whom see Chap. 21, *infra*.

[4] H. W. Randall, *Critical Theory of Lord Kames* (1940), pp. 77–81.

[5] *Fogo* v. *Fogo* (1842) 4 D.1063 at p. 1084.

[6] Reprinted in *Scots Magazine*, 28 (1766), pp. 15–27.

[7] His earlier views are contained in *Essays on the Principles of Morality and Natural Religion* (1751) and *Principles of Equity* (2nd ed., 1767).

[8] For Hutcheson and Adam Smith see Chap. 18, *infra*.

[9] *Theory of Moral Sentiments* II, ii, 1.4–2.4.

[10] D. Lieberman, "The legal needs of a commercial society: the jurisprudence of Lord Kames," in I. Hont and M. Ignatieff, *Wealth and Virtue* (1983), pp. 211–12.

[11] J. S. Shaw, *The Management of Scottish Society*, 1707–1764 (1983), p. 67.

[12] (1754–1835, advocate 1775, barrister 1782). See DNB; Anderson, S.N., III, p. 463; Chambers, BDES; Rosalind Mitchison, *Agricultural Sir John*.

[13] (1741–1820); DNB.

[14] The volumes were published as the parish reports came in, so that the parishes for any county are very scattered. A reprint in 20 volumes in 1974–84 rearranged the parish accounts under counties.

[15] Preface, pp. vii, ix, xiii.

[16] F. A. Pottle, *Boswell in Holland* (1952), p. 43. The reference is to Boswell's plan for employing the hours of the day.

[17] Ross, *op. cit.*, pp. 316–322.

[18] John Walker, *An Economical History of the Hebrides and Highlands* (2 vols., 1808).

[19] Andrew Wight, *The Present State of Husbandry in Scotland* (4 vols., 1778–84).

[20] Ross, *op. cit.*, pp. 322–328.

[21] Ross, *op. cit.*, pp. 328–329.

[22] Ross, *op. cit.*, pp. 329–331; T. McCrae "Lord Kames and the North Bridge: Notes on the Scheme of 1754," *Book of the Old Edinburgh Club* 23 (1940), p. 147; A. J. Youngson, *The Making of Classical Edinburgh, 1750–1840* (1966).

[23] He attacked them in *Elucidations, Essays concerning British Antiquities, Equity* and, above all, *Sketches*. See Tytler, *Memoir*, I, pp. 210, 222; Lehmann, *Henry Homes, Lord Kames*, pp. 327. On the campaign to abolish entails see also N. Phillipson, "Lawyers, Landowners and the Civic Leadership of Post-Union Scotland," 1976 J.R. 97.

[24] *Historical Law Tracts*, v.

[25] Stewart, *Works*, I, p. 69; X, p. 34; A. S. Skinner, "Natural History in the Age of Adam Smith," *Political Studies*, 15 (1967), p. 32.

[26] *Historical Law Tracts*, p. 23.

[27] On this aspect see Leslie Stephen, *History of English Thought in the Eighteenth Century* (1876); J. McCosh, *Scottish Philosophy; Biographical, Expository and Critical* (1875); H. Laurie, *Scottish Philosophy in its National Development* (1902); Lehmann, *op. cit.*, pp. 162, 270.

[28] It should be made clear that by "common sense" the adherents of this philosophic group did not mean the views of the man in the street, but taking prevailing judgment or appreciation of intelligent persons as the ultimate rule of standard, *i.e.* "common" means "generally held." They believed that persons generally have a prevalent sense of right and wrong based on intuition more than on reason.

[29] Laurie, *supra*, p. 103.

[30] See also Lehmann, *op. cit.*, p. 195.

[31] *Intellectual Powers of the Human Mind* (1785), Dedication.

[32] *Scotland and Scotsmen in the Eighteenth Century*, I, p. 194.

[33] *Private Papers of James Boswell* (G. Scott and F. A. Pottle ed., 1928), I, p. 55.

[34] F. Brady and F. A. Pottle, *Boswell in Search of a Wife* (1957), p. 161.

[35] C. M. Weis and F. A. Pottle, *Boswell in Extremes*, 1776–78, pp. 330–331.

[36] F. A. Pottle, *Boswell's London Journal* (1950), p. 255.

[37] Smellie, *Literary and Characteristic Lives*, p. 128.

[38] John Adams, *Works* (1962), II, pp. 146–148; III, pp. 445–464; *Diary and Autobiography of John Adams* (ed. L. H. Butterfield), I, p. 253.

[39] Thomas Jefferson, *Papers*, (ed. F. Donovan, 1963), pp. 209, 214, 217; *Commonplace Book*, (ed. G. Chinard, 1926), pp. 95–135.

[40] James Wilson, *Works* (ed. J. Andrews, (1896), I, p. 38; see also II, pp. 133–135.

[41] *Inquiries in the Science of Law* (1847), p. 49. Reddie had been a student under Millar, who had been Kames's protégé and tutor to his children.

[42] *Lectures* (ed. Paton, Stair Soc.), I, pp. 15, 358.

[43] (1885) 12 R. 722, at p. 755. The reference seems to be to Lord Fraser's criticism of him at p. 759.

CHAPTER 15

JOHN MILLAR

THE teaching of law in Glasgow was undistinguished in the years between Forbes and Millar. John Millar[1] was the son of the minister of Shotts and was born on June 22, 1735. He was educated by an uncle and then at Hamilton grammar school. In 1746 he went to Glasgow, entered the College and lived in the College chambers and dined with William Cullen, his mother's cousin, then lecturer in chemistry. He became familiar with James Watt[2] and attended the lectures of Adam Smith on moral philosophy.[3] "His intelligence and ardour soon attracted Dr. Smith's notice, and at this time was laid the foundation of that mutual esteem, which, during the few years they were afterwards professors in the same university,[4] produced lasting intimacy and friendship."[5] He had been destined for the church, but had some scruples about the profession of faith which was necessary and, encouraged by an uncle, John, who had been a Writer to the Signet, he turned to the law. He attended Hercules Lindsay's lectures on law. After completing his studies he spent two years in the household of Lord Kames as tutor to the latter's son George.

> "Lord Kames found in young Millar a congenial ardour of intellect, a mind turned to philosophical speculation, a considerable fund of reading, and what above all things he delighted in, a talent for supporting a metaphysical argument in conversation with much ingenuity and vivacity. The tutor of the son became the pupil and companion of the father; and the two years before Mr. Millar was called to the bar, were spent, with great improvement on his part, in acquiring those enlarged views of the union of law with philosophy, which he afterwards displayed with uncommon ability in his academical lectures on jurisprudence."[6]

He there met David Hume the philosopher, and came under the influence of Hume's metaphysical views. Hume was so greatly impressed by Millar that he later, in 1775, sent his nephew David Hume, the later professor and Baron of Exchequer, to Glasgow to be under Millar's charge. Millar may have spent some of the years 1755 to 1760 in legal study and as an apprentice in a legal office which was, if not a formal requirement, a customary training for prospective advocates.

In 1760 Millar passed advocate[7] but only a year later, supported in his candidacy by Smith and Kames, at the age of 26, accepted the post of Regius Professor of Law in the University of Glasgow. He was appointed through the interest of the guardians of the Duke of Hamilton. The post was not exclusive of professional practice and he acquired some reputation for the defence of persons indicted before the circuit court of justiciary, and was also frequently employed in commercial arbitrations.[8] He held the chair for 40 years, until his death in 1801.[9] He had a family of 13; a son, James, became professor of mathematics in Glasgow, and a grandson, Allen Thomson, became a distinguished biologist and professor of anatomy in Glasgow. The Millars' home, Milheugh, near

Blantyre, passed into the hands of his descendant Andrew Millar Banna-tyne of the Glasgow law firm of Bannatyne, Kirkwood, France & Co., but is now demolished.[10]

Millar's predecessor, Hercules Lindsay, had, despite protests from the Faculty of Advocates, abandoned the practice of lecturing in Latin in favour of English[11] and Millar continued this practice.

According to Craig, previous to Millar's appointment the students of law seldom exceeded four or five a year and sometimes fell short even of that number. But he effected a rapid improvement: "he had, frequently, about forty students of Civil Law; while those who attended his lectures on Government, often amounted to a much greater number. To establish and maintain the reputation of his classes became with him the principal object of his life; and never, perhaps, was an object followed out with more ardour and perseverance."[12]

Millar's fame spread rapidly and he attracted students from all parts of the country.[13]

"Amongst these were David Hume, professor of Scots Law in the University of Edinburgh and a judge of the Court of Exchequer[14]; David Boyle of Shewalton, Lord Justice General of Scotland and Lord President of the Court of Session[15]; Lord Gillies, Lord Reston and Lord Pitmilly, Judges of the Court of Session and Sir Patrick Murray, one of the Barons of Exchequer; the Right Hon. Sir David Rae of St. Catherines, Lord Advocate and M.P., the friend of Sir Walter Scott; Sir John Anstruther, Chief Justice of Bengal; James Kerr, Chief Justice of the Court of King's Bench at Quebec and Speaker of the Legislative Council of Quebec; Lord Cardross, afterwards Earl of Buchan; James Maitland, afterwards eighth Earl of Lauderdale,[16] on whose recommendation the Hon. William Lamb, afterwards second Viscount Melbourne,[17] and his brother Frederick Lamb, afterwards third Lord Melbourne, became students under Professor Millar[18]; William Windham (1750–1810) the celebrated statesman, the friend of Dr. Johnson; the Hon. Thomas Fitzmaurice, son of the Earl of Shelburne; Richard Wing-field, afterwards Lord Powerscourt; Thomas Douglas, fifth Earl of Selkirk, Commissioner to Canada for the settlement of the Colonies; Charles Stuart, afterwards Lord Rothesay, British Ambassador to many of the courts of Europe; Charles Kinnaird, afterwards the eighth Earl Kinnaird; Sir Archibald Grant of Monymusk, afterwards Lord Saltoun; Robert Ferguson of Raith, M.P. for several Scottish constituencies; Sir James Grant Suttie, baronet, of Prestongrange, a member both of the Scottish and of the English Bar. A large number of young men who intended to be called to the Scottish bar studied under Professor Millar, often eight in a session, many of whom rose to eminence and judicial positions. Graduates of Oxford and of Cambridge, some of whom had already entered one of the Inns of Court, came to Glasgow to attend Professor Millar's lectures. James Reddie, afterwards the eminent Town Clerk of Glasgow, also studied under him, as did Thomas Campbell the poet and the unfortunate Thomas Muir of Huntershill, who attended his class for two sessions[19]."[20]

Indeed it was said[21] that: "On his account the University of Glasgow was attended by all the most talented and distinguished of the high Whig aristocracy, among whom attendance upon the lectures of Professor Millar was regarded as a necessary portion of sound political education. He may be considered as having formed the minds of many of those who have been distinguished in the political world on the liberal side during the last fifty or sixty years."

Others who sat under him included

"Thomas Thomson,[22] Sir James Moncreiff (Lord Wellwood), Dean of the Faculty of Advocates, active on the *Edinburgh Review*; Sir George Cranstoun, later Lord Corehouse, prominent Whig lawyer, also an Edinburgh Reviewer; Lord William Craig of the Court of Session, eminent jurist of his time; William Adam, Lord Chief Commissioner of the Scottish Jury Court, member of the King's Council, Solicitor General and later, Attorney-General to the Prince of Wales; Sir William Rae, third baronet of Eskgrove and Lord Advocate; Simon Jefimovich Desnitsky, Professor of Roman Law and Russian Jurisprudence in the University of Moscow, said to be the first to lecture on civil law in any Russian university and 'one of the most influential professors of the Moscow University in the late eighteenth century,' a member of the Russian Academy; also Ivan Andreevitch Tretiakov, professor of legislative science in the University of Moscow."[23]

The two Russians are of particular interest. Semyon Efimovich Desnitsky and Ivan Andreyevich Tret'yakov studied in Glasgow from 1761 to 1767,[24] attended Adam Smith's lectures on ethics and jurisprudence and attended for three years John Millar's classes of civil law.[25] From the evidence in Desnitsky's later works "it is possible to be fairly certain that he also attended Millar's classes on Scottish law, as well as his pioneering 'lectures on government.' Desnitsky and Trek'yakov undoubtedly worked more closely with John Millar than with any other Glasgow professor and when the University agreed to their request to submit doctoral dissertations,[26] it was Millar who was allocated the task of supervising them."[27] Millar had to examine them privately and reported that they were qualified to undergo public examination. They were examined publicly and each was prescribed a title of the Pandects for a thesis to be read and defended in public.[28] The theses were read aloud, examined by professors, Millar being one, and after some delay, the degree of Doctor of Law conferred.[29]

Both in 1768 became professors of law in Moscow, the first Russians to hold chairs of law in Russia's first university. Desnitsky quickly achieved prominence as a scholar and by 1783 was giving courses on the history of Russian law, on Justinian's Pandects from the compendium of Heineccius, and a comparison between Roman and Russian law. He was elected a founding member of the Russian Academy in 1783.[30] It is plain that the teaching of Millar and Adam Smith influenced both Russians. Many points in Desnitsky's *A Legal Discourse on the Beginning and Origin of Matrimony* (1775) are found in Millar's *Observations concerning the Distinction of Ranks in Society* (1771). So too in *A Legal Discourse about the Different Ideas which People Have concerning the Ownership of*

Property in different Conditions of Society (1781) Desnitsky draws on Millar and Smith.[31] But apart from specific citations Desnitsky's entire concept of jurisprudence and the study of man in society were shaped by his years in Glasgow; it was from Millar and Smith that he acquired his approach to legal studies.[32] Desnitsky is considered "the founder of Russian jurisprudence," and as the founder of a particular school of jurisprudence whose approach can best be described as comparative-historical, a description which well describes the approach of Smith in his lectures on jurisprudence and of Millar in his lectures on law and government.

In particular Desnitsky's key tool of analysis, used in both the works of 1775 on marriage and 1781 on property, is the theory of the four stages of the development of society, hunting and gathering, pastoralism, agriculture, and commerce, which is found in variant forms in the work of several Scottish thinkers of the later eighteenth century but explicitly stated by Millar and Smith as a valuable basis for the comparison of different societies, institutions and customs.[33] Desnitsky held his chair for 19 years, till 1787, and died in 1789. Tret'yakov resigned in 1773 and died in 1776.

As was the practice common at that time Millar pretty regularly took some students into his house as boarding students, usually three or four at a time. There is evidence that Millar selected them on the basis of ability and promise of future achievement,[34] and he devoted a considerable amount of time to discussions with them and encouraging them in their work.[35] Among these were William Lamb, later second Viscount Melbourne[36] and Prime Minister, and his brother Frederick, later third Viscount,[37] James Maitland, eighth Earl of Lauderdale,[38] later a strong advocate of Parliamentary reform and writer on political and economic topics, and young David Hume, later professor in Edinburgh and Baron of Exchequer, sent to Glasgow by his uncle, the philosopher and historian.[39]

Doubtless he also invited other students into his home from time to time and engaged in discussion with them. "No young man admitted to his house ever forgot him, and the ablest used to say that the discussions into which we led them, domestically and convivially, were the most exciting and most instructive exercises in which they ever took part."[40]

Millar seems also to have taken an active part in university management, frequently acting as chairman of committees or Clerk of Senate and at one time as Vice-Rector. He not infrequently took an unpopular or minority view and, consistently with his concern for students, frequently took their part to secure fair dealing when some of them were charged with misbehaviour.[41]

On April 10, 1784, Millar was one of a party, along with Lord Daer, Professor Dalzel, Dugald Stewart and Adam Smith who breakfasted with Edmund Burke on the day when Burke was in Glasgow to be installed as Lord Rector of the University. James Boswell came to pay his respects to Burke and was invited to join them.[42]

It was probably Millar who initiated the proposal to confer the honorary LL.D. on William Wilberforce, the opponent of the African slave trade; this was done in 1791.[43]

Several sets of students' notes of his lectures survive.[44] These show that his courses included (1) The Institutes, founded on Heineccius as a textbook,[45] in 64 lectures; (2) Jurisprudence. This was styled a second Course of Institutes and embraced six introductory lectures on Ethics and Jurisprudence or Law and 39 on the Personal and Domestic Relations, Property, Exclusive Privilege, Servitudes, Pledge, Contracts and Quasi contracts, crimes and delinquencies and criminal procedure. (3) The Pandects in 46 lectures. (4) Government in 46 lectures. (5) Scots Law in 50 lectures. Several of these' courses were given in a session. Thus in 1776–77 he gave the courses on the Institutes, the Pandects, and on Government; in 1783–84 he gave the Institutes, the Pandects, Public Law and the Law of Scotland.[46] Some years before his death he offered a course on English law alternating with that on Scots law.[47] According to his successor, Davidson,[48] Millar lectured twice a week on Scots law in alternate sessions, but did not lecture on criminal law at all.

Surviving sets of students' notes of Millar's lectures on Scots law show general similarity but substantial variation in detail from one session to another, suggestive of a teacher who did not stick to his notes every session but elaborated on points and varied the precise points he dealt with.[49] The general pattern seems to have been: 1–9: Husband and wife, parent and child, master and servant, guardian and ward; 10–26: Feudal property, casualties, transfer of property, servitudes, tithes, wadsets; 27–31: Personal rights arising from contracts, pledge, bills, society, cautionry; 32–39: Obligations arising from crimes and delinquencies; 40–41: Rights and obligations arising from equity, without intervention of contract or delinquency; 42–45: Extinction and transmission of personal rights; prescription; 46–49: Succession and executors; 50–52: Actions, appeal and review; diligence. This order is generally that of Mackenzie and Erskine. There appears to have been rather fuller treatment of criminal law and procedure than was given by his predecessors. Mackenzie's *Matters Criminal* was by this time largely outdated and Erskine's treatment of that branch of law in his *Principles*, and even in his *Institutes* (published only in 1773), was only a sketch and did not deal with procedure. There were moreover no reports of criminal cases. Hume later adopted a similar practice in Edinburgh, giving a short course on criminal law in the summer.

But even more interesting and important was Millar's inclusion of a course on Government, or what we would now call Public Law.[50] The first 15 or so lectures were devoted to outlining what he saw as the general principles of government, a presentation of his general view of society, government, the evolution of property and family institutions, and of social and political institutions. They reflected a broadly historical or historico-sociological approach and there was no hard line drawn between society and social controls on the one hand and government in a formal sense on the other. In the second part of the course he applied these general principles to the development of political institutions in Athens and Sparta, and among the Romans, and then passed to medieval and modern times, and considered their evolution in France, Germany and Britain.[51] In the third part, again of about 15 lectures, he gave an exposition of the present state of government in Great Britain, the constitution and powers of Parliament and its three branches, King, Lords, and Commons, the structure of courts, including the differences between Scottish and English courts.

But the lectures go beyond the conventional scope of a course on public law, and mention the economic ordering of society, the institutions of property, the ranks of society and the distribution of power in society, family structure, the origin and development of feudal institutions, religious institutions and ecclesiastical policy, the development of the arts and sciences, the consequences of the division of labour, servitude, slavery and liberty. His lectures changed after the publication of Smith's *Wealth of Nations*.[52]

> "Mr. Millar never wrote his lectures; but was accustomed to speak from notes, containing his arrangement, his chief topics, and some of his principal facts and illustrations. For the transitions from one part of his subject to another, the occasional allusions, the smaller embellishments, and the whole of the expression, he trusted to that extemporaneous eloquence which seldom fails a speaker deeply interested in his subject."[53]

Tytler,[54] though politically opposed to Millar, conceded that, "The reputation of the university, as a school of jurisprudence, rose from that acquisition [*i.e.* of Millar as professor] ... there were few who attended those lectures, without at least an increase of knowledge; or who have perused his writings, without deriving from them much valuable information." Ramsay of Ochtertyre, though even more opposed politically to Millar's views, also accepted that, "Whatever may have been his demerits ... it is agreed that he made many excellent scholars. In fact, his general views of jurisprudence were masterly."[55]

A traveller in Scotland[56] noted that, "It is to hear his [Millar's] lectures ... that students resort hither from all quarters of Britain ... Glasgow is, in short, famous as a school for law, as Edinburgh is as a school for medicine."

Thomas Campbell, the poet, was in his class in 1793–94:

> "I heard him, when I was but sixteen, lecture on Roman law. A dry subject enough it would have been in common hands; but in his hands Heineccius was made a feast to the attention. His eyes, his voice, his figure, were commanding; as if nature had made him for the purpose of giving dignity and fascination to oral instruction. Such was the truth, cheerfulness and courage, that seemed to give erectness to his shapely bust, he might have stood to the statuary for a Roman orator; but he was too much in earnest with his duty, and too manly to affect the orator; but keeping close to his subject, he gave it a seriousness that was never tiresome, and a gaiety that never seemed for a moment unillustrative or unnecessary. His cheerfulness appeared as indispensable as his gravity, and his humour was as light as his seriousness was intense. But he was the contrast of those weak men who suffer either their gaiety or gravity to run away with them – he was master of both. His students were always in the class before him, waiting as for a treat. It was rumoured that he was coming. There was a grave look of pleasure on every face when he began; and

I thought – it might be imagination – that there was a murmur of regret when the time was at an end."[57]

Elsewhere Campbell wrote:

"To say that Millar gave me liberal opinions would be understating the obligation which I either owed, or imagined I owed, to him. He did more. He made investigations into the principles of justice, and the rights and interests of society, so captivating to me, that I formed opinions for myself, and became an emancipated lover of truth.

"I will not take upon me to say that Millar's tuition was profound; for his mind, with all its natural strength, had grown to maturity in an age, when, with the exception of Adam Smith and a few others, there appears to me to have been a dearth of deep-thinking men . . . But John Millar had the magic secret of making you so curious in inquiry, and so much in love with truth, as to be independent of his specific tenets. Every lecture that he gave was a treat from beginning to end. . . .

"The impulse which Millar's lectures had given to my mind, continued to act long after I had heard them . . . Poetry itself, in my love of jurisprudence and history, was almost forgotten. . . ."[58]

Campbell also described him[59]:

"He was a fine muscular man, somewhat above the middle size, with a square chest and shapely bust, a prominent chin, grey eyes that were unmatched in expression, and a head that would have become a Roman senator. He was said to be a capital fencer, and to look at his light elastic step, when he was turned of sixty, disposed you to credit the report."[60]

Francis Jeffrey commented later:

"Mr. Millar is the only public lecturer we have known who seems to have been fully aware of [the need to work with and encourage students], and by attending to them, he certainly delivered a series of most instructive lectures in a more attractive and engaging manner than any other teacher we have heard of; commanding the attention of all descriptions of hearers, at the same time that he convinced their understandings; and not only putting them in possession of knowledge, but making it familiar and serviceable to them."[61]

Cockburn wrote[62]:

"His lectures were admirable; and so was his conversation; and his evening parties; and his boxing (gloved) with his favourite pupils. No young man admitted to his house ever forgot him; and the ablest used to say that the discussions into which he led them, domestically and convivially, were the most exciting and the most instructive exercises in which they ever took a part. Jeffrey says that his books, excellent though they be, 'reveal nothing of that magical vivacity which made his conversation and his lectures still more full of delight than of instinction; of that frankness and fearlessness which led him to engage, without preparation, in every fair contention, and neither to dread nor disdain the powers of any opponent; and still less, perhaps, of that remarkable and unique talent, by which he was enabled to clothe, in concise and familiar expressions, the most profound and original views of the most complicated questions; and thus to render the knowledge which he communicated so manageable and unostentatious, as to turn out his pupils from the sequestered retracts of a college, in a condition immediately to apply their acquisitions to the business and affairs of the world."

He seems to have examined daily[63]:

"Every morning, before he began his address from the chair, he endeavoured to ascertain, by putting a number of questions to his pupils, whether they had been able to follow his reasoning on the preceding day, and it was his custom, when the lecture was over, to remain some time in his lecture-room to converse with those students who were desirous of further information on the subject. By engaging with them in an easy dialogue, he contrived to remove obscurities, and to correct any errors into which they might have fallen."[64]

By all accounts Millar was a man of outstanding personality, of intellectual vigour and of advanced and daring views. He was clearly an expositor of the very first distinction, as is evidenced by his ability to attract students from afar. James Mill considered his lectures as "probably among the most instructive things that ever were offered to the minds of youth"[65]; Francis Jeffrey of the *Edinburgh Review* considered his classroom teaching to be in several respects unique in the whole history of education; "Millar's classes were ... the great training school for the lawyers and statesmen of the next generation; and many of them in after life owned that Millar's prelections had first given the impulse that stimulated them through life. . . . There can be no question that the bold lines of thought on which the *Edinburgh Review* was afterwards constructed, were first laid down by his masterly hand."[66] David Murray formed the opinion from the views expressed that he was "the most celebrated and most successful teacher of his time."[67]

Kames was critical of the law teachers of his time as men who "husband their reasoning faculty as if it would rust by exercise" and "load the weak mind with a heap of interesting facts without giving any exercise to the judgment," but added in a footnote: "I should merit censure equal to what I do liberally bestow on others, did I not except Mr. John Millar, Professor of Roman law in the College of Glasgow."[68]

It is clear that Millar did not regard the teaching of law as limited to instruction in the technicalities, practicalities and mechanics of the working lawyer's skills; nor was law confined to private law, between man and man; public law was important; the study of law was an aspect of the study of men interacting in society, as were politics and economics and what we now call sociology, and that study could be enormously enlightened by an approach through history. "He was not merely desirous to convey to his students just views and accurate information; but he was anxious to convey them in a manner most likely to seize the attention, and to produce habits of original thought and philosophical investigation;

thus rendering lectures, formerly considered as useful only to lawyers, the most important schools of general education."[69]

> "To many of his students . . . who, without any intention of becoming practical lawyers had been sent to the University as to a seminary of liberal education, a course of lectures on Public Law seemed more important than on almost any other science. In a free country every man may be said to be a politician; and the higher classes of society, those who chiefly resort to universities as general students, are frequently obliged, by their situation in life, to give opinions on various subjects of Government, which may have considerable influence on the welfare of their country. To them a knowledge of Public Law must be an object of the first importance, whether they look forward to the degree of estimation in which they would wish to be held in their respective countries, or listen to the voice of honourable ambition, which calls them to add lustre to their names, by defending the rights and augmenting the happiness of their fellow men."[70]

> "The general student was delighted with the acuteness of the observations, the sagacity of the antiquarian researches, the number and elegance of the analogies, the comprehensiveness and consistency of the doctrines: the young lawyer by tracing the progress and views of the government was instructed in the spirit and real intention of the laws: but to the future statesman were opened up views of human society, of the nature and ends of Government, and of the influence of Public Institutions on the prosperity, morals and happiness of states; views which could hardly fail to impress a veneration for liberty on his heart, and which, through his exertions, might essentially promote the welfare of his country."[71]

Millar's first publication was *Observations Concerning the Distinction of Ranks in Society*, published in 1771; an enlarged second edition came out in 1773, and a third, corrected and enlarged, and renamed as *The Origin of the Distinction of Ranks, or an Enquiry into the Circumstances which Gave Rise to Influence and Authority in the Different Members of Society*, was published in 1779.[72] A fourth edition in 1806 had prefixed "An Account of the Life and Writing of the Author" by John Craig, Esq. It was translated into German at least twice, into French and Italian. The revised title and sub-title were suggested by the title of Section III, chapter II, of Adam Smith's *Theory of Moral Sentiments* – Of the origin of Ambition, and of the distinction of Ranks – published in 1759.[73] In his introduction Millar described the book as "intended to illustrate the natural history of mankind . . . by pointing out the more obvious and common improvements which gradually arise in the state of society, and by showing the influence of these upon the manners, the laws, and the government of a people." The work was clearly based on his lectures on jurisprudence and government, and draws on a large number of published works, notably the Bible, classical authors, legal sources, books on travel and non-European history, modern history, and modern literary and philosophic works, including Montesquieu, Hume, Kames, Adam Smith and several others. It evidences wide reading and deep reflection on the conclusions which may be drawn from the information gathered. Montesquieu's *Esprit des Lois* had been published in 1748 and in translation in 1750. Rousseau's *Origin of Inequality* had appeared in 1754, his *Social Contract* and *Emile* in 1762, Hume's *Essays* in 1754, Adam Smith's *Moral Sentiments* in 1759, Robertson's *History of Scotland* in 1759 and his *View of the Progress of Society in Europe* in 1769, Ferguson's *History of Civil Society* in 1767 and Antoine Y. Goguet's *Origin of Laws, Arts and Science, etc.*, which Millar referred to repeatedly, in 1758, and in an Edinburgh-published translation in 1761, so that thought on the general theme of the evolution of society was prevalent. The *Origin* comprises seven chapters dealing respectively with the rank and condition of women in different ages, the jurisdiction and authority of a father over his children, the authority of a chief over the members of a tribe or village, the authority of a sovereign and of subordinate officers, over a society composed of different tribes or villages, the changes produced in the government of a people by their progress in arts and in polished manners, and the authority of a master over his servants. The most original and interesting part of the work is the history of sexual relations within the family, the place of women and the impact of commercial society on their condition and on family authority.[74]

The *Origin* has been rediscovered in recent years and Millar hailed as a founding father of what is now called sociology. "A strong case can be made for the claim that this man was a seminal thinker who did more than any of the others (David Hume, Adam Smith, Adam Ferguson, Thomas Reid, Francis Hutcheson and William Robertson) to advance the area of knowledge we now call sociology."[75]

In his teaching and writing Millar showed an historical and sociological approach to the problems of justice, law and government, not a narrow or merely positivist approach.

Jeffrey summed up his view of Millar in this way: "It was the leading principle ... of all his speculations on law, morality, government, language, the arts, sciences and manners – that there is nothing produced by arbitrary or accidental causes; that no great change, institution, custom or occurrence could be ascribed to the character or exertions of an individual, to the temperament or disposition of a nation, to occasional policy, or peculiar wisdom or folly; everything, on the contrary, he held, arose spontaneously from the situation of the society, and was suggested or imposed irresistibly by the opportunities or necessities of their condition."[76] Again later: "It was the great object of [Millar and such others as Kames and Adam Smith] to trace back the history of society to its most simple and universal elements – to resolve almost all that had been ascribed to positive institution into the spontaneous and irresistible development of certain obvious principles – and to show with how little contrivance or political wisdom the most complicated and apparently artificial schemes of policy might have been erected."[77]

Millar's other book was *Historical View of the English Government from the Settlement of the Saxons in Britain to the Accession of the House of Stewart*, published in 1787, with a second edition in 1790. In the dedication to Charles James Fox, Millar speaks of his work as an attempt "to write a constitutional history of England." A third edition followed in 1803 in four volumes octavo, including additional material culled from his manuscripts. The first two volumes contained the original work. There was added to the title *To which are subjoined some Dissertations connected with the History of the Government from the Revolution to the Present Time*. There was a fourth edition in 1818, and a German translation in 1819–21.

This is a work of considerable interest and importance as being the first constitutional history of Britain or of England, with which it is principally concerned. This shows him as clearly an original thinker. The central theme is the growth and diffusion of liberty[78] through a multitude of people, spread over a wide extent of territory. "As the government which we enjoy at present has not been formed at once, but has grown to maturity in a course of ages, it is necessary in order to have a full view of the circumstances from which it has proceeded, that we should survey with attention the successive changes through which it has passed. In a disquisition of this nature, it is hoped that, by considering events in the order in which they happened, the causes of every change will be more easily unfolded, and may be pointed out with greater simplicity."[79] Book I (volume I) deals with the English government from the settlement of the Saxons in Britain to the reign of William the Conqueror, Book II (volume II) covers the period 1066–1603. Volume III deals with the seventeenth century to 1689. It opens with a review of the government of Scotland from Roman times to 1603. From 1603 began what Millar called the Commercial Government of England. "The progress of commerce and manufactures had now begun to change the manners and political state of the inhabitants. Different arrangements of property had contributed to emancipate the people of inferior condition, and to undermine the authority of the superior ranks."[80] Volume IV deals with the English government from the reign of William III to the then present time and contains a review of the government of Ireland. Volume IV is notable also for its wide-ranging chapters, such as V – the Separation of the different Branches of Knowledge; and the Division of the liberal Arts and of the Sciences, and VII – the Progress of Science relative to Law and Government, and VIII – the Gradual Advancement of the Fine Arts, Their Influence upon Government. Though the papers printed in Volume IV are certainly by Millar it is probable that they were not in their final state, and possible even that they were not intended for publication.

According to the Advertisement to the third edition, part of the materials for the history of the second period from the Revolution of 1688 to his own time, containing the rise and progress of the influence of the Crown, as well as for an account of the present state of the English Government, had been collected and partly arranged by him, but required editorial attention before publication.

Hallam, who recognised the book's pioneering nature, criticised it[81] as pleasing from its liberal spirit, but thought that Millar was too fond of theorising upon an imperfect induction, and very often upon a total misapprehension of particular facts.

By modern historical standards it is unscholarly, there being very few references to authorities and little evidence of having searched in original or primary sources, even available printed ones. But there are valuable insights which compensate. He appreciated the interrelations and interactions of social, political and economic facts, and the relationships of power in society. The dissertation on "The Advancement of Manufactures, Commerce and the Arts"[82] shows a competent acquaintance with economic theory, and an awareness of the significance of communications and transport. He laid stress, moreover, on the importance of the role of capital in production and in making profit.[83]

In 1796 he published in the *Scots Chronicle* of Edinburgh under the pseudonym "Crito" a series of 15 letters. These were reprinted as a pamphlet later in the same year, as the *Letters of Crito*, with a preface and dedication to Fox. It is a political pamphlet attacking the war policies of Pitt's government.

A series of 18 letters were also published in the *Scots Chronicle*, partly overlapping on, partly following the *Letters of Crito* and reprinted as a pamphlet under the title *Letters of Sidney on Inequality of Property* and making an attack on the dangerously increasing inequality in the distribution of property. These have been attributed to Millar.[84] He may have been the author also of some letters to the same journal on an adult education movement, and some review articles in the *Analytical Review* between 1788 and 1792 or 1793, some signed "M."

It is essential for an understanding of Millar's attitude to society, law, government and politics to remember that he lived his years of maturity, the years of his tenure of the chair, in a time of a ferment of social and political ideas, of political upheaval and rising political consciousness.[85] The American War of Independence fell in the first half of his tenure and the French Revolution in the second. There were numerous publications urging parliamentary reform and sometimes more extreme changes. Joseph Priestley's *Essay on the First Principles of Government* was published in 1768, Richard Price's *Observations on Civil Liberty and the Justice and Policy of the War with America* in 1776, Tom Paine's *Rights of Man* appeared in 1791, Godwin's *Political Justice* in 1793. Nearer home, Adam Ferguson produced his *History of Civil Society* in 1767, William Robertson published a *View of the Progress of Society in Europe* (1769) as an introductory volume to his *History of Charles V*, Lord Kames his *Sketches of the History of Mankind* in 1774, Gilbert Stuart, a *View of Society in Europe through its Progress from Rudeness to Refinement* (1778), James Dunbar an essay on the *History of Mankind in Rude and Cultivated Ages* (1780), all showing a strongly historical approach to the analysis of contemporary societies. Moreover, thought generally moved very much from concentration on theology and man's relations to God to interest in politics and economics and man's relations with the state and with men; methodologically thought took an historical and empirical approach instead of one deferring to scriptural or traditional authority. It was a time of questioning and challenging formerly accepted views and values.

Millar was an ardent Whig and was looked upon by many contemporaries as a radical and even as a dangerous man, and even "did not perhaps bear any great antipathy to the name of republican."[86] Indeed we know that he was croupier at a dinner held by the "Friends of Liberty"

in Glasgow on the second anniversary of the Fall of the Bastille.[87] Some
professional colleagues were also there, and it was not really a conspira-
torial celebration. It is plain, however, whence some like young Thomas
Muir of Huntershill got their ideas.[88] Millar later became a member of the
Friends of the People and active in promoting Parliamentary reform.[89]
But on the other hand Millar was not a Utopian socialist:

> "There never was a mind, perhaps, less accessible to the illusions of
> that sentimental and ridiculous philanthropy which has led so many
> to the adoption of popular principles. He took a very cool and
> practical view of the condition of society; and neither wept over the
> imaginary miseries of the lower orders, nor shuddered at the
> imputed vices of the higher. He laughed at the dreams of perfectibi-
> lity, and looked with profound contempt at those puerile schemes of
> equality that threatened to subvert the distinctions of property, or to
> degrade the natural aristocracy of virtues and of talents."[90]

While Millar ardently believed in liberty, it was not freedom from all
restraints but freedom under law and protected by law, freedom from
subserviency to other men not justified by the general interest. Liberty to
him required the guarding and improving of free institutions such as an
independent judiciary and just laws, and protection against the irrespon-
sible rule of the ignorant. Millar accordingly approved the disappearance
of serfdom and slavery, the victory of reason over superstition and
clerical intolerance, and constitutional guarantees of liberty. He welcomed the decline of feudalism in face of the development of industry and
commerce, the intellectual awakening and the extension of education in
his own day.

Millar was, naturally, sharply criticised by some for his views.
"Jupiter" Carlyle was critical of the "democratic principles and sceptical
philosophy which young noblemen and gentlemen of legislative rank
carried into the world with them from his law class . . . though some sound
heads might find antidote to this poison before they went into the world
. . . yet, as it was connected with lax principles of religion, there might be
not a few of such contexture of understanding as not to be cured."[91]

It is apparent that during his professorship his thinking about law
broadened very considerably, from an initial concern with Roman law
and Scots law to a concern with historical and comparative law, with
government and public policy, with law in society. In the *Historical
View*[92] he observed:

> "The attempts to delineate systems of jurisprudence . . . opened at
> length a new source of speculation, by suggesting an enquiry into the
> circumstances which have occasioned various and opposite imper-
> fections in the law of different countries and which have prevented
> the practical system, in any, from attaining that improvement which
> we find no difficulty in conceiving. In the prosecution of this inquiry,
> more especially by President Montesquieu, by Lord Haines [*sic*] and
> by Dr. Smith, the attention of speculative lawyers has been directed
> to examine the first formation and subsequent advancement of civil
> society; the rise, the gradual development, and cultivation of arts
> and sciences; the acquisition and extension of property in all its

different modifications, and the combined influence of these and other political causes, upon the manners and customs, the institutions and laws of any people. By tracing in this manner the natural history of legal establishments, we may be enabled to account for the different aspect which they assume in different ages and countries, to discover the peculiarity of situation which has, in any case, retarded or promoted their improvement, and to obtain, at the same time satisfactory evidence of the uniformity of those internal principles which are productive of such various and apparently inconsistent operations.

"The system of law, in every country is divided into that part which regulates the power of the state, considered as a corporation or body politic; and that which regulates the conduct of the several members of which this corporation is composed. The former is the government, the law which constitutes; the latter, the law which is constituted. The former may with propriety, though not in the common acceptation be called the public; the latter the private law."

In substance Millar moved increasingly to what would now be called a sociological view of law, looking not so much at what the rules are but at what men do and how they behave in their relations with one another. He was also deeply conscious of the way society and its legal system naturally evolved. "It was the leading principle ... of all his speculations on law, morality, government, language, the arts, sciences and manners – that there is nothing produced by arbitrary or accidental causes; that no great change, institution, custom or occurrence could be ascribed to the character or exertions of an individual, to the temperament or disposition of a nation, to occasional policy, or peculiar wisdom or folly: everything, on the contrary, he held, arose spontaneously from the situation of the society, and was suggested or imposed irresistibly by the opportunities or necessities of their condition."[93] In the light of twentieth century experience of consciously-effected changes in social structure, government and law this view seems very dated.

His sociological approach, analysing in particular two themes in the structure and functions of personal relationships in society, its rank structure and its system of power-relations, comes out most strongly in his *Distinction of Ranks* but appears also in the *Historical View*, where he discusses the military, the peasantry and the clergy in Anglo-Saxon England, the military, the husbandmen, the craftsmen and manufacturers, and the clergy of feudal society, landlords, capitalists and labourers of industrial and commercial society. He even writes of the labouring classes, the middling ranks and the superior classes. Interpersonal relations are regarded by him as mainly power-relations; men were and are always seeking power and authority over their fellowmen, in families, in wider kinship-groups, in employment, in government. Dominance and subordination were a major aspect of society, particularly political society.

Mention has been made of the impact of Millar's personality on his students, many of whom attained distinction in Parliament, law, letters or elsewhere, and in some of these cases there is reason to believe that they were influenced by Millar's teaching in their activities or writing.[94] His wider influence was not immediate; indeed his works were quite quickly forgotten, save by a few,[95] but never completely so. His influence is quite clearly visible in his nephew and biographer John Craig's *Elements of Political Science* (1814), in repeated references and acknowledgments of indebtedness and in the views expressed. James Mill repeatedly pays tribute to Millar's influence[96] and prescribed his works to young John Stuart Mill, who refers favourably to Millar's *Historical View*.[97] James Wilson,[98] in his course on law in 1790–91 in the new College (later University) of Pennsylvania cites Millar's *Historical View* some 45 times as his source on English constitutional history and constitutional law. President Madison owned a copy of the *Distinction of Ranks*.

The *Distinction of Ranks* was translated into German (1772), French (1773) and there is thought to have been an Italian translation.[99] The *Historical View* was translated into German. Herder gave a lengthy review to the *Distinction of Ranks*[1] and Millar's works were widely known in Germany and may possibly have been known to Savigny, Neibuhr and to Marx.[2] Some later scholars have seen him as a pioneer of the materialist interpretation of history,[3] others as a father of mainstream sociology.[4] It is clear that his contribution to thinking was more than the stimulating exposition of Roman or current law.

NOTES

[1] DNB; Anderson, S.N., III, p. 157; Chambers, BDES.; *Int. Encyc. Soc. Sc.* X, 348; "Account of [his] Life and Writings," by John Craig (his nephew) in 4th ed. of *Origin of the Distinction of Ranks*; Obituary in *Scots Magazine* LXIII (1801) 527; Lehmann, *John Millar of Glasgow* (1960).

[2] Letter from Watt quoted in Strang, *Glasgow and its Clubs*, p. 156.

[3] His description of these lectures is quoted in Dugald Stewart's *Life of Smith* in *Trans. R.S.E.* 3 (1794) 61.

[4] They were fellow-professors from 1761 to 1764, when Adam Smith was succeeded by Thomas Reid.

[5] Craig, p. iv.

[6] Tytler, *Memoir of Kames*, I, p. 199; Craig, p. vii.

[7] He is said by Craig (*Life* p. ix) to have been accorded, presumably by Kames's influence, the privilege of pleading not only in the Outer House, but in the Inner House before the full court, a privilege then usually granted to advocates of considerable experience.

[8] Craig, *Life*, pp. lxxxvii, lxxxix.

[9] On Millar's private and family life see Lehmann, p. 26.

[10] *The Old Glasgow Houses of the Old Glasgow Gentry* (1870) contains a representation of Milheugh as it then was.

[11] A. Carlyle, *Autobiography*, p. 80.

[12] *Life*, p. xi.

[13] In the early years (to 1764) some students may have been attracted as much by the fame of Adam Smith.

[14] Chap. 19, *infra*.

[15] 1841–52.

[16] Later a strong advocate in Parliament of parliamentary reform.

[17] Prime Minister, 1834, 1835–41. On this see further L.C. Sanders (ed.), *Lord Melbourne's Papers* (1881), pp. 4–8, 14, 19; W.M. Torrens, *Memoirs of the Rt. Hon. William Lamb, Second Viscount Melbourne* (1878), I, p. 39; Lord David Cecil, *The Young Melbourne* (1939), pp. 65–67.

[18] They lived in Millar's house in 1799–1800.

[19] On his influence on this student see Christina Bewley, *Muir of Huntershill* (1981), pp. 3–6.

[20] Murray, *Memories of the old College*, pp. 221–222.

[21] J.H. Gray, *Autobiography of a Scottish Country Gentleman* (1868).

[22] Cosmo Innes, *Memoirs of Thomas Thomson* (1854), pp. 3–15. Millar encouraged Thomas Thomson to try his fortune at the Bar, not in the church.

[23] Lehmann, *John Millar*, p. 37. On the Russians see also W.R. Scott, *Adam Smith as Student and as Professor*, App. VII.

[24] A.H. Brown, "Adam Smith's First Russian Followers," in *Essays on Adam Smith* (ed. A.S. Skinner and T. Wilson, 1975), p. 247.

[25] Brown, *op. cit.*, p. 252.

[26] For the degree of LL.D. In 1765 they had petitioned the Faculty, *i.e.* what later became the Senate, to be accepted as candidates for the degree of doctor of law.

[27] Brown, *op. cit.*, p. 253.

[28] This process of private examination, public examination and public defence of a Latin thesis on a title of the Pandects is reminiscent of the procedure followed until recently in the examination of an Intrant to the Faculty of Advocates, though in modern times the private examination has usually been satisfied by production of a university degree diploma and the public examination and defence of the Latin thesis have been ceremonies rather than serious tests of knowledge.

[29] Brown, *op. cit.*, p. 259.

[30] Brown, *op. cit.*, p. 260. The Royal Society of Edinburgh also was chartered in 1783.

[31] Brown, *op. cit.*, p. 269. Desnitsky frequently cites Adam Smith's *Theory of Moral Sentiments* and also the works of Hume, Robertson and Kames. He probably quoted Millar from his lecture notes as he does not mention the book.

[32] A.L. Macfie, "John Millar: A Bridge between Adam Smith and Nineteenth Century Social Thinkers?" in *The Individual in Society: Papers on Adam Smith* (1967), p. 149.

[33] Brown, *op. cit.*, pp. 270–271; *cf.* R.L. Meek, "Smith, Turgot and the 'Four Stages' Theory," in *History of Political Economy*, 3 (1971) 9.

[34] Lehmann, *op. cit.*, p. 23; *cf.* Scott, *Adam Smith as Student and Professor*, pp. 292, 306.

[35] Craig, p. lxv.

[36] DNB.

[37] DNB.

[38] DNB.

[39] See J.T.Y. Greig, *Letters of David Hume* (1932), letters 507, 512.

[40] Francis Jeffrey, Rectorial Address, in Hay. *Inaugural Addresses*, 6.

[41] Lehmann, *op. cit.*, pp. 46–47.

[42] Boswell, *The Applause of the Jury*, 1782–85 (ed. Lustig and Pottle), p. 204.

[43] Lehmann, *op. cit.*, p. 50.

[44] David Murray (*Memories*, p. 222) had two sets of such notes. They are now in the David Murray Collection in Glasgow University Library. See also Lehmann, *John Millar of Glasgow*, App. III.

[45] *Element Juris Civilis Secundum Ordinem Institutionum* by Johannes Gottlieb Heineccius (1681–1741), professor at Halle, published in 1725. Heineccius also wrote a larger *Elementa juris civilis secundum ordinem Pandectarum* (1727) and various other texts.

[46] Murray, *Memories*, p. 223; University advertisements quoted by Lehmann, p. 22. Millar must have lectured at least twice a day throughout the session.

[47] Craig, *supra*.

[48] Evidence to University Commissioners (1826), Vol. II (Glasgow), p. 145.

[49] There are in Glasgow University Library the following:
Lectures on Scots private law, 1776–77 (MS. Gen. 347);
Lectures on the Law of Scotland, 1783 (MS. Gen. 178);
Lectures on the Law of Scotland, 1789–90 (MS. Murray 83–87);
Lectures on the Law of Scotland, 1790 (MS. Gen. 181/1–3);
Lectures on Scots law, 1792 (MS. Gen. 1078).
There are also sets of notes of his lectures on the *Institutes*, jurisprudence and English law, and also some in Edinburgh University Library and the National Library of Scotland.

[50] The following sets of notes are preserved in Glasgow University Library:
Lectures on the Public Law of Great Britain (undated) (MS. Gen. 203);
Lectures on Government (1783) (MS. Gen. 179);
Lectures on Government (1787–88), 3 vols. (MS. Gen. 289–91);
Lectures on Government taken down by William Rae (1789), 3 vols. (MS. Gen. 18/1–3);
Lectures on Government taken by David Royle (1789–90), 3 vols. (MS. Murray 88–90);
Lectures on the Science of Government 1797–98 (MS. Hamilton 116).
There are also extant the following others:
Lectures on Government delivered by Mr. J. Millar, an. 1771–72, extended by George Skene, 2 vols. (Mitchell Library, Glasgow, MS. 99);
Notes from Professor Millar's Lectures on Publick Law or Government, 1780–81, (NLS MS. 3931); A Course of Lectures on Government, 1782 (Aberdeen University Library, MS. 133);
Lectures on Government taken by James Moncreiff (Moncreiff of Tulliebole Collection, NRA (Scotland) Survey 0333, Box 12).

[51] Millar, regrettably, seems to have used the terms British and English, Great Britain and England, pretty indifferently.

[52] I. Hont, "The rich country – poor country debate in Scottish classical political economy", in I. Hont and M. Ignatieff, *Wealth and Virtue* (1983), pp. 271, 309; A.L. Macfie, "John Millar: A Bridge between Adam Smith and the 19th century Figures," in *The Individual in Society: Papers on Adam Smith* (1967).

[53] Craig, *supra*.

[54] *Memoir of Lord Kames*, I, pp. 199, 200–201.

[55] Ochtertyre MSS., III, 1860, in N.L.S., quoted by Lehmann, *op. cit.*, p. 36.

[56] R. Heron, *Journey through Western Scotland in 1792* (1793) II, p. 418.

[57] C. Redding, *Literary Reminiscences and Memoirs of Thomas Campbell* (1860), I, p. 20.

58 Beattie, *Life and Letters of Thomas Campbell* (1849), I, pp. 157–160.

59 W. Beattie, *ibid.*, p. 158.

60 There is a Tassie medallion of him, a photograph of which is the frontispiece in Lehmann's *John Millar of Glasgow*. He is represented also in one of the carved stone heads which are the crowns of the arches above the ground-floor windows of Charles Wilson's Royal Faculty of Procurators' Hall in St. George's Place, Glasgow. Millar's head is the second from the left on the frontage facing St. George's Place.

61 *Edinburgh Review*, IX, p. 86.

62 *Life of Jeffrey*, I, pp. 10–11.

63 Craig, p. xiii.

64 George Jardine, *Outlines of Philosophy of Education* (1818), p. 465.

65 Quoted by Lehmann, *op. cit.*, p. vii.

66 *Edinburgh Review* 135 (1872), p. 406.

67 *Memories of the Old College of Glasgow* (1927), p. 221.

68 *Elucidations respecting the Common and Statute Law of Scotland* (1777) Introduction, p. vii.

69 Craig, *Life*, p. xii.

70 Craig, *Life*, p. xlii.

71 *Ibid.*, p. lvi.

72 There is a reprint of the third edition in Lehmann, *John Millar of Glasgow*, pp. 165–322.

73 This work is fully discussed in the edition of 1974 by D.D. Raphael and A.L. Macfie.

74 See discussion in M. Ignatieff, "John Millar and Individualism," in I. Hont and M. Ignatieff, *Wealth and Virtue* (1983), p. 317, 332.

75 R.M. MacIver, Foreword to Lehmann, *John Millar of Glasgow*, p. xi; Lehmann, "John Millar: Historical Sociologist," *Brit. Jo. Sociology*, 2 (1952), pp. 30–46.

76 *Edinburgh Review*, III (1803), 157.

77 *Ibid.*, IX (1806), 184.

78 The work is dedicated to Charles James Fox.

79 Vol. I, Intro., pp. 5–6.

80 Vol. III, Intro., pp. 1–2. Chapter 3 of Vol. IV, Bk. II, is entitled: "The Advancement of Manufactures, Commerce and the Arts since the reign of William III, and the tendency of this Advancement to diffuse a spirit of Liberty and Independence."

81 *View of the State of Europe during the Middle Ages*, (1818) preface. Millar's use of the phrase "constitutional history of England" in his dedication to Charles James Fox was said to have antedated by 40 years Hallam's use of the phrase in 1827 in the title of his *Constitutional History of England*: J.D. Mackie, *History of the University of Glasgow* (1951), p. 214. But Millar had been anticipated by Gilbert Stuart's *Observations concerning the Public Law and the Constitutional History of Scotland with remarks concerning English Antiquity*, published in 1779.

82 Vol. IV, p. 102.

83 Craig draws attention to the similarity between Millar's view and that of Millar's former student Lauderdale, in the latter's *Inquiry into the Nature and Origin of Public Wealth and into the Means and Causes of its Increase*, showing how both advanced beyond Adam Smith's position on this matter. They had probably discussed the problem together.

84 Lehmann, *op. cit.*, App. II, states the view that there is strong internal evidence to support such a claim. But it has also been suggested that they were written by his nephew and biographer, Craig: M. Ignatieff, "John Millar and Individualism," in I. Hont and M. Ignatieff, *Wealth and Virtue* (1983), 317, 323.

85 On this background see generally Gladys Bryson, *Man and Society: The Scottish Inquiry of the Eighteenth Century* (1945); C.R. Fay, *Adam Smith and the Scotland of His Day* (1956); H.W. Meikle, *Scotland and the French Revolution* (1912) Lehmann, *John Millar*, pp. 91–121; A.L. Macfie, "The Scottish Tradition in Economic Thought," *Scottish Journal of Political Economy* 2 (1955), p. 81; Duncan Forbes, "Scientific Whiggism: Adam Smith and John Millar," *Cambridge Journal* VII (1954) 643, and "Sceptical Whiggism, Commerce and Liberty," *Essays on Adam Smith* (ed. A.S. Skinner and T. Wilson, 1975), p. 179.

86 Jeffrey, *Edinburgh Review*, III, 158; Craig's *Life*, pp. xcix-cxx; He is included in J.O. Baylen and N.J. Gossman, *Biographical Dictionary of Modern British Radicals*. 1770–1830.

87 J. Strang, *Glasgow and its Clubs* (1857), p. 167; H.W. Meikle, *Scotland and the French Revolution*, p. 71. The Friends of Liberty were not the same as the Friends of the People.

[88] C. Bewley, *Muir of Huntershill* (1981), p. 3.

[89] Craig, *Life*, p. cxiv.

[90] Jeffrey, *supra*.

[91] Alexander Carlyle, *Autobiography*, pp. 516–518.

[92] Vol. 4, Chap. 7, "The Progress of Science relative to Law and Government", 266 at pp. 284–285.

[93] Jeffrey in *Edinburgh Review*, 3 (1803) 157; *cf.* Tytler, *Memoir of Kames*, I, p. 200, on Millar.

[94] John Rae, *Life of Adam Smith* (1895) p. 53, called him "the most effective and influential apostle of liberalism in Scotland in that day."

[95] McCulloch, *Political Economy* (1829), p. iv; C. Innes, *Memoir of Thomas Thomson* (1854), p. 10; J.F. McLennan, *Studies in Ancient History* (1876), p. 420; W. Sombart, "Die Anfange der Soziologie" in M. Palyi (ed.), *Hauptprobleme der Soziologie Erinnerungsgabe an Max Weber* (1923), I, p. 11.

[96] Translation of Charles Viller's *Spirit and Influence of the Reformation of Luther* (1805), pp. 176, 232; *History of British India* (1848) I, pp. 182, 196; II, p. 156; Alex. Bain, *James Mill* (1882), pp. 56, 176.

[97] *Westminster Review*, 6 (1826), 95, 102; *System of Logic* (1843), Bk. VI, Chap. 9, on "Logic of the Social and Moral Sciences"; Duncan Forbes, "Scientific Whiggism," *Cambridge Journal*, 7 (1954) 669. J.H. Millar, *Literary History of Scotland* (367) points to similarities of style in Millar's and J.S. Mill's work.

[98] On him see *D. Amer. Biog.*; C.P. Smith, *James Wilson: Founding Father (1742–98)* (1956); Charles Warren, *History of the American Bar* (1911), p. 340.

[99] Millar is included in Michaud's *Biographie Universelle Ancienne et Moderne* (nouvelle ed.), Vol. 28.

[1] J.G. Herder, *Sämtliche Werke* (1877) 5, 452.

[2] Lehmann, *op. cit.*, pp. 157–158; R.L. Meek, "The Scottish Contribution to Marxist Sociology," in *Economics and Ideology and Other Essays* (1967).

[3] R. Pascal, "Property, or Society: The Scottish Historical School of the 18th century," *Modern Quarterly* 1 (1938), 167; Meek, *supra*.

[4] Lehmann, *op. cit.*; L. Schneider, "Tension in the Thought of John Millar," in *Studies in Burke and His Time*, 13 (1972), 2083.

CHAPTER 16

SIR DAVID DALRYMPLE, LORD HAILES

SIR David Dalrymple (*c.* 1665–1721, advocate 1688)[1] was the youngest son of the first Viscount Stair[2] and younger brother of Sir John Dalrymple (1648–1707, advocate 1672, Lord Advocate 1689–92), created in 1703 the first Earl of Stair[3], and of Sir Hew Dalrymple of North Berwick (1652–1737, advocate 1677, Dean, 1695), Lord President 1698–1737[4], and was himself Lord Advocate 1700–11 and 1714–20. His son, Sir James Dalrymple of Hailes (1692–1751), was auditor of the Exchequer in Scotland, and married Lady Christian Hamilton, a direct descendant of Thomas Hamilton, Secretary of State 1612–16 and Lord President of the Court of Session 1616–37.[5] The eldest of their 16 children was David,[6] who was born on October 28, 1726, educated at Eton and Utrecht, became a barrister of the Middle Temple in 1744[7] and passed advocate in 1748. He was not a good speaker but pleading was then largely in writing and he attained a good reputation as a learned and accurate lawyer.

In 1766 he was made a Lord of Session and in 1776 a Lord of Justiciary also, and was well regarded as a sound and humane judge. Having been rejected by a Miss Whyte, reported to have a fortune of £30,000[8], he married twice, firstly Anne, daughter of George Brown, Lord Coalston, and, secondly, Helen, daughter of Sir James Fergusson, Lord Kilkerran[9]; his daughter by his second marriage became ancestress of the Fergussons of Kilkerran and the Dalrymples of New Hailes. He lived at New Hailes near Inveresk within sight of the Forth and went there whenever he could to pursue studies and maintain correspondence with men of letters. He died in 1792 and "Jupiter" Carlyle, minister of Inveresk, eulogised him in a funeral sermon.

Boswell admired Hailes because he was a man of letters; he had contributed to the *Gentleman's Magazine* and *The World* and was a correspondent of Horace Walpole.[10] "Before I left Scotland [in 1763] I had a long conversation with Sir David Dalrymple on my future schemes of life. Sir David is a man of great ingenuity, a fine scholar, an accurate critic, and a worthy member of society. From my early years I used to regard him with admiration and awe, and look upon him as a representative of Mr. Addison. Since I came to London I have found his name much respected in the literary world. He is also a great friend of my father's, is one of two witnesses to an important transaction between my father and me, and is a sincere well-wisher to the family of Auchinleck. Upon all these considerations, I thought his advice and correspondence would be of service to me and also give me pleasure. I therefore wrote to him. . . ."[10] He advised Lord Auchinleck, for whom he had high regard, to send James Boswell to Utrecht to study civil law, and Boswell looked up to him as a model to be followed; his diary contains frequent self-admonitions to be like Sir David Dalrymple, among others. Boswell and Hailes corresponded extensively. Hailes frequently mediated between Boswell and his father and advised Boswell.[13] In 1767 Hailes ·

read Boswell's *Journal of a Tour to Corsica* in manuscript and made suggestions for revision.[14]

Through Hailes, Boswell secured his wish to meet Dr. Johnson and by July 1763 Boswell and Johnson were drinking Dalrymple's health.[15] On July 22 of that year Johnson "drank a bumper to Sir David Dalrymple, whom he considers a very worthy man, a scholar, and a man of wit. He never heard of him but from me. But he bid me let Sir David know his opinion, as he did not show himself much in the world, and so should have the praise of the few who hear of him."[16] When Johnson was in Edinburgh in August 1773, Boswell had to dinner with him Hailes, Mr. Maclaurin, advocate (later Lord Dreghorn), and others. Hailes pleased Johnson very much and Maclaurin's learning and talents enabled him to do his part very well in Dr. Johnson's company.[17] In November, before departing for London, Johnson dined with both Hailes and Maclaurin, along with Principal Robertson and others.[18] In 1775 Hailes wrote to Boswell praising Boswell's *Journal of a Tour to the Hebrides*.[19]

Later, through Boswell, Hailes sent his *Annals of Scotland* for Johnson's comments.[20] Johnson in turn sought Hailes' opinion as that most worth having on any matter of Scottish law or history. Hailes also corresponded with Burke, Horace Walpole and numerous bishops, who were grateful to him for his writings, refuting Edward Gibbon's views on the rise of Christianity.

Hailes wrote very extensively, though many of his publications are slight; many relate to religion and the early history of Christianity, but it is for his contributions to Scottish legal history that he is mainly remembered, and only these are mentioned here.

His first legal work was an edition of a small book, *A Discourse of the Unnatural and Vile Conspiracy attempted by John, Earl of Gowry, and his brother against His Majesty's Person at St. Johnstoun upon the 5th August 1600*, published in 1757. It was followed by *Memorials and Letters relating to the History of Britain in the reign of James I, published from the originals*, an edition of source-materials from the Balfour of Denmilne papers in the Advocates' Library. It appeared in 1762 and there was an enlarged edition in 1766, in which year appeared a companion volume dealing with the reign of Charles I, chiefly collected from the manuscripts of the Reverend Robert Wodrow, historian of the Church of Scotland. In the same year he published *An Account of the Preservation of Charles II after the Battle of Worcester drawn up by himself: To which are added, his Letters to Several Persons*. These were drawn from Pepys MSS., the account dictated to Pepys by the King, and the letters drawn from various sources. Also in the same year there came out *The Secret Correspondence between Sir Robert Cecil and James VI*.

The following year saw the publication of *A Catalogue of the Lords of Session, from the Institution of the College of Justice to 1752, with Historical Notes*. This was based on a manuscript abridgment of the Books of Sederunt formerly belonging to Seton, Lord Pitmedden. The catalogue gives in four columns the date, name of the judge, judicial title, and whom he succeeded. There was a later edition bringing the list down to 1799. This work formed the basis of the later account by George Brunton and David Haig, who added the biographical notes relative to each judge. The notes give further information about some of the Lords. There is appended a "Catalogue of the Faculty of Advocates from the Institution of the College of Justice to the Revolution in 1688," taken from Aikman's manuscript collection in the Advocates' Library.

More important was *An Examination of Some of the Arguments for the High Antiquity of Regiam Majestatem and an Inquiry into the Authenticity of Leges Malcolmi*, a pamphlet published in 1769. Hailes starts by observing that, "I would not willingly derogate from the labours of others, but truth obliges me to observe, that to all appearance, Skene was a careless, if not an unfaithful publisher,"[21] a criticism which he proceeds to justify by examination of particular passages from the MSS. "It was judged proper to make these observations on Skene's edition of *Regiam Majestatem*, that it may not on every occasion be appealed to as correct, and unexceptionably authentic."[22] He then deals with some of the arguments for antiquity, that David I was a lawgiver, the argument from mention of the *Regiam* in the Chronicle of the Abbey of Kinloss, and that *Regiam Majestatem* is quoted as authentic in our statute book, and shows that none of these is conclusive or even convincing. He does not, however, express positively his own views on its date, beyond accepting that clearly it drew on Glanvill. Similarly in respect of the *Leges Malcolmi*, he criticises the attribution of these to Malcolm III and their authenticity; the early chapters "are all the composition of some illiterate forger,"[23] in the later chapters "the author seems rather to have copied than invented."[24] Hailes was the first scholar with the competence, and the interest, to examine the MSS. critically and reveal some of the deficiencies of Skene's editions.

At this time Hailes corresponded with Adam Smith. On January 15, 1769, Smith wrote to Hailes[25] thanking him for the use of his collection of papers concerning the prices of corn in ancient times, and again on March 5[26] requesting papers on the prices of provisions in former times and also commenting on the statutes of James I of Scotland which Hailes had sent him for comparative consideration. Hailes replied the next day[27] sending the papers requested, which are notes made from old charters and cartularies from 1243 onwards. This gives further evidence of Hailes's extensive reading in the early (and unprinted) records and of his careful noting of matters of interest, not only those of legal concern but points of economic interest also. Smith acknowledged on March 12[28] and on May 16 wrote again [29] to say with what great pleasure he had read Hailes's *Examination of Regiam Majestatem* and agreeing that the *Leges Malcolmi* were spurious. A week later he wrote again[30] commenting on Skene's understanding of a passage in the *Leges Malcolmi*.

Hailes's *Remarks on the History of Scotland*, published in 1773, is a slight work, not now remembered.

His major historical work appeared in 1776. It was the *Annals of Scotland from the accession of Malcolm III to the accession of Robert I; with an Appendix containing eight Dissertations*. Three years later came *Annals of Scotland from the accession of Robert I, sirnamed Bruce, to the accession of the House of Stewart; with an Appendix containing Nine Dissertations*. There was a later edition in three volumes in 1819. Each volume consists of notes under the heading of each year of the significant events of that year with marginal references to the chronicles or other early histories which are authorities for his statement and dates. It evidences extensive acquaintance with these ancient sources of information, nearly all, it should be remembered, then unprinted, and a well-developed critical faculty. It must have been a most laborious compilation. The *Annals* is still a valuable repository of information and references and has been a quarry for many historians. Hailes does not draw inferences or generalise, but states facts and gives his authority for them. It is a collection of the basic materials of history, but not history as a form of literature. Dr. Johnson observed to Boswell[31]:

> "Lord Hailes's *Annals of Scotland* are very exact, but they contain mere dry circumstances. They are to be considered as a dictionary. You know such things are there and may be looked at when you please. When you have read them, you close the book, and find you have nothing in your head. Robertson[32] paints; but the misfortune is you are sure he does not know the people whom he paints, so you cannot suppose a likeness. Characters should never be given by an historian unless he knew the people whom he describes or copies from those who knew them."

Minor historical works include *Historical Memoirs concerning the Provincial Councils of the Scottish Clergy*, (1769), *Canons of the Church of Scotland drawn up in the Provincial Councils held at Perth, anno 1242-69*, contributed to Wilkins' *Concilia Magnae Britanniae*, *Remarks on the History of Scotland* (1773), and *Disquisitions concerning the Antiquities of the Christian Church* (1783). The first two of these in particular show his appreciation of the fact that medieval history cannot be written or understood without appreciating the influence of the church.

To Hailes are attributed also some undated and scarce works, *A Specimen of Notes on the Statute Law of Scotland*, and *A Specimen of Notes on the Statute Law during the reign of Mary Queen of Scots*. These are probably notes made towards a more substantial work on the lines of Mackenzie's *Observations on the Statutes*, and circulated among friends to secure comments with a view to the fuller work.[33]

In 1826 Mungo Ponton Brown, advocate, printed from Hailes's papers two volumes of *Decisions of the Lords of Council and Session from 1766 to 1791*, collected by Hailes. These cover, accordingly, practically the whole of Hailes's time on the Bench and during the whole period he must have industriously noted what he and his fellow-judges said. Most of the reports are of cases also reported in the *Faculty Collection* for that period, but they usefully supplement these other reports in that they give notes of the judges' opinions whereas the reports in the *Faculty Collection* rarely do so. Many are not in the *Faculty Collection* and were not printed by Brown as being not worth reporting. Some are also in Kames's *Select Decisions*. But they have considerable interest and value because of the frequently substantial notes of individual judges' opinions, and give something of the flavour of the court and of the personality of individual judges. Thus the important copyright case of *Hinton v. Donaldson* in 1773 is reported in Morison[34] in nine lines from Kames and Woodhouselee's *Folio Dictionary*,[35] but runs to more than seven pages in Hailes.[36] For the facts and pleas of the parties one has to resort to the *Faculty Collection* reports as Brown prints the opinions only. Hailes's *Decisions* are not reprinted in Morison's *Dictionary*, being later in date of publication, nor in Brown's own *Supplement* to Morison, and tend therefore to be overlooked.

Again one cannot but be struck by the assiduity of the man, regularly recording the substance of what the judges all said in every case of substance and also working away in his leisure hours at religious tracts and historical investigations. From Boswell's Journals he appears as a level-headed, restraining, mediating influence, well-regarded by everyone. Despite Dr. Johnson's somewhat grudging view of it, his *Annals of Scotland* is still, two centuries later, a valuable source-book. Apart from the *Decisions*, Hailes's importance is as a legal and general historian, but in that field his importance is great. He was a careful record scholar and critic and many subsequent writers have been indebted to him. It is a great pity he did not essay a narrative history of Scots law.

NOTES

[1] DNB; *Scots Peerage*, VIII, 143; Omond, *Lord Advocates*, I, p. 281.

[2] Chap. 8, *supra*.

[3] DNB; *Scots Peerage*, VIII, 147; Omond, *Lord Advocates*, I, p. 236.

[4] DNB; *Scots Peerage*, VIII, 125; Brunton & Haig, p. 465; Omond, *Lord Advocates*, I, p. 241;

[5] Chap. 10, *supra*.

[6] DNB; Anderson, S.N., II, p. 9; Chambers *BDES*; Brunton & Haig, p. 529; Tytler, *Memoir of Lord Kames* I, pp. 181–183; H. G. Graham, *Scottish Men of Letters in the 18th Century* (1901), p. 198; W. F. Gray, *Some Old Scots Judges* (1914), p. 123; Kay's *Edinburgh Portraits* I, 364.

[7] 17 S.H.R. 106.

[8] F. A. Pottle, *James Boswell, The Earlier Years*, 36. Boswell, too, had a passion for her. She married Charles Bruce, fifth Earl of Elgin and ninth Earl of Kincardine, and became ancestress of the present line of Elgin and Kincardine: *Scots Peerage*, III, 491.

[9] Chap. 18, *infra*.

[10] Pottle, *op. cit.*, p. 36.

[11] F. A. Pottle, *Boswell's London Journal* (1950), p. 187. Correspondence continued for a considerable time.

[12] *Ibid.*, p. 277.

[13] F. A. Pottle, *Boswell on the Grand Tour: Germany and Switzerland* (1953), p. 236.

[14] Pottle, *James Boswell*, p. 339; F. Brady and F. A. Pottle, *Boswell in Search of a Wife* (1957), p. 77.

[15] F. A. Pottle, *Boswell's London Journal*, p. 292.

[16] *Ibid.*, p. 310; C. Ryskamp and F. A. Pottle, *Boswell: The Ominous Years*, pp. 112–113. "He said, 'Does Lord Hailes love me? I love him'."

[17] F. A. Pottle and C. H. Bennett, *Boswell's Journal of a Tour to the Hebrides*, (1961), pp. 30–31.

[18] *Ibid.*, pp. 385–389. "Dr. Johnson also one day visited the Court of Session. He thought the mode of pleading there too vehement, and too much addressed to the passions of the judges. 'This,' said he, 'is not the Areopagus' ": *Ibid.*, p. 389.

[19] *Ibid.*, p. 394.

[20] W. K. Wimsatt and F. A. Pottle, *Boswell for the Defence*, p. 215; Ryskamp and Pottle, *supra*, p. 112.

[21] p. 4.

[22] p. 10.

[23] p. 50.

[24] p. 51.

[25] E. C. Mossner and I. S. Ross, *The Correspondence of Adam Smith* (1977), p. 139.

[26] *Ibid.*, p. 141.

[27] *Ibid.*, p. 143.

[28] *Ibid.*, p. 151.

[29] *Ibid.*, p. 152.

[30] *Ibid.*, p. 154.

[31] October 4, 1779: J. W. Reed and F. A. Pottle, *Boswell: Laird of Auchinleck* (1977), p. 141.

[32] Principal Robertson, whose *History of Scotland* appeared in 1759.

[33] Tytler, *Memoir of Lord Kames*, I, p. 209.

[34] Mor. 8307.

[35] III, 388.

[36] I, 535. James Boswell, who was of counsel in the case, published in 1774 *The Decision of the Court of Session upon the Question of Literary Property, in the cause John Hinton of London, Bookseller, Pursuer: against Alexander Donaldson and John Wood, Booksellers in Edinburgh and James Meurose, Bookseller in Kilmarnock, Defenders*.

CHAPTER 17

WALTER ROSS

THE study and teaching of land law and conveyancing was for long done by the teachers of Scots law, supplemented by instruction in offices aided by the use of some of the books of styles. But in the later eighteenth century various proposals were made in Edinburgh for systematic instruction in this branch of law and practice.

Walter Ross was born on September 28, 1738, admitted to the Society of Writers to the Signet on June 25, 1764, and died on March 11, 1789.[1] His health appears to have failed some years before his death so that he had to leave Edinburgh, and he then felt that he could not employ his time with more advantage to the profession or more pleasure to himself than by dedicating it to the study of the practical part of the law of Scotland and to the instruction of young men entering the legal profession. In 1782 he published a *Discourse upon the Removing of Tenants, published to serve as a specimen of the Lectures intended to be delivered upon the Practice of the Law of Scotland*. In 1783 and 1784 he taught a private class in Edinburgh and the substance of his lectures was published in 1792 by an unknown editor as *Lectures on the History and Practice of the Law of Scotland relative to Conveyancing and Legal Diligence*. A revised edition, with the *Discourse upon the Removing of Tenants* reprinted as an appendix, came out in 1822.

To the first volume is prefaced an introductory essay, "To the Members of the College of Justice," critical of the defects of apprenticeship in a writer's chambers as the sole training of a young solicitor. Styles and forms, Ross observes, cannot be comprehended "without some acquaintance with ancient customs, manners and history both civil and ecclesiastical." He quotes Lord Kames's statement that law becomes only a rational study, when it is traced historically, and applies it to the practice of the law. "Let this branch likewise be treated historically. Let every part of it be traced from its origin. Let illustration be borrowed from Law – from history – from antiquity – from manners. No science will refuse its aid to embellish the rugged path. . . . Is it not a shame to see people, during the whole course of their lives, writing words, nay whole clauses of Deeds, they do not understand. . . ." He continues that the arrangement of the subject is to follow the order of practice, and that he is going to treat every branch of his subject in the order adopted by Dallas of St. Martin,[2] and to treat each subject historically.

Later[3] he observes: "My province is to teach you, what my brethren the Writers would teach the gentlemen committed to their care, if the other duties of their profession could possibly admit of it." Even then masters in offices seem to have neglected their apprentices.

Volume I consists of 18 essays[4] dealing with moveable rights, personal bonds, assignation, discharge and various forms of diligence. Volume II contains an "Introductory Discourse" and nine essays dealing with heritable rights, original charter, sasine, registration, voluntary alienation, voluntary securities upon land and related topics.

As was common in the eighteenth century the style is leisurely, allusive and replete with classical references and he may be thought slow in coming to the point, which is the analysis of the then current deeds and forms and practice generally.

Ross was clearly a very scholarly and learned writer, with an extensive knowledge of the origins, history and development of the kinds of transactions he dealt with, and well acquainted with the earlier books of the law. He is not afraid to criticise, and Kames comes in for a fair amount of criticism. He refers to a small number of cases and, of course, to relevant statutes. Much of each essay is devoted to analysis of and commentary on the clauses of the relevant kind of deed.

His work is clearly invaluable for information on and explanation of some of the older forms such as caption and wadset, but is also always worth examining for his elucidation of the origins and development of surviving bodies of rules such as those as to poinding. When the course of lectures was delivered it must have been a revelation to the young hearers, who had nothing better to guide them than Dallas's and other books of styles, many of which must have frequently been copied uncomprehendingly, and possibly inappropriately. Ross's lectures were the first attempt to make conveyancing understandable and explain much of it.

Ross has always been considered of high authority and his views treated with respect. The *Lectures* have been cited many times in argument, in judgment and in later writings.

NOTES

[1] *History of the Society of Writers to H.M. Signet* (revised ed., 1936), p. 306.
[2] Chap. 10. *supra.*
[3] p. 3.
[4] The editor in his Advertisement, p. vi, wishes the volumes to be considered rather as consisting of so many practical essays, or law tracts, than as being a complete course of Lectures, of which indeed they were intended to be only a part.

CHAPTER 18

THE MINOR JURISTS OF THE EIGHTEENTH CENTURY

THE picture of the minor jurists in the eighteenth century differs considerably from that of the seventeenth. Legal history and jurisprudence make an appearance. The editors of the statutes have gone but there are abridgers of the statutes; there are no more practicks; reports are getting better and the series more continuous; and there are many more treatises and books on particular branches of the law as well as the more general books.

HISTORY

Scottish historiography, as distinct from chronicles, emerged with George Buchanan's[1] *Rerum Scoticarum Historia* (1582) and Thomas Innes's[2] *Critical Essay on the Ancient Inhabitants of the Northern Parts of Britain or Scotland* (1729). There were numerous publications in the eighteenth century.

William Nicolson (1655–1727), Bishop of Carlisle and later of Derry,[3] wrote a *Scottish Historical Library*, published in 1702, which surveys the sources and authorities on Scottish history and the various writers' works. Chapter 7 deals with records and law-books. "The first authentic body of laws of Scotland (if even that may be justly esteemed so) is their *Regiam Majestatem*:" Nicolson had his doubts.

He mentions the "Practiques (as they call them, a word of the same import with that of Reports in England)," Skene, Mackenzie and "the incomparable Th. Craig's *Ius Feudale*," but not Stair. Nicolson had certainly examined his sources and the MSS. and books which he mentions, and he produced, for its time, a useful and helpful bibliographical guide. It was later reissued with companion works as *English, Scotch and Irish Historical Libraries* in 1736. But he also produced in 1705 and in 1747 *Leges Marchiarum: or Border-Laws Articles and Treaties made by the Commissioners of the Kings of England and Scotland for the better preservation of Peace and Commerce upon the Marches of both Kingdoms, from the reign of Henry III to the Union of the two Crowns in James I.* This includes an Appendix of Charters and Records.

A much more important scholar was James Anderson (1662–1728, W.S. 1691),[4] an antiquary and genealogist, who published an *Historical Essay, showing that the Crown and Kingdom of Scotland is Imperial and Independent* in 1705, as a reply to William Atwood's *Superiority and Direct Dominion of the Imperial Crown of England over the Crown and Kingdom of Scotland, the true foundation of a compleat Union, reasserted* (1704 and 1705), a book which revived Edward I's claim to sovereignty over Scotland and derided that country's independence. Anderson's reply is clear and convincing. The Scottish Parliament found Anderson's work so acceptable that it ordered him to be rewarded and their thanks to be given him by the Lord Chancellor in presence of the Queen's Commissioner and the Estates. This was done, and Atwood's work ordered to be burned by the common hangman at Edinburgh.

Anderson, encouraged by this success and by the Scottish Parliament, gave up his profession, turned to scholarship and devoted years of work to his great work, *Selectus Diplomatum et Numismatum Scotiae Thesaurus*, a still-valuable collection of facsimiles of ancient charters, seals, coins and other muniments. In the interval he published *Collections relating to the History of Mary, Queen of Scotland* (4 vols., 1727–28). The *Diplomata* were published only after his death, in 1739. The Introduction may be by Thomas Ruddiman,[5] who issued a translation of the *Introduction*, to which he added notes, in 1773. Cosmo Innes recommended the *Diplomata* to young lawyers "as a fitting commencement to your charter studies."[6]

In 1723 Anderson offered his books on British history to the Faculty of Advocates, which purchased a substantial part of his collection.[7]

Scottish history sprang into the limelight with the work of William Robertson (1721–93),[8] minister of Gladsmuir and then of Lady Yester's chapel in Edinburgh, who was a member of the Select Society with Adam Smith, Hume, Wedderburn (later Lord Chancellor Loughborough), Adam Ferguson, Monboddo, Kames and Woodhouselee, and in 1759 published a *History of Scotland during the Reigns of Queen Mary and of James VI till his Accession to the Crown of England*. It was an instant success and Robertson moved to Old Greyfriars and became in 1762 Principal of Edinburgh University and in 1763 Moderator of the General Assembly, which body he controlled for 16 years, and also Historiographer for Scotland. His later works included a *History of the Reign of the Emperor Charles V with a View of the Progress of Society from the subversion of the Roman Empire to the Beginning of the Sixteenth Century* (1769), which won him a European reputation. The Introduction was a brilliant generalised account on the basis of massive accumulations of fact. He also published a *History of America* (1777) and a *Historical Disquisition concerning the knowledge which the Ancients had of India* (1791). He played a major part in the foundation of the Royal Society of Edinburgh in 1783. He was a liberal and one of the major figures of the Enlightenment. His eldest son, William (1753–1835, advocate 1775),[9] became Lord Robertson in 1805 and sat on the Bench until 1826.

In Glasgow University a lectureship in civil and ecclesiastical history had been established as early as 1692 but this was transformed in 1716 into a chair in ecclesiastical history alone. In Edinburgh University on the other hand the study of history was from the outset linked with the Faculty of Law. In 1719 the town council established a "profession of universal history," possibly on the initiative of Principal Carstares, to complete the provision made for the liberal arts and sciences.[10] But appointment came to be virtually on the nomination of the Faculty of Advocates, which tended to choose one of themselves, and such an incumbent naturally tended to give pride of place to legal antiquities. The first professor, Charles Mackie (?–1765) professor 1719–65,[11] was a nephew of Carstares, and was expected to lecture on the history of Scotland and on Roman, Greek and British antiquities. His main interests seem to have been Roman law and antiquities, and chronology. From

1753 he had John Gordon[12] as joint professor, but within a year Gordon resigned so as to be in a position to accept the chair of civil law, for which he thought himself better qualified, but which he did not get. William Wallace[13] was then made joint professor with Mackie until appointed to the chair of Scots law in 1765 (which he held until 1786). It is said that no lectures were given from about 1760.

Wallace was succeeded by John Pringle (1741–1811, advocate 1763) (professor 1765–80), who also is not known to have lectured. Then came Alexander Fraser Tytler (1747–1813, advocate 1770, Lord Woodhouselee 1802) (professor 1780–1801),[14] who revived historical study, published the substance of his course as *Elements of General History* (1801), and wrote a valuable biography of Lord Kames (1807). He was an accomplished and scholarly man, active in the Royal Society of Edinburgh, and was succeeded in the chair by his son William.[15] The legal hold on the chair was continuous, but none of the holders before Tytler contributed anything to the subject.

LEGAL HISTORY

Legal history, however, lagged behind more general history. Alexander Bayne (?–1737, advocate 1714),[16] the first professor of Scots law at Edinburgh (1722–37), appended to his 1726 edition of Sir Thomas Hope's *Minor Practicks* a *Discourse on the Rise and Progress of the Law of Scotland and the Method of Studying It, For the Use of the Students of the Municipal Law*. This is a mere essay of 35 pages. It seems to have been Bayne's introductory discourse to his students. The oldest laws we have account of, according to Bayne, are these of Kenneth II who began to reign about 834, then those of Malcolm II. But the first considerable body of laws are those in *Regiam Majestatem*. Bayne thought the proofs of these laws being collected in the time of David I were very lame, and that they were clearly later. The chief sources from which our law had sprung were the feudal law and the civil law. Our law gradually received improvements by Acts and decisions and became what it now was. This does not carry one very far, though it shows Bayne's belief that law must be studied historically.

The second half of the essay is devoted to advice on the method of studying.

> "The text I choose is Sir George Mackenzie's *Institutions*, which is the most complete work of its kind of anything that that ingenious and learned author has left us."[17] "My first business will be shortly to give you our author's meaning in other words and a little more copiously. . . . It will therefore be your care, Gentlemen, to take down these notes as accurately as you can, and to endeavour to make them your own; but I am not to expect that you are, during the first year, to examine the authorities to which I refer with any great measure of study. . . . Your next care would be to read the Acts of Parliament. . . . But you, Gentlemen, who are further advanced in the study of our law, and who have already gone one course with

me.... . But when you are at home, I'm to look for a closer and more extensive application from you than from the first year's students. Your business it ought to be to consult the authorities I refer you to, with care and exactness; and from thence to extend your notes.... ."[18]

Bayne concludes his advice by paying tribute "to the man who laid the first foundation of reducing our municipal law into a system ... Sir Thomas Craig of Riccartoun.... . Such was the state of our law, and such the unhappy condition of its students, when first Sir Thomas Craig like another Justinian (to use the words of the publisher of his book) *lucem e tenebris eruit*."[19] To pay such tribute to Craig and not to mention Stair was surely a strange attitude.

To George Crawfurd (?–1748)[20] we are indebted for two tall folios. The first is *The Peerage of Scotland, Containing an Historical and Genealogical Account of the Nobility of that Kingdom*, published in 1716. This is founded on vast and painstaking research in unpublished materials, and deals with each noble family in alphabetical order, from Abercorn to Yester, and is the basis of most later work on the Scots peerage. The second is *The Lives and Characters of the Officers of the Crown and of the State in Scotland from the Beginning of the Reign of King David I to the Union of the Two Kingdoms* (1726). It bears to be Volume I but no further volume seems to have appeared. This also is the product of Herculean research in original sources. Crawfurd deals with the Chancellors of Scotland, the Chamberlains and the Treasurers, giving a detailed account of each holder of these offices in chronological order. In an appendix he prints some relevant original documents. Crawfurd deserves to be better remembered. His works are still valuable historical sources and all later workers in these fields are indebted to him.

One of the less popular consequences of the Union was the creation of a new Court of Exchequer in Scotland, on English lines, with English names, terminology and forms. Sir John Clerk, Bt., of Penicuik (1676–1755, advocate 1700)[21] and John Scrope (?1662–1752, barrister (Middle Temple) 1692)[22] were both appointed Barons of the Court of Exchequer when that court was established after the Union of 1707. Scrope resigned in 1714 but Clerk held office till his death. At some time, probably about 1720, they collaborated in the writing of an *Historical View of The Forms and Powers of the Court of Exchequer in Scotland*, which lay in manuscript in the King's Remembrancer's office until 1820 when it was published; there is no indication of by whose initiative this was done, but the appendices containing Rules of Procedure in His Majesty's Court of Exchequer, Additional Rules to be observed in the Court of Exchequer in Scotland, and Minutes of Court are later additions. The book is of great historical value and our principal authority for the powers and work of the new court established in 1707 and merged in the Court of Session in 1856. It is said[23] that the editor was Sir Henry Jardine, W.S., King's Remembrancer, and that it was printed for private circulation by the Barons of the Exchequer.

The history of the feudal system also attracted attention at this time. Hailes's collateral, Sir John Dalrymple (1726–1810, advocate 1748),[24] a descendant of the great Stair's second son, fourth baronet of Cousland

and later, by right of marriage, Sir John Dalrymple Hamilton Macgill, was solicitor to the Board of Excise and from 1776 to 1807 was a Baron of Exchequer. He published in 1757 an *Essay towards a General History of Feudal Property in Great Britain*, which was widely commended, in 1765 a pamphlet *Considerations on the Policy of Entails in Great Britain* and in 1771 in three volumes a *Memoirs of Great Britain and Ireland from the Dissolution of the Last Parliament of Charles II until the Sea Battle of La Hogue*, illustrated by collections of state papers.[25] He wrote also a number of less important historical works and engaged in chemical experiments. His fourth and sixth sons became in succession eighth[26] and ninth[27] Earls of Stair.

Another who wrote on the feudal theme was W. Borthwick who wrote a small *Origin and Limitations of the Feudal Dignities of Scotland* (1775) and a *Remarks on British Antiquities and Feudal Dignities* (1776).

George Wallace (1727–1805, advocate 1754) was son of Robert Wallace,[28] Moderator of the General Assembly and an authority on population; he put out a *Thoughts on the Origin of Feudal Tenures and the descent of Ancient Peerages in Scotland* in 1783, and in 1785 a revised version, *Nature and Descent of Ancient Peerages connected with the State of Scotland, the origin of tenures, the succession of fiefs and the constitution of Parliament in that country*. He became a commissary of Edinburgh in 1792. He also published in 1760 Volume I of a *System of the Principles of the Law of Scotland*.[29]

Two other writers commenced the literature on constitutional history. Gilbert Stuart (1742–86)[30] was the son of George Stuart, Professor of Humanity at Edinburgh, and studied there. As early as 1768 he published an anonymous *Historical Dissertation on the Antiquity of the English Constitution*, tracing it to a German source. There was a second edition in 1770 and others in 1778 and 1790. After a period engaged in journalism in London he promoted the *Edinburgh Magazine and Review* which ran from 1773 to 1776. Smellie, the printer, had constantly to be checking Stuart's verbal excesses and libels. In 1778 appeared his most important work, *A View of Society in Europe in its Progress from Rudeness to Refinement, or Inquiries concerning the history of law, government and manners*, a work several times reprinted and translated into French. It is sociology based on empiricism and owes a good deal to Montesquieu. About 1779 Stuart was an unsuccessful candidate for the chair of public law at Edinburgh and it may be thought that the Crown made the wrong choice.[31] In that year also Stuart published *Observations on the Public Law and Constitutional History of Scotland* and in it (at page 175) attacked Principal Robertson, apparently attributing to him his lack of success in the competition for the chair.

In 1780 appeared his *History of the Establishment of the Reformation in Scotland*, several times reissued, and in 1782 *The History of Scotland from the Establishment of the Reformation till the Death of Queen Mary*, in which he attacked the view of the Queen's guilt put forward by Principal Robertson. Thereafter he worked again in London. Stuart alternated periods of hard work and of gross dissipation. He has been described as brilliant but violent and dissipated. Many of his works are spoiled by the strain of spite and prejudice running through them but he was clearly a good scholar.

Alexander Wight (?–1793, advocate 1754, Solicitor-General 1783–84) published in 1773 a *Laws concerning the Election of the different Representatives sent from Scotland to the Parliaments of Great Britain with a Preliminary View of the Constitution of the Parliaments of England and Scotland before the Union of the two Kingdoms* and in 1784 brought out a greatly enlarged and improved edition under the title of *An Inquiry into the Rise and Progress of Parliament Chiefly in Scotland*. This deals with the development and structure of the Scottish Parliament, and the manner of election of peers, and representatives to the Commons. An appendix includes various documents, forms, warrants and other specimens. It is a valuable work on a subject with many complexities and obscurities. There was a later edition, in two volumes, in 1806, with cases arranged by W. M. Morison, the compiler of the *Dictionary of Decisions*.

By 1800 accordingly there was a substantial volume of literature on legal and constitutional history, some of it still of importance and value.

JURISPRUDENCE

The influence of Grotius on Stair has previously been mentioned. We know that Wiliam Scott, one of the regents, was lecturing at Edinburgh University in the first decade of the eighteenth century on the basis of Grotius' works. In 1707 he produced *Hugonis Grotii De Iure Belli ac Pacis Librorum III Compendium, Annotationibus et Commentariis Selectis Illustratum. In usum Studiosae Iuventutis Academiae Edinensis.*

The first emergence of the study of what is now called jurisprudence, however, nominally appeared with the creation in 1707 of the Regius Chair of Public Law and the Law of Nature and Nations in the University of Edinburgh. But the first professor, Charles Areskine (1680–1763, advocate 1711),[32] who had been a regent in philosophy from 1700 (at the age of 20!) made no impact. The creation of the chair may have been a job; the only evidence of his activity is an inaugural address, in Latin, on God as the foundation of law. He apparently used the salary to enable him to study law at Utrecht and qualify for the Bar. He passed advocate in 1711, was made Lord Advocate in 1737, and later (1744) became Lord Tinwald and (1748) Lord Justice-Clerk. The chair accordingly came to be looked on as a sinecure and the second holder, William Kirkpatrick (1705–78, advocate 1728, professor 1734–35), sold it to the third in 1735 for £1,000. The third holder, George Abercromby of Tullibody (1705–1800, advocate 1728, professor 1735–59), is said to have lectured on Grotius' *De Jure Belli ac Pacis* and in 1759 made over the chair to his son-in-law Robert Bruce (1718–85, advocate 1743, professor 1759–64), later (1764) Lord Kennet.[33] His successor James Balfour (1705–95, advocate 1730, professor 1764–79) is not known to have lectured at all and he sold the chair to Allan Maconochie (1748–1816, advocate 1773),[34] later (1796) Lord Meadowbank, for £1,522 18s. 2d. Maconochie is said to have lectured but without attracting a class and his successor Robert Hamilton (1763–1831, advocate 1788, professor 1796–1831) was a Principal Clerk of Session from 1822, and also treated the post as a total sinecure and never lectured. The chair indeed fell into abeyance between 1831 and 1862 when it was revived and Lorimer appointed.[35] Clearly this sorry tale cannot count as study or teaching of jurisprudence.

Jurisprudential topics were however included by the moral philosophers in their schemes of teaching and many of those who attended the courses on law of Forbes, Millar and others at Glasgow, or of Bayne, Erskine or Hume at Edinburgh would also attend the lectures of one of the philosophers. And it was in the eighteenth century that there took place that extraordinary efflorescence of penetrating thinking that we have come to call the Scottish Enlightenment, stimulated by that extraordinary, marvellous, group of Scottish philosophers comprising Gerschom Carmichael, Francis Hutcheson, Thomas Reid, David Hume, Adam Smith, Adam Ferguson and Dugald Stewart. Hutcheson is by common consent the man who above all began the Enlightenment by his eloquent advocacy of liberal ideas.

Much more important accordingly than the contributions of the incumbents of the Public Law chair were the teachings and writings of various Scottish philosophers, the group whose work collectively contributed so much to the Scottish Enlightenment, and who cannot be ignored in a survey of the Scottish jurists though most of them were not, strictly speaking, lawyers or law teachers.[36] They thought and wrote much about law and legal matters though it was only a part of their thinking. Consequently young men studying in a university, or in touch with current thinking, would get from philosophers much of what they now get from teachers of jurisprudence, indeed possibly more broadly and profoundly. In consequence also, anomalous though it may seem, figures of the first importance in the history of social, moral, or economic thought fall to be considered as minor figures in legal thought, among the minor jurists. A matter of much significance is that all of these philosophers were interested in social and moral philosophy rather than metaphysics, logic or other branches of philosophy, and with justice through law in human relations. Their thinking was highly relevant to the study of law, and their influence cannot be ignored.

This can be seen from the start. The first figure to be noted is Gerschom Carmichael[37] who had taught under the old regenting system in Glasgow, under which a professor took an intake of students through the four years' curriculum, before he became the first specialist professor of moral philosophy in 1727. His published work shows that he was a man of powerful intellect, wide learning and well-informed as to current thinking in his subject. He introduced Grotius and Pufendorf to Scottish students, discussed the fundamentals of the law of nature and produced an annotated edition of Pufendorf's *De Officio Hominis et Civis iuxta Legem Naturalem* (1718 and 1724), which remained a standard work for many years and was used by his successor, Francis Hutcheson, till 1742, and elsewhere. Later editions of his notes and supplements to Pufendorf were published in Switzerland and Holland. He established the natural jurisprudence tradition in the Scottish universities, insisting that natural religion and natural jurisprudence were inseparable and the former the foundation for the latter. The end or aim of the study of the law of nature was knowledge of how one must conduct one's life if one would enjoy eternal happiness.[38] This principle was also the efficient cause for observance of the law of nature. Carmichael was an original thinker in seeking to found natural jurisprudence in natural theology and in his modification of John Locke's political thought, namely the theory of the original contract, by founding it on an exchange of promises and believing that the original contract theory was corroborated by history and experience. Though he took Pufendorf as his textbook he gave his students a radically revised version of Pufendorf's philosophy.

Gerschom Carmichael was succeeded in 1729 by Francis Hutcheson.[39] He inaugurated lecturing in English and covered natural religion, morals, jurisprudence and government in his daily lectures.[40] At first he used Pufendorf and Carmichael's *Compend* but later departed from these.[41] His natural jurisprudence was very largely taken over from Carmichael.[42] Hutcheson had wide influence as a teacher of philosophy but also, and more importantly, is generally recognised as the initiator of the Scottish Enlightenment. He was an apostle of liberal ideas, not only in the classroom but in public lectures, in the management of the university and in public affairs, and sent out students who were convinced that the cultivation of the intellect and refinement of the feelings were preferable to spiritual bigotry. He belonged to the school of psychological moralists, which accepted that moral distinctions are founded in the nature of man, and his acknowledged master was Shaftesbury,[43] particularly in holding as a central doctrine that there is a special moral sense inherent in man, an internal capacity, whereby he can discern good and bad in conduct without having regard to its consequences, and that the conduct which the moral sense thus approves is in fact coincident with the conduct which would best promote the general happiness, that benevolent impulses are as integral a part of the natural constitution of man as are selfish impulses, and that, in the long run, the way of life most conducive to the general happiness is the same as the way of life which will bring to the agent his own greatest happiness. To him is attributed the phrase "the greatest happiness of the greatest number," which foreshadows utilitarianism.[44]

The moral sense was a capacity to experience feelings of approval and disapproval, and moral sense theory is contrasted with the view that moral distinctions are perceived by reason.[45] The theory was taken up by Hutcheson and Hume, though Hume uses the word sentiment rather than sense. Kames also presented himself in his *Principles of Morality* as a supporter of the moral sense theory and like Shaftesbury, Hutcheson and Hume compares moral sense with aesthetic feeling, though he criticises them for giving inadequate attention to the idea of duty and obligation which, like the rationalists, he regarded as the central concept of morality. Adam Smith however was critical of the theory of moral sense.

Hutcheson's *Inquiry into the Original of Our Ideas of Beauty and Virtue* (1725), *An Essay on the Nature and Conduct of the Passions and Affections with Illustrations on the Moral Sense* (1728) (both published before he came to the Glasgow chair) and *System of Moral Philosophy* (1755) entitle him to a high place in the school of thinkers to which he belongs, but he was not a very original thinker. Most of his ideas are derived from Shaftesbury though his later work modifies and to some extent moves away from Shaftesbury's position.[46]

He propounded a theory of moral sense by which we perceive and approve virtue and condemn vice, and sought to counter Hobbes's claim that all human action was self-interested and contended that men were capable of disinterested love. Indeed benevolent affection was the spring of virtue; this was the basis of his utilitarianism.

Hutcheson utilised, primarily against the earlier philosophers Samuel Clarke[47] and William Wollaston,[48] arguments which in effect challenge Stair's contention[49] that law was the dictate of reason: "Since reason," he wrote,[50] "is understood to denote our power of finding out true propositions, reasonableness must denote the same thing with conformity to true propositions, or to truth." Reason in this sense cannot determine the justification for conduct. But he distinguishes between actions which, if permitted generally, would bring about misery, and actions which promote general happiness or at least, if neglected, do not produce misery. The former include assault, contract-breaking, dishonesty and much more against which men have perfect rights; the latter include the duties of charity, benevolence and gratitude, which give rise to merely imperfect rights. This is not much different from Stair's view; Hutcheson's perfect and imperfect rights are in substance Stair's legal rights and natural (but legally unenforceable) rights. Kames also held a variety of the moral sense theory[57] but differed from Hutcheson as to the content and operation of that sense; he held that the moral sense comprehended a sense of duty and a sense of propriety, and that benevolent conduct went beyond what duty enjoined. Kames also rejected Hutcheson's utilitarian views as an adequate explanation of the duties held enforceable by courts; to promote the general benefit is no doubt virtuous, but it is not the only moral end to be sought. In his *Equity*, Kames contended that courts of equity must supplement the common law by reference to two major principles, justice and utility.

Hutcheson also discussed the state of nature, where there are no civil laws with a visible power to execute their sanctions, and defined right as that which tends to the universal good, and then gives a list of the rights which exist in the state of nature by reference to consideration of the desires, fulfilment of which is necessary for personal happiness. These include the rights to life, liberty, our own opinions, to acquire property and to commerce.

He was willing to see the principle of utility applied as a legislative principle. To determine the proper content of law we have to discover the rules and policies which conduce to the happiness of all. He would, however, restrict the proper content of positive law to more precise formulations of the dictates of natural law which are needed for the existence of society. He was concerned for the interests of women, servants and animals and opposed to slavery.

Hutcheson corresponded regularly with Hume and exercised a major influence on Hume's ethics and epistemology; his lectures on government aroused Adam Smith's interest and many of the elements in Adam Smith's analysis of sympathy as the basis for moral, legal and economic theories and in his economic theories are derived from Hutcheson,[52] and he influenced Reid, Adam Ferguson and others.

Hutcheson was highly regarded by his students and it is recorded that some attended his lectures four, five or even six sessions.[53] Adam Smith warmly admired him and spoke of him as the "never to be forgotten Hutcheson." Jupiter Carlyle[54]

"attended Hutcheson's class this year with great satisfaction and improvement. He was a good-looking man of an engaging countenance. He delivered his lectures without notes, walking backwards and forwards in the area of his room. As his elocution was good and his voice and manner pleasing, he raised the attention of his hearers at all times; and when the subject led him to explain and enforce the moral virtues and duties, he displayed a fervid and persuasive eloquence which was irresistible. Besides the lectures he gave through the week, he, every Sunday at six o'clock, opened his class-room to whoever chose to attend, when he delivered a set of lectures on *Grotius de Veritate Religionis Christianae* which, though learned and ingenious, were adapted to every capacity; for on that evening he expected to be attended, not only by students, but by many of the people of the city; and he was not disappointed, for this free lecture always drew crowds of attendants."

Carlyle also observed[55] that Hutcheson and Leechman, the professor of divinity, "opened and enlarged the minds of the students, which soon gave them a turn for free inquiry," and[56] that Hutcheson's fame "had filled the College with students of philosophy."

Hutcheson's influence extended also to America and played a part in the thinking which led to the American Revolution.[57]

David Hume (1711–76)[58] was a grandson of Lord President Sir David Falconer and was pressed to study law but found it not to his taste. He failed to secure the Edinburgh chair of moral philosophy in 1744 and in 1751 failed to obtain the succession to Adam Smith in Glasgow; accusations of heresy or even atheism blocked his candidature. He succeeded Thomas Ruddiman as Keeper of the Advocates' Library (1752–57) and was later private secretary to the British ambassador in Paris (1763–66) and under-secretary of state for the Northern Department from 1767 to 1768. He is undoubtedly a philosopher of the first importance and also an historian of considerable importance.[59]

Hume's theory of morals was derived from Hutcheson. He ascribed moral decisions to sentiment or sense, which is pleasant if it is a feeling of approval, and unpleasant if one of disapproval. He differed, however, from Hutcheson in finding the basis of the sense of moral obligation in utility to society whereas Hutcheson had seen it in dispositions to action, such as benevolence. Hume contended that reason alone cannot decide moral questions but moral sentiment does, and this is actuated only by what is either pleasant or useful.

Hume devoted space in his *Treatise*[60] and the second *Enquiry* to proving that principles of justice depended entirely on inventions and traditions of men and that obligation to observe and enforce them arose solely from their utility.

Part II is divided into 12 sections, the first six dealing with justice, whether it is a natural or an artificial virtue, the origin of justice and property, the rules which determine property, the transference of property by consent, the obligation of promises, and further reflections concerning justice and injustice. Also interesting is section II,"Of the Laws of Nations." In section 1, Hume rejects the view adopted in different degrees by Locke, Butler and others that justice is something natural, part of the nature of things, that its edicts are eternal and immutable and discernible by reason, and attempts to put forward an empiricist theory of justice, that justice is an artificial virtue, a matter of observing conventions and rules of human invention, so that our acquisition of knowledge of justice is a matter of ascertaining what these rules or conventions are. He accordingly describes justice as an artificial virtue. Rules of justice were invented to remedy a defect in human nature, the defect that nature had not instilled in man any motive for a number of different kinds of actions, such as abstaining from taking the possessions of others. Man accordingly has to introduce rules stigmatising such conduct as unjust and providing sanctions against it.

Hume thought that the habit of keeping promises was another artificial virtue and the rules enjoining it were artificial. The problem was to see how, by promising, one could place oneself under a moral obligation. Promises could not be intelligible without human conventions. Even if there could be promises without human conventions, they could not do what promising must do if it is to be successful, namely, alter our obligations. Self-interest was in his view the first natural obligation to the performance of promises.[61]

In section 6 Hume repeats that it is on the observance of three fundamental laws of nature, that of the stability of possession, of its transference by consent, and of the performance of promises, that the peace and security of human society entirely depend. Justice cannot be defined as giving every man his due because man's due must be defined in terms of justice; making rules of justice actually created the rights, which do not exist until after they have been made.

In sections 7 to 11 of the *Treatise* Hume discusses some other topics of legal relevance, the origin of government, the source of allegiance, the measure of allegiance, the objects of allegiance, and the laws of nations, and finally he discusses the problem of chastity and modesty.

Hume also treated of justice in *An Enquiry Concerning the Principles of Morals*, section III. He sets out there to show that the mere existence of rules of justice depends on their being useful and then goes on to seek to show that the fact that we have certain rules as opposed to others is due also to their utility. The civil law can extend or limit or modify any rule of natural justice, but where the civil law is harmful we may be guided by natural justice in setting it aside, according to which is more useful. Utility, he concludes, must be the source of a considerable part of the merit ascribed to the natural virtues, and the sole source of the moral approbation paid to fidelity, justice, veracity, integrity, and the other artificial virtues.

In his examination of all these topics Hume makes very little reference to any known system of law; there are a few mentions of Roman law doctrines such as the difference between confusion and commixtion, but he seems to have made surprisingly little use of his family and personal connections with lawyers. What effect his cogent, if difficult, reasoning had on younger contemporary lawyers is problematical, though there seems to be no evidence of direct influence.

Adam Smith (1723–90)[62] was not only the founding father of political economy. He studied at Glasgow, where he was powerfully influenced by Francis Hutcheson, and went with a Snell Exhibition to Oxford, where he pursued a course of self-education. After his return to Scotland the support of Lord Kames enabled him to give a series of public lectures in Edinburgh in 1748–51 on a variety of subjects including rhetoric, belles-lettres and some political and economic theory.[63] In 1751 he was appointed professor of logic at Glasgow, transferring in 1752 to the chair of moral philosophy. In 1751–52 he took the jurisprudence part of the course for Craigie, the professor of moral philosophy, who died in November 1751. His colleagues in the chair of law were successively Hercules Lindsay (till 1761) and then his former pupil John Millar. He also took an active part in university affairs and is reported to have been a good teacher.

He was friendly not only with Hume but with Black, the pioneer chemist, James Watt, Robert Foulis the printer and publisher and many of the Glasgow merchants engaged in the colonial trade. He resigned in 1763, travelled on the Continent as tutor to the young Duke of Buccleuch, and met Voltaire, Quesnay and the physiocrats, and returned to Kirkcaldy in 1768, where he worked on *The Wealth of Nations*, which was published in 1776. He died in 1790.

According to John Millar,[64] Smith's teaching fell into four parts, concerning natural theology, ethics, jurisprudence and political economy.

"In the third part he treated at more length of that branch of morality which relates to justice, and which being susceptible of precise and accurate rules is for that reason capable of a full and particular explanation.... In the last part of his lectures he examined those political regulations which are founded, not upon the principle of justice, but that of expediency, and which are calculated to increase the riches, the power and the prosperity of a State. Under this view, he considered the political institutions relating to commerce, to finances, to ecclesiastical and military establishments. What he delivered on these subjects contained the substance of the work he afterwards published under the title of An Inquiry into the Nature and Causes of the Wealth of Nations."

In his private class, additional to his ordinary or public class of moral philosophy, Smith lectured on rhetoric and belles-lettres, using the material he had prepared in Edinburgh.[65]

Smith's first book, *The Theory of Moral Sentiments*, represents his teaching on ethics.[66] The primary influence on his thought was Stoic philosophy to which he added Hutchesonian benevolence. Like Hume he regards sympathy as the ultimate element into which moral sentiments may be analysed, and denies any justification for assuming a "moral sense." Approval of conduct does not arise from perception of utility but, in the cases of prudence, justice and benevolence our sense of the agreeable effects of virtue constitutes always a large, frequently the greater part, of our approbation. This sense of propriety is the most essential and universal element of our moral judgments and arises from direct sympathy or fellow-feeling with the passions of others. Sympathetic indignation, impelling us to approve and demand the punishment of an injury done to another, is the primary constituent of what we call the sense of justice.

The book was well received by scholars and brought Smith an international reputation. It was translated into French and German. Appreciation of its importance, as an advance on the theories of Hutcheson and Hume, is now growing.

A clearer idea of what Smith dealt with under the head of jurisprudence is given by the sets of students' notes on his lectures on that subject now printed as Adam Smith: *Lectures on Jurisprudence*.[67] According to John Millar,[68] Smith's lectures fell into four parts, concerning natural theology, ethics and then:

> "In the third part, he treated at more length of that branch of morality which relates to justice and which, being susceptible of precise and accurate rules, is for that reason capable of a full and particular explanation.
>
> "Upon this subject he followed the plan that seems to be suggested by Montesquieu; endeavouring to trace the gradual progress of jurisprudence, both public and private, from the rudest to the most refined ages, and to point out the effects of those arts which contribute to subsistence, and to the accumulation of property, in producing correspondent improvements or alterations in law and government. This important branch of his labours he also intended to give to the public; but this intention, which is mentioned in the conclusion of *The Theory of Moral Sentiments* he did not live to fulfil."

Smith defined jurisprudence as "the theory of the rules by which civil governments ought to be directed,"[69] or "that science which inquires into the general principles which ought to be the foundation of the laws of all nations."[70] Four things would be the design of every government, to maintain justice, the opulence of the state, or police,[71] the revenue of the government and protecting the state from foreign injuries, or arms and the laws of peace and war.[72]

The content of Smith's course in 1762–63[73] seems to have been as follows:

Division of the subject.

Part I – Justice

Introduction

1. Private Law – Occupation, accession, prescription, succession, voluntary transfer, servitudes, pledges and mortgages, exclusive privileges, contract, quasi-contract, delinquency and crimes,

2. Domestic Law – Husband and wife, parent and child, master and servant,

3. Forms of government, republican governments, military monarchy, the feudal system, the English Parliament, the English courts, the rights of sovereigns, citizenship and the rights of subjects, the doctrine of the

original contract.

Part II – Police

Cleanliness and security, cheapness or plenty, the division of labour, money and the balance of trade.

In 1763–64[74] he adopted a different order,[75] *viz.*:

Introduction and division of the subject.

Part I – Justice

1. Public jurisprudence.
2. Domestic law.
3. Private law.

Part II – Police

Part III – Arms

Part IV – The Laws of Nations.[76]

This is clearly more a generalised survey of legal institutions and some of the constituent elements of a legal system than a course on jurisprudence in the modern sense.[77] It is descriptive rather than analytic. It owes a good deal to Roman law but Smith clearly had a reasonable general knowledge of Scots and English law. But it is proper to remember that this was a course given by a philosopher, not a lawyer, and to students attending a course on moral philosophy as part of a general liberal education, not part of a course on law, though doubtless some prospective lawyers were among the students.

The lectures do not, however, adequately bring out the points that the Roman law was itself a series of layers of law laid down over a thousand years from the Twelve Tables at Rome to Justinian's legislation at Constantinople, and all of it was the product of a different society and different times, and that contemporary systems, notably the Scots and English, were each the product of a further thousand years of development from different origins and had diverged from each other in that time. In historical perspective Smith's lectures were accordingly defective. Frequently he seems insensible of differences between Scots and English law.

In Smith's lectures, as recorded, there were mentions of sources and examples but not specific references to sources, though many have been traced by the modern editors. Clearly he expected of his students a general understanding but not a knowledge of the specific sources justifying particular points, nor can he have expected them to look for themselves at the sources from which he drew his propositions. He draws examples much more from English than from Scottish history and law. He mentions classical authors, Justinian, Grotius and Pufendorf, various English statutes, *Regiam Majestatem* and "Glannmore's book" (*sic*) – *i.e.* Glanvill's *Tractatus*. There is reference to the Great Cause of 1291–92 in which Edward I of England awarded the crown of Scotland to Balliol in preference to Bruce. There is no reference to Stair, Bankton, or Erskine, though Smith must have known of, and had probably looked at, these works; there is a mention of Mackenzie and Forbes.[78] There is one reference to a case dealing with assythment.[79]

However there are in Smith's lectures some points of great interest. Speaking of contract he said: "The origin of this right is the expectation raisen in him to whom the promise was made that the promiser will perform what he has undertaken. Thus if one promises to give another five pounds, this naturally creates an expectation that he will receive five pounds from him at the time promised; and here the promiser must be bound to make up to him any loss he has suffered by this expectation."[80] Here we have the reliance on expectation theory of contract long before it was invented by modern jurists.

Again, before considering the obligations which arise from contract or agreement, "it will be proper to consider what it is in a contract which produces an obligation to perform the thing contracted." The bare declaration of will cannot. "The only thing that can make an obligation in this manner is an open and plain declaration that he desires the person to whom he makes the declaration to have a dependance on what he promises."[81] The obligation arises, that is, not from the promise but from reliance thereon being requested. In exploring this point Smith was far in advance of British jurisprudents. He points out that the laws with regard to property necessarily differ with the stage of economic development of the particular society, and he distinguishes four main stages, hunting, pastoral, agricultural and commercial. He is critical of the privileges of patents and copyrights.

On the other hand the course seems disappointingly blank on some of the topics which one might have expected a philosopher to discuss in a general, non-legal, course of this kind, such as the relations of law and morality, and of law and politics or government, the nature and sources of rights and duties, the purpose of law, and, above all, the nature of law; is it the expression of the revealed will of God, or an emanation of the spirit of the people, or the command of the secular sovereign for the time being, or what? To say, "Now we may observe that the original of the greatest part of what are called natural rights, or those which are competent to a man merely as a man, need not be explained. That a man has received an injury when he is wounded or hurt any way is evident to reason, without any explanation,"[82] is imperceptive. Again: "the origin of natural rights is quite evident. That a person has a right to have his body free from injury . . . no body doubts."[83] The existence of a body of rules of natural law is simply accepted without question. Even justice is not analysed. "Justice is violated whenever one is deprived of what he had a right to and could justly demand from others, or rather, when we do him any hurt or injury without a cause"[84] and, in the other set of lectures: "The object of justice is the security from injury, and it is the foundation of civil government."[85] Even Justinian's *suum cuique tribuere* is not quoted.

In the shorter report of the 1762–63 lecture course it is recorded that Smith concluded the major part of his course by saying: "Having considered the laws of nature as we proposed, as they regard Justice, Police, Revenue and Arms, we shall proceed to the last part of our plan, which is to consider the Law of Nations or the claims which one nation may have upon another."[86] This is followed by a lecture, possibly two, on the latter subject, mainly concerned with warlike relations, concluding with the phrase: "Thus we have considered both the laws of nature and the laws of nations."[87] Smith accordingly seems to have conceived of his course as one on the law of nature and nations, precisely the field supposed to be dealt with by the incumbents of the Regius Chair in Edinburgh.

The third branch of Adam Smith's teaching, dealing with political economy, gave rise to the famous *An Inquiry into the Nature and Causes of the Wealth of Nations*.

Adam Smith was succeeded in the Glasgow chair in 1764 by Thomas Reid (1710–96),[88] who had had his attention turned to philosophy first by Hutcheson's *Inquiry*, who was a moral philosopher of great distinction, and who deserves to be remembered for his original contributions in the field of theory of knowledge. Throughout his time in Glasgow his legal colleague was John Millar. He is familiarly known as founder of the Common Sense School of philosophy. But by common sense he did not mean the judgments of men in the streets, but rather principles with characteristics which no vulgar prejudice possessed.

Reid greatly admired Butler and he carried on Butler's combination of religion, epistemology and ethics into an argument against Hume's scepticism, empiricism and utilitarianism. He attacked Hume's sceptical conclusions by challenging Hume's assumption that what we apprehend in perception is only a sensation or impression, arguing that in perception the sensation is only an element in a complex experience which comprises certain judgments, of which the most important are that a sensible quality characterises an existing external thing, and that there exists a subject or self by which the external thing is being apprehended. These are natural judgments immediately inspired by our constitution. The propositions corresponding to them must be accepted by us as true, as first principles, because the nature of our minds is such that we cannot but accept them. Being principles which flow from the very constitution of our minds, they are principles of common sense.

Reid seems to have said little directly about legal problems, but included a discussion on justice in the *Essays on the Active Powers*[89] in which he argues against Hume for the view that different kinds of injuries, to person or family, liberty, reputation, breach of contract and the like, are perceived intuitively to be violations of natural rights, without conscious reference to the public good, and that though the right of property is not innate but acquired it is a necessary consequence of the natural right to life, and to liberty, which imply rights to the means of life and the fruit of labour. But he does not seek to lay down axioms of justice, for the decision of rights in concrete cases, without reference to an ultimate standard in public utility. He also, in the *Active Powers*, included a useful and perceptive examination of the concepts of right and duty, stressing their connection and correspondence.[90]

Reid had numerous disciples, notably James Beattie[91] but, most importantly, Dugald Stewart. He also influenced the great Scottish religious leader, Thomas Chalmers,[92] and Alexander Smith.[93]

Adam Ferguson (1723–1816)[94] the next important figure, became a minister, chaplain to the Black Watch, and fought at Fontenoy in 1745. In 1757 he succeeded David Hume as Keeper of the Advocates' Library and in 1759 he became professor of natural philosophy at Edinburgh and in 1764–85 professor of moral philosophy. His legal contemporaries were James Balfour and Allan Maconochie in the Public Law chair, Robert Dick in the Civil Law chair, and Erskine and William Wallace in the Scots Law chair.

He adhered to the common-sense school of philosophy but was a forerunner of modern sociology in his insistence on individual and social interaction. His publications include an *Essay on the History of Civil Society* (1766), which was widely read and translated, *Institutes of Moral Philosophy* (1769), *History of the Roman Republic* (3 vols., 1783) and *Principles of Moral and Political Science* (1792).

In the *Essay*[95] he inquired into the nature and origin of society and its evolution from a rude to a polished state. He first gives an account of the general characteristics of human nature and then traces the progress of society from rudeness to refinement. Civil society was civilised society, with government and political organisation, as distinct from a state of nature; the criterion of civilisation was legal and political. He does not utilise Adam Smith's fourfold scheme of development, from hunting and fishing, through pastoral, and agricultural to the commercial stage, but distinguishes savagery and barbarism. There are other important differences between Ferguson's description of the progress of society and those of Smith and Millar; to him social organisation and government emerge instinctively out of the natural differences between men and constitutional government arises from the clash of parties.

His doctrine of ethics was an attempt to establish a comprehensive system based on a perfectionist principle of moral approbation. The sanctions of this are of two kinds, those which need to be enforced and those left to the agent's free will.

In his *Principles of Moral and Political Science*,[96] Part II, Chapter III, Ferguson dealt with Jurisprudence or Compulsory Law, including sections on the term right, occupancy and the species of right that may result from it, contract or the principle of conventional obligation, in which he explores the basis of the obligation of compact or contract and sees it in the expectation created in the one party's mind by the doing of something sufficient to justify such an expectation.

In Chapter IV, entitled "Jurisprudence, Part II, Respecting the Defences of Men," he discusses the means that may be opposed to injustice in general such as self-defence and, as between nations, war, and in Chapter V he discusses the characteristics of goodness or justice but without reference to its legal applications.

These chapters are in the most general terms, shallow and without reference to specific problems or cases which have arisen, still less to legal authorities save for a reference to Blackstone's *Commentaries* and mentions of Hobbes and Beccaria. One cannot but think that he might have written more interestingly if he had asked his colleagues of the chair of Scots law, Erskine (till 1768) and then William Wallace, for some examples.

James Beattie (1735–1803),[97] professor of moral philosophy and logic in Marischal College, Aberdeen, 1760–1803, in his *Elements of Moral Science* (2 vols., 1790–93) based on his lectures, deals in Volume II under the head of moral philosophy with "Ethicks, Economicks, Politicks and Logick," and under the third of these heads treats of the general nature of law which he defines as:

"Law is a rule of civil conduct, prescribed by the supreme power in a state, commanding what is right and prohibiting what is wrong.[98] But taking the word Law in a more general sense, and considering ourselves as subject to the laws of God, as well as of man, we may rather say, that Law is the declared will of a person, or persons, in authority, (that is having a right to govern), commanding some things, and forbidding others, with a promise, expressed or implied, of reward or convenience to those who obey, and a denunciation of punishment or inconvenience to those who disobey. The good thus promised, and the evil thus denounced, are called the Sanctions of the law. They who obey the law enjoy the advantage of being protected by it, and sometimes other positive rewards. They who transgress are liable to the punishment or penalty denounced. That, under equitable government, the protection of the law is an unspeakable advantage, will appear to those who consider, that a good citizen has the whole power of the state engaged on his side, to vindicate his rights, and guard him from injury."

He goes on to distinguish law of God, comprising natural or moral law, and positive or revealed law; the divine moral law in relation to states is called the law of nations; and the civil or municipal law of the nation. The Roman civil law, in Scotland, serves as a kind of supplement to the municipal law of the land, and great regard is had to its authority. He mentions Glanvill and *Regiam Majestatem*, the canon law, the obligation of law, equity and strict law, and goes on to consider human rights, and particularly property, before coming to contracts: "A contract is the consent of two or more persons, in the same design, mutually expressed or signified, in order to constitute some right and obligation."

As a philosopher Beattie is a lesser figure than the others mentioned in these pages, but he gives a better exposition of jurisprudence; he was either more interested in these questions or knew more about law.

Dugald Stewart (1753–1828)[99] studied under Reid in Glasgow and boarded in the same house as Archibald Alison. In 1785 he succeeded Adam Ferguson in the chair of moral philosophy at Edinburgh and followed Reid as a leading exponent of the common sense philosophy. He retired in 1810. Throughout his time his contemporary in the chair of Scots law was David Hume.[1] His books made the influence of the ideas he shared with Reid felt in France and America. "To me his lectures were like the opening of the heavens."[2]

He held liberal opinions and taught some political economy on Smithian lines but made little direct mention of law in his teaching and writings. He did not put forward a separate theory of natural jurisprudence. He stressed the obligation of justice as distinct from benevolence[3] but in defining justice he does not get beyond the general principle of impartiality. He discusses also veracity and fidelity to promises but does not arrive at any principles manifestly and absolutely binding, but yet sufficiently precise to give practical guidance. He criticises the tendency of writers on natural jurisprudence to rely exclusively on Roman law, but failed himself to draw anything from the system of law being so thoroughly taught by his colleague Hume.

Whatever the merits or defects of these teachers and their systems of thought the important point is that lawyers, and particularly young men attending the universities with a view to entering the legal profession, had throughout most of, and particularly the latter part of, the eighteenth century the opportunity of listening to distinguished and stimulating teachers who were discussing *inter alia* some of the theoretical issues relevant to law, questions of right and wrong, obligation, justice and similar matters. To think that there was then no study of what we now call jurisprudence is accordingly quite wrong. Modern jurisprudence, like modern economics, modern sociology and modern political science, has separated out from the philosophy taught by these notable figures, and indeed in the later nineteenth century, under English influence, became almost wholly distinct from philosophy.

What is surprising, and disappointing, is that none of them takes up and examines Stair's views of law. Or had the positivist views of Erskine, who equally is never mentioned, become already so accepted that law was already deemed mainly a matter outside philosophic comment? Again, why was Blackstone looked at rather than any Scottish text-writer?

Mention deserves also to be made at this point of one who was a Scot by origin but supported the liberal side in England.

Sir James Mackintosh (1765–1832)[4] was the son of an army officer. He could not afford to go to the Bar but instead studied medicine at Edinburgh. He moved to London in 1788 and became known in debating societies. In 1791 he published *Vindiciae Gallicae*, a reasoned reply to Edmund Burke's *Reflections on the French Revolution*, and became honorary secretary to the Friends of the People. In 1795 he was called to the English Bar and, his views on the Revolution having changed, he became a friend of Burke. In 1798 he planned a series of lectures on "The Law of Nature and Nations" and an introductory discourse showed how far he had moved from his position of 1791. His course of 39 lectures in 1799 and 1800 was very successful, being attended by many distinguished persons, and he developed a substantial practice in cases involving constitutional or international law. In 1803 he was made Recorder of Bombay but in 1813 returned to England and entered Parliament, where he was a notable liberal. In 1818 he became part-time professor of law and general politics at Haileybury, the East India Company's college, was offered the chair of moral philosophy at Edinburgh in 1820, and he held minor office in Canning's government of 1827. He wrote on the English revolution of 1688, but this has been superseded by later work.

MUNICIPAL LAW

The Abridgments of the Statutes

After the Restoration, and even more so after the Union, the volume of statute law increased steadily. It is a pity that nobody then undertook a complete edition of the Acts of the Parliaments of Scotland, even from 1424 and ignoring the very difficult problems of what earlier materials could be called authentic legislation. But nobody did. Instead several writers made abridgments of the statutes for various periods.

Sir James Steuart of Goodtrees (1635–1713, advocate 1661),[5] Lord

Advocate 1692–1709 and 1711–13 and author of the *Answers to Dirleton's Doubts*, published an *Index or Abridgment of the Acts of Parliament and Convention from the Reign of King James the First* [of Scotland] in 1702 and 1707. It follows his Index or Abridgement of the Acts to 1681 and summarises the legislation under alphabetical headings.

Alexander Bruce (?–1729, advocate 1702) published in 1726 a small duodecimo being an *Index or Abridgment of such Acts of the British Parliament as either equally concern the whole United Kingdom or particularly relate to Scotland from 1707 to 1726, being a continuation of Sir J. Steuart's Abridgment of the Scots Acts of Parliament*. He also published in 1728 *An Explication of the XXXIX Chapter of the Statutes of King William*, with notes.[6]

As one of his many contributions to legal literature, Lord Kames, as already mentioned,[7] produced a *Statute Law of Scotland Abridged, with Historical Notes* in 1757, with other editions in 1767 and 1769. It summarises the Acts under alphabetical headings, and follows, in general, the order of his *Dictionary of Decisions* and is a more substantial volume than any of the previous ones.

John Swinton (?–1799, advocate 1743, Lord Swinton 1781–99)[8] made an *Abridgment of the Public Statutes in Force and Use relative to Scotland from the Union (1707) in the fifth year of Queen Anne, to the 27th. year of his present Majesty King George II inclusive* [1754], published in two volumes in 1755. As before, the Acts are collected under alphabetical headings.

He later published an *Abridgment of Statutes in Force relative to Scotland, from the Union to 27 George III* [1787] in two volumes in 1788. There was a supplement in two parts in 1788–89. This was continued by William Forsyth's *Abridgment of the Statutes relative to Scotland in continuation of Swinton's Abridgment*, 1789–1827, in three volumes, published in 1827 with a supplement in 1829. Swinton also published proposals on reform of the law of entails, uniformity of weights and measures and the revival of jury trial in civil causes.

The Reporters

In the eighteenth century reports of decisions become commoner, better, and more important as sources of principles for decision of new cases.

Sir Hew Dalrymple of North Berwick (1652–1737)[9] was the third son of Viscount Stair. He passed advocate in 1677 and became Dean of the Faculty of Advocates in 1695. In 1698 he was made a baronet of Nova Scotia and Lord President of the Court of Session in succession to his father but after a vacancy of three years. He sat in the last Scottish Parliament of 1702 and supported the union with England, being one of the commissioners who negotiated the treaty. One contemporary expressed the view that "he is believed to be one of the best presidents that ever was in the chair, and one of the completest lawyers in Scotland; a very eloquent orator, smooth and slow in expression, with a clear understanding, but grave in his manner."[10] It was said of him that "if he inherited not the distinguished talents of his father, the Viscount of Stair, and his elder brother, the secretary, he was free from that turbulent ambition and crafty policy which marked the characters of both; and with sufficient knowledge of the laws was a man of unimpeached integrity and of great private worth and amiable manners."[11] His *Decisions of the Court of Session from 1698 to 1718, Collected by The Right Honourable Sir Hew Dalrymple of North Berwick, President of that Court* was published in a tall quarto of 252 pages in 1758. The cases are chronological and the reports are substantial, usually giving the substance of the argument and the interlocutor is frequently given verbatim. Most of the reports are reprinted in Morison's *Dictionary*.

Part of the same period, namely 1705–13, was also covered by William Forbes's *Journal of the Session*.[12]

Alexander Bruce (?–1729), called in 1702, was appointed by the Faculty of Advocates collector of decisions in succession to William Forbes and held the appointment until dismissed for negligence in 1723.[13] But the volume he published in 1720 contains the decisions of 1714–15 only.[14] This is sometimes found bound separately and referred to as Bruce, Volume I, but is usually found bound up with the first (1728) edition of Lord Kames's *Remarkable Decisions* and entitled on the spine Bruce and Home's *Decisions*. It extends to 178 pages and 136 decisions. Later decisions, covering 1716–17, collected by Bruce are printed at the end of *Faculty Decisions*, Volume 3 (1760–64), published in 1772, and are sometimes called Bruce, Volume 2. In 1718 he professed to be compiling a complete dictionary of decisions from 1532 to 1720 and sought permission to borrow manuscript decisions for that purpose from the Advocates' Library.[15] There are mentions of this in 1725,[16] and in 1728 a bookseller petitioned the Faculty stating that Bruce's *Dictionary of Decisions* was now ready for the press and praying the Faculty to augment a committee already appointed for reviewing that work.[17] The Faculty did so, but no more is heard of the *Dictionary* and Bruce died in 1729.[18] The work was taken up by Henry Home, later Lord Kames, and became his *Dictionary of Decisions*.[19]

John Edgar (?–1744), called in 1716, was appointed collector of decisions by the Faculty of Advocates in 1724 in succession to Bruce[20] and though he held the post until his death in 1744,[21] he published only a slim volume of 208 pages in 1742 containing reports of 1724–25.[22] In 1730 the Faculty pressed him for progress[23] and in 1743 Thomas Walker and Thomas Ruddiman petitioned the Faculty, narrating that they had published Edgar's *Decisions* but not been paid, and seeking to be paid from arrears due to Edgar's salary as collector of decisions.[24] It is not clear whether they ever were so paid.

The periods 1716–28 and 1730–52 are also covered by Kames's *Remarkable Decisions*.[25]

Patrick Grant of Easter Elchies (1690–1754)[26] became an advocate in 1712 and was promoted to the Bench in 1732 with the title of Lord Elchies. According to Fraser Tytler[27] Elchies owed his eminence at the Bar to the pure force of natural abilities and his genius developed the most intricate points of law as by a species of intuition. He made a collection of *Decisions of the Court of Session from the year 1733 to the year 1754 collected and digested into the form of a Dictionary*. The reports are frequently brief but many are valuable; there are more than 1600 cases. He has been described as "the best reporter of Scotch decisions."[28]

This collection remained unknown until the early nineteenth century when it was edited and published in 1813 by Morison, editor of Morison's *Dictionary*. Morison published at the same time, as Volume II, the Notes from which Elchies compiled his dictionary, printed in the same order as the cases in the dictionary. The Notes in many cases give a fuller statement of the arguments and opinions than appears in the dictionary and the cases must be read along with the notes. Both volumes are uniform with the volumes of Morison's *Dictionary*.

Elchies is also credited with the anonymous volume entitled *Annotations on Lord Stair's Institutions* published in 1824[29] and has been said to be "one of our greatest lawyers and judges."[30]

The reporter usually known as Clerk Home was truly one Alexander Home, Clerk of Session. His collection contained the decisions from 1735 to 1744 and was published, as his preface narrates, to supply the deficiency in reports of the period 1728 to 1744. The sheets were composed from a parcel of printed papers which occasionally came into the author's possession, and form a quarto volume of 441 pages containing 274 cases. An interesting feature is the appearance of short headnotes to cases stating the principle or point laid down by the decision. It is a good collection and bears to have been well edited.

Sir James Fergusson of Kilkerran, second baronet, (1689–1759)[31] was called in 1711, and raised to the Bench as Lord Kilkerran in 1735. He is said to have been "undoubtedly one of the ablest lawyers of his time."[32] Though by the standards of the time deemed abstemious,[31] he was a devotee of claret and afflicted by gout. The second youngest of his children was George Fergusson, later Lord Hermand.[34] In 1775 was published the father's *Decisions of the Court of Session from the year 1738 to the year 1752*, a quarto of 619 pages. These are under dictionary headings, and have head-notes. It has been said that it "exhibits the clearest comprehension of jurisprudence, and will for ever serve as a model for the most useful form of law reports."[35] The volume was published by "his son," who may have been Adam, an advocate and Member of Parliament, but more probably George, later Lord Hermand.[36] Additional cases noted by Kilkerran over 1735–59 are printed in Brown's *Supplement*, Volume 5.

James Burnett (1714–99),[37] born at Monboddo in the Mearns on October 25, 1714, was descended from a younger son of the Burnetts of Leys, whose seat was Crathes Castle on Deeside. He was tutored at home by Francis Skene, later professor of civil and natural history at Marischal College, who instilled in him a love of classical literature, and he went on to King's College, Aberdeen,[38] Groningen and possibly Leyden. He passed advocate in 1737 and was promoted to the Bench, as Lord Monboddo, in 1767. He declined appointment to the Court of Justiciary because it would have interfered with his studies. Young Boswell was a close friend and frequently sought Monboddo's advice, notably on his choice of a wife,[39] and took Dr. Johnson to visit him in 1773. Monboddo wrote extensively on philosophical subjects. His main published works were *Of the Origin and Progress of Language* (eventually six volumes, published between 1773 and 1792) in which he argued, on the basis of wide acquaintance with classical and modern languages, that they all had a common ancestor and established practical techniques for examining accurately the relationships between languages. Gilbert Stuart[40] reviewed the second and third volumes intemperately, indeed abusively, and at great length in the *Edinburgh Magazine and Review*,[41] largely if not entirely without factual justification.

His *Antient Metaphysics* came out in six volumes between 1779 and 1799; his purpose was to revive ancient theism, particularly that of Plato and Aristotle, and he founded heavily on Aristotle. In the fourth volume he suggests that man and the ape must have had some common ancestor similar in form, structure and appearance to the great apes; he accordingly had the germ of the idea of evolution of species, though it is uncertain whether Darwin knew of Monboddo.

Among Monboddo's papers which came into the possession of M. P. Brown was a substantial collection of reports of nearly 900 cases covering 1738 to 1768 in chronological order. They were probably not intended for publication but had been carefully prepared and it was right to publish them. The collection fills almost 300 pages of Brown's Supplement to *Morison's Dictionary*, Volume V. Many of the cases are also in other collections.

Monboddo was also an improving and benevolent landlord, and for many years went annually to London to meet some of his correspondents. He was clearly a considerable scholar with very wide interests and extensive reading; he knew some Sanskrit and corresponded with Sir William Jones, the great orientalist.

Monboddo and Kames very much overlapped in interests and if Monboddo did not publish on all the topics on which Kames did, he seems to have thought, frequently to have written, and to have intended to publish on most of them. On practically every matter Monboddo disagreed with Kames and they were long-standing rivals and opponents.[42]

Monboddo was a "character," indeed rather an eccentric, but he expressed some ideas which have been developed by others and become accepted wisdom.

George Fergusson (1743–1827)[43] son of Sir James Fergusson, Bt., Lord Kilkerran (1735–59),[44] passed advocate in 1765, was appointed one of the four Commissaries for Edinburgh in 1775 and was promoted to the Court of Session Bench in 1799, when he took the title of Lord Hermand. He resigned in 1826. In his old age he acquired the reputation of being something of an eccentric and was certainly fond of company and good wine; he was a blunt and straightforward speaker[45] and has frequently been regarded as the best of the old kind of Scots judges, blunt and homely, "who combined a respect for tradition with a taste for Tory politics, studied literature, philosophy or agriculture in their spare time, and drank claret by the quart."[46] "With very simple tastes and rather a contempt of epicurism, but very gregarious, he was fond of the pleasures, and not least of the liquid ones, of the table; and he acted in more of the severest scenes of old Scotch drinking than any man at last living. Common-place topers think drinking a pleasure; but with Hermand it was a virtue."[47] One of his sisters became the second wife of Sir David Dalrymple, Lord Hailes.

He made a collection of *Consistorial Decisions in the Order of a Dictionary* covering the years from 1684 to 1777, published by the Stair Society in 1940 as *Lord Hermand's Consistorial Decisions*.[48] The cases are collected under headings arranged alphabetically, from "Adultery" to "Witness," and have been drawn from a larger collection known as the Abridgment, apparently now lost, but also with references to the volume of the Edinburgh Consistorial Decreets now in H.M. General Register House, Edinburgh, together with the date, names, of the parties and sometimes the page in the volume. From these references further information about the case can frequently be found.[49]

The collection is interesting not least because of the extensive reference to foreign jurists which shows that, long after and notwithstanding the Reformation, the Commissary Court and on appeal, the Court of Session, sought guidance from Catholic canonists and continental jurists who had written on matrimonial law. The matrimonial law of Scotland and all the Western European countries had a common origin in the canon law and this continued to influence them all powerfully.

This is a valuable collection, later used by James Fergusson in his *Reports of some Recent Decisions by the Consistorial Court of Scotland*[50] and judicially described as "the most valuable and instructive record known to me of our former law and practice."[51]

David Falconer (1712–76) was called in 1732 and succeeded Edgar as Faculty collector of decisions in 1744.[52] He displayed more ability and diligence than his two predecessors and published two volumes of *The Decisions of the Court of Session from the month of November, 1744*. Volume I covers 1744 to July 1748 in 380 pages and Volume II covers from November 1, 1748, to December 1751 in 309 pages. The reports are chronological and have no head-notes but are clear and give the arguments and, frequently, the authorities referred to in the debate.

The next reports in chronological sequence are Kames's *Select Decisions*, 1752–68.[53]

Ilay Campbell of Succoth (1734–1820)[54] became an advocate in 1757, acquired a large practice and was Solicitor-General briefly in 1783 and Lord Advocate in 1784. In 1789 he was appointed Lord President and held that office until 1808 when the Court of Session sat undivided for the last time, being then divided into First and Second Divisions. "As a lawyer, and in every department of the science he was inferior to none of his brethren in depth or learning, and was greatly superior to them all in a genuine and liberal taste for the law's improvement. Of all the old judges he was the only one whose mind was thoroughly opened to the comprehension of modern mercantile jurisprudence.... Bell's recorded acknowledgments of the assistance he derived from him, in the construction of his great work [the *Commentaries*] are not merely complimentary, but express the simple fact."[55] On retirement he was made a baronet and thereafter presided over two commissions inquiring into the state of the courts of law in Scotland. A son became a judge as Lord Succoth.[56] He was jointly responsible for *Decisions of the Court of Session from the end of the year 1756 to the end of the year 1760. Collected by Mr. John Campbell, Junr. and Mr. Ilay Campbell, advocates*, which was published in 1765. This book is very scarce and very little known. There is a copy in the British Library.[57]

He published also in 1811 *The Acts of Sederunt of the Lords of Council and Session from the Institution of the College of Justice in May 1532 to January 1553* with a long preface, and pamphlets explanatory of a Bill of 1785 respecting the Judges in Scotland, and Hints on the Question of Jury Trial as applicable to the proceedings in the Court of Session in 1809.

Hailes' *Decisions*, 1766–91, and Professor (later Baron) David Hume's *Decisions*, 1781–1822, belong at this point in the sequence of reports, and are examined separately.[58]

Robert Bell (?–1816) Writer to the Signet, 1784, advocate 1812, brother of George Joseph Bell,[59] and the W.S. Society's lecturer on Conveyancing, was responsible for two separate collections, *Cases decided in the Court of Session from November 1790 to July 1792*, an octavo volume of 563 pages in which the cases are collected under alphabetical headings, published in 1794 and known as "Bell's Octavo Cases," and *Cases decided in the Court of Session during Summer Session 1794, Winter Session 1794–5 and Summer Session 1795*, a quarto volume of 238 pages, in which the cases are noted chronologically, published in 1796 and known as "Bell's Folio Cases." The reports give the sederunt of judges and the authorities cited in argument. Bell also wrote a number of useful works on conveyancing noted later.

Throughout the eighteenth century the Faculty of Advocates was concerned about the reporting of decisions. In 1692 it recommended to the curators to speak to Sir Patrick Hume[60] anent the collections of the Lords' decisions,[61] and in 1698 agreed payments to the Clerks of Sessions' first servants for collecting the Lords' interlocutors towards completing the collection of decisions made by Sir Patrick Hume and carrying it on.[62] In 1705 William Forbes was appointed to observe and collect the Lords' decisions,[63] and in 1712 the Faculty, having no money to spare to print Forbes's volume, allowed him to do so at his own expense.[64] Forbes was succeeded in 1714 by Bruce,[65] who published only one year's decisions and was ultimately dismissed in 1723 for non-performance of his duties. Bruce was followed in turn in 1724 by Edgar,[66] and Edgar in 1744 by David Falconer.[67]

The gaps thus left by the official Faculty reports were to some extent filled by other collections, by Kames's *Remarkable Decisions*, 1716–28, and Volume II, 1730–52, Elchies' *Decisions*, 1733–54, Clerk Home's *Decisions*, 1735–44, and Kilkerran's *Decisions*, 1738–52, but several of these were not published till long after, and the judges and pleaders of the mid-eighteenth century must have been hampered by inability to find reports of decisions.

On the resignation of David Falconer in 1752, a meeting of Faculty was held to discuss the problem, and four members offered to do the work gratuitously. This system stumbled along till 1769 when a committee reported that no decisions had been published since 1760, that publication even prior thereto had been dilatory and slow, that fewer cases had been reported than should have been, and that hardly any decisions of the Court of Teinds and none of the High Court of Justiciary had been included.[68]

While the volumes containing the Faculty Collection of Decisions provide a continuous record, the volumes were not published in serial order. Volume V (1769–72) did not appear until 1803 and Volume VII not until 1810.

Alexander Tait (?–1781, Writer to the Signet, 1756) a Principal Clerk of Session 1760–81, was appointed a Faculty reporter in 1770 but resigned on account of ill-health in 1772. He compiled a collection of reports covering 1761–80 under headings in the form of a dictionary. It is a substantial collection of nearly 300 pages and is printed in Volume V of Brown's Supplement to *Morison's Dictionary*.

"There were no judicial reporters or 'collectors of decisions' formerly, except two advocates, who were appointed and paid by the Faculty for doing this work. Right reporting was attended then with some risk. It had never been the practice to give any full and exact account of what passed on the Bench, but only results. The public, or at least the independent portion of the legal profession, had begun to require something more, and their Lordships were very jealous of this pretension. They considered it as a contempt; and the contempt was held to be aggravated by the accuracy of the report. Mr. Robert Bell, afterwards lecturer on conveyancing to the Society of Writers to the Signet, was the first who adventured on independence in this matter; and he announced that he meant to report without any official appointment, and to give the opinions of the judges. This design was no sooner disclosed than he met with many threatening hints, and as much obstruction as could be given in an open court. The hated but excellent volume at last appeared; and though the judges were only denoted by letters, he was actually called into the robing room, and admonished to beware. Eskgrove's objection was 'the fellow taks doon ma' very words' – a great injury to his Lordship, certainly. More than ten years passed before it was acknowledged by rational judges that the offensiveness of publishing each opinion was no inconsiderable proof of its utility. Fear lest the Faculty should assert its right generally disposed the court in favor of submissive and unambitious collectors; and this, it was thought, operated against Jeffrey, who, in 1801, dared to aspire to the office."[69]

THE TEXT-WRITERS

Public Law

The great text-writers of the eighteenth century, Bankton and Erskine, and even the writers of the second rank, such as Forbes, neglected public law. But the Union of 1707 stimulated interest in this branch of the law.

Daniel De Foe (?1661–1731) journalist and pamphleteer,[70] is today remembered almost entirely for *Robinson Crusoe*, but he wrote *Six Essays at Removing National Prejudices against a Union with Scotland* (1766–7) and a *History of the Union between England and Scotland* (1709, 1712 and later editions). In 1706 he was sent to Edinburgh by the English government as a secret agent with the party favouring union, and he exerted himself vigorously to promote the union. His *History* is not objective but contains some useful historical documents and is valuable for its contemporary comments and arguments for the union.

Gilbert Stuart's *Observations concerning the Public Law and the Constitutional History of Scotland, with occasional remarks concerning English antiquity*, published in 1779, has already been mentioned. It deals with the feudal law, the revenue of the sovereign, the members of the King's court, the national council, the Union of 1707 and its consequences. More than half of the book is taken up with notes on particular topics, such as the possessions of the Scottish kings in England, Thanes and Thane-land, the Lords of the Articles, and other points. This is important as a pioneering work and though modest in size and scope, shows an unprecedented appreciation of the importance and interest, and of the importance of the historical development, of public law.

The Reverend George Logan (1678–1755),[71] one of the ministers of Edinburgh, and Moderator of the General Assembly in 1740, published in 1746–47 *Two Treastises on Government; showing that the right of the Kings of Scotland to the Crown was not strictly and absolutely hereditary*. This provoked in 1747 from Thomas Ruddiman *An Answer to The Reverend Mr. George Logan's late Treatise on Government in which (Contrary to the manifold Errors and Misrepresentations of that Author) The ancient Constitution of the Crown and Kingdom of Scotland, and the hereditary succession of its Monarchs are asserted and vindicated*. This runs to 400 pages and is a minute dissection and criticism of the unfortunate Mr. Logan's observations. Ruddiman was a much better scholar than Logan and convincingly refutes him on all points. Logan, however, replied to Ruddiman in *The Finishing Stroke; or Mr. Ruddiman self-condemned, being a Reply to Mr. Ruddiman's Answer (1748); The doctrine of the jure-divino-ship of hereditary indefeasible monarchy enquired into and exploded, in a Letter to Mr. Thomas Ruddiman* (1749); and *A Second Letter to Mr. Thomas Ruddiman, vindicating Mr. Alexander Henderson from the vile Aspersions cast upon him by Messieurs Sage and Ruddiman* (1749). The controversy is now forgotten but that it arose shows the interest, and heat, which discussion of the subject then provoked.[72]

One James Carmichael is believed to be the author of *Various Tracts concerning the Peerage of Scotland; collected from the public records with appendix of original papers, among others, an account of the foundation of the Principality of Scotland*, a small quarto published in 1791.

Henry Curson, an English barrister, is believed to be the author of a large *Compendium of the Laws of Government, Ecclesiastical, Civil, and Military, of England, Scotland and Ireland and Dominions, etc. thereunto belonging, with the Maritime Power thereof and Jurisdiction of Courts therein*, which appeared in 1699 and 1716.

Walter Stewart of Pardovan was the author of *Collections and Observations Methodised: concerning the Worship, Discipline and Government of the Church of Scotland* [with] *the form of Process in the Judicatories of the Church of Scotland, also an Abridgment of the Acts of Parliament relating to the Reformation* (1773 and later editions).

Alexander Bruce, the Faculty reporter, produced *The Institutions of Military Law, Ancient and Modern*, in 1717. It deals with war, declaring and managing a war, the immunities and privileges competent to soldiers, military crimes, courts-martial and related topics. Some of this would now be regarded as falling under international law. It shows considerable learning and acquaintance with continental jurists.

Criminal Law

After Mackenzie's *Matters Criminal*, there was not much advance in the study of criminal law. The second volume of William Forbes's *Institutes* (1730) deals with the criminal law. The first part, in five books, deals successively with crimes in general, crimes against God, crimes against the state, crimes against the person and crimes relating to offices. The second part, in two books, deals with criminal courts and jurisdiction, and with the order of judicial proceedings. It is a very sound brief account.

Alexander Bayne of Rires (?–1737, advocate 1714)[73] first professor of Scots law at Edinburgh (1722–37) clearly used Mackenzie's works as his textbooks and supplemented them by an *Institutions of the Criminal Law of Scotland* (1730, 1748), despite its title a small book of 70 pages, dealing, after Preliminary Observations on crimes generally, with particular crimes, and a slim *Notes on the Criminal Law* (1748). Bayne clearly lectured on criminal law at some length, as the *Institutions* bears to "contain the chief heads of discourse which are treated of at large in my lectures upon the criminal law;" they were printed to save students the trouble of taking them down in writing. The lack of criminal reports is evidenced by the almost complete lack of citation of decisions.

John MacLaurin (1734–96)[74] the son of Colin MacLaurin,[75] the eminent mathematician, professor successively at Aberdeen and Edinburgh, was educated at Edinburgh University and passed advocate in 1756. He was raised to the Bench as Lord Dreghorn in 1788 and died on December 24, 1796. He published two minor works, *Observations on some Points of Law; with a System of the Judicial Law of Moses* in 1759 and *Considerations on the Nature and Origin of Literary Property* in 1767. His main work, however, was *Arguments and Decisions in Remarkable Cases before the High Court of Justiciary, and other Supreme Courts in Scotland*, published in 1774. It is a large book of nearly 800 pages. His intention, he tells us, was "to publish only some few remarkable or leading cases which I had either argued or attended to particularly." But he extended the scope of his work. "In this country but few trials have been printed; no treatise of merit has yet appeared on its criminal law; and it is irksome to search the record of the court of justiciary." He narrates also that he went through "two voluminous, though but partial abridgments of the record, the one from 1536 to 1674, the other from 1694 to 1730."[76]

The Introduction contains much valuable historical material extracted from the old justiciary records. There follow reports of 100 cases extending from 1670 to 1770. They are good reports, frequently narrating the indictment, and giving the names of the counsel involved. Some of the cases are quite notorious, such as the trial of Rob Roy for the abduction of

Jean Key in 1750 and the important assythment case of *Machargs* v. *Campbell* in 1767.

Shortly thereafter in 1785 Hugh Arnot (1749–86 advocate 1772)[77] published *A Collection and Abridgment of Celebrated Criminal Trials in Scotland from* A.D. *1536 to 1784 with Historical and Critical Remarks*. The cases are collected under legal heads but are presented more for their interest than their importance as legal authorities. They include such historically interesting trials as the Gowrie conspirators, Chiesly of Dalry for murdering Lord President Lockhart, James Stewart for the murder of Colin Campbell of Glenure (the Appin murder),[78] Captain Green, master of the "Worcester," for piracy,[79] John Ogilvie (later canonised), for saying Mass, and other notable cases.

John Louthian, Writer in Edinburgh, published in 1732 *The Form of Process before The Court of Justiciary in Scotland containing the Constitution of the Sovereign Criminal Court, and the Way and Manner of their Procedure*. There was a second edition in 1752, substantially revised. It deals with procedure in trials before the Justiciary Court at Edinburgh and procedure of the judges in their justice airs or circuit-courts. An appendix to the second edition deals with the form of procedure before the sheriff and stewart courts in civil and criminal causes. It gives specimens of all the writs in ordinary use, such as criminal letters, citations, oaths, and so on.

Private Law

The minor writers on private law are mostly unimportant.

In 1710 one John Dundas[80] published a small *Summary View of the Feudal Law with the differences of the Scots Law from it, together with a Dictionary of the Select terms of the Scots and English Law by way of Appendix*.

Alexander Bruce the reporter produced in 1713 a *Principia Juris Feudalis, Institutionum Imperialium Methodo (quantum materiae feudalis ratio patitur) disposita; accedunt notae et observationes practicae, ad mores patrios tam antiquos quam hodiernos, singulis titulis annexae*. To seek to explain the feudal law according to the model of Justinian's *Institutions* was surely not the most useful way of expounding it. Bruce also published, in 1714, a *Tutor's Guide, or Principles of Civil and Municipal Laws and Customs relating to Pupils and Minors and their Tutors and Curators*.

Alexander Nisbet (1657–1725)[81] having written an *Heraldic Essay on Additional Figures and Marks of Cadency* (1702) and an *Essay on the Ancient and Modern Use of Armories* (1718), produced in 1722–42 in two folios his *System of Heraldry speculative and practical: with the true art of blazon*. In 1699 he had sought encouragement from the Faculty of Advocates for this project, and the use of their library, which was granted,[82] and in 1703 he got a grant from Parliament,[83] though it was never paid. Volume 2 was edited by Robert Fleming. There was a later edition in 1804 and another in 1816 and a reprint in 1984. He left also various manuscripts on heraldry.[84] Nisbet's *System* is a very learned work, still a great authority and a mine of information.[85]

There has also been attributed[86] to him a *Decisions of the Court of*

Session from 1655 to 1687 (1718) but this seems a mistake. Such a book has not been traced.

A related topic was dealt with by William Robertson in his *Proceedings relating to the Peerage of Scotland*, 1707–88, of 1790.

Sir James Steuart or Stewart of Goodtrees or Gutters (1635–1713, advocate 1661, Lord Advocate 1692–1709 and 1711–13),[87] published in 1715 *Dirleton's Doubts and Questions in the Law of Scotland Resolved and Answered*. According to the Advertisement, "his superior knowledge in the laws (which was but the best part of his character) and his singular faculty of resolving difficulties, did render him fully equal for an undertaking of this kind: And, if this essay shall be found to bear any proportion to the reputation of the author, it will certainly be very acceptable to all that can use it. The manuscript was revised once by himself; But he designed a second review before publication." The topics are arranged alphabetically and under each Nisbet's (Dirleton's) question is printed, followed by Stewart's answers. The answers appear convincing; no authority is cited for them, but they are reasoned, not merely dogmatic pronouncements.

James Innes of Symonds Inn (?) lived and worked in London and published there in 1773 *Idea Juris Scotici, or a Summary View of the Laws of Scotland*. In his preface he states that the work was written at the request of a young gentleman, who, after studying English law, was intending to travel abroad and wished to be informed about the law in north Britain, so as to be able to answer questions he came across about the law of the whole of Britain.[88] He stated that the subject consists in three words, *viz.* Persons, Rights and Actions, "and the laws of any Nation may be properly wrote upon the same theme."[89] Innes makes a good attempt to explain Scots law in an elementary way, including some aspects of public law and an elementary account of criminal law and procedure. There was a second edition in 1747. The work is today almost completely forgotten.

Alexander Bayne of Rires produced *Notes for the use of Students of the Municipal Law in the University of Edinburgh, Being a Supplement to Sir George Mackenzie's Institutions* (1731, 1749). This is a small book of 187 pages. It consists of notes supplementing Mackenzie, under the same title and section numbers; there are references to Stair, statutes and some cases. Bayne seems to have had a genuine concern for his students as this book and his *Institutions* and *Notes* on the criminal law were all written to aid their studies.

Later in the century, in 1760, George Wallace (1727–1805, advocate 1754) a Commissary of Edinburgh, published a *System of the Principles of the Law of Scotland*. Only Volume I was ever published and the work, apart from being incomplete, has never attained any reputation. It seems to have been a disastrous failure. It is said that only 40 copies were sold and that the author bought up the rest of the edition himself, either to avoid having it remaindered, or to conceal his own defective presentation.[90] Wallace's father fell out of favour with Lord Advocate Dundas and only after his death was Wallace appointed a Commissary.[91]

In *Kerr* v. *Martin*,[92] a most interesting case of legitimation *per subsequens matrimonium*, Wallace's work was cited and varying views were expressed about it. "Though Mr. Wallace may not, perhaps, have been a very eminent general lawyer, he had great experience as a judge of the Consistorial Court, and his statement must therefore be entitled to respect, as it shows how the law was understood to stand in his time on a subject with which he was familiar."[93] "But it is the first time I ever heard of that worthy man as an authority of any weight. He is more, I think, of a speculative philosopher than a lawyer."[94] "The comparatively slender authority of Wallace."[95] And Lord President Hope: "Your Lordships have, I think, undervalued the weight of the opinion of Professor Wallace; for it will be observed that it is more likely that this was not only his individual opinion, but I think it is not possible to believe that while he so states the law he was not also stating the opinion of his brother Commissaries, and the opinion and understanding of the Commissary Court at that time.... I studied under Mr. William Wallace, the predecessor of the late Baron Hume in the chair of Scotch law and if my memory does not fail me, he laid down the same doctrine. I am sorry now that I have not kept my notes taken in his class; and my reason for not keeping them was that I had access to notes of Baron Hume's lectures, who laid down the same doctrine."[96] It seems here that the Lord President may have been confusing George Wallace (1727–1805), advocate 1754, Commissary 1792, with William Wallace (?–1786), advocate 1752, Professor of History 1755, and of Scots Law 1765–86. The latter is not recorded as having published anything, and nothing attributable to him is mentioned in the report as having been cited to the court.

George Wallace also published *Thoughts on the Origin of Feudal Tenures and the descent of ancient peerages in Scotland* (1783) and, a revised version, *Nature and Descent of Ancient Peerages connected with the State of Scotland, the Origin of Tenures, the Succession of fiefs and the constitution of Parliament in that country* (1785).

Robert Boyd published a *Judicial Proceedings before the High Court of Admiralty and Supreme Consistorial or Commissary Court of Scotland, also before the Sheriff, Bailie, Dean of Guild, Justice of Peace, and Baron Courts, with the Styles of Summonses etc. in use before these Courts, and Observations in Law thereon*, which was clearly useful as it went through five editions between 1770 and 1814, and an *Office, Powers and Jurisdiction of His Majesty's Justices of the Peace and Commissioners of Supply* in two volumes and over 1000 pages (1787 and 1794) dealing with their respective jurisdictions in various matters, which was doubtless a most useful work for persons of these ranks.

A work occasionally referred to in the reports is the *Theory of Conveyancing* (1788 and 1791) by John Russell (?1753–1792, Writer to the Signet 1774), an attempt to digest the principles of that branch into a system for one of his sons and quite a sound work.

A number of further collections of conveyancing styles were published in the eighteenth century. The earliest was the *Compend or Abbreviat of the most important ordinary Securities of and concerning Rights, personal and real, redeemable and irredeemable, of common use in Scotland* attributed to J. Carruthers and published in 1702 and 1709.[97] It is a small book but contains a considerable variety of forms and in the preface he attempts to sketch the evolution of our legal deeds.

John Spotiswoode (1665–1728, advocate 1696),[98] grandson of Lord President Spottiswoode, was trained in the chambers of James Hay of Carriber (?–1702, Writer to the Signet 1671), reputed the ablest conveyancer of his day. About 1703, in default of any public teaching of law in Edinburgh, he established Spotiswoode's College of Law and himself became "professor." He conducted the college in his own house for 26 years. He used Mackenzie's *Institutions* as textbook but himself compiled an *Introduction to the knowledge of the Stile of Writs* (1708 and many later editions) and to him is sometimes attributed *A Compend or Abbreviate of the most important ordinary Securities of and concerning Rights, personal and real, redeemable and irredeemable, of common use in Scotland* (1700 and later editions) but his work is also attributed with greater probability to one Carruthers (?Hay of Carriber) or sometimes to Sir Andrew Birnie, Lord Saline (?–1688, advocate 1661)[99] and known as Carruthers' *Styles* or *Saline's Styles*.

Spotiswoode's collection was followed by a volume, published in 1711 and 1718, entitled *The Form of Process before the Lords of Council and Session observed in Advocations, Ordinary Actions, and Suspensions, to which is prefixed the Present State of the College of Justice*. The *Form of Process* is stated to be 'written for the use of students in Spotiswoode's College of Law, by John Spotiswoode of that Ilk, Advocate." This appears to be a clear account of procedure for student. Other works by Spotiswoode included *The Law covering the Election of Members for Scotland to sit and vote in the Parliament of Great Britain* (1710) and *Treatise concerning the Origin and Progress of Fees* (1731), and he edited for publication the collections of *Decisions* by Presidents Gilmour and Falconer (1701). He also edited and published his grandfather's *Practicks* (1706) and Hope's *Minor Practicks* (1734). He left in manuscript, and refers in his works to, a *Scots Law-Lexicon* and a work *Spotiswoode's Practical Titles*. He was clearly a diligent and scholarly man, with an interest in communicating practical guidance on legal practice.

In 1734 appeared James Mackenzie's *Treatise concerning the Origin and Progress of Fees: or the Constitution and Transmission of Heritable Rights. A Supplement to Spotiswood's Introduction to the Knowledge of the Style of Writs*. There were further editions to 1781. This is intended more for students than practitioners and gives preliminary dissertations on matters of law illustrated by typical forms of writs rather than a practitioner's collection of styles. He also published, anonymously, in 1750, *The General Grievances and Oppression of the Isles of Orkney and Shetland*, which was reprinted by A. Groat and H. Cheyne in 1836.

Akin to these style of books is *Ars Notariatus* or *The Art and Office of a Notary Publick as the same is practised in Scotland, In two parts: I Rise and Institution of the office and ancient and present state thereof: II Notarial instruments of all kinds, to which is added by way of conclusion an advice to Notaries attaching the right discharging of their office*. Published in 1740, there were numerous editions down to 1821. The author is unknown but the book was in heavy use.

One Anthony Macmillan published a number of books on conveyancing, a *Forms of Writings used in the most common cases in Scotland with such parts of the The Principles of the Law as appears connected therewith*

(1784, and Supplement 1786). *In so far as relates to Moveables or Personal Rights and Securities* (1786, and Supplement 1790), a *Notarial Instruments, connected with Forms of Writings* in 1787 and *A Complete System of Conveyances of, and Securities upon Land: or Heritable Rights according to the practice of Scotland, including Freehold Qualification*, in 1787.

At the end of the century there appeared the *Juridical Styles*, which was the standard reference book of its kind for a century. Correctly this work is the *Juridical Society of Edinburgh Collection of Styles or Complete System of Conveyancing*. Volume I on Heritable Rights appeared in 1787, Volume II, Signet Letters, came out in 1790, and Volume III, Moveable Rights, in 1794. There were many later editions of all the volumes. The Juridical Society was established in 1773, membership being open to advocates and Writers to the Signet and their intrants and apprentices. The Library was taken over by the Faculty of Advocates in 1925 and latterly housed at 40 Charlotte Square, but discontinued about 1970.

Robert Bell (?–1816, Writer to the Signet 1784 and advocate 1812), brother of George Joseph Bell, was the first lecturer on conveyancing appointed by the W.S. Society and gave his first full courses in 1795–96. From 1797 he gave two courses in alternate years.[1] He published *Lectures on the Solemnities used in Scotland in the Testing of Deeds* (1795),[2] *System of the Forms of Deeds* (1797, 7 vols. 1802–15 and 1811–17); *Outline of Lectures on Conveyancing* (1800–1807); *Treatise on Leases* (1803, 1825–26); *Laws of Election* (1812); *Abstract of the Forms of Deeds relating to Heritable Rights* (1814); *The Conveyance of Land to a Purchaser and on the Manner of Completing his Title* (1815, 1830); and a *Dictionary of the Law of Scotland* (1807–08) taken up and amplified by his son William Bell (?–1839, advocate 1824) as *Dictionary and Digest of the Laws of Scotland* (1838, 7th ed. 1890).

He also issued Bell's "Octavo Cases" and "Folio Cases" and a *Report of a Case of Legitimacy, under a Putative Marriage, tried before the Court of Session in 1811* (1825).

Apart from these published works there are known to be many collections of styles still in manuscript,[3] and there may well be other manuscript collections in offices or private houses. These seem to fall into two groups, collections prepared by conveyancers for their own use, and collections of drafts or copies of deeds actually used and kept for future reference. Some of these include writs of much earlier date, and some deserve to be published.

NOTES

[1] 1506–1582.

[2] 1662–1744.

[3] DNB.

[4] DNB; Anderson, S.N., I, p. 125; Chambers, BDES; portrait in Signet Library.

[5] Ruddiman was Keeper of the Advocates' Library for nearly 50 years, 1702–52. On Ruddiman and the Ruddiman Press see Douglas Duncan, *Thomas Ruddiman* (1965). App. III lists the publications of the Ruddiman Press, which include many legal works.

[6] *Lectures on Scotch Legal Antiquities* (1872), pp. 288–289.

[7] *Faculty of Advocates Minute Book* (ed. Pinkerton), II, 64.

[8] DNB; Anderson, S.N., III, p. 349; Chambers, BDES; Dugald Stewart, *Biographical Memoirs of Adam Smith, William Robertson and Thomas Reid* in Stewart's *Works*, Vol. X; H. G. Graham, *Scottish Men of Letters in the 18th Century*, p. 78; Kay's *Edinburgh Portraits*, I, 93; J. B. Black, *The Art of History* (1926); J. P. Kenyon, *The History Men* (1983), p. 57.

[9] Brunton & Haig, p. 546.

[10] Grant, *History of the University of Edinburgh*, I, pp. 230, 285.

[11] L. W. Sharp, "Charles Mackie, the first Professor of History at Edinburgh University", S.H.R. 41 (1962) 23. Grant, *History*, p. 367, says Mackie was an advocate.

[12] 1715–75, advocate 1737; joint editor of 3rd ed. (1759) of Stair's *Institutions*.

[13] ?–1786, advocate 1752, Sheriff of Ayr, 1775–86.

[14] DNB; Anderson, S.N., III, p. 587. The Tytlers were descended from a Seton who assumed the name of Tytler in the 16th century.

[15] 1777–1853, advocate 1799, Sheriff of Inverness 1810. On later members of the Tytler family, see Chap. 25, *infra*.

[16] On him see chap. 9, *supra*. and p. 303, 305, *infra*.

[17] p. 168.

[18] It is apparent that students normally attended Bayne's course for at least two sessions, and that the lectures were the same each year. See also his broadsheet of 1725, *To the gentlemen who have attended his college of prelections*.

[19] p. 185.

[20] DNB; Anderson, S.N., I, p. 707. His wife was the daughter of Anderson, author of the *Diplomata Scotiae*.

[21] DNB; Anderson, S.N., I, p. 653. Clerk sat in the Scottish Parliament of 1702–07, was a commissioner for the Union, and a noted antiquarian. He was author also of *Money and Trade considered, with a proposal for supplying the Nation with Money* (1705), and various writings on antiquities. On him see *Memoirs of the Life of Sir John Clerk of Penicuik*, ed. J. M. Gray. (S.H.S., 1892). His son, of the same name (1728–1812; DNB), wrote a famous *Essay on Naval Tactics* (1790) which is believed to have been influential during the Napoleonic Wars. His grandson, of the same name (1757–1832, advocate 1785; DNB), became Solicitor-General for Scotland and a judge as Lord Eldin in 1823; he resigned in 1828. On him see also Brunton & Haig, p. 551; Cockburn's *Memorials* and *Life of Lord Jeffrey*, I, p. 199; Kay's *Edinburgh Portraits*, II, 438.

[22] DNB. He was an M.P. from 1722 till his death, a commissioner of the Great Seal in 1710 and a strong supporter of Walpole. He was author also of a treatise against papal power, *Exercitatio Politica de Cive Protestante in Republica Pontificia* (1686).

[23] DNB, *s.v.* "Clerk."

[24] DNB; *Scots Peerage*, VIII, 121.

[25] On Dalrymple as an historian see J. P. Kenyon, *The History Men* (1983), pp. 53, 64, who commends the "careful and accurate transcripts he published of these and other key documents."

[26] DNB; *Scots Peerage*, VIII, 158.

[27] *Scots Peerage*, VIII, 159.

[28] DNB; Chambers, BDES;

[29] On this see p. 305, *infra*.

[30] DNB; Anderson, S.N., III, p. 539; Chambers, BDES.

[31] In 1779 James Balfour (1705–95, advocate 1730) sold the Regius Professorship of Public Law to Allan Maconochie (1748–1816, advocate 1773), later the first Lord Meadowbank. Stuart might have made more of the post than did Maconochie, but might well have caused more trouble.

[32] DNB; Omond, *Lord Advocates*, II, p. 1; Brunton & Haig, p. 513.

[33] Brunton & Haig, p. 528.

[34] DNB; Anderson, S.N., III, pp. 60, 634; Brunton & Haig, p. 542.

[35] Grant, *History of the University of Edinburgh*, II, pp. 313–317; Lorimer, "The Story of The Chair of Public Law in the University of Edinburgh" (1888) 4 L.O.R. 139. On Lorimer see Chap. 23, *infra*.

[36] C. Camic, *Experience and Enlightenment* (1983), examines the backgrounds of Hume, Adam Smith, Ferguson, John Millar and William Robertson, the historian. L. Schneider, *The Scottish Moralists*, reprints passages from them, as well as Kames and Monboddo. See also D. Kettler, "History and Theory in the Scottish Enlightenment," *Jl. Modern History* 48 (1976), p. 95.

[37] (1672–1729) Anderson, S.N., I, p. 592. He was a regent at St. Andrews, 1693, and then at Glasgow, 1694–1727, and first professor of moral philosophy at Glasgow, 1727–29. He published also *Breviuscula Introductio ad Logicam* (1722) and *Synopsis Theologiae Naturalis* (1729). Sir William Hamilton (Thomas Reid, *Works*, ed. Hamilton, I, p. 30) held the view that Carmichael might on good grounds be regarded as the true founder of the Scottish School of philosophy. On his teaching and reputation see also R. Wodrow, *Analecta: Or Materials for a History of Remarkable Providences* (1842–43), IV, p. 95; H. G. Graham, *Scottish Men of Letters in the 18th Century*, p. 30; David Murray, *Memories of the Old College of Glasgow* (1927), p. 506; J. Moore and M. Silverthorne, "Gerschom Carmichael and the natural jurisprudence tradition," in I. Hont and M. Ignatieff (ed.), *Wealth and Virtue* (1983); J. Moore and M. Silverthorne, "Natural Sociability and Natural Rights in the Moral Philosophy of Gerschom Carmichael," in V. Hope (ed.), *Philosophers of the Scottish Enlightenment* (1984).

[38] *De Officio*, Supplement I, pp. i-xi; "Greeting to the Reader," p. xvii, and notes to author's preface, sec. 6.

[39] (1694–1746) DNB; Chambers BDES; *Ency. Soc. Sc.*, VII, p. 561; Leslie Stephen, *English Thought*, Chap. IX, p. 56. T. Fowler, *Shaftesbury and Hutcheson* (1882); W. R. Scott, *Francis Hutcheson* (1900); H. G. Graham, *Scottish Men of Letters in the 18th Century* (1901), p. 31; H. T. Buckle, *On Scotland and the Scotch Intellect* (ed. Hanham, 1970), p. 244; D. D. Raphael, *The Moral Sense* (1947); C. Reto, *Die Problematik des Moral Sense in der Moralphilosophie Hutchesons* (1950); W. K. Frankena, "Hutcheson's Moral Sense Theory," *Jl. Hist. Ideas* 16 (1955), p. 356; H. Jensen, *Motivation and Moral Sense in Francis Hutcheson's Ethical Theory* (1971); W. T. Blackstone, *Francis Hutcheson and Contemporary Ethical Theory* (1975); T. D. Campbell, "Francis Hutcheson: Father of the Scottish Enlightenment," in R. H. Campbell and A. S. Skinner (ed.), *The Origins and Nature of the Scottish Enlightenment* (1982), p. 167. He was Professor of Moral Philosophy at Glasgow, 1720–46, author of *An Inquiry into the Original of our Ideas of Beauty and Virtue* (1725), *An Essay on the Nature and Conduct of the Passions and Affections* (1728), *Philosophiae Moralis Institutio Compendiaria Ethices et Jurisprudentie Naturalis Elementa Continens Libri III* (1742), *A Short Introduction to Moral Philosophy* (1747), (a translation of the *Institutio*) and *System of Moral Philosophy* (2 vols., 1755), with biographical introduction by Principal William Leechman. All his works went through several editions. A facsimile reprint, mainly of the first editions, *Collected Works of Francis Hutcheson*, appeared in 1971.

[40] Leechman, *Life of Hutcheson*, p. xxxvi.

[41] Wodrow, *Analecta*, IV, p. 185.

[42] Scott, *op. cit.*

[43] Anthony Ashley Cooper, 3rd Earl of Shaftesbury (1671–1713), the first to use the term "moral sense." His essays were collected as *Characteristics of Men, Manners, Opinions, Times* (3 vols., 1711). On him see Leslie Stephen, *History of English Thought in the Eighteenth Century* (1876), Chap. IX, p. 20.

[44] Hutcheson's *Inquiry*, sec. iii, § 8. On this see Scott, *op. cit.* p. 273.

[45] H. Jensen, *Motivation and the Moral Sense in Francis Hutcheson's Ethical Theory* (1971).

[46] H. Sidgwick, *History of Ethics* (1931), p. 201; C. A. Campbell, "Philosophy," in *Fortuna Domus* (1951), pp. 97, 104.

[47] 1675–1729, author of *Works of Samuel Clarke* (4 vols., 1738–42).

[48] 1659–1724; author of *Religion of Nature Delineated* (1722).

[49] *Inst.*, I, 1, 1.

[50] *Illustrations Upon the Moral Sense*, in D. D. Raphael (ed.), *British Moralists, 1650–1800* (1969), I, p. 307.

[51] *Principles of Morality and Natural Religion*, II, ii.

[52] Scott, *Francis Hutcheson*, p. 230; W. I. Taylor, *Francis Hutcheson and David Hume as Predecessors of Adam Smith* (1965).

[52] Leechmann, *Life of Hutcheson*, p. xxxiii; Dugald Stewart, *Works of Adam Smith*, V, p. 523; Ramsay of Ochtertyre, *Scotland and Scotsmen*, I, p. 276; Scott, *Francis Hutcheson*, p. 74.

[54] *Autobiography*, p. 78.

[55] p. 94.

[56] p. 91.

[57] Caroline Robbins, *The Eighteenth Century Commonwealthman* (1968); H. F. May, *The Enlightenment of America* (1976); A. Hook, *Scotland and America* (1975); D. F. Norton, "Francis Hutcheson in America," in *Studies in Voltaire and the Eighteenth Century* 154 (1976) 1547.

[58] DNB; Anderson, S.N., II, p. 504; Chambers, BDES; *Encyc. Soc. Sc.* VII, p. 550; *Int. Encyc. Soc. Sc.* VI, p. 546; J. H. Burton, *Life and correspondence of David Hume* (2 vols., 1846); H. G. Graham, *Scottish Men of Letters in the 18th Century* (1901), p. 35; E. C. Mossner, *The Life of David Hume* (1954); D. G. C. MacNabb, *David Hume: His Theory of Knowledge and Morality* (1966); J. V. Price, *David Hume* (1968); Leslie Stephen, *English Thought*, Chap. IX, p. 92; H. T. Buckle, *On Scotland and the Scotch Intellect* (ed. Hanham, 1970), p. 277; J. B. Stewart, *Moral and Political Philosophy of David Hume* (1963). His published work comprises *Treatise of Human Nature* (1739–40), *Essays, Moral and Political* (1741–42), *An Enquiry Concerning Human Understanding* (1748, revised 1758), *An Enquiry Concerning the Principles of Morals* (1751) and also a standard *History of Great Britain* (6 vols., 1754–62).

[59] On Hume as an historian see J. P. Kenyon, *The History Men* (1983), p. 41.

[60] Bk. III, Pt. II. This branch of Hume's thought is analysed by J. Harrison, *Hume's Theory of Justice* (1981). See also K. Haakonssen, *The Science of a Legislator: The Natural Jurisprudence of David Hume and Adam Smith* (1981).

[61] On this topic see further P. S. Ardal, "Hume and Reid on Promise, Intention and Obligation," in Hope (ed.), *Philosophers of the Scottish Enlightenment* (1984), p. 47.

[62] DNB; Anderson, S.N., III, p. 480; Chambers, BDES; *Ency. Soc. Sc.* XIV, p. 112; *Int. Ency. Soc. Sc.* XIV, p. 322; Dugald Stewart, *Biographical Memoir of Adam Smith*, in *Trans. R.S.E.* 3 (1794) 55; also in Stewart, *Biographical Memoirs of Adam Smith, William Robertson and Thomas Reid* (1811); Stewart, *Works of Adam Smith* (1811), V, 403; and Stewart, *Collected Works* (ed. Sir William Hamilton, 1858), X, 1, reprinted in Adam Smith, *Essays on Philosophical Subjects* (ed. Wightman, Bryce and Ross, 1980), p. 269; John Rae, *Life of Adam Smith* (1895); W. R. Scott, *Adam Smith as Student and Professor* (1937); C. R. Fay, *Adam Smith and the Scotland of His Day* (1956); H. G. Graham, *Scottish Men of Letters in the 18th century* (1901), p. 148; R. H. Campbell and A. S. Skinner, *Adam Smith* (1982); Leslie Stephen, *English Thought*, chap. IX, p. 73; H. T. Buckle, *On Scotland and the Scotch Intellect* (ed. Hanham, 1970), p. 255; Kay's *Edinburgh Portraits*, I, 73, 75; Duncan Forbes, "Scientific Whiggism: Adam Smith and John Millar," *Cambridge Journal*, 7 (1954) 643; and "Sceptical Whiggism, Commerce and Liberty," in A. S. Skinner and T. Wilson (ed.), *Essays on Adam Smith* (1975), p. 179; W. P. D. Wightman, "Adam Smith and the History of Ideas," in the same, p. 44; A. S. Skinner, *A System of Social Science, Papers relating to Adam Smith* (1979).

[63] Scott, *op. cit.* 50, 54, gives evidence for lectures on civil law.

[64] Dugald Stewart, *Memoir*, in *Essays on Philosophical Subjects*, p. 274. Stewart identified Millar as his informant in his *Account of Smith* as reprinted in his edition of Smith's *Works* (1811), V, p. 412n.

[65] Now printed as *Lectures on Rhetoric and Belles-Lettres* (ed. J. C. Bryce, 1983).

[66] See D. D. Raphael and A. L. Macfie (ed.), *The Theory of Moral Sentiments* (1976); A. L. Macfie, *The Individual in Society* (1967); T. D. Campbell, *Adam Smith's Science of Morals* (1971); "Scientific Explanation and Ethical Justification in the *Moral Sentiments*," in A. S. Skinner and T. Wilson (ed.), *Essays on Adam Smith* (1975), p. 68; J. R. Lindgren, *The Social Philosophy of Adam Smith* (1973); H. Mizuta "Moral Philosophy and Civil Society," in A. S. Skinner and T. Wilson (ed.), *Essays on Adam Smith* (1975), p. 114; N. Phillipson, "Adam Smith as Civic Moralist," in L. Hont and M. Ignatieff, *Wealth and Virtue* (1983); V. Hope, "Smith's Demigod," in Hope (ed.), *Philosophers of the Scottish Enlightenment* (1984), p. 157; G. Morice, "Opinion, Sentiment and Approval in Adam Smith", *ibid.*, p. 168.

[67] (ed. Meek, Raphael and Stein, 1978). This comprises (pp. 5–394) notes of his lectures

given in 1762–63, and (pp. 397–554) notes of his lectures given in 1763–64, the latter previously published by E. Cannan in 1896 as *Lectures on Justice, Police, Revenue and Arms delivered in the University of Glasgow by Adam Smith*. The two sets of lectures cover very much the same topics but in a different order. See also P. G. Stein, "Adam Smith's Theory of Law and Society," in R. R. Bolgar (ed.), *Classical Influences on Western Thought* (1978) and "Adam Smith's Jurisprudence – Between Morality and Economics" (1979) 64 Cornell L.R. 621; T. D. Campbell "Economic Analysis of Law," in Hope (ed.), *Philosophers of the Scottish Enlightenment* (1984), p. 133.

[68] Communicated to Dugald Stewart and printed by the latter in his "Account of the Life and Writings of Adam Smith," and in Smith, *Essays on Philosophical Subjects* (ed. Wightman, Bryce and Ross), p. 275.

[69] *Lectures* (1978 ed.), p. 5.

[70] *Ibid.*, p. 397.

[71] Police is used in the Greek and French senses of the regulation of government in general.

[72] *Ibid.*, pp. 5–7.

[73] *Lectures*, pp. 5–394.

[74] *Ibid.*, pp. 397–554.

[75] The two courses are collated and commented on in *Lectures*, Introduction, pp. 27–32. There are both substantial and minor differences at many points but it is only a poor professor who says the same things in the same order each year.

[76] Arms and the Law of Nations are not included in the report of the previous session's lectures. They may not have been discoursed on, or no notes may survive.

[77] Some of the books of modern English analytical jurisprudence were however not much more than generalised surveys of law, founded mainly on Roman and English law.

[78] p. 133. Smith's library included copies of Bankton, Erskine's *Principles*, Grotius, Hale's *Pleas of the Crown*, Heineccius, Kames's *Historical Law Tracts* and *Equity*, Madox's *Exchequer*, Montesquieu, Pufendorf, *Regiam Majestatem*, Stair. See J. Bonar, *Catalogue of the Library of Adam Smith* (1932); H. Mizuta, *Adam Smith's Library* (1967).

[79] p. 109.

[80] *Lectures*, p. 12; similarly p. 472.

[81] *Ibid.*, p. 87; see also p. 92. On this see further Atiyah, *Promises, Morals and Law* (1982).

[82] p. 13.

[83] p. 401; similarly p. 459.

[84] p. 7.

[85] p. 398; *cf.* p. 399.

[86] *Lectures*, p. 544.

[87] *Ibid.*, p. 545.

[88] DNB; Anderson, S.N., III, p. 334; Chambers, BDES; Dugald Stewart, *Memoir of Thomas Reid* in *Biographical Memoirs of Adam Smith, William Robertson and Thomas Reid* (1811); A. C. Fraser, *Thomas Reid* (1898); H. G. Graham, *Scottish Men of Letters in the 18th Century* (1901), p. 242; Thomas Reid, *Works* (ed. Sir Wm. Hamilton and H. C. Mansel, 1846–63); O. M. Jones, *Empiricism and Intuitionism in Reid's Common Sense Philosophy* (1927); S. A. Grave, *The Scottish Philosophy of Common Sense* (1960); H. T. Buckle, *On Scotland and the Scotch Intellect* (ed. Hanham, 1970), p. 293; M. T. Dalgarno, "Reid's Natural Jurisprudence – The Language of Rights and Duties," in Hope (ed.), *Philosophers of the Scottish Enlightenment* (1984) p. 13. He became a Presbyterian minister, 1737–51, a regent in King's College, Aberdeen, 1751–64, and then Professor of Moral Philosophy at Glasgow, 1764–96. His main works were *An Inquiry into the Human Mind on the Principles of Common Sense* (1764); *Essays on the Intellectual Powers of Man* (1785); *Essays on the Active Powers of Man* (1788).

[89] V, Chap. v.

[90] On this see particularly Dalgarno, "Reid's Natural Jurisprudence" in Hope (ed.), *Philosophers of the Scottish Enlightenment* (1984), p. 13, examining unpublished works of Reid.

[91] *Infra.*

[92] (1780–1847); *Sketches of Moral and Mental Philosophy* (1841).

[93] (?1794–?); *The Philosophy of Morals* (1835).

[94] 1723–1816; DNB; Anderson, S.N., II, p. 202; Chambers, BDES; *Ency. Soc. Sc.*, VI, 184; *Int. Ency. Soc. Sc.*, V, 369; J. Small in *Trans. R.S.E.* 23 (1864); H. G. Graham, *Scottish Men of Letters in the 18th Century*, p. 104; W. C. Lehmann, *Adam Ferguson and the*

Beginnings of Modern Sociology (1930); D. Kettler, *The Social and Political Thought of Adam Ferguson* (1965); D. G. MacRae, "Adam Ferguson," in T. Raison (ed.), *The Founding Fathers of Social Science* (1969), p. 17; J. A. Bernstein, "Adam Ferguson and the Idea of Progress," in *Studies in Burke and his Time*, 19 (1978), p. 99.

[95] See 1966 ed. with introduction by Duncan Forbes. Also D. Kettler, "History and Theory in Ferguson's *Essay on the History of Civil Society*: A Reconsideration, "*Political theory*" 5 (1977) 437.

[96] D. Kettler, "Ferguson's *Principles*: Constitution in Permanence," in *Studies in Burke and His Time*, 19 (1978), p. 208.

[97] DNB; Anderson, S.N., I, p. 263; Chambers, BDES; Sir William Forbes "Account of the Life and Writings of James Beattie," *Edinburgh Review* 19 (1806); Sir William Forbes, *Life and Writings of James Beattie* (2 vols., 1806); H. G. Graham, *Scottish Men of Letters in the 18th century* (1901), p. 259. He was schoolmaster of Fordoun near Laurencekirk, where he became acquainted with Lords Gardenstone and Monboddo, before appointment to the chair at Marischal. He wrote also poetry.

[98] He refers to Blackstone. The passage is in *Commentaries*, I, 2 (1st ed., I, p. 44).

[99] DNB; Anderson, SN, III, p. 518; Chambers, BDES; His major works are *Elements of the Philosophy of the Human Mind* (3 vols., 1792–1827); *Outlines of Moral Philosophy* (1793); *Philosophical Essays* (1810); and *Philosophy of the Active and Moral Powers of Man* (1828). An edition of his *Works* by Sir William Hamilton, with a memoir of the author, appeared in 10 vols. in 1855–57. See also K. Haakonssen, "From Moral Philosophy to Political Economy: The Contribution of Dugald Stewart," in Hope (ed.), *Philosophers of The Scottish Enlightenment* (1984), p. 211. For a case about copyright in Stewart's works see *Stewart* v. *A. & C. Black* (1846) 9 D. 1026.

[1] Chap. 19, *infra*.

[2] Cockburn, *Memorials*, p. 20.

[3] *Active and Moral Powers*, Bk. IV, Chap. II.

[4] DNB.

[5] DNB; Anderson, S.N., III, p. 509; Omond, *Lord Advocates*, I, p. 242. On him see also p. 305, *infra*.

[6] On him see also p. 296, *infra*.

[7] Chap. 14, *supra*.

[8] DNB; Anderson, S.N., III, p. 547; Brunton & Haig, p. 536; Cockburn's *Memorials*, p. 103.

[9] DNB; Brunton & Haig, p. 465; Omond, *Lord Advocates*, I, p. 260; *Scots Peerage*, VIII, 125.

[10] Mackay, *Memoirs*, p. 211.

[11] Fraser Tytler, *Memoir of Lord Kames*, I, pp. 42–43.

[12] Chap. 11, *supra*.

[13] He was in the Tolbooth for debt in Jan. 1722; *Faculty of Advocates' Minute Book*, II, 47; and seems to have been constantly in financial trouble. He died in poverty: *ibid.*, II, 119.

[14] Ms. vols. for 1713–14 and 1716–17 are in the Advocates' Library. The Faculty appointed a committee in 1720 to revise his first year's collection of decisions: *Faculty of Advocates' Minute Book*, II, 33, 34, 36, and again in Jan. 1728 to review his work and added to the committee in July: *Faculty of Advocates' Minute Book*, II, 110, 112.

[15] *Faculty of Advocates' Minute Book*, II, 20. In 1721 The Faculty nominated a committee to advise and assist Bruce: *ibid.*, 39.

[16] *Ibid.*, II, 92.

[17] *Ibid.*, II, 112.

[18] *Ibid.*, II, 119.

[19] Chap. 14, *supra*.

[20] *Faculty of Advocates' Minute Book*, II, 72, 84.

[21] *Faculty of Advocates' Minute Book*, II, 199.

[22] A committee reported unfavourably on his work in Jan. 1743: *Faculty of Advocates' Minute Book*, II, 189.

[23] *Ibid.*, II, 124, 125, 128.

[24] *Ibid.*, II, 189–190.

[25] Chap. 14, *supra*.

[26] DNB; Anderson, S.N., II, p. 365; Brunton & Haig, p. 503; Fraser Tytler, *Memoir of Lord Kames*, I, pp. 39–40; *Letters of Patrick Grant, Lord Elchies*, with memoir by H. D. MacWilliam (1927). Easter Elchies house, high above the Spey between Aberlour and Craigellachie, but on the other (west) side of the river, is now the Visitors' Reception Centre

for Macallan-Glenlivet Distillery and deserves a visit by pious lawyers for its associations. Elchies lived at Carberry in Inveresk parish and was an elder while Jupiter Carlyle was minister of Inveresk: see Carlyle's *Autobiography*, p. 220. William Grant (1752–1832), born at Elchies but not related, became Master of the Rolls in England 1801–17.

[27] *Memoir of Lord Kames*, I, p. 39.

[28] *Heron* v. *Espie* (1856) 18 D. 917, at p. 935.

[29] See Bell, *Commentaries*, I, 24.

[30] *Kippen's Trs.* v. *Kippen* (1856) 18 D. 1137, at p. 1164, *per* Lords Handyside and Mackenzie.

[31] DNB; Anderson, S.N. II, p. 195; Brunton & Haig, p. 505. James Fergusson, "Lord Hermand: A Biographical Sketch," in Walton (ed.), *Lord Hermand's Consistorial Decisions* (Stair Soc. 1940), p. 2; Fergusson, "Background to a Lord of Session," 1974 S.L.T. (News) 1.

[32] Tytler, *Memoir of Lord Kames*, I, p. 36.

[33] Ramsay of Ochtertyre, *Scotland and Scotsmen in the Eighteenth Century* (1888) I, p. 93n.

[34] *Infra*, p. 298.

[35] A. F. Tytler, *Memoir of Lord Kames*, I, p. 36.

[36] Fergusson, *ibid.*, p. 10.

[37] DNB; Anderson, S.N., I, p. 494; Chambers, BDES; Brunton & Haig, p. 531; W. A. Knight, *Lord Monboddo and Some of His Contemporaries* (1900); G. Burnett, *The Family of Burnet of Leys* (1901); H. G. Graham, *Scottish Men of Letters in the Eighteenth Century* (1901), p. 188; W. Forbes Gray, *Some Old Scots Judges* (1914), p. 41; E. L. Cloyd, *James Burnett, Lord Monboddo* (1972); Cockburn, *Memorials*, p. 102; Kay's *Edinburgh Portraits*, I, 18, 17, 247; II, 135.

[38] Cloyd, p. 6.

[39] F. Brady and F. A. Pottle, *Boswell in Search of a Wife* (1956), p. 215.

[40] On whom see p. 280, 302.

[41] Vol. 5 (1776); the attacks extend over 64 pp. and seven issues of the periodical, and led John MacLaurin and others to cancel their subscriptions. The periodical failed shortly thereafter.

[42] J. Ramsay, *Scotland and Scotsmen of the Eighteenth Century* (ed. Allardyce, 1888), I, p. 356; E. B. Ramsay, *Reminiscences of Scottish Life and Character* (1874), p. 152.

[43] DNB; Anderson, S.N. II, p. 196; Brunton & Haig, p. 544; W. F. Gray, *Some Old Scots Judges* (1914), 188; James Fergusson, "Lord Hermand: A Biographical Sketch," in Walton (ed.), *Lord Hermand's Consistorial Decisions* (Stair Soc., 1940), pp. 1–40; Kay's *Edinburgh Portraits*, I, 392; II, 380.

[44] *Supra* p. 297.

[45] Cockburn, *Memorials*. His style is imitated in "The Diamond Beetle Case" by George Cranston, Lord Corehouse, printed in Kay's *Edinburgh Portraits*, II, 385–6; see also Maidment, *Court of Session Garland*, p. 103.

[46] James Fergusson, *supra*, p. 33.

[47] Cockburn, *Memorials*, p. 123.

[48] On the grounds for attributing it to George Fergusson see Walton, Introd. to Stair Soc. Ed., pp. x–xii.

[49] The Scottish Record Society published an index to *Consistorial Processes and Decreets*. 1658–1800, from which cases can be traced.

[50] 1817.

[51] *Burman* v. *Burman*, 1930 S.C. 262, *per* Lord Murray at p. 271.

[52] *Faculty of Advocates' Minute Book*, II, 199.

[53] Chap. 14, *supra*.

[54] DNB; Anderson, S.N., I, p. 570; Brunton & Haig, pp. 539, 547; Omond, *Lord Advocates* II, pp. 65, 174; Kay's *Original Portraits*, II, 89, 380. A grandson was Archibald Campbell Tait, Archbishop of Canterbury.

[55] Cockburn, *Memorials*, pp. 115–117.

[56] Brunton & Haig, p. 547.

[57] It is a different book from *Faculty Collection*, Vol. III, which also covers 1756–60. Neither of the Campbells is mentioned as a reporter on the title page of that volume.

[58] Chaps. 16, *supra*, and 19, *infra*.

[59] Chap. 20, *infra*. On Robert Bell see further p. 308, *infra*.

[60] Sir Patrick Home of Renton.

[61] *Faculty of Advocates' Minute Book*, I, 109.

[62] *Ibid.*, I, 182.

[63] *ibid.*, I, 261.

[64] *Ibid.*, I, 298–299.

[65] *Ibid.*, II,9.

[66] *ibid.*, II, 71, 72, 83. His salary was stopped in 1743 for failure to lodge decisions in the library: *ibid.*, II, 190.

[67] *Ibid.*, II, 199.

[68] R. Hannay, *Address to the Right Hon. Lord President Hope and to the Members of the College of Justice on the Method of Collecting and Reporting Decisions* (1821) p. 21.

[69] Cockburn, *Memorials*, p. 158.

[70] DNB.

[71] DNB; Anderson, S.N., II, p. 689.

[72] On the controversy see Douglas Duncan, *Thomas Ruddiman*, pp. 135–138.

[73] DNB; Anderson S.N., I, p. 262.

[74] DNB; Anderson, S.N., III, p. 38; Brunton & Haig, p. 538.

[75] DNB.

[76] He attributes one of these abridgments at least in large part to Lord Roystoun (Sir James Mackenzie (1771–1744, advocate 1698, Lord Roystoun 1710), the other to "a learned lawyer, lately deceased."

[77] DNB; Anderson, S.N., I, p. 158; Chambers, BDES; Kay's *Edinburgh Portraits* I, 16, 25, 157, 324; He published also a *History of Edinburgh*, 1779 and 1816.

[78] See also *The Trial of James Stewart*, Printed for G. Hamilton and J. Balfour, 1753, and *Supplement* (1754); *The Trial of James Stewart* (ed. D. N. Mackay, 1907).

[79] See also Sir R. Temple, *New Light on the Mysterious Tragedy of the "Worcester," 1704–5* (1930).

[80] Possibly John Dundas of Philipston, advocate 1698, Procurator for the Church 1706–31 and Principal Clerk of the General Assembly. BL catalogue calls him "of Arniston" but there is no known John Dundas of Arniston connected with law.

[81] DNB; Anderson, S.N. III, p. 255.

[82] *Faculty of Advocates' Minute Book* (ed. Pinkerton), I, 197. See also 238.

[83] APS, XI, 50, 85, 195, 203.

[84] Andrew Ross and F. J. Grant published in 1892, *Alexander Nisbet's Heraldic Plates originally intended for his "System of Heraldry"*, with introduction and notes.

[85] See, *e.g.* Stewart Mackenzie v. Fraser-Mackenzie, 1920 S.C. 764 at pp. 788, 791, 792; 1922 S.C. (H.L.) 39 at p. 48. *Maclean of Ardgour v. Maclean*, 1941 S.C. 613 at pp. 631, 657, 676, 683, 685, 706.

[86] In Anderson, S.N., III, p. 255.

[87] On him see also p. 294, *supra*.

[88] Preface, p. i.

[89] *Ibid.*, p. ii.

[90] J. Balfour to G. Wallace, July 9, 1779, and receipt dated September 29, 1779, in Edinburgh Univ. Library, Laing Papers, MS. La.II, 694/6.

[91] A. Carlyle, *Autobiography*, p. 334.

[92] (1840) 2 D. 752.

[93] At p. 776, *per* Lord Justice-Clerk Boyle and Lords Glenlee, Meadowbank, Medwyn and Moncreiff.

[94] At p. 792, *per* Lord Mackenzie.

[95] At p. 799, *per* Lord Fullerton.

[96] At p. 801, *per* Lord President Hope.

[97] David Murray, *Legal Practice in Ayr and the West of Scotland* (1910), p. 34, attributes Carruthers' *Styles* to Sir Andrew Birnie, Lord Saline; H.P. (later Lord) Macmillan ("The Old Scots Conveyancers" (1898) 10 J.R. 425; (1899) 11 J.R. 41) doubts this attribution. The second edition, sometimes attributed to Birnie, has the same title and appears to be the same book. Walter Ross refers to it as *Carruthers' Stiles*.

[98] DNB; Anderson, S.N., III, p. 496, H. P. Macmillan, "The Old Scots Conveyancers" (1899) 11 J.R. 44, 46.

[99] Anderson, SN, I, p. 302; Brunton & Haig, p. 407.

[1] *History of the Society of Writers to H. M. Signet* (1890 ed.) p. cix.

[2] Described judicially as an "authoritative treatise:" *Smith* v. *Chambers' Trs.* (1877) 5 R. 97, at p. 114 *per* Lord Deas.

[3] A list of MS. style books is in *Sources and Literature of Scots Law*, pp. 314–316, and some of these are described there at pp. 303–310.

CHAPTER 19

DAVID HUME

WHEN Lord President Sir David Falconer of Newton (?1639–1685, advocate 1661) died his widow married one John Hume of Ninewells in Chirnside parish, Berwickshire. His third daughter Katherine later married Joseph, son of John Hume. Joseph (?–1713, advocate 1705) and Katherine's children included another John (1709–86) and David (1711–76), who grew up to become the famous philosopher and histor- ian.[1] John became an active and enterprising Border laird and was held in good repute in the district.[2] He had a large family and his third son and fourth child was also named David. This younger David[3] was born in February 1757 and baptised on the 27th of that month. He was sent to Edinburgh High School[4] and Edinburgh University, where he attended the lectures of, *inter alios*, Adam Ferguson and Hugh Blair, and in 1774 Roman law under Robert Dick.

But in 1774 young David wrote to his uncle David, who was looking after his education, expressing an inclination to go to Glasgow to study under John Millar, whom he had heard much about and esteemed highly. Dick, it may be surmised, he did not find inspiring. Uncle David agreed and arranged with Millar to take young David, and young David accord- ingly matriculated at Glasgow in 1775.[5]

Uncle David had good reports of young David from Millar but was warned that while Mr. Millar was very well pleased with him, he thought young David was working too hard, and might damage his health.[6] One feature of Millar's teaching, probably significant for young David's later interests and work, was that Millar gave a short summer-term course on criminal law and procedure, which was then a novelty.[7]

In the summer of 1776 young David returned to Edinburgh. His uncle died that summer; apart from a close and affectionate family relationship David's uncle had been a most valuable adviser on David's education, had got him in as a student of Millar, and paid for his studies in Glasgow. He left David a legacy of £1000, if David's father survived him, which he did, "to assist him in his education," and left most of his property to David's father, John, whom failing to David. The manuscript of Hume's *Dialogues* was left by codicil to William Strahan, printer and publisher, as literary executor, with the provision that failing publication by him within two and a half years (which in fact he did not do) the property therein was to vest in young David who was to publish them. When they were published in 1779 he was presumed to have been responsible.[8] Young David was also pressed to publish his uncle's letters but did not do so, from regard, it was said, of his memory, and he ultimately bequeathed them to the Royal Society for Edinburgh.[9]

Hume[10] spent the session 1776–77 again with Millar, boarding with him at his house, No.1 The College,[11] and in session 1777–78 attended the Scots Law class in Edinburgh University under Professor William Wallace (*c.* 1725–86, Professor 1765–86). He was admitted an advocate on July 13, 1779, and elected F.R.S.E. in 1783.

He appears to have had a fair practice from the beginning and in March 1783 he was appointed part-time Sheriff of Berwickshire. He must moreover have acquired the reputation among the advocates of being of a scholarly kind. In December 1786 his was one of the two names put forward to the Town Council, as was the statutory requirement for filling the post, to fill the vacancy in the Chair of Scots Law caused by the death of Professor William Wallace. The other name submitted was Robert Dundas,[12] a son of the second Lord President Dundas, and nephew of Henry Dundas, a man of moderate talents who by reason of his family connections later became Solicitor-General (1784), Lord Advocate (1789) and Chief Baron of Exchequer (1801). Hume was presented to the University and the Senate admitted him as Professor of Scots Law on December 19, 1786. This was then a part-time post but the duties of the chair, of his researches, and of his sheriffship can have left little time for private practice.

Yet his huge collection of *Session Papers*, now bound in 135 volumes, shows that he regularly attended the court and took notes, sometimes verbatim, of the judgments.[13] At that time proceedings were conducted mainly in writing and there seemed hardly a limit to the pleadings and counter-pleadings which might be delivered. Cockburn, only a little later,[14] remarked: "The great mass of the business was carried on by writing – not merely by written pleadings, but by the whole circumstances and legal merits of every cause being laid before the judges in the form of written or of printed statement and argument." Some of these pleadings might, moreover, be in themselves substantial dissertations on the relevant law.

Hume continued to play an active part in the life of the Faculty of Advocates, as a curator of the Library 1785–90 and 1792–95,[15] a member of the Dean's Council from 1797 to 1822 and a representative of the Faculty on charitable bodies. In 1793 he was appointed Sheriff of Linlithgow and Bathgate and resigned the office of Sheriff of Berwickshire. As the sheriff-substitutes of these days were either unqualified legally or, even if qualified, not permitted to judge in cases of difficulty or importance, whole bundles of processes came weekly and he had to decide, write out the interlocutors and orders and return them to be signed in court by the substitute, if indeed he was made to attend personally.[16]

Hume was a strong Tory and was one of the ringleaders of the movement which prevented Henry Erskine from being re-elected to the office of Dean of Faculty in 1795 for having presided at a meeting in Edinburgh which, though expressing loyalty to the Crown, had passed a resolution moved by him condemning, as striking at the very existence of the British constitution, two Bills then before Parliament, one extending the law of treason[17] and the other[18] giving the Lords of Justiciary power to dissolve seditious assemblies or meetings without the reading of the Riot Act.[19] Young advocates sometimes had a written test presented to them, that they did not support the Whig or Liberal party. "I have heard George Cranstoun say that the test was put to him, and by a celebrated Professor of Law acting for the Tory party."[20]

The W.S. Society had in 1793 at the instance of Robert Bell[21] instituted a lectureship in conveyancing and were anxious to have this raised to the rank of a chair; sometime in 1795 or 1796 they sought the concurrence of the Lords of Session for a petition to the Crown to effect this. Hume was strongly opposed to this and got the Senate of the University to disapprove of the move as "neither conducive to the improvement of the course of Law Studies nor consistent with the due regard to the rights and interests of the established Professor of Scots Law," and appointed a committee to oppose the plan. The Faculty of Advocates also opposed it, and it was not until 1825 that the Town Council acceded to the W.S. Society's renewed proposal and MacVey Napier was appointed professor.

Hume was also involved in advising the Senate in 1810 on the relative powers of the Senate and the Town Council to make regulations and prescribe fees for degrees.[22] Some years later the Senate disregarded his opinion and the Town Council obtained declarator that it had the sole right to prescribe regulations for studies and the course of study.[23] Later still the Senate raised the matter again.[24] Hume's opinion was printed as part of the pleadings and approved in all the courts. On appeal Lord Brougham referred[25] to "another high authority – an authority, in my opinion, of the greatest weight – I mean that of the late most learned Professor Hume, Professor of Scotch Law...."

Hume became a member of the Speculative Society, a prominent literary and debating society, in 1774, was President from 1777 to 1781 and raised to honorary member in 1779. He took a prominent part in the society's activities.[26] As a young man he contributed to *The Mirror* and *The Lounger*, short-lived literary journals. At the first meeting of the Literary Class of the Royal Society of Edinburgh, in November 1783, he was elected to Fellowship[27] and in 1789 he delivered before the Society an appreciation of the life and work of Sir Thomas Miller, Lord Glenlee, successively Lord Justice-Clerk (1766–87) and Lord President (1787–89) and a Fellow of the Society.[28] He also served in the Edinburgh Volunteers and attained the rank of major.[29]

In 1804 Hume received the honorary degree of Doctor of Laws from the University of Glasgow.[30]

In March 1811 he was appointed a Principal Clerk of Session and resigned the office of Sheriff of Linlithgow; as a Principal Clerk he had as a colleague Walter Scott, and relations between them seem to have been very harmonious. According to Scott,[31] Hume "repeatedly declined high promotion in the Court of Session where his eminent legal talents and legal knowledge might be employed successfully." In another letter[32] Scott stated that he knew that Hume was "a most worthy and respectable man and has repeatedly refused a situation of a judge." Scott's *Journal* shows that in the latter 1820s he and Hume were very friendly and dined at each other's houses.

In January 1822, Hume was appointed a Baron of Exchequer,[33] an office he had long desired, and in the same month resigned his chair and his offices of Principal Clerk of Session and Clerk of the King's Processes in Scotland. For the remainder of the session his lectures were read by J. H. Forbes (1776–1854, advocate 1799) later (1825) Lord Medwyn.[34]

George Joseph Bell was appointed Professor in February[35] and commenced to teach in November.[36]

During his long tenure of the Chair many students attended his lectures who later attained distinction. These included Henry Brougham, later Lord Chancellor, David Boyle and Duncan McNeill, later Lords President, John Hope, later Lord Justice-Clerk, Adam Anderson, Archibald Campbell, Henry Cockburn, John Cowan, John Cunningham, George Deas, David Douglas, John Hay Forbes (Medwyn), John Fullerton, Robert Handyside, Alexander Irving (Newton), Francis Jeffrey, Joshua Henry Mackenzie, Alexander Maconochie (Meadowbank), John Marshall (Curriehill), James Wellwood Moncrieff, David Monypenny (Pitmilly), Alexander Murray (Henderland), Charles Neaves, Henry Robertson (Benholme), Patrick Robertson, Andrew Rutherford, Alexander Wood, all later Lords of Session, Archibald Alison, writer on criminal law and Sheriff of Lanark, George Joseph Bell, who succeeded Hume, John Schank More and George Moir, the next two professors of Scots law, and Robert Davidson who succeeded John Millar in Glasgow, George Brodie who edited Stair, Mungo Ponton Brown who produced Brown's *Synopsis* and Brown's *Supplement*, Adam Duff, writer on conveyancing, Cosmo Innes, the historian, and John Riddell, the antiquary, Thomas Carlyle, Sir Walter Scott and John Gibson Lockhart, all men of letters, Sir William Hamilton and John Wilson (Christopher North) philosophers, and many others who made some mark in their lives.

Hume received many honours on and after his retirement. Edinburgh University conferred on him an LL.D. The Faculty of Advocates passed a resolution expressing appreciation of his scholarship and services. The students of his last session gave him a piece of silver plate.[37] The W.S. Society[38] and S.S.C. Society[39] did similarly; the former body also presented him with his portrait by Raeburn;[40] judges and advocates who had been among his students presented him with his bust by Chantrey. Cockburn was asked by some of Hume's friends to move that the gift be accepted by the Faculty of Advocates and placed in the library. "I never thought that I should find myself eulogising David Hume. I specially bargained that I should not be expected to approve of his lectures, or the public principles of his book. This being guarded against, there was plenty to praise, and honestly, and I believe that even his friends were satisfied."[41]

In July 1823 he was appointed one of a Royal Commission set up by statute[42] to investigate the simplification and shortening of the forms of pleading and proceeding in the Court of Session, including the conducting of more of the pleading orally, the extending of the application of jury trials, and the system of appeals. The report[43] resulted in the Court of Session Act 1825.

Hume resigned his judicial office on February 20, 1834. The curtailment of the powers of the Court of Exchequer had already been begun[44] and vacancies on the Bench of that court were not to be filled. His health seems to have been failing and he died on July 27, 1838, and was buried in the Old Calton Cemetery. In 1832 he had, on the death of his elder brother, succeeded to the estates of Ninewells and Castle Fairney, and these passed to his daughter Elizabeth.[45]

When Hume commenced to teach Scots law Erskine's *Institute* was only 13 years old and his *Principles* only 32 years old, though already in its sixth edition. But he prepared a most thorough set of lectures which, as now printed, read more like a leisurely treatise than notes for lectures. If he spoke the text exactly or substantially as it was written the lectures would be very agreeable to listen to, but contain far more than need ever have been noted or remembered, and lectures read verbatim lack the spontaneity which characterises the best oral exposition.

From the surviving manuscript it is plain that Hume regularly revised his material to take account of changes in the law, new decisions, changes of his opinion and of his view as to the best arrangement of material and the best order of presentation. Notes on the manuscript indicate that in some years he omitted some chapters or parts of chapters.[46] The order of some of the topics seems to have varied. Bankruptcy seems to have been dropped after about 1800 and the notes were not updated.

In his introductory lecture he depreciated the Roman law.

> "For although our Municipal Law is in many respects founded on that of the Romans, which is our highest authority where our own statutes and customs are silent; yet the instances in which those customs and statutes differ from it are so numerous, and the alterations they make so very considerable, that it is frequently far less difficult to understand the original doctrines of Justinian, than to perceive their application to our own practice. This is in particular the case with that branch of our Law which is derived from the Feudal System. . . .
>
> "But although thus useful on such occasions or, as I have already said, necessary, may be a knowledge of the Civil Law, it is however far from being sufficient. . . ."[47]
>
> "The law, under which this or any other nation lives, was not contrived by metaphysicians. It is the assemblage of those customs and regulations, which mankind, according to the state of society they are in, feel to be just or find to be convenient, and their sentiments in those respects will ever be the controlling principles in judicial decisions.
>
> "In a certain degree indeed, by a careful investigation of what is, in fact, the system adopted, we may discover various principles that pervade it, the knowledge of which will facilitate our progress to an acquaintance with its several parts. But it were vain to imagine that we can chain it down, in rules as simple and constant, as those in which Sir Isaac Newton has bound the phenomena of the heavenly motions. . . . You are here to be made acquainted with the special laws of your own country, as they actually stand; and must not expect to find everywhere the beauty and harmony of a Philosophical System."[48]
>
> "The person who holds this Chair ought not, I think, to regard himself as called upon to furnish his pupils with a complete digest of the Law, perfect in all its parts, and which they are to keep by them as a repository of authorities to be resorted to for their direction in practice. It were indeed impossible to give an entire system of so

intricate a science, in lectures, delivered *viva voce*, during the proper period of our course. Nor indeed, if it were otherwise, would this method of teaching prove truly beneficial to my hearers. For there is no want of books in which the various parts of the law are fully and accurately treated, and where this kind of knowledge may to better advantage be gained. What young men stand in need of is an elementary view of the subject, such as may enable them to understand these works, and to peruse them profitably. Indeed it would not be right, even if it were practicable, to relieve the student from the wholesome office of seeking for knowledge by the efforts of his own attention; nor is it the tutor's business to save him the trouble of private research and of thinking for himself, but guide him only in the direction of his industry, and enable him to turn it to account. In short, to use the words of an English author, equally eminent as an able lawyer, and an elegant writer,[49] 'he should consider his course as a general map of the law, marking out the shape of the country, its connexions and boundaries, its greater divisions and principal cities; it is not his business to describe minutely the longitude and latitude of every inconsiderable hamlet'."[50]

"One thing which seems in a peculiar manner to be part of his duty is to lay before his hearers the history of the law tracing its progress to its present state, through the successive changes it has undergone, and pointing out the causes and motives of these alterations. . . . Besides, to such as have any love of knowledge, those inquiries are for their own sake of some value, which connect the study of the law with the history of past times, and of manners and morals of our forefathers."[51]

"But above all it lies upon the teacher of law properly to methodise and distribute the study, to divide the whole subject of the law into the due number of distinct heads, and to arrange these in a luminous manner. It is, perhaps, in this respect chiefly that the printed systems of our law are to be reckoned defective. Lord Stair, it is true, does propose what upon the whole is a just enough order of arrangement, but he is very apt to deviate from it in the detail of execution. Sir George Mackenzie again (whose order is followed by Erskine) has generally been accounted somewhat unfortunate in this important article."[52]

"On that account and certainly on that only, I do not make use of Erskine's lesser work – his *Principles of the Law of Scotland* – as a text both to be commented upon and expounded from this Chair. That treatise is, however, certainly one of the most useful law books that we have and comprises within very moderate bounds a great deal of sound intelligent doctrine and accurate information; and I mean therefore every day before dismissing to direct you to those passages of it where the subject of next day's study is to be found."[53]

"In regard to this principle of any arrangement of our system of law – this is to be found in the nature of the several objects to which law relates. Our books inform us that these are three in number, namely, Persons, Things and Actions. It is, however, obvious that the persons or the things themselves are not in any proper sense the objects of attention to the lawyer. He is rather employed in considering the connections formed by mankind with the things round them and the rights, the claims and obligations which arise among the several orders or classes of persons. The correct division of the objects of the law is, therefore, into Rights and Actions; into Rights and the means of prosecuting and enforcing Rights in the course of law, for it is in this juridical sense that the term Actions is here employed."[54]

Hume then spoke of the sources of Scots law.

"The Law of Scotland is of two sorts, the *Lex non Scripta*, the unwritten, customary or common law, and the *Lex Scripta*, the written or statutory law. The former of these, the common or customary law, is so termed by reason of its origin – because it does not derive its authority from any positive act, or record, or declaration of the supreme power, but from the tacit consent of the inhabitants of the land, implied in their observance of it, time out of mind, as a rule of conduct. This was in fact the original Law of Scotland and at present the greater part of our law is what has been formed in that way. It was not till about the time of James the First that Acts of Parliament began to touch upon Private Rights; before that time they seem rather to have had for their object the remedying some abuse or inconvenience in the Public Law. Some general principles have existed in our law from time immemorial which seem consistent with material justice and are not established by any positive enactment, such as a child succeeding to the property of his father, a widow being provided from the funds of her husband, a husband succeeding to the estate of his wife."[55]

The basis of these practices is, he held, feelings of natural justice. Another cause which had a powerful influence was the imitation of the feudal customs which became a sort of common law to all Europe, particularly the Norman customs which gradually made their way into Scotland through England. Then there was the introduction of the Roman law:

"in many kinds of business it was long ago adopted by our Judges as their model and rule of decision. And so far – in those particular departments of business – having been incorporated into our practice, by a long and uniform train of decisions, the Civil Law has certainly become a proper integral part of our common or customary law, so as to constrain and bind us, and from which, on no pretence of better reasoning, or greater convenience, our Judges are now at liberty to swerve.

"Not only so but generally speaking, and more especially in such matters as are analogous, or related to those in which the Civil Law has been naturalised (if I may say so) our Courts have been trained for several centuries to a habit of respect and deference for that system, as an example fit to be regarded, and an authority before others, if there is no strong consideration of justice or convenience on the other side to outweigh it.

"Thus much seems to be certainly true. I cannot, however, with some authorities, go still further, and say generally that the entire system of the Civil Law is truly our law, and equally binding on us (independently of reception by a course of judgments) as our own statutes, or ancient customs themselves. I must rather be of opinion, along with Stair and Craig (two not incompetent judges certainly) that the obeisance we pay to the Civil is now, and always has been, a voluntary obeisance and matter of courtesy, such as depends, in the main, on its agreement with equity and reason, its analogy to the rest of our practice, and its suitableness to our state of things and kinds of business. . . ."[56]

"Certainly while I thus refuse allegiance to the Civil Law, as having dominion over us, I have no purpose of discouraging the study of that most enlightened, ingenious and elegant system. Doubtless an acquaintance with it is the best possible instruction for a young man in the general principles of right and wrong, and in the method of reasoning on matters of law; and indeed as I have already said, the knowledge of it is in many points the knowledge of our own established and municipal practice."[57]

Hume then went on to talk about the repositories of the common law, the collections of reports and the writings of learned lawyers.

"The delineations of doctrine given by such men, when they are explicit and in unison with one another, have justly much weight as evidence of the strain and tenor of our common law; and they are quoted in that view, by our pleaders, as of little inferior authority to the judgments even of Court. Among those authors Sir Thomas Craig is entitled to our thanks; but he who has done most for us, and stands certainly in the highest place, is Lord Stair, an acute reasoner certainly, and a profound and intelligent lawyer, who has given us a complete system of our law, from which all later authorities have drawn, and were obliged to draw, a great part at least of what is most valuable in their works."[58]

Among the reporters Hume mentioned Kilkerran and Kames, and then spoke of the statutory law. *Regiam Majestatem* he considered to be "undoubtedly an ancient compilation, not much later probably than the time of Alexander III and never could have grown into that degree of credit which it had long ago gained with our people, and even with the legislature, unless it had borne a strong resemblance at least to the actual usages and laws of the country."[59]

This account of the sources and repositories is surprisingly inadequate; Mackenzie and Erskine surely deserved a mention, even if Bankton did not get one. Decisions of courts are not accorded any authority, save as evidence of common law. It may be that Hume was relying on students to read little Erskine and supplement what he said.

Then follows the exposition of the private law in the order which he had outlined, as follows:

Part I (Chaps. 2–5)	Husband and wife; parent and child; guardian and ward; voluntary servants.[60]
Part II (Chaps. 1–16)	Things, personal rights, sale; location-tack; charter-party; loan, mandate; society; cautionry; bills of exchange;[61] assignation of personal claims; extinction of obligations by payment; compensation and retention; novation; prescription; obligations *ex delicto*; obligations *quasi ex contractu*; obligations *quasi ex delicto*.[62]
Part III (Chaps. 1–5)	The right of property; servitudes;[62] pledge and hypotheck; exclusive privilege; tacks.[63]
Part IV (Chaps. 1–18)	The feudal investiture; the superior's estate; the vassal's estate; transmission of feudal rights; infeftments in conjunct fee; liferent; wadset; heritable bonds; real liens; adjudication; judicial sale; prescription; heritable and moveable;[63] heritable succession; settlements and tailzies; privileges of apparency; service of heirs; moveable succession.[64]
Part V (Chaps. 1–16)	Jurisdiction; jurisdiction of Supreme Courts; jurisdiction of inferior courts; summons and execution; proof by oath of party; proof by witnesses;[65] probation by writing; decrees; process of review in Court of Session; inhibitions; poinding; arrestment; confirmation qua creditor; personal diligence; *meditatio fugae* and liberation; *cessio bonorum*.[66]

This was clearly a most extensive and thorough conspectus of the subject. There are quite frequent references in the text to cases, many of them noted only in Hume's own *Session Papers*.

It was also a logical structure; the misguided split between Scots law (so-called) and mercantile law had not emerged, and while not dealing with practical conveyancing Hume dealt extensively with the principles of land law, topics of substantive law which have in modern times been annexed by the teachers of conveyancing, and with evidence and procedure.

In many respects his lectures show the changing emphasis of the law since Erskine's time; master and servant is much more fully treated than by Erskine; his discourse on insurance, mainly marine insurance, is the earliest Scottish consideration of the subject apart from J. Millar's *Elements of the Law of Insurance* of 1787; his consideration of benevolence under the general head of "Quasi-Contract" is probably owed to Kames's *Principles of Equity*.

On the other hand the substance of the lectures is still remarkably older-fashioned and showing little of the impact of industrialisation and the increasing importance of commerce. "Companies" does not figure as a heading; trusts are barely mentioned; negligence by the mishandling of vehicles is unknown; moveable property is still wholly unimportant as compared with heritage.

Hume's own manuscript notes on the manuscript show that the order of the topics was sometimes varied, and that some topics were omitted in some years, others in others; bankruptcy seems to have been omitted altogether after about 1800.

It appears that during his term of office, numbers in the Scots Law class rose from about 100 to at least 200, but at that time some students attended for two or even three sessions. The students were drawn from all over the country and comprised both youngsters just beginning the study of law and more mature students, in their twenties or more, who had come in from country places to acquire a better, or possibly, for the first time, a proper, understanding of the law.[67]

The class met at 2 p.m., five days a week, over a session from the end of October to the end of April. Christmas Day and New Year's Day were holidays, and this gave about 27 or 28 weeks or about 130–140 meetings in all. Each lecture must have covered about 15 pages of the printed text. The similarity of sets of students' notes to the text now printed indicates that Hume must have read his text with little or no extempore deviation, and at a pace which permitted the taking of full notes.

Hume's lectures were very highly regarded. Walter Scott attended them in 1790–92 and later wrote:[68]

"But the Scotch Law lectures were those of Mr. David Hume, who still continues to occupy that situation with as much honour to himself as advantage to his country. I copied over his lectures twice with my own hand, from notes taken in the class, and when I have had occasion to consult them, I can never sufficiently admire the penetration and clearness of conception which were necessary to the arrangement of the fabric of law, formed originally under the strictest influence of feudal principles, and innovated, altered, and broken in upon by the change of times, of habits and of manners, until it resembles some ancient castle, partly entire, partly ruinous, partly dilapidated, patched and altered during the succession of ages by a thousand attritions and combinations, yet still exhibiting, with the marks of its antiquity, symptoms of the skill and wisdom of its founders, and capable of being analyzed and made the subject of a methodical plan by an architect who can understand the various styles of the different ages in which it was subjected to alteration. Such an architect has Mr. Hume been to the law of Scotland, neither wandering into fanciful and abstruse disquisitions, which are the more proper subject of the antiquary, nor satisfied with presenting to his pupils a dry and undigested detail of the laws in their present state, but combining the past state of our legal enactments with the present, and tracing clearly and judiciously the changes which took place, and the causes which led to them."

Scott's second manuscript copy was bound and presented to Scott's father; this both gratified him as giving proof of his son's assiduous attention to Hume's instruction and afforded him "very pleasant reading for leisure hours."[69]

According to Thomas Carlyle, who had thought of becoming an advocate and took the class in 1819–20, "The Professor, Dr. Hume, a nephew of the philosopher . . . speaks in a voice scarce audible; and his thinking has yet to show all its points of similarity with the penetrating genius of his uncle."[70] Later: "I am at the Scots Law class; and the professor (a nephew of the historian Hume) is most perspicuous; but law is to me an untrodden path and much toil will be requisite for mastering it. . .".[71] Later again: "[Mr. Hume] is very plain hitherto. . .".[72] But by March: "Alas! David Hume owns no spark of his uncle's genius; his lectures on law are (still excepting Erskine's *Institute*) . . . the dullest piece of study I ever saw or heard of. Long-winded dry details about points not of the slightest importance to any but an Attorney or Notary Public; observations upon the formalities of customs which ought to be instantly and for ever abolished; uncounted cases of Blockhead A versus Blockhead B, with what Stair thought upon them, what Bankton, what the poor doubting Dirleton; and then the nature of actions – *O infandum.*[73] By degrees I got disheartened."[74] This is a fairly standard response of one not born to be a lawyer. Against this is the unanimous tribute of those who took to and liked law that Hume was a lucid expositor.

After he resigned the chair Hume was strongly pressed to publish his lectures, by unanimous resolution of the Faculty of Advocates, which however he declined: "In their present shape and condition those praelections certainly do not to myself appear to be by any means worthy to be laid, as a printed work, before the public; as to the conversion of them into some more careful and better digested shape such as that of a system or an Institute of the Law of Scotland which has now grown to be so large and so various a code, this is a great and a very arduous undertaking such as ought not to be engaged in hastily or indeed without the most serious and mature deliberation."[75] The University Senate also requested him to publish his lectures, as did deputations from the W.S. Society[76] and the S.S.C. Society.[77] In all cases Hume declined in similar terms. Not only did he never do so but by his settlement of July 31, 1832, he provided: "And further, with the exception aftermentioned, I hereby expressly prohibit the publication of my Lectures or any part of them, or any other composition of mine, in any shape or on any account whatever; and I enjoin my heirs and executors to take all proper and competent measures in course of law, to prevent any publication of the substance of my Lectures, or any Notes or Abstracts or copies of the same, in case any attempt or proposal of that nature shall be made on the part of any person, in any shape whatever."[78]

Many sets of students' notes of his lectures, however, were in existence and were carefully preserved, referred to and came to be preserved in university and legal libraries. The lectures were sometimes cited in judgment by judges, particularly by Lord Deas, from their own copies, and given as much weight as a printed book.[79]

In particular in *Kerr* v. *Martin*[80] in which all the major text writings on Scots law were cited and considered, Hume's lectures were treated as on a par with published institutional writings.

> "It has now been ascertained that Mr. Baron Hume, while Professor of the Law of Scotland, delivered the very same doctrine as the law of

Scotland, according to his understanding of it. We cannot but consider this as authority of very great weight. Independent of the deep study by which those lectures were prepared, Mr. Hume was in the daily observation of all the proceedings of the Court, and of all the cases which occurred during the very long period in which he held the chair in the University; and standing, as it is admitted that this question does, besides the great weight of his own opinion, if it were only his opinion, there could not be more decisive evidence of the general and understood state of the law, than this express and constant delivery of it year after year affords."[81]

After the other judges had been consulted, "the pursuer stated, that the purport of the lectures of Baron Hume had been erroneously assumed, in the opinions of some of the consulted judges, to be in favour of the defender and she obtained leave to put in the notes taken by various lawyers while attending the class of Baron Hume, in evidence of their alleged actual import. After these were put in, the cause was advised."[82] At this stage Lord Mackenzie remarked: "For I find such not only in the notes which have been printed,[83] but in the notes taken by myself in attending his lectures,[84] and written out at large day by day. And these notes were corrected by another person, who attended the lectures after a good many years. Yet this passage is not changed."[85] Finally Lord President Hope said: "I studied under Mr. William Wallace, the predecessor of the late Baron Hume in the chair of Scotch law and, if my memory does not fail me, he laid down the same doctrine. I am sorry now that I have not kept my notes taken in his class; and my reason for not keeping them was, that I had access to notes of Baron Hume's lectures, who laid down the same doctrine."[86]

Reference was also made to the *Lectures*, either from the manuscript in the Advocates' Library or from students' notes, by later text-writers, by Brodie in his notes on Stair,[87] Baird on *Master and Servant*,[88] Lord Fraser on *Master and Servant*,[89] Napier on *Prescription*,[90] Borthwick on *Libel and Slander*,[91] and Tait on *Evidence*.[92]

The original manuscript of Hume's *Lectures* was presented to the Faculty of Advocates in 1873 by J. H. A. Macdonald, later Lord Justice-Clerk Kingsburgh, whose father had married, as his third wife, Hume's second daughter.[93] Finally, with the consent of Hume's then living heir, the *Lectures* were edited by Dr. G. Campbell H. Paton and published by the Stair Society in six volumes over the years 1939–58.

The manuscript bears many additions, corrections and interpolations resulting from Hume's regular revision to take account of new statutes, decisions and changes in his own views. There are many notes giving the dates where he began or ended particular topics in particular years.

Since their publication by the Stair Society the *Lectures* have become more generally available and have been cited in modern cases.[94] In a case before the Whole Court in 1942 in which Volume I had been cited,[95] the consulted judges in their opinion said:

"We are, however, unable to treat Hume's lectures as a book of institutional authority, and, since they may be referred to in other cases hereafter, and their publication may be followed by other similar publications of manuscripts hitherto unpublished, we take this opportunity of stating the reasons for our opinion on this point. Baron Hume was a very distinguished lawyer, and his treatise on the Criminal Law (published in 1797) ranks along with the other institutional works to which we pay homage in our law. But these lectures were not prepared for publication by Baron Hume, and they are not *in pari casu* with a treatise written with a view to publication, although published posthumously.[96] They are not, in our opinion, of comparable authority with his treatise on the Criminal Law, because they do not come into the world with his final approval and authority. Their historical value is high, and they are of great value in ascertaining what the law was supposed to be at the date when they were delivered by a lawyer of great eminence. In *Kerr* v. *Martin*,[97] notes taken by his former students were referred to by learned judges as evidence of the general and understood state of the law, but they were not put upon the same plane as the works of the recognised institutional writers. Baron Hume left the chair of Scots Law in 1822 and became a Baron of Exchequer. He survived till 1838. He published his Reports of Decisions in 1829.[98] If he had desired to publish his lectures, he had ample opportunity for doing so, and from these dates alone the inference should be drawn that he was averse to publishing them, even if this were not known with much greater certainty from other circumstances.[99] The publication of the lectures a century after his death by the Stair Society, for which we should be grateful, cannot be held to have made available to us and our successors a new and authoritative source of Scots law."

Similarly Lord Justice-Clerk Cooper observed:[1]

"I attach importance to the views expressed by Mackenzie in his Observations on the Act 1573, cap. 55, More in his Notes to Stair, and Lord Ivory in his Notes to Erskine; and in the same category I would place the Lectures of Baron Hume, with regard to which I agree with your Lordship in the chair in thinking that, while they have no claim to the veneration attaching to our recognised institutional works, they are entitled to be regarded in the light in which they were viewed by the consulted judges in *Kerr* v. *Martin*, that is, as 'authority of very great weight' and as 'decisive evidence of the general and understood state of the law' at the time when Baron Hume lectured."

Lord Mackay[2] concurred in these observations.

While thus denying institutional rank to the lectures, whether as recorded by students or as printed, the court did not prohibit or even deprecate citation of them, but they have the same weight of persuasive authority as highly-regarded contemporaneous textbooks. The lectures have in fact been cited as authority in a number of later cases.[3] In *Wills' Trs.* v. *Cairngorm School Ltd.*[4] Lord President Emslie discusses Hume's view under the heading of "the authoritative commentators or text book writers"[5] and Lord Cameron observed,[6] "While the authority and respect due to writers of the stature of Professor Bell and Baron Hume is great. . . ."

The *Lectures* appear accordingly by their posthumous publication to have taken rank as one of the standard textbooks, though not of institutional rank, as are his *Commentaries* in matters of criminal law.

Hume must also from early in his academic career have begun research into and writing on the criminal law, and following John Millar's example, offered a summer course on criminal law. There was published in 1797 in two volumes *Commentaries on the Law of Scotland respecting the Description and Punishment of Crimes.* "I now offer to the public," he stated in the Introduction,[7] "the substance of those observations on the description and punishment of crimes, which, in the discharge of my duty, as Professor of the Law of Scotland in the University of Edinburgh, I have for some years had occasion to deliver, as part of a course of Academical lectures." Mackenzie's *Matters Criminal* "was a valuable present to the lawyers of his day, but later times have added almost nothing to our stock of knowledge in this department."[8] Erskine's *Institute* professes to treat of criminal law. "But of this part of his work which at any rate is much too brief to be of any material service in real business I may be allowed to say (for in this I am not pretending to lead, but am following the public opinion) that it is not of the same high authority as the other. . . . The same remark is no less applicable to Mr. Forbes's *Institute of the Criminal Law*; which is little more than a set of hasty notes of the contents of our statutes, without any enquiry into what has been argued or decided."[8] "In this penury therefore, of information, having, in the course of my duty as Public Teacher of the Law, particularly directed my attention to the department of Crimes; and having gone over the whole series of the Books of Adjournal (for so the records of the Court of Justiciary are called); I hope I may at least be excused for the attempt of saving others the labour of the like research, for which not many persons can be supposed to have either leisure or inclination."[9] He adverts also to his desire "of rescuing the law of my native country from that state of declension in the esteem of some part of the public, into which, of late years, it seems to have been falling; owing, I am persuaded, to this more than any other cause, that they are ignorant of what it really is. This disposition, in particular, appears in those multiplied references to the Criminal Law of England, and those frequent and extravagant encomiums on the English practice, in preference to our own."[10] Hume was not at all an Angliciser.

He observes in relation to capital crimes:
"I am certain that I am within the truth, when I mention, that on an average of thirty years preceding the year 1797, the executions for all Scotland have not exceeded six in a year. For a period of fifteen years, preceding the 1st May 1782, the number of persons who suffered death at Edinburgh (where by far the greater number of capital trials take place) amounted only to twenty-three. . . ."[11]
"In regard to the sources from which my information has been drawn. I shall begin with a word or two respecting the Law of Rome; which some may think deserving of notice, not only as being the law of a great and civilized people, but even as having pretensions to some sort of authority in our Courts. But it seems to be the better opinion (and such are the sentiments of Sir Thomas Craig, and of

Lord Stair) that even in the civil department, the Roman Law never attained to a binding authority, like that of our own customs or statutes; nor came to be in any other sense our law, than as it was long ago, in particular matters, made a rule of judgment, and thus incorporated into our common law by the decisions of our Courts; or farther than is agreeable to equity and reason, or suitable to our situation, and analogous to the rest of our system."[12] "The main store from which I have drawn the materials of this treatise, is therefore the books of adjournal (or records of the Court of Justiciary) containing the pleading of the Bar and the judgments of Court and which extend (though with several interruptions in the sixteenth century and one of six years [1655 to 1661] in the seventeenth), from November 1524, down to the present time. I have gone over the whole with attention. . . . There is, in the Advocates' Library, a manuscript abridgment of the records of Justiciary; and of this I have also made use (but never without marking it as my authority), for those periods of which the original records have perished; for this abridgment must have been made at a time when the books of adjournal were more complete than they are now. These memorials of our custom, along with Lord Royston's[13] manuscript Notes upon Mackenzie, which contain many judicious remarks and much valuable information, have been the main ground-work of this undertaking."[14]

In Chapter 1, Hume treats of the nature of crimes, dealing with dole, the pleas of minority, insanity, sudden frenzy, intoxication, subjection, compulsion, superior orders, and compulsion by want, and then proceeds in successive chapters to discuss all the main kinds of crimes. Most of the authorities are statutes, and cases, referred to by date only, from the Books of Adjournal.

In 1800 there appeared, also in two volumes, a companion work, *Commentaries on the Law of Scotland respecting Trial for Crimes*. He deals with courts of criminal jurisdiction, arrest and precognition, commitment and bail, and so on to verdict, sentence and execution, pardon and process of review.

In 1814 Hume published a *Supplement* bringing both works up-to-date, and in 1819 a second edition in two volumes (sometimes bound in one) each containing a revised version of one of the earlier works, and re-titled *Commentaries on the Law of Scotland respecting Crimes*. There was a third edition in 1829 and a fourth, with a Supplement by Benjamin Robert Bell,[15] in two volumes, in 1844. The supplemental notes are extensive, running to 300 pages.

The *Commentaries* were obviously the biggest and the most detailed and thorough examination of Scottish criminal law and procedure hitherto published, and founded on the most painstaking examination of the unpublished records of the Court of Justiciary, a labour never before undertaken and unlikely ever to be repeated. They were immediately accepted as of high authority, and every subsequent textbook on the subject regularly cites Hume as the authority for many propositions.

Cockburn observed[16] that it and Bell's *Commentaries* were works "that will ever hold their places in our system"; he continues, however:

"Hume's work was composed in a great measure for the purpose of vindicating the proceedings of the Criminal Court in the recent cases of sedition,[17] and was therefore hailed with the loudest acclamations by the friends of those whose proceedings stood so much in need of defence. But we are far enough now from the passions of those days to enable us to appreciate its merits more candidly. And the judgment of the public is right in having decided that, for ordinary practice, it is a most useful work, the importance of which can scarcely be understood by those who have never had to grope their way amidst the darkness which he removed, and that there its merits end. But his admirers disdain this praise, and maintain it to be a great work of original thought, and the model of a criminal system, the supposed imperfections of which the author has shown not to exist. They will not allow his style to be heavy and affected, his delineation of principle superficial, his views on all matters of expediency or reason narrow, indeed monastic. The proceedings of the savage old Scotch Privy Council are held up by him as judicial precedents, even in political cases, at the end of the eighteenth century. The impeachable domineering of Braxfield in 1794 is just as commendable in his pages as if the times had been moderate, and the judge impartial. As an institutional writer, he certainly could not exclude either ancient or modern proceedings from his view; and he was perfectly entitled to put his own value on them. So was any mere chronicler of legal events. But before any one can deserve the praise of being an enlightened expounder of a system of law not previously explained or methodised, and of first delivering to the people the rules which they must obey, and ought to admire, the past actings of courts ought not to be merely stated, but to be criticised and appreciated, so that future tribunals may be guided, and the public instructed, on defects and remedies. On such matters there is no book that has worse stood the test of time. There is scarcely one of his favourite points that the legislature, with the cordial assent of the public and of lawyers, has not put down."

Lord Justice-Clerk Hope said that Hume was one "whose authority is so great, and whose services to the law are so incomparably beyond any writer on any branch of the law of Scotland except Lord Stair."[18]

Hume's *Commentaries* were cited in a number of cases in the early nineteenth century, while he was still in the chair of Scots Law.

Hume's views have been canvassed in all the leading criminal cases, such as *Greenhuff*,[19] which accepted his proposition that the High Court had an inherent power to punish every act of a criminal nature even though in the past it has never been the subject of prosecution,[20] *Sugden*,[21] which examined whether prescription applied to crime, and *Brennan*,[22] which considered whether self-induced intoxication could amount to diminished responsibility. It is quite pointless to list all the innumerable cases in which Hume's statements have been accepted as authoritative or at least as a guide to the decision of the matter before the court.

The *Commentaries* did not escape criticism. Hill Burton,[23] Cockburn[24] and the *Edinburgh Review*[25] criticised the style; the *Edinburgh Review* and the *North British Review*[26] found an absence of philosophy or general principle, such as Stair had provided for civil law, a lack of insistence on civil and religious liberties, a conservative attitude towards change, and a politically unacceptable view of public law.[27]

In his testamentary settlement of July 31, 1832, Hume excepted from the prohibition on publication of his manuscripts "a large collection of Reports of Decisions" which only required to be arranged alphabetically to be published in the form of a dictionary, and he committed the care of the publication and revisal to John Hay Forbes, Lord Medwyn,[28] and Adam Urquhart, advocate.[29] These literary executors complied with their instructions and published Hume's *Decisions* in 1839, a volume of 900 pages. The decisions extend over 1781–1822 and cover every subject of the law of Scotland, are mostly cases otherwise unreported, and are valuable, apart from the actual record of facts and decision, for the frequently lengthy notes added by Hume to many cases. They are also notably clear reports, with catchwords indicating the points at issue and mention of the counsel engaged.

It has became apparent that the notes are frequently very similarly worded to the treatment of the same topic in Hume's *Lectures*. The reports have sometimes been criticised[30] and it has been observed[31] with reference to Lord Deas's dissenting opinion in an earlier case[32] that "professional opinion of Hume's *Reports* is not so high as was Lord Deas's respect for his notes of Hume's *Lectures*."

Hume had in his copies of the Session Papers frequently made careful manuscript annotations on judges' opinions or observations, and not only did these provide materials for his *Lectures* and his *Decisions* but they have themselves been founded on by later scholars.[33] In *Adams* v. *McWilliam, Thomson* v. *Lindsay*[34] Lord Justice-Clerk Hope observed that "the other counsel on the same side, the late Baron Hume, when going over his Session Papers in later life, with a view to the volume of Reports which he drew up, and for each volume of which papers he prepared a very neat and careful index thus enters the papers for [a case under consideration]." In *Wills' Trs.* v. *Cairngorm School Ltd.*[35] Lord Wilberforce mentions among "weighty material" put before the House of Lords excerpts from the Hume collection bearing upon later causes which threw light on what was truly decided in an important but inadequately reported precedent.

Hume accordingly, quite apart from his great influence as a teacher, stands in the front rank of the Scottish jurists. He is the supreme text-writer on the criminal law, compiler of a valuable dictionary of decisions, and by virtue of the posthumous editing and publication of his lectures, has taken rank as author of a valuable text on civil or private law also.

NOTES

[1] On him see Chap. 18, *supra*.

[2] J. Y. T. Greig, *David Hume* (1931), pp. 63, 265. See also Kay's *Edinburgh Portraits*, II, 72.

[3] DNB; Anderson, S.N., II, p. 507; G. C. H. Paton, *Biography of Baron Hume* in *Baron Hume's Lectures, 1786–1822* (Stair Soc.) VI, p. 327.

[4] W. Steven, *History of the High School of Edinburgh* (1849), pp. 14, 122, 208.

[5] W. I. Addison, *Matriculation Albums of the University of Glasgow* 1728–1858 (1913), p. 112.

[6] Hill Burton, *Life and Correspondence of David Hume* (1846), II, p. 479; J. Y. T. Greig, *The Letters of David Hume* (1932) II, p. 305.

[7] D. Murray, *Memories of the Old College of Glasgow* (1927), p. 223.

[8] Hill Burton, II, p. 454; Mossner, pp. 593, 606.

[9] There is a calendar of the letters in (1932) 52 *Proc. R.S.E.* 3. Many are printed in Hill Burton, and Greig.

[10] He may henceforth be so designated as the chance of confusion between the historian-philosopher uncle and the lawyer-nephew is minimal from this point.

[11] This house was situated in the High Street: David Murray, *Memories of the Old College*, pp. 227, 397.

[12] (1758–1819, advocate 1779); DNB; Omond, *Lord Advocates*, II, p. 178; Omond, *Arniston Memoirs* (1887), Chaps. 11–12.

[13] "Hume was in the daily observation of all the proceedings of the Court and of all the cases which occurred during the very long period in which he held the chair": *Kerr* v. *Martin* (1840) 2 D. 752, at p. 777, opinion of the consulted judges.

[14] *Life of Jeffrey*, I, p. 87.

[15] Walter Scott was a colleague: Lockhart, *Life*, I, p. 206.

[16] R. Robertson, *History and Present Constitution of the Sheriff Courts of Scotland* (1863); see also (1899) 6 S.L.T. (News) 18.

[17] Passed as the Treason Act 1795, later mostly repealed.

[18] Passed as the Seditious Meetings Act 1795, and repealed 1869.

[19] On the whole affair see further DNB, *s.v.* Erskine, Henry; Cockburn, *Life of Jeffrey*, I, p. 94; H. Brougham, *Life and Times of Henry Brougham* (1871), I, p. 229; Omond, *Lord Advocates*, II, p. 168; A. Fergusson, *The Hon. Henry Erskine* (1882), pp. 354, 544.

[20] Cockburn, *Memorials*, p. 84, Cranstoun later became Lord Corehouse.

[21] On him see Chaps. 20 and 24, *infra*.

[22] On the dispute see A. Grant, *History of the University of Edinburgh* II, p. 8.

[23] *Edinburgh Magistrates* v. *Edinburgh Professors* (1829) 7 S. 255.

[24] *University of Edinburgh* v. *Edinburgh Magistrates* (1851) 14 D. 74; (1854) 17 D. (H.L.) 8; I Macq. 485.

[25] I Macq. at p. 503.

[26] *History of the Speculative Society* (1845), p. 22.

[27] *Trans. R.S.E.*, I, 83.

[28] *Trans. R.S.E.*, II, 63–75.

[29] J. H. A. Macdonald, *Life Jottings of an Old Edinburgh Citizen*, p. 112; *Fifty Years of It*, p. 80; Macdonald, later Lord Justice-Clerk, a zealous volunteer, had Hume's sword.

[30] W. I. Addison, *Roll of Graduates of the University of Glasgow, 1727–1897* (1898), p. 277.

[31] *Letters of Sir Walter Scott* (ed. H. J. C. Grierson, Centenary ed.), IV, 313.

[32] *Ibid.*, IV, 443.

[33] *Caledonian Mercury*, January 10, 1822; *Edinburgh Advertiser*, January 11, 1822.

[34] *Ross* v. *Macleod* (1861) 23 D. 972, at p. 994, *per* Lord Deas.

[35] *Scotsman*, March 2, 1822; *Caledonian Mercury*, March 2, 1822.

[36] *Scotsman*, November 16, 1822.

[37] *Edinburgh Advertiser*, April 16, 1822; *Scotsman*, April 20, 1822.

[38] *Caledonian Mercury*, January 24, 1822.

[39] *Caledonian Mercury*, January 31, 1822.

[40] In Signet Library, copy in Parliament Hall. T. Grainger Stewart, *The Portraits in Parliament House* (1907), No. 38.

[41] Cockburn, *Journals*, I, pp. 57–58.

⁴² Process in Courts of Law (Scotland) Act 1823.

⁴³ *Report of the Commissioners for Inquiring into the Forms of Process in the Courts of Law in Scotland and the Course of Appeals from the Court of Session to the House of Lords*, 1824 (C. 241).

⁴⁴ Exchequer Court (Scotland) Act 1832.

⁴⁵ The mansion was rebuilt in 1740 and 1841, in each case after a fire. It is described in R. Chambers, *The Book of Days*, I, p. 555, and there is a drawing in Drummond, *History of Noble British Families*, Vol. II.

⁴⁶ Paton, *Biography*, p. 400, gives examples.

⁴⁷ *Lectures* I, 2.

⁴⁸ *Ibid.*, I, 6.

⁴⁹ Blackstone, *Commentaries on the Law of England*, I, 22.

⁵⁰ *Lectures*, I, 7–8.

⁵¹ *Ibid.*, I, 8.

⁵² *Ibid.*, I, 8–9.

⁵³ *Ibid.*, I, 9.

⁵⁴ *Ibid.*, I, 9–10. This is in effect merely the distinction between substantive law and procedure.

⁵⁵ *Ibid.*, I, 11–12.

⁵⁶ *Ibid.*, I, 13.

⁵⁷ *Ibid.*, I, 14.

⁵⁸ *Ibid.*, I, 14–15.

⁵⁹ *Ibid.*, I, 16–17.

⁶⁰ Stair Soc. ed., Vol. I.

⁶¹ Vol. II.

⁶² Vol. III.

⁶³ Vol. IV.

⁶⁴ Vol. V.

⁶⁵ Vol. V.

⁶⁶ Vol. VI.

⁶⁷ Paton, *Biography*, pp. 404–405. It should be remembered that there were no degrees in law, no curricula, no examinations required, and attendance on the class was entirely voluntary. While there were other law classes there was no prescribed order of study. Men seeking to be called to the Bar had to be examined in the civil law or the Scots law and attendance on the courses was valuable preparation; men becoming writers or law agents were examined by a few senior men of the local Faculty of Procurators.

⁶⁸ Autobiographical fragment, "The Ashiestiel Memoir," in Lockhart's *Life of Scott* (Macmillan's Library of English Classics ed.), I, p. 45.

⁶⁹ *Ibid.*, I, p. 157.

⁷⁰ C. E. Norton, *Early Letters of Thomas Carlyle* (1886), I, 249.

⁷¹ *Ibid.*, I, 254.

⁷² *Ibid.*, I, 261.

⁷³ Possibly a reference to Virgil's *infandum, regina, iubes renovare dolorem*: *Aeneid*, II, 3.

⁷⁴ *Ibid.*, I, 300.

⁷⁵ Report in *Caledonian Mercury*, January 31, 1822, quoted in Paton, *Biography* p. 392.

⁷⁶ *Caledonian Mercury*, January 24, 1822.

⁷⁷ *Caledonian Mercury*, January 31, 1822; *Edinburgh Advertiser*, February 1, 1822.

⁷⁸ Quoted in Advertisement to Hume's *Decisions* (1839).

⁷⁹ *e.g. Rose* v. *Ross* (1827) 5 S. 605, at p. 636 (594 N.E.) *per* Lord Meadowbank: "of one of the highest authorities in the law of Scotland"; *Sim* v. *Miles* (1829) 8 S. 89, at p. 98, *per* Lord Pitmilly; *Walker's Trs* v. *Mansfield* (1832) 11 S. 830; 1 Sh. & McL. 203, at p. 245 *per* Lord Craigie; *Murray* v. *Maclachlan* (1838) 1 D. 294, at p. 298 *per* Lord MacKenzie; *Kerr* v. *Martin* (1840) 2 D. 752, at p. 777, *per* consulted judges; 785 (narrative); 792–793, *per* Lord MacKenzie; 801, *per* Lord President Hope; *Barns* v. *Barns' Trs.* (1857) 19 D. 626, at p. 651, *per* Lord Deas – "that eminent lawyer"; *Henderson* v. *Burt* (1858) 20 D. 402, at p. 405, *per* Lord Handyside; *Grant* v. *Grant's Trs.* (1859) 22 D. 53, at p. 72, *per* Lord Deas: "I studied under that great lawyer"; *Lindsay* v. *L.N.W. Ry* (1860) 22 D. 571, at p. 598, *per* Lord Deas; *Ross* v. *McLeod* (1861) 23 D. 972, at p. 994, *per* Lord Deas; *Thompson* v. *Whitehead* (1862) 24 D. 331, 336; *Christie* v. *Ruxton* (1862) 24 D. 1182, at p. 1186, *per* Lord Benholme; note also Lord Cowan's reference to "our venerable instructor"; *Morris* v. *Riddick* (1867) 5

M. 1037, 1044, *per* Lord Deas; 1046, *per* Lord Ardmillan; *Agnew* v. *Lord Advocate* (1872) 11 M. 309, at p. 327, *per* Lord Cowan; *Kermack* v. *Kermack* (1874) 2 R. 156, at p. 161, *per* Lord Deas; *Auld* v. *Hay* (1880) 7 R. 663, at p. 673–674, *per* Lord Deas; *Biggart* v. *City of Glasgow Bank* (1879) 6 R. 470, 475 *per* Lord Deas; "one of the most learned lawyers of his day"; *Reid* v. *Reid* (1897) 11 S.L.T. 529, at p. 531, *per* Lord Kincairney. See also reference back in *Surtees* v. *Wotherspoon* (1873) 11 M. 384, 386.

[80] (1840) 2 D. 752.

[81] *Ibid.*, at p. 777, *per* the consulted judges. They add that the late Lord Newton (Mr. Irving) while professor of civil law laid down the same doctrine in his lectures both on the *Institutes* and the *Pandects*. (Alexander Irving, 1766–1832, advocate 1788) was professor of Civil Law 1800–26 and judge as Lord Newton 1826–32. This is much lower authority. The judges refer also to the then Professor of Law (Bell) and to More's notes on Stair.

[82] *Ibid.*, 785.

[83] In the pleadings.

[84] Lord Mackenzie took the class in 1797–99.

[85] *Ibid.*, pp. 792–793.

[86] *Ibid.*, p. 801.

[87] (1826), p. 28.

[88] (1840), pp. 51, 58, 60.

[89] (3rd ed., 1882) pp. 84, 163.

[90] (1854), p. 648.

[91] (1826), p. 94. This book is dedicated to Baron Hume.

[92] (1824, 1827 and 1834).

[93] Macdonald, *Life Jottings of an Old Edinburgh Citizen*, p. 113; *Fifty Years of It*, p. 80.

[94] *e.g. Bell* v. *Bell*, 1940 S.C. 229, at p. 261, *per* Lord Wark.

[95] *Fortington* v. *Kinnaird*, 1942 S.C. 239, at p. 253 *per* consulted judges.

[96] This is a reference to Erskine's *Institutes*. The same is true of Hume's own *Decisions*, though this is a dictionary of decisions, not a treatise.

[97] (1840) 2 D. 752.

[98] This is a mistake. They were by his authority prepared for publication by literary executors and published posthumously, in 1839.

[99] *i.e.* from the prohibition in his settlement.

[1] at p. 265.

[2] at p. 276.

[3] *Sinclair* v. *Juner*, 1952 S.C. 35, at p. 43, *per* Lord President Cooper; *Pettigrew* v. *Harton*, 1956 S.C. 67, 73, 74, 77; *MacLennan* v. *MacLennan*, 1958 S.C. 105, at p. 108 *per* Lord Wheatley; *Thomson* v. *St. Cuthbert's Co-operative Assocn. Ltd.*, 1958 S.C. 380, 394, 398; *N.C.B.* v. *Thomson*, 1959 S.C. 353, at pp. 381–382, *per* Lord Strachan; *Cole-Hamilton* v. *Boyd*, 1962 S.C. 247, at p. 257; *Mill's Trs.* v. *Mill's Trs.* 1965 S.C. 384, at p. 394 *per* Lord Migdale; *Balshaw* v. *Balshaw*, 1967 S.C. 63, at p. 83, *per* Lord Migdale; *Wills' Trs* v. *Cairngorm School Ltd.* 1976 S.C. (H.L.) 30, at p. 48 *per* Lord Maxwell; 76, 80 *per* Lord President Emslie; Hume's *Lectures* were cited also in the House of Lords (pp. 113, 126, 141, 146, 164) and referred to among "the writers" (p. 121); *Sloan's Dairies* v. *Glasgow Corpn.*, 1977 S.C. 223, at p. 240, *per* Lord Dunpark; *Wolifson* v. *Harrison*, 1977 S.C. 384, at p. 392 *per* Lord Justice-Clerk Wheatley, at pp. 391–392 *per* Lord Stott.

[4] 1976 S.C. (H.L.) 30.

[5] at pp. 79–80.

[6] at p. 98, also pp. 99, 100.

[7] p. xxxvii.

[8] p. xxxviii.

[9] p. xli.

[10] p. xlii

[11] p. 1. This is very important in view of the common misapprehension that hanging was an everyday penalty at that period.

[12] pp. lvii-lviii

[13] Sir James Mackenzie of Royston (?1670–1744, advocate 1698), son of Sir George Mackenzie, first Earl of Cromarty, and husband of Elizabeth, youngest daughter of Sir George Mackenzie of Rosehaugh, was a Lord of Session and Justiciary 1710–44. He is said to have been "a person of vast learning . . . justly ranked among the first judges, in criminal causes, of the age. . . .": Brunton & Haig, p. 490.

[14] p. lxii.

[15] 1810–86, advocate 1832.

[16] *Memorials*, pp. 56–57.

[17] It hardly seems credible that any author would have undertaken such a large book, founded on infinite research, to justify some particular trials. This can at most have been a subsidiary purpose.

[18] *H.M. Advocate* v. *Grant* (1848) J. Shaw 17, at p. 92. This is a bit hard on Erskine and Bell.

[19] (1838) 2 Swinton 236.

[20] For the exercise of this power see *Strathern* v. *Seaforth*, 1926 J.C. 100.

[21] 1934 J.C. 103.

[22] 1977 J.C. 38.

[23] *Life and Correspondence of David Hume*, II, p. 402.

[24] *Memorials*, p. 156.

[25] (1846) Vol. 83, pp. 196–223 (this was written by Cockburn).

[26] (1846) IV, pp. 313–346 (said to be by James Crawford, Lord Ardmillan).

[27] *Scotsman*, January 26 and November 16, 1822.

[28] 1776–1854, advocate 1799, Lord Medwyn 1825–54.

[29] 1794–1860, advocate 1815, Sheriff of Wigton 1843–60.

[30] *e.g. Wilson* v. *Wright* (1816) Hume 537, criticised in *Wilson's Trs*. v. *Wilson* (1856) 18 D. 1096, at pp. 1103, 1104, 1114: "he had entirely mistaken the case".

[31] *Johnston* v. *Tillie, Whyte & Co.*, 1917 S.C. 211, at p. 223, *per* Lord Johnston. He observes also that Lord Deas' "reliance on Hume is matter of notoriety."

[32] *Thomson* v. *Stiven* (1868) 6 M. 777, at p. 782.

[33] Thus Bell in his *Commentaries*, and George Ross in his *Leading Cases*, frequently make reference to notes in Hume's *Session Papers*. So too Lord Fraser on *Husband and Wife, e.g.* (2nd ed., 1876), I, 28.

[34] (1849) 11 D. 719, at p. 733.

[35] 1976 S.C. (H.L.) 30 at p. 118; see also pp. 136, 161, 162.

CHAPTER 20

GEORGE JOSEPH BELL

THE Reverend William Bell, an Episcopalian clergyman resident in Edinburgh in the latter part of the eighteenth century, had six children, four of whom attained distinction. The eldest son Robert (?–1816) became a Writer to the Signet in 1784, lecturer in conveyancing to the W.S. Society, and author of many books on property law[1]; he became an advocate in 1812. The second son John (1763–1820)[2] became a distinguished surgeon, the third son George Joseph became a notable jurist, and the youngest of the family, Charles (1774–1842)[3] became a famous anatomist and surgeon, who made fundamental discoveries about the human nervous system, was knighted, and became professor of surgery at Edinburgh in 1836.

George Joseph Bell,[4] the brother with whom we are concerned, was born in Fountainbridge, Edinburgh, on March 26, 1770, and is said to have been mainly self-educated at home. He attended Hume's lectures on Scots law at Edinburgh University in 1787–88, passed advocate on November 19, 1791, and devoted himself seriously to the study of the subject of his profession. In 1806 he married Barbara Shaw of Ayr; his youngest brother Charles married her younger sister; and their brother was Patrick Shaw (1796–1872, advocate 1819),[5] reporter, editor of some editions of Bell's works, and Sheriff of Chancery 1848–69.

In 1800–04 Bell published a two-volume *Treatise on the Law of Bankruptcy in Scotland* and reshaped this in its second edition in 1810 into a *Commentaries on the Law of Scotland in relation to Mercantile and Maritime Law, Moveable and Heritable Rights and Bankruptcy*. Further editions followed in 1816–19 and 1821. In 1816–18, after the death of his brother Robert, he gave the latter's lectures on conveyancing to the W.S. apprentices, prior to the appointment of MacVey Napier (1776–1847, W.S. 1799)[6] as lecturer (till 1824 and thereafter, till 1847, as the first professor of conveyancing).

This work brought him a reputation for scholarship but success in practice did not follow, though his name appears among counsel in a number of cases in the first years of the nineteenth century, and in January 1822, on David Hume's resignation, Bell was unanimously nominated by the Faculty of Advocates to the Town Council to fill the vacant chair. He was almost 52 and several junior to him had already gone on the Bench. The nomination was moved by John Clerk of Eldin, leader of the Bar, and seconded by Sir Walter Scott. As author of the *Commentaries*, already in its fourth edition, he was the obvious candidate. The Town Council appointed him on February 27[7] and he gave his inaugural lecture on November 12 when he spoke with becoming diffidence of his own powers and exaggerated in some degree those of his predecessor.[8] In the same year Bell was elected F.R.S.E.

In 1823 he was made a member of a commission appointed to inquire into the forms of process in the courts and the course of appeals from the Court of Session to the House of Lords and he drafted the report which was the basis for the Court of Session (Judicature) Act 1825. This gave rise to a book *An Examination of the Objections stated against the Bill for better regulating the Forms of Process in the Courts of Scotland*. In 1832 he succeeded Scott as one of the Principal Clerks of Session and in 1833 was made chairman of the royal commission appointed to make proposals for what became the Bankruptcy (Scotland) Act 1839 and he is believed to have been the chief draftsman of the Act.[9]

Bell "projected a course of lectures on criminal and constitutional law, but he never carried his design into effect."[10] There was accordingly no teaching of criminal law in his time.

Bell was very friendly with Francis Jeffrey and dedicated later editions of the *Principles* to him. In a letter to Bell of November 1830[11] Jeffrey wrote: "I love and esteem you beyond any man upon earth." As Lord Advocate, Jeffrey (who held that office from December 1830 to May 1834) "thought himself almost sufficiently rewarded for having taken office, by the power which it gave him of obtaining one of the principal Clerkships in the Court of Session for George Joseph Bell. He would have made him a judge if there had been a vacancy; and certainly no man had ever a stronger claim, so far as such claims depend on eminent fitness, than Mr. Bell had for a seat on that Bench, which his great legal work had been instructing and directing for above thirty years."[12]

Bell died on September 23, 1843. Cockburn heard of Bell's death on October 1:

> "When here [Bonaly] I received intimation of the death of my old friend, George Joseph Bell, Clerk of Session, and Professor of Scotch Law, and destined to be known to posterity as the author of the book on Bankruptcy.[13] His death was not to be regretted – old, blind, poor and getting poorer and never forgetting the disgraceful treatment which excluded him from the Bench because he would not be dishonest,[14] life for him had lost most of its attractions. There could not possibly be a better man, and he is the greatest legal writer in Scotland next to Stair.[15] It is not, perhaps, too much to say that his work is the greatest practical book on Mercantile Jurisprudence that has been produced in modern times."[16]

It has been said of Bell that he was "of a genial disposition and courteous manners, and appears to have had a larger culture than is common among lawyers."[17] His manuscripts were entrusted to his brother-in-law Patrick Shaw, who had been involved in the later editions of Bell's works and himself produced the first editions of both the *Commentaries* and the *Principles* after Bell's death.

Bell's first book, as has been mentioned, was *A Treatise on the Law of Bankruptcy in Scotland*, renamed in the second edition (1810) as *Commentaries on the Law of Scotland and on the Principles of Mercantile Jurisprudence*. He himself edited further editions (all in two volumes) in 1816–19 and 1821 and, after bring appointed to the Chair, again in 1826. After his death, his brother-in-law Patrick Shaw produced a sixth edition in 1858[18] and in 1870 John McLaren, Sheriff of Chancery, and later a judge,[19] edited in two volumes the definitive edition, extensively annotated to bring the law up-to-date.

"During the latter half of the eighteenth century Scottish commercial enterprise had been steadily growing with increasing vigour. . . . But Scotland was still virtually devoid of any system of Mercantile Law worthy of the name. . . . By the time Bell first turned his attention to the question, the need for the development and elaboration of Commercial Law was clamant; and he determined to collect and to systematise the universal Law Merchant, to extract its principles and practice from English and foreign sources, and to reconcile these principles with the fundamental doctrines of Scots law. This ambitious and exceptionally difficult project required that the learned author should not merely set out the law as it had been declared to be, but the law as it probably was, and as it ought to be; for he had practically no detailed and technically authoritative precedent upon which to rely."[20]

In his Preface, Bell observed that the mercantile branch of law had been comparatively neglected in Scotland until the latter part of the eighteenth century. The first bankrupt law was passed in 1772.

"It is from that time only that the rise of the mercantile law in Scotland is to be dated, and that the attention of our lawyers and judges began to be directed judicially to commercial dealings. . . . In the dearth of materials afforded by the books of the Scottish law, it was natural, or necessary, to look abroad for aid – to the writings of foreign lawyers, and the decisions of foreign courts: And the occasion was such as to justify the use of such authorities.

"The Law Merchant[21] is universal: It is a part of the law of nations, grounded upon the principles of natural equity, as regulating the transactions of men who reside in different countries, and carry on the intercourse of nations, independently of the local customs and municipal laws of particular states. For the illustration of this law, the decisions of courts, and the writings of lawyers in different countries, are as the recorded evidence of the application of the general principle; not making the law, but handing it down; not to be quoted as precedents, or as authorities to be implicitly followed, but to be taken as guides towards the establishment of the pure principles of general jurisprudence.

"This general law merchant is, in England, said to form part of the common law: . . . But the same principle operates as in England; and our courts are daily in the habit of proceeding on this Law-Merchant as fully authoritative in Scotland, and of allowing the decisions of courts, and the writings of lawyers, to be cited in illustration of it . . . the English books afford valuable aid in cultivating the subject of mercantile law."

It seems a serious over-statement to say that the law merchant was universal, part of the law of nations. There was no defined body of law merchant, but only a good deal of more or less common practices, of borrowing and adaptation, of widespread acceptance of rules and usages and absence of technicality. It was never put together authoritatively as were the Roman law and the canon law, but was a body of practices, often different from local law but acquiesced in for mercantile transactions and frequently enforced by tribunals outside the official system of courts of the territory. These usages might be recognised and accepted in particular countries, as they were by the King's Bench under Lord Mansfield, and ultimately embodied in legislation such as the Bills of Exchange Acts, but there never was a universal law-merchant. Bell did, however, perform an important function in suggesting to Scottish judges and lawyers, on the basis of foreign treatises and decisions on mercantile topics, how problems arising out of commercial relations might be solved. He helped to bring to the notice of Scots lawyers such texts as Beawes' *Lex Mercatoria* (1720), Domat's *Civil Law* (1722), Casaregis' *Discursus Legales de Commercio* (1719); Emerigon's *Traité des Assurances* (1783), Malynes' *Consuetudo vel Lex Mercatoria* (1622); Millar on *Insurance* (1787); Park on *Marine Insurance* (1787); Pardessus's *Cours de Droit Commercial* (1825); Pothier's works, Valin's *Nouveau Commentaire sur l'Ordonnance de la Marine* (1760) and, of course, the decisions of the English courts.[22]

He refers to the work of Lord Mansfield in developing a system of mercantile jurisprudence,[23] and continues:

> "But in the use of those materials a task of great delicacy remained to be performed. England and Scotland were, by the Articles of Union, placed so entirely on the same footing in all the regulations respecting trade, that the system of mercantile jurisprudence in the two countries is truly to be considered as the same; and of late years, the judgments of Westminster Hall and those of the Court of Session have, in both countries, been allowed to be quoted as the decisions of British Courts upon the mercantile law of Great Britain. Still much caution is to be observed in the adopting of English judgments as authorities in Scotland, and I state this the rather, that I think there has appeared of late some danger lest the purity of this part of jurisprudence, and the integrity of our own system of law, should be impaired by too indiscriminate a use of English authorities."

Again Bell seriously overstates the identity or even similarity between the two systems; no doubt there were and are substantial areas of similarity but on many matters there were, and still are, differences. The Union assimilated the regulation of trade in the two countries, but it did not assimilate the rules of law relative to trade. There were differences in the fundamental mercantile transaction, sale. The Mercantile Law Amendment Act (Scotland), 1856, was necessary to produce assimilation in certain areas and this was in turn largely replaced by the Bills of Exchange Act, 1882, the Factors Act 1889 and the Factors (Scotland) Act 1890, the Partnership Act 1890, and the Sale of Goods Act 1893 (now 1979). Even today there is not complete identity.

"But this book was not meant to be a commentary on mercantile law alone. In every branch of the law there has been a very remarkable progress since Mr. Erskine's time. The necessity even for a new Institute has been strongly felt. . . ." He mentions the suggestion that a modern digest or code be prepared co-operatively. "At other times we have cherished the hope as less visionary, that a very eminent person, peculiarly qualified for so great an undertaking, and in possession of invaluable materials for the purpose, might be induced to think that he should best discharge that debt which every man is said to own to his profession, by the publication of an Institute."[24] There is accordingly a good deal in the *Commentaries* which goes beyond the general understanding of a book on mercantile law.

Book I of the *Commentaries* reviews briefly and generally the law of debtor and creditor, Book II deals with the several kinds of estate which may be attached for debt, land, leaseholds, incorporeal rights and corporeal moveables, Book III with the rights of creditors by personal obligation or contract, including maritime and mercantile contracts, Book IV with preferences by securities, voluntary or judicial, over the heritable estate, Book V with real securities over the moveable estate, including diligence, Book VI with the system of the bankrupt laws, including sequestration, trust deeds for creditors and division of assets, and Book VII with partnership. Under every head there is a great deal of valuable exposition of the relevant law and of citation of earlier case law, but the treatise as a whole is most strangely organised and the law most strangely presented. A great deal of the exposition is in fact subsidiary to and explanatory of another principle, the principle of the insolvent debtor's liability. Book II,[25] for example, is headed: Of the several kinds of estate *which may be attached for debt*. Restitution against deeds granted in pupillarity or minority comes under the head of Faculties or Rights of Restitution *available to Creditors*.[26] The whole exposition of the principles of obligation and contract, extending to nearly 400 pages, commences[25]: "It will be the object of this Book to inquire into the nature and effect of those obligations from which the *jus ad rem* arises: the object of personal actions, and the ground of *demands by creditors in bankruptcy*." This is a strangely biased view: no doubt refusal or inability to pay, or insolvency, gives rise to the disputes and litigations which produce case law and highlight legal principles, but the great majority of commercial relationships are satisfactorily performed and validly paid for and discharged. Bell has a pathological approach to commercial relations; he views every relationship as a potential or actual bankruptcy. "The dark spectre of insolvency broods over every chapter, and constantly reminds the reader of the initial and abiding object with which the author wrote."[28] The fact that today one usually searches in the *Commentaries* for guidance on a particular point, and cites a particular proposition or sentence, tends to conceal the very defective structure of the work as a whole.

Even in its fifth edition of 1826, the version finally revised by him, and taken by McLaren as the basis of his standard 1870 edition,[29] Bell's *Commentaries* is seriously flawed as a systematic treatise by its development from a treatise on bankruptcy. When he remodelled it from a treatise on bankruptcy into a treatise on Scottish mercantile law it would have been much better if he had changed its structure radically. A systematic treatise on mercantile law might have dealt with mercantile persons – sole traders, firms[30] and incorporations,[31] and their agents,[32] with mercantile property,[33] with mercantile transactions, notably contracts[34] and the kinds of contracts of mercantile importance, particularly sale,[35] with rights in security,[36] with payment by bills and cheques,[37] and with mercantile remedies, including bankruptcy.[38] But Bell did not do this. He observed in a prefatory page to the fifth edition that he had "been led on gradually from edition to edition to extend this work by adding Commentaries on subjects or questions not formerly discussed. But in thus following up my original design, I have been guided invariably by what, in a practice at the Bar of five-and-thirty years, I have experienced to be chiefly useful in application to the existing state and transactions of the country, as occurring in consultation or in judicial discussion." But to the end his book still looked at everything from the standpoint of bankruptcy, and every edition brought accretions. The work was never rethought, reshaped or restructured, but just added to.

His *Commentaries on Some Detached Branches of the Law of Scotland* (1828) consists of chapters on a variety of topics, included in the fifth edition but also published separately to serve as a supplement for users of the fourth edition.

He founds extensively on Stair and Erskine and much less so on other jurists, but where Bell differs sharply from all earlier text-writers is in his extensive citation of English case law as well as of Scottish cases. Where he was dealing with statutes common to the two countries this was inevitable. But in other contexts it raises the question whether he was not too much of an Angliciser, indeed an assimilationist. It is very difficult to resist the conclusion that Bell too frequently and too readily not merely mentioned English authorities as indications of the view taken elsewhere on a point but cited them as authorities equally applicable in Scotland and to be taken as guides in Scotland.

The work was, however, well received from the start. Bell's *Commentaries* and Hume's *Commentaries* are "works that will ever hold their places in our system. Bell's is the greatest work on Scotch jurisprudence that has appeared since the publication of Lord Stair's *Institute* [sic].[39] Its authority has helped to decide probably eighty out of every hundred mercantile questions that have been settled since it began to illuminate our courts; and it has done, and will do, more for the fame of the law of Scotland in foreign countries than has been done by all our other law books put together."[40]

> "The work displays throughout a mastery of the vast and previously unknown stores of legal lore contained in the case law of England, and particularly the decisions of the new school of commercial lawyers of whom Lord Mansfield was the founder. Bell thus paved the way for that process of rapprochement between the two systems which has since enured so greatly to the advantage of both. He has been called 'the lawyer of precedent'; but the description is unjust if it suggests that undue and invertebrate dependence upon the leading strings of authority which is too often seen today; for no one ever used precedents as they ought to be used with more sagacity and discrimination than Bell. His style, though possessing no outstanding literary pretensions, has the crisp precision of a mathematical treatise, and many of his polished maxims and definitions have passed into the current coin of legal speech. A century of multifarious progress has familiarised us with ideas and doctrines undreamt

of in Bell's philosophy; but his work stands to this day as a unique and permanently valuable contribution not merely to the exposition, but to the creation of the latest and most important chapter of our law. It is not too much to say that the work of Bell was an essential link in the chain of causation which rendered possible the great expansion of Scottish industry, commerce, and banking which took place during the latter half of the nineteenth century."[41]

From an early date too the *Commentaries* were being cited in court along with Stair, Bankton and Erskine. The first reference noted is *Broadfoot* v. *Leith Banking Co.*,[42] where there is mention in judgment of "the doctrine laid down and cases quoted in Bell's *Commentaries on the Bankrupt Law*, vol. i, p. 163." In *Wrights* v. *Findlater*[43] the Lord Justice-Clerk observed: "Mr. Bell's opinion in his *Treatise on the Bankrupt Law* is against us . . . but his reasoning is overthrown by the case of. . . ." There are references to his work repeatedly in the later volumes of the Faculty Collection and the early volumes of Shaw's reports, which make it evident that he was being cited as an authority while still himself at the Bar.[44] He was cited increasingly in matters of mercantile law and bankruptcy, if only because the earlier writers had treated these topics so lightly and their views had been overtaken by the development of commercial practices and law.

This attitude continued. In *Matthew's Trs.* v. *Matthew*[45] Lord Deas, having cited Bell's *Commentaries*, observed: "I cannot forget that for more than half a century Mr. Bell's work has been the great standard of authority in this branch of the law, and it seems to me impossible to doubt, that upon this branch his opinion has been acquiesed in, and has regulated the practice in innumerable instances." In *Morrison's Trs.* v. *Webster*[46] Lord Ormidale said: "Professor Bell, the highest authority that could be appealed to on the subject states in his *Commentaries*. . . ." In *Royal Bank* v. *Commercial Bank*[47] the First Division followed a principle laid down in Bell's *Commentaries* and declined to import an English principle enunciated by Lord Chancellor Eldon.

Bell has not of course escaped criticism. In *Scott* v. *North of Scotland Banking Company*[47] Lord Ivory said: "I was at first staggered by the conflicting authority that exists in the work of Mr. Bell, whom I have looked up to with great respect. On the other hand, I felt myself under the necessity of looking into the authorities, and having gone through them all, I find that there is not enough in them to support the doctrine of Mr. Bell. Therefore I must lay aside even his authority, where I find a mere dictum unsupported by older authority or decision."

One of the unfortunate consequences of Bell's *Commentaries* and his view of the law merchant has been to foster the mistaken view that mercantile or commercial law is something distinct from civil or private law. This has been the development in some European legal systems, notably French and German law, with distinct codes for civil and commercial law, though Italian law has moved towards a unified system. But in Scots, and in English, law, mercantile or commercial law is not a branch of law but is only a convenient collective name for a number of topics of private law of particular relevance in commercial relations, some of which have been influenced historically by the law merchant, just as the law regulating other sets of legal relations has been particularly influenced historically by the civil law, or the canon law, or the feudal law. In modern times it frequently happens that topics compendiously called commercial law have to be taught to and studied by persons concerned with those topics for practical purposes and not needing or wishing to know other parts of the private law so that there are books on these topics alone, which fosters the mistaken view that it is a distinct branch of law. This unjustifiably breaks the unity of the private law. The first book in Scotland with the title Mercantile (or Commercial or Business) Law seems to have been R. Vary Campbell's *Principles of Mercantile Law* (1881). Bell did not fall into the same error in his *Principles* where sale, bills, partnership, carriage, insurance are dealt with as specific kinds of contracts, patents, trade marks and rights in security as kinds of property, and insolvency as a means of enforcement of rights.

When in 1822 Bell succeeded Hume as Professor of Scots Law at Edinburgh University, his students presumably still used Erskine's *Principles* as their textbook. Shortly thereafter he issued, for the use of the students, Outlines of his lectures. He must almost at once have set himself to write a new students' textbook, partly to suit his approach and the greater emphasis on contracts and commercial law, partly because little Erskine must already have been showing signs of being old-fashioned, outdated and already something of an old book. In 1829 accordingly there appeared Bell's *Principles of the Law of Scotland, for the use of Students in the University of Edinburgh*. The Dedication, to the Students of the Law of Scotland in the University of Edinburgh, expresses the "hope it will render your study of a very difficult science more easy, by supplying you with a brief statement of the leading rules and exceptions, and a correct list of the authorities relied on in support of the several propositions, or useful in illustrating them." It was initially, that is, a rather extensive "hand-out." He recommends to students "carefully to consult the Authorities to which I have referred, to verify the propositions which they accompany; and to take note of the practical observations, or difficulties, which arise to you in the perusal of the cases. For you may be assured that no man can become a lawyer by hearing the prelections or lessons of another, without severe study; and that none ever yet became eminent in the Law, who was not his own teacher."

His purpose, he later said, was "to exhibit for the use of students, and for the sudden occasions of practice, a concise and clear statement of the principles and rules of the law, with proofs and illustrations from decided cases of their practical application in the actual business of the bar."[49]

The book in its first edition is a substantial octavo of 584 pages, divided into four Parts, dealing respectively with Rights arising from Contract, Express or Implied, Rights of Property and Possession, of both heritage and moveables, Rights arising from Marriage and the Constitution of a Family, including succession, and Rights of Persons. There is at the end a General View of Actions and Diligence. The book is subdivided into 896 numbered sections, varying in length from two or three lines to about a couple of pages. To each section or paragraph therein is appended a list of the relevant authorities. The authorities he cites are most frequently Stair, Erskine and sometimes Pothier or occasionally some of the European writers on mercantile topics, such as Emerigon or Casaregi. Bankton, Kames and other texts are mentioned occasionally. Blackstone is also cited sometimes. He cites also statutes and Scottish reports and, on mercantile topics, such as affreightment, English cases also. It is an admirable book for its purpose, concise, clear and to the point, plain, dogmatic and not discursive.

It is interesting that Bell had departed completely from the order of treatment of Justinian, Stair and all his predecessors. Order indeed does not seem to have been very important to him. Similarly he wholly disregards philosophic issues, and even preliminary matters such as the sources of the law and their handling. Nowhere, for example, does he say whether previous decisions are binding or merely illustrative.

The *Principles* proved a very successful book. The second edition in 1830 was expanded to some 2400 sections and cited many more authorities. Two more editions followed in 1833 and 1839. By this time the last section had become Part V dealing with evidence, sentences and their execution, and bankruptcy. The sections on procedure in the third edition were dropped in the fourth because that branch had become so complicated.

In the fourth edition he wrote in the Advertisement: "In this work, and in the three volumes of *Illustrations*, I have completed my original design. My purpose was to exhibit for the use of students, and for the sudden occasions of practice, a concise and clear statement of the principles and rules of the law; with proofs and illustrations from decided cases of their practical application in the actual business of the bar." The book now ran to 900 pages and 2354 sections. The sections had become longer and the citation of authority was much more extensive, including many more English cases.

Admittedly Bell had more decided cases to rely on than his main predecessors but the advance which he made on them in systematic analysis is very striking. His classification of contracts for the purpose of proof of consent, for example, into consensual, real and written contracts, the last subdivided into writings attested, holograph and privileged, is much clearer than in the work of any previous text-writer.

After Bell's death in 1843 a further edition was produced by his brother-in-law, Patrick Shaw, who introduced the division into Books and Chapters, and then followed five other editions by William Guthrie, later Sheriff of Lanarkshire, the last in 1899. By this time the *Principles* was a very large book in double-column with a very extensive citation of authority to every numbered section. It had ceased to be a students' textbook, though it was still used as such, and become a practitioners' reference book. The text had, of course, been in many respects altered by editors to take account of developments in the law.[50] But it retained to the end the merits of clear, direct and plain statement. So much had it been accepted as a standard work for students that a *Synopsis of Bell's Principles* was published by F. H. Morrison in 1903.

Like the *Commentaries* the *Principles* were soon being referred to in judgment. As early as 1832[51] a Lord Ordinary made a passing reference to Bell's *Principles* and soon it was among authorities cited.[52] Before Bell's death it had been cited repeatedly and by mid-century it was being quoted in the same paragraph as Stair, Bankton and Erskine.[53]

In the House of Lords in *Stewart* v. *Kennedy*[54] Lord Watson founded on and approved Bell's analysis[55] of the effect of error in substantials affecting the consent of a party entering into a contract.

Certainly accordingly by the latter part of the nineteenth century Bell's works were regarded as authoritative, and of institutional rank. Fraser[56] refers to "the institutional writers on Scottish law" but does not mention Bell among them and cites him sparingly in the footnotes, though admittedly Bell deals less fully with Domestic Relations than with Commercial Relations. But the citation of both of Bell's works is common from the mid-nineteenth century onwards.

Today there is no doubt as to the standing of the *Principles*. Thus in *Fortington* v. *Kinnaird*[57] it was cited among the institutional writers. In *Sinclair* v. *Juner*[58] the Lord President mentioned the *Principles* along with Hume's *Lectures* mildly critically, but distinguishing them from "modern textbooks" and noted how Bell had altered his statement on the point in question in the fifth edition of his *Commentaries*.

In 1826 Bell gave evidence to the Commissioners for Visiting the Scottish Universities appointed under the Universities Act 1825. He said[59] that Hume began the hour with examination, *i.e.* oral questions to members of the class, but he was against examination and had no examinations whatever because many of the students were young men "generally pretty far advanced in life." His students were aged, he continued, between 17 and 24 or 25. He had about 250 in the class. He could not even find sufficient time in the course for the civil part of our jurisprudence and had not yet entered on the criminal law. [It is understood that he never did]. The principles of conveyancing were included in the course, though it was useful for students also to attend the lectures on conveyancing.[60] He spoke his lectures from full notes. There should in his view be two courses over two years. He went on[61]: "I take a general view of the principles giving all the authorities I think necessary for enabling the students in private study to understand the subject fully. Towards the end of the course I take up more particularly doctrines which require a more full commentary – elections, mercantile law, maritime law." Conveyancing he regarded as an auxiliary class. His evidence gives the impression of a man with no ideas; he could not suggest any desirable improvements in the system and had no proposals for developments. He may have been a better scholar than professor, better on paper than in the lecture-room. If so, he was not unique among professors. Indeed Bell was criticised about this time in a university student journal[62] for talking too much about English or French law, and quoting these rather than expounding the principles of Scots law and quoting Scots authorities, and for "not having his lectures prepared beforehand. This allegation, I am aware, was more applicable to him during other sessions than during this [1824–25]; but he still is, at times, almost unprepared upon the subject he means to lecture on. This may be attributed to his time being so much occupied by his professional business; but that ought not to prevent him from dedicating a portion of his time to prepare himself for his class." The same critic also commented that his "mode of speaking, too, is rather mincing and affected, which is a pity as it prejudices his students against him."

Some years later a student, Thomas Fraser, who attended in 1831–32, noted in his diary[63]:

"I attended both the Law of Scotland class taught by the celebrated legal author George Joseph Bell; and the Conveyancing class taught by MacVey Napier,[64] who was less known as a lawyer than as a literateur. He had I believe little or no practice in his profession of W.S. but he had been the Editor of the Edinburgh Encyclopaedia and Editor of that periodical when Jeffrey became Lord Advocate. Strange to say, however, the lectures of Mr. Bell notwithstanding his high legal reputation were generally considered profitless, and his class were most inattentive. While the lectures of Napier, who as a lawyer was unknown, were deemed most instructive and always commanded the utmost attention from his students. The explanation however is easy. The subject of Mr. Bell's lectures was a very wide one embracing the whole law of Scotland, with the exception of conveyancing which he left to Napier, and criminal law, which he rarely touched on, and his mode of treating it was extremely desultory consisting almost entirely of verbal commentaries, with little attempt at system or arrangement, upon his own very excellent textbook, the Principles of the Law of Scotland. Napier's department on the other hand was very limited and admitted of being treated in an elaborate and complete manner: and he went through it in a series of lectures arranged in the clearest and most satisfactory manner and written in a style marked by extreme conciseness and precision and by as much elegance as was compatible with those predominating characteristics . . . I paid as much attention as I could to Mr. Bell's class and worked hard at Mr. Napier's."

The same student considered that the oral examinations in class which Bell had by this time introduced, following the advice of his brother Charles, long experienced in teaching medical students, "were vague and desultory and the questions were frequently expressed with so little precision that it was not easy for a student to know what really was the precise point involved in the question which he had to answer."

The breadth of the field which Bell had to cover in his course is not really an excuse. Once the *Principles* were available in print Bell could have omitted some topics and lectured more fully on others, or divided the course into two. Lack of system or arrangement is a serious criticism of lectures. It may be that he was simply not a good oral expositor. On the other hand he provided "a private library, purchased at great cost by the Professor, and open to the students morning and evening, for the purpose of consulting and verifying the authorities referred to."[65]

In 1836–38 Bell published, in three volumes, *Illustrations from Adjudged Cases of the Principles of the Law of Scotland*. This is a very early specimen of the "Cases on . . ." genus of book, which has become so common in the twentieth century. As he said in the Preface: "in this work my design is to give a short analysis of the cases cited in the 'Principles of the Law of Scotland' as illustrative of the doctrines in that work." Both Scottish and English cases are included. Under section numbers corresponding to those of the *Principles* hundreds of cases are summarised in from half-a-dozen to 20 or 30 lines. The labour of making the summaries must have been considerable. The summaries are, as one would expect from Bell, concise and very clear. There are no quotations from the judgments but it is always made clear what the case was about, and what the decision was and the ground for it. Sometimes Bell appended a concise note on the case, as where he observes that one "was a very doubtful decision." The third volume contains a supplement of omitted and recent cases. The books must have been a godsend to the students of his time.[66] Sometimes even today the concise narrative of a case found in Bell's *Illustrations* has been found preferable to the full report of the case.[67]

Later works were *Commentaries on the recent Statutes relative to Diligence or Execution against the Moveable Estate; Imprisonment, Cessio bonorum; and Sequestration in Mercantile Bankruptcy*, published in 1840 and reissued in 1870, a slim book, rather a supplement to the *Commentaries* than a distinct work, and a short *Inquiries into the Contract of Sale of Goods and Merchandise as Recognised in the judicial decisions and mercantile practice of modern nations*, published posthumously in 1844, which have both not survived in legal literature. The *Inquiries* is stated in the preface to have been one of a series of books Bell had been preparing before his death on specific branches of law but to have been the only one sufficiently finished to be worth publishing.

Bell is very much a text-writer in the modern mould. There is no philosophising or reference to the Mosaic Law and the Bible, and no more than necessary to the Roman law. Pothier, Pardessus, Valin, Emerigon are more important. One is left to guess at his philosophy of law; pretty certainly he was a positivist, regarding law as the dictate of the sovereign, expressed through legislation or delegated power of judicial decision. He does not discuss the sources of the law or their relative weights.

Possibly his greatest quality was his ability to formulate concisely but accurately a definition. Thus: "Abandonment is a relinquishment to the underwriter in a case of loss constructively total, of all right, title and claim to what may be saved; leaving it to him to make the most of it for his own benefit."[68] "Parts and pertinents are such accessory parts, and fixtures, and appendages to land, or houses, or such separate possessions, or privileges, as accompany the occupation and use of the land, or have for forty years been so enjoyed along with it."[69] His verbal formulation of the principle of *rei interventus*[70] has been quoted judicially many times, and made the basis of judgment[71]; Lord Macmillan[72] said, "In the words of Professor Bell, which have now classical authority and have been expressly approved in this House, *rei interventus*. . . ."

His greatest weakness is in systematic arrangement of his material. One can never remember where in the *Commentaries* to find anything. It is a badly arranged book. The arrangement of the *Principles* is rather better but breaks away from the order adopted, with variations, by all his predecessors, presumably to put in the forefront the commercial relationships created by contracts, but without any other apparent advantage. He there[73] says that the object of jurisprudence [a system of law] is the protection and enforcement of civil rights; rights which may be vindicated by judicial aid may be distinguished into those which relate to property or things external, and those which relate to the person. This gives rise to the order of treatment adopted, *viz.* rights personal, from obligation or contract; rights real in property; rights arising from marriage and the family, and by succession; rights relative to the person – safety, freedom and reputation; and the evidence and enforcement of these rights. But there is much to be said for the older view – that the status of persons is logically prior to their rights against each other and over things and it is a mistake to separate rights arising from obligation or contract so far from rights relative to the person, which also arise from obligation.

Bell's works became better known abroad than those of practically any of his predecessors. Chancellor James Kent[74] in his *Commentaries on American Law* makes numerous references to Bell and in the preface to his second (1832) edition Kent refers[75] to the continuous improvements in the successive editions of Bell's work. Conversely, in his final (fourth) edition of the *Principles* Bell makes reference to Kent's *Commentaries* and also to Story.[76] Story, in his *Bailments* (1832) makes frequent reference to Stair, Erskine and Bell's *Commentaries*; in his *Conflict of Laws* (1834) there are many references to Erskine, Kames, Fergusson's *Consistorial Reports* and Bell's *Commentaries*.

These is extant[77] a letter from Charles Sumner to Story, written from Stirling on October 7, 1838, in which he writes:

> "Among others, I saw Professor Bell, the venerable author of the work on Commercial Law. He came out to Lord Jeffrey's at dinner, though, poor man, he ate nothing, as his physician had cut him off from dinner; he afterwards came to Sir William Hamilton's where he ate nothing. I breakfasted with him and he was so good as to go with me over the courts, and explain to me their different jurisdictions. I assure you a worthier or more warm-hearted old gentleman does not exist in either hemisphere. He is advanced in life – say seventy – and, I fear, quite weak, even for his years. He told me that he was the first person in Scotland who imported a copy of Pothier. His works, in a pecuniary sense, I understand, have been losing affairs. He was well acquainted with Kent's *Commentaries*, and inquired after the Chancellor as if for an old friend."

Probably in consequence of Sumner's visit Bell wrote to Story on December 12, 1838, sending him copies of his *Principles* and the three volumes of *Illustrations*:

> "I have to acknowledge many obligations to you for knowledge imparted and views opened of great consequence, and you will easily believe me in expressing my respect for your labours, when I tell you that, in learning from your friend, Mr. Sumner, your intention of writing on the Law of Agency, I at once abandoned a half-completed work on that important subject.[78]
>
> "I have ventured to send you two books, which, from a sense of duty to my pupils, I have lately published – one on the Principles of the Laws of Scotland, another of illustrations of these principles from decided cases. You will, of course, receive them, as they were

intended, not for the perusal of the masters in jurisprudence, but for the initiation of students."[79]

Story responded on June 8, 1839, as follows:

"A short time ago I had the pleasure of receiving the volumes on the *Principles of the Law of Scotland* and the Illustrations thereof, which you were so obliging as to send me. I beg leave to return you my most sincere thanks for this truly acceptable present. These volumes have great intrinsic value, not merely for Scottish lawyers, but for all who cultivate the law as a rational and comprehensive science. They ought to be in the library of every common law Advocate to teach him a just respect for foreign jurisprudence, and to abate somewhat of that exclusive reverence for his own particular department of the profession, which (I am sorry to say) in past times has not added either to the honour or to the wisdom of the profession. For myself, I am free to confess, that imperfect as, from my constant engagements, have been my studies of foreign jursiprudence, and incomplete as have been my researches, I have never failed to find a great deal of most important instruction in them, and I have been alternately struck with admiration at the variety of new views suggested by them, and with profound reverence for the depth and vigour of the reasoning of many of the leading authors of that jurisprudence. It was many years ago that my attention was first attracted to the highly cultivated state of jurisprudence in Scotland by possession of a copy of Erskine's *Institute*; and the liberal use of your own excellent *Commentaries on Commercial Law*. Allow me to express to you my deep obligations to this latter. I have used it constantly in the preparation of all my works upon topics connected with the law of contracts, and especially of commercial law and I have derived many of the most valuable illustrations from it. I can therefore truly say that though I have not a personal acquaintance with you, yet I feel that you are among my most familiar friends.

"It has been a matter of no small surprise, as well as of regret, to me, that the Bar of Westminster Hall have not hitherto directed more time to the study of Scottish jurisprudence, and to a more thorough estimate of the great value of your judicial authors. On the subject of international jurisprudence you have been altogether ahead of them. And I cannot but persuade myself, that in all cases of the conflict of laws they will find, as I have found, the most extensive information and accurate researches in the doctrines and decisions of your country. In the next age I cannot doubt, but that in England and America the writings of Scottish jurists will be as much consulted and as highly esteemed as are now your authors in the general walks of literature. . . ."[80]

Possibly because of these American links there was a Philadelphia edition of Bell's last work, his *Inquiries into the Contract of Sale of Goods*. Cockburn wrote of Bell[81]:

"But his true distinction consists in his being the author of the Commentaries on the Law of Bankruptcy [sic], an institutional work of the very highest excellence, which has guided the judicial deliberations of his own country for nearly fifty years, and has had its value acknowledged in the strongest terms by no less jurists than Story and Kent. With a stiff and sometimes a hard manner, he was warm-hearted and honourable, a true friend and excellent in all the relations of life. No-one ever knew him well without respect and regard."

NOTES

¹ On him see Chap. 18, *supra*.

² DNB.

³ DNB; Anderson, S.N., II, p. 278.

⁴ DNB; Anderson, S.N., I, p. 277; G. W. Wilton, *George Joseph Bell* (1929); Lord Justice-Clerk Moncrieff in *Edinburgh Review* (1872), quoted in *Journal of Jurisprudence*, XVI, 428; Grant, *History of the University of Edinburgh*, II, p. 374; Kay's *Edinburgh Portraits*, II, 464.

⁵ DNB; and see Chap. 25, *infra*.

⁶ DNB. See also *History of the Society of Writers to H.M. Signet* (1890 ed.).

⁷ *Scotsman*, March 2, 1822; *Caledonian Mercury*, March 2, 1822.

⁸ *Scotsman*, November 16, 1822.

⁹ *Littlejohn* v. *Black* (1855) 18 D. 207 at p. 215, *per* Lord President McNeill.

¹⁰ J. S. More, *Lectures on the Law of Scotland* (ed. John McLaren, 1864), I, 15.

¹¹Cockburn, *Life of Jeffrey* (1852), II, p. 231.

¹²Cockburn, *Life of Jeffrey*, I, p. 327. There was no vacancy on the Bench between June 1829 and May 1834 when Jeffrey promoted himself. Why Jeffrey would have been willing to elevate Bell in 1830 but did not do so in 1834 is unexplained. By 1833, however, he had wished respite from the work and worry of the office of Lord Advocate and when the vacancy arose, he was eager to take it himself. See Omond, II, p. 336.

¹³ *i.e.* The *Commentaries*.

¹⁴ The point of this comment is unknown.

¹⁵ This is unfair to Erskine.

¹⁶ Cockburn, *Circuit Journeys* (1889), p. 203 (engraving of Bonaly on title-page).

¹⁷ DNB.

¹⁸ Shaw called his edition *Commentaries on the Law of Scotland in relation to mercantile and maritime law, moveable and heritable rights, and bankruptcy*.

¹⁹ Chap. 23, *infra*.

²⁰ Lord Cooper, "Some Classics of Scottish Legal Literature," in *Select Papers* (1955), 39, at pp. 49–50.

²¹ See generally W. A. Bewes, *Romance of the Law Merchant* (1923); F. R. Sanborn, *Origins of the Early English Maritime and Commercial Law* (1930); On the Law-Merchant in Europe and England see Holdsworth, *History of English Law*, V, 60–154; VIII, 99–300. A notable feature in Scotland, England and Europe, was the extent to which mercantile and maritime disputes were dealt with in lower, local courts, such as fair and staple courts; see C. Gross and C. Hall, *Select Cases concerning the Law Merchant*, 1239–1633 (3 vols., Selden Soc., 1908–32).

²² In the earliest years of the 19th century, as can be seen from the relevant volumes of the Faculty Collection, Blackstone and English decisions were not infrequently cited in the Court of Session, and Malynes and Molloy rub shoulders with Pufendorf and Voet. See also G. Gorla, "Bell, one of the Founding Fathers of the 'Common and Comparative Law of Europe' during the Nineteenth Century," 1982 J.R. 121.

²³ On this see Holdsworth, *History of English Law*, XII, 464–78, 524–42, 549–60.

²⁴ *Commentaries*, Preface, xv. Was Bell by this reference trying to induce Hume (who was then still alive and well) to develop his lectures into a new Institute?

²⁵ (5th ed.), p. 19; (7th ed.), p. 18.

²⁶ (5th ed.), p. 132; (7th ed.), p. 127.

²⁷ (5th ed.), p. 293; (7th ed.), p. 312.

²⁸ Lord Cooper, "Some Classics of Scottish Legal Literature," in *Selected Papers* (1955), p. 51.

²⁹ McLaren disregarded Patrick Shaw's sixth edition and "republished the text and notes of Professor Bell without alteration and has added notes adapting the work to the present state of the law," save that he excised Bell's chapter on the now-repealed Bankruptcy Acts and substituted Shaw's chapter on the then current Bankruptcy Act. McLaren's additions to the notes are enclosed in square brackets.

³⁰ (7th ed.), II, 499–544.

³¹ II, 545–546.

³² I, 278, 448, 506.

[33] I, 145.

[34] I, 312.

[35] I, 457.

[36] II, 19; II, 87.

[37] I, 412.

[38] II, 155. These citations show how far the *Commentaries* departs from a logical ordering. The order suggested is generally that adopted by the major English book, J. W. Smith's *Compendium of Mercantile Law* (1834, 13th ed. 1931).

[39] This is unduly hard on Erskine.

[40] Cockburn, *Memorials*, p. 156. Cf. p. 246 "George Joseph Bell, our greatest modern institutional writer."

[41] Lord Cooper, "Some Classics of Scottish Legal Literature," Selected Papers (1955), 39, 51.

[42] December 9, 1808, F.C.

[43] January 19, 1809, F.C.

[44] The citations are far too numerous to be worth listing. This makes plain that the doctrine that an author is not an authority until dead or on the Bench was not followed in Scotland at that time, nor is it now. In *Mansfield* v. *Walker's Trs*. (1833) 11 S. 813 both Hume (p. 830) and Bell (probably the *Commentaries*) (p. 841) were cited. Both authors were then still alive.

[45] (1867) 5 M. 957, at p. 966.

[46] (1878) 5 R. 800, at p. 806; see also p. 814.

[47] (1881) 8 R. 805; affd. (1882) 9 R. (H.L.) 67.

[48] (1855) 17 D. 292, at p. 299.

[49] Bell's Advertisement to his own last (fourth) edition (1839).

[50] The major changes are indicated in the Prefaces to Shaw's (fifth) edition, Guthrie's eighth edition and Guthrie's tenth edition, all printed in the tenth edition.

[51] *Montrose Magistrates* v. *Scott* (1832) 10 S. 211.

[52] *Duke of Portland* v. *Gray* (1832) 11 S. 14, at p. 18; *Moffat* v. *Robertson* (1834) 12 S. 369, at p. 373; *Buchan* v. *Risk* (1834) 12 S. 511, at p. 512; *Creighton* v. *Rankin* (1838) 16 S. 447, at p. 451; *Kerr* v. *Martin* (1840) 2 D. 752, at pp. 756, 758, 771.

[53] *Gordon* v. *Grant* (1850) 13 D. 1, at p. 24; *Commissioner of Woods and Forests* v. *Gammell* (1851) 13 D. 854, at p. 858; *Rossmore's Trs.* v. *Brownlie* (1877) 5 R. 201, at p. 218; *Morrison's Trs.* v. *Webster* (1878) 5 R. 800, at p. 814.

[54] (1890) 17 R. (H.L.) 25, at p. 28.

[55] *Prin.*, §11.

[56] *Husband and Wife* (2nd ed., 1876), I, p. 3.

[57] 1942 S.C. 239, at pp. 246–247, 253, 276, 288.

[58] 1952 S.C. 35, at p. 43.

[59] *Evidence*, Vol. I (Edinburgh), p. 186. He later changed his mind and from 1829–30 introduced examinations.

[60] Given at this time by MacVey Napier.

[61] p. 189. Davidson, his Glasgow counterpart, gave evidence (*Evidence*, Vol. II (Glasgow), p. 145) that his appointment was for Roman law but he lectured also on Scots law. He examined "minutely" on the relevant passages in the "Abridgment of Erskine." Alexander Dauney, Professor of Civil Law at King's College, Aberdeen, admitted (*Evidence*, Vol. IV (Aberdeen), p. 45) that he had been incumbent since 1793 and had never been called on to give, nor had he given, any lectures! The students had a lecturer on Scots law named by their society, but not above five or six attended him.

[62] *The New Lapsus Linguae* or *The College Tattler* (Edinburgh, 1825), February 11, 1825, quoted in T. N. Bates, "Mr. McConnachie's Notes and Mr. Fraser's Confessional," 1980 J.R. 166, 176.

[63] Bates, *loc. cit.*

[64] Napier (1776–1847, W.S. 1799) edited the Supplement to the 6th ed. of the *Encyclopaedia Britannica* (6 vols., 1814–24) the 7th ed. (22 vols., 1827–42), and became editor of the *Edinburgh Review* in 1829 in succession to Jeffrey.

[65] Royal Commission, *Evidence*, Vol. I (Edinburgh), p. 257.

[66] The *Illustrations* were cited in court as early as *Johnstone* v. *Johnstone* (1839) 2 D. 73, at p. 77.

[67] *Sinclair* v. *Juner*, 1952 S.C. 35, at p. 43, examining *McDonnel* v. *Ettles*, December, 15, 1809, F.C. "better reported in" *Bell's III.*, I, 170.

[68] *Prin.*, §484.

[69] *Prin.*, §739.

[70] *Prin.*, §26.

[71] *Kirkpatrick* v. *Allanshaw Coal Co.* (1880) 8 R. 327, at p. 342.

[72] *Mitchell* v. *Stornoway Trs.*, 1936 S.C. (H.L.) 56, at p. 63.

[73] *Prin.*, §1–4.

[74] (1763–1847) first professor of law at Columbia, 1794–98 and again 1824–26; Chief Justice of New York (1804–14); and Chancellor of New York (1814–23). His *Commentaries on American Law* (4 vols., 1826–30), modelled on Blackstone, was America's first legal classic and very influential. On him see W. Kent; *Memoirs and Letters of James Kent, LL.D.* (1898); G. Goldberg, "Kent – The American Blackstone," in Harding (ed.), *Law Making and Law Makers in British History* (1980) 120.

[75] Kent, I, xi.

[76] Joseph Story (1779–1845), an Associate Justice of the U.S. Supreme Court, 1812–45 and also Dane Professor of Law at Harvard, 1829–45, author of *Commentaries on Bailments* (1832), the *Constitution of the United States* (1833), *The Conflict of Laws* (1834), *Equity Jurisprudence* (1836), *Equity Pleadings* (1838), *Agency* (1839), *Partnership* (1841), *Bills of Exchange* (1844), *Promissory Notes, Checks and Bankers* (1845). On him see W. W. Story, *Life and Letters of Joseph Story*.

[77] K. H. Nadelman, "Joseph Story and George Joseph Bell," 1959 J.R. 31, 37.

[78] Story's *Commentaries on the Law of Agency, as a branch of Commercial and Maritime Jurisprudence, with occasional illustrations from the civil and foreign law* appeared in 1839.

[79] W. W. Story, *Life and Letters of Joseph Story* (1851), II, p. 302, quoted in 1959 J.R. 36.

[80] 1959 J.R. 38–39.

[81] *Life of Jeffrey*, I, p. 108.

CHAPTER 21

SIR ARCHIBALD ALISON

THE Reverend Archibald Alison (1757–1839)[1] was a son of Patrick Alison, at one time Lord Provost of Edinburgh and descended from the Alisons of Newhall in Fife. He was educated at Glasgow and Oxford, entered Anglican orders and in 1790 published an *Essay on the Nature and Principles of Taste* which attracted much attention and went through several editions. In the same year he was presented by Sir William Pulteney to the perpetual curacy of Kenley in Shropshire. (Pulteney was born William Johnstone (1729–1805), passed advocate in 1751 and in his young days completed the third edition of Stair's *Institutions*, which had been begun by John Gordon, advocate. Being a prudent young advocate, he married a rich heiress, Frances Pulteney, and assumed her name. He was later Member of Parliament for Forfar burgh and Cromartyshire 1768–74 and for Shrewsbury 1775–1805.)

In 1800, however, largely to give his children the benefit of Scottish education, Alison returned to Edinburgh as priest in charge of the Episcopal chapel, Cowgate, Edinburgh, which later removed to St. Paul's, York Place. He was a Fellow of the Royal Societies of London and Edinburgh (1783) and contributed to the transactions of the latter[2] a memoir of the Life and Writings of the Hon. Alexander Fraser Tytler, Lord Woodhouselee, the biographer of Kames. He was friendly with many distinguished men of the time, Woodhouselee, Dugald Stewart, Adam Smith, Adam Ferguson, Principal Robertson and others. By his wife, the eldest daughter of the famous Dr. James Gregory, he had several children. His oldest son, William Pulteney Alison (1790–1859),[3] became a distinguished physician and professor successively of forensic medicine (1820–22), of institutes of medicine or physiology (1822–42), and of practice of medicine (1842–56) in the University of Edinburgh. He became F.R.S.E. in 1817. It is said that he was so distinguished in philosophy that Dugald Stewart wanted Alison to succeed him. He wrote extensively on medical subjects.

His second son, Archibald[4] was born at Kenley on December 29, 1792. After the family removed to Edinburgh he was educated by a private tutor and at Edinburgh University, where he attended Hume's lectures. He is said to have been intelligent and hard-working but not brilliant.

He was called to the Scottish Bar in 1814 and made good progress from the outset. In 1825 he married a niece of Fraser Tytler, Lord Woodhouselee. In 1828 he became an advocate-depute and Sir William Rae, the Lord Advocate, promised to recommend him for appointment as Solicitor-General when next a vacancy occurred. He assisted Rae in the prosecution of Burke and McDougal for the Burke and Hare murders. He was elected F.R.S.E. in 1830. He indulged regularly in Continental travel but the fall of the Duke of Wellington's government in 1830 lost him his post in the Crown Office and the hope of becoming a Law Officer. This, and the collapse of two firms of solicitors who had been his steadiest providers of briefs, threw him into comparative idleness, which he employed by writing his two books, *Principles of the Criminal Law of Scotland* (1832) and *Practice of the Criminal Law of Scotland* (1833), both drawing on his experience in the Crown Office.

He also wrote extensively for *Blackwood's Magazine* and by 1829 had begun work on his *History of Europe during the French Revolution*. By 1834 historical literature was a greater interest than professional advancement and when Wellington resumed the premiership and Sir William Rae resumed the office of Lord Advocate he declined Rae's offer to nominate him for·the office of Solicitor-General and accepted instead the office of Sheriff of Lanarkshire. He took up residence at Possil House on the north side of Glasgow[5] and applied himself diligently to the manifold duties of his post but also kept some time each day for reading, to form his style, and for historical writing. He remained sheriff till his death, on May 23, 1867. In that time, apart from the onerous ordinary duties of his office, he had to cope several times with industrial unrest which required the presence of military forces in aid of the civil power. He is also known to have been a member of the National Association for the Vindication of Scottish Rights, a body formed in 1853 to assert the distinctness, within the United Kingdom, of Scottish institutions, practices and problems, and the distinctive national existence of the Scottish people.

His elder son, Sir Archibald Alison (1826–1907) entered the army, served in the Crimea, the Indian Mutiny and led the Highland Brigade at Tel-el-Kebir in 1882. He attained the rank of general in 1887 and in 1889 was made military member of the Council of India. His younger son, Frederick, also served in the Crimea and the Mutiny.

His *History of Europe*, covering the period from the French Revolution to the restoration of the Bourbons in 1815 appeared in ten volumes over the years 1833 to 1842, acquiring a steadily growing reputation all the time; it was translated into many other languages and further editions appeared. An essay on *Population*, contradicting and refuting the views of Malthus, published in 1840, did not make any great impact. In 1847 there appeared a *Life of Marlborough*, founded on articles he had published in *Blackwood's Magazine*; it reappeared, rewritten and enlarged, in 1852. A continuation of his *History*, *Europe from the Fall of the First to the Accession of the Third Napoleon*, appeared in four volumes between 1852 and 1859 but was unfavourably treated by the critics. It did not, it was said, show enough of the popular democratic spirit, but it sold well. In 1861 he published *Lives of Lord Castlereagh and Sir Charles Stewart*, and at various times lesser works and collections of his essays and papers from *Blackwood*.

In 1845 he was elected rector of Marischal College, Aberdeen, defeating Macaulay, and in 1850 rector of Glasgow University, defeating Palmerston. In 1852 he was made a baronet. He died in 1867. His *Autobiography*, edited by his daughter-in-law, appeared in 1883.

Alison's historical and other works are now long superseded but his reputation among Scots lawyers continues, based on the *Principles* and *Practice*. The *Principles* (1832), an octavo of almost 700 pages, dedicated to his friend Sir William Rae, late Lord Advocate, professed to be a treatise "of more immediate application to the business which actually comes before the Court" than Hume's work, particularly in view of the

> "vast increase of criminal business [which] has brought prominently forward a complete new set of delinquencies, of which little is to be found in the records prior to the last twenty years. . . . To remedy this defect, and render the law, as explained in books, applicable to the daily practice of the Court, is the object of the following work . . . besides embodying every decision in Hume and Burnett on the subjects on which it treats of practical application at this time, this Volume contains above a thousand unreported cases . . . and above five hundred decisions upon the analogous points in English practice."[6]

The book is accordingly not an abridgment of or supplement to Hume, but an independent work, and is severely practical. There is no examination of the theory of criminal law or the nature of crime in general, nor of the general requisites of criminal liability, art and part liability, nor of the effect of non-age, mistake, unsoundness of mind or diminished responsibility or similar factors, though insanity and idiocy, intoxication, minority and pupilage, and subjection to others are treated in the final chapter under the head of "Defences against Crimes arising from state of Pannel." There are 34 chapters dealing with specific crimes and a final one on defences. The writing is pleasantly plain and direct; each crime is defined clearly and succinctly. The main propositions are stated concisely in numbered paragraphs, each followed by comment and illustration from decided cases.

The authorities cited are most commonly Hume and Burnett, frequently recent unreported cases, occasionally Mackenzie, and to a very minor extent, vouching points where the law was the same, such as treason, and there is justification for it, comparative references to English law, Hawkins, Russell and English authorities. Statute was then still an unimportant authority.

The work was clearly conceived rather as a handier, more concise, more modern, complement to Hume than as a completely self-sufficient work. Judged as the latter it can only be criticised as inadequate and defective.

The *Practice* (1833) is a slightly larger volume. It opens with an admirable non-technical Introduction outlining the main stages in prosecution, in both Scotland and England. Then follow 12 chapters dealing with jurisdiction, prosecutors, arrest, indictment and related matters. Chapter 13 dealing with parole proof itself extends to 160 pages and deals with many matters now obsolete, such as infancy, enmity and partial counsel, interest and undue influence. The remaining five chapters deal with declarations and confessions, written evidence, proof in exculpation, verdict and sentence.

As in the *Principles* the pattern is generally to state propositions in numbered paragraphs, followed by comment and illustration. The authorities cited are again mainly Hume, Burnett and unreported cases. Nearly 1000 unreported cases are cited, and on many points, especially on evidence and the examination of witnesses, English cases are quoted "not as authorities to be obeyed, but as rules to be considered, and adopted or not according as they seem consonant to the dictates of justice, and in unison with the principles of our jurisprudence."[7]

One cannot but wonder why such handy and useful volumes were not revised and brought up to date. It may simply be that Alison himself lacked the time and the interest to do so and that, just at the time he died, in 1867, there appeared the more up-to-date but much inferior *The Criminal Law of Scotland* by J. H. A. MacDonald (later Lord Justice-Clerk Kingsburgh) which in turn cited Hume and Alison on every page.

But even without having ever gone into a second edition Alison's work has taken a place and achieved esteem second only to Hume as an authority on the criminal law, and in every criminal case raising a significant point of principle or common law it is examined. In many ways it is complementary to Hume. Hume was the scholar who searched the Justiciary records and extracted principles from evolving practice; Alison is the experienced advocate-depute who states what recent and current practice is, what the courts currently do, without bothering much about the history or theory of the matter. The *Practice* is now mainly of historical value but there remains much of value in the *Principles*, while there are recorded many cases for which Alison's work is our sole authority.

NOTES

[1] DNB; Anderson, S.N., I, p. 113; Chambers, BDES.

[2] *Trans. R.S.E.*, VIII (1818), 515.

[3] DNB; Anderson, S.N., p. 113; Grant, *Story of the University of Edinburgh*, II, pp. 407, 412, 447.

[4] DNB; Anderson, S.N., I, p. 113; *Some Account of my Life and Writings: An Autobiography*, edited by his daughter-in-law, Lady Alison (2 vols., 1883); *Memoirs and Portraits of One Hundred Glasgow Men* (1886), with portrait.

[5] It is said to have been a large but plain edifice whose finely wooded grounds had a quiet secluded aspect. In and after the 1870s the area was developed as the industrial and tenement district of Possilpark as industry, notably ironworks, such as the Saracen Foundry, and potteries, spread north of the Forth and Clyde Canal.

[6] Preface, pp. v–vi.

[7] Preface, p. vii.

CHAPTER 22

PATRICK FRASER, LORD FRASER

THE Lords of Session were not to be outdone in legal writing in the nineteenth century by mere professors. The first to make a notable contribution was Lord Fraser.

Patrick Fraser[1] was born on September 18, 1817, third son of a Perth merchant, and educated at Perth Grammar School and St. Andrews University. He served in writers' offices in Edinburgh before in 1843 being called to the Bar. Three years later he published his first book, *A Treatise on The Law of Scotland as applicable to the Personal and Domestic Relations*, in two volumes, which attracted favourable attention and promoted his practice. Thereafter he made speedy progress, being appointed Sheriff of Renfrewshire in 1862 and elected Dean of Faculty in 1878. He was engaged in many of the major cases of the period such as *Longworth* v. *Yelverton*,[2] *Udny* v. *Udny*,[3] and some of the cases arising out of the failure of the City of Glasgow Bank.[4] His practice seems to have been mainly in consistorial and trust cases. The breadth of his scholarship is apparent in some of his arguments where numerous unfamiliar authorities are cited.[5] In *Biggart* v. *City of Glasgow Bank*,[6] in which he was counsel, Lord Shand observed in judgment that various cases "were cited and discussed in the argument, and are collected and commented on in Fraser on Husband and Wife, vol. i, p. 535, and subsequent pages ... it was fairly conceded in the argument for the petitioner by the learned Dean of Faculty [Fraser], who has so intimate and complete an acquaintance with this branch of law, that. .. ." In *Ralston* v. *Ralston and the Lord Advocate*[7] in which, as Dean, he appeared for the pursuer, both parties founded on Fraser on *Husband and Wife*! His book was repeatedly cited in argument and decision while he was still at the Bar: "The dissertation by Mr. Fraser on the point in the first volume of his work on the law of Personal Relations has been particularly referred to, and is extremely able; and no one can apply to the study of the subject without deriving the greatest benefit from that dissertation."[8]

In 1871 he received the honorary degree of LL.D. from the University of Edinburgh for his "historical research, the vigour of thought, and boldness of criticism which characterise his work on personal and domestic relations." In 1881 he became a judge, as Lord Fraser, and was well regarded, as was evidenced by the large number of cases set down for him. (At that time parties could choose which Lord Ordinary should hear their case.) His judicial career was, however, unfortunately brief as he died suddenly on March 27, 1889, and he had never escaped from the Outer House. His scholarly nature might have been seen to better advantage in the Inner House, but as Lord Ordinary he delivered some important judgments such as in relation to condonation of adultery in *Collins* v. *Collins and Eayres*,[9] a characteristically scholarly opinion citing Sanchez, Lupus, Voet, Sande, Pothier and other unfamiliar authorities, in relation to minority and lesion in *Cooper* v. *Cooper's Trs.*,[10] and as to land law in *Cassels* v. *Lamb*.[11] His only son, William Edmund (1859–1904) was called to the Bar in 1886, but made no mark in the law.

His first book, on the *Personal and Domestic Relations* (1846), was later split into three separate treatises, each substantially rewritten and much enlarged, namely *A Treatise as the Law of Scotland relative to Parent and Child and Guardian and Ward*, in which he was assisted by Hugh Cowan and R. V. Campbell (1866), with a posthumous third edition by James Clark (1906), *A Treatise on Husband and Wife according to the Law of Scotland*, in two volumes (1876), and *A Treatise on the Law of Scotland relative to Master and Servant and Master and Apprentice*, in 1872 (with a third edition by William Campbell, later Lord Skerrington, in 1882). Until well into the twentieth century these three works remained standard authorities, though the progress of the law has now almost completely superseded them all. All three books are notable for careful statement and the wide range of authorities cited and remain valuable statements of the law of their times. *Husband and Wife* in particular is founded on examination of the decisions of the Scottish consistorial courts from the earliest times, the pre-Tridentine canon law, and refers to many European authorities[12] such as Brouwer, Carpzovius, Van Espen, Sanchez and Thomasius, whose names even are now unknown to too many Scots lawyers. Some of his views on points of legal history have been criticised, but it is undeniable that he had searched deeper than any previous writer on the topics for the origins and underlying principles of his propositions.

Fraser also published a small book on *The Conflict of Laws in Cases of Divorce* in 1860, a *Sketch of the Career of Duncan Forbes of Culloden, 1737–47*[13] in 1875, and a few other unimportant works.

His major works were being cited in court during his lifetime[14]; while he was still at the Bar Lord Ardmillan observed[15]: "The dissertation by Mr. Fraser on the point in the first volume of his work on the law of Personal Relations has been particularly referred to and is extremely able; and no one can apply to the study of the subject without deriving the greatest benefit from that dissertation." Shortly after his death Lord Shand said in one case:[16] "I desire to treat with much respect the authority of one so learned in the law of marriage as the late Lord Fraser"; and in the same case[17] Lord McLaren remarked: "But in consulting Lord Fraser's work it must be kept in mind that his Lordship, following the example of some illustrious predecessors, intended his book to be not merely a textbook of Scots law but also a philosophical work in which illustrations are drawn from general principles of jurisprudence and from foreign sources of authority. It is very necessary, therefore, in reference to this work to distinguish between what the author means to lay down as the law of Scotland and what he states as matter of principle or by way of historical illustration." The book continued to be an authority until well into the twentieth century.

Fraser well exemplifies the modern trend in text-writing, which became established both in Scotland and England, away from general treatises on the private law to more thorough and detailed examinations of the law of particular major branches. This was attributable to the greater variety of problems coming before the courts and the resultant greater volume of case law, the need to examine the relevant law more thoroughly and the desire of scholars to do so. Not much of what he wrote has survived, but that must not detract from the credit due to him for his thorough and scholarly volumes, which were standard authorities for many years.

NOTES

[1] DNB; *Scotsman* and *Glasgow Herald*, March 29, 1889.

[2] (1862) 1 M. 161; (he was not of counsel in the appeal: (1864) 2 M. (H.L.) 49).

[3] (1866) 5 M. 164; (1869) 7 M. (H.L.) 89.

[4] *e.g. Muir* v. *City of Glasgow Bank* (1879) 6 R. 392; *Biggart* v. *City of Glasgow Bank* (1879) 6 R. 470 and *McDougall* v. *City of Glasgow Bank* (1879) 6 R. 1089 in which he persuaded the First Division to overrule a statement in Bell, *Comm.*, I, 638 about the *jus mariti.*

[5] *e.g.* Domat and Voet in *Douglas* v. *Douglas* (1876) 4 R. 105; many canonists in *Lockyer* v. *Ferryman* (1876) 3 R. 882, at p. 890; Sanchez in *Munro* v. *Munro* (1876) 4 R. 332, at p. 342.

[6] (1879) 6 R. 470.

[7] (1881) 8 R. 371, at p. 374.

[8] *Fraser* v. *Walker* (1872) 10 M. 837, at p. 844, *per* Lord Ardmillan.

[9] (1882) 10 R. 250.

[10] (1885) 12 R. 473, at pp. 486–490.

[11] (1885) 12 R. 722, at pp. 757–769.

[12] See the Authorities cited in Vol. II, pp. xxxiii–li.

[13] Duncan Forbes was Lord President of the Court of Session during these years. On him see DNB and G. Menary, *Life and Letters of Duncan Forbes of Culloden, 1685–1747* (1936).

[14] *e.g.* in the House of Lords in *C.B.* v. *A.B.* (1885) 12 R. (H.L.) 36; in *Auld* v. *Auld* (1884) 12 R. 36, at p. 39; *Maloy* v. *Macadam* (1885) 12 R. 431, at p. 451; *Campbell* v. *Maquay* (1888) 15 R. 784, and other cases.

[15] *Fraser* v. *Walker* (1872) 10 M. 837, at p. 844.

[16] *Strain* v. *Strain* (1890) 17 R. 297, at p. 300.

[17] at p. 302.

CHAPTER 23

JAMES LORIMER

IN Lorimer we meet the first Scot who, in modern times, at least to date, made an international reputation in jurisprudence and international law. James Allan Lorimer[1] was born at Aberdalgie, Perthshire, on November 4, 1818, a son of James Lorimer, the factor on the Kinnoul estates and Rothesay Herald. Educated at Perth High School, he proceeded to Edinburgh University (M.A. 1856) where he attended Sir William Hamilton's lectures on philosophy, an experience to which he attributed his abiding interest in philosophy, and studied also at Berlin, Bonn and the Academy of Geneva. He first tried briefly to make a career in commerce in Glasgow but it was not to his taste and in 1845 he was called to the Scottish Bar. He does not appear to have made much of practice though his name appears occasionally in the reports.[2] He became principal Lyon Clerk in 1848 and wrote a small popular *Handbook of the Law of Scotland* (1859 and five further editions to 1894). He also contributed essays to the *Edinburgh Review* and *North British Review* on historical and political subjects, and particularly on matters of educational and university reform, as his years in Germany had impressed him with that country's cultural and intellectual standards.

In 1852 he founded an Association for Extension of the Scottish Universities, which was concerned to promote the development of the Scottish universities along their established lines of a broadly-based education, in opposition to those who wished to reform them on English lines, by the development of honours schools concentrating narrowly on particular subjects, particularly classics and mathematics, or of schools of higher research like those in Germany.[3] The Association's policy was based on a pamphlet by Lorimer, its secretary, entitled *Scottish Universities, Past, Present and Possible* (1854). His analysis of the prospects of the Scottish universities was connected with a report produced by the Faculty of Advocates recommending a new attitude to the study of law, and the Association was supported not only by leading Scottish academics such as Sir David Brewster but by leading lawyers, including Lord Justice-Clerk (later Lord President) Inglis. His fundamental argument was that Scotland lacked a learned class, and that the universities must be a magazine and a laboratory of thought; learning must be fostered and advanced as well as communicated. The Association believed that developments should be modelled on what had been happening on the Continent rather than in England. Lorimer was satisfied in principle with the tradition of a basic general arts course, a seven-subject M.A., but wanted a higher standard, though without weakening the traditional bias towards general ideas and philosophical culture. Accordingly the old general education must lead on to a specialist training, and this required the creation of new chairs and the development of post-graduate schools and research.

Lorimer was concerned with the fate of the Scottish academic heritage in an increasingly complex, industrialised, world, and his ideas were not empty or impracticable; he saw, for example, the increasing diversification of subjects. His ideas were influential and he attracted powerful support, in particular from the legal profession.

The Faculty of Advocates' report of 1854[4] approved the national tradition of breadth in education; it prescribed that intrants must be graduates in arts or pass an equivalent examination.[5] "No circumstance has indeed tended so much to the formation of a single and intelligible system of Scotch law, as the liberal training of the judges who in former days made it. The *Institutions* of Lord Stair are largely indebted to the circumstance that its author was once a professor of philosophy." A broad basis for law was essential and the idea of a Continental-type law school had survived from the eighteenth century. These were in fact the ideas which Lorimer later, as a professor, sought to include in the compass of the Scottish law degree. The ideas of Lorimer and the Association were also interwoven with the maintenance of Edinburgh as a leading city of culture, an intellectual capital. The Association's ideas were, however, strongly criticised in and from London and a policy recommended from there of rapid and ruthless anglicisation; Scotland was to be educationally and culturally subordinated to England. This was the background to the Royal Commission on the Scottish Universities, the Universities (Scotland) Act 1858 and the curricula established by the commissioners appointed thereunder to implement the Act, though in the result the commissioners adopted a moderately pro-Scottish line, in that they recommended a system of honours degrees but by way of specialisation superadded on the general degree and not *ab initio* specialisation.[6]

Lorimer's Association produced numerous circulars, reports and memorials,[7] and became a vigorous pressure-group for legislation. In 1857, at the request of Lord Advocate Moncreiff, he drafted a Bill on the basis that the government would endow the universities to the extent of £20,000 per annum, providing for a national board of examiners, a compulsory entrance examination for those intending to graduate,[8] and a graduating curriculum. But the government fell and Lord Advocate Inglis in 1858 introduced the Bill which became the Universities (Scotland) Act 1858. It was mainly concerned with constitutional matters but established an executive commission empowered to make ordinances on many academic matters. Among these was one regulating the new degree of LL.B., for which only graduates in arts were eligible, and for which, in fact, only Edinburgh could offer all the required courses. Lorimer had ambitious ideas for making a law degree, as on the Continent, the normal course for those aiming at politics, the diplomatic service or the civil service, but this did not come about and by 1870 Lorimer was himself of the view that the LL.B. degree had failed.[9] In the end nothing came of the Association's bold ideas and its leading members were deeply disappointed. Lorimer himself spoke of English jealousy of Scottish prowess in education as the cause of the setback.

Lorimer was later associated, along with Moncreiff, Inglis, Principal Grant of Edinburgh, Donaldson of Edinburgh High School (later Principal of St. Andrews) and others in the foundation of an Association for Promoting Secondary Education in Scotland, seeking to carry out John

Knox's scheme of schools or colleges intermediate between the parish schools and the universities.[10]

He held strong, and not quite orthodox, political views which found expression in *Political Progress not necessarily Democratic* (1857) and *Constitutionalism of the Future* (1865). Thus he favoured the enfranchisement of women, a very advanced view for that time, and some other measures, such as basing the franchise on educational qualification, which have great merit but would today be damned as élitist and not "democratic." He was intellectually hostile to democracy. It is said that these books attracted the attention of Sir George Cornwell Lewis, and led to his appointment to the Regius Chair of Public Law and the Law of Nature and Nations at Edinburgh.

Lorimer, however, found his true métier when in 1862 he was appointed to that post. The chair had been founded in 1707 and held by a series of sinecurists;[12] it was even in abeyance between 1831 and Lorimer's appointment, which was prompted partly by the fact the commissioners under the Universities (Scotland) Act 1858, who created the degree of LL.B. and devised the curriculum, made jurisprudence, general or comparative, and the law of nations or public international law subjects for the degree and ordained that the Professor of Public Law should give at least 40 lectures on the latter subject annually. Lorimer's appointment was "a most fortunate event for the University and for the credit of Scottish juridical science, for he stands alone in his century so far as the Philosophy of Law in Scotland is concerned."[13] Not content with the 40 lectures required by the commissioners he undertook a full winter course divided between the philosophy of law or general jurisprudence or natural law, and public international law.[14]

He devoted himself also to developing legal studies as both a liberal and a professional education. He cultivated friendly relations with politicians and diplomats and tried to develop legal studies so as to qualify graduates not only for legal practice but for the public service, the diplomatic service and public life generally.[15] He held the chair until 1889.

In 1872 he published his first major work. *The Institutes of Law, A Treatise of the Principles of Jurisprudence as determined by Nature.* A revised and enlarged second edition came out in 1880 and it was abridged and translated into French by Ernest Nys in 1890. By the 1870s the positivist jurisprudence of Bentham and, more especially, John Austin, had become the prevalent one in England and, to a large extent, throughout the English-speaking world. Amos's *Systematic View of the Science of Jurisprudence* was published in 1872 and his *The Science and Art of Law* in 1874. Markby's *Elements of Law* appeared in 1871, Heron's *The Principles of Jurisprudence* in 1873, Holland's *Elements of Jurisprudence* in 1880. All had substantially the same approach; law was a body of rules made by the state; the function of jurisprudence was to classify the principles, analyse the concepts employed, such as rights and duties, and provide a logic of the legal system. Lorimer, however, drew on a much older tradition. He was a follower of Thomas Reid and Sir William Hamilton. Apart from ancient and medieval proponents of natural-law thinking he derived his thought particularly from Krause's

Abriss des Systems der Philosophie des Rechts (1825) and Ahrens's *Cours de droit naturel* (1837).

In his dedication to the Dean and Faculty of Advocates he describes the book as "this attempt to vindicate the necessary character of jurisprudence by exhibiting it as a branch of the science of nature," and in his preface he says that he has given the name of Natural Law to the rule of Life gradually recognised, as faith becomes more reasonable and reason becomes more faithful: "before another decade elapses, the preference for the older and grander traditions which Grotius inherited from Socrates, 'the great lawyer of antiquity,' as Lord Mansfield called him, through the Stoics and the Roman jurists, over those which Bentham transmitted to Austin, will, I hope, be as universal and unequivocal as that for classical and medieval architecture over the architecture of the Georgian era has already become."

He rejected the view that one could derive a complete and adequate understanding of law from theology and divine revelation, and insisted that all that we know of the law of nature must be learned inductively, by the ordinary processes of conscious observation and reasoning. As a natural lawyer, Lorimer aimed at establishing the fundamental principles for the right ordering of human communities; positive law is, ideally, whatever compulsory ordering of a community is in accordance with these fundamental principles, an expression of the rational will of a community.

The book is divided into four Books dealing respectively with the sources of natural law, the objects of natural law and jurisprudence in general, the sources of positive law or special jurisprudence, and the objects of positive law. It draws heavily on German philosophy and the discussion is throughout at a highly abstract level with little apparent relevance to any actual legal system or problem situation.[16]

Indeed Lorimer himself wrote later:[17] "A course devoted exclusively to the Philosophy of Law would probably drift away into those abstract and subtle metaphysical speculations the bearing of which on Positive Law is of too indefinite and disputed a kind to render them acceptable in this country, and which, even in Germany, in recent years, have almost banished the subject from the academical area." Was he, by 1889, changing his mind, or even rather disillusioned? Because his text is open to many of the criticisms he mentions. He ignores the fact that, whatever the ultimate moral source of legal principles and rights and duties may be alleged to be, the immediate practical source is in codes and statutes, executive orders and court decisions and it is only the latter which are enforceable.

The law of nature, in the jural sense, he says,[18] "is not the whole scheme of the universe, but the branch of that scheme which has reference to human relations." The modern division of law is into natural law, or permanent and universal laws of the human relations, and positive law, or variable and particular laws of the human relations and the latter is itself divided into municipal law, public and private, and international law, public and private.[19] "The modern division proceeds on the hypothesis that the question to what extent the limits of positive law shall be made, for the time and place under consideration, co-extensive with those of natural law – that is to say, to what extent natural law shall be enforced, or left to vindicate itself indirectly – is a question of what is vulgarly called expediency; and this hypothesis, as we shall afterwards see, is warranted by the results of the science of jurisprudence."[20] When he comes to discuss the rights and duties which nature reveals[21] Lorimer asserts that in our relation to creation nature reveals rights, notably the right to be, and from this fundamental right he deduces such other rights as the right to reproduce and multiply, the right to dispose of the fruits of being, and so on, which are logical deductions but wholly unproveable assertions. Does a man have a "right to be" in any legal sense; or does he merely in fact exist? Lorimer reaches the conclusion that all human laws are declaratory,[22] and that the function of the judge, as such, is limited to the interpretation and application of written or of consuetudinary law. This was, and is, incorrect.

To a modern lawyer the book is heavy going and not at all enlightening. "This work is probably the best English exposition of the idea of a Law of Nature in the special form which that idea has received at the hands of German jurists and moralists who have adopted the principle of *Naturrecht* as the basis of their systems. Having decided that monogamy is the system approved by the law of nature, because, among other reasons, the sexes are on the whole equal in numbers, Professor Lorimer sees possible difficulties. . . ."[23] This illustrates Lorimer's constant difficulty; what grounds are there for asserting that the law of nature approves, or prescribes, monogamy or that Scots law in prescribing and enforcing monogamy is giving effect to the law of nature, or legislating in accordance with the law of nature? The fact is that, given that the number of males and females of a given age in society are approximately equal, monogamy seems the most simple and sensible and workable system and that least likely to provoke quarrels and that monogamy is customary. Some of Lorimer's natural rights, moreover, are surprising: he speaks of aggression as a natural right, the extent of which is measured by the power which God has bestowed on the aggressor or permitted him to develop; it may be that he does not mean by this more than a natural right of self-defence, but he consistently uses the word "aggression."[24]

Lorimer was insistent that fact is the basis of law. When we ask: what is law? he bids us turn to human nature for our answer. The ultimate appeal is to human nature as a whole and by human nature as a whole Lorimer meant the existence of the individual with its fundamental qualities and radical impulses. He replaces Kant's maxim, Follow the universal, by the maxim, Follow nature as a whole.[25]

It is possibly hardly surprising that Lorimer's theory did not catch on or survive him. It is exactly the kind of theorising which appears to have no foundation in reality and no relation to any living system of law. He does not even exemplify or illustrate or test his theorising by reference to any actual situations or cases or statutes. Lord Mansfield and Stair rate a mention apparently only because they acknowledged their obligations to heathen prophets such as the Stoics and the Roman jurists. Though the natural law of Grotius and Stair was a different thing from the *Naturrecht* of Ahrens, Krause and Lorimer, it is surprising and disappointing that he ignores Stair. Even his former student W. Galbraith Miller, who taught jurisprudence at Glasgow at the end of the century, did not follow Lorimer closely and criticises him sharply.[26] His hope that natural-law thinking would triumph over positivism was not to be realised.

In 1883–84 he published, in two volumes, *The Institutes of the Law of Nations, A Treatise of the Jural Relations of Separate Political Communities*. In the preface he speaks of his anxiety to place international law on deeper and more stable foundations than comity or convention and to vindicate for international jurisprudence the character of a science of nature which he had elsewhere claimed for jurisprudence as a whole. This book is similarly pitched on a highly theoretical and abstract plane, with only limited reference to actual instances of inter-state relations. The work is divided into an Introduction and five Books, dealing with Sources, the Recognition of State-existence, The Normal Relations of States, The Abnormal Jural Relations of States, and the Ultimate Problem of International Jurisprudence. Not surprisingly he viewed the law of nations as the law of nature realised in the relations of separate nations. Part of the book is devoted to private international law, based on the work of Savigny but adapted by Lorimer to accord with his own views. He states that[27]: "a doctrine of rights and duties, logically deducible from the doctrine of recognition, is a branch of the science of nature," but fully recognises that the rules of private international law form part of every municipal system enforceable by the municipal executive.[28] Lorimer's *Law of Nations* was from the start much too abstract to have any success or influence and quietly passed into legal history. The roughly contemporary Phillimore's *Commentaries upon International Law* (1852, third edition 1879–89) and Hall's *Treatise on International Law* (1880, eighth edition 1924) far outstripped it. Some of his annual introductory lectures were collected as *Studies, National and International* and published after his death, in 1890.

His colleague Professor Flint[29] wrote of his two books:[30]

"They are constituent parts of a self-consistent scientific whole. The first treats of the law of nature, and of positive law in general, of their sources, and of their relations to each other; or in other words of the universal principles of jurisprudence. The second treats of the law of nature as realised in the relations, both normal and abnormal, of separate political communities; it consequently implies the principles exhibited in the former treatise, while setting forth international law as derived from, and declaratory of, natural law. Together they present a comprehensive view of jurisprudence as a whole, and a developed view of a most important and difficult department of it."

Flint saw[31] as among the more general characteristics of Lorimer's system of thought its philosophical spirit, its religious spirit ("The primary source of law, he holds, is God"), his accurate and comprehensive insight into the connections and distinctions between ethics and jurisprudence and its method of investigation, giving due place to deduction but placing chief reliance on induction.

Lorimer was one of the founders and an original Member of the Institute of International Law in 1873 and on terms of personal friendship with leading jurists all over Europe. He became F.R.S.E. in 1861, Honorary LL.D. of Glasgow in 1882, and received many other honours from universities and learned societies. He died on February 13, 1890. He was personally very highly regarded: "No one could know him without respecting the elevation and integrity of his character and being won by the general courtesy of his manner."

Lorimer and his wife had six children. They used to holiday in Fife where the sea breezes were considered good for Lorimer's asthmatic chest. In 1877 they came across Kellie Castle, three miles inland from Pittenweem, a house dating from about 1360 with a long but not stormy history, then lying derelict and empty, almost a ruin. It stands in farmland amidst trees but with a splendid distant view of the Firth of Forth, the Bass Rock and the hills of Lothian beyond.[33] The Lorimers fell in love with the castle and saw its potential, and persuaded the Earl of Mar and Kellie, the owner, to let it to them for 38 years as improving tenants at the modest rent of £25 per annum. It became their country home and a major influence in their lives and to them we owe the saving of the castle from neglect and ultimate destruction. There are many relics of the Lorimers, many the products of their own skills, still in Kellie.

The Lorimer children were all very gifted artistically; John painted canvases which hang in major galleries all over the world.[34] Robert, the youngest, became an architect, the greatest Arts and Crafts architect who practised in Edinburgh, imbued by William Morris with a detailed and passionate interest in all the elements of craftsmanship which went to make up a building – stone carving, woodwork, ironwork, plasterwork, stained glass, furniture, bedspreads and curtains.[35] He was deeply influenced by the Scottish vernacular tradition in building. He designed great new buildings and country houses, such as Rowallan in Ayrshire, Ardkinglas in Argyll, and Formakin in Renfrewshire, restored a number of great houses and castles, such as Earlshall in Fife, Balmanno in Perthshire, Dunderave in Argyll, Dunrobin in Sutherland, Marchmont in Berwickshire and Hill of Tarvit in Fife. A beautiful smaller house is Briglands in Kinrossshire, executed for J. A. Clyde, later the first Lord President Clyde. Not least he was responsible for the Thistle Chapel added to St. Giles Cathedral, the restoration of Paisley Abbey and the Place of Paisley, and for the design of the Scottish National War Memorial in Edinburgh Castle. He was knighted in 1911. Sir Robert's second son, Hew, became an outstanding sculptor. He took on Kellie Castle and in 1958 bought it. In 1970 it was acquired by the National Trust for Scotland.[36] One of Hew Lorimer's works is the fine stone tablet set in the wall of the lower entrance hall of Glasgow University from which the staircase rises to the Court and Senate rooms and the main offices. The tablet commemorates Viscount Stair.

Lorimer's works have unfortunately not withstood the passage of time and changing ideas on jurisprudence and law. The great revival of belief in natural law which he hoped for has not come about, and though positivism as a creed has been modified and retreated it is a more sociologically-based jurisprudence that has filled the void. His writings are now virtually forgotten and their influence spent; he is never mentioned save in historical footnotes.[37] They were a late product of purely philosophical theorising about law, totally divorced from actuality. The theoretical problems, the moral difficulties, thrown up by cases and legislation are not looked at, and deduction of principles of law from metaphysical postulates must be checked by examination of what legislatures and executives and courts do. Probably his most enduring work has been his attempts to vitalise the study and teaching of jurisprudence and law in Scotland, and his emphasis on a broadly-based study of law. He did restart, or probably more truly, start the study of jurisprudence in Edinburgh and influenced the start of the modern concept of the Scottish Law Faculties. He would have been undoubtedly gratified, and surprised, if he could have seen the Law Faculties of the Scottish Universities a century after his time, with their great variety of courses, with teaching to Honours level, with research students and staff thinking and writing; he dreamed of it, and did something to make it possible.

NOTES

[1] DNB; R. Flint, "Professor Lorimer," (1890) 2 J.R. 113 (portrait): *Quasi Cursores* (Edinburgh University third centenary celebration volume, 1883); Memoirs by Rolyn Jacquemyns and Ernest Nys in *Revue de Droit International*.

[2] *e.g.* McNaughton v. *Caledonian Ry.* (1858) 21 D. 160, a claim for assythment.

[3] The controversy is fully discussed in G. E. Davie, *The Democratic Intellect* (1961) and R. D. Anderson, *Education and Opportunity in Victorian Scotland: Schools and Universities* (1983).

[4] Lorimer, *The Universities of Scotland*, App. A. Lorimer was a member of the committee and probably wrote the report.

[5] There was still, be it remembered, no degree of LL.B. in existence, only classes in Scots law and conveyancing and, at Edinburgh, in civil law.

[6] Davie, *op. cit.*, p. 58.

[7] There is a bound collection of reports, pamphlets and other papers in the Lorimer papers in Edinburgh University Library.

[8] At this time only a small proportion – less than 10 per cent – of those who attended the universities proceeded to graduation; most only attended a few classes.

[9] The LL.B. attracted only a handful of students. In 1874 Edinburgh created the B.L. degree, obtainable on two years of study and not requiring the prior full arts degree. Glasgow did so also in 1878. But the B.L. was not much more successful. See Lorimer, *On the sphere and functions of an academical Faculty of Law* (1864). Compare W. Galbraith Miller of Glasgow, *The Faculty of Law in the University of Glasgow* (1889).

[10] Anderson, *op. cit.*, p. 170.

[11] His inaugural lecture, on the Law of Nature and Nations, was published in 1863.

[12] Grant, *Story of the University of Edinburgh*, II, p. 313; Lorimer "The Story of the Chair of Public Law in the University of Edinburgh" (1888) 4 L.Q.R. 139 (his introductory lecture for 1887–88).

[13] R. Flint "Professor Lorimer" (1890) 2 J.R. 113, at p. 116.

[14] Lorimer, "The Story", *supra*.

[15] See his expression of his views in "The Faculty of Law" (1881) 1 J.R. 4 (his introductory lecture for 1888–89).

[16] On his views see also P. J. H. Grierson, "The *De Facto* Principle in Jurisprudence" (1890) 2 J.R. 245; A. Thomson, "Lorimer's Juristic Theory" (1896) 8 J.R. 242; Singh, "The Jurisprudence of Lorimer," 44 Int. Jl. of Ethics, 332; D. N. MacCormick, "The Idea of Liberty: Some Reflections on Lorimer's Institutes," in Hope (ed.), *Philosophers of the Scottish Enlightenment* (1984), p. 233.

[17] "The Story . . ." (1889) 4 L.Q.R. 139, at p. 156.

[18] p. 3.

[19] p. 16.

[20] pp. 16–17.

[21] pp. 204–255.

[22] p. 255.

[23] D. G. Ritchie, *Natural Rights* (1894), 3rd ed. (1916), p. 92.

[24] *Institutes of Law*, p. 414. Ritchie (*op. cit.*, p. 233) criticises Lorimer on this point.

[25] See this elaborated in P. F. Hamilton-Grierson, "The *De Facto* Principle in Jurisprudence" (1890) 2 J.R. 245.

[26] Miller, *Lectures on the Philosophy of Law* (1884), dedicated to Lorimer.

[27] I, p. 357.

[28] I, p. 390.

[29] (1834–1910) Professor of Divinity at Edinburgh, 1876–1903.

[30] "Professor Lorimer" (1890) 2 J.R. 113, at p. 118.

[31] *Ibid.*, p. 119.

[32] Note: (1891) 6 L.Q.R. 230.

[33] On the connection of the Lorimers with Kellie see Magnus Magnusson, *Treasures of Scotland* (1981), pp. 181 *et seq.*

[34] A portrait by John of his father hangs in Edinburgh University.

[35] On him see Christopher Hussey, *The Work of Sir Robert Lorimer* (1931); Peter Savage, *Lorimer and the Edinburgh Craft Designers* (1980).

[36] There are now in Kellie Castle a room devoted to Professor Lorimer, and another containing a display of the work of Sir Robert Lorimer, supplemented by an audio-visual display on the Lorimer family.

[37] He is not referred to in F. Berolzheimer (trs. Jastrow), *The World's Legal Philosophies* (Modern Legal Philosophy Series, Vol. II, 1912) or in C. J. Friedrich, *The Philosophy of Law in Historical Perspective* (1958). He is mentioned in Roscoe Pound, *An Introduction to the Philosophy of Law* (revised, 1954), p. 121; W. G. Friedmann, *Legal Theory*, (3rd ed., 1953), p. 52; and G. del Vecchio, *Philosophy of Law* (H. S. Martin, 1953), p. 200, but not in C. G. Haines, *The Revival of Natural Law Concepts* (1930), nor in John Finnis, *Natural Law and Natural Rights* (1980), nor, in general, in modern books on jurisprudence, legal theory or legal philosophy, nor in books on international law. Though he does not acknowledge any debt to Lorimer Ronald Dworkin's views in *Taking Rights Seriously* (1978) in fact resemble Lorimer's.

CHAPTER 24

JOHN McLAREN, LORD McLAREN

IN the Edinburgh of the mid-nineteenth century one of the most notable men was Duncan McLaren,[1] bailie, treasurer, and from 1851 to 1854 Lord Provost and then Liberal Member of Parliament for the city from 1865 to 1881. He acquired such a reputation in the Commons that he was sometimes called the Member for Scotland.

His eldest son, John,[2] was born on April 17, 1831. He was never physically robust, indeed nearly died in 1843, had to live abroad for his health in 1845–47, and all his life was afflicted with a cough. He was never strong enough for school and was educated at home. Later, however, he was able to attend Edinburgh University and he passed advocate in 1856.

Within a short time he published two books, a *Collection of Public General Statutes and Acts of Sederunt relating to Procedure Acts in the Courts of Exchequer, Session and Teinds from the Union, including a reprint of sixty of the leading Procedure Acts* (1861) and a *Treatise on the Law of Trusts and Trust Settlements*, in two octavo volumes in 1862.

In 1864 he issued in two volumes the *Lectures on the Laws of Scotland by John Schank More*. More[3] had succeeded Bell in the Scots Law chair at Edinburgh from 1843 to 1861. McLaren's preface states:

> "For a considerable time past the legal profession had experienced the want of a systematic treatise on the Law of Scotland, which, without departing from the general method and scope of the existing textbooks, should at the same time offer the advantages of being written by a lawyer of the present age, and with special reference to the state of the existing law of our country."[4] "In the hope that an edition of Professor More's Lectures on the Law of Scotland would be found to supply the want of a modern textbook, the Lectures were ... placed, with a view to publication, in the hands of the editor....
> The author's arrangement is generally simple and perspicuous; and as a whole, it will bear a favourable comparison with that of other systematic treatises."

McLaren's annotations were confined to brief notices of recent decisions and statutes. The *Lectures* did not in fact establish themselves as a textbook. Comparison with the contemporary editions of little Erskine and Bell's *Principles* suggests that they were too diffuse and general to be of practical use in competition with the concise, and more fully vouched, statements of propositions of Erskine and Bell.

At this point in his career McLaren had to spend a winter in Algiers for his health and in consequence lost much practice. On his return he set himself to revise and extend his book on *Trusts* so as to comprehend the whole of succession, testate and intestate. It is said that when working on this book he latterly worked through the whole of each alternate night! This was published in two volumes in 1868 as *The Law of Scotland relating to Wills* and at once took its place as the leading textbook. It was being cited in court while McLaren was at the Bar.[5] It was later very largely rewritten for the third edition in 1894, as *The Law of Wills and Succession as administered in Scotland, including Trusts, Entails, Powers and Executry*. A supplementary volume by D. Oswald Dykes appeared in 1934, noting changes in the law since 1894.

In 1869 McLaren was appointed part-time Sheriff of Chancery, an office for which his studies on trusts and wills fitted him well. In that year also he became F.R.S.E.

He had by then also turned to a fresh major undertaking. The fifth edition of Bell's *Commentaries* had been published by Bell himself in 1826, with a Supplement in 1828. There was a sixth edition in 1858 by Patrick Shaw, but this had never attained acceptance. In 1870 McLaren produced a large, handsome, edition in two volumes of the *Commentaries*, based on Bell's fifth edition, republishing Bell's text and notes unaltered,[6] but carefully revised, with extensive and valuable new notes clearly distinguished from the author's notes indicating changes in the law and referring to later cases and fresh interpretations of Bell's text. "To bring the work up to date was Mr. McLaren's object; and this he did with such skill that it was said at this time that though he could not have written the *Commentaries*, there were few men, perhaps not even Professor Bell himself, who could have annotated them so well."[7] This was a major work of scholarship and it too was regularly used in court while McLaren was still in practice. It has proved the definitive version of the *Commentaries* and McLaren's notes and revisions have high authority in their own right. It confirmed that, though he may not have had a large practice, he was a very learned lawyer with a great capacity for expounding the law in writing.

McLaren had of course been brought up a radical by his father and between 1874 and 1880 he took a very active part in the reorganisation of the Scottish Liberal Party. In 1880 he was elected to Parliament for Wigtown and appointed Lord Advocate. This was a stroke of luck because the two leaders in legal practice who had stood as Liberals, John Blair Balfour (later Lord President Kinross) and Alexander Asher, had been defeated. McLaren was the only Liberal lawyer who had been returned. As was then the rule, having accepted office he had to stand for re-election, and was defeated. He suffered defeat shortly afterwards in another constituency and accordingly had to act as Lord Advocate without a seat in the Commons, though the Solicitor-General (J. B. Balfour) had by this time obtained a seat at a by-election. McLaren's father, however, applied for the Chiltern Hundreds early in 1881 and the son was elected in his stead. Of the Scottish legislation which he shepherded through Parliament the most notable was the Married Women's Property (Scotland) Act, 1881, which proceeded on the report of a Select Committee of which he had been chairman.

In 1881 a vacancy occurred on the Court of Session Bench by the death of Lord Gifford and McLaren submitted two names but was pressed himself to take the place, and eventually reluctantly did do. He sat as a judge for nearly 30 years, till 1910, and obtained a high reputation as a judge, for legal ability, courtesy, patience and fairness. His judicial opinions are clear and concise, qualities doubtless derived from his experience in legal writing. For some years he was one of a particularly strong First Division with Lord President Dunedin and Lords Adam and Kinnear. In 1908–09 he presided over a temporary Third Division of the Inner House, set up to clear off arrears of Inner House business. He died on April 6, 1919; the sickly boy had survived to his 78th year!

McLaren was an amateur scientist of distinction, devoted to botany, mathematics and astronomy. He was elected F.R.S.E. in 1869, read papers to the society, and served three terms as a Vice-President.[8] He was intimate with Lord Kelvin and other leading contemporary scientists. He received the honorary degree of LL.D. from Edinburgh (1882), Glasgow (1883) and Aberdeen (1894) universities.

McLaren's standing as a jurist rests on two works, his *Wills and Succession* and his edition of Bell's *Commentaries*. The former has been from its first publication the standard text on the subject and, despite having become increasingly obsolete as statutes and decisions have changed the law, it has not been replaced. The latter is a great work of editorship, in which the editorial contribution is a major part of the value of the whole work, and the editor's notes are treated as authoritative almost as much as is the text.

NOTES

¹ DNB; J. B. Mackie, *Life and Works of Duncan McLaren* (2 vols., 1888).

² DNB, 2nd Supp.; Omond, *Lord Advocates of Scotland* (2nd ser.), p. 316; Obituary in *Proc. R.S.E.* 31 (1910–11), 694; (1897) 5 S.L.T. 1 (portrait); 1910 S.L.T. (News) 37 (portrait); N. J. D. Kennedy, "Lord McLaren" (1910) 22 J.R. 181; *Scotsman* and *Times*, April 7, 1910. John's half-brother (by his father's third wife, who was the sister of John Bright, the radical politician), Charles Benjamin Bright McLaren (1850–1934), became Lord Aberconway in 1911. He was a leading industrialist and chairman of John Brown & Co. Ltd., shipbuilders, Clydebank.

³ On him see Chap. 25, *infra*.

⁴ This is a rather strange statement. "Little Erskine" was by then in its 13th ed. and Bell's *Principles* in its 5th. Both had been brought up to date by editors. In fact both outlived More's *Lectures* by many years and many editions.

⁵ *e.g.* in *Sillars' Trustees* v. *Stewart* (1872) 11 M. 160, at p. 162; *Jack* v. *Rennie* (1874) 1 R. 828, at p. 830; *Bryce's Trustee* (1878) 5 R. 722, at p. 726.

⁶ Save, as he explains in his Preface, that he omitted Bell's chapter on the now-repealed Bankruptcy Act and substituted Patrick Shaw's chapter on the then current Act, which embraced Bell's observations so far as applicable to the present state of the law.

⁷ Omond, *op. cit.*, p. 300.

⁸ *Trans. R.S.E.*, Vol. 31, pt. 5, p. 695. There is, at p. 696, a list of scientific papers by him.

CHAPTER 25

THE MINOR JURISTS OF THE NINETEENTH CENTURY

IN the nineteenth century there was a great deal of text-writing, from institutional texts[1] and further editions of older institutional writings, through large standard treatises[2] to lesser, but still substantial and valuable, contributions to legal literature. Works appeared on most of the major, and some of the minor, branches of the law, and some works were replaced by others in the course of the century. Many of these nineteenth-century books were not only standard texts in their time but are still valuable for their picture of what the law was believed to be at their several dates and in some cases embody statements still of relevance and value. Some are by no means wholly superseded.

JURISPRUDENCE

In the nineteenth century, unlike the eighteenth, the philosophers do not seem to have devoted any great attention to matters of law. Legal philosophy was left to the lawyers and in the nineteenth century, apart from Lorimer,[3] Scots did not make much contribution to jurisprudence. William Galbraith Miller (1848–1904, advocate 1885),[4] the first lecturer on Public Law and Public International Law (1878–92) and Philosophy of Law (1893–1904) in Glasgow University, published *Lectures on the Philosophy of Law* (dedicated to Lorimer) in 1884, a short *Law of Nature and Nations in Scotland* in 1896 and *The Data of Jurisprudence* in 1903.[5] The *Lectures* formed the course which he gave as introductory to the course of Public Law, *i.e. Jus Naturae*. Though philosophic the work is much less so than was Lorimer's and comes closer to an examination of some fundamental concepts. Thus he treats of obligation, the family, the state, contract, succession and the like. He sees a legal institution corresponding to each logical form: thus to propositions in respect of quantity correspond legal judgments as to person or property. In this he founds on Kant. His *Law of Nature and Nations* comprises only three essays, on jurisprudence in Glasgow, what is international law, and the law of nations in the Scottish courts. His *Data* is said in the preface to be the first instalment of a larger treatise, though complete in itself, but no more ever appeared. He said that he had generally adopted the standpoint of the common-sense man. It sets out the basis of his Glasgow course. The book evidences wide scholarship and shows the influence of the English analytical jurists, in that it deals with right, obligation or duty, law, custom, and the aim of law. Though there is merit in the *Lectures* and the *Data*, neither was ever influential and both are now forgotten.

In 1878 James Hutchison Stirling published *Lectures on the Philosophy of Law*, merely a summary of Hegel's *Philosophy of Right*. At the end of the century W. A. Watt produced a brief *Outline of Legal Philosophy* (1893), in which the subject never emerged from cloudy Hegelian abstractions, and a *Theory of Contract in its Social Light* (1897), and W. R. Herkless a *Lectures on Jurisprudence or Principles of Political Right*

(1901), similarly obscure Hegelianism. Both writers are deservedly forgotten. William Hastie (1842–1903), a clergyman, who despite a very chequered career was Professor of Divinity at Glasgow, 1895–1903, made a number of translations from German, *The Philosophy of Law* by Immanuel Kant (1887), *Outlines of the Science of Jurisprudence*, being translations from the Juristic Encyclopaedias of Puchta, Friedlander, Falck and Ahrens (1887), *The Sources of the Law of England* by Heinrich Brunner (1888), and *The Philosophy of Right* by Diodato Lioy, translated from Italian (1891). None of these have other than historical interest, and there is no evidence that they were even influential in their times. Robert Campbell (1832–1912, advocate 1856 and barrister), however, revised and edited John Austin's *Lectures on Jurisprudence* (1869) on the basis of notes of the original lectures taken by John Stuart Mill, and produced an abridgment, the Student's Edition, in 1882. His editions played a vital part in the transmission of Austin's thought to the line of English analytical jurists who followed Austin, such men as Amos, Clark, Markby, Hearne, Holland and Salmond.

It is doubtful whether to number James, Viscount Bryce (1883–1922),[6] among Scottish jurists or not. He held the Regius Chair of Civil Law at Oxford from 1870 to 1893 and began the revival of the study of Roman law there. Of his brilliance and distinction in many fields there is no doubt, but though a Scot his fame was won outside Scotland and not in relation to any branch of Scots law; he was primarily a political thinker, statesman and commentator on world affairs.

LEGAL HISTORY

In legal history in the nineteenth century the most important and valuable work was that done by sorting, editing and printing records and original source-materials, an essential preliminary to the writing of satisfactory narrative history. Despite the building in 1789 of the beautiful new Register House at the junction of North Bridge and Princes Street in Edinburgh, the records of Scotland were in total disorder, but in 1806 Lord Frederick Campbell, the Lord Clerk Register, who took his responsibilities seriously, made a brilliant appointment as Deputy Clerk Register of one Thomas Thomson. Thomas Thomson (1768–1852, advocate 1793)[7] was a son of the manse and destined for the ministry but chose rather to pursue law. As a young man he was fortunate in being patronised by Lord Hermand, who gave him a collection of law books, and Lord Hailes, who made him free of his splendid library at New Hailes, and the latter in particular may have influenced Thomson towards what became his consuming interest in legal antiquities.

He was a close friend of Walter Scott, who was called in the same year, and helped Jeffrey and Horner found the *Edinburgh Review*, in which he published a few papers. Later he collaborated with Scott in founding the Bannatyne Club in 1823 for the "printing and publication of works illustrative of the history, literature and antiquities of Scotland," and he was its guiding spirit, vice-president and, after Scott's death in 1832, its president. (The club was ultimately dissolved, having published 118 volumes, in 1861.[8])

His real lifework commenced with his appointment as Deputy Clerk Register in 1806 when he began the gargantuan and still unfinished task of getting the national records into order, edited and printed. He had to find and train staff, recover and sort out the records, and repair and preserve fragile, decayed and damaged materials. Then he could begin to prepare calendars and indexes, and to edit and print. He worked in Register House for 33 years and many of his rules and practices survive there to this day. He was elected F.R.S.E. in 1807 and appointed a Principal Clerk of Session in 1828. He was however careless in keeping accounts and Register House accounts got into disorder and were even confused with his private funds. After an inquiry he was dismissed in 1839 though there is no ground for inferring more than carelessness and muddle.

His own most learned work is the *Memorial on Old Extent*, a paper arising out of a disputed vote in the election of 1812 which gave rise to a protracted and complicated litigation.[9] It is "at once a paper on a case at law and an historical monograph," in which Thomson drew on his unequalled knowledge of feudal law and the public records and investigated the whole history of taxation of land in Scotland and the basis of the right to vote, as it then was. Lord Glenlee declared "that to read Thomson's Old Extent was to him like reading a lost decade of Livy."

Of more general interest and value, however, were the works he edited. These included the *Abridgment of Retours, Inquisitionum ad capellam Domini Regis retornatorum ... abbreviatio* (three volumes, 1811–16); *Registrum Magni Sigilli Regum Scotorum*, Vol. I, 1306–1424 (1814);[10] *The Acts of the Lords of Council in Civil Causes* (*Acta Dominorum Concilii*) 1478–1495 (1839); *The Acts of the Lords Auditors of Causes and Complaints* (*Acta Dominorum Auditorum*) 1466–94 (1839) and *Accounts of the Great Chamberlains of Scotland*, 1326–1453 (three volumes, 1841–45).

He was mainly responsible for the editing and publishing, over the years 1814–24, of Volumes II to XI of the massive Record edition of the *Acts of the Parliaments of Scotland*, covering 1424–1707.[11] The first volume, the most difficult one, dealing with the pre-1424 fragments, was long delayed, ultimately taken out of his hands and published by his successor, Cosmo Innes, in 1844. The index volume did not appear until 1875. The *Acts of the Parliaments of Scotland* alone would justify the eternal gratitude of lawyers and historians. It corrects many of the errors which Skene and Glendook made in their editions of the statutes.

He edited also many volumes for the Bannatyne and other publishing clubs.

Thomson was a fine record scholar, undoubtedly the greatest legal antiquary of the time, and it is to him, more than anyone else, that we owe the institution of the orderly preservation of the public records of Scotland, and major steps towards their editing and publication. His 14 annual reports as Deputy Clerk Register themselves contain much historical information. His successor, Cosmo Innes (1798–1874, advocate 1822, Sheriff of Moray 1840, F.R.S.E. 1858),[12] succeeded Thomson as a principal Clerk of Session also in 1852. As succeeding editor of the *Acts of the Parliaments of Scotland* he wrote the important introduction to, and brought out Volume I in 1844. He was a skilled record scholar and edited many monastic cartularies and other records for the publishing clubs such as the Bannatyne and the Maitland. He published also *Scotland in the Middle Ages* (1860), *Sketches of Early Scotch History* (1861), *Ancient Laws and Customs of the Burghs of Scotland* (1868) and *Lectures on Scotch Legal Antiquities* (1872), which all contain matter still of interest and value. From 1846 until his death he was professor of constitutional law and history at Edinburgh.

Robert Pitcairn (1793–1855, Writer to the Signet 1815)[13] long an assistant to Thomas Thomson in Register House, published in ten parts, usually bound as three volumes in seven, over the years 1829–33, *Ancient Criminal Trials in Scotland*, a fascinating, important and valuable collection of criminal trials of the period 1488–1624. They are much more historically interesting than reported for their legal content but there is much of legal relevance as well and they are an invaluable source of both social and legal history. Cases include the murder of David Rizzio, the Gowrie conspiracy, cases of sorcery and witchcraft, slaughter, mutilation and demembration, high treason and much more.

William Tytler (1711–92, Writer to the Signet 1744),[14] was professionally successful and acquired the estate of Woodhouselee, but his major interests were archaeology and history. His principal work was *The Inquiry, Historical and Critical, into the Evidence against Mary Queen of Scots, and an Examination of the Histories of Dr. Robertson and David Hume with respect to that Evidence* (1759), a strong defence of the unfortunate Queen's conduct. His son, Alexander Fraser Tytler (1747–1813, advocate 1770),[15] published two supplementary volumes to Kames's *Dictionary of Decisions* in 1778, and became in 1780 joint, and in 1786, sole professor of universal history at Edinburgh. The fruit of this employment was *Elements of General History, Ancient and Modern* (two volumes, 1801). In 1790 he became judge-advocate of Scotland, which resulted in 1800 in the publication of an *Essay on Military Law and the Practice of Courts-martial*. In 1802 he went on the Bench as Lord Woodhouselee and in 1807 he produced his *Memoir of the Life and Writings of the Hon. Henry Home, Lord Kames*, a dull but useful account of his late friend. He published a number of other non-legal works. One of his sons, James, became father of James Stuart Fraser Tytler (1820–91, Writer to the Signet 1849),[16] professor of conveyancing at Edinburgh, 1866–91. Another son, Patrick (1791–1849, advocate 1813),[17] was a friend of Archibald Alison and, like him, interested in history, and did not obtain much practice. In 1822 he collaborated with Walter Scott in founding the Bannatyne Club, and on Scott's suggestion took up the writing of a history of Scotland. It covered 1265–1603 and appeared over the years 1828–43. Despite being criticised severely by Patrick (later Lord) Fraser in the *North British Review* as being written from an aristocratic, Tory and episcopalian point of view and neglecting to regard the development of the Scottish people it became accepted, and there were several later editions. The real value of the work is that, far more than any previous history, it is based on an examination of original sources and materials, and Patrick Tytler was largely instrumental in securing acceptance of a plan for publishing the state papers held in the British Museum. In 1823 he published *An Account of the Life and Writings of Sir Thomas Craig of Riccarton* (reprinted from *Black-wood's Magazine*). He wrote other historical works but, for political reasons, was not appointed Historiographer-royal for Scotland in 1836, George Brodie, the editor of the 1826 edition of Stair, being unjustifiably preferred.

James Reddie (1775–1852, advocate 1797)[18] was a scholarly man who served as town clerk of Glasgow 1804–52 and published *Inquiries, Elementary and Historical in the Science of Law* (1840, 1847), which shows a detailed knowledge of the history of jurisprudence in modern Europe, *Historical View of the Law of Maritime Commerce* (1841), *Inquiries in International Law* (1842, 1851), and *Researches, Historical and Critical, in Maritime International Law* (two volumes, 1844–45), all works now unjustly forgotten as containing much valuable historical matter.

John Riddell (1785–1862, advocate 1807)[19] made a special study of genealogy and Scottish peerage law; his main works were *Remarks upon Scottish Peerage Law* (1833), later developed into his *Inquiry into the Law and Practice in Scottish Peerages before and after the Union, involving the Questions of Jurisdiction and Forfeitures; with an Exposition of our original Consistorial Law* (two volumes, 1842), which is still a standard authority on this esoteric topic, *Tracts Legal and Historical* (1835), and *Stewartiana: being more about the case of Robert II and his Issue* (1843).

Another lawyer who wrote on general history was John Hill Burton (1809–81),[20] who passed advocate in 1831, but never had much practice. Apart from journalism he published in 1839 a *Manual of the Laws of Scotland* (1829; second edition in two volumes, 1847), edited Bentham's works, in conjunction with Bowring, wrote a biography of Hume the philosopher, biographies of Lord Lovat of the Forty-five and Lord President Duncan Forbes of Culloden (1847), *Narratives from Criminal Trials in Scotland* (two volumes, 1852), a *Treatise on the Law of Bankruptcy Insolvency and Mercantile Sequestration in Scotland* (1853) and a large *History of Scotland*, completed in 1870. He became secretary to the Prison Board for Scotland, married the daughter of Cosmo Innes, and was Historiographer-royal from 1867 to 1881, in which capacity he was first editor of the *Register of the Privy Council of Scotland*.

Sir Stair Andrew Agnew (1831–1916, advocate 1860) became secretary to the Lord Advocate and Queen's and Lord Treasurer's Remembrancer, but also wrote *The Agnews of Lochnaw: A History of the Hereditary Sheriffs of Galloway* (1864) and *The Hereditary Sheriffs of Galloway* (two volumes, 1891, 1893), which cast light on one by-way of legal history.

William Forbes Skene (1809–92, Writer to the Signet 1832),[21] clerk of the bills in the Bill Chamber of the Court of Session, Celtic scholar and Scottish historian, F.R.S.E. 1859, wrote *The Highlanders of Scotland* (two volumes, 1836), edited the *Chronicles of the Picts and Scots* (1867), translated John of Fordun's chronicle in the "Historians of Scotland" series (1871) and wrote *Celtic Scotland* (three volumes, second edition 1886–90), all of which, particularly the last, though now superseded on some points, cast much light on the early organisation of the Scottish state. *Celtic Scotland* was a great achievement of scholarship; it is criticised but no one has improved on it as a survey of a very dark age. In 1872 a young man who was intending to go to the Bar was in Skene's office for a time learning conveyancing; the young man's name was Robert Louis Stevenson.[22] From 1879 to 1892 Skene was Historiographer-royal for Scotland in succession to Hill Burton.

The most notable legal antiquary at the end of the century and in the early twentieth century was George Neilson (1858–1923). He became a solicitor in 1881, procurator fiscal of police in Glasgow in 1891 and was stipendiary magistrate there from 1910 till shortly before his death. He had a zeal for learning in legal history and made himself a palaeographer and charter scholar. He was encouraged by Maitland to publish *Trial by Combat* (1890) which is a classic, still not superseded as a careful study of a fascinating and involved theme. Maitland constantly sought his views on Scottish aspects of feudal law and practice, and Neilson was on friendly terms with such other leading medievalists as Mary Bateson, J. H. Round, H. C. Lea, and F. Liebermann as well as F. J. Haverfield, Andrew Lang and others. He was active in archaeology and was a leading protagonist of, first editor of, and a regular contributor to the *Scottish Historical Review* from its foundation in 1904. In 1918, after delay due to the war, there was published *Acta Dominorum Concilii*, 1496–1501, edited by himself and H. M. Paton, with a valuable scholarly introduction by Neilson, following on a volume edited by Thomas Thomson in 1839. He published also in the field of Middle Scots verse and corresponded with literary and linguistic scholars. He failed in an attempt to secure the chair of Scottish History at Edinburgh in 1901 (P. Hume Brown was appointed), but gave a series of lectures on Scottish history and literature in Glasgow University in 1902 and very justifiably received an honorary LL.D. from that university in 1903. In 1913 he delivered the Rhind Lectures of the Society of Antiquaries of Scotland on "Scottish Feudal Traits." Neilson is a classic example of the self-taught historical scholar; till 1903 he had no degree.

A valuable adjunct to legal history was legal biography. George Brunton (1799–1836) an advocate's first clerk, and David Haig, assistant librarian to the Faculty of Advocates, published in 1832 their invaluable *Historical Account of the Senators of the College of Justice from its institution in 1532*, giving a brief account of each judge. It amplifies Lord Hailes's work and is invaluable but requires correction, particularly for the early period.[24] John Hill Burton wrote, *inter alia*, a short biography of Lord President Duncan Forbes (1847). Aeneas James George Mackay (1839–1911),[25] professor of constitutional law and history at Edinburgh, 1875–81, Sheriff of Fife 1886–1901, one of the founders of the Scottish History Society and active also in the Scottish Text Society, published a useful *Memoir of Sir James Dalrymple, First Viscount Stair* (1873) and also contributed the entries on many Scots, not least Scots lawyers, to the *Dictionary of National Biography*. He also wrote important books on Court of Session practice. In 1875 John Murray Graham issued in two volumes *Annals and Correspondence of the Viscount and the First and Second Earls of Stair*, which is however not so strong on the founder of the family as on his successors. Eighteen eighty-two witnessed the publication of Alexander Fergusson's *The Honourable Henry Erskine*, which deals also with other members of the Erskine family and legal affairs of the period, and of George Seton's *Memoir of Alexander Seton, Earl of Dunfermline, Lord President and Lord Chancellor*, concerned with a much earlier period.

George William Thomson Omond (1846–1929, advocate 1871) published a most valuable *The Lord Advocates of Scotland from the close of the Fifteenth Century to the Passing of the Reform Bill* in two volumes in 1883, which deals with the holders of that great office from its first appearance in 1483 to 1832. He followed it with *The Lord Advocates of Scotland, Second Series, 1834–1880* (1914). This work is well founded historically, makes fascinating reading, and is very well regarded. Omond also wrote *Arniston Memoirs, 1571–1838* (1887) dealing with that interesting family, the Dundases of Arniston, which produced in direct and immediate succession two Lords of Session, two Lords President and a Lord Chief Baron of Exchequer, not to speak of Henry Dundas, Lord Advocate and later Viscount Melville, Treasurer of the Navy, brother of the second Lord President Dundas. He also wrote a rather slight *The Early History of the Scottish Union Question* (1906).

In 1893 James Crabb Watt (1853–1917, advocate 1890)[26] contributed an essay in hagiography rather than in biography in his *John Inglis, Lord Justice-General of Scotland, A Memoir*. It nevertheless contains much information about that outstanding judge.

Scotland also made some contributions to Roman Law scholarship. David Irving (?) produced *Observations on the Study of the Civil Law* (1820, third edition 1823) and *Introduction to the Study of the Civil Law* (fourth edition 1837). Donald Mackenzie (1818–75, advocate 1842, Lord of Session (Lord Mackenzie) 1870) published *Studies in Roman Law, with comparative views of the Laws of France, England and Scotland* which came out in 1862 and ran through seven editions by 1898 with a reprint of the last in 1911. Though now quite obsolete the book had a modern attitude in seeing the civil law as the basis of comparative law and of a family of modern systems.

James Muirhead (1830–89, advocate 1857, barrister 1857), was professor of civil law at Edinburgh 1862–89 and also an advocate-depute 1870–80, Sheriff of Chancery 1880–85 and Sheriff of Stirling 1885–89.[27] He wrote an *Historical Introduction to the Private Law of Rome* (1886), founded on an article on the subject written for the *Encyclopaedia Britannica*, and also produced an edition of the *Institutes of Gaius and Rules of Ulpian*, with translation and notes, a work of much learning (1880, 1895, 1904). Muirhead believed strongly in instilling a proper understanding of the history of legal institutions, and was highly regarded among civilians as a scholar and by students as an expositor. His favourite pupil and successor Henry Goudy (1848–1921, advocate 1872)[28] was the son of an Ulster clergyman and educated at Glasgow, Edinburgh and Konigsberg. His health was poor and he hardly practised. He tried for the chair of Scots law in 1888 but Rankine was preferred. After having held Muirhead's chair from 1890 to 1893 he moved to the Regius Chair of Civil Law at Oxford in succession to Bryce. His inaugural lecture was published as "The Fate of Roman Law North and South of the Tweed" (1894).

"He was a Roman lawyer of the old school, bred in the old Pandectist tradition, before much attention was paid to the problem of interpolations in the *Corpus Juris*. He was an excellent lecturer who spoke with great clarity and distinction. He was the first President of the Society of Public Teachers of Law (1909–10)[29] and the principal founder of the Grotius Society,[30] and performed many useful services in Oxford and elsewhere. Before coming to Oxford he had written a book on the Scottish law of bankruptcy. Later he brought out a second edition of Muirhead's *Historical Introduction to the Private Law of Rome*.[31] Otherwise he published only a slight book on *Trichotomy in Roman Law*."[32]

Comparative study of legal systems was not yet a regular approach, so that James Paterson's *Compendium of English and Scotch Law stating their Differences* (1860, 1865) was a novelty and seems to have been found useful. Paterson was also the reporter of Scottish appeals to the Lords, 1851–73.

SCOTS LAW GENERALLY

First one must notice some useful reference books. Robert Bell (?–1816, Writer to the Signet 1784, advocate 1812), brother of George Joseph Bell, compiled a useful *Dictionary of the Law of Scotland* (1807–08), the entries in which were long enough to make it truly a concise legal encyclopaedia. After three editions it was expanded by his son, William Bell (?–1839, advocate 1824) into a *Dictionary and Digest of the Laws of Scotland* (fourth edition 1838; seventh edition by George Watson, 1890), which is full of still-valuable information on nineteenth century law. John, later Lord, Trayner (1834–1929, advocate 1858, Lord of Session 1885–1904),[33] compiled a useful *Latin Maxims and Phrases*, collected from the institutional writers and other sources, with translations and illustrations (1861, fourth edition 1894). Prepared mainly for students, it has been more widely used and provided the basis for many arguments.

In 1841 William Alexander, Writer to the Signet, published an *Abridgment of the Acts of the Parliaments of Scotland, 1424–1707* which included a verbatim reprint of all the Acts then in force and use, with notes and references. In 1827–29 William Forsyth published *An Abridgement of the Public General Statutes in force and use relative to Scotland, from 1789, when Swinton's Abridgment ends, till 1826* in three volumes. The value of this and Swinton's works, before there had been Statute Law Revision Acts, and before there were either an *Index to the Statutes* or a *Chronological Table* of them must have been very great. Apart from any other advantage they made the substance of the statutes available in small compass.

There were numerous editions in the nineteenth century of Acts of Sederunt for various periods. The Acts for 1628–1740 had been published in 1740–42, those for 1739–1753 in 1753 and those for 1553–1790, collected by William Tait, in 1790. In 1800 there appeared those for 1790–1800, in 1810 those for 1800–1810, then in 1811 those for 1532–53, collected by Ilay Campbell, with an excellent historical review in his long preface, in 1821 those for 1810–21, and in 1832 those for 1821–31. Finally between 1838 and 1852 there came out William Alexander's three-volume *Abridgment of the Acts of Sederunt, 1532–1851*. This was followed by Edwin Adam's (1862–1931, advocate 1885) *Abridgment of the Procedure Acts containing the Acts of Sederunt, 1852–86* (1886). Adam was Principal Clerk of Session from 1907 to 1927. These works made available the mass of subordinate rules regulating procedure.

The early part of the nineteenth century was notable for the great printing and reprinting of the older reports, many of which had become scarce. William Maxwell Morison (?–1821, advocate 1784) set out to put together, from all available sources, under dictionary headings, a reprint of the decisions of the Court of Session from its beginnings down to the division of the Court into two Divisions in 1808. The full title of his work is *The Decisions of the Court of Session from its Institution until the Separation of the Court into Two Divisions in the year 1808, Digested under Proper Heads in the Form of a Dictionary*. Morison followed the general classification adopted by Kames in the *Folio Dictionary* and followed by Fraser Tytler, Lord Woodhouselee, in his continuation volumes. But he reprinted in full, whereas they had abridged. The period covered by the *Dictionary* is accordingly conventionally taken as 1540 to 1808, but there are a few cases, mainly drawn from Balfour's *Practicks*, of earlier date. Where, as is not uncommon, a case is reported by more than one reporter, both or all reports are reprinted. Morison not only collected all the printed series but drew on the manuscript collections of Spotiswoode, Auchinleck (Lord Balmanno), McGill (Lord Foord), Baird (Lord Newbyth) and Wedderburn (Lord Gosford). But Morison did not print all the cases in these, or even in the previously printed reports. Tait, author of the *Index* (*infra*), calculated that Morison omitted 2804 cases contained in the printed and accessible collections such as Stair's *Decisions* and Fountainhall's *Decisions*, 5210 decisions contained in the manuscript collections from which he drew some cases, such as Haddington's *Practicks*, about 1700 cases in Balfour's *Practicks*, and some others, a total of over 10,000 cases. Tait implies that Morison had relied too much on Kames's *Dictionary* and should not have trusted to the accuracy of anyone, however eminent. "He had almost completed the Dictionary before he discovered that, by following Lord Kames without any examination of the completeness of his Lordship's work, a number of the decisions contained in the printed collections had been omitted."[34]

The work is paginated consecutively throughout and accordingly cited as M. or Mor. with the page number. It was planned and originally published in 38 volumes but these are normally bound as 19. There are two Appendices. Appendix I comprises mainly cases reported while the *Dictionary* was going through the press and is usually bound up with the *Dictionary*, each title of the Appendix following the corresponding main title. It includes also some cases from Kames's *Select Decisions* and from *Faculty Decisions*. Appendix II consists of the reports of cases by Patrick Grant, Lord Elchies, but, though uniform with it, this is usually separated from the *Dictionary* and bound and backed up as *Elchies' Decisions*. A Branch II of Appendix II is said to have been contemplated but was never published. Volumes 20 and 21 consist of a Synopsis or Digest of the cases reported in the main *Dictionary* but omitting the cases in Appendix I.

There is also a so-called Synopsis, sometimes bound as Volume 23 and 24 of the Dictionary, and different from the true Synopsis (Volume 20 and 21). This is a continuation of the Dictionary to 1816; Volume I includes cases from 1808 to 1812, Volume II cases from 1812 to 1816, but is incomplete, ending at the title "Sale." Volume 22 is a Supplemental Volume containing 819 cases omitted in the Dictionary and an Abstract, taken from the Journals of the House of Lords, of the cases decided on appeal by the House from the Union to 1773.

While the work was very far from faultlessly executed and the scheme of Appendices, Synopsis and Synopsis (continuation) seems ill-planned, the labour involved must have been enormous and the enterprise reflects enormous credit on Morison and his publisher. His diligence, in the days before computers, photocopiers or even typewriters, must have been herculean. Few lawyers now look further back than Morison for the older reports and his work has been invaluable to jurists and judges since it was published. But it is important to appreciate the very substantial omissions he made, and a serious researcher after old law must search elsewhere as well as in Morison's Dictionary.

Mungo Ponton Brown (?–1832, advocate 1816) carried on Morison's enterprise by publishing in five volumes a Supplement to Morison's Dictionary of Decisions containing the unpublished Decisions, 1622–1760, in 1826. This purports to print all the cases in the printed and MS. reports which Morison omitted and also cases collected by Alexander Tait, Clerk of Session, covering 1762–80, and a selection of reports for the period 1738–68 made by James Burnett, Lord Monboddo. The cases are not grouped under dictionary heads but each reporter's cases are kept together, being themselves arranged chronologically. Brown also brought out in 1827–29 in four volumes a General Synopsis of Decisions of the Court of Session, including House of Lords Appeals, 1540–1827. This is a synopsis or digest of the cases in Morison's Dictionary, Brown's Supplement, the decisions of Elchies, Hailes, Bell and the Faculty Decisions down to 1827, cases appealed to the House of Lords, so far as reported down to 1827, and some unprinted decisions. The reports are conveniently abridged to four or five lines each and arranged under alphabetical headings. This is a most useful work, virtually a Digest of all the pre-1827 cases.

William Tait (1793–1864),[35] who had been articled to a Writer to the Signet, opened a bookshop with his brother, became a publisher and supplied an invaluable reference tool by producing in 1823 an Index to the Decisions of the Court of Session contained in all the Original Collections and in Mr. Morison's Dictionary of Decisions, of all the cases contained in the printed reports and in Morison's Dictionary. It is arranged alphabetically under pursuers' names, showing defenders' names, the date of the decision, the reference to the original report and the page of Morison's Dictionary. The notes at the end give a great deal of information about law-reporting and reporters in Scotland. Tait's Index is accurate and very useful.

Peter Halkerston, ssc,[36] published in 1819, with a supplement in 1820, a Compendium or General Abridgment of the Faculty Collection of Decisions of the Lords of Council and Session from 1752–1817, which is a most useful digest of the *Faculty Decisions* and complements Morison's *Dictionary*. It received the thanks and commendation of the Lords of Session. In 1841–42 Sydney S. Bell, barrister, produced a two-volume *Dictionary of Decisions* digesting all the reported decisions of the Court of Session between 1808 and 1833.

As ancillary to his reports Patrick Shaw published two successive volumes of a digest of decisions, which covered from 1800 to 1852, and which were continued by a volume from 1852 to 1862 by Norman Macpherson, Andrew Beatson Bell and William Lamond, and finally revised, consolidated into a single work and continued to 1868 by Bell and Lamond and published in three volumes in 1869. This digest includes House of Lords appeals from 1726 to 1868; it became a recognised standard work of reference and remains the best source of information on the cases of its period, being concise and accurate. The *Faculty Digest of Decisions* starts at 1868 and follows on this edition of Shaw's *Digest*. By mid-century accordingly the lawyer was well-equipped for finding case law relevant to a problem.

In the nineteenth century the reporting of current decisions passed completely out of the hands of individuals who collected decisions over a period of time and finally put them in a volume. The transitional stage was represented by the *Faculty Decisions*, reported year by year by the team of Faculty reporters, though the volumes were not published until some time after the last case reported and the reports were accordingly considerably in arrears. The establishment of a system of annual volumes was urged by several critics, not least by Robert Hannay (1789–1868, advocate 1814) who published as a pamphlet an *Address to Lord President Hope and to the members of the College of Justice on the Method of Collecting and Reporting Decisions* (1821) and a *Letter to the Dean of the Faculty of Advocates, relative to a plan which has been proposed for reporting the Decisions of the Court of Session* (1823).

In 1821 Patrick Shaw (1796–1872, advocate 1819, later Sheriff of Chancery 1846–69), a brother-in-law of George Joseph Bell, commenced to issue annual volumes of decisions, and this began the practice which has continued ever since.[37] There were eventually five series of such reports, known by the names of the leading reporters, namely Shaw (16 volumes, 1821–38), Dunlop (24 volumes 1838–62), Norman Macpherson[38] (11 volumes, 1862–73), Middleton Rettie (25 volumes, 1873–98) and Hugh Fraser (eight volumes, 1898–1906).[39] In 1906 the reports were taken over by the Faculty of Advocates and entitled *Session Cases*.

House of Lords appeals, however, remained in the hands of private reporters, whose volumes covered the cases of several years.[40] From 13 Dunlop (1851) House of Lords appeals are reported also in Dunlop, Macpherson, Rettie and Fraser's reports and *Session Cases*, but paginated separately from the Court of Session reports.[41] Some English series of reports included also some Scottish appeals, and when the *Law Reports* were begun in England in 1866 two volumes of their first series (1866–75) of reports were devoted to Scotch and Divorce appeals. In their second (1875–90) and third (1890 to date) series the *Law Reports* include some Scottish appeals among the English as they occur.

The reporting of criminal cases continued even longer in the hands of private reporters who issued volumes as and when they had enough materials to make a volume.[42] There are overlaps and gaps in the early nineteenth century but from 1835 the record is continuous. From 1874 criminal cases were reported also in the volumes of Rettie's and Fraser's reports but paginated separately from the House of Lords and Court of Session reports in the same volume.[43]

There were also some concurrent series: George (later Lord) Deas ((1804–87, advocate 1828) and James Anderson (?–1888, advocate 1828) issued five volumes of Court of Session cases, 1829–33, and Robert Stuart (1816–96, advocate 1840, barrister 1856, Chief Justice of the N. W. Frontier Province of India, 1871–74), James S. Milne (1823–83, advocate 1847), and William Peddie (1824–52, advocate 1851, barrister 1849) published two volumes in 1851–53. William Buchanan (1780–1863, advocate 1806) published in 1813 *Reports of Certain Remarkable Cases in the Court of Session and Trials in the High Court of Justiciary*; Joseph Murray (1786–1876, advocate 1808) produced five volumes of *Jury Court Reports* and Robert Macfarlane (1802–80, advocate 1838, later Lord Ormidale) a volume of *Reports of Cases in the Court of Session by Jury Trial*, 1838–39, in 1841. More important are the *Scottish Jurist*, 45 volumes and five Parts, 1829–73, the *Scottish Law Reporter*, 61 volumes, 1866–1924, and the *Scots Law Times*, 1893 to date. All these include some cases not found in *Session Cases*.

There were also two good collections of leading cases. George Ross (1814–1863, advocate 1835), who succeeded More in the chair of Scots Law in Edinburgh in 1861, published two valuable collections of cases, *Leading Cases in the Law of Scotland (Land Rights 1638–1849)* in three volumes, 1849–51, and *Leading Cases in the Commercial Law of England and Scotland*, in three volumes, 1853–57. They were intended for students. Both are still valuable collections, bringing together reports not always readily available. The cases are systematically arranged, the reports prepared from the pleadings, and many of the opinions are nowhere else printed. Ross was "respectably eminent in conveyancing work. In his life he was known as a stiff counsel and a bad pleader, with a profound knowledge of case-law. His fame rests upon his *Leading Cases* and an edition of Bell's *Dictionary*."[43] He held the chair three years only, being succeeded in 1864 by George Moir, whose tenure was only one year.

PUBLIC LAW

The comparative unimportance of the public or governmental law in the nineteenth century is seen in the paucity of literature on that aspect of Scots law. One W. Ritchie was responsible for *Essays on Constitutional Law and the Forms of Process in the Courts of Scotland* in 1824 but this was not a systematic treatise on constitutional law. Judges and counsel probably made reference to English books, of which a number were published in the eighteenth and nineteenth centuries. Blackstone's *Commentaries* are all too frequently referred to in Scottish cases in the late eighteenth and early nineteenth centuries. Election law was the subject of a work by Arthur Connell (1794–1863, advocate 1817) who wrote a *Treatise on the Election Laws in Scotland* in 1827, dealing with the

election of representative peers, representatives of shires, and representatives of royal boroughs (*sic*). The book is historically valuable and
contains in the Appendix forms which are most interesting. Much later in
the century J. Badenach Nicolson produced a *Law of Parliamentary
Elections in Scotland* (1865, 1879) and several lesser works on elections.

Local government was a nineteenth-century growth while administrative authorities were still largely unknown. Burghal government was
reformed from 1833 onwards but there was no literature until James
Muirhead's *Law and Practice relating to Police Government in Burghs in
Scotland* (1893). County government was in the hands of sheriffs, justices
of the peace, commissioners of supply and lords lieutenant until 1889.[45]
Several of these categories were the subject of books. Thus Robert Clark,
a writer, published *A View of the Office of Sheriff in Scotland* in 1824,
sketching both the criminal and civil jurisdiction and powers of that
office.

Gilbert Hutcheson (?–1824, advocate 1790) was responsible for a
*Treatise on the Offices of Justice of Peace; Constable; Commissioner of
Supply and Commissioner under Comprehending Acts in Scotland*, which
expanded from two volumes in 1806 to four volumes in the 1809 and 1815
editions. It is now only of, but of considerable, historical value. George
Tait (?–1865, advocate 1807) published a *Summary of the Powers and
Duties of a Constable in Scotland* (1812 and several later editions) and a
Summary of the Powers and Duties of a Justice of the Peace in Scotland
(1815 and several later editions) while Hugh Barclay published, among
many works, a *Digest of the Law of Scotland with Special Reference to the
Office and Duties of a Justice of the Peace* in 1852–53, with later editions.
It has been said of him[46] that he was "a sound judge and an able lawyer
... his opinion on this matter is well worthy of attention."

The first attempts at general books in this field seem to have been
Henry Goudy and Will C. Smith's *Local Government in Scotland* (1880)
and J. Badenach Nicolson and W. J. Mure's *Handbook to the Local
Government (Scotland) Act, 1889* (1889).

There was a good deal of literature about the poor laws, such as R.
Burn's *Historical Dissertations on the Law and Practice of Great Britain
and particularly of Scotland with regard to the Poor* (1819) and Alexander
Dunlop's *Poor Laws of Scotland* (1825 and later editions).

CRIMINAL LAW

Apart from the later editions of Hume[47] and the works of Alison[48] the
most valuable contribution to criminal law was John Burnett's
(1763–1810, advocate 1785, F.R.S.E.) *Criminal Law of Scotland* (1811),
frequently cited by Alison. Later in the century John Hay Athole
Macdonald (1836–1919, advocate 1859, later Dean of Faculty 1882–85,
Lord Advocate 1885–88, and Lord Justice-Clerk (Kingsburgh)
1888–1919)[49] wrote a *Practical Treatise on the Criminal Law of Scotland*
(1867) which undeservedly reached a fifth edition in 1948. The author
tells us:[50]

> "At that time (1860) there was practically no instruction given at the
> University in this branch of the law, and even later it was treated as
> only a side subject, to which but a few perfunctory lectures were

devoted at the close of the session, when weariness had set in. [James, later Lord] Adam's words made a strong impression on me. I knew that the available criminal textbooks were only the great and valuable – but somewhat out of date – treatise of Baron Hume, and a not altogether satisfactory book by Sir Archibald Alison, and it occurred to me that a practical and condensed exposition of the law brought down to date would be useful, and help to supply to myself the equipment which might enable one to be efficient in the practice of the Criminal Courts. I am grateful to my friend James Adam to this day. Without delay I began, and for three years I had abundance of work to occupy my time of attendance at the Parliament House. The labour of ransacking for and laying down material took much time and some patience, and I found the task of putting it together not so difficult. At last my *Practical Treatise*, as I made bold to call it, passed through the press, and was well received by the critics. It brought in a nice little sum at the time when a young man is the better of a financial uplifting. . . ."

According to his own preface, Macdonald's purpose was "to supply the legal practitioner with a brief summary of the criminal law" and to provide "some handy means of reference to the existing authorities." While Macdonald made use of manuscript notes of a number of judges he relies very heavily on Hume and Alison. The book was, however, open to serious criticism. Apart from a brief discussion in the introduction, there was no adequate attempt at analysis of the most general principles of liability, of the effect of non-age, insanity, compulsion and other general matters. Thereafter, moreover, the book simply deals with a series of specific crimes, theft, robbery, piracy, wrecking, breach of trust and so on. The crimes were not even grouped into major categories such as crimes against the person, against property, against public order, and so on. It was a completely shapeless book and in this respect it represented a retrogression from the works of Hume and Alison. It was discreditable to Scots law that this was the standard book on the subject for nearly a century. Its survivance probably owed more to the office attained by the author than to the intrinsic merits of his book.

Criminal procedure was neglected after Hume and Alison though dealt with quite extensively by Macdonald. Henry James Moncrieff (1840–1909, advocate 1863, later Lord Wellwood), wrote a *Law of Review in Criminal Cases* in 1877. In 1890 Robert Wemyss Renton[51] published a book on *Summary Criminal Procedure and Appeal* and in 1895 Henry Hilton Brown published a *Principles of Summary Criminal Jurisdiction according to the Law of Scotland*. They later collaborated to produce *Criminal Procedure according to the Law of Scotland* (1909), still standard in later incarnations, heavily revised.

One of the works of John Hill Burton (1809–81, advocate 1831, F.R.S.E.) was two volumes of *Narratives from Criminal Trials in Scotland* (1852). He deals there with some historically notable cases such as the trial of James Stewart (the Appin murder), the trial of Captain Green, witchcraft trials, and proceedings against the Covenanters and the Episcopalians. They are good reading but do not add to knowledge of law or history.

PRIVATE LAW

Literature on private law swelled to a flood in the nineteenth century. In the first place there were the new editions of the institutional writings.

A new edition of Stair was brought out in two volumes in 1826–27 by George Brodie (?1786–1867, advocate 1811).[52] He had no success at the Bar and no special qualifications for the task. He professed to have collated the three former editions with various manuscripts, a fact which gave him confidence in the accuracy of the edition of 1693 (*i.e.* Stair's own second edition), and in general he followed the 1693 text more faithfully than did Gordon and Johnstone in 1759, but in some places took considerable liberties with it. He added references to Morison's *Dictionary* to the cases cited and added footnotes, mostly not of particular value. He added a Supplement on mercantile law, in fact only on sale and shipping, probably only a part of the promised "large Supplement, comprising a treatise on mercantile law which I had prepared with a view to separate publication." The work might have been more successful had it not been soon overtaken by More's edition. Brodie was later in dispute with his publisher over the edition.[53] He published also a *History of the British Empire from the accession of Charles the First to the Restoration* (1823), a partisan work of no historical value, attacking the Stewarts and supporting the Puritans, but reissued in 1866 as *A Constitutional History of the British Empire*, and a pamphlet, *Strictures on the Appellate Jurisdiction of the House of Lords*, in 1856. Yet, by political influence, being an ardent Whig, he was appointed Historiographer-royal for Scotland in 1836.

Shortly thereafter, in 1832, John Schank More (1784–1861, advocate 1806, F.R.S.E.)[54] published a fifth edition of Stair in two volumes. It has been recorded of More that,

> "he was what was known as a plodding lawyer, and never attempted to pose as anything else. His acquaintance with case-law was prodigious, as all students of his editions of Erskine's *Principles* and *Stair's Institutes [sic]* must know. It was remarked of him that he knew so many cases, and had studied so many decisions, that he could not tell what the law really was, and lost the power or had not the presumption to take the matter into his own hands and boldly declare it. His great erudition pointed him out as the most fit successor to George Joseph Bell, and he succeeded him in 1843 after he had been nearly forty years at the Bar. Promotion was slow then! A most encouraging example to young men conscious of power and content to labour and to wait! More was not so successful as a writer. He had no consecution; that is, his remarks were so copiously interlarded with cases that one could follow his meaning only with great difficulty. His mind when too full became chaotic. He had not keenness enough to master what he had read. In this respect he was like Story, who is said by someone to have bought a pile of continental jurists for little purpose other than quotation. Kind, modest and unassuming, More died in the year 1861, when he had almost attained the dignity of father of the Faculty."[55]

In his preface[56] More observed: "The text of the second edition [of 1693] seems, on the whole, the best, but as the third edition [of 1759] has

has been said by a very competent judge to be 'deemed far preferable to the rest,' as it is undoubtedly that which is best known, and has been most esteemed by the profession, the text of the present edition has been reprinted from it ... most of the material alterations between the text of the third edition and of the first or second have been pointed out in marginal notes. So that the text of this edition embraces all the advantages of any of these three editions." The text of Gordon and Johnstone's third edition of 1759 was intended, according to their preface, "to remove, by the help of several manuscripts, the obscurity which everywhere occurred in the former editions of this valuable system of law. That the established authority of the book might suffer no diminution, by the alterations in the text, which were judged proper to be made in this edition, all these alterations are printed in italics; And such of them as have been made without the authority, either of the manuscripts, or of the decisions referred to in the book, are besides, inclosed by crotchets; and the former reading is placed at the bottom of the page."

Gordon and Johnstone's text offends accordingly against the principle that where an author has himself had printed and published a revised edition of his own work, that should be taken as the copy-text and the manuscripts (which are in any event not Stair's manuscripts, but manuscript copies of a text, not necessarily authentic) be deemed superseded thereby. Also they admittedly made changes without the authority either of the manuscripts, or of the decisions referred to. The latter changes are equally unjustifiable. If Stair misunderstood cases or misstated their effect, that may be made the subject of editorial comment in a note, but should not justify altering the text as he finally left it.

Moreover, More's statement that the third edition had been said by a very competent judge to be far preferable to the rest is unjustified. In 1811 in the case of *Dalrymple* v. *Dalrymple* (which in fact concerned a descendant of Stair and raised a question of marriage by declaration *de presenti*) and which was heard in the London Consistorial Court before Lord Stowell,[57] evidence was given on commission by various Scots lawyers on the relevant law; all referred to Stair, and Robert Craigie, advocate, in doing so observed that the 1759 edition was deemed far preferable to the rest.[58] The dictum was accordingly uttered by a witness, not by Lord Stowell, and in any event he is no authority on the merits of editions of Stair. Also it was uttered when there were in existence only the first three editions of Stair, and the third was in 1811 pretty certainly the best printed, the most readily available, and the commonly used one. The dictum is no authority for preferring the text of the third edition.

The consequence of this, however, is that More printed an inaccurate text, containing matter from manuscripts and matter altered by Gordon and Johnstone, despite his own statement that the text of the second edition seemed, on the whole, the best. This was surely an error of judgment.

More, however, added to his edition not merely references to the pages of Morison's *Dictionary* on which the cases referred to by Stair are printed, and some footnotes, but long and learned Notes, designated by letters, at the end of each volume, amplifying the doctrines stated in the text and very largely bringing the statement of the law down to nearly the time of publication. The value of these Notes goes far to redeem the defects of his text and they have a substantial independent value. They have repeatedly been considered and referred to as independent authorities.[59] In *Fortington* v. *Kinnaird*[60] Lord Justice-Clerk Cooper attached importance to his views expressed by More in his Notes to Stair, and Lord Mackay[61] personally assigned "a good deal of special weight" to More's Notes, and said that "the work carries almost the authority of a separate Institution." More's edition held the field for a century and a half, and the Notes were and still are of great importance and value, and More's most enduring claim to fame.

Patrick Shaw, the reporter, published in 1863 a *Principles of the Law of Scotland in Lord Stair's Institutions with Notes and References to modern law*. It acquired no reputation.

There were also several editions of Erskine's *Institute*, from the fourth in 1805, none very fully annotated. There have never been problems about the text of Erskine. In 1824–28 James Ivory (1792–1866, advocate 1816, later Lord Ivory, 1840–62)[62] published a good (sixth) edition in two volumes, with very extensive notes, which also have an independent value and have been referred to as authority.[63] After an undistinguished seventh edition by Alexander Macallan (?–1840, advocate 1825) in 1838 James Badenach Nicolson (1832–1899, advocate 1855)[64] published in 1871 the definitive edition, in which he reprinted nearly all Lord Ivory's notes and himself added further good and substantial notes to both the text and Ivory's notes; these too have independent value.

Throughout the century editions of Little Erskine continued to appear regularly, from the eighth in 1802 to the 19th in 1895.

Of Bell's *Commentaries* there were in the nineteenth century five editions by Bell himself, a sixth by Patrick Shaw, and the seventh, the best, by John McLaren in 1870.[65] After Bell's death the *Principles* appeared in regular revised and enlarged editions, the fifth (1860) by Patrick Shaw, and the sixth to tenth (1899) by William Guthrie.

General statements of the substantive private law were accordingly numerous. Yet McLaren in his Preface to his edition of More's *Lectures on the Law of Scotland* (two volumes, 1864) wrote:

"For a considerable time past, the legal profession has experienced the want of a systematic treatise on the Law of Scotland, which, without departing from the general method and scope of the existing textbooks, should at the same time offer the advantages of being written by a lawyer of the present age, and with special reference to the state of the existing law of our country. It appeared to some of the friends of the late Professor More, that the Lectures which had for many years been delivered by that accomplished jurist with so much acceptance, had strong claims to the confidence of the lawyers of the present time; many of whom have been indebted to his prelections for the acquirement of the principles of the law and the method of legal investigation which they have applied to the prosecution of the business of practical jurisprudence. Upon these considerations, and in the hope that an edition of Professor More's Lectures on the Law of Scotland would be found to supply the want of a modern textbook, the Lectures were, about the commmencement of last year, placed, with a view to publication, in the hand of the editor. . . ."

McLaren printed the lectures with only minor alterations, brief notices of recent decisions and statutes.

More's own Introductory Lecture distinguished the municipal law into written and unwritten, or statute and common law, the latter derived chiefly from the Roman or civil law but in part also from the feudal and canon laws. The civil or Roman law was the great foundation on which the municipal law of Scotland, as of almost every modern state, had been built.

> "Our Jurisprudence both in its theory and in its administration, rests more on the principles of natural justice and expediency, than upon any artificial rules or statutory enactments and that, accordingly, it is more elastic, and accommodates itself more easily to the changes in the state and manners of society than some other systems. It is distinguished from that of our sister country of England by the comparative ease with which obsolete laws and usages are held to be abrogated by disuse, without the interposition of any express enactment of the Legislature. Even acts of the Legislature itself, like other laws, fall under the operation of this principle, which pervades our whole system; while in England no act of the Legislature, nor even any established rule of the Common Law, how absurd so ever it may become, or however long it may have been forgotten or in disuse, can be abrogated or rendered ineffectual till it has been formally replaced by an Act of Parliament"[66]. . . . "In this country the most positive enactments of the Legislature, as well as the rules of the Common Law, may be abrogated by disuse, and by a contrary usage more in conformity to the existing state of the times and to the rules of justice and expediency."[67]

More recommended to his students the works of Stair, Erskine, Bankton, "which, though it has never stood so high in public estimation as either of the two former works, is a publication of considerable merit,"[68] Bell, Walter Ross, Menzies, Hume and Alison. He also recommended students to "peruse carefully" Craig, Balfour's *Practicks*, Mackenzie's and Kames's works. "Though much of what is antiquated and perhaps incorrect, will be found in these works, they are of great use in exploring the history and progress of our law, and in enabling the student to trace the foundation on which many of the rules of our modern practice are built."[69]

Not only of these but he recommended[70] a careful perusal of the works of Pothier,[71] Troplong,[72] Chancellor Kent[73] and Justice Story[74] on *Equity Jurisprudence*, and Serjeant Stephen's *Commentaries on the Law of England*.[75] Much of this exhortation seems not only optimistic but liable to produce confusion in young students' minds. It must be questioned whether reference to these non-Scottish authorities would not have been more baffling and confusing than helpful.

More remarked also:

> "After Baron Hume published his *Commentaries on Criminal Law*, about the close of the last century, no lectures on this branch of law

were delivered from this chair. Before the publication of that valuable work Professor Hume was in the use of delivering a separate course of lectures on Criminal Law during the summer session, and these lectures formed the substance of his *Commentaries*. His successor, Professor Bell, projected a course of lectures on Criminal and Constitutional Law, but he never carried his design into effect. As no course of lectures on the Law of Scotland can be deemed complete where the Criminal Law is entirely omitted, I have endeavoured, in the concluding lecture, to embody the more important principles of our criminal code."[76]

But the conclusion of his Introductory Lecture is as true today as in the 1860s:

"But you will greatly err if you should imagine that public lectures, however full or complete, could ever dispense with your own private study, or that by means of such lectures a full and correct knowledge of law or of any other science could be acquired. The chief use of lectures is to stimulate and direct your private studies, and your success in acquiring an accurate and extensive knowledge of any branch of science will depend wholly on your own private exertions. And when you keep in view the important interests which may be committed to your trust and the duty of diligently preparing for their discharge, I cannot too strongly urge upon you the indispensable necessity of the most sedulous private study."[77]

More adopted the traditional order of treatment, partly because[78] it had long been the familiar order[79] and partly because it had some advantages lost by following a different order. He dealt successively with social or domestic relations, contracts or obligations, including the commercial contracts but with no examination of the general issues, such as of capacity and power, formalities, validity and the like, applicable to contracts generally, quasi-contracts, obligations arising from delinquency or quasi-delinquency, including under this head, oddly enough, breach of contract, assignation of obligations and extinction of obligations. He then dealt with the distinction between heritable and moveable rights, real or heritable rights, including leases, succession, election law, actions and diligence, including sequestration, and criminal law and procedure (which, as it extends to over 100 pages, was clearly a fuller account than what he dealt with in his concluding lecture).

The lectures proceed in an easy narrative style, not much loaded with references to cases, two or three only to a page. But the book never attained any reputation and was never reprinted or re-edited. It failed to displace Little Erskine and Bell's *Principles*. J. H. A. Macdonald, later Lord Justice-Clerk Kingsburgh, who attended the law classes in the 1850s, reported[80] that,

"with the exception of the Civil Law [Professor Campbell Swinton] I found the law lectures very dry ... and the Scots Law lectures were also terribly humdrum in character. Only one touch of relief do I remember, when the law on slavery was stated, and the dear old modest Professor More, who never looked at the class, but glanced up at the end of every utterance to the upper left-hand corner of the class-room, said in a most sober tone: 'And so' (head up) 'as the sun can never set on the British Dominions', (head up) 'so that sun can never rise upon a British slave'. The worthy gentleman blushed as he looked for the last time at the corner, when for once the room resounded with a round of applause, possibly ironical to some extent, but kindly as well."

Increasingly, however, in the nineteenth century there were published books on individual branches of the law. There were more statutes and cases to take account of, and the quality of analysis was improving.

In the sphere of the personal and domestic relations James Fergusson (1769–1842, advocate 1791), who became a judge of the Commissary Court in 1811, published *Reports of Some Recent Decisions by the Consistorial Courts of Scotland in Actions of Divorce*, 1811–17 (1817), which was reprinted in his *Consistorial Law of Scotland, with reports of decided cases* (1829). The major works in this field were, of course, those of Patrick Fraser.[81]

Francis W. Clark (1827–86, advocate 1851), later Sheriff of Lanarkshire, produced *The Law of Partnership and Joint Stock Companies* (two volumes, 1866), which continued, at least as to the first branch of its subject, the standard authority for a century.

In the field of obligations, Patrick Shaw produced a *Law of Obligations and Contracts* (1847), not of any lasting value, Mungo Ponton Brown, apart from his *Supplement* to and *Synopsis* of Morison's *Dictionary*, wrote a *Treatise on the Law of Sale* (1821) which is the best book on the common law of sale, and George Joseph Bell his small *Inquiries into the Contract of Sale of Goods and Merchandise* (1844). Much later came Richard Brown's[82] *Sale of Goods Act 1893* with a very extensive citation of authority (1895, 1911). Robert Thomson (1791–1857, advocate 1812) wrote a good book on *Bills of Exchange* (1825, 1837, 1865) and William D. Thorburn (1846–88, advocate 1870) another. Carriage was treated by Francis Deas (1839–74, advocate 1862) in the *Law of Railways applicable to Scotland* (1873, 1896).

Delict or reparation for harm became important with the rise of industrial and railway accidents in the nineteenth century. But there were no individual books until John Guthrie Smith's (1831–95, advocate 1854)[83] *Law of Damages: the Reparation of Injuries as administered in Scotland* (1864, 1889) and at the end of the century Arthur Thomson Glegg's (1858–1914, advocate 1883)[84] *Law of Reparation in Scotland* (1892); though ill-arranged and very defective in analysis of basic concepts and principles it reached a fourth edition in 1956. John Borthwick (1787–1845, advocate 1810) published a *Law of Libel and Slander in Scotland with Appendix of 48 unreported cases* in 1826 and Frank T. Cooper (1863–1915, advocate 1886)[85] a very unsatisfactory *Defamation and Verbal Injury* in 1894, revised in 1906, in which these two kinds of laws are treated as separate species instead of as one species and the genus respectively, as the institutional writers had appreciated. J. C. C. Brown produced a small *Law of Nuisance* in 1891.

There were no adequate books on land law generally until John Rankine's[86] *Law of Land Ownership* in 1879, but particular branches were better covered. Robert Hunter's *Law of Landlord and Tenant* (1833) reached a fourth edition, by William Guthrie, in 1876, but thereafter was superseded by Rankine's[86] *Law of Leases in Scotland* (1887, 3rd ed. 1916). Erskine D. Sandford (1793–1861, advocate 1816) wrote a *History and Law of Entails* (1822, 1842) and a *Law of Heritable Succession* in two volumes (1830). There was a good deal of writing about parishes, churches and teinds. Sir John Connell's (1765–1831, advocate 1788)[87] *Law of Scotland respecting Parishes* (1818), *Law of Scotland relating to Ministers' Glebes, Patronage, etc.* (1818) and *Law of Scotland regarding Tithes and the Stipends of Parochial Clergy* (three volumes, 1815; two volumes, 1830) still have value. Alexander Dunlop (1793–1880, advocate 1817)[88] also known as a reporter, wrote a *Parochial Law* (1830, third edition 1841) and a *Law of Patronage* (1833). Later William Buchanan (1780–1863, advocate 1806) wrote a *Law of Teinds* (1862) and William G. Black a *Parochial Ecclesiastical Law of Scotland* (1888 and later editions), *Parochial Law of Scotland other than Ecclesiastical* (1897) and *What are Teinds? A History of Tithes in Scotland* (1893). Nenion Elliot, the Clerk of Teinds, was author of *Teind Papers* (1874) and of *Teinds or Tithes and Procedure in the Court of Teinds in Scotland* (1893), described as a "standard work."[89] Many of these books still have considerable historical value.

Security rights were, surprisingly enough, not treated individually until Gloag and Irvine's book[90] in 1897. The subject was, however, covered in books on conveyancing. David Robertson, a barrister of the Middle Temple, published an interesting *Treatise on Personal Succession* in 1836, treating of both Scots and English law and, quite importantly, dealing with problems of foreign and international succession.

Trusts received a substantial amount of attention from textwriters. Charles Forsyth (1816–49, advocate 1837) published his *Law of Trusts and Trustees in Scotland* in 1844. Then came Lord McLaren's book, *Law of Trusts and Trust Settlements* which appeared in two volumes in 1862, and was later incorporated in his *Wills and Succession* (third edition, 1894).[91] Charles R. A. Howden (1862–1936, advocate 1886) wrote a handy *Trusts, Trustees and the Trust Acts* in 1893, and his contemporary Alexander John Pople Menzies (1863–1943, advocate 1886)[92] published on the *Law of Scotland affecting Trustees* (two volumes, 1893–97; one volume, 1913). George H. Thoms (1831–1903, advocate 1855) wrote on *Judicial Factors, Curators Bonis and Managers of Burghs* in 1859 and 1881.

Conveyancing was very well-served. Robert Bell (?–1816, Writer to the Signet 1784, advocate 1812)[93] who in 1793 proposed a scheme for public instruction in conveyancing, published *Lectures on the Solemnities used in Scotland in the Testing of Deeds* (1795); *System of the Forms of Deeds* (two volumes, 1797; seven volumes, 1802–05 and 1811–17); *Outline of Lectures on Conveyancing* (1800–07); *A Treatise on Leases explaining the Nature, Form, etc. of the Contract of Lease and Legal Rights of the Parties* (1803; fourth edition, two volumes, 1825–26); *Laws of Election* (1812); *Abstract of the Forms of Deeds relating to Heritable*

Rights (1814); *The Conveyance of Land to a Purchaser and on the Manner of Completing his Title* (1815; third edition 1830). Later Alexander Duff (1800–50, Writer to the Signet 1823, advocate 1848) published several valuable books, a *Treatise on Deeds and Forms used in the Constitution, Transmission and Extinction of Feudal Rights* (1838), a *Treatise on Deeds, Chiefly affecting Moveables* (1840), *Recent Statutes relative to Conveyancing* (1847 and 1848), and a *Treatise on the Deed of Entail* (1848). These are classics on conveyancing as it was before the reforming and consolidating Acts transformed the subject.

The *Lectures* of three professors of conveyancing in Edinburgh University were published, those of Allan Menzies (1804–56, Writer to the Signet 1829)[94] in 1856, described judicially as a "very reliable authority"[95] with a fourth edition, revised and extended by James S. Sturrock in 1900, of Alexander Montgomerie Bell (1809–66, Writer to the Signet 1835)[96] in two volumes in 1867, with a third edition in 1882, and of John Philp Wood (1847–1906, Writer to the Signet 1871)[97] in 1903. John Craigie's (1857–1919, advocate 1884)[98] books *Scottish Law of Conveyancing: Heritable Rights* (1887, third edition 1899) and *Scottish Law of Conveyancing: Moveable Rights* (1888 and 1894) were less diffuse, more concise and useful. Craigie also compiled a valuable volume of *Conveyancing Statutes, 1214–1894* (1895).

There were many other books connected with conveyancing, such as J. Hendry's *Manual of Conveyancing* (1859; fourth edition, 1888) in question-and-answer form for students; one of the most useful was J. Henderson Begg's (1844–1911, advocate 1870) *Conveyancing Code* (1879) bringing together all the legislation affecting conveyancing. At the end of the century John Burns, Writer to the Signet, published his *Handbook of Conveyancing* (1889) a learned but very ill-composed work for students, and his *Conveyancing Practice* (1894) a valuable but badly-written book of practical guidance. Both continued in use until the mid-twentieth century.

Incidental rights of landownership were examined by A. Grigor in *Game Laws relating to Scotland* (1834, 1837), Alexander Forbes Irvine (1818–92, advocate 1843) in the *Game Laws of Scotland* (1850, 1856, 1883), while Charles Stewart (1840–1916, advocate 1862) wrote on *Laws and Rights of Fishing in Scotland* (1809, 1892).

Throughout the nineteenth century successive editions of the *Juridical Styles*, or *Juridical Society of Edinburgh's Collection of Styles or Complete System of Conveyancing* remained an invaluable practitioner's standby.

Prescription was thoroughly examined by Mark Napier (1798–1879, advocate 1820)[99] in his *Law of Prescription in Scotland* (1839–54) and by John Hepburn Millar (1864–1929, advocate 1889, professor of constitutional law and history at Edinburgh, 1909–25)[1] in his *Handbook of Prescription according to the law of Scotland* (1893).

In the rather specialised field of heraldry George Seton (1822–1908, advocate 1846, F.R.S.E. 1872)[2] published his *Law and Practice of Heraldry in Scotland* in 1863, a recension of which was incorporated in J. H. Stevenson's *Heraldry in Scotland* (two volumes, 1914).

Henry Goudy (1848–1921, advocate 1872),[3] who was the unsuccessful rival to John Rankine for the Edinburgh Chair of Scots Law in 1888 before he succeeded James Muirhead as Professor of Civil Law at Edinburgh (1890) and then departed in 1893 to succeeed James Bryce in the Regius Chair of Civil Law at Oxford, wrote a *Law of Bankruptcy* (1886, fourth edition 1914) which has not yet been superseded as the standard text.

In the field of international private law William Guthrie (1835–1908, advocate 1861) published a translation of F. C. von Savigny's *Treatise on the Conflict of Laws* (1869, 1880) and G. R. Gillespie (1851–92, advocate 1875) a translation of Ludwig von Bar's *Private International Law* (second edition, 1892). Both were valuable works in their time but have been almost completely superseded by the progress of international conventions and decisions and the developing sophistication of scholarship in this field.

Further mention deserves to be made of William Guthrie (1835–1908, advocate 1861)[4] who had little practice and wrote nothing of his own but diligently edited. He edited the *Journal of Jurisprudence* 1867–74 and was then successively sheriff substitute (1874–1903) and sheriff principal of Lanarkshire 1903–08. He received an LL.D. from Edinburgh in 1881. He translated and annotated Savigny's *Conflict of Laws* (1869, 1880), published two volumes of *Select Cases in the Sheriff Courts*, 1861–78 (1879) and 1879–85 (1894),[5] edited a fourth edition of Hunter's *Landlord and Tenant* (1876), three editions of Erskine's *Principles* (1870, 1874, 1881) and the last five editions of Bell's *Principles* (1872, 1876, 1885, 1889 and 1899). He was a very capable lawyer and his editions of these writers were always highly regarded.

In the sphere of adjective law, evidence was first treated as a distinct subject by James Glassford (1771–1845, advocate 1793), who published a *Principles of Evidence* in 1820, and by George Tait (?–1865, advocate 1807) in a *Law of Evidence in Scotland* (1824). Both were superseded by William Gillespie Dickson's (1823–1876, advocate 1847) *Law of Evidence in Scotland* (two volumes, 1855, 1864) which, particularly as revised in the third edition (1887) by Philip J. Hamilton Grierson (1851–1927, advocate 1880, later Solicitor of Inland Revenue and knighted),[6] was recognised as the standard authority and still, more than a century later, regularly consulted.

Court of Session practice and procedure, and the forms of process attracted many writers. J. Watson produced a *New Form of Process before the Court of Session* in 1799, James Ivory a *Form of Process before the Court of Session* (two volumes, 1815–18), T. Beveridge a *Forms of Process before the Court of Session, Teinds and Jury Court* (two volumes, 1826) and J. J. Darling a *Practice of the Court of Session* (two volumes, 1833) which was taken as the basis of Charles Farquhar Shand's (1812–89, advocate 1834, barrister 1876, Chief Justice of Mauritius 1860)[7] *Practice of the Court of Session* (two volumes, 1848, with Appendix 1858). William Adam, the first Lord Chief Commissioner of the Jury Court wrote several books on the practice of that court, notably a *Practical Treatise and Observations on Trial by Jury in Civil Cases* (1836). Robert McFarlane also produced a *Practice of the Court of Session in Jury Court Civil Causes* (1837), and also a volume of reports of cases in the Court of Session by Jury Trial, 1838–39 (1841). Among his many works Patrick

Shaw produced a *Forms of a Process in the House of Lords, Court of Session, Jury Court, Teind Court and Sheriff Court* (two volumes, 1843).

In 1877–79, however, Aeneas J. G. Mackay published his magisterial two-volume *Practice of the Court of Session* which superseded all the previous works. In 1893 he produced a more concise *Manual of Practice in the Court of Session*. Both were in constant use for many years and are still worth looking into. There were also some lesser works on practice such as J. P. Coldstream's *Procedure in the Court of Session* (1878; fourth edition, 1889).

There was similarly a series of books on sheriff court practice. J. McGlashan's *Practice in the Sheriff Courts* went through four editions between 1831 and 1868. It was described judicially as "a very accurate and useful treatise on the practice of sheriff courts, published by Mr. McGlashan."[8] John Dove Wilson's (1833–1908, advocate 1857)[9] *Practice of the Sheriff Courts of Scotland in Civil Causes* did the same between 1869 and 1891. This in turn was replaced by William J. Lewis's[10] *Handbook of Sheriff Court Practice* (1896; eighth edition 1939). The specialised area of sheriff court work dealing with confirmation of executors was well treated by James Geddes Currie, Depute Commissary Clerk of Edinburgh,[11] in a book with that title which, published in 1884, continues, revised, in regular use. It replaced W. Alexander's *Practice of the Commissary Court of Scotland* (1859).

The various forms of diligence were treated of in J. Parker's *Notes on the Diligence of Adjudication* (1845), R. Campbell's *Law and Practice of Citation and Diligence* (1862), W. Spinks' *Procedure and Redress at Law* (1879), and some other books before the whole subject was thoroughly examined by John Graham Stewart (1860–1917, advocate 1887)[12] in his *Law of Diligence* (1898) which has remained the standard work for nearly a century.

John Montgomerie Bell (1804–62, advocate 1825) published a *Law of Arbitration in Scotland* described judicially as "his excellent Treatise on Arbitration."[13]

In the later nineteenth century the solicitor's profession began to be organised nationally and John Henderson Begg (1844–1911, advocate 1870), wrote *The Law of Scotland relating to Law Agents* (1873, 1883), now much outdated but unreplaced and on many points still valuable.

Accordingly during, and particularly by the latter part of, the nineteenth century the student and the practitioner of law were, in general, well supplied with literature in most fields. Some of the books were not very good, but some were very sound; some had still before them a long period of utility.

NOTES

¹ Chaps. 19, 20, 21, *supra*.

² Chaps. 22, 24, *supra*.

³ Chap. 23, *supra*.

⁴ (1898) 5 S.L.T. 197 (portrait).

⁵ He also published anonymously a pamphlet *Points of Leading Cases in Private International Law done into Doggerel* in 1896.

⁶ DNB Supp., 1922–30; H. A. L. Fisher, *James Bryce* (1927); Memoir by H. A. L. Fisher in *Proc. British Academy* 12 (1926), 297. (Bryce was an original Fellow when the British Academy was chartered in 1901, and was President 1913–17.) See also F. H. Lawson, *The Oxford Law School, 1850–1965* (1968), pp. 29–30.

⁷ DNB; Chambers, BDES; portrait and biographical notice by David Laing (Bannatyne Club, 1854); Cosmo Innes, *Memoir of Thomas Thomson* (Bannatyne Club, 1874).

⁸ A list of its publications is in C. S. Terry, *Catalogue of the Publications of Scottish Historical and Kindred Clubs and Societies, 1780–1908* (1909).

⁹ Edited by J. D. Mackie and published by the Stair Society in Vol. 10 (1946). The case is *Cranston* v. *Gibson*, May 16, 1818, F.C.

¹⁰ Later continued by Sir James Balfour Paul and others, from 1882 onwards.

¹¹ There is a new edition of Vol. VI (1643–60) in two Parts, published in 1870–72, superseding the Vol. VI of 1819.

¹² DNB; *Memoir* (1874) founded on various obituaries; A. Grant, *Story of the University of Edinburgh*, II, p. 370.

¹³ DNB; Chambers, BDES; *History of the Writers to H.M. Signet*; references in Lockhart's *Life of Scott*.

¹⁴ DNB; Henry Mackenzie, in *Trans. R.S.E.* (1796).

¹⁵ DNB; Brunton & Haig, p. 545; Chambers, BDES; Rev. Archd. Alison in *Trans. R.S.E.* 8 (1816–17) 515.

¹⁶ A. Logan Turner, *History of the University of Edinburgh, 1883–1933*, p. 98; W. Hole, *Quasi Cursores* (1884) p. 195 (portrait).

¹⁷ DNB; J. W. Burgon, *Life of Patrick Fraser Tytler* (1859); biographical sketch prefixed to 4th vol. of 1864 ed. of his *History*.

¹⁸ DNB.

¹⁹ DNB.

²⁰ DNB; memoir by his widow in one edition of *The Book Hunter*, 1882; *Blackwood's Magazine*, 1881.

²¹ DNB; obituary in *Proc. RSE*, 20 (1893–94) viii.

²² On Stevenson see (1903) 11 S.L.T. 1 (portrait); C. J. (Lord) Guthrie, "Robert Louis Stevenson" (1919) 31 J.R. 89, 161; (1920) 32 J.R. 7, 129; Rosaline Masson, *Life of Robert Louis Stevenson* (1923), p. 92.

²³ DNB 1922–30; (1898) 6 S.L.T. 29 (portrait); D. Baird Smith, *Trans. Glasgow Archaeological Soc.* (N.S.) vii (1924) 351; E. L. G. Stones and T. I. Rae, *George Neilson; The March Laws* in *Stair Society Miscellany* I (1971) (portrait); E. L. G. Stones, *F. W. Maitland: Letters to George Neilson* (1976) (portrait).

²⁴ See P. G. B. McNeill, "Senators of the College of Justice, 1569–1578," 1960 J.R. 120; "Senators of the College of Justice, 1532–69," 1978 J.R. 209.

²⁵ DNB Supp., 1901–11; (1894) 1 S.L.T. 487 (portrait); (1901) 9 S.L.T. 17 (portrait); 1911 S.L.T. (News) 102. He wrote also a *Memoir of John Major* (1892) and contributed a history of *Fife and Kinross* (1896) to Blackwood's *County Histories of Scotland* series.

²⁶ (1900) 8 S.L.T. 41 (portrait).

²⁷ A. L. Turner, *History of the University of Edinburgh, 1883–1933*, p. 92; W. Hole, *Quasi Cursores* (1884) 175 (portrait); G. Carle, "James Muirhead" (1890) 2 J.R. 27 (portrait).

²⁸ A. L. Turner, *op. cit.*, p. 93; *The Times*, March 4, 1921; *Oxford Magazine*, April 29, 1921.

²⁹ A. D. Bowers, "The Founding of the Society" (1959) 5 J.S.P.T.L. (N.S.) 1.

³⁰ Lord Reay was President. Goudy as Vice-President wrote the introduction to Vol. I of what became (from Vol. IV) the *Transactions of the Grotius Society*, giving the aims of the society.

³¹ There was a third edition by Alexander Grant in 1916.

[32] F. H. Lawson, *The Oxford Law School, 1850–1965*, p. 82.

[33] 1929 S.L.T. (News) 21 (portrait).

[34] Tait's *Index, Notes*, p. 517.

[35] DNB.

[36] He also produced a *Translation of the Technical Phrases in Erskine's Institutes* (1820–1829), a *Collection of Latin Maxims* (1823), a *Digest of the Law of Scotland relating to Marriage*, 1827–31, and a *History, Law and Privileges of the Palace and Sanctuary of Holyrood House, with List of Cases* (1831).

[37] He also edited reports of House of Lords cases 1821–38, a volume of Justiciary cases 1819–31, and a Digest of Cases 1800–62.

[38] Later Professor of Scots Law in Edinburgh University, 1865–88.

[39] Though the series are known as Shaw, Dunlop, Macpherson, Rettie and Fraser, these reporters were not in office for the same periods as the reports which bear their names. Shaw was a reporter from 1 S. to 13 S., Dunlop joined him in 2 S. and they were joined by others to 16 S. Hence these volumes are sometimes known as Shaw and Dunlop's reports, cited S. & D. Dunlop dropped out after 3 D. and others carried on to 24 D. Hence these volumes are sometimes called Dunlop, Bell and Murray's reports, cited D.B. and M. Alexander Colquhoun-Stirling-Murray-Dunlop (1798–1870, advocate 1820; (DNB) published also a treatise on the *Poor Laws of Scotland* (1825 and two later editions), *Parochial Law* (1830 and two later editions), and a *Law of Patronage* (1833). He was much involved in the controversies preceding the Disruption of 1843 and was an M.P., 1852–67. Macpherson became one of the reporters from 1853 (16 D.) and continued to 2 M. and then dropped out, and in that year Rettie joined the team; by 4 M. Rettie was senior reporter, and he continued, to 11 M. and throughout the whole series which bears his name. Rettie continued chief reporter throughout the Fraser series and on to 1910 S.C. (55 years!) when he was replaced by J. S. Leadbetter. Only from 1 F. is anyone designated "editor"; till then there are merely teams of reporters. In 1 F. Rettie became "editor" and Hugh Fraser senior reporter. The change to *Session Cases* in 1907 was made when the Faculty of Advocates assumed responsibility for the reports.

[40] These are:

Reporter	Vols.	Period	Published
David Robertson	1	1707–27	1807
Thomas S. Paton	6	1726–1821	1849–56
Patrick Shaw	2	1821–26	1826–28
James Wilson and Patrick Shaw	7	1825–35	1829–39
Patrick Shaw and Charles H. Maclean	3	1835–38	1836–39
Charles H. Maclean and Geo. Robinson	1	1839	1840
Geo. Robinson	2	1840–41	1840–42
Sydney S. Bell	7	1842–50	1843–52
John F. Macqueen	4	1851–65	1855–66
James Paterson	2	1851–73	1879, 1895

Patrick Shaw also edited the Session Cases 1821–38, a volume of Justiciary cases 1891–31, and a Digest of Cases 1800–1862.

[41] They are distinguished as *e.g.* (1874) 1 R. (H.L.) 20, which is accordingly a different case from 1 R. 20.

[42] The series are as follows:

Reporter	Vols.	Period	Published
Patrick Shaw	1	1819–31	1832
David Syme	1	1826–29	1829
Archibald Swinton	2	1835–41	1838–42
Archibald Broun	2	1842–45	1844–46
Patrick Arkley	1	1846–48	1849
John Shaw	1	1846–51	1853
Alex Forbes Irvine	5	1851–68	1855–68
Charles T. Couper	5	1868–85	1871–87
James C. White	3	1885–93	1888–93
Edwin Adam	7	1893–1916	1894–1917

Patrick Shaw also edited the Session Cases, 1821–38 and volumes of House of Lords cases 1821–38 and a Digest of Cases 1800–62.

[43] They are distinguished as, *e.g.* (1874) 1 R. (J.) 20, the J. standing for "Justiciary." From 1907 to 1916 they are known as S.C. (J.) and from 1917 *Justiciary Cases* (J.C.).

[44] J. Crabb Watt, *John Inglis* (1893), p. 45.

[45] A. E. Whetstone, *Scottish County Government in the Eighteenth and Nineteenth Centuries* (1981).

[46] *Butter* v. *McLaren*, 1909 S.C. 786, at p. 791 *per* Lord Ardwall. See also p. 800.

[47] Chap. 19, *supra*.

[48] Chap. 21, *supra*.

[49] DNB; his own *Life Jottings of an Old Edinburgh Citizen* (1915) (portrait); *Who Was Who*, 1908–29; (1896) 3 S.L.T. 207 (portrait); (1900) 12 J.R. 217 (portrait); 1915 S.L.T. (News) 69 (portrait); (1919) 40 *Proc. R.S.E.* 5.

[50] *Life Jottings*, p. 316.

[51] 1912 S.L.T. (News) 125 (portrait).

[52] DNB; *Scotsman*, January 31, 1867.

[53] See *Brodie* v. *Clark* (1859) 21 D. 634.

[54] More published also an edition of Erskine's *Principles* in 1827 and succeeded Bell in the chair of Scots Law at Edinburgh in 1843. On his *Lectures* see Chap. 24 and also *infra*. See obituary in *Proc. RSE* (1861); A. Grant, *Story of the University of Edinburgh*, II, p. 375.

[55] J. Crabb Watt, *John Inglis* (1893), p. 45.

[56] Preface, p. xvi.

[57] (1811) 2 Hagg. Consist. Rep. 54; 161 Eng. Rep. 665.

[58] 2 Hagg. C.R. (Appendix) 42; 161 Eng. Rep. 802.

[59] *e.g.* in *Kerr* v. *Martin* (1840) 2 D. 752, at pp. 771, 777; *Orlandi* v. *Castelli*, 1961 S.C. 113, at p. 119.

[60] 1942 S.C. 239, at p. 265.

[61] at p. 276; Lord Jamieson at p. 289 also cited More's Notes.

[62] DNB; Brunton & Haig, p. 554.

[63] *e.g. Fortington* v. *Kinnaird*, 1942, S.C. 239, at p. 265.

[64] (1899) 7 S.L.T. 84.

[65] On this see Chap. 24, *supra*.

[66] *Lectures*, i, pp. 6–7.

[67] *Ibid.*, p. 8.

[68] *Ibid.*, p. 13.

[69] *Ibid.*, p. 14.

[70] *Ibid.*, p. 14.

[71] Robert Joseph Pothier (1699–1772), the greatest French jurist, wrote *Pandectae Justinianae in novum ordinem digestae* (1748), *Traité des Obligations* (1761), translated by Evans as *Pothier on Obligations* (1806), *Traité du Contrat de Vente* (1762) and treatises on many other particular contracts, and on other branches of French customary (pre-Code Civile) law. On Pothier see Dupin, *Dissertation sur la vie et les ouvrages de Pothier* (1825); Frémont, *Vie de Robert Joseph Pothier* (1859); de Montmorency, in *Great Jurists of the World* (ed. Macdonell and Manson, 1913), p. 447.

[72] Raymond Théodore Troplong (1795–1869) became first president of the court of appeal in Paris (1848), president of the Senate and first president of the Court of Cassation in 1852. He wrote a large number of works, including a *Commentaire du contrat de société en matière civile et commerciale* (1843), all part of a series entitled *Le droit civil expliquée suivant l'ordre des articles du Code.* (It is held by Advocates', Signet and Edinburgh University Libraries.) On Troplong see further Larousse, *Dictionnaire Universel du XIX me siècle.*

[73] James Kent (1763–1847) became Professor of Law in Columbia College, New York (now Columbia University) in 1793–97, became a judge of the New York Supreme Court in 1798, and Chancellor of that state (whence he is called Chancellor Kent). In 1823, having retired from the Bench, he again became Professor of law at Columbia and held the office actively till 1826 and nominally till 1847. Basing himself on the model of Blackstone he used his lectures as the basis of a systematic exposition of the common law of the United States. Published over 1826–30 the *Commentaries on American Law* were a huge success and undoubtedly the most important American law book of the 19th century. On Kent see *Dictionary of American Biography*; Duer, *Discourse on the Life of James Kent* (1848); Goebel, *The School of Law, Columbia University* (1955).

[74] Joseph Story (1779–1845) sat in Congress and served as an Associate Justice of the U.S. Supreme Court (1811–45). From 1829 to 1845 he was also Dane Professor of Law at Harvard

and wrote numerous *Commentaries* on various branches of American law, notably *Equity Jurisprudence* (1836), *Agency, Partnership, Bills of Exchange* and other topics. Apart from Kent no one has had greater influence on American law. See *Dictionary of American Biography*; W. W. Story, *Life and Letters of Joseph Story*; Warren, *The Supreme Court in U.S. History*; Sutherland, *The Law at Harvard*; Harno, *Legal Education in the U.S.* (1958).

75 Henry John Stephen (1787–1864, serjeant-at-law) wrote a *New Commentaries on the Laws of England partly founded on Blackstone*, in four vols. (1841–45), modelled on Blackstone and as a more modern version of that work. It was very successful and reached a 21st edition, very radically changed, in 1950. A. Gibson and A. Weldon produced a *Guide to Stephen's Commentaries* (1879, 17th ed. 1928) and there were other students' guides to that work. On Stephen see DNB.

76 *Lectures*, I, p. 15.

77 *Ibid.*, p. 16.

78 *Ibid.*, p. 14.

79 Though departed from by Bell's *Commentaries* and *Principles*.

80 *Life Jottings of an Old Edinburgh Citizen* (1915), p. 234.

81 Chap. 22, *supra*.

82 (1896) 4 S.L.T. 141 (portrait).

83 (1895) 3 S.L.T. 50, 53 (portrait).

84 (1900) 8 S.L.T. 149 (portrait); 1914 S.L.T. (News) 3.

85 (1899) 7 S.L.T. 37 (portrait); 1915 S.L.T. (News) 89 (portrait).

86 See further, Chap. 26, *infra*.

87 DNB; Kay's *Edinburgh Portraits*. He was the last judge of the Scottish Court of Admiralty.

88 DNB.

89 *Galloway* v. *Earl of Minto*, 1920 S.C. 354, at p. 391, *per* Lord Guthrie.

90 See further, Chap. 27, *infra*.

91 On this see Chap. 24, *supra*.

92 1914 S.L.T. (News) 33 (portrait).

93 Anderson, S.N., I, p. 275. He was a brother of George Joseph Bell and Sir Charles Bell, the distinguished anatomist and Professor of Surgery at Edinburgh, 1836–42.

94 Grant, *Story of the University of Edinburgh*, II, p. 377: "Professor Menzies, whose word on any matter of practice, is law. . . ." *Lord Advocate* v. *Earl of Zetland*, 1920 S.C. (H.L.) 1, at p. 31 *per* Lord Shaw (rather extravagant praise).

95 *Lumsden* v. *Buchanan* (1864) 2 M. 695, at p. 745, *per* Lord Deas.

96 Grant, *op. cit.*, II, p. 378.

97 A. L. Turner, *History of the University of Edinburgh, 1883–1933*, p. 98; (1894) 2 S.L.T. 129 (portrait); (1906) 14 S.L.T. 137 (portrait).

98 (1897) 5 S.L.T. 145 (portrait).

99 DNB. He wrote also *Memoirs of John Napier of Merchiston* (his ancestor) (1834); *Montrose and the Covenanters* (1838); *Life and Times of Montrose* (1840); *Memorials of Montrose and his Times* (1848–50); *Memoirs of the Marquis of Montrose* (1856); *Memorials of Graham of Claverhouse, Viscount Dundee* (1859–62) and edited Spotiswood's *History of the Church of Scotland*, Vols. ii and iii, for the Bannatyne Club.

1 *Who Was Who*, 1929–40; Turner, *History of the University of Edinburgh* 1883–1933, p. 95. He was a son of Lord Craighill and grandson of Lord Neaves. He wrote also *The Mid-Eighteenth Century* (Blackwood's *Periods of English Literature*) (1902); *A Literary History of Scotland* (1903) and *Scottish Prose of the Seventeenth and Eighteenth Centuries* (1912). The last two are still well-regarded. His inaugural lecture as professor is printed in (1909) 21 J.R. 219.

2 (1908) 16 S.L.T. 133 (portrait).

3 (1893) 1 S.L.T. 113 (portrait); *The Times*, March 4, 1921; *Oxford Magazine*, April 29, 1921; J. Mackintosh, "Henry Goudy" (1922) 34 J.R. 53.

4 DNB, 2nd Supp.; *Who Was Who*, 1897–1915; (1893) 1 S.L.T. 17; (1903) 10 S.L.T. 149; (1908) 16 S.L.T. 77 (each with portrait).

5 After 1885 sheriff court cases were reported in the Sheriff Court Reports published in the *Scottish Law Review* and some after 1893 in the *Scots Law Times*.

6 (1895) 3 S.L.T. 139 (portrait).

7 He was the plaintiff in the leading case of *P. & O. S.N. Co.* v. *Shand* (1865) 3 Moo. P.C. (N.S.) 272, when his luggage was lost on the voyage to Mauritius.

⁸ *Faculty of Procurators in Glasgow* v. *Douglas* (1851) 14 D. 280, at p. 289, *per* Lord Cunninghame.

⁹ He was sheriff substitute at Kincardine 1861–70 and Aberdeen 1870–90, and Professor of Scots Law at Aberdeen University 1891–1901. See (1908) 15 S.L.T. 149. The 4th edition was by his son John Carnegie Dove Wilson (1865–1935, advocate 1888; judge and later President of the Supreme Court, Natal); see 1911 S.L.T. (News) 193 (portrait).

¹⁰ 1931 S.L.T. (News) 38 (portrait).

¹¹ (1906) 13 S.L.T. 161 (portrait).

¹² (1898) 6 S.L.T. 105 (portrait).

¹³ *Thomson's Trs.* v. *Muir* (1867) 6 M. 145, at p. 149, *per* Lord Justice-Clerk Patton.

CHAPTER 26

SIR JOHN RANKINE

JOHN Rankine[1] was born at Sorn in Ayrshire on February 18, 1846, and educated at the local school there, Edinburgh Academy and the Universities of Edinburgh (M.A. 1865) and Heidelberg, where he studied under Vangerow, whom he thereafter always called "my revered teacher." Called to the Bar in 1869, he became an advocate depute in 1885 and, having published two major books, was appointed Professor of Scots Law in the University of Edinburgh in 1888. He received an Honorary LL.D. from the University of Glasgow in 1892, was elected F.R.S.E., took silk in 1897 when the Scottish order of Q.C.s was created, was knighted in 1921, and resigned his chair in 1922. He died later the same year, on August 8.

Rankine was clearly more interested in heritable property than in obligations or commercial relations. "It was perhaps not difficult to discover from his lectures that, as with the older school of Scots lawyers, commercial law possessed less attraction in his eyes than these topics which are associated with the law of heritable property; but no student could fail to admire the skill with which, in the comparatively brief time at his disposal, he contrived to present so complete an outline of all the main principles."[2]

In 1879 he published *The Law of Land Ownership in Scotland*. In this he was concerned neither with heritable conveyancing nor with landlord and tenant but with the principles regulating the use and enjoyment of lands and other heritages by their owner in possession. The main divisions of his subject are accordingly possession and ownership generally, restrictions in favour of the Crown and the public, restrictions in favour of individuals, and public burdens. It is a scholarly book and the propositions are well buttressed by references to authority. It reached a fourth edition in 1909. The book is original in theme, plan and execution. It remains of great value and is still regularly referred to, though the statutory restrictions and burdens on a landowner's use of his land have increased greatly since Rankine's day.

Eighteen eighty-seven witnessed the publication of the *Law of Leases*. This theme was not novel but Hunter on *Landlord and Tenant*[3] was by now somewhat outdated and Rankine wrote a fresh and very thorough examination of the subject, supported by a very full citation of authority. It took the place of Hunter, became the recognised authority, and went into a third edition in 1916. It too, despite much statutory change, is still a standard authority and supplemented rather than replaced by modern works.

Rankine was responsible for several editions of "Little Erskine," including the last (the 21st) in 1911, in which he had several collaborators, and editor of the *Scots Revised Reports* and joint consulting editor of the *Scots Style Book*.

At the very end of his career he published a small book on personal bar, *A Treatise on the Law of Personal Bar in Scotland, collated with the English law of estoppel in pais*, which brings together the variety of principles which all have the underlying rationale that a person may not be heard to deny what he has previously affirmed by his conduct, such principles as *rei interventus*, mora, taciturnity and acquiescence, homologation, adoption, holding out and some other related principles. Again it is an entirely novel work in that these principles had not previously been examined as a group or in relation to one another, but it has never won the acclaim of either of his other books, partly because it deals with a rather subsidiary group of principles rather than with major branches of private law, though it remains a quite distinctive contribution to legal literature and is the only book on these principles in Scotland.

Rankine had a long tenure of his chair, was a good lecturer and regarded with affection by his students, and became a respected father-figure to a whole generation of lawyers, and he contributed two major books to the corpus of standard Scottish works which are both, after a century, still in regular use.

NOTES

[1] *Who Was Who*, 1916–28; A. L. Turner, *History of the University of Edinburgh, 1883–1933*, p. 97; (1893) 1 S.L.T. 147 (portrait); 1919 S.L.T. (News) 61 (portrait); 1921 S.L.T. (News) 97 (portrait); 1922 S.L.T. (News) 123 (portrait); (1922) 42 *Proc. R.S.E.* 371; J. Balfour Paul, "The late Sir John Rankine KC" (1923) 34 J.R. 305 (portrait).

[2] Turner, *supra*, p. 97.

[3] On this book see Chap. 25, *supra*.

CHAPTER 27

WILLIAM MURRAY GLOAG

AFTER John Millar[1] the Regius Chair of Law at Glasgow was held by several undistinguished persons. But this changed when Gloag came. William Murray Gloag[2] was born on March 16, 1865, the only son of William Ellis Gloag (1828–1909, advocate 1853)[3] who was elevated to the Bench as Lord Kincairney in 1889 and retired in 1905. He was educated at Edinburgh Academy and Balliol College, Oxford, (B.A., 1888) and was called to the Bar in 1889.

From 1899 to 1905 he was an Assistant (to Rankine) in Scots Law and from 1902 to 1905 part-time lecturer in evidence and procedure in the University of Edinburgh. Then in 1905 he was appointed Regius Professor of Law in the University of Glasgow. He took silk in 1909 and received an honorary LL.D. from Edinburgh in 1915. He was active in the University, a Senate Assessor in the University Court for eight years and University representative on various boards. He died quite suddenly on February 5, 1934; he never married, and a sister kept house for him at his residence, 3 The University.

Gloag was of slight build, small and dapper, with a slightly withered hand.

> "The figure and gait could never be mistaken – the bald egg-shaped dome of a head, the resolute, slightly choleric, slightly pugnacious, Churchillian mien, the foreshortened arm, with its curious curving movement, clutching a bundle of lecture notes, the vigorous jerky gait as he propelled himself forward on the tip of one toe. The peculiarities of this hereditary gait inevitably recalled the story of Gloag and his father, Lord Kincairney. One day young Gloag followed his father up the Mound in Edinburgh to the Court of Session. The son's gait so resembled the father's that a passer-by, possessed of a wholesome respect for Senators of the College of Justice, conceived that the youth following the judge was deliberately mimicking him, and gave young Gloag a cuff on the ear, exclaiming: 'Take that for imitating a Court of Session judge. Don't you know that that's Lord Kincairney?'."

In his teaching Gloag

> "covered a wide field with precision and point, and his wit and his rather mordant comment delighted his classes. He regarded his course as a general introduction to the study of law, but naturally emphasised the importance of those fields in which he was a master. . . . His comments on men and institutions were flavoured with Attic salt, but they were delivered with a disarming smile. He was a familiar figure in the Western Club and on Prestwick golf course and he played bridge and golf with equal mastery and

deliberation. He was a faithful son of Balliol College and like all Balliol men he believed that Oxford was Balliol College."[5]

Gloag had a very distinctive personality and made a profound impression on his students, most of whom remembered him with affection and revered his memory all their lives. Nearly all regarded him as the best teacher they encountered in all their days at university. His speech tended to be staccato, but his lectures were concise, omitting all irrelevancy. He had tremendous enthusiasm for his subject, based on encyclopaedic knowledge, and could communicate that enthusiasm to his students. He spoke extempore without reference to notes, save for citation of authorities; he had great skill in illustrating legal principle by apt example of actual circumstances, and moreover with considerable humour. Even at eight in the morning, when he lectured, he roused and stimulated.[6] "The average student would quickly have forgotten the decision in *Heaven* v. *Pender* (1883) 11 Q.B.D. 503 (except that it related to the liability of one supplying a defective article to the person who was injured by using it) had not Gloag added the remark that Heaven climbed a defective staging provided by Pender and then "Heaven fell" – a pre-Copernican observation which always caused delight."[7] After sources, procedure, relevancy, right, obligation and duty he went on to contract, which he said was the basis of the law. Some special topics, such as workmen's compensation and rent restriction, he dealt with in special lectures in successive years, not annually. His treatment of criminal law had to be, and was, very brief, in the last two or three lectures of the session. (It has to be remembered that he had what was even then the impossible task of covering the main topics of the whole private law in less than 100 lectures, Tuesday to Saturday weekly from October to March. Other courses occupied the summer term.) He held strong and fearless views about decisions which were in his view questionable and was not prevented from criticising them by deference to their authority. He was a keen golfer at the Old Course, Prestwick, a good after-dinner speaker and very humorous, not pompous but sociable, though he found it rather difficult to unbend with individual students, save with the favoured groups whom he occasionally invited to breakfast after the lecture.[8]

His first major publication, in 1897, while he was still at the Bar, jointly with J. M. Irvine (1852–1945, advocate 1889),[9] then part-time lecturer on civil law in Glasgow University, was a large volume on *Rights in Security and Cautionary Obligations*, dealing with real securities over property, heritable and moveable, and personal securities by guarantee for the payment of money or other performance of obligations. In this Gloag was responsible for the chapters on rights in security over heritage and moveables and some other topics. The book is original in that real and personal security had not previously been examined together. This book has never been re-edited, possibly because of its sheer bulk, but despite changes in the law it is still highly respected as the leading book on the subject containing a valuable analysis of the law, and as the repository of many important statements of principle.

In 1914 he produced *The Law of Contract: A Treatise on the Principles of Contract in the Law of Scotland.* In 1929 there appeared a re-arranged and partially rewritten second edition. This was a major work, long and detailed, with a very full citation of authority, which at once superseded all existing writings on the subject, apart from the relevant portions of the institutional writings, and won high professional regard. It has continued to be so regarded and indeed has been frequently quoted or cited with the deference normally accorded only to institutional writers, or even accorded something approaching the authority of statute or code. It is undoubtedly a classic. Nevertheless the book contains many flaws. The ordering of the material seems strange and illogical. Error, misrepresentation and illegality, though prerequisites of validity of a contract or grounds for challenge of validity, are not dealt with till half-way through the book and after impossibility of performance, interpretation and assignability of contractual rights, which are all material only if the contract is valid. The treatment of the effect of error is unclear and gives the impression of a series of sets of circumstances which have not been reduced to instances falling within general principles; it is a gross over-simplification to group all cases of error under error in expression or error in intention; the latter category covers a wide range of sub-groups of cases and grounds of challenge. But the book's merits far outweigh its defects.

In *Carmina Legis* (1920), a collection of witty and clever light verses about topics of Scots law, Gloag showed his lighter side. In it he narrates a number of leading Scottish cases in light verse, such as the sad tale of the will of McCaig,[10] the Oban banker whose bequest is still marked by the unfinished monument known as McCaig's Folly on the hill above Oban Bay. The will was ultimately set aside by the court as contrary to public policy, being productive of no benefit to anyone. It may be that only a Scots lawyer can savour the cleverness of the verses but at least to such a readership the verses have great appeal.

From its publication in 1754, Erskine's *Principles* had been the main textbook in the Scots Law classes in the Scottish Universities. It had been repeatedly revised by editors to take account of changes in the law but that process had reached its limit. Bell's *Principles* had outgrown its original scope as a students' book and became a large practitioners' treatise. By the mid-1920s the last (21st) edition of Little Erskine was out of print and Gloag and his Edinburgh counterpart, Robert Candlish Henderson (1874–1964, advocate 1898, professor of Scots Law at Edinburgh, 1922–47)[11] sought in collaboration to supply a replacement. They produced in 1927 Gloag and Henderson's *Introduction to the Law of Scotland*.

> "On the whole it appeared to us that it would be unwise to attempt a new edition [of Erskine]. In the later editions Erskine's original work had been extensively altered by the inclusion of new material rendered necessary by the development of the law: and the addition of this new material in a book within the compass of a student's textbook was possible only at the cost of such compression as to make it extremely difficult for readers at the outset of their legal studies. As the present book is less comprehensive in its scope, we have been enabled to treat more fully the subjects embraced.
>
> "We have confined our work to those branches of the law which are usually dealt with in classes of Scots and of Mercantile Law."[12]

The order of their treatment seems to owe more to Bell's *Principles* than to any other predecessor, as it deals first with contracts generally, some of the specific contracts and other mercantile transactions, then with leases, reparation, property, legal rights and succession, trusts, domestic relations, diligence, bankruptcy and criminal law. The book was, however, an immediate success and has continued to be so, but it cannot be said to be a satisfactory book at all.

It fails to make clear to the student the basic structure, the plan or pattern or layout of the major topics of the private law in the way Erskine and Bell did. The limitation mainly to topics dealt with in particular university courses, the classes of Scots Law and Mercantile Law, a division then misguided and today meaningless, results in property and, in particular, land law being inadequately treated, the chapter failing to make clear the complex relationships in feudal land tenure. The treatment of error in contract does not seem to discern general principles and gives the impression of merely a list of instances, and the chapter on the role of writing in contract is also open to criticism. The chapter on reparation for harm also does not clearly state the general principles, nor distinguish the general principles from the particular sets of circumstances in which liability may arise, such as occupier's liability and employer's liability, while that on rights in security does not satisfactorily distinguish security rights over land, over moveables, and over incorporeal rights.

Had Gloag lived longer the book might have been improved, but after only two editions it fell into the hands of editors.

Gloag is nevertheless the outstanding jurist of the century.

"Gloag was an outstanding jurisprudent. In lecturing, his rather dry, nervous style was mordant and memorable. He was a master of elegant and accurate compression. His lectures and he himself were most popular. There were some excellent lecturers amongst the lawyers in my undergraduate day, but Gloag was easily the best. Fortunately his fame rests on more than the evanescent word of mouth. His great treatise on the *Law of Contract*, which is a classic, is the finest text book on a single subject which has ever been added to the literature of our law. It seems to me to yield at no point even to such a masterpiece as Pollock's work on the English Law of Contract. And the *Contract* was not Gloag's only work. His two collaborations, one in the *Law of Rights in Security* and the other in his *Introduction to the Law of Scotland* are notable, the latter having actually ousted Bell and the 'little Erskine' from the field as students' textbooks. I regard Gloag as beyond all question the most remarkable legal scholar who has ever held this Chair, and the University ought to be proud of him."[13]

NOTES

[1] Chap. 15, *supra*.

[2] *Who Was Who*, 1929–40; (1901) 9 S.L.T. 101 (portrait); 1934 S.L.T. (News) 25 (portrait); *Glasgow Herald*, February 6, 1934; *Scotsman*, February 6, 1934; *College Courant* 7 (1955) 83.

For personal recollections I am greatly indebted to Dr. G. Campbell H. Paton, Q.C., Emeritus Reader in Scots Law in the University of Edinburgh, who sat under him, and to Dr. Robert T. Hutcheson, Secretary of Court Emeritus of the University of Glasgow, who recalls Gloag as a Professor and member of the University Court.

[3] DNB, 2nd Supp.; (1895) 2 S.L.T. 539 (portrait); (1903) 15 J.R. 1 (portrait); (1905) 13 S.L.T. 61 (portrait); 1909 S.L.T. (News) 117 (portrait).

[4] *College Courant*, 83.

[5] *Glasgow Herald*, February 7, 1934.

[6] In those days the Scots Law classroom was on the south front of the university, back to back with the Conveyancing classroom. The space was converted in the 1970s into the university internal printing department.

[7] *College Courant*, 84.

[8] See further J. M. Halliday, 29 J.L.S. 453.

[9] Professor of Law at Aberdeen, 1907–19, and Sheriff of Renfrew and Bute 1918.

[10] *McCaig* v. *Glasgow University*, 1907 S.C. 231; *McCaig's Trustees* v. *Lismore Kirk Session*, 1915 S.C. 426.

[11] 1964 S.L.T. (News) 59.

[12] Gloag and Henderson, *Introduction*, Preface to 1st ed.

[13] Andrew Dewar Gibb (1888–1974, advocate 1914, barrister 1919), Gloag's successor as Regius Professor of Law, in *Fortuna Domus* (Lectures in Commemoration of Glasgow University's Quincentenary) (1952), pp. 166–167.

CHAPTER 28

THE MINOR JURISTS OF THE TWENTIETH CENTURY

THIS chapter is and must be incomplete and unsatisfactory. When the twentieth century has not yet fully run its course and some who may ultimately deserve to be ranked as minor, or even as major, jurists of that century are still alive it is impossible properly to describe or evaluate the juristic achievements of the century. The chapter is accordingly confined to the work of those who have finished their course, with bare mentions of the work of living writers; the work of the living cannot yet be fairly assessed or seen in context, but not to mention it at all would leave the picture very distorted and imply that the living are doing nothing to continue the traditions of their predecessors.

Down to the latter part of the twentieth century Scotland gave nothing of any significance to legal philosophy. W. R. Herkless's *Lectures on Jurisprudence* (1901) were not original but summaries of the then prevalent cloudy Hegelian philosophy. It is not very enlightening for a practical lawyer to be told that jurisprudence is "the science of the human will, in the distinction of the particular from the universal, and in the relation of the particular to the universal,"[1] or that "Right ... [is] the correspondence or harmony of the will of the individual with the universal will."[2] But unfortunately no one in Scotland thought or wrote to any substantial extent or in an original way about jurisprudence, not even by making a Scottish contribution to the current analytical and positivist thinking about law.

In Roman law, Frederick Parker Walton (1858–1948, advocate 1886)[3] who taught Roman law at Glasgow and at McGill, Montreal, and was Director of the Royal School of Law, Cairo, as well as being for a time Legal Secretary to the Lord Advocate, produced four editions of an *Historical Introduction to the Roman Law* (1903–20), a not very original but useful book which, however, has since been totally replaced by more modern books. He also wrote a small book on *Husband and Wife* (1893), with Sir Maurice Amos, an *Introduction to French Law* (1935), and edited *Lord Hermand's Consistorial Decisions*, 1684–1777, for the Stair Society (1940).

The situation was better in the field of legal history. William Sharp McKechnie (1863–1930),[4] lecturer in constitutional law and history (1894–1916) and then professor of conveyancing (1916–1927) at Glasgow University, is deservedly remembered for his book on *Magna Carta* (1905, revised 1914) which presented that charter as a feudal document, a compact between king and barons, only accidentally serving the interests of persons outside the class of the barons, and not as a great grant of liberties to subjects generally; that latter view was based on what later politicians read into it and the purposes for which they quoted it. McKechnie regarded Magna Carta from a lawyer's standpoint and wrote a learned commentary on it, article by article, and was concerned to pursue its provisions through subsequent legal developments. He was not so concerned with the circumstances in which the charter was produced as medieval historians are.[5] But his work remains essential reading for any student of the agreement between king and barons which is still looked upon in England as a great constitutional document.

The bicentenary of the Union of the Parliaments of 1707 attracted the attention of some notable historians. James Mackinnon wrote *The Union of England and Scotland* in 1896, a good study, while Peter Hume Brown, professor of Scottish History at Edinburgh, discussed the subject in *The Legislative Union of England and Scotland* (1914). Then Albert Venn Dicey, later Vinerian Professor at Oxford and author of *Introduction to the Study of the Law of the Constitution, Conflict of Laws* and *Law and Opinion in the 19th Century*,[6] collaborated with Robert (later Sir Robert) Sangster Rait, in *Thoughts on the Union between England and Scotland* (1920), an important study which also casts much light on the last century of the Scottish Parliament. James Mackinnon, by this time Professor of Ecclesiastical History in Edinburgh, published in 1924 *The Constitutional History of Scotland*, a pedestrian work which comes down to the Reformation only. Rait's own *chef d'oeuvre* was *The Parliaments of Scotland* (1924), an important study, criticised but not yet bettered. The interesting last century of the Parliament's existence was studied by Charles Sanford Terry, professor of history at Aberdeen, in *The Scottish Parliament: Its Constitution and Procedure, 1603–1707* (1905).

George Neilson[1] and Henry M. Paton took up the work begun by Thomas Thomson and published an edition of the *Acta Dominorum Concilii, Acts of the Lords of Council in Civil Causes* 1496–1501, with a valuable introduction (1918) and this series was continued by James A. Crawford in Stair Society, volume 8, with a volume covering 1501–03 (1943). Robert Kerr Hannay published in 1932 a companion volume *Acts of the Lords of Council in Public Affairs*, 1501–54, being selections introductory to the Register of the Privy Council of Scotland, which was already printed from 1545. Publication continued of other records important for legal history, the Registers of the Privy Council, of the Privy Seal (*Registrum Secreti Sigilli*), of the Great Seal (*Registrum Magni Sigilli*), the *Treasurer's Accounts, Exchequer Rolls* and other records. This too was further execution of Thomas Thomson's plans.

In purely Scottish legal history Sir Archibald Campbell Lawrie (1837–1914, advocate 1860),[8] who was for most of his career a judge in Ceylon, while a young man at the Bar compiled the Index to Thomson and Innes's *Acts of the Parliaments of Scotland*, and published in 1905 *Early Scottish Charters prior to A.D. 1153*, collected from the chartularies printed by the Bannatyne Club, Maitland Club and other publishing clubs, and from a few other similar sources. There are valuable notes, and Lawrie's *Charters* is an essential source book for anyone researching into early Scots law. Lawrie published also an *Annals of the Reigns of Malcolm and William, Kings of Scotland*, A.D. 1153–1214, which is scarcely less valuable. This work was taken up again from 1951 in the project of *Regesta Regum Scottorum*, in which it is hoped to publish in eight volumes the surviving written Acts of the sovereigns of Scotland from 1153 to the return of James I from captivity in England in 1424 (at which point Thomson and Innes's *Acts of the Parliaments of Scotland* commence). These royal Acts comprise charters, grants, confirmations and many

THE MINOR JURISTS OF THE TWENTIETH CENTURY

other kinds of royal writs, and are not confined to legislative Acts. In those days, in any event, the lines between legislative, administrative and other acts were not clearly drawn. The completion of the series will make much more material readily available to the legal historian. David Murray (1842–1928)[9] became head of a notable Glasgow firm of solicitors but still found the time to write a *Law relating to the Property of Married Persons* (1891) and, more importantly, *Legal Practice in Ayr and the West of Scotland in the 15th and 16th Centuries* (1910) and *Early Burgh Organisation in Scotland as Illustrated in the History of Glasgow and of some Neighbouring Burghs* (two volumes, 1924–32), which is an important study of the subject, not least because Murray was naturally interested in the legal as much as the economic aspects of burghal history. He also wrote a most interesting *Memories of the Old College of Glasgow* (1926). Alan Orr Anderson in *Scottish Annals from English Chroniclers* (1908) and *Early Sources of Scottish History*, 500–1286 (two volumes, 1922) made available in print much early matter relevant to legal origins and development.

The Scottish History Society and the Scottish Record Society continued to publish books many of which contain material relevant to legal history. The foundation of the Stair Society in 1934 was a noteworthy event and that society has secured the editing and publishing of several works of importance, notably Lord President Clyde's[10] edition of Hope's *Major Practicks* (two volumes, 1937–38) and Dr. G. Campbell H. Paton's edition of Hume's *Lectures*, 1786–1822 (six volumes, 1939–58). Some volumes have been disappointing. Its difficulty has been to find editors with the time and the skill to edit texts. Lord President Clyde also published a valuable translation of Craig's *Jus Feudale* (two volumes, 1934).

A subject of central interest to legal historians is the origin and early development of the supreme court and R. K. Hannay made a valuable contribution on this theme in *The College of Justice: Essays on the Institution and Development of the Court of Session* in 1933 and dealt with a related topic in the "Early History of the Scottish Signet" in the revised (1936) edition of the *History of the Writers to Her Majesty's Signet.*

Thomas Mackay Cooper (1892–1955, advocate 1915),[11] later Lord Advocate, Lord Justice-Clerk (1941) and Lord President (1947) was deeply interested in legal history and published *Select Thirteenth Century Cases*, 1203–94 (1944), and edited *The Register of Brieves* for the Stair Society in 1946, but in his *Regiam Majestatem* (Stair Society, 1947) made no advance on Skene's work of 1609, taking the view that Skene's edition was the received text of Scots lawyers, but this merely perpetuates Skene's mistakes.

The tercentenary of the first publication of Stair's *Institutions* was marked in 1981 by the publication of a handsome tercentenary (sixth) edition which reprinted Stair's final (second edition) text with modern references to the sources he referred to, but without annotations.

In legal biography a good deal has been published in the twentieth century. Samuel Cowan published a two-volume *The Lord Chancellors of Scotland 1124–1707* (1911), which is unscholarly and does not advance knowledge very much. George Menary's *The Life and Letters of Duncan*

Forbes of Culloden, 1685–1747 (1936) greatly advanced understanding of the career of that distinguished Lord President. Kames was studied in William C. Lehmann's *Henry Home, Lord Kames, and the Scottish Enlightenment* (1971), which views him in the context of the history of ideas, and in Ian S. Ross's *Lord Kames and the Scotland of his Day* (1972), which gives a more balanced picture, and Monboddo by E. L. Cloyd in *James Burnett, Lord Monboddo* (1972).

George Omond added a "second series," (one volume covering 1834–84), to his *Lord Advocates of Scotland* (1914)[12] and Andrew Lang discussed the career of one of them in his *Sir George Mackenzie, His Life and Times* (1909). Cyril Matheson produced a useful *Life of Henry Dundas, First Viscount Melville* (1933) and David Marshall in *Sir Walter Scott and Scots Law* (1932) added a legal appreciation to the literary ones in the numerous biographies of Scott. But the Scots lawyer who has had far and away the most attention has been James Boswell, not so much as lawyer, for he was of no significance as that, but as friend and biographer of Dr. Johnson, writer and diarist. His career, which casts light on Kames, Hailes and the life of the Parliament House in the eighteenth century, is laid bare in detail by himself in his *Journal* and by F. A. Pottle in *James Boswell: The Earlier Years*, 1704–69 (1966). Most of this output has, however, been made by non-lawyers and it is not, strictly speaking, Scottish jurists' work; but it cannot be ignored when considering legal scholarship and one must welcome assistance from scholars in other disciplines.

Mention deserves also to be made of the work of William Roughead (1870–1952, Writer to the Signet 1893) who, at the instigation of Andrew Lang, began to write some entertaining essays, mainly on criminal trials, in the *Juridical Review*. They were, however, based on scholarly investigation of the sources and records and not mere journalism. They proved very popular and were reprinted with some other pieces in book form, ultimately running to 12 volumes.[13] They are highly readable, but also a contribution to the byways of legal history. He also edited several volumes[14] in the *Notable British Trials* series published by William Hodge & Co. Ltd.

In dogmatic exposition of Scots law itself the twentieth century was a period of inadequate activity, particularly during the years 1914 to 1945. Thereafter activity varied, stimulated by the greatly increased emphasis put by the law faculties of the Scottish universities on legal studies as distinct from lectures to law apprentices and by the foundation in 1960 of the Scottish Universities Law Institute, a co-operative enterprise of the universities' law faculties and schools to secure the writing and publication of modern standard textbooks, backed by a guarantee against loss on publications given by the Carnegie Trust for the Scottish Universities. The Institute sponsored a number of new and valuable books. But writers were faced more than ever, particularly since 1945, with rapidly changing and developing bodies of rules, and rules more detailed, voluminous and complicated than ever, and simultaneously with sharply rising costs of publication and consequently rising prices, which inhibited sales.

Several large co-operative works appeared. Green's *Encyclopaedia of the Laws of Scotland* first appeared in 14 volumes in 1896–1904; there was a revised edition in 12 volumes in 1909–14 and a new edition in 16 volumes in 1926–35 with supplementary volumes to 1952. The articles, by various hands, are of uneven quality; some are very good, others poor. A *Scots Style Book* in eight volumes appeared over the years 1902–11 and superseded the ageing *Juridical Styles*. An *Encyclopaedia of Scottish Legal Styles* in nine volumes appeared in 1935–45. The *Faculty Digest*, a digest of decisions from 1868–1922 (continuing Shaw's *Digest*, but better planned and with much fuller summaries of cases) appeared in six volumes in 1924–26 and was continued by four volumes of supplements to 1960. The *Scots Digest* covers House of Lords appeals from 1707 and cases in the Scottish superior courts from 1800 to 1944 in 11 volumes (1800–73 in four volumes, 1908–12; 1873–1904 in 2 volumes, 1905; single volumes for 1904–14, 1914–23, 1923–30, 1930–37 and 1937–44). Thereafter annual volumes of *Current Law* from 1948 and, more recently, information from computer sources have to be looked to for information about modern case law.

The most useful new kind of publication was *Current Law*, a monthly summary of legal materials from every source, consolidated annually in volume form. It started in England in 1947 and was extended to Scotland in 1948, the Scottish including both United Kingdom and English, and purely Scottish, materials.

Messrs. W. Green & Son Ltd., the Edinburgh law publishers, which incorporated the very old-established firm of Bell and Bradfute, founded in 1734, stimulated by the vigorous Charles Edward Green[15] published the *Encyclopaedias* and many textbooks, and established *The Scots Law Times*, a weekly, in 1893, containing current news, articles and reports of cases in all the courts. Till 1948 it included the texts of statutes. Greens also published *The Scots Statutes Revised*, 1424–1900, in 10 volumes (1899–1907), *The Scots Statutes*, 1901–1948, in 12 volumes (1908–48), and *Scottish Current Law Statutes* annually from 1949. In this last series many of the statutes have useful annotations. *The Scottish Law Review*, including sheriff court cases, which had run from 1885, stopped publication in 1964. A new, specialised series, *Scottish Criminal Case Reports*, began in 1981.

In public law Arthur Berriedale Keith (1879–1944, barrister 1904, advocate 1921),[16] who at various times taught ancient history and Sanskrit and was a civil servant in the Colonial Office, produced a number of works valuable in their time, such as *Responsible Government in the Dominions* (1912), *Imperial Unity and the Dominions* (1916), *The Sovereignty of the British Dominions* (1929), *Constitutional History of the First British Empire* (1930), *The Constitutional Law of the British Dominions* (1933), *The Governments of the British Empire* (1935), *The King and the Imperial Crown* (1936), *The Dominions as Sovereign States* (1938), *The British Cabinet System, 1830–1938* (1939). He edited also part of W. R. Anson's *The Law and Custom of the Constitution* and collaborated with A. V. Dicey in the third edition of Dicey's *Conflict of Laws*. He had prodigious learning and endless energy, and his books were highly authoritative though now mainly of historical value. John D. B. Mitchell wrote a *Constitutional Law* (1964, 1968; SULI) which stressed Scottish problems and attitudes and dealt less fully with some of the more traditional topics of the subject, so that it could only really be read as a supplement to the standard English texts on the subject.

In criminal law Andrew Macbeth Anderson (1862–1936, advocate 1889, Lord of Session 1913)[17] wrote a useful *The Criminal Law of Scotland* (1892; 1904). Though a better-planned book it failed to displace Macdonald's *Criminal Law*. An infinitely better book came in the form of Gerald Henry Gordon's (1929– , advocate 1953) *Criminal Law of Scotland* (1967, 1978; SULI), which contained the most thorough examination of the general questions of criminal liability since Hume, as well as analyses of the specific crimes. Gordon also re-edited and largely rewrote Renton and Brown's *Criminal Procedure* (1972, 1983).

The present writer sought to innovate for students in producing *The Scottish Legal System* (1959, fifth edition 1980) as an introduction for students to the study of the law rather than to the law itself, dealing with history, sources, literature, divisions and classification, the elements of procedure and the ways of finding the law, and in *The Oxford Companion to Law* (1980) sought to provide a very wide-ranging compendium of information on persons, concepts and many other matters met in reading. Gloag and Henderson's *Introduction to the Law of Scotland* (1927),[18] though defective, despite improvements made in later editions by editors, continued to be a commonly-used first book for students, though it became increasingly inadequate for the rising standards of knowledge expected following the introduction in 1960 of compulsorily full-time study of law in the Scottish universities.

Thomas Broun Smith (1915– , advocate 1947, barrister 1938) published *A Short Commentary on the Law of Scotland* (1962) and James John Gow a complementary *The Mercantile and Industrial Law of Scotland* in 1964, and the present writer published a *Principles of Scottish Private Law* (two volumes, 1970, 1975; four volumes, 1982–83).

There was little development in the law of persons. Two more editions of F. P. Walton's handbook on *Husband and Wife* (1922, 1951) appeared but it was superseded in 1974 by E. M. Clive and J. G. Wilson's *Husband and Wife* (1974, 1982; SULI). In obligations Gloag on *Contract* (1914, revised 1929), though recognised as a classic was not re-edited, and important developments led to the present writer's *Law of Contracts and Related Obligations in Scotland* (1979, 1985). In delict A. T. Glegg's unsatisfactory *Law of Reparation* (1892, fourth edition 1956) was replaced by the present writer's *Law of Delict in Scotland* (1966, 1981; SULI).

The law of property was rather neglected. Nothing followed on Rankine on *Land Ownership* (fourth edition, 1909) and his *Leases* (third edition, 1916) was supplemented rather than replaced by G. C. H. Paton and J. G. Cameron's *Law of Landlord and Tenant* (1967; SULI). William Jardine Dobie (1892–1956) published in 1941 a handy *Manual of the Law of Liferent and Fee in Scotland*. James Ferguson (1857–1917, advocate 1879)[19] published useful textbooks on *Law of Roads and Streets* (1904), *Law of Water and Water Rights in Scotland* (1907) and several books on railway law. In its own rather esoteric field Robert Candlish Henderson's *Principles of Vesting in the Law of Succession* (1905, 1938) proved very valuable and was much relied on in courts.

Trusts were discussed usefully by Alexander Mackenzie Stuart (1877–1935, advocate 1903, professor of law at Aberdeen 1919),[20] (1932) and by William A. Wilson (1928-) and A. G. M. Duncan (1975; SULI) and *Judicial Factors* by Norman M. L. Walker (1889–1975, advocate 1920).

The present writer sought to plough a new field in his *Law of Damages* in Scotland (1955) later incorporated, in revised form, in his broader *Law of Civil Remedies in Scotland* (1974; SULI). William Wallace (1860–1923, advocate 1888) produced a sound *Law of Bankruptcy* in Scotland (1907, 1914) which complements Goudy on that subject.

Statutory charges made the older books on prescription obsolete and the present writer sought to fill the gap by his *Law of Prescription and Limitation of Actions in Scotland* (1973; third edition, 1981).

In the area of jurisdiction and international private law George Duncan (1847–1949, advocate in Aberdeen)[21] and David Oswald Dykes (1876–1942, advocate 1903)[22] later (1925–42) professor of constitutional law and history at Edinburgh produced a valuable *Principles of Civil Jurisdiction in the Law of Scotland* (1911) which won regard as a standard text. Andrew Dewar Gibb (1888–1974, advocate 1914, barrister 1919),[23] later professor of law at Glasgow, 1934–58, published an *International Law of Jurisdiction in England and Scotland* (1926) and an interesting *International Private Law of Scotland in the 16th and 17th centuries* (1928) and Alexander Elder Anton (1922-) wrote a scholarly *Private International Law* (1967; SULI).

William John Lewis (1858–1943)[24] published a handy *Manual of the Law of Evidence in Scotland* in 1925 and a new book on that subject by Allan Grierson Walker (1907- , advocate 1931, later Sheriff of Lanark) and Norman Macdonald Lockhart Walker (1889–1975, advocate 1920) came out in 1964.

Procedure was dealt with fully by James Anderson MacLaren (1866–1926, advocate 1888)[25] in *Bill Chamber Practice* (1915) and *Court of Session Practice* (1916), sketchily by G. R. Thomson and J. T. Middleton in *Manual of Court of Session Procedure* (1937), and the latter topic more fully again by David Maxwell in *The Practice of the Court of Session* (1980).

Sheriff court practice was expounded by William Wallace (1860–1922, advocate 1888) (1909), Thomas Alexander Fyfe (1852–1928) (1913)[26] William John Lewis (1887; eighth edition, 1939),[24] and William Jardine Dobie (1892–1956) (1948) who also produced a useful book of *Sheriff Court Styles* (1951). John McKie Lees (1843–1926, advocate 1867)[27] wrote several useful small books on sheriff court and small debt court practice.

Increasingly, however, in the twentieth century the Parliamentary imposition of the same rules on Scotland as on England and the tendency to assimilate the rules in the two jurisdictions has led to steadily increasing reference in Scotland to English books, which frequently ignore Scottish decisions and specialities of Scots law. The same reasons have frequently made it not worth while for a Scottish writer to seek to write a distinctively Scottish book on a theme, such as company law or carriage or employment or shipping, where the law is largely common to the two systems and the majority of the cases are English. The same reasons have led to steadily increased citation of English cases in Scottish courts, frequently without adequate appreciation of the different background from which those English cases emerged, and the different context, historical, doctrinal and procedural in which they were decided.

NOTES

[1] Herkless, *op. cit.*, p. 1.

[2] *Ibid.*, p. 69.

[3] 1914 S.L.T. (News) 21 (portrait).

[4] DNB, Supp.; *Who Was Who*, 1929–40; 1911 S.L.T. (News) 9 (portrait); 1916 S.L.T. (News) 89. His son, Hector McKechnie, Q.C., was a prime mover in the formation of the Stair Society in 1934 and its first literary editor.

[5] J. C. Holt, *Magna Carta* (1965), passim.

[6] On Dicey see H. G. Hanbury, *The Vinerian Chair and Legal Education* (1958), pp. 98–163; F. H. Lawson, *The Oxford Law School, 1850–1965* (1968), pp. 69–71. Rait wrote a *Memorials of Albert Venn Dicey*.

[7] On Neilson see Obituary (1924) 21 S.H.R. 144; DNB 1922–30; memoir in Stair Soc. *Miscellany* I (1971), 1–10.

[8] Obituary (1915) 12 S.H.R. 113 (portrait).

[9] *Who Was Who*, 1916–28; (1894) 1 S.L.T. 471 (portrait). Murray's library, now in the Special Collections of Glasgow University Library, includes many rare items of value for Scottish legal history.

[10] James Avon Clyde (1863–1944), advocate 1889, Dean of Faculty 1915–18, Lord Advocate 1916–20, Lord President of the Court of Session 1920–35. See (1897) 5 S.L.T. 61 (portrait); 1920 S.L.T. (News) 61 (portrait). His son James Latham McDiarmid Clyde, (1898–1973, advocate 1924, Lord Advocate, 1951–55) was Lord President 1955–72.

[11] DNB, 1951–60; *Who Was Who*, 1951–60. See also his *Selected Papers* (1957) which include many of his shorter pieces.

[12] On this see p. 384, *supra*.

[13] These are: *Twelve Scots Trials* (1913); *The Riddle of the Ruthvens* (1919, revised 1936); *Glengarry's Way* (1922); *The Fatal Countess and Other Studies* (1924); *The Rebel Earl and Other Studies* (1926); *Malice Domestic* (1928); *Bad Companions* (1930); *In Queer Street* (1932); *Rogues Walk Here* (1934); *Knave's Looking Glass* (1935); *Mainly Murder* (1937); *The Seamy Side* (1938).

[14] Namely *Dr. Pritchard*; *Deacon Brodie*; *Captain Porteous*; *Oscar Slater*; *Mrs. McLachlan*; *Mary Blandy*; *Burke and Hare*; *Katharine Nairn*; *John Donald Merrett*; *John Watson Laurie*.

[15] Lord Guthrie, "C. E. Green: Personal Reminiscences" (1920) 32 J.R. 1; 1920 S.L.T. (News) 5 (portrait); (1938) 50 J.R. 1 (portrait).

[16] DNB, 1941–50; *Who Was Who*, 1941–50.

[17] (1906) 14 S.L.T. 65 (portrait); 1936 S.L.T. (News) 121 (portrait).

[18] On the genesis of this, see Chap. 27, *supra*.

[19] (1897) 5 S.L.T. 45 (portrait); 1917 S.L.T. (News) 49 (portrait).

[20] 1919 S.L.T. (News) 81; 1920 S.L.T. (News) 113 (portrait). His son Alexander John Mackenzie Stuart became a judge of the Court of Session (1973) and the first British Judge of the Court of Justice of the European Communities (1973–).

[21] *Who Was Who*, 1940–50.

[22] 1925 S.L.T. (News) 153 (portrait); *Who Was Who*, 1940–50.

[23] 1934 S.L.T. (News) 114, 117 (portrait); 1974 S.L.T. (News) 38; *Who Was Who*, 1970–80. He also edited some English books, notably Marsden on *Collisions at Sea* and Beven on *Negligence*.

[24] 1931 S.L.T. (News) 33 (portrait).

[25] 1916 S.L.T. (News) 97 (portrait).

[26] 1928 S.L.T. (News) 81 (portrait).

[27] 1926 S.L.T. (News) 209 (portrait).

CHAPTER 29

THE CONTRIBUTIONS OF THE SCOTTISH JURISTS TO THE SCIENCE OF LAW

WHAT have been the importance and the value of the various contributions to the science of law made by those whom we have identified as Scottish jurists? How are these qualities to be judged? A jurist's reputation, and the importance and value of his contribution to scholarship, depend on the esteem in which his writings were held professionally and among scholars in the same field; were they regularly referred to, cited in argument, relied on in judgment and regarded as valuable? Obviously law is an evolving body of doctrine and works become superseded, but are still entitled to be remembered as valuable in their time. It is also proper to remember that some works can have been held in high repute without much of that being apparent in later books, judgments or other public evidences. To answer the first question one must look at the different major fields or areas of jurisprudence or legal science.

In the field of jurisprudence, in the narrow, modern, sense, or legal philosophy or legal theory, Scotland has made disappointingly little contribution. Lorimer has been the only name of note and he and his work made little impact in their time and are now largely forgotten.

In legal history the situation is not much better. In Roman law the work of Mackenzie, Muirhead, Walton and Mackintosh is largely superseded. Despite the connection with the civil law of Rome, Scotland, it seems, has yet to produce a civilian fit to rank with those from other Western European countries. Neilson's *Trial by Combat* and McKechnie's *Magna Carta* are still authoritative for scholars working in the medieval field and have a broader than solely or merely Scottish relevance; indeed McKechnie's work has little Scottish relevance. A great deal of materials for a history of law in Scotland has now been printed but no attempt has yet been made to synthesise the available materials and construct a narrative history.

In comparative legal studies Scotland has made no mark despite the necessity of Scottish lawyers having a comparative approach to their studies.[1] Nor have Scots yet achieved anything in European Community Law.

In public international law Lorimer is again the only man who has stood in the first rank and been recognised worldwide, and his work has not lived. In the twentieth century Arnold Duncan McNair[2] was in the first rank but, though of Scottish origins, he was an English lawyer, and all his noteworthy work was done from Cambridge.

It is only, it seems, in the field of national or municipal law, of the native law of Scotland, that Scotland has produced a number of jurists whose work, though not as well known in the wider world as some who have worked in bigger jurisdictions, can fairly be ranked with those of the great jurists of other national systems. There is a distinct similarity in the pattern of development of distinct legal literatures as the nation states of Western Europe established themselves after the Reformation and the

424

religious wars. Roman law as a *jus commune* was declining; half of Europe had rejected the authority of the canon law (though its influence long continued); feudalism was increasingly taking divergent forms. In the seventeenth and eighteenth centuries in many countries jurists were writing institutes of national law. These tended to be called Institutions or Institutes, indicating that the work was an attempt at a systematic, ordered exposition.[3] As in some other European countries the task of the jurists down to the latter eighteenth century was to create a systematic corpus of unified national law. Some of these foreign works were sometimes mentioned in Scotland.[4]

Divergence from the European tradition became more marked as time went on. The Napoleonic wars cut off the long-standing Scottish connection with the Continent and the Napoleonic Codes gave France a fresh start, and the need for a new legal literature based on commentaries on the Codes. But the works of Aubry et Rau, Planiol et Ripert and others were no more useful in Scotland than were Erskine and Bell in France. It was the same as most other European countries codified their main bodies of law at various times in the nineteenth century: Scotland and they were drifting further apart.

From about the end of the eighteenth century accordingly Scottish jurists have necessarily been concerned with the restatement of their distinct system in the light of legislation increasingly shaped for and in England and, increasingly intended to, or at least having the effect of assimilating their law to English law.

Evaluation of the works of the different Scottish jurists is a matter of some difficulty. It is impossible to determine how frequently at different periods different books have been referred to in library or office or study, or used to base a view or found an argument. Some indications may be derived from the extent of citation of particular works in later books and reported cases but direct evidence of the reputation attaching to different writers and different works may be scanty, and is certainly hard to find, particularly before the nineteenth century. But from the beginning of the eighteenth century the writings of jurists are beginning to be cited in the reports of decisions, in argument and in judicial opinion.[5]

Particular interest and importance attaches to those jurists who in Scottish legal parlance have been designated "institutional writers." This raises the related questions of what is meant by "institutional" and which writings are properly called "institutional."[6]

The noun "institution(s)" and the adjective "institutional" are obviously taken from the Latin *institutio(nes)*, itself deriving from the verb *instituere*, to arrange or instruct. The Latin noun was used in the singular signifying instruction or training, as by Quintilian in his *Institutio oratoria* (*c.* A.D. 95), and, much later, by Erasmus in his *Institutio Principis Christiani* (1516). It was used in the plural as the title for elementary instructional works, or textbooks, as by Florentinus, who wrote an *Institutiones* in 12 books,[7] Gaius, whose *Institutiones* in four books has survived almost complete,[8] Paul, Callistratus, Ulpian and Marcian (two, three, two and 16 books respectively).[9] Most importantly the word was used as the title of the authorised textbook issued by Justinian's commissioners in 533. The word was not appropriated exclusively to legal textbooks: Lactantius wrote a *Divinae Institutiones* (c. 310).

From this source the word is found in its different language formulations in all the legal systems which have drawn substantially from the civil law of Rome as an appropriate title for a book covering a substantial range, expository and instructional.[10] The word (in English) was taken into the titles of their works by Stair, Mackenzie and Forbes. The variant, "institute," in singular or plural, which is probably merely a translation with no independent connotations,[11] was used by Bankton and Erskine and, in relation to criminal law, by Bayne, and varieties of both words by text-writers in England, such as Coke's *Institutes of the Lawes of England (1628–44)*, J. Cowell's *Institutiones Iuris Anglicani ad Methodum et Seriem Institutionum Imperialium Compositae et Digestae* (1605 and later editions), M. W. Bohun's *Institutio Legalis, or an Introduction to the Study and Practice of the Laws of England* (1708 and later editions), and in T. Wood's *An Institute of the Laws of England* (1720 and later editions). It was used also by theologians, as in John Calvin's *Institutiones Religionis Christianae* (1536), and by philosophers as in Francis Hutcheson's *Philosophiae Moralis Institutio* (1742), Adam Ferguson's *Institutes of Moral Philosophy* (1769) and, somewhat later, Lorimer's *Institutes of Law* (1872) and *Institutes of the Law of Nations* (1883–84). The term "institutes of medicine" was the former term for what is now called physiology.

While many of these works were educational many of them were not elementary, in the way Gaius's and Justinian's works were intended to be.

In some of these works indeed "institution" or "institute" is possibly shifting to its second significance, of an established principle, custom or organisation, as used in such phrases as "the peculiar institution of slavery," or "the institution of property," "the institution of marriage." Thus in *Harvey* v. *Farquhar*[12] Lord Westbury refers to "a rule or principle which appears to have been long incorporated into the law of Scotland and to have become an established rule and institution in the marriage law in that country." This usage leads on the third significance, an established organisation of persons, such as the Royal Institution, or the Institution of Civil Engineers. In relation to the second significance, "institution," "institute" and "institutional" may mean not so much "institutional" as "dealing with established rules, customs and elements of organisation."

The adjective "institutional" was used by Blackstone,[13] Bentham,[14] and by Austin, in relation to the Roman institutional writers.[15]

It is not clear when the work "institutional," used both of writers, and of particular works, came to be used in Scotland in the sense not merely as meaning "of an *Institutions* (or *Institute*)" but in the more refined sense of meaning "authoritative" or at very least "of high standing, of special weight and value." This use of the adjective, moreover, is open, whether the book in question is entitled "Institutions," "Institute" or bears another title such as "Commentaries," "Principles," "Treatise" or other. In this sense "institutional" is distinguished from "the text-writers" (whose views may be helpful or persuasive, and even be approved or accepted or followed, but are not authoritative); "institutional writings" rank as sources of the law, whereas text-writings rank only as legal literature, as expressions of opinion by scholars on what they believe the law to be.

It is plain from early in the series of reports of Scottish decisions that relevant passages in books were being cited to the court in argument for their persuasive effect and in the earlier years there was no discrimination between institutional writers and others.

Down to about the end of the eighteenth century the word "institutional" does not appear to be used in the refined sense, and the phrase "institutional writers" was not in regular use.

The phrases found in the reports are more neutral, such as "the authorities,"[16] "the law books,"[17] "lawyers,"[18] "all the authors in our law,"[19] "writers," "writers on our law,"[20] "text writers,"[21] "law writers of authority,"[22] "the writers upon the law of Scotland,"[23] "the most respectable authorities,"[24] and similar words. Rather later one meets the phrase "Stair, Erskine, or any of the fathers of the law."[25]

In *McDonells* v. *Carmichael* in 1772[26] it was contended that:

> "where a series of decisions have run counter to the opinions even of the most eminent writers in our law, it may be a good reason for rejecting their opinions upon these points; but, where the decisions of the court are silent, the opinions of our lawyers must be considered as of the highest authority; because, where the writers upon our law have laid down the law in any particular, and where in the course of ages, no decision of the supreme court is to be found upon the point, it is the strongest declaration possible of the sense of the whole nation, and that they had acquiesced in such opinions as law."

Moreover at that time weight seemed to attach not so much to particular writings as to the consensus of opinion.[27] Hume in his *Lectures*[28] says that "the delineations of doctrine given by such men, when they are explicit and in unison with each other, have justly much weight as evidence of the strain and tenor of our common law."

Even before the concept of "institutional writers" was developed the essence of their status is sometimes visible; in *Meuse* v. *Craig's Exors*[29] the report observes: "what principally seemed to move them was the *authority* of Lord Stair (II, 1, 4) and of Mackenzie (II, 2, 9)." In *Cameron* v. *Boswell*[30] a rule was stated as appearing "both by decisions and authorities: Durie ... Bankton ... and Erskine." In *Henderson* v. *Makgill*[31] there was mention of "the following authorities, Craig ... Lord Stair ... Lord Bankton ... Erskine...." and one case. Again in *Ross* v. *Heriot's Hopital Governors*[32] the Lord Ordinary (Meadowbank) said in his note: "The Ordinary conceives it quite desperate of the defenders to think they are to get the better ... of the *authority* of Stair, Bankton and Erskine, without an adverse authority of any description; even Craig being also hostile," and Lord Justice-Clerk Boyle, having referred to "our law writers" went on to say:[33] "Their *authority* on this point is as much to be rested on as any other dictum in the works of these writers. Lord Bankton and Mr. Erskine are quite clear about it, as well as Stair; and I fairly confess that I am not bold enough for one to set my opinion against the great luminaries of our law, even if I differed from them." He clearly regarded the opinions of the jurists as authoritative. Later he concludes: "and I never can be of opinion, that the *authority* of Stair, Bankton and Erskine, ought to be departed from. . . ."

Accordingly it seems to have been accepted in the eighteenth century that the writings of certain jurists had authority, or were authorities, just as much as were decisions of the court.[34] It is also interesting to note on this matter of authorities that the phrase *ratio decidendi* appears quite frequently in reports of the latter years of the eighteenth century: the point of what was the authoritative or persuasive element in a prior decision was recognised.[35]

The concept of the "institutional writers" seems to have arisen at the beginning of the nineteenth century. Hume in his *Lectures* used the phrase,[36] but not in the lecture dealing with sources, though he does mention[37] "the writings of these learned and eminent persons, skilled in the law." Cockburn in his *Memorials*[38] wrote of Hume: "As an institutional writer . . ." and again:[39] "George Joseph Bell, our greatest modern institutional writer. . . ."

Lord Fraser[40] remarked: "The institutional writers on Scottish law were all advocates or judges in the Court of Session . . . Balfour, the earliest institutional writer. . ." and he later refers to Craig, Stair, Bankton and Erskine, and seems by implication to include Dirleton under this head. Cosmo Innes[41] uses the variant "institutionalist."

The title was also applied judicially. An early instance was in *Campbell* v. *McKellar*,[42] in argument, a reference to "the opinion of the best institutional writers" where the books referred to were Stair, Bayne's Notes on Mackenzie, Bankton, and Erskine. In *Forbes' Trs.* v. *Welsh*[43] Lord Justice-Clerk Boyle referred to "passages in our institutional writers" and went on to quote Stair, Bankton and Erskine. In *Yuille* v. *Scott*[44] reference was made to Hume's lectures in argument and Lord Justice-Clerk Boyle[45] referred to the "opinions of our institutional writers and adopted by the eminent instructor of the students of law in our university whose opinion has been referred to and whose authority I regard as very important." In *Cowie* v. *Fleming*[46] he referred to "the authority both of Stair and Erskine." In *Creightons* v. *Deans*[47] it is reported that: "More, for pursuers, contended that all the institutional writers. . . ." In *Dawson* v. *Muir*[48] Lord Murray (Ordinary) said in his note: "The Lord Ordinary has chiefly proceeded on the doctrines laid down by Lord Stair and other institutional writers. . ." but it is not stated which he referred to. In *Fenton* v. *Livingstone*[49] Lord Ardmillan stated: "The institutional writers on Scottish law concur in stating that. . .," and he cites Stair, Erskine, Mackenzie, Bankton and Bell's *Principles*.

In *Miller* v. *Milne's Trs.*[50] Lord Ardmillan stated that: "the same rule of law . . . has been laid down by all the institutional writers since the date of the decision. . .," and he refers to Erskine, Erskine's *Principles*, Bell's *Principles*, More's Notes to Stair, and Menzies' *Lectures on Conveyancing*, while Lord President McNeill[51] based his opinion "on the authority of nearly all our institutional writers. I find it in Erskine and Bell – and I think it is to be found in Professor More's edition of Stair; and I find that the doctrine was taught from the chair of conveyancing;" and later:[52] "This appears to be the doctrine of Stair. It is, at all events, clearly the doctrine of Erskine, as stated in his *Principles*, published for the use of his students and was afterwards repeated and illustrated by him in his *Institutes*. The same doctrine is stated in Professor Bell's *Principles*, in Professor More's Notes on Stair, and in Professor Menzies's *Lectures on Conveyancing*."

In *Fenton* v. *Livingstone*[53] Lord President McNeill said:[54] "It is the opinion which is expressed without hesitation by Stair, and by Erskine, and by Bankton and by Mackenzie. It is also mentioned by Forbes, and by Wallace, who had a good deal of experience in such matters, and was himself a commissary. But still more, I think it is the opinion which is expressed by Professor Bell, and by Professor More. It is the opinion also which is expressed by a gentleman of great experience in consistorial law, Mr. Ferguson. It is therefore the doctrine which has been taught by all our institutional writers. It is the doctrine which has been taught from the chair of law." Lord Curriehill observed: "we do not have institutional writers anterior to the Reformation to let us see very clearly into it [the common law of marriage]." Later he concludes:[56] "Bankton and Erskine are so; and then we have Professors Bell and More to the same effect. We have, therefore, this statute interpreted, by a practice of three centuries, by all the institutional writers. . . ." Lord Deas said:[57] "But when we come to the institutional writers . . . we find an entire coincidence of opinion. . .," and he mentions Stair, Bankton, Erskine, Bell's *Principles*, and Hume.

In *The Ministers of Old Machar* v. *The Heritors*[58] Lord Curriehill asked himself: "Let us first see how the institutional writers deal with this matter. Forbes, Mackenzie and Erskine did state. . .," while Lord Ardmillan[59] refers to "the authority of Sir George Mackenzie, and Forbes, and of Erskine. . . ."

In *Harvey* v. *Farquhar*[60] Lord Chelmsford observed that certain decisions "have been acquiesced in for many years and that such institutional writers as Lord Stair, Lord Bankton, Erskine and Bell have treated the law upon the subject as settled," while Lord Westbury[61] refers to "the established rule in Scotland, which is evidenced not only by decisions, but by a long series of writers who have taught the law to generations of lawyers. . . ."

Again in *Haldane* v. *Speirs*[62] Lord Ardmillan remarked that a rule "is clearly laid down by our great institutional writers, and has been recognised as law since the days of Lord Stair."

In *Sandeman* v. *Scottish Property Investment Co.*[63] Lord Watson said: "All the institutional writers, from Lord Stair downwards, are agreed. . . ." In *Samson* v. *Davie*[64] Lord Craighill mentioned "passages in the *Corpus Juris Civilis* and in our own institutional writers," and Lord Justice-Clerk Moncreiff[65] used the words "the authorities – whether institutional writers or judicial decisions."

Over the nineteenth century accordingly this usage of "institutional" seems to have become well established, connoting writers of works recognised as authoritative, and there was also substantial consensus as to who the recognised institutional writers were.

Lord President Normand stated in 1941:[66] "Stair, Erskine and Bell are cited daily in the courts, and the court will pay as much respect to them as to a judgment of the House of Lords, though it is bound to follow a judgment of the House of Lords whatever the institutional writers may have said." This ranks the institutional writings very high, as high as a judgment of the House of Lords but less authoritative than an actual judgment, in point, of the House.

So too in *Fortington* v. *Kinnaird*[67] Lord Wark observed that the court had had "an exhaustive discussion of the authorities, both the institutional writers and the decisions."

Similarly in *Lord Advocate* v. *Aberdeen University*[68] Lord Patrick[69] quoted Bell's *Principles* and said that, "Bell's statement has the support of the other institutional writers, as Stair, Erskine and Bankton;" Lord Mackintosh[70] relied on "the relevant passages in the institutional writers (all of which have been cited by the Lord Ordinary)," which refers back to references to Craig, Stair, Bankton, Erskine and Bell's *Principles*, while Mackenzie was also referred to; later[71] he referred to "our institutional writers from Stair to Bell inclusive."

In *Wills' Trustees* v. *Cairngorm Canoeing and Sailing School*[72] Lord President Emslie[73] said: "I look first of all at the institutional writers . . . Stair . . . Bankton . . . Erskine. . .," and later:[74] "There remain for consideration the commentators and text book writers . . . Hume's *Lectures* . . . Bell's *Illustrations* . . . Rankine, *Land Ownership* . . . Ferguson, *Law of Water*. . . ." In the same case in the House of Lords Lord Wilberforce said:[75] "The Institutional writers of authority whose work appeared before 1772 were Craig, Stair, Bankton and Erskine's *Principles*. Erskine's *Institute* appeared in 1773 but must have been completed in 1768 when he died."

Similarly Lord Fraser[76] mentioned: "The institutional writers . . . Craig, Stair, Bankton, Erskine. . . ."

It appears accordingly that from the early nineteenth century there has been recognition of a group of jurists as "institutional writers," whose works have been regarded as not merely usefully stating a view on the law but having authority which a judge should defer to, akin to the authority of a superior court decision. Any passage in an institutional writing is, however, deferred in authority to a legislative rule and to a binding decision of a superior court. In *Macdonald* v. *Hall*[77] Lord Watson, speaking of one interpretation of a passage in Erskine, said that if Erskine did understand the law in that sense, "I should regard it as matter of little consequence, because Bankton's rule had been judicially recognised and applied, not only by the Court of Session, but by this House many years before Erskine wrote, and authority of that kind cannot be impaired by the dicta of an institutional writer, however eminent."

In *Fothergill* v. *Monarch Airlines*[78] Lord Diplock remarked, *obiter*: "To a court interpreting the convention subsequent commentaries can have persuasive value only; they do not come into the same authoritative category as that of the institutional writers in Scots law."

There is no authoritatively settled list of what writings are to be treated as "institutional"; we have nothing corresponding to the Theodosian Law of Citations of A.D. 426 which named five jurists as authoritative; one can only look at judicial dicta to see what the consensus of judicial opinion is. The high status of "institutional" seems always to have been accorded to

Craig, Stair, Mackenzie, Bankton, Erskine's *Institutes* and Bell's *Commentaries* and *Principles*.[79] It has sometimes been given to other works, such as Forbes's *Institute*, Kames's *Equity*, Erskine's *Principles*, Alison and some other works such as Dirleton's. Particularly in the eighteenth century Mackenzie was ranked high, as was Dirleton, but today Dirleton would not be likely to be put in the "institutional" class.[80] In *H.M. Advocate* v. *Graham*[81] Lord Justice-Clerk Hope referred to "all these great lawyers," having mentioned Hope, Mackenzie, Dirleton and Stair. In criminal law the status is certainly accorded to Hume, probably to Mackenzie and sometimes to Alison.

A characteristic of an institutional work is that it deals with the whole private law or criminal law, or at least with a very major part thereof; no work dealing only with a branch, such as the law of contract, seems ever to have been regarded as institutional.[82]

The original characteristic of an institutional work, that it be educational or instructional, has been rather departed from; it can hardly be contended that any of the larger works were intended or suitable for instructional use, if only on account of their size, save in the broad sense, that any treatise is instructional. On the other hand Mackenzie, Forbes, Erskine's *Principles* and Bell's *Principles* were so intended, but the second and third are by no means accepted as institutional.

The extent of reliance in later cases on institutional writings has varied at different times. Down the mid-eighteenth century Stair was frequently cited alone, but in the latter years of that century there is heavier reliance on Erskine, as being more recent and up-to-date, and possibly more readily available. In the nineteenth century there appears to be heavier reliance on Bell, as the most recent writer, but he scrupulously cites Stair and Erskine, wherever relevant, as his authorities and there is accordingly a measure of reliance on them also by implication.

The term "institutional" in the modern sense of "authoritative" has been used also in relation to specialised areas of the law. In a heraldry case, *Stewart Mackenzie* v. *Fraser Mackenzie*,[83] Lord Sumner observed that a particular "proposition is asserted by many institutional writers, by Mackenzie, Nisbet and Seton." But this seems to be an isolated dictum.

The acceptance in the nineteenth century that works of institutional rank were authoritative does not imply that every word or phrase or opinion has been accepted as if divinely inspired. On particular points many of the institutional writers have been held to be inaccurate, or passages have had to be explained,[84] and in various respects later writers have disagreed with earlier. Erskine quite frequently differs from Stair or criticises his view. Kames's *Elucidations* contains many detailed criticisms of Stair's views on particular points, and his *Historical Law Tracts* turn a cold light of rational analysis on Stair's work. But from the 1840s there has developed a tendency to comment on the fact if a view of an institutional writer is not being accepted or followed; this corresponds to the increasing acceptance of the institutional writings as authoritative.

From quite early times, of course, pleaders cited to the court texts other than those of the institutional writers, particularly the civil law and to a lesser extent the canon law and the *Libri Feudorum*, and the major European commentators on one or other of these systems, particularly

Vinnius and Voet.[85] In the eighteenth century there were not infrequent citations of Beawes' *Lex Mercatoria*, Magens on *Insurance*, Molloy *de iure maritimo*, Malynes' *Lex Mercatoria* and some other classics of mercantile or maritime law. Domat and Pothier were sometimes referred to.

From shortly after its publication Blackstone's *Commentaries* were cited, without, it frequently seems, due regard to the unreliability of that work as any sort of authority in Scotland, and sometimes also decisions reported in the old English private reports such as Burrow's.

Moreover though a jurist at least one of whose works has been recognised as "institutional" may be referred to as "an institutional writer" this does not mean that all his works are equally entitled to enjoy the distinguished status of "institutional writings." In *Fortington* v. *Kinnaird*[86] Lord President Normand said:

> "We were referred to the lectures delivered by Baron Hume in 1821–1822 when he held the chair of Scots Law at Edinburgh, and recently published by the Stair Society ... Baron Hume was a very distinguished lawyer, and his treatise on the Criminal Law (published in 1797) ranks along with the other institutional works to which we pay homage in our law. But these lectures were not prepared for publication by Baron Hume, and they are not *in pari casu* with a treatise written with a view to publication, although published posthumously.[87] They are not, in our opinion, of comparable authority with his treatise on the Criminal Law, because they do not come into the world with his final approval and authority. Their historical value is high, and they are of great value in ascertaining what the law was supposed to be at the date when they were delivered by a lawyer of great eminence. In *Kerr* v. *Martin*,[88] notes taken by his former students were referred to by learned judges as evidence of the general and understood state of the law, but they were not put upon the same plane as the works of the recognised institutional writers. Baron Hume left the chair of Scots Law in 1822 and became a Baron of Exchequer. He survived till 1838. He published his Reports of Decisions in 1829.[89] If he had desired to publish his lectures, he had ample opportunity for doing so, and from these dates alone the inference should be drawn that he was averse to publishing them, even if this were not known with much greater certainty from other circumstances."

Similarly Lord Justice-Clerk Cooper said:[90]

> "I attach importance to the views expressed by Mackenzie in his Observations on the Act 1573, cap. 55, More in his Notes to Stair, and Lord Ivory in his Notes to Erskine; and in the same category I would place the Lectures of Baron Hume, with regard to which I would agree with your Lordship in the chair in thinking that, while they have no claim to the veneration attaching to our recognised institutional works, they are entitled to be regarded in the light in which they were viewed by the consulted judges in *Kerr* v. *Martin*,[91] that is, as 'authority of very great weight' and as 'decisive evidence of

the general and understood state of the law' at the time when Baron Hume lectured.''

So too Lord Mackay:[92]

"I desire also to concur fully in the observations of your Lordship in the chair as to the value of Hume's Lectures. . . . I personally assign a good deal of special weight . . . to the place in that tradition of Mr. John S. More, advocate and antiquary, whose Notes on Stair were published to the world in 1832 . . . the work carries almost the authority of a separate Institution. . . . I place a similar stress upon the position and date of Professor Bell, who was responsible for editions of the Principles up to the 4th, 1839, the next edition being that of Shaw in 1860.''

In *Wills' Trustees* v. *Cairngorm Canoeing and Sailing School*[93] Lord President Emslie adopted the same approach. Having examined the institutional writings he said: "There remain for consideration the commentators and text book writers . . . Hume's *Lectures* . . . Bell's *Illustrations* . . . Rankine, *Land Ownership* . . . Ferguson, *Law of Water*." Lord Cameron drew the same distinction.[94]

But in the same case in the House of Lords[95] Lord Wilberforce said: "The Institutional writers of authority whose work appeared before 1772 were Craig, Stair, Bankton and Erskine's *Principles*. Erskine's *Institute* appeared in 1773 but must have been completed in 1768 when he died;" and later:[96] "Of the writers, Hume's *Lectures*, Bell's *Principles*, Rankine on *Land Ownership*, Green's *Encyclopaedia*, s.v. Water and Water Rights. . . ." It is surely mistaken to include Erskine's *Principles* along with Craig, Stair and Bankton. Though the *Institute* certainly has, Erskine's *Principles* has never elsewhere been deemed a work of institutional standing and authority, probably because it is not so much a work distinct from the *Institutes* as an abridgment of it. Conversely Bell's *Principles* is normally ranked higher than among "the writers." Lord Fraser[97] similarly refers to "subsequent writers of authority in the law of Scotland" and mentions Hume's *Lectures*, Bell's *Principles*, Rankine on *Land Ownership*, and Green's *Encyclopaedia*.

What has been the function, and the achievement, of these "institutional" writers, at least in their writings recognised as of institutional rank?

In the first place, in the absence of codes or similar very wide-ranging legislation, it has been the function of the major institutional writings to establish a systematic structure or planned layout of the private law or of the criminal law into which the different principles fit, as distinct from *e.g.* statements under a series of headings listed alphabetically. This latter arrangement is admirable for reference purposes, as in an encyclopedia, or *Current Law*, but it is usable only by a person who understands the systematic structure of the law. It is of course obvious that not all writers adopted the same structure or layout, and indeed Bell's *Commentaries* suffers severely from its defective structure or even lack of structure. But that case apart, all the great institutional works have sought to exhibit the law as a systematic body of principles and rules, not just a collection or congeries of specific rules.

In the second place they had to integrate the materials drawn from different sources, from native custom, Roman law, canon law, feudal law, law merchant and maritime, and English law into a more or less coherent and consistent body of doctrines and principles. Naturally in some areas of the law a writer draws more from one source than from another.

In the third place, particularly in the earlier writings, they had to fill gaps and to suggest principles which could be adopted, and applied or adapted in default of native materials, to provide a rule for circumstances not yet covered by an accepted rule. Stair in particular did this, and the full extent of his creative function has not yet been adequately explored.

Fourthly, they had to seek to extract principles and general rules from particular pieces of legislation, the decisions on particular kinds of disputes and the other sources and to put these forward as the basic propositions which explained and justified various decisions.

The institutional writings in effect built and developed the common law (including in that the fairly modest amount of statutory addition and modification made down to about the early nineteenth century), and it is in topics still mainly governed by common law that their influence is still important. It is necessarily excluded in topics where the law has been created or reshaped by legislation, such as the law of divorce, of companies, of trade unions, of hire-purchase, and some other topics.

Is the class of "institutional writings" closed, probably by the last works of Bell? Probably yes. There seems to be no instance of the application of the term "institutional writing," or of the attribution of authority, to any writing later than those of Bell and possibly Alison.

It has to be acknowledged that, fundamentally important and valuable though the contributions of the institutional writers has been, their function has now very largely been served and been exhausted. It is mainly in matters of common law that their views have been and are valuable. The rules of law, and sometimes even the fundamental principles, have changed or been changed in many respects and a great deal of the issues giving rise to disputes today spring from matters governed by modern statutes, and from whole areas of law created by modern legislation, such as unjust dismissal, taxation, social security, town and country planning and many others on which the institutional writers can afford us no guidance. Moreover even where a principle is still fundamentally that expounded by an institutional writer, it has normally been discussed and explained in more modern cases, so that the latter, rather than the institutional writer's exposition, are, and must be, now referred to as the authority for a modern decision. The principle that if a breadwinner is killed by fault, the person in fault is liable to compensate surviving relatives who suffer by reason of the death, is enunciated by Stair and all the institutional writers, but its present form depends on qualifications introduced by later cases and statutes. These factors conspire to reduce the extent of express reference to and citation of the institutional texts in modern practice. But conversely they increase the need for, and importance of, modern textbooks restating the law in the light of modern changes.

Increasingly, accordingly, among the Scottish writers, a distinction has been drawn between institutional writings, which, in default of a binding decision of a court on the point, are authoritative, and passages in those textbooks accepted as standard works, which are not in themselves authoritative, but may be regarded as valuable and highly persuasive. Thus in *Fortington* v. *Kinnaird*[98] Lord Justice-Clerk Cooper said of Baron Hume's *Lectures* that "while they have no claim to the veneration attaching to our recognised institutional works" they were entitled to be treated as authority of very great weight. In *Annan* v. *Annan*[99] Lord Sorn referred to "institutional writers and textbooks"; in *Thomson* v. *St. Cuthbert's Co-operative Association*[1] Lord Patrick mentioned a principle "commented on by Judges, institutional writers and text writers." In *Orlandi* v. *Castelli*[2] Lord Cameron said: "I turn now to consider the views of the institutional and text writers," and he examined More's Notes to Stair, Erskine, Bell's *Principles*, Hume's *Lectures*, Fergusson's *Consistorial Law* and Fraser on *Husband and Wife*. In *Dundee Corporation* v. *Marr*[3] Lord President Clyde spoke of "our institutional writers (*e.g.* Bankton ... Bell's Principles ... Bell's Commentaries ...) and in our standard text-books (Rankine on Leases ... and Hunter on Landlord and Tenant ...)" while Lord Cameron[4] referred to "authorities or text-writers," mentioning Bell's *Principles*, Hunter, and Rankine.

It is again a question determined by the practice and general esteem of the profession what are in any given field of law the books which are regarded as standard works, which can be cited and will be looked at as persuasive, as distinct from the many lesser manuals, which may be accurate and even helpful in elucidating a difficulty but which a court would not accept as a standard book fit to be cited. Any substantial new book may be accepted on its merits and come to be accepted as standard, and older books may be dropped from the class and be treated as mainly historical, evidence of the former state of the law, only.

The functions, and the achievements, of the text-writers since the early eighteenth century have been, in some respects, similar to those of the institutional writers. They have had a rather lesser role in systematising the law as a whole, or in incorporating external sources, or in suggesting how gaps might be filled. The steadily developing bulk, complicated nature and difficult verbal embodiment of modern principles and rules indeed is such that it has become practically impossible to see or to state the law as a whole. Text-writers have increasingly been driven not to essay general books on the law as a whole but to work in smaller areas of the whole field, for example, in contract or delict or trusts, or even in the field of the employment relationship. The modern jurist is driven to confine his analysis and exposition to limited areas, while the working lawyer needs to look at books which try to bring together and render understandable and usable the jumble of relevant materials on particular topics. The great danger is that the public or criminal or private law will cease to be seen or thought of by students and working lawyers as a systematic, ordered body of related principles, subordinate detailed rules and exceptions, but be regarded as merely a vast collection of the aggregate of the particular rules on special topics such as leases or bankruptcy or consumer credit. Yet within the limited areas examined by most modern jurists their task is fundamentally the same, to systematise the materials relevant to the particular topic, to bring out and formulate the general principles, the qualifications and exceptions, to fit the statutory provisions and rationes of decisions into a coherent pattern, to criticise the unclear or mistaken and suggest solutions for the problems which are foreseeable but have not been decided.

As the twentieth century approaches its close, is the jurist's function still necessary?

In the major theoretical branches of legal science, legal philosophy, legal history, and comparative study of law, the continuing need for juristic activity is quite cleár. It is no less so in the more practical branches, public international law, European law, and the municipal law of Scotland.

In the three major divisions of the domestic or municipal law of Scotland, public, criminal and private, the need for the jurist still exists. The reason is, fundamentally, to bring together, and make sense of, the materials supplied by the sources of the law. Propositions of law on any matter are formulated in the forms of, or may be extracted from, one or more, frequently several, of, a medley of Acts of Parliament, statutory instruments, Acts of Sederunt or of Adjournal, and codes of practice, the *rationes* of cases decided by Scottish courts of varying ranks and compositions and to some extent by some foreign courts, statements in books of varying dates and authority, practices, customs and usages, ideas of morality, social policy and other sources. So long as this is so it is essential that some persons in each generation set out to put down on paper a synthesis of the propositions which can be extracted from the sources and used to regulate conduct or decide controversies, to restate the law in terms of the current materials. Computers can efficiently store, find and reproduce source materials, but cannot synthesise them or extract general principles. Encyclopedias, digests and data-banks have their value in containing information on points but do not present the law of Scotland, or even any particular branch of that law, as a systematised body of principles and exceptions any more than does a volume of statutes or a volume of reports of decisions.

Furthermore if the synthesis of particular propositions and rules is to be more than a collection, the writer must try to make sense of his materials, to impose shape and order on them, to extract generalisations and leading ideas, in short, principles, and to present the rules on each matter in the form of general principles, subordinate or more limited principles, detailed rules, qualifications and exceptions. It is of the utmost importance for the understanding of the whole corpus of national law, for its exposition and teaching, for the discovery of the norm relevant to a particular set of facts and its application to them, that the principles be put in order. Various models of order exist, those of Justinian's *Institutions*, of the major institutional writers, the French and German Civil Codes, and others can be devised.[5]

It is noteworthy that, in modern times, most of the major and many of the minor jurists have been academic lawyers, professors in one or other of the universities. The same is true of most Western legal systems. This is partly because today academic lawyers are expected to think and research and write about the law they profess as well as to teach it, and partly because on the whole they have more time and better opportunities to do so than have judges or persons engaged in professional practice of law. A writer's holding an important academic position has indeed been held to enhance the standing of his work. "And, I may add, that my confidence in the general principle, stated by Lord Newton[6] as the ground of the judgment in the case of Lady Dunmore,[7] is much strengthened by the circumstance that the eminent judge was for a considerable time professor of civil law in the University of Edinburgh."[8] The task of the jurist falls more and more to be discharged by the academic lawyer.

Since the mid-nineteenth century this task has in every field been becoming steadily more difficult. The volume of materials has been growing with increasing rapidity. The complex nature of the propositions and the detail in which they are stated has been developing; propositions formulated by legislation are verbose, full of exceptions and qualifications. Increasingly legal development has been irrational, the *ad hoc* reaction of Parliament or department of state to particular conditions, pressures or felt needs. Even reform committees are concerned with particular difficulties, amendment and patching. We are moving away from, rather than towards, a rational systematic body of law which even the lawyer can comprehend.

Courts in Scotland have never been accustomed to being limited, in relation to the treatises and textbooks cited in argument and judgment, to Scottish ones. But the citation of French, Dutch, German and other European books common in the eighteenth and earlier nineteenth century has been replaced in the twentieth century by citation of English and, to a much lesser extent, United States and Commonwealth literature. This has been partly due to the lesser availability of European materials, and partly the shift of Scots law from a civil-law type system towards being in some measure a common-law type system. While in some branches of law, where the principles, particularly if largely statutory, may be the same as or similar to those applicable in England, this is understandable, it is regrettable and liable to have unfortunate consequences if in branches of law mainly based on common law there is uncritical regard to English textbooks. But this practice is long-established. It is remarkable how often Blackstone's *Commentaries* are referred to in Scottish reports in the century after they were published. Today too often English textbooks are quoted not merely for comparative guidance or cross-reference or corroboration but as persuasive authority, which they cannot properly ever be.

The movements for law reform have frequently not been beneficial. Even where one agrees with the necessity for and the policy underlying reform, reform seems so frequently merely to take the form of introducing exceptions to or qualifications of hitherto accepted principles.

The municipal law is becoming more and more an unprincipled jumble of particular rules, qualifications, amendments, exceptions. The role of the jurist is becoming more frustrating and difficult and less satisfying; but it is not becoming less necessary or important but more so. It is essential if Scotland is to survive as a national entity and its law to survive as an ordered rational body of principles that there continue to be scholars to carry on the tradition of the Scottish jurists.

NOTES

[1] *Cf.* Lord Cooper, "The Importance of Comparative Law in Scotland," in *Selected Papers* (1957), p. 142.

[2] (1885–1975) Professor of International Law, Cambridge, Judge (1946–55) and President (1952–55) of the International Court of Justice, author of many books on international law.

[3] K. Luig, "The Institutes of National Law in the Seventeenth and Eighteenth Centuries," 1972 J.R. 193. See also Note (1984) 5 Jl. Legal Hist. 179.

[4] *e.g.* *McInnes* v. *Moore*, December 20, 1781, F.C. ("Institute par M. Argen"); *Ross* v. *Heriot's Hospital Governors*, June 6, 1815, F.C. (Argou and Don Ignacio Jorden de Asso and Don Miguel de Manuel). Argou is Gabriel Argou, author of *Institution au droit français* (1692); Jordan de Asso is Ignacio Jordan de Asso y del Rio who with Miguel de Manuel y Rodriguez wrote *Instituciones del derecho civil de Castilla* (1771).

[5] On the extent of citation of Stair see J. W. G. Blackie in *Stair Tercentenary Studies* (1981), pp. 212–227.

[6] See also J. W. Cairns, "Institutional Writings in Scotland Reconsidered" (1983) 4 Jl. Legal Hist. 76.

[7] F. Schulz, *History of Roman Legal Science*, p. 158.

[8] *Ibid.*, p. 159.

[9] *Ibid.*, p. 171.

[10] Cairns, *op. cit.*, *supra.*, p. 80. Mackenzie in particular stressed the instructional factor. Erskine's and Bell's *Principles* were professedly instructional.

[11] Cowell's *Institutiones Juris Anglicani* (1605) was translated as *Institutes of the Lawes of England* (1651) and Moyle translated Justinian's *Institutiones* as *Institutes*.

[12] (1872) 10 M. (H.L.) 26, at p. 32.

[13] *Commentaries* (1765), I, Intro., §3 (p. 73): "Coke's ... institutes ... have little of the institutional method to warrant such a title."

[14] *Chrestomathia*, 210.

[15] *Lectures on Jurisprudence* (1832) I, xv, 392.

[16] *Johnston* v. *Smiths*, November 18, 1766, F.C. (p. 82).

[17] *Kempt* v. *Watt*, January 28, 1779, F.C. (p. 111).

[18] *Hog* v. *Tennant* (1760) M. 4780, 4781; *Dobie* v. *Richardson*, July 17, 1765, F.C. (p. 41); *Maxwell* v. *Maxwell*, January 21, 1767, F.C.; *Machargs* v. *Campbell*, February 24, 1767, F.C. (p. 285); *Montier* v. *Baillie*, June 29, 1773, F.C. (p. 189); *Montgomery-Agnew* v. *Agnew* February 28, 1775, F.C. (p. 57).

[19] *Mowat* v. *Fordyce*, August 11, 1772, F.C. (p. 69).

[20] *Wright* v. *Taylor*, February 24, 1768, F.C.; *Lowther* v. *McLaine*, December 15, 1786, F.C.

[21] 1 Rob., Intro. xiv.

[22] *Ibid.*

[23] *Dreghorn* v. *Hamilton*, August 5, 1774 F.C. (p. 348).

[24] *McMillan* v. *Tait*, August 4, 1775, F.C. (p. 127).

[25] *Monteith* v. *Robb* (1844) 6 D. 934, at p. 937.

[26] November 20, 1772, F.C. (p. 78).

[27] *Schaw* v. *Schaw and Houston* (1718) 1 Rob. 203, 206; *Carlyle* v. *Lyon's Creditors* (1725) M. 147; *Wades* v. *Heir of Marshall Wade* (1760) M. 221, 223; *Pringle* v. *Murray* (1760) M. 1639, 1640; *Sibbald* v. *Inglis* February 23, 1785, F.C. (p. 316).

[28] I, 14.

[29] (1748) M. 5506, 5509. Emphasis added by present writer.

[30] February 28, 1772 F.C. (p. 27).

[31] February 21, 1782, F.C.

[32] June 6, 1815, F.C. (p. 395). Emphasis added.

[33] *Ibid.* at p. 412. Emphasis added. *Cf. Thomson* v. *James* (1855) 18 D. 1, 12, *per* Lord President McNeill: "The *authority* of Lord Stair was appealed to...."

[34] *Cf.* T. B. Smith, "Authors and Authority" (1972) 12 J.S.P.T.L. (N.S.) 3.

[35] *e.g. Paterson* v. *Speirs*, November 29, 1782, F.C., where the Lord Ordinary's interlocutor bears "that the precedent established by the court ... ought to be followed." The earliest use of the phrase *ratio decidendi* appears to be in Kames's Prefaces to his *Dictionary of Decisions* (1741) and his *Remarkable Decisions*, vol.2 (1766).

36 IV, 359.
37 *Lectures*, I, 14.
38 p. 157.
39 p. 246.
40 *Husband and Wife* (2nd ed., 1876), I, 3.
41 *Scotch Legal Antiquities*, 6.
42 March 2, 1808, F.C., at p. 122.
43 (1827) 5 S. 497, at p. 499.
44 (1827) 6 S. 137, at pp. 141, 143.
45 at p. 145.
46 (1828) 7 S. 146, at p. 148.
47 (1832) 11 S. 30, at p. 31.
48 (1851) 13 D. 843, at p. 848.
49 (1856) 18 D. 865, at p. 873.
50 (1859) 21 D. 377, at p. 386. In *Heron* v. *Espie* (1856) 18 D. 917, at p. 954 Lord Ardmillan also referred to "our institutional writers."
51 at p. 393. At pp. 396–397 he cites Stair, Bankton and Erskine.
52 at p. 399.
53 (1861) 23 D. 366, at p. 372 (argument).
54 p. 374.
55 p. 376.
56 p. 378. Earlier he mentions Stair and Mackenzie.
57 p. 384.
58 (1868) 6 M. 489, at p. 531 (a teind case).
59 p. 536.
60 (1872) 10 M. (H.L.) 26, at p. 31.
61 p. 32.
62 (1872) 10 M. 537, at p. 560.
63 (1885) 12 R. (H.L.) 67, at p. 68.
64 (1886) 14 R. 112, at p. 115.
65 *Ibid.*, at p. 119.
66 "The Scottish Judicature and Legal Procedure" (Presidential Address, Houldsworth Club, University of Birmingham).
67 1942 S.C. 239, at p. 282.
68 1963 S.C. 533.
69 at p. 554.
70 at p. 558.
71 at p. 563.
72 1976 S.C. (H.L.) 30.
73 p. 77.
74 p. 80.
75 p. 117.
76 p. 156.
77 (1893) 20 R. (H.L.) 88, at pp. 95–96.
78 [1980] 2 All E.R. 696, at p. 708.
79 See, *e.g. Fenton* v. *Livingstone* (1856) 18 D. 865, at p. 873. *Cf.* Lord Cooper, "Some Classics of Scottish Legal Literature," in his *Selected Papers* (1955) 39, who describes Stair's *Institutions*, Erskine's *Institutes* and Bell's *Commentaries* as "three outstanding master-pieces."
80 In *Stewart* v. *Duke of Montrose* (1860) 22 D. 755, at p. 794, Lord Curriehill refers to "all our institutional writers, from Craig, the earliest, to Professor Menzies, the latest. . . ." So too in *Hope* v. *Hope* (1864) 2 M. 670, at p. 675. This seems unwarranted.
81 (1844) 7 D. 183, at pp. 192–193; see also Lord Moncrieff at p. 208.
82 A. C. Black, "The Institutional Writers, 1600–1826," in (Stair Soc.) *Sources and Literature of Scots Law*, 59, observes: "Readers must decide for themselves whether or not the field covered by the writers to be noticed is in each case sufficiently wide."
83 1922 S.C. (H.L.) 39, at p. 52.
84 See, *e.g. Carmichael* v. *Carmichael* (1719) Mor. 2677; *Maxwell* v. *McCulloch* (1738) Mor. 2550; *Macdonald* v. *Hutchison* (1744) Mor. 10070; *Earl of Morton* v. *Officers of State* (1753) Mor. 10672; *Dobie* v. *Richardson* (1765) Mor. 6183; *Lord Blantyre* v. *Kennedy* (1838) 1 D. 148; *Watt* v. *Watson* (1897) 24 R. 330, at p. 336; (all criticising Stair); *Skene* v.

Greenhill (1825) 4 S. 25, at p. 26 (Bankton and Erskine dissented from); *Courtenay* v. *Edinburgh Tramways* 1909 S.C. 99, at p. 105 (definition in Bell's *Principles* criticised); *Highland Engineering Liquidators* v. *Thomson*, 1972 S.C. 87, at p. 91 (Bell's *Commentaries* disapproved).

[85] There is an impressive citation of European commentators in *Kerr* v. *Martin* (1840) 2 D. 752.

[86] 1942 S.C. 239, at p. 253.

[87] The Lord President had in mind Erskine's *Institute*.

[88] (1840) 2 D. 752, at pp. 771, 785.

[89] This is a mistake. Hume's *Decisions* were put in final shape and published by J. H. Forbes (later Lord Medwyn) and Adam Urquhart (later Sheriff of Wigton) in 1839.

[90] at p. 265.

[91] (1840) 2 D. 752.

[92] at p. 276.

[93] 1976 S.C. (H.L.) 30, at p. 80.

[94] at pp. 92–93.

[95] at p. 117.

[96] at p. 121.

[97] at p. 163.

[98] 1942 S.C. 239, at p. 265.

[99] 1948 S.C. 532, at p. 536.

[1] 1958 S.C. 380, at p. 394.

[2] 1961 S.C. 113, at p. 118.

[3] 1971 S.C. 96, at p. 100.

[4] at p. 108.

[5] The present writer in his *Principles of Scottish Private Law* has sought to organise the whole private law under 10 heads: (1) Introductory and general; (2) International private law; (3) Persons, natural and legal; (4) Obligations; (5) Property; (6) Trusts; (7) Succession; (8) Civil remedies; (9) Diligence; and (10) Insolvency. This excludes the adjective law of evidence and procedure.

[6] Alexander Irving (1766–1832, advocate 1788) was part-time Professor of Civil Law at Edinburgh, 1800–26, and a judge as Lord Newton, 1826–32.

[7] *Countess of Dunmore* v. *Alexander* (1830) 9 S. 190.

[8] *Thomson* v. *James* (1855) 18 D. 1, at p. 23, *per* Lord Curriehill.

REPORTS OF DECISIONS OF THE COURT OF SESSION

Reporter	Period	Vols.	Published	Abbreviation
John Sinclair	1540–48	—	MS.[1]	Sinc. Pr.
Sir James Balfour of Pittendreich	1540–1679	1	1759	Balf. Pr.
Sir Richard Maitland of Lethington	1550–69	—	MS.[1]	Mait. Pr.
Alex. Colvil of Culross	1570–84	—	MS.[1]	Colvil
Thos. Hamilton, Earl of Haddington	1592–1624	—	MS.[1]	Hadd.
Sir Thomas Nicolson of Carnock	1610–32	—	MS.[1]	Nicolson
Sir Thomas Hope	1608–33	2	1937–38	Hope, Maj. Pr.
Sir George Erskine of Inverteil	1621–42	—	MS.	Ersk.
Sir Alex. Gibson, Lord Durie	1621–42	1	1690[2]	Durie
Sir Robert Spottiswood of Pentland	1623–36	1	1701[2]	Spot.
Sir George Auchinleck of Balmanno	1628–35	—	MS.[2]	Balm.
Robert McGill, Lord Foord	1649–50	—	MS.[1,2]	McGill
Decisions of the English Judges during the Usurpation	1655–61	1	1762	Eng. Judg.
Sir John Gilmour of Craigmillar, Ld. Pres.	1661–66	1	1701[2]	Gil.
Sir David Falconer of Newton, Ld. Pres.	1681–86			Pres. Falc.
Sir James Dalrymple of Stair, Ld. Pres.	1661–81	2	1683[3] 1687	Stair 1 Stair 2
Sir John Baird of Newbyth	1664–67	—	MS.[1,2]	Newbyth
Sir John Nisbet, Lord Dirleton	1665–77	1	1698[2]	Dirl.
Sir Peter Wedderburn of Gosford	1668–77	—	MS.[1,2]	Gosford

Sir John Lauder, Lord Fountainhall	1678–1712	2	1759[3,4] 1761	Fount.
Sir Patrick Home of Renton	1681–88	—	MS.[1]	P. Home
George Fergusson, Lord Hermand	1684–1777	1	1940	Hermand
Sir Roger Hog, Lord Harcarse	1681–91	1	1757[3]	Harc.
Sir Hew Dalrymple of North Berwick, Ld. Pres.	1698–1720	1	1758	Dalr.
William Forbes, Faculty Reporter (Journal of the Session)	1705–13	1	1714[5,6]	Forbes
William Forbes	1713–14	—	MS.	Forbes MS.
Alex. Bruce, Faculty Reporter	1714–15	1	1720[5,7]	Bruce
Henry Home, Lord Kames	1716–28	1	1728	Kames, Rem. Dec. I
John Edgar, Faculty Reporter	1724–25	1	1742	Edgar
Henry Home, Lord Kames	1730–52	1	1766	Kames, Rem. Dec. II
Patrick Grant, Lord Elchies	1733–54	2	1813	Elchies
Alex. Home, Clerk of Session	1735–44	1	1757	Clk. Home.
Sir James Fergusson, Lord Kilkerran	1738–52	1	1775[8]	Kilk.
James Burnett, Lord Monboddo	1738–68	—	MS.[9]	Monboddo
David Falconer, Faculty Reporter	1744–51	2	1746, 1753	D. Falc.
Henry Home, Lord Kames	1752–68	1	1780	Kames, Sel. Dec.
Ilay Campbell	1756–60	1	1765[10]	Camp.
Alex. Tait	1762–79	1	1826[10]	Tait
Sir David Dalrymple, Lord Hailes	1766–91	2	1826	Hailes
David Hume	1781–1822	1	1839	Hume
Robert Bell, w.s.	1790–92	1	1794	Bell, Oct. Cas.
Robert Bell, w.s.	1794–95	1	1796	Bell, Folio Cas.
Faculty Reporters	1752–1825	21	1760–1823[11]	F.C.
Faculty Reporters	1825–41	16	1825–41	Fac. Dec.[12]

Private Reporters

1st Series (Shaw)	1821–38	16	1822–38	S.[13]
2nd Series (Dunlop)	1838–62	24	1839–62	D.[14]
3rd Series (Macpherson)	1862–73	11	1863–73	M. or Macph.
4th Series (Rettie)	1873–98	25	1873–98	R.
5th Series (Fraser)	1898–1906	8	1899–1906	F.
6th Series	1907 to date		1907–	S.C.

Collateral Series

Reporter	Period	Vols.	Published	Abbreviation
Buchanan's *Remarkable Cases*, Court of Session and High Court of Justiciary	1800–13	1	1813	Buch.
J. S. Anderson, *Agricultural Decisions*	1800–83	1	1883	And. Agr. Dec.
Star Session Cases	1824–25	1	1825	Star Sess. Cas.
George Deas and James Anderson	1829–33	5	1829–33	Deas and And.[15]
Scottish Jurist	1829–73	45	1829–73	Sc. Jur.
Robert Stuart, J. S. Milne and William Peddie	1851–53	2	1852–53	Stuart: or Stuart, M. & P.
Scottish Law Reporter	1866–1924	61	1866–1924	S.L.R.
Scots Law Times	1893 to date		1893–	S.L.T.

NOTES

[1] Some cases printed in Morison's *Dictionary*.

[2] Some cases printed in Brown's *Supplement*, Vol. I.

[3] Some cases printed in Brown's *Supplement*, Vol. II.

[4] Some cases printed in Brown's *Supplement*, Vols. III and IV.

[5] Some cases printed in Brown's *Supplement*, Vol. V.

[6] Further reports by Forbes covering 1713–14 were included by Lord Kames in his *Folio Dictionary*.

[7] Further reports by Bruce covering 1716–17 are appended to *Faculty Collection*, Vol. 3 (1772).

[8] Further reports by Kilkerran covering 1735–59 are printed in Brown's *Supplement*, Vol. V.

[9] Printed in Brown's *Supplement*, Vol. V.

[10] Printed in Brown's *Supplement*, Vol. V.

[11] Cases are cited by the date of the decision with the suffix F.C.

[12] Cases are cited by volume and page.

[13] Volumes are sometimes cited as S. and D. (for Shaw and Dunlop).

[14] Early volumes are sometimes cited as D., B. and M. (for Dunlop, Bell and Murray).

[15] Vol. 1 includes Jury Court cases and Justiciary cases; Vol. 5 includes Justiciary cases.

REPORTS OF DECISIONS OF THE HIGH COURT OF JUSTICIARY

Reporter	Period	Vols.	Published	Abbreviation
Robert Pitcairn, *Scottish Criminal Trials*	1488–1625	3	1833	Pitcairn
Hugh Arnot, *Celebrated Criminal Trials in Scotland*	1536–1784	1	1785, 1812	Arnot
Stair Gillon (Vol. I) and J. Irvine Smith (Vols. II and III) (ed.), *Selected Justiciary Cases* (Stair Soc.)	1624–1650	3	1953–74	Sel. Just. Cas.
W. G. Scott-Moncrieff (ed.), *Records of the Proceedings of the Justiciary Court, Edinburgh* (S.H.S.)	1661–1678	2	1905	Scott-Moncrieff
John MacLaurin, *Arguments and Decisions in Remarkable Cases before the High Court of Justiciary*	1670–1773	1	1774	MacLaurin
Patrick Shaw	1819–31	1	1831	P. Shaw or Shaw Just.
David Syme	1826–29	1	1829	Syme
Archibald Swinton	1835–41	2	1838–42	Swin.
Archibald Broun	1842–45	2	1844–46	Broun
Patrick Arkley	1846–48	1	1849	Arkley
John Shaw	1848–51	1	1853	J. Shaw
Alex. Forbes Irvine	1851–68	5	1855–68	Irv.
Charles T. Couper	1868–85	5	1871–87	Coup.
James C. White	1885–93	3	1888–93	White
Edwin Adam	1893–1916	7	1895–1919	Adam

From 1874 Justiciary cases have also been included in the annual volumes of *Session Cases*, but paginated separately. These reports, from 1917, are also sometimes found bound separately, five years to a volume, and backed as *Justiciary Cases*. Justiciary cases are also included in the *Scottish Law Reporter*, 1866–1924, and the *Scots Law Times*, 1893 to date.

OTHER COURTS

Reporter	Period	Vols.	Published	Abbreviation
Jury Courts				
J. Murray	1815–30	5	1818–31	Mur.
R. MacFarlane	1838–39	1	1841	MacF.
Consistorial (Commissary) Court				
J. Fergusson	1811–17	1	1817, 1829	Fergusson
Teind Court				
P. Shaw	1821–31	1	1831	Shaw, Teind
Lyon Court				
Scots Law Times (Lyon Court)	1959 to date	—	1959–	S.L.T. (Lyon Ct.)
Land Court				
Scottish Land Ct. Reports	1913–63	—	1913–63	S.L.C.R. or L.C.
Scots Law Times (Land Ct.)	1964 to date	—	1964–	S.L.T. (Land Ct.)
Sheriff Courts				
William Guthrie, *Select Cases in the Sheriff Courts.*	1861–78 1879–85	2	1879, 1894	Guthrie
Scottish Law Review	1885–1963	78	1885–1963	Sh. Ct. Rep.
Scots Law Times (Sheriff Court)	1893 to date	—	1893–	S.L.T. (Sh. Ct.)

Scottish Appeals to the House of Lords

Reporter	Period	Vols.	Published	Abbreviation
David Robertson	1707–27	1	1807	Rob. or Robert.
John Craigie, John S. Stewart and Thomas S. Paton	1726–1821	6	1849–56	Pat.
Patrick Shaw	1821–26	2	1826–28	Sh. App.
James Wilson and Patrick Shaw	1825–35	7	1829–39	W. & Sh.
Patrick Shaw and Charles H. Maclean	1835–38	3	1836–39	Sh. & Macl.
Charles H. Maclean and Geo. Robinson	1839	1	1840	Macl. & R.
George Robinson	1840–41	2	1840–42	Rob. or Robin.
Sydney S. Bell	1842–50	7	1843–52	Bell
John F. Macqueen	1851–65	4	1855–66	Macq.
James Paterson	1851–73	2	1879, 1895	Paters.

From 1850, from 13 D. onwards, House of Lords decisions are also reported in volumes of *Session Cases*, but separately paginated. From 1893 House of Lords decisions are also reported in *Scots Law Times*.

From 1719 some Scottish House of Lords decisions are also reported in some of the English private reports, in the *Law Reports*, in *All England Reports Reprint* (1558–1935) and *All England Reports* (1936 to date).

Collections, Reprints, Synopses and Digests

Reporter	Period	Vols.	Published	Abbreviation
Kames and Woodhouselee's Folio Dictionary				
Henry Home, Lord Kames: *The Decisions of The Court of Session Abridged and Digested under proper Heads in Form of a Dictionary*	1540–1748	2	1741	*Fol. Dict. or K. & W. Dict.*
The same with additional matter	1540–1770	5	1774	
The same, second edition	1540–1728	2	1791	
Alex. Fraser Tytler, Lord Woodhouselee:				
The same, supp. vol.	1728–76	1	1778	As above
The same, Vols. 3 and 4	1728–96	2	1797	
Thomas McGrugor: *Supplement to Volumes Third and Fourth of the Dictionary of Decisions containing all the omitted cases*	1728–96	1	1804	As above
Morison's Dictionary of Decisions				
William Maxwell Morison: *The Decisions of the Court of Session Digested under Proper Heads in the Form of a Dictionary*	1540–1808	38 in 19	1801–04	M. or Mor.
Appendix (usually bound in with Dictionary)				M. Appx.
Synopsis of Morison's Dictionary	1540–1808	2 (Vols. 20–21)	1804	
Supplemental Volume (omitted cases)		1 (Vol. 22)	1815	M. Supp.
Morison's Synopsis (continuation of the Dictionary)	1808–12 1812–16	2 (Vols. 23–24)	1814, 1817	M. Syn.

Brown's Supplement				
Mungo Ponton Brown: *Supplement to the Dictionary of Decisions*	1628–1794	5	1826	B.S.
Tait's Index				
William Tait: *Index to the Decisions of the Court of Session contained in all the original collections and in Mr. Morison's Dictionary of Decisions*	1540–1820	1	1823	Tait, Index
Brown's Synopsis				
Mungo Ponton Brown: *General Synopsis of the Decisions of the Court of Session from its Institution until Nov. 1827*	1540–1827	4	1829	B. Syn.
The Scots Revised Reports	1540–1873	45		Sc.R.R.
Kinnear's Digest				
John Boyd Kinnear: *Digest of House of Lords Cases on Appeal from Scotland*	1709–1864	1	1865	Kinnear
Halkerston's Compendium				
Peter Halkerston, s.s.c.: *A Compendium or General Abridgment of the Faculty Collection of Decisions of the Lords of Council and Session 1752–1817*	1752–1817	1	1819	Halk. Comp.
Bell's Dictionary of Decisions				
Sydney S. Bell, barrister: *Dictionary of the Decisions of the Court of Session, 1808–1833*	1808–33	2	1842	Bell's Dict.

Shaw's Digest				
Patrick Shaw, continued by A. B. Bell and W. Lamond: *Digest of Cases decided in the Supreme Courts of Scotland, 1800–68, and by the House of Lords, 1726–1868*	1726–1868	3	1869	Shaw's Dig.
The Faculty Digest				
An Analytical Digest of Cases decided in the Supreme Courts of Scotland and in the House of Lords 1868 to 1922	1868–1922	6	1924–26	Fac. Dig.
Supplementary Volumes	1923–60	4	1932–65	
The Scots Digest				
The Scots Digest of Scots Appeals in the House of Lords from 1707 and of the cases decided in the Supreme Courts of Scotland, 1800–73.	1707–1873	4	1908–12	Scots Dig.
The Scots Digest of the Cases decided in the Supreme Courts of Scotland	1873–1904	2	1905	
The same	1904–1914	1	1915	
The same	1914–23	1	1924	
The same	1923–30	1	1931	
The same	1930–37	1	1938	
The same	1937–44	1	1946	
Scottish Current Law Yearbooks				
(Annually)	1948–		1949–	C.L.Y.

BIBLIOGRAPHY

1. Works of Reference

Aldis, H. G., *A List of Books Printed in Scotland before 1700* (1904).

Anderson, W., *The Scottish Nation*, 3 vols. (1863).

Brunton, George, and Haig, David, *An Historical Account of the Senators of the College of Justice* (1832).

Catalogue of the Printed Books in the Library of the Faculty of Advocates, 7 vols. (1867–79).

Chambers, R., *Biographical Dictionary of Eminent Scotsmen*, 3 vols. (1868–70).

Cokayne, G. E., *The Complete Peerage*, 2 ed., 14 vols. (1910–59).

Cowan, S., *The Lord Chancellors of Scotland*, 2 vols. (1911).

Dickinson, W. C., Donaldson, G., and Milne, I. A., *A Source Book of Scottish History*, 3 vols. (1958–61).

Dictionary of National Biography, ed. L. Stephen, 63 vols. and Supps. (1885–1970).

Donaldson, G., *Scottish Historical Documents* (1970).

Donaldson, G., and Morpeth, R. S., *Dictionary of Scottish History* (1977).

—— *Who's Who in Scottish History* (1973).

Encyclopaedia Britannica, 14th and 15th editions (1970; 1974).

Encyclopaedia of Philosophy, ed. P. Edwards, 8 vols. (1967).

Encyclopaedia of the Social Sciences, ed. E. R. A. Seligman, 15 vols. (1930–35).

Ferguson, J. P. S., *Scottish Family Histories* (1960).

Gouldesbrough, P., Kup, A. P., and Lewis, I., *Hand List of Scottish and Welsh Record Publications* (1954).

Grant, Sir Francis J., *The Faculty of Advocates in Scotland, 1532–1943*, Scottish Record Soc. (1944).

Groome, F. H. (ed.), *Ordnance Gazetteer of Scotland*, 6 vols. (1882–85).

Hancock, P. D., *A Bibliography of Works Relating to Scotland*, 1915–50, 2 vols. (1960).

History of the Writers to H.M. Signet (1890; 1936).

International Encyclopaedia of the Social Sciences, ed. D. L. Sills, 17 vols. (1968).

Livingstone, M., *Guide to the Public Records of Scotland deposited in H.M. General Register House, Edinburgh* (1905).

Matheson, Cyril, *A Catalogue of the Publications of Scottish Historical and Kindred Clubs and Societies, 1908–27* (1928).

Maxwell, W. H. and L. F., *A Legal Bibliography of the British Commonwealth of Nations*: Vol. 1 – English Law to 1800 (1955); Vol. 2 – English Law, 1801–1954 (1957); Vol. 5 – Scottish Law and Roman Law (1957).

Mitchell, Sir A., and Cash, C. G., *A Contribution to the Bibliography of Scottish Topography*, 2 vols. (s.h.s.) (1917).

Omond, G. W. T., *The Lord Advocates of Scotland*, 2 vols. (1883).

—— *The Lord Advocates of Scotland*, Second Series (1914).

Paul, Sir James Balfour (ed.), *The Scots Peerage*, 9 vols. (1904–14).

Powicke, Sir M., and Fryde, E. B., *Handbook of British Chronology*, 2 ed. (1961).

Speirs, J. N., "A Catalogue of the Senators of the College of Justice" (1834–1972), 1972 S.L.T. (News) 233.

451

—— "A Catalogue of the Senators of the College of Justice" (1972–1979), 1979 S.L.T. (News) 323.

[These lists also include Lords of Appeal, Lords Advocate, Solicitors-General, Deans and Vice-Deans of Faculty]

Stuart, M., and Paul, J. Balfour, *Scottish Family History* (1929).

Terry, C. S., *A Catalogue of the Publications of Scottish Historical and Kindred Clubs and Societies, 1780–1908* (1909).

—— *An Index to the Papers relating to Scotland described or Calendared in the Historical MSS. Commission's Reports* (1908).

Who Was Who, 1897–1980, 8 vols.

2. HISTORICAL RECORDS

Accounts of the Lord High Treasurer of Scotland, 1473–1580, ed. T. Dickson and others, 13 vols. (1877–1978).

Acta Dominorum Auditorum, Acts of the Lord Auditors of Causes and Complaints, 1466–94, ed. T. Thomson (1839).

Acta Dominorum Concilii, Acts of the Lords of Council in Civil Causes, 1478–95, ed. T. Thomson (1839).

Acta Dominorum Concilii, Acts of the Lords of Council in Civil Causes, 1496–1501, ed. G. Neilson and H. M. Paton (1918).

Acta Dominorum Concilii, 1501–1503, ed. J. A. Clyde (1943).

Acta Dominorum Concilii et Sessionis, Selected Cases, 1532–33, ed. I. H. Shearer (1951).

Acts and Ordinances of the Interregnum, ed. C. H. Firth and R. S. Rait, 3 vols. (1911).

Acts of the Lords of Council in Public Affairs, 1501–54, ed. R. K. Hannay (1932).

Acts of the Parliaments of Scotland, 1124–1707, 12 vols. in 13, ed. T. Thomson and Cosmo Innes (1814–75).

Calendar of Documents relating to Scotland, 1108–1509, 4 vols., ed. J. Bain (1881–88).

Calendar of State Papers, Domestic Series, 1547–1704, 100 vols., ed R. Lemon and others (1856–1972).

Calendar of State Papers relating to Scotland, Scottish Series, 1509–1603, 2 vols., ed. M. J. Thorpe (1858).

Calendar of State Papers relating to Scotland and Mary Queen of Scots, 1547–1603, 13 vols., ed. Joseph Bain and others (1898–1969).

Register of the Great Seal of Scotland (Registrum Magni Sigilli) 1306–1668, ed. J. Maitland Thomson and others, 11 vols. (1890–1914).

Register of the Privy Council of Scotland, 1545–1625, ed. J. H. Burton and David Masson, 14 vols. (1877–98).

Register of the Privy Council of Scotland, Second Series, 1625–60, ed. David Masson and P. Hume Brown, 8 vols. (1899–1908).

Register of the Privy Council of Scotland, Third Series, 1660–91, ed. P. Hume Brown and others, 16 vols. (1908–70).

Registrum Secreti Sigilli, Register of the Privy Seal, 1488–1584, ed. M. Livingstone and others, 8 vols. (1908–82).

3. PARLIAMENTARY PAPERS

Three Reports of the Commissioners appointed to inquire into the Administration of Justice in Scotland (1810) (P. P., 1810 (6, 109, 238), Vol. 9).

Twelve Reports of the Commissioners on the Courts of Justice in Scotland (1816–22) (P. P. 1816 (419) – 1822 (595), Vols. 7–11).

Report of the Commissioners for enquiring into the Forms of Process in the Courts of Law in Scotland (1824) (P. P. 1824 (241) Vol. 10).

Report made to His Majesty by a Royal Commission of Enquiry into the State of the Universities of Scotland (1831) (P. P. 1831 (310) XII).

Evidence, oral and documentary, taken and received by the Commissioners . . . for visiting the Universities of Scotland, 1826–30.
    I.   *University of Edinburgh* (1837) (P. P. 1837, (92) XXXV);
    II. *University of Glasgow* (1837) (P. P. 1837, (93) XXXVI);
    III. *University of St. Andrews* (1837) (P. P. 1837 (94) XXXVII);
    IV. *University of Aberdeen* (1837) (P. P. 1837, (95) XXXVIII).

Report of the Select Committee on the Supreme Court of Judicature (Scotland) with minutes of evidence, appendix and index (1840), P. P. 332, XIV.

Scottish Universities Commission: General Report of the Commissioners under the Universities (Scotland) Act, 1858. With an Appendix (1863) (P. P. 1863, 3174, XVI).

Report of the Royal Commissioners appointed to inquire into the Universities of Scotland, with Evidence and Appendix.
    I.   *Report with Index of Evidence* (1878) (P. P. 1878, [C. 1935] XXXII);
    II. *Evidence – Part I* (1878) (P. P. 1878, [C. 1935–II] XXXIII);
    III. *Evidence-Part II* (1878) (P. P. 1878, [C. 1935–II] XXXIV);
    IV. *Returns and Documents* (1878) (P. P. 1878, [C. 1935–III] XXXV).

General Report of the Commissioners under the Universities (Scotland) Act, 1889. With an Appendix (1900) (P. P. 1900, [Cd. 276] XXV).

4. WRITINGS OF SCOTTISH JURISTS

It has been thought unnecessary to set out here alphabetically the significant works of all the Scottish jurists as they are all referred to in the text, and can be found through the Index.

5. BOOKS AND ARTICLES

Abraham, J. H., *Origins and Growth of Sociology* (1973).

Album Studiosorum Academiae Lugduno Batavae (1875).

Alison, Archibald, *Essays on the Nature and Principles of Taste* (1790).

Alison, Sir Archibald, *An Autobiography*, 2 vols. (1883).

Allardyce, A. (ed.), *Scotland and Scotsmen in The Eighteenth Century*, 2 vols. (1888).

Allen, J. W., *History of Political Thought in the Sixteenth Century*, 3 ed. (1951).

Alsop, J. D., "William Welwood, Anne of Denmark and the Sovereignty of the Sea" (1980) 59 S.H.R. 171.

Anderson, R. D., *Education and Opportunity in Victorian Scotland* (1983).

Arnot, Hugo, *History of Edinburgh* (1780).

Aron, R., *Main Currents in Sociological Thought*, 2 vols. (1965–68).

Ashley, Maurice, *James II* (1977).

B[rown], R. S., "James, First Viscount Stair" (1906) 14 S.L.T. 21.

Baillie, Robert, *Letters and Journals, 1637–1662*, ed. D. Laing, 3 vols. (1841–42).

Balfour-Melville, E. M. W. (ed.), *An Account of the Proceedings of the Estates in Scotland, 1689–90* (s.h.s.) 2 vols. (1954–55).

Barrow, G. W. S., *Feudal Britain, 1066–1314* (1956)

—— "Beginnings of Feudalism in Scotland," *The Kingdom of the Scots*, Ch. 10 (1973).

Barty, J. W., *Ancient Deeds and Other Writs in the Mackenzie – Wharncliffe Charter-Chest* (1906).

Bates, T. St. J. N., "Mr. McConnachie's Notes and Mr. Fraser's Confessional," 1980 J.R. 166.

Beattie, James, *Philosophical and Critical Works*, 4 vols. (1975).
Becker, Carl L., *The Heavenly City of the Eighteenth Century Philosophers* (1932).
Becker, Howard, and Barnes, H.E., *Social Thought from Lore to Science*, 3 vols. (1966).
Bell, A. S. (ed.), *The Scottish Antiquarian Tradition* (1981).
Berlin, Isaiah, *The Age of Enlightenment* (1956).
Bernstein, J. A., "Adam Ferguson and the Idea of Progress," *Studies in Burke and His Time*, 19 (1978) 99.
Black, G. F., *A Calendar of Witchcraft Cases in Scotland, 1511–1727* (1938).
Black, J. B., *The Art of History: A Study of Four Great Historians of the Eighteenth Century* (1926).
Blackstone, Sir William, *Commentaries on the Law of England*, 4 vols. (1765–69).
Blackstone, William T., *Francis Hutcheson and Contemporary Ethical Theory* (1965).
Blair, Hugh, *Lectures on Rhetoric and Belles Lettres*, 2 vols. (1783).
Bonar, James, *A Catalogue of the Library of Adam Smith* (1932).
Boswell, James, *The Decisions of the Court of Session upon the Question of Literary Property in the Cause John Hinton . . . against Alexander Donaldson . . . John Wood . . . and James Meurose* (1774).
—— *The Essence of the Douglas Cause* (1767).
—— *A Letter to Lord Braxfield* (1780).
—— *Boswell's London Journal, 1762–63*, ed. F. A. Pottle (1950).
—— *Boswell in Holland, 1763–64*, ed. F. A. Pottle (1952).
—— *Boswell on the Grand Tour: Germany and Switzerland, 1764*, ed. F. A. Pottle (1953).
—— *Boswell on the Grand Tour: Italy, Corsica and France, 1765–66*, ed. F. Brady, and F. A. Pottle (1953).
—— *Boswell in Search of a Wife, 1766–69*, ed. F. Brady and F. A. Pottle (1957).
—— *Boswell for the Defence, 1769–74*, ed. F. A. Pottle and W. K. Wimsatt (1959).
—— *Journal of a Tour to the Hebrides, 1773*, ed. F. A. Pottle and C. H. Bennett (1963).
—— *Boswell: The Ominous Years, 1774–76*, ed. C. Ryskamp and F. A. Pottle (1963).
—— *Boswell in Extremes, 1776–78*, ed. C. McC. Weis and F. A. Pottle (1971).
—— *Boswell, Laird of Auchinleck, 1778–82*, ed. J. W. Reid and F. A. Pottle (1977).
—— *Boswell, The Applause of the Jury, 1782–85*, ed. I. S. Lustig and F. A. Pottle (1981).
    See also Brady; Pottle.
Bower, A., *The History of the University of Edinburgh*, 3 vols. (1817–30).
Brady, F., *James Boswell, The Later Years*, 1759–95 (1984).
    See also Pottle.
Brown, H. H., "Lord Hailes," 1924 S.L.T. (News) 1.
Brown, Henry H., "Lord Kames, A Judicial Historian" (1911) 23 J.R. 180.
—— "Sir George Mackenzie: A Study of Old Scots Crime" (1901) 13 J.R. 261.
—— "An Old Scots Law Book" [Mackenzie] (1901) 8 S.L.T. 105, 113, 130, 138, 145, 154, 157; (1902) 9 S.L.T. 9.
—— "Lord Monboddo: A Judicial Metaphysician" (1905) 17 J.R. 267.
—— "Sir George Mackenzie of Rosehaugh" (1902) 9 S.L.T. 1.
—— "A Master of Equity" (1904) 20 L.Q.R. 308.
—— "Equity" (1914) 26 J.R. 338.
—— "Lord Monboddo's Correspondence" (1902) 9 S.L.T. 59, 61, 69, 79, 89, 101, 113, 118, 125, 133.

—— "Lord Kames's Principles of Equity" (1903) 10 S.L.T. 94, 111, 127, 159, 173, 181; (1904) 11 S.L.T. 7, 22.

Brown, P. Hume, *George Buchanan* (1890).

—— *John Knox*, 2 vols. (1895).

—— *History of Scotland*, 3 vols. (1899–1909).

—— *The Legislative Union of England and Scotland* (1914).

—— and others, *The Union of 1707* (1907).

Bruce, George (ed.), *Edinburgh in the Age of Reason* (1967).

Bryce, James, *Studies in History and Jurisprudence*, 2 vols. (1901).

Bryson, Gladys, *Man and Society: The Scottish Inquiry of the Eighteenth Century* (1954).

Buchanan, George, *Rerum Scoticarum Historia* (1583).

Buchanan, John, "The MSS of *Regiam Maiestatem*" (1937) 49 J.R. 217.

Buckle, H. T., *On Scotland and the Scotch Intellect*, 1861, ed. H. J. Hanham (1970).

Buckroyd, Julia, *Church and State in Scotland, 1660–1681* (1980).

Bulloch, J. M., *A History of the University of Aberdeen*, 1495–1895 (1895).

Burnet, Gilbert, *History of His Own Time*, ed. O. Airy, 6 vols. (1823).

Burn-Murdoch, H., "English Law in Scots Practice" (1908) 20 J.R. 59, 148; (1909) 21 J.R. 59, 148.

Burns, J. H., "The Political Ideas of George Buchanan" (1951) 30 S.H.R. 60.

Burton, John Hill, *History of Scotland*, 8 vols. (1873).

—— *Life and Correspondence of David Hume*, 2 vols. (1846).

Cairns, Huntington, *Legal Philosophy from Plato to Hegel* (1949).

Calderwood, David, *History of the Kirk of Scotland* [1545–1625], ed. T. Thomson and David Laing, 8 vols. (1842–49).

Cameron, John, "James Dalrymple, 1st Viscount of Stair," 1981 J.R. 102.

Camic, G., *Experience and Enlightenment: Socialization for Cultural Change in Eighteenth-Century Scotland* (1983).

Campbell, A. H., "The Structure of Stair's Institutions," David Murray Lecture, Glasgow, 1954.

Campbell, John, Lord, *Lives of the Chancellors*, 4 ed., 10 vols. (1856).

Campbell, R. H., *The Rise of an Industrial Society: Scotland since 1707* (1965).

—— "Stair's Scotland, The Social and Economic Background," 1981 J.R. 110.

—— and Skinner, A. S., *The Origins and Nature of the Scottish Enlightenment* (1982).

Campbell, T. D., *Adam Smith's Science of Morals* (1971).

Cant, R. G., *The University of St. Andrews: A Short History* (1946).

—— "The Scottish Universities and Scottish Society in the Eighteenth Century," *Studies on Voltaire and the Eighteenth Century*, lviii (1967) 1953.

Carlyle, Alexander, *The Autobiography of Alexander Carlyle of Inveresk*, ed. J. H. Burton (1910).

—— *Anecdotes and Characters of the Times*, ed. J. Kinsley (1973).

Carlyle, R. W. and A. J., *History of Medieval Political Theory in the West*, 6 vols. (1902–36).

Carnie, R. H., "Lord Hailes: A Study," unpub. Ph.D. thesis, St. Andrews (1954).

Cassirer, Ernst, *The Philosophy of the Enlightenment* (1951).

Chalmers, George, *Life of Thomas Ruddiman* (1794).

Chitnis, Anand C., *The Scottish Enlightenment: A Social History* (1976).

Clive, John L., *Scotch Reviewers: The Edinburgh Review, 1802–1815* (1957).

Cloyd, E. L., *James Burnett, Lord Monboddo* (1972).

Cockburn, Henry, Lord, *Circuit Journeys 1837–1854* (1888).

—— *Journal of Henry Cockburn, 1831–1854*, 2 vols. (1874).

—— *Life of Lord Jeffrey*, 2 vols. (1852).

—— *Memorials of His Time* (1856).

Colville, James, "The Diary of Sir Thomas Hope" (1906) 3 S.H.R. 423.

Cooke, C. A., "Adam Smith and Jurisprudence" (1935) 51 L.Q.R. 326.

Cooper, T. M. (Lord), *Selected Papers, 1922–54* (1957).

—— *Selected Scottish Cases of the Thirteenth Century* (1944).

—— *The Scottish Legal Tradition* (1949).

—— "A Scottish Lawyer's Library in the Seventeenth Century" (1954) 66 J.R. 1.

—— "Cromwell's Judges and their Influence on Scots Law" (1946) 58 J.R. 20.

—— "Early Scots Statutes Revisited" (1952) 64 J.R. 197.

—— "The Liber *De Judicibus*," 1941 S.L.T. (News) 21.

—— "Stair the Scientist" (1955) 67 J.R. 23.

Couper, W. J., "Mrs. Anderson and the Royal Prerogative in printing," *Proc. Royal Phil. Soc. of Glasgow*, 48 (1918).

Coutts, J., *History of the University of Glasgow* (1909).

Craig, John, "The Character of the late Professor Millar," *Scots Magazine*, 63 (1801) 527.

Craik, Sir Henry, *A Century of Scottish History*. 2 vols. (1901).

Crawfurd, Donald (ed.), *Journal of a Foreign Tour in 1665 and 1666 by Sir John Lauder, Lord Fountainhall*.

Crawford, George, *The Lives and Characters of the Officers of the Crown and of the State in Scotland* (1726).

—— *The Peerage of Scotland* (1716).

Daiches, David, *The Paradox of Scottish Culture: The Eighteenth Century Experience* (1964).

—— (ed.), *A Companion to Scottish Culture* (1981).

Dalrymple, Sir David, Lord Hailes, *Annals of Scotland*, 3 vols. (1819).

David, Hélène, "Deux Contemporains: Stair et Domat," 1982 J.R. 68.

—— *Introduction a l'étude du droit écossais* (1972).

Davie, G. E., *The Democratic Intellect*, 1961.

—— "Hume, Reid and the Passion for Ideas," *Edinburgh in the Age of Reason*, ed. Bruce (1967).

Dawson, J. P., *The Oracles of the Law* (1968).

D'Entrèves, A. P., *Natural Law* (1951).

Dicey, A. V., and Rait R. S., *Thoughts on the Union between England and Scotland* (1920).

Dickson W. K., "The Advocates Library" (1902) 14 J.R. 1, 113, 214.

—— "The National Library of Scotland" (1923) 40 J.R. 172.

—— "David Hume and The Advocates Library" (1932) 44 J.R. 1.

Dickinson, W. C., *Scotland from the Earliest Times to 1603*, 3 ed. by Duncan (1975).

—— "The Advocates' Protest against the Institution of a Chair of Law in the University of Edinburgh" (1926) 23 S.H.R. 205.

Diurnal of Remarkable Occurrents [1513–75] ed. T. Thomson (1833).

Dobie, W. G. M., "Law and Lawyers in the Waverley Novels," (1920) 32 J.R. 244, 317.

Donaldson, Gordon, *Scotland, James V to James VII* (1965).

—— "The Legal Profession in Scottish Society in the 16th and 17th centuries," 1976 J.R. 1.

—— "Stair's Scotland: The Intellectual Inheritance," 1981 J.R. 128.

Douglas, Sir Robert, *The Baronage of Scotland* (1798).

—— *The Peerage of Scotland*, 2 ed. by J. P. Wood, 2 vols. (1813).

Dow, E. F., *Cromwellian Scotland* (1979).

Dunbar, Sir Arch. H., *Scottish Kings*, 2 ed. (1906).

Duncan, A. A. M., *Scotland, The Making of the Kingdom* (1975).

—— "Regiam Maiestatem: A Reconsideration," 1961 J.R. 199.

Duncan, Douglas, *Thomas Ruddiman* (1965).

Duncan, J. Lindsay, "Life and Times of Viscount Stair" (1934) 46 J.R. 103.

Dunlop, A. I. (ed.), *Acta Facultatis Artium Universitatis Sanctiandree, 1413–1588*, 2 vols. (S.H.S.) (1964).

Durkan, John, and Kirk, J., *The University of Glasgow, 1415–1577* (1977).

Dwyer, J., Mason, R. A., and Murdoch, A. (ed.), *New Perspectives on the Politics and Culture of Early Modern Scotland* (1980).

Erskine of Carnock, Diary of the Col. the Hon. John, 1683–87, ed. W. Macleod (S.H.S.) (1893).

Fay. C. R., *Adam Smith and the Scotland of His Day* (1956).

Feenstra, R., and Waal, C., *Seventeenth Century Leiden Law Professors and Their Influence on the Development of the Civil Law* (1976).

Ferguson, Adam, *An Essay on the History of Civil Society*, 1767, ed. Forbes (1966).

—— *Institutes of Moral Philosophy* (1769).

—— *Principles of Moral and Political Science: being chiefly a retrospect of lectures delivered in the College of Edinburgh*, 2 vols. (1792).

Ferguson, F. S., "Bibliography of the Works of Sir George Mackenzie, Lord Advocate, Founder of the Advocates' Library," *Trans. Edin. Bibliographical Socy.*, XIV (1935) 1.

Ferguson, William, *Scotland, 1689 to the Present* (1968).

—— *Scotland's Relations with England* (1977).

Fergusson, A., *The Honourable Henry Erskine* (1882).

Fergusson, James, "Sir James Fergusson: Background to a Lord of Session," 1974 S.L.T. (News) 1.

Fifoot, C. H. S., *Judge and Jurist in the Reign of Queen Victoria*, (1959).

Finnis, J. M., *Natural Law and Natural Rights* (1980).

Firth, C. H. (ed.), *Scotland and the Commonwealth* (S.H.S.) (1895).

—— *Scotland and the Protectorate* (S.H.S.) (1899).

—— *The Last Years of the Protectorate* (1909).

Flint, R., "Professor Lorimer" (1890) 2 J.R. 113.

Forbes, Duncan, *Hume's Philosophical Politics* (1975).

—— "'Scientific' Whiggism: Adam Smith and John Millar," (1953) VII *Cambridge Journal* 643.

Fortuna Domus: A series of Lectures delivered in the University of Glasgow in commemoration of the fifth centenary of its foundation (1952).

Franklin, J. H., *Jean Bodin and the Sixteenth Century Revolution in the Methodology of Law and History* (1963).

—— *Jean Bodin and the Rise of Absolutist Theory* (1973).

—— *John Locke and the Theory of Sovereignty* (1978).

Fraser, A. C., *Thomas Reid* (1898).

Fraser, Antonia, *Mary, Queen of Scots* (1969).

—— *Cromwell, Our Chief of Men* (1973).

—— *King Charles II* (1979).

Fraser, J. A. Lovat, "Lord Chancellor Erskine" (1906) 18 J.R. 357.

—— "Henry Erksine" (1912) 24 J.R. 51.

—— "A Famous Lord Advocate" [H. Dundas] (1902) 14 J.R. 350.

—— "The Impeachment of Lord Melville" (1912) 24 J.R. 235.

Friedrich, C. J., *The Philosophy of Law in Historical Perspective* (1958).

Furber, Holden, *Henry Dundas, First Viscount Melville* (1931).

Ganshof, F., *Feudalism*, trs. Grierson (1952).

Gardiner, S. R. (ed.), *Charles II and Scotland, 1650* (S.H.S.) (1894).

Gardiner, J. C., "Judicial Decisions as a Source of Scots Law" (1941) 53 J.R. 33.

Gay, Peter, *The Enlightenment: An Interpretation*, 2 vols. (1966–69).

—— (ed.), *The Enlightenment: A Comprehensive Anthology* (1973).

General Survey of Events, Sources, Persons and Movements in Continental Legal History (Continental Legal History Series, Vol. I) (1912).

Gierke, O. von, *Natural Law and the Theory of Society, 1500–1800*, trs. Barker (1934).

Gilbert, J. M., *Hunting and Hunting Reserves in Medieval Scotland* (1979).

Gilmour, R., *Samuel Rutherford* (1904).

Giuliani, A., "Adamo Smith, filosofo del diritto," *Riv. int. filosofia del diritto*, 31 (1954) 505.

Glanville, R., *De Legibus et Consuetudinibus Angliae*, ed. G. E. Woodbine (1932); ed. G. D. G. Hall (1965).

Goldmann, L., *The Philosophy of the Enlightenment* (1973).

Gordon, W. M., "Stair's Use of Roman Law," in Harding (ed.), *Law Making and Law Makers in British History* (1980).

Gorla, Gino, "Bell, one of the Founding Fathers of the 'Common and Comparative Law of Europe' during the 19th Century," 1982 J.R. 121.

Goudy, H., "Lord Fraser" (1889) 1 J.R. 178.

Graham, H. Grey, *Scottish Men of Letters in the Eighteenth Century* (1908).

—— *The Social Life of Scotland in the Eighteenth Century* (1928).

Graham, J. M., *Annals and Correspondence of the Viscount and First and Second Earls of Stair*, 2 vols. (1875).

Grant, Sir A., *The Story of the University of Edinburgh*, 2 vols. (1884).

Grave, S. A., *The Scottish Philosophy of Common Sense* (1960).

Gray, W. Forbes, *Some Old Scots Judges* (1914).

Greig, J. A., *Francis Jeffrey of the Edinburgh Review* (1948).

Greig, J. Y. T., *David Hume* (1934).

—— (ed.), *The Letters of David Hume*, 2 vols. (1932).

Guthrie, C. J. (Lord), "Charles Edward Green" (1920) 32 J.R. 1.

—— "Robert Louis Stevenson" (1919) 31 J.R. 89, 161; (1920) 32 J.R. 7, 129.

Haakonssen, Knud, "John Millar and the Science of a Legislator," 1985 J.R. 12.

Haldane, A. R. B., "The Society of Writers to Her Majesty's Signet" (1970) 15 J.L.S. 35.

Hamilton, Henry, *An Economic History of Scotland in the Eighteenth Century* (1962).

—— *The Industrial Revolution in Scotland* (1932).

Hamilton Grierson, P. J., "The De Facto Principle in Jurisprudence" (1890) 2 J.R. 245.

Hampshire, Stuart, *The Age of Reason* (1956).

Hampson, Norman, *The Enlightenment* (1976).

Hanbury, H. G., *The Vinerian Chair and Legal Education* (1958).

Handley, J. E., *Scottish Farming in the Eighteenth Century* (1953).

—— *Agricultural Revolution in Scotland* (1963).

Hannay, R. K., *The College of Justice* (1933).

—— "Scotland and the Canon Law" (1937) 49 J.R. 25.

Harding, A (ed.), *Law Making and Law Makers in British History* (1980).

Hayek, F. A., "The Legal and Political Philosophy of David Hume," in *Studies in Philosophy, Politics and Economics* (1967), 106.

Hazard, Paul, *European Thought in the Eighteenth Century: from Montesquieu to Lessing* (1954).

—— *The European Mind, 1680–1715* (1964).

Heatley, D. P., "Pollock and Lorimer" (1944) 56 J.R. 6.

Heineccius, J. G., *Elementa Iuris Civilis secundum Ordinem Institutionum Commoda Auditoribus methodo Adornata* (1738).

—— *Elementa Iuris Civilis Secundum Ordinem Pandectarum commoda auditoribus methodo adornata* (1731).

—— *Historia Iuris Civilis Romani ac Germanici* (1733).

Henderson, J. S., "Sir Thomas Craig's *Ius Feudale*" (1934) 50 L.Q.R. 585.
—— "The Scottish College of Justice in the 16th Century" (1934) 50 L.Q.R. 120.
—— "James Boswell and His Practice at the Bar" (1905) 17 J.R. 105.
Heron, R., *Journey through Western Scotland in 1792*, 2 vols. (1793).
Hewitt, G. R., *Scotland under Morton* (1982).
Higgins, A. Pearce, "James Lorimer (1818–90)" (1933) 45 J.R. 239.
Holdsworth, Sir William S., *Essays in Law and History* (1946).
—— *History of English Law*, 17 vols. (1936–66).
—— *Sources and Literature of English Law* (1925).
Hole, William, *Quasi Cursores* (1884).
Hont, I., and Ignatieff, M., *Wealth and Virtue: The Shaping of Political Economy in the Scottish Enlightenment* (1983).
Hope, V. (ed.), *Philosophers of the Scottish Enlightenment* (1984).
Horn, D. B., *A Short History of the University of Edinburgh, 1556–1889* (1967).
—— "The Universities (Scotland) Act of 1858" (1958–60) XIX *Univ. of Edin. Jl.* 169.
Hume, David, *History of England*, 6 vols. (1754–62).
—— *Letters of David Hume*, ed. J. Y. T. Greig, 2 vols. (1932).
—— *My Own Life* (1777) [reprinted in Greig, and Mossner].
—— *New Letters of David Hume*, ed. R. Klibansky and E. C. Mossner, (1954).
—— *Philosophical Works of David Hume*, ed. T. H. Green and T. H. Grose, 4 vols. (1874–75).
—— *Life of*; *see* Mossner.
Hume, Sir David, of Crossrig, *Dairy of the Proceedings in the Parliament and Privy Council of Scotland, 1700–1707* (1828).
Hutcheson, Francis, *An Essay on the Nature and Conduct of the Passions and Affections, With Illustrations on the Moral Sense* (1728).
—— *An Inquiry into the Original of our Ideas of Beauty and Virtue, in Two Treatises: I. Concerning Beauty, Order, Harmony, Design; II. Concerning Moral Good and Evil* (1725).
—— *De Naturali hominum socialitate* (1756).
—— *A Short Introduction to Moral Philosophy*, trans. from the Latin (1764).
—— *Synopsis metaphysicae* (1749).
—— *System of Moral Philosophy*, with an account of the author by William Leechman, 2 vols. (1755).
—— *Collected Works*, 6 vols. (1969–71).
Innes, Cosmo, *Lectures on Scotch Legal Antiquities* (1872).
—— *Memoir of Thomas Thomson, Advocate* (1854).
—— *Scotland in the Middle Ages* (1860).
—— *Sketches of Early Scotch History* (1861).
—— (ed.), *Ancient Laws and Customs of the Burghs of Scotland, 1124–1424* (1868).
Jeffrey, Francis, *Contributions to the Edinburgh Review*, 3 vols. (1846).
Jessop, I. E., *A Bibliography of David Hume and of Scottish Philosophy from Hutcheson to Balfour* (1938).
Johnston, C. N. (Lord Sands). "Lord Justice-Clerk Macdonald and His Edinburgh" (1923) 35 J.R. 107.
Jolowicz, H. F., and Nicholas, J. K. B. M., *Historical Introduction to the Study of Roman Law*, 3rd ed. (1972).
Kay, John, *A Series of Original Portraits and Caricature Etchings*, 2 vols. (1837); new ed. (1887).
Kennedy, N. J. D., "Lord McLaren" (1910) 22 J.R. 66, 181.
Kenyon, J. P., *The History Men* (1983).
Kettler, David, *The Social and Political Thought of Adam Ferguson* (1965).
Knight, William, *Lord Monboddo and some of His Contemporaries* (1900).

Knox, John, *History of the Reformation in Scotland*, ed. W. C. Dickinson, 2 vols. (1949).
—— *Works*, ed. D. Laing, 6 vols. (1895).
Kunkel, Wolfgang, "On the Origins and Social Position of the Roman Jurists" (1954) 66 J.R. 148.
Laing, D., *Portrait and biographical notice of Thomas Thomson* (1853).
Lamont, Claire, "William Tytler, His Son Alexander Fraser Tytler (Lord Woodhouselee) and The Encouragement of Literature in Late 18th Century Edinburgh": unpub. B. Litt. thesis, Oxford (1968).
Lang, Andrew, *Sir George Mackenzie, King's Advocate, of Rosehaugh: His Life and Times, 1636(?)–1691* (1909).
Lauder, Sir John, *The Journals of Sir John Lauder, Lord Fountainhall*, ed. D. Crawford (S.H.S.) (1900).
—— *Historical Notices of Scottish Affairs*, ed. D. Laing, 2 vols. (1848).
Laurie, H., *Scottish Philosophy in its National Development* (1902).
Law, George, "*Cragii Ius Feudale*" (1898) 10 J.R. 177, 334.
—— "Fountainhall" (1897) 9 J.R. 59, 173.
Lawson, F. H., *The Oxford Law School, 1850–1965* (1968).
Lee, Maurice, *John Maitland of Thirlestane* (1959).
—— *Government by Pen* (1980).
Lehmann, William C., *Adam Ferguson and the Beginnings of Modern Sociology* (1930).
—— "Some Observations on the Law Lectures of Professor Millar at the University of Glasgow (1761–1801)," 1970 J.R. 56.
—— "The Historical Approach in the Juridical Writings of Lord Kames," 1964 J.R. 17.
—— "John Millar, Professor of Civil Law at Glasgow, 1761–1801," 1961 J.R. 218.
—— *John Millar of Glasgow, 1735–1801* (1960).
—— *Lord Kames and the Scottish Enlightenment* (1971).
Lenman, B. P., *Integration, Enlightenment and Industrialisation* (1981).
Levack, B. P., "The Proposed Union of English Law and Scots Law in the 17th Century," 1975 J.R. 97.
Levie, W. E., "Alison's History of Europe" (1942) 54 J.R. 144.
—— "The Place of the War of Independence in Scottish Legal History" (1943) 55 J.R. 121.
Lewis, J. V., "The Moral Character of Positive Law in Stair's *Institutions*," 1976 J.R. 127.
Lindgren, J. R., *The Social Philosophy of Adam Smith* (1973).
Lochhead, Marion, "Scots Law and Letters" (1954) 292 *Quarterly Review* 465.
—— "Parliament House and the Lords of Session" (1955) 293 *Quarterly Review* 62.
Lockhart, George, *Memoirs concerning the Affairs of Scotland from Queen Anne's Accession . . . to the Union* (1714).
Lockhart, John Gibson, *Memoirs of Sir Walter Scott*, 5 vols. (1900).
Luig, Klaus, "Institutes of National Law in the Seventeenth and Eighteenth Centuries," 1972 J.R. 193.
Lorimer, James, "The Story of the Chair of Public Law in the University of Edinburgh" (1889) 4 L.Q.R. 139.
—— "The Faculty of Law" (1889) 1 J.R. 4.
MacCormack, G., "Note on Stair's Use of the term Pollicitatio," 1976 J.R. 121.
McCormick, D. N., "The Rational Discipline of Law," 1981 J.R. 146.
McCosh, James, *The Scottish Philosophy from Hutcheson to Hamilton* (1875).
McCrae, Thomas, "Lord Kames and the North Bridge: Notes on the Scheme of 1754" (1940) 23 *Book of the Old Edinburgh Club* 147.

Macdonald, J. H. A. (Lord Kingsburgh), *Life Jottings of an Old Edinburgh Citizen*, 1915.

Macdonell, Sir John, and Manson, Edward (ed.), *Great Jurists of the World* (1913).

McElroy, D. D., *Scotland's Age of Improvement: A Survey of Eighteenth-Century Clubs and Societies* (1969).

McFarlane, I. D., *Buchanan* (1981).

Macfie, A. L., *The Individual in Society: Papers on Adam Smith* (1967).

McGuiness, A. E., *Henry Home, Lord Kames* (1970).

MacKay, A. J. G., *Memoir of Sir James Dalrymple, First Viscount Stair* (1873).

McKechnie, Hector (ed.), *An Introductory Survey of the Sources and Literature of Scots Law* (Stair Soc.) (1936).

—— "Balfour's Practicks" (1931) 43 J.R. 179.

Mackenzie, W. C., *The Life and Times of John Maitland, Duke of Lauderdale, 1616–1682* (1923).

Mackie, J. B., *The Life and Work of Duncan McLaren (1800–86)*, 2 vols. (1888).

Mackie, J. D., *The University of Glasgow, 1451–1951* (1954).

Mackinnon, F. D., "The Origins of Commercial Law" (1937) 52 L.Q.R. 30.

Mackinnon, James, *The Union of England and Scotland* (1896).

Mackintosh, James, "Henry Goudy" (1922) 34 J.R. 53.

Macleod, W. (ed.), *Diary of Col. the Hon. John Erskine of Carnock, 1683–87* (S.H.S.) (1893).

Macmillan, A. R. G., *Evolution of the Scottish Judiciary* (1941).

—— "Judicial System of the Commonwealth in Scotland" (1937) 49 J.R. 232.

—— "The Scottish Court of Admiralty" (1922) 34 J.R. 38, 164.

Macmillan, A. D., *Letters of Patrick Grant, Lord Elchies, with Memoir* (1927).

Macmillan, Hugh P. (Lord), *A Man of Law's Tale* (1952).

—— "The Old Scots Conveyancers I: Dallas of St. Martin's" (1898) 10 J.R. 425.

—— "The Old Scots Conveyancers II: Carruthers & Spotiswood" (1899) 11 J.R. 41.

—— "The Court of Session in 1629" (1900) 12 J.R. 137.

McNeill, P. G. B., "Sir James Balfour of Pittendreich," 1960 J.R. 1.

—— "Senators of the College of Justice, 1569–78," 1960 J.R. 120.

—— "Senators of the College of Justice, 1532–69," 1978 J.R. 209.

—— "The Passing of the Scottish Privy Council," 1965 J.R. 263.

Macpherson, Hector, *The Intellectual Development of Scotland* (1911).

MacRae, D. G., "Adam Ferguson," in T. Raison (ed.), *The Founding Fathers of Social Science* (1969).

Maidment, James, *The Court of Session Garland* (1888).

Malcolm, C. A., "Was Lord Durie Twice Kidnapped?" (1913) 25 J.R. 33.

—— "The House of Lords and Appeals from Scotland" (1910) 22 J.R. 295.

Marshall, J., "John Erskine" (1895) 3 S.L.T. 171, 179.

—— "Lord Monboddo" (1900) 7 S.L.T. 1, 9.

Matheson, Cyril, *The Life of Henry Dundas, First Viscount Melville* (1933).

Mathew, David, *Scotland under Charles I* (1955).

Mathieson, W. Law, *The Awakening of Scotland, A History from 1747 to 1797* (1910).

—— *Church and Reform in Scotland, 1797–1843* (1916).

—— *Politics and Religion*, 2 vols. (1902).

—— *Scotland and the Union, 1695–1747* (1905).

Meek, R., "The Scottish contribution to Marxist Sociology," *Democracy and the Labour Movement*, ed. Saville (1954), 84.

Megaw, B. R. S., "The 'Moss Houses' of Kincardine, Perthshire, 1792" (1962) 6 *Scottish Studies* 87.

Meikle, Henry W., *Scotland and the French Revolution* (1912).

—— *Some Aspects of Later Seventeenth Century Scotland*, David Murray
    Lecture, Glasgow (1947).
Melville, James, *Autobiography and Diary* [1556–1601], ed. R. Pitcairn (1842).
Melville, James, of Halhill, *Memoirs of his Own Life* [1549–93] ed. T. Thomson
    (1827).
Menary, George, *The Life and Letters of Duncan Forbes of Culloden,
    (1685–1747)* (1936).
Menzies, W., "Alex. Bayne of Rires, Advocate" (1924) 36 J.R. 60.
Merryman, J. H., *The Civil Law Tradition* (1969).
Millar, A. H., (ed.), *A Selection of the Forfeited Estates Papers* (s.h.s.) (1909).
Millar, John, *A Course of Lectures on Government: given annually in the
    University of Glasgow* (1783).
—— *An Historical View of the English Government: From the Settlement of the
    Saxons in Britain to the Accession of the House of Stewart* (1787); 3rd ed.,
    4 vols. (1803).
—— *Observations Concerning the Distinction of Ranks* (1771), as *The Origin of
    the Distinction of Ranks*, 4th ed. (1806), including An Account of the Life
    and Writings of the Author by John Craig.
Millar, J. H., *A Literary History of Scotland* (1903).
Miller, W. G., *Lectures on the Philosophy of Law* (1884).
Montesquieu, Charles de Secondat, Baron de, *L'Esprit des Lois* (1748).
More, J. W., "The Second Founder of the Advocates' Library" [Ruddiman],
    1928 S.L.T. (News) 117.
Morrow, G. R., *The Ethical and Economic Theories of Adam Smith* (1923).
Mossner, Ernest C., *The Life of David Hume* (1954).
Moysie, David, *Memoirs of the Affairs of Scotland* [1577–1603], ed. J. Dennis-
    toun (1830).
Murdoch, A., *The People Above* (1980).
Murray, Athol, "Sinclair's Practicks," in Harding (ed.), *Law Making and Law
    Makers in British History* (1980).
Murray, David, *Legal Practice in Ayr and the West of Scotland in the Fifteenth and
    Sixteenth Centuries* (1910).
—— *Memories of the Old College of Glasgow* (1927).
Nadelmann, K. H., "Joseph Story and George Joseph Bell," 1959 J.R. 31.
Neilson, G., *Trial by Combat* (1890).
—— "The Study of Early Law" (1891) 3 J.R. 12.
—— "Sir John Skene's MS." *Memorabilia Scotica* and revisals of *Regiam Maies-
    tatem, Trans. Glasgow Archaeological Soc.* (N.S.) 7 (1924).
Nicholas, J. K. B. M., *An Introduction to Roman Law* (1962).
Nicholson, R., *Scotland, The Later Middle Ages* (1974).
Nicoll, John, *Diary of Public Transactions, 1650–67* (1836).
Norton, David F., "Thomas Reid and the History of Scottish Common Sense
    Philosophy," unpub. Ph.D. thesis, California, La Jolla (1966).
Omond, George W. T., *The Lord Advocates of Scotland*, 2 vols. (1883).
—— *The Lord Advocates of Scotland*, Second series (1914).
Pascal, Roy, "Property and Society: The Scottish Historical School of the
    Eighteenth Century" (1938) 1 *Modern Quarterly* 167.
Paton, G. Campbell H. (ed.), *An Introduction to Scottish Legal History* (Stair
    Soc.) (1958).
Paul, J. Balfour, "The late Sir John Rankine, K.C." (1923) 34 J.R. 305.
Phillipson, N. T., "The Scottish Whigs and the Reform of the Court of Session,
    1785–1830," unpub. Ph.D. thesis, Cambridge (1967).
—— "Lawyers, Landowners and the Civic Leadership of Post-Union Scotland,"
    1976 J.R. 97.
—— "The Social Structure of the Faculty of Advocates in Scotland, 1661–1840,"

in Harding (ed.), *Law Making and Law Makers in British History* (1980).
—— and Mitchison, Rosalind (ed.), *Scotland in the Age of Improvement* (1970).
Pinkerton, J. M., *The Faculty of Advocates' Minute Book*, 2 vols. (1976–80).
Plamenatz, John, *Man and Society*, 2 vols. (1963).
Plant, Marjorie, *The Domestic Life of Scotland in the Eighteenth Century* (1952).
Pollock, F., "A History of The Law of Nature," *Essays in the Law* (1922).
Pollock, F., and Maitland, F. W., *History of English Law before the Time of Edward I*, 2 vols. (1898).
Pottle, F. A., *James Boswell, The Earlier Years, 1740–1769* (1966).
    See also Brady.
Pound, Roscoe, *Introduction to the Philosophy of Law* (1954).
Priestly, Joseph, *Examination of Dr. Reid's Inquiry into the Human Mind on the Principles of Common Sense, Dr. Beattie's Essay on the Nature and Immutability of Truth, and Dr. Oswald's Appeal to Common Sense in behalf of Religion* (1774).
Pryde, George S., *Scotland from 1603 to the Present Day* (1962).
Rae, John, *Life of Adam Smith* (1895).
Rait, R. S., *The Parliaments of Scotland* (1924).
—— *The Universities of Aberdeen* (1895).
Ramsay, James, "Eighteenth Century Advocates and their Study of Legal and General Literature" (1939) 51 J.R. 23.
Ramsay, John, of Ochtertyre, *Letters*, 1799–1812, ed. B. L. H. Horn (s.h.s.) (1966).
—— *Scotland and Scotsmen in the Eighteenth Century*, ed. A. Allardyce, 2 vols. (1888).
Rankine, John, "Professor Muirhead" (1890) 2 J.R. 27.
Raphael, D. D., *The Moral Sense* (1947).
—— (ed.) *British Moralists, 1650–1800*, 2 vols. (1969).
Rashdall, H., *The Universities of Europe in the Middle Ages*, 2 ed. by F. M. Powicke and A. B. Emden, 3 vols. (1936).
Reid, Thomas, *An Inquiry into the Human Mind on the Principles of Common Sense* (1764).
—— *Essays on the Intellectual Powers of Man* (1785).
—— *Essays on the Active Powers of Man* (1788).
—— *Works*, ed. Sir Wm. Hamilton, 2 vols. (1846–63).
Reisman, D. A., *Adam Smith's Sociological Economics* (1976).
Rendall, Jane, *The Origins of the Scottish Enlightenment, 1707–76* (1978).
Richardson, H. G., "Roman Law in *Regiam Maiestatem*" (1955) 67 J.R. 155.
Riley, P. W. J., *King William and the Scottish Politicians* (1979).
—— *The Union of England and Scotland* (1978).
—— *The English Ministers and Scotland, 1707–1727* (1964).
Ritchie, D. G., *Natural Rights* (1916).
Robertson, William, *History of Scotland*, 2 vols. (1759).
Robertson, William, *Proceedings relating to the Peerage of Scotland, 1707–1788* (1790).
Ross, Ian S., *Lord Kames and the Scotland of His Day* (1972).
Sabine, G. H., *History of Political Theory* (1937).
Salmond, J. W., "Law of Nature" (1895) 11 L.Q.R. 121.
Sands, C. N. Johnston, Lord, "Lord Justice-Clerk Macdonald and his Edinburgh" (1924) 35 J.R. 107.
Saunders, L. J., *Scottish Democracy, 1815–1840: The Social and Intellectual Background* (1950).
Schneider, L., *The Scottish Moralists on Human Nature and Society* (1967).
Schulz, Fritz, *Classical Roman Law* (1951).
—— *History of Roman Legal Science* (1946).

Scott, W. R., *Adam Smith as Student and Professor* (1937).
—— *Francis Hutcheson* (1900).
Scott Moncrieff, W. G., "Upon Some of Lord Cockburn's Opinions" (1912) 24
    J.R. 302.
Senior, W., "Early Writers on Maritime Law" (1921) 37 L.Q.R. 323.
Seth (Pringle-Pattison), Andrew, *Scottish Philosophy* (1885).
Seton, George, *Memoir of Alexander Seton, Chancellor of Scotland* (1882).
Sharp, L. W., "Charles Mackie, The First Professor of History at Edinburgh
    University," (1962) 41 S.H.R. 23.
Shaw, J. S., *The Management of Scottish Society, 1707–1764* (1983).
Simpson, T. B., "Boswell as an Advocate" (1922) 34 J.R. 201.
Skene, W. Forbes, *Memorials of the Family of Skene of Skene* (1887).
Skinner, Andrew S., *A System of Social Science: Papers relating to Adam Smith*
    (1979).
—— "Economics and History – The Scottish Enlightenment" (1965) 12 *Sc. Jl.
    Pol. Econ* 1.
—— and T. Wilson (ed.), *Essays on Adam Smith* (1975).
Skinner, Quentin, *Foundations of Modern Political Thought*, 2 vols. (1978).
Small, John, "Biographical Sketch of Adam Ferguson," in *Trans. R.S.E.* 23
    (1864) 599.
Smellie, William, *Literary and Characteristical Lives of J. Gregory, M.D., Henry
    Home, Lord Kames, David Hume and Adam Smith, LL.D.* (1800).
Smith, Adam, *An Inquiry into the Nature and Causes of the Wealth of Nations*
    (1776), ed. R. H. Campbell, A. S. Skinner and W. B. Todd, 2 vols.
    (1976).
—— *Correspondence of Adam Smith*, ed. E. C. Mossner and I. S. Ross (1977).
—— *Essays on Philosophical Subjects*, ed. W. Wightman, J. C. Bryce and I. S.
    Ross (1980).
—— *Lectures on Jurisprudence*, ed. R. L. Meek, D. D. Raphael and P. G. Stein
    (1978).
—— *Lectures on Rhetoric and Belles Letters*, ed. J. C. Bryce (1983).
—— *Theory of Moral Sentiments* (1759), ed. D. D. Raphael and A. L. Macfie
    (1976).
Smith, Annette, *Jacobite Estates of the Forty-Five* (1982).
S[mith], D. B., "Characteres Quorundam Apud Scotos Advocatorum," 1961
    S.L.T. (News) 73.
—— "Mr. Erskine's Lectures," 1962 S.L.T. (News) 74.
—— "Practicks," 1962 S.L.T. (News) 147.
Smith, David Baird, "Sir Thomas Craig, Feudalist" (1915) 12 S.H.R. 271.
—— "William Barclay" (1914) 11 S.H.R. 136.
Smith, D. Nichol, *Literary Criticism of Francis Jeffrey* (1910).
Smith, Norman Kemp, *The Philosophy of David Hume* (1949).
Smith, Preserved, *The Enlightenment, 1687–1776* (1934).
Smith, T. B., "Authors and Authority" (1972) 12 J.S.P.T.L. (N.S.) 3.
—— *Judicial Precedent in Scots Law* (1952).
—— "English Influences on the Law of Scotland," in *Studies Critical and
    Comparative*, 116.
—— "The Contribution of Lord Cooper of Culross to the Law of Scotland"
    (1955) 67 J.R. 249 and in Lord Cooper's *Selected Papers*.
—— "Scots Law and Roman Dutch Law: A Shared Tradition," 1961 J.R. 32.
Smith, Will C., "The Sources of Scots Law" (1904) 16 J.R. 375.
Smout, T. C., *A History of the Scottish People*, 1560–1830 (1969).
Spottiswoode, John, *History of the Church of Scotland*, ed. M. Russell and M.
    Napier, 3 vols. (1847–51).
Stair Society, *Introduction to Scottish Legal History*, ed. G. C. H. Paton (1958).

—— *Miscellany*, Vol. 1 (1971).

—— *Stair Tercentenary Studies*, ed. D. M. Walker (1981).

—— *The Sources and Literature of Scots Law*, ed. H. McKechnie (1936).

Stein, Peter, "Influence of Roman Law on the Law of Scotland," 1963 J.R. 205.

—— "Law and Society in Eighteenth-Century Scottish Thought," in *Scotland in the Age of Improvement* (ed. Phillipson and Mitchison) (1970), 148.

—— "Legal Thought in Eighteenth-Century Scotland," 1957 J.R. 1.

—— Osservazioni intorno ad Adamo Smith, filosofo del diritto," *Riv. int. filosofia del diritto*, 32 (1955) 97.

—— *Regulae Juris* (1966).

—— "Roman Law in Scotland" *Ius Romanum Medii Aevi*, V, 13 b, 23.

—— The General Notions of Contract and Property in Eighteenth Century Scottish Thought, 1963 J.R. 1.

—— "The Source of the Romano-Canonical Part of *Regiam Maiestatem*" (1969) 48 S.H.R. 107.

Stephen, Leslie, *History of English Thought in the Eighteenth Century*, 2 vols. (1902).

Steuart, Sir James, of Coltness, *An Inquiry into the Principles of Political Economy*, ed. A. S. Skinner, 2 vols. (1966).

Stewart, W. D., "The Lockharts of Lee" (1928) 40 J.R. 142.

Stevenson, D., "The Covenanters and the Court of Session, 1637–1650," 1972 J.R. 227.

Stevenson, J. H., *Heraldry in Scotland*, 2 vols. (1914).

Stewart, Dugald, *Biographical Memoirs of Adam Smith, William Robertson and Thomas Reid* (1811).

—— *Works*, ed. Sir William Hamilton, 11 vols. (1854–60).

Stewart, John B., *The Moral and Political Philosophy of David Hume* (1963).

Stones, E. L. G., *Anglo-Scottish Relations*, 1174–1328. (1965).

Stronach, G., "A forgotten Incident in the Court of Session" [A. Wedderburn] (1911) 23 J.R. 346.

Taylor, W. L., *Francis Hutcheson and David Hume as Predecessors of Adam Smith* (1965).

Terry, C. S., *The Scottish Parliament: Its Constitution and Procedure*, 1603–1707.

—— (ed.), *Papers Relating to the Army of the Solemn League and Covenant 1643–47* (s.h.s.) (1917).

—— (ed.), *Sir Thomas Craig's De Unione Regnorum Britanniae Tractatus* (s.h.s.) (1909).

—— (ed.), *The Cromwellian Union, Negotiations for a union between England and Scotland, 1651–52* (s.h.s.) (1902).

Teulet, A. (ed.), *Papiers d'État . . . relatifs à l'histoire de l'Écosse au XVIe siècle*, 3 vols. (1852–60).

—— *Relations Politiques de la France et de l'Espagne avec l'Ecosse au XVIme siècle*, 5 vols. (1862).

Thomson, A., "Lorimer's Juristic Theory" (1896) 8 J.R. 242.

Thomson, J., "Harry Erskine" (1934) 46 J.R. 266.

—— "The First Viscount Stair" (1924) 36 J.R. 33.

Thomson, J. Maitland, *The Public Records of Scotland* (1922).

Thomson, T. (ed.), *Diary of the public correspondence of Sir Thomas Hope* (1843).

Turner, A. Logan, *History of the University of Edinburgh, 1883–1933* (1933).

Twining, W. L., "Treatises and Textbooks," (1973) 12 J.S.P.T.L. 267.

Tytler, Alexander Fraser, Lord Woodhouselee, *Elements of General History, Ancient and Modern* (1853).

—— *Memoirs of the Life and Writings of the Honourable Henry Home of Kames*, 2 vols. (1807); *Supplement* (1809); 3 vols. (1814).

—— *Universal History from the Creation of the World to the Beginning of the Eighteenth Century*, 6 vols. (1834).

Tytler, Patrick Fraser, *History of Scotland* [1249–1603], 9 vols. (1841–43).

—— "Account of the assassination of Sir George Lockhart," *Archaeologia Scotica*, IV (1857).

"Venio," "Sir David Dalrymple, Lord Hailes," 1926 S.L.T. (News) 161.

Vinogradoff, Paul, "Origins of Feudalism," 2 *Camb. Med. Hist.*, Chap. 20.

—— "Feudalism," 3 *Camb. Med. Hist.*, Chap. 18.

Walker, David M., "Equity in Scots Law" (1954) 66 J.R. 103.

—— "The Importance of Stair's Work for the Modern Lawyer," 1981 J.R. 161.

—— *The Scottish Legal System*, 5th ed. (1981).

—— (ed.), *Stair Tercentenary Studies* (Stair Soc.) (1981).

Walton, F. P., "The Humours of Hailes" (1894) 6 J.R. 223.

—— "Lord Monboddo" (1896) 8 J.R. 360.

Watson, Alan, *Law Making in the Later Roman Republic* (1974).

Watt, J. Crabb, *John Inglis* (1893).

Wellwood, Sir Henry Moncrieff, *An Account of the Life and Writings of John Erskine*, D.D. (1818).

Whetstone, A., *Scottish County Government in the 18th and 19th Centuries* (1981).

Whyte, J. F., "Henry Goudy – An Appreciation" (1921) 33 J.R. 161.

Williams, A. M., "Sir George Mackenzie of Rosehaugh" (1915) 13 S.H.R. 138.

Wilson, J. Dove, "The Sources of the Law of Scotland" (1892) 4 J.R. 1.

—— "Historical Development of Scots Law" (1896) 8 J.R. 217.

—— "The Reception of the Roman Law in Scotland" (1897) 9 J.R. 361.

—— "The Study of the History of Law in Scotland" (1904) 16 J.R. 54.

Wilton, G. W., "Pothier (1699–1772)" (1947) 59 J.R. 208.

Winch, D., *Adam Smith's Politics* (1978).

Winfield, Percy H., *The Chief Sources of English Legal History*, (1925).

Wodrow, Robert, *History of the Sufferings of the Church of Scotland from the Restoration to the Revolution*, ed. R. Burns, 4 vols. (1828–36).

Young, G. B., "Sir George Mackenzie of Rosehaugh" (1907) 19 J.R. 266.

—— "Sir John Nisbet of Dirleton" (1909) 21 J.R. 170.

—— "James Stewart, Lord Advocate" (1909) 21 J.R. 249.

INDEX